D1566650

WHO
INVENTED
THE COMPUTER?

John V. Atanasoff

Foreword by
DOUGLAS HOFSTADTER
author of the Pulitzer Prize–winning
Gödel, Escher, Bach:
An Eternal Golden Braid

ALICE ROWE BURKS

WHO
INVENTED
THE COMPUTER?

THE LEGAL BATTLE
THAT CHANGED
COMPUTING HISTORY

 Prometheus Books
59 John Glenn Drive
Amherst, New York 14228-2197

Published 2003 by Prometheus Books.

Inquiries should be addressed to
Prometheus Books
59 John Glenn Drive
Amherst, New York 14228–2197
VOICE: 716–691–0133, ext. 207
FAX: 716–564–2711
WWW.PROMETHEUSBOOKS.COM

07 06 05 04 03   5 4 3 2 1

Library of Congress Cataloging-in-Publication Data

Burks, Alice R., 1920–
    Who invented the computer? : the legal battle that changed computing history /
Alice Rowe Burks ; foreword by Douglas R. Hofstadter.
        p. cm.
    Includes bibliographical references and index.
    ISBN 1–59102–034–4 (alk. paper)
    1. Computers—United States—History. 2. Computers—United States—Patents.
3. Patent suits—United States. I. Title.

QA76.17.O45 1996
004'.9—dc21

                                                          2002036720

Printed in the United States of America on acid-free paper

CONTENTS

A. NOTHING BUT THE TRUTH

B. THE COURT OF PUBLIC OPINION

C. CLOSING ARGUMENT

FIGURES AND TABLES

CHAPTER 1. MAUCHLY ON THE STAND

CHAPTER 2. MAUCHLY IN DEPOSITION

CHAPTER 3. ATANASOFF AS WITNESS

CHAPTER 4. MAUCHLY BEFORE ATANASOFF

CHAPTER 5. LARSON FROM THE BENCH

ACKNOWLEDGMENTS

I want to thank four longtime friends for reading and responding to early drafts of my manuscript: Maurita Holland, Nathan Houser, Edward Jenner, and Richard Laing. I recently reviewed my file of their comments, together with my own margin notes for the needed repairs, and I am newly amazed at the attention both to detail and to overall presentation that these "critics" brought to their task. All of them are masters of the concept of constructive criticism.

My husband Arthur Burks served as abiding critic-in-residence, discussing basic issues throughout and reading and commenting on successive chapters as the book took shape. Our daughter Nancy Burks served as final critic, studying the entire work and offering several further helpful suggestions along with her own insightful overview.

I have special thanks for Douglas Hofstadter, who graciously accepted my invitation, with the enthusiastic concurrence of Prometheus Books, to write the foreword.

I want to express my gratitude to those people who provided the photographs reproduced here: Alice Atanasoff, for the frontispiece of her husband, John Vincent Atanasoff, with permission from photographer Carolyn Caddes, and also for the snapshot of him and her together at an Iowa celebration; Cecill Larson, for the photo of her husband, Judge Earl R. Larson; Raymond Mollenhoff for the photo of his father, Clark R. Mollenhoff; Thomas K. Sharpless, for the photo of his father, T. Kite Sharpless; and Marina v. N. Whitman, for the photo of her father, John von Neumann. In this regard, I am also indebted to my good neighbors, Melvyn and Muriel Gluckman, for contributing their expertise in old-photo restoration—fittingly, through modern computer magic.

9

FOREWORD

Typically, in the case of a revolutionary invention that comes to pervade society, most of us have a knee-jerk reflex answer to the question "Who invented it?" Thus for the light bulb, the automobile, the airplane, and the telephone, we Americans would tend to reply, rightly or wrongly: "Thomas Edison," "Henry Ford," "Wilbur and Orville Wright," and "Alexander Graham Bell." In a way, such knee-jerk answers (which I have here once again unwittingly propagated) are nothing more than simplistic myths that fill a psychological need in the public's mind for easy answers to complicated questions, and, perhaps even more, for the existence of uncomplicated hero figures. The existence of such mythic heroes in the collective human mind, as well as the power of belief in the tales that swirl around them, tends to be reinforced ever more clearly over time thanks to many subtle and intangible pressures in society.

This book is about the hidden social pressures to create such "mythic hero" figures for the computer—the general-purpose electronic digital computer—a device that today pervades our lives as much as does the light bulb, the automobile, the airplane, or the telephone. The computer lurks everywhere, both overtly and behind the scenes, and its overt and hidden presence will continue to increase over the next decades.

As of this time, although in the public mind there are a few names that might be vaguely associated with the computer (Alan Turing and John von Neumann, perhaps), there is no "mythic name" that pops out in the same ritualistic, iconic fashion as do those mentioned above—and this is fortunate, for simplistic myths are nearly always wrong. There is, however, a strong collective pressure pushing today toward the buildup of one pair of "mythic names" responsible for the existence of the computer. That pair of names is J. Presper Eckert and John W. Mauchly, and their mythical Model T computer is the ENIAC, unveiled in early 1946. Alice Burks's book is intended to serve as a breakwater to the powerful waves that would wash away all of the competition to Eckert and Mauchly and that would reduce the story of the computer to this simple and handy formula, thereby instituting an enduring and appealing, yet enormously distorted, myth.

<<<>>>

Perhaps the most frequently repeated phrase during the Watergate Senate investigation in 1973–74 was Senator Howard Baker's question: "What did the President know, and when did he know it?" This query concerned President Nixon in the White House on Pennsylvania Avenue, of course, and what he had heard from his underlings about the Watergate break-in. A very similar query could be posed about J. Presper Eckert at the Moore School of Electrical Engineering at the University of Pennsylvania, who was known to his friends as "Pres": "What did Pres know, and when did he know it?"

Indeed, during those same Watergate years, a parallel trial was taking place in the United States District Court in Minneapolis, and its central purpose was to determine the nature of the ideas that were brought back from Iowa to Pres Eckert in Pennsylvania by his underling John Mauchly, who in the summer of 1941 had gone to visit "one John V. Atanasoff" at the Iowa State University in Ames, and who had spent a few days there observing the "ABC," as it subsequently came to be called (short for "Atanasoff-Berry Computer").

The brief visit by physicist Mauchly to his physicist colleague Atanasoff is today shrouded in mystery, and for this reason it recalls, in my mind, the mysterious brief visit paid by the outstanding German physicist Werner Heisenberg to his Danish mentor, colleague, and close friend Niels Bohr in Copenhagen—also, ironically in the year 1941. Heisenberg's visit, whose purpose seems plausibly linkable with the German hope of building an atomic bomb, has been dramatized by playwright Michael Frayn in the famous play "Copenhagen," and indeed the central question of the play is precisely why Heisenberg visited his old mentor, what he hoped to learn, and what Bohr told him.

In the court case concerning Mauchly's 1941 visit to Atanasoff, the central question was whether Mauchly was exposed to a new kind of electronic machine whose underlying principles radically affected his notion of how vacuum-tube circuits could carry out complex series of mathematical calculations, or whether, contrariwise, he merely saw "a little piece of junk," "a little gismo," "a gadget," "a pile of tubes," "a monstrosity," "a complete joke," "a few tubes hooked up," "a crude little machine," "some little thing which he [Atanasoff] never finished and which wouldn't have worked if he had finished it." Or perhaps, as Pres at one point claimed, Mauchly never saw anything at all, but merely heard some fantasizing about Atanasoff's hopes for the future.

Like Heisenberg's visit to Bohr, Mauchly's visit to Atanasoff is of disputed duration, but both seem to have lasted on the order of three to five days. Also, in both cases, the visitor was lodged in his host's home, and in both cases, the only other adult present was his host's wife.

What ideas did Mauchly take home to Pres in Pennsylvania? This book is largely about that question. But it is also about the deep desire of the vast majority of humanity to accept the "standard version" of stories, the desire not to rock the boat with alternate versions—the profound desire, in short, for building and propagating simple and appealing myths. On the other hand, this book is just as much about exceptional people who refuse to accept myths and who insist on investigating things for themselves, risking their reputations and their jobs.

A leitmotiv that pervades the second half of this book is the increasing (and increasingly insidious) infiltration of corporations and commercialism into American society, propagating ideas and opinions that are beneficial to their own interests alone, irrespective of the truth of the matter.

A wonderful example is the 1979 advertisement for a new computer built by Sperry Univac (a division of Sperry Rand, which had acquired all of the Eckert-Mauchly patent rights). Posed leaning against the new 1100/60 computer is an elderly Pres Eckert, with a photo in the background of the enormous hulk of the 1946 ENIAC machine, and the text says, "WHO WOULD HAVE THOUGHT THAT THE FATHER OF GOLIATH WOULD BE INTRODUCING DAVID?" This ad appeared in the *Wall Street Journal* some six years after Eckert and Mauchly's patent for the ENIAC had been struck down by the United States District Court's unappealed decision.

The following year, at a meeting of the Association for Computing Machinery in Nashville, a Special Awards Luncheon honored Eckert and the late Mauchly for "building the first electronic computer," after which a bronze medallion was handed out to all conference registrants, courtesy of Sperry Univac.

Then there was a television series about the invention and evolution of computers, called "The Machine that Changed the World," coproduced in 1992 by WGBH (the Boston PBS affiliate) and the BBC. This series, which never once mentioned John Atanasoff, had one sole corporate sponsor—Unisys (formed when Sperry Rand merged with Burroughs)—to the tune of $1.9 million. It is important to point out that whereas 86 percent of PBS funding had come from federal sources in 1980, by 1992 that amount had fallen to roughly 20 percent. When Alice Burks and her husband, Arthur, a distinguished computer scientist and philosopher, objected to the omission of any reference to John Atanasoff, the executive producer of the TV series, Jon Palfreman, wrote in a letter to the *Ames Daily Tribune*: "They [the Burkses] perpetrate falsehoods and distortions. . . . Atanasoff was undoubtedly a great man, but regretfully has become a pawn in the hands of a group of fanatics who use intimidation rather than serious intellectual argument to further their case."

A final example of this deplorable tendency to blur the lines between objective and biased information involves a display about the evolution of computers put up in 1990 at the Smithsonian Institution in Washington. This display, underwritten in part by Unisys, blatantly featured the ENIAC as the key invention and ignored the role of the ABC. When pressed on this strange omission, Museum Director Roger Kennedy claimed, "Not one of the sponsors ever made any attempt to influence our staff." Oddly enough, on the other hand, the 1989 Smithsonian Museum Bulletin thanked the exhibit's sponsors for contributing not just money but also "ideas and advice."

The cast of characters in this story is filled with vivid and very real personalities. Some are oddballs and some are squares; some are honest, some are dishonest, and some are opportunists, floating halfway between. It is a genuine drama, written with flair and a supreme attempt at objectivity. The deep involvement of Arthur Burks not only in the development of the ENIAC computer at the University of Pennsylvania but also as a coworker of John von Neumann, in the development of a computer for the Institute for Advanced Study in Princeton, renders the book far more intriguing, since Alice Burks's writing is informed by her husband's personal experiences that stretch back to the earliest days of computing machinery.

What we have in *Who Invented the Computer?* is a classic battle between a little-known underdog and a massively backed "easy winner." Alice Burks has taken on formidable opponents, but she has done a formidable job of building and defending her case. You, the readers of this book, are now the jury.

Douglas Hofstadter
Director, Center for Research on Concepts and Cognition
Indiana University, Bloomington

Bologna, Italy
June 2002

ALL RISE

Our story of the invention of the electronic computer takes us back more than sixty years, to the 1930s. Recent developments have been so rapid-fire, with ever new possibilities emerging faster than they can be realized, that we forget how slowly it all began, how gradually it progressed from an arithmetic rate of advancement to our present exponential pace.

Imagine a time when "word processing" a report or a term paper or a manuscript meant feeding paper sheet by sheet onto the roller of a typewriter, pounding out text on a mechanical keyboard, throwing a shift lever at the end of each line—upon the ping of a bell—and correcting errors with a special eraser that always left a noticeable trace.

Imagine the satisfaction of advancing from the mechanical to the electrical models, with keys so responsive that one had to develop a new light touch to avoid repeating letters, and with a narrow paper tape that allowed errors to be whited out and corrections typed in. But imagine, even then, having to retype major portions of a document if revisions extended beyond a line or two here and there—or resorting to patching over with strips of paper in an actual "cut and paste" operation that has its counterpart in today's word processing toolbar.

So accustomed have we become to the electronic word processor, with its screen and keyboard and mouse, that we hardly realize how recent it really is. Word processing on the personal computer was launched not quite three decades ago, in 1975, and it would be many more years before such computers became commonplace.

Imagine the almost giddy sense of power those who had lived by the typewriter experienced, once they had mastered a headful of processing rules—their sense of power growing as they wondered whether, maybe, there was some way of doing some new thing and found that, yes, of course there was.

In the world of business and commerce, the electrically operated punched-card machines had become extremely fast and flexible long before they were finally abandoned, in the 1960s, for electronic devices. These calculators were also adapted, to a limited extent, for scientific applications as early as the 1930s. And some privileged scientists had access to one of the few models of the electrically driven differential analyzer, a room-sized mechanical analog machine for solving differential equations that came into existence in the 1930s and endured into the 1950s.

In the main, however, the scientific researcher had to rely on an electrically driven, hand-operated "desk calculator," a machine that produced arithmetic results through a system of meshing gears. Imagine here a scientist in the mid-1930s, a university professor guiding graduate students through doctoral theses when complex problems had to be solved with only the aid of this device. Imagine the student tediously recording a long series of intermediate results, step-by-step via pencil and paper, making little hand calculations along the way to determine what next to enter on the machine's keyboard.

The depth to which one could probe in this fashion was severely limited, not only by time constraints but by the occurrence of human errors that, once made, could be ruinously compounded. Many a professor was intensely frustrated, as well, by the amount of time promising young researchers were spending in this mind-numbing procedure rather than in original, creative thinking and learning. It was, in fact, to facilitate such scientific calculations that, between 1939 and 1942, the first electronic computer was invented.

Here we turn to the particular professor of physics and mathematics at Iowa State College who, in 1973, was declared by a federal judge to have been the inventor of that first machine: the inventor, indeed, from whose work a later electronic computer had been derived. This inventor, ruled District Judge Earl R. Larson, was "one Dr. John Vincent Atanasoff," from whose prior "automatic electronic digital computer" the world-acclaimed ENIAC of J. Presper Eckert and John W. Mauchly had been derived through Mauchly's direct contact with Atanasoff and his ABC. Judge Larson accordingly invalidated the Eckert-Mauchly patent on the ENIAC.

Atanasoff had set himself the goal of finding means to solve the large sets of algebraic linear equations that he and his students were encountering in a wide variety of physical problems. Starting in 1935, he made a thorough study of the current computing technology, both as it stood and as he could adapt it. He considered, for example, "ganging" or interconnecting some thirty desk calculators and running them simultaneously—and repeatedly—through a solution procedure, or algorithm, for sets of up to thirty equations. But this proved mechanically impractical. He then considered adapting the punched-card tab-ulators. But their capacity was inadequate.

Atanasoff also considered the differential analyzer, but as an analog device it could not provide the accuracy he needed. His explorations had led him to the distinction between the analog and the digital modes, *and* to the possibility of computing electronically, with vacuum tubes, in the binary mode. Realizing that he would have to invent such a computer himself—and fired by enthusiasm for his novel concepts—he set about designing what was to be the world's first elec-tronic computer.

My purpose in this book is twofold: first, to develop this story, largely through the ENIAC trial proceedings themselves; second, to explore the trial's aftermath, the effective widespread *rejection* of its verdict, with very little atten-tion to the hard evidence and the copious testimony (even that of Mauchly him-self) elicited in that courtroom setting. In an earlier, more technical book, my hus-band Arthur and I described Atanasoff's computer in great detail; we also placed his special-purpose ABC, the general-purpose ENIAC, and the ensuing stored-program EDVAC and Institute for Advanced Study Computer in their historical perspective.[1]

In our introduction to that work, we noted the failure of computer historians to respond to the substance of the court case, even as they faulted Judge Larson's decision. We deplored this odd bypassing of what we termed "a researcher's dream," federal trial transcripts constituting "an immense public treasure" of closely scrutinized data in "a contest over many millions of dollars." In our concluding chapter, we again remarked on this failure of purveyors of the history to avail themselves of the court record. There we found the stance of these scholars "the more reprehensible in that they have elected to *oppose* the strong, unappealed decision of that court."

The sad fact is that our 1988 charge could be made almost as well today. While the Atanasoff cause has certainly gained ground, it is still the decision, rather than the particulars on which that decision was based, that is usually cited—and usually as still *controversial* (a favorite term). Particularly regrettable is the fact that the ABC, even when recognized as a prior electronic computer, is rarely credited with its influence on the ENIAC and so with its critical role in starting today's computer revolution.

In part A of this book, I present the court proceedings from the angles of John Mauchly, John Atanasoff, and Judge Earl Larson. Then, in part B, I delve into the story behind this widespread disregard for the true history by so many in posi-tions of authority and trust.

As my title for this introduction, "All Rise," indicates, I have envisioned the present work as something of a trial in itself. Part A is, accordingly, titled "Nothing but the Truth"; part B is "The Court of Public Opinion"; and part C, the conclusion, is "Closing Argument." I offer this work as a challenge to scholars concerned with the accuracy of our history and with properly crediting major contributors to that history: a challenge either to accept the conclusions of one of our nation's highest courts, or to show how, based on the evidence, Judge Larson could have reached any other decision.

My fervent hope is, of course, that serious researchers will ultimately recognize Atanasoff both for his invention and for his influence, and that in the process they will come to see this successful functioning of our justice system as cause for celebration. Not incidentally, I take up the role of another man, as well, one whose ideas Eckert and Mauchly also misappropriated as they moved beyond the ENIAC. This is John von Neumann, whose contributions to the concept of the stored-program computer arose from his consultations with the principals of the ENIAC team. His part in the history has been poorly understood and poorly differentiated, especially from that of Eckert. What von Neumann accomplished is also revealed to a considerable extent by the ENIAC trial proceedings, and to an even larger extent by documents from the 1940s.

A note on the times in which all these events occurred is in order. The Great Depression that started with the stock market crash of 1929 still prevailed in this country—and throughout the world, actually—when in the fall of 1939 Atanasoff proved out his principles of electronic digital computing in a test model. By the time he and his graduate assistant, Clifford E. Berry (the "B" of ABC, or Atanasoff-Berry Computer), had built the computer itself in the spring of 1942, the United States had entered World War II.

The impact of both the depression and the war cannot be emphasized too strongly in viewing this history. Funding for research projects during the depression was extremely scarce, most of it coming from private foundations. But the depression also saw an infusion of federal money into many enterprises not previously supported at that level, both for public works and for private cultural pursuits. Toward the end of the depression, with war on the horizon, modest "defense" investments in technology were made. And then, the events of December 1941 initiated a dramatic increase in funding for military purposes that was to continue after the war and, as we know, become a major portion of our national budget.

So it was that Atanasoff in 1940 was able to secure funding for his projected computer from the private Research Corporation, of New York City, to the impressive tune of $5,000. For its part, Iowa State College provided a start-up sum of about $1,500, certain facilities and services, and, of course, his professor's handsome salary of $5,000 a year. And then the ENIAC, proposed in 1943 with the promise of calculating artillery firing tables, was completely financed by the U.S. Army, to the truly astounding tune of $500,000! The EDVAC likewise was funded, after the war, by the army, and the Institute for Advanced Study Computer was funded primarily by the three branches of the military.

It seems clear that our current level of funding for the military, for the arts, for the sciences, and for medicine, among other areas, has its roots in those initial public projects of the depression and the requirements of World War II.

Finally, I want to alert my readers that my husband and I have of necessity become players in certain aspects of this story. Arthur was one of the chief designers of the ENIAC at the University of Pennsylvania, working with Eckert and Mauchly. He also went on after the war to work with von Neumann on the design of the Institute for Advanced Study Computer. And he pursued a long professorial career at the University of Michigan, where he taught, did research, and directed doctoral dissertations in both computer science and philosophy. I have relied on him for technical material, which I do try to keep to a minimum, and also for an historical accounting of events in which he participated.

I was what was called a "computer" working on firing tables at the University of Pennsylvania before the ENIAC project got under way. More significantly, I became caught up in the recording of this history in the late 1970s and have been at it ever since. And so both Arthur and I are directly involved in seeking proper recognition for Atanasoff, first as writers but also as advocates in matters of publication and of the public presentation of this history.

In all cases, whether we are involved or not, I take care to differentiate opinion from demonstrable fact. And I document the events portrayed, citing and quoting from reports and papers of that seminal decade, 1939 to 1948; from ENIAC patent trial materials; from writings both critical and supportive of my position; and from exchanges with such institutions as the Smithsonian and Public Broadcasting. I have stepped on some toes, unavoidably. But my interest—and Arthur's—lies in the preservation of an accurate history. I welcome whatever refinements or corrections may be offered in this same spirit.

A.

NOTHING BUT THE TRUTH

ONE

MAUCHLY ON THE STAND

I t was Monday, November 8, 1971, five months into the trial of Case 4-67 Civil 138 pitting Honeywell against Sperry Rand in the matter of the ENIAC patent. Although the University of Pennsylvania had unveiled the ENIAC (Electronic Numerical Integrator and Computer) in 1946, the patent was not issued until 1964. In the meantime, patentees J. Presper Eckert and John W. Mauchly had sold their rights—and their company—to Remington Rand, and Remington Rand had merged with Sperry Gyroscope to form Sperry Rand.

Now Sperry Rand, ENIAC patent in hand, was demanding huge royalties on *all* the electronic data processing sales of *all* its large competitors, except IBM and Bell Telephone Laboratories, with whom it had signed cross-licensing agreements. And Honeywell, one of those competitors, was challenging the patent's validity, claiming derivation from John V. Atanasoff, among other charges.

The place was Courtroom Number 2, United States Court House, Minneapolis, District Judge Earl R. Larson presiding. John Mauchly was testifying for defendant Sperry Rand. He would come through this direct examination by attorney H. Francis DeLone unscathed, of course. Later, he would have a rougher time under cross-examination by plaintiff Honeywell's attorney.

The issue was this: Just what had Mauchly learned about a computer being built at Iowa State College when he traveled to Ames in June of 1941? What had he learned of that machine being built there by John Atanasoff and his graduate assistant Clifford Berry—less than a year before their electronic computer would be finished and nearly two years before work on the ENIAC would even begin?

The burden of Mauchly's testimony to the Sperry Rand attorney was that he had learned very little, that he now remembered even less, and that, for his own purposes, he had found the Atanasoff-Berry Computer, or ABC, disappointing after what he had been led to expect in an earlier meeting with Atanasoff.[1]

DeLone began by alluding to that first and only prior meeting between Mauchly and Atanasoff, at the University of Pennsylvania in December 1940. Atanasoff had attended a session of the American Association for the Advancement of Science in which Mauchly had given a paper on weather analysis. Afterwards, these two physicists talked about their mutual interest in computing machines, and Atanasoff invited Mauchly to come to Iowa State and see his invention. DeLone queried Mauchly at length about his experience of the ABC.

> *DeLone:* And while you were there did you go to the physics building to see a device which he was developing, the one he had told you about in Philadelphia but without telling you any of the details?
>
> *Mauchly:* Yes, I did.
>
> . . .
>
> *DeLone:* Could you describe for us what it was you saw there?
>
> *Mauchly:* Well, I can. The description is not a very detailed one. The clearest thing I remember is that there was a large frame made out of angle iron and that within that there was . . . a rotating drum which was studded with contacts, which presumably were connected to condensers [capacitors] inside that drum. Although I never took it apart I had every reason to believe there were condensers inside that drum.
>
> . . .
>
> *DeLone:* Now, when you went there, can you recall anything else about what it was you saw there, when you went to the laboratory, or the physics building on Saturday morning [June 14], if it was Saturday?
>
> *Mauchly:* Well, there were other pieces, you might say, hung on this framework that I spoke of. The drum was not the only thing there. I can't remember now exactly what other pieces, but there were chassis which were intended for working in cooperation with the drum to produce the results that he was expecting to get from this machine. Now, I can't remember clearly exactly what chassis or what they looked like or exactly what they were or how many of them there were. Details of that I have no recollection of.
>
> *DeLone:* Did the chassis have tubes? Were there tubes connected with the machine in some way?
>
> *Mauchly:* Well, it's hard at this time for me to—I don't have a photographic memory of these things—it's hard for me now to answer that in sort of a direct recollection way. I know that he was proposing using tubes and he showed me things with tubes in them, but I don't know whether they were hanging on the machine at the time I saw the machine or whether they were across the room on a table or just where they were.
>
> . . .
>
> *DeLone:* Do you recall what was done with the machine itself [on subsequent visits to the laboratory]? Was it operated? Did you see it compute?

Mauchly: I guess my difficulty is you are talking about the machine as if this describes—you mean that to apply to what I saw at that time?

DeLone: To what you saw at that time, yes.

Mauchly: Yes, because there was another entity you might call the machine, which is really what he intended to build, which I didn't see.

. . .

Mauchly: Well, . . . the motor was turned on, the drum rotated—that I believe I saw. How much further a demonstration could have been made with what I saw there I can't really recall now, because of a, you might say, slight confusion in this respect. My memory tells me that there was another table in that room, I believe and, so, some of the parts of this machine could be demonstrated by tests made when the equipment was off the machine. So what I can't remember is how much was demonstrated off the machine and how much was demonstrated on the machine. But whatever was demonstrated was demonstrated in a very non-automatic way, you might say, by specific operations of buttons or with some way not—maybe the simplest way to say this is it did not have any way of putting in numbers or taking out numbers in any automatic way. If you wanted to demonstrate anything, you had to apply electric charges to wiring elements or something in the machine in order to even get a small set of digits in there so that you could demonstrate that anything happened.

DeLone: . . . You indicated [earlier—p. 11,818] that your interest in going to Ames was kindled in part by the suggestion of a cost of $2.00 per digit, the suggestion that Dr. Atanasoff had made to you back in December of 1940? . . . What did you learn about that?

Mauchly: I didn't learn a great deal about that, as I didn't really try to do the cost accounting to say is this $2.00 per digit, but what I did learn was, you might say, the essence of what I wanted to know. It was a disappointment because there had been nothing said, so far as I can remember, in my meeting with him at the University of Pennsylvania which indicated that this machine was not a fully electronic machine. That's why my great curiosity, my great wonderment, how in the world did he do this for $2.00 a digit, because I was thinking in terms of all electronic things, which make use of electronic speeds, and almost immediately, of course, when I got out there I began to learn, even though the machine was not operative, for instance, on Saturday, you could see the drum idea and you could begin to put together the picture that this is a mechanical gadget which uses some electronic tubes in operation, but it's still restricted in speed and was not what I was interested in from the point of view of electronic speed gadgets. The fact that it was also being built specifically to solve a special class of problems, rather than a general class, was quite obvious, of course, but that wasn't the thing that really worried me because what I had been looking for were ways of getting high speed electronic things without paying too much for them and—sure, this was electronic in part, but it became perfectly clear without much examination or talking that it wasn't electronic in whole and it was sacrificing too much of the electrical end. So I think that a lot of the conversa-

tion that we had out there was really going over this point of "Why don't
you do this and why didn't you do that."

DeLone: . . . what do you mean by a special class of problems, not a general
class?

. . .

Mauchly: What I meant was that his machine was specifically, deliberately constructed with the idea that when finished it would solve simultaneous linear
algebraic equations, which is a very special class of problems, class of
problems that occurs over and over again in many places: statistics,
physics, engineering, whatnot, but there are many other problems which
cannot be handled in this way and my interest was in solving some problems which couldn't be handled this way. So my general interest was in
trying to get computers which would be versatile and not restricted to some
one class of problems. That did not worry me about his machine, the fact
that he was designing that. That was his privilege, if that's what he wanted
to do. The thing that I was really interested in was how did he have—what
kind of way could he devise something at very low cost, but I figured if I
could understand that, why, there would be ways of going on to general
purpose machines at a very low cost also.

DeLone: And when you say "What ways could he design something at a very
low cost," you have reference, as I understand your testimony, to something
which was all-electronic?

Mauchly: Yes.

DeLone: And you didn't find that?

Mauchly: I didn't find that, no.

. . .

DeLone: When you were at Ames, Iowa, do you recall . . . whether you were
given anything to read?

Mauchly: Yes. . . . I believe I was, yes.

DeLone: What do you believe you were given to read?

Mauchly: I don't remember much about it. My main memory on this is, you
might say, a little—or the other way around, in that what impressed itself
on my memory was that I was not allowed or given anything that I could
take home to read. In other words, anything that I was given to read, I had
to read there. He did not want any information in written form to leave his
laboratory offices, and so he made it very clear to me. I mean, it wasn't
any—no bashfulness, you know, about this. It was a clear understanding
that "We do not want this material circulated, and so, to prevent this from
happening, why we will not let any written material be taken away."

DeLone: So that are you able to testify with assurance now that you did not take
away from Dr. Atanasoff—

Mauchly: I am absolutely sure on that point. I didn't take anything away, no.

DeLone: I was asking you if you recall what, if anything, you did read, and do
you recall whether you read anything, and, if so, what it was?—while you
were there as distinguished from whether you took anything away.

Mauchly: Well, my general memory is that while I was there, he gave me to read

some material, which I think was prepared originally to describe what he was proposing to do to any organization that might be available to give him a grant to help him do it. In other words, it was something like a proposal.
DeLone: Do you have any specific recollection of the contents of the document?
Mauchly: Not specific, no. I mean, the general idea was just describing the utility of wanting to solve certain classes of problems, and here was a way of doing it, and then some detail—but not very much—as to how you would do it.

Honeywell attorney Henry Halladay's rather stern cross-examination of Mauchly, begun three days later in the presence of a large drawing of the ABC, prompted an accelerating recall of much greater detail.[2] Indeed, the most critical portion, on the electronics of the ABC, brought two responses that may have surprised DeLone as well as Halladay. The first was Mauchly's admission of his distinct memory of the computer's binary adders, those "chassis" to which he had vaguely alluded in direct testimony. The second was his admission of an understanding of these adders that went far beyond his earlier sworn statements. It was one of several times that this court was to see an impetuous Mauchly cross a seemingly carefully drawn line into dangerous territory.

Atanasoff's add-subtract mechanisms, as he called them, had not been identified in the direct testimony, either as adders or as add-subtract mechanisms. Mauchly called them "pieces . . . hung on this framework that I spoke of," "chassis which were intended for working in cooperation with the drum to produce the [expected] results." He could not remember exactly "what they looked like or exactly what they were or how many of them there were." As to whether they were electronic, Mauchly recalled that Atanasoff "was proposing using tubes and he showed me things with tubes in them," but he could not remember "whether they were hanging on the machine [or] were across the room on a table or just where they were." DeLone did not inquire further into their function.

Halladay began his inquiry into this topic by asking if Mauchly recalled that the ABC "had vacuum tubes on it mounted in modular chassis."

Mauchly: Well, I recall that that was the intention and I believe that probably there were some vacuum tubes mounted on it while I was there. As I say, these things could be put on or removed. I was perfectly aware of what the machine was supposed to do and the general idea that he was going to use vacuum tubes, that he was going to mount them there, and it is a little hard for me to remember now which of the things I might have seen as the way the machine existed at a particular point in time and which of the things I merely understood, because he described them to me verbally.
. . .
Halladay: Do you recall, Dr. Mauchly, while you were there in Ames, Iowa, in June of 1941, . . . seeing and being informed about the existence of some

thirty so-called add-subtract mechanisms which were pluggable in or removable from the main frame of this ABC . . . ?

Mauchly: You have touched upon something which now I can very distinctly remember, and in a sense you asked if I had seen 30 of these. I know that I understood that there were going to be 30 such things, but I didn't see them. [italics added]

. . .

Halladay: But you did see at least a number of the add-subtract mechanisms in place on the machine, did you not?

Mauchly: I know that I saw some number of them, and I can't recall now when they were in place and when they weren't. They might even have been put on or removed in my presence—

Halladay: Yes.

Mauchly:—and that's why I say I know that these things were removable and could be put back on. Lots of these things were built in modular form and you could make these changes.

Halladay: And as you were getting acquainted with the machine and talking about it, conducting a dialogue connected with it, it wouldn't be surprising, would it, for you to take off your coat and actually participate in removing one of these removable modules or plugging one back in?

Mauchly: Well, the first part would not be unusual. That is, considering it was summer, I might well have taken off my coat. It strikes me . . . that it would be unlike me to be taking apart or putting together somebody else's equipment.

Halladay: Your purpose, of course, was to learn as much as you could about it, was it not?

Mauchly: I think, yes, that purpose is so, but I wondered whether you realize that my method of learning is not by handling apparatus.

Halladay: Well, I don't know what your method of learning is, but I am trying to find out how good your recollection is, and you now tell me that it's not impossible that being hot, you took off your coat, and you are also telling me, if I understand you, that you wouldn't deny actually participating in either unplugging or plugging one of these demountable modules that Atanasoff was calling an add-subtract mechanism, or an ASM for short?

Mauchly: Yes, I certainly wouldn't deny that. It's perfectly possible that Cliff Berry or somebody said, "Here, will you help me, hold this end of this for me?"—or something else. I wouldn't deny that. It's a perfectly natural thing to happen.

Halladay, having established thus far that the modular chassis referred to earlier were the "so-called add-subtract mechanisms," that there were to be thirty of them in the ABC, and that they were somehow to use vacuum tubes, moved off to other aspects of Mauchly's experience of Atanasoff's computer. But later, in a summation of that experience, he returned to these binary adders, this time pressing Mauchly on his observation of them in action.

Figure 1. Front view of the ABC as of August 1940. This photograph, taken for inclusion in Atanasoff's descriptive proposal, shows the ABC's main memory—*two* drums, actually, on a common axle—and four of its add-subtract mechanisms. The modular add-subtract mechanisms, all thirty of which had already been built, were to be mounted on the vertical racks of the machine's angle-iron frame, fifteen from the front and fifteen from the back.

The space between the two storage drums at the top rear of the picture was for a timing drum, yet to be built, and the space to their left was for a base-conversion drum, also yet to be built. At the lower right is a voltage-regulated power supply, with its filament transformer just behind it. Behind that is the motor that turned the drum axle.

Halladay: And there is no doubt, is there, Dr. Mauchly, that while there in Ames, Iowa, you actually observed the add-subtract mechanisms adding, did you not?

Mauchly: It's my belief, the best recollection I can summon at this time, that I saw these add-subtract mechanisms demonstrated in one way or another. Whether they were on the machine or on a test bench, I don't remember. I say that I believe that I did see them demonstrated.

Halladay: There isn't any question, is there, Dr. Mauchly, that at that time Dr. Atanasoff had a device for a static test of the add-subtract mechanism modules, . . . is there?

Mauchly: You are asking me if there is any doubt that he had such a thing?

Halladay: Any doubt in your mind that you saw such a thing?

Mauchly: Oh. . . . I am saying that I know that there was something by which he was testing what he was doing there.

. . .

Halladay: And demonstrating that the ASM would in fact add or subtract in the binary mode?

Mauchly: That was the only mode in which it could. Yes, I agree.

Halladay: And you in fact observed this occurring there at Ames, Iowa, did you not?

Mauchly: I believe I did, yes.

Halladay: And you observed, did you not, on the face of a cathode ray tube oscilloscope the shape of the pulses involved in the Atanasoff-Berry Computer, did you not?

Mauchly: Well, this I have no direct recollection of. I am sure he had an oscilloscope there.

Halladay: And you are sure, are you not,—

Mauchly: I think I saw one. What the shape of the pulses were that might have been shown on that I am not sure.

Halladay: Are you sure that you looked at the face of an oscilloscope with Dr. Atanasoff or Clifford Berry, or both of them, and learned to distinguish on the face of that oscilloscope between the appearance or representation of a 0 and the figure 1?

Mauchly: I have been looking at oscilloscopes for many years—

Halladay: I submit that is not an answer, Your Honor.

DeLone: May the witness be allowed to finish the answer?

Judge Larson: Had you finished?

Mauchly: No, I hadn't.

Judge Larson: You said you had been looking at oscilloscopes for many years.

Mauchly: That was sort of a prefatory statement to qualify my answer. If I looked at an oscilloscope there, and I believe I did, why, I would have asked what did these things represent. And if they represented 0s and 1s, why, so they would be, yes.

Halladay: Well, then is it not fair to say that you do have a memory of seeing that particular sort of a demonstration on an oscilloscope so that you did in fact at that time see 0s and 1s in the binary mode in which addition was accomplished by the Atanasoff-Berry Computer?

Mauchly: There was an "if" in my answer and that "if" translated into this context means I am not saying that I recollect now distinctly seeing exactly such a demonstration and I am not denying that I saw such a one. *In either case, whether I saw it or didn't see it, I was perfectly convinced by what Dr. Atanasoff said and what I saw at that time that his add-subtract mechanism did in fact work.* [italics added]

Halladay: And did in fact accomplish addition electronically?

Mauchly: Work in this case means that it did produce a result which was the result of adding two binary digits and getting an answer, or subtracting two binary digits and getting an answer.

Halladay: And doing so electronically, correct?

Mauchly: It used vacuum tubes, yes.

So here was Mauchly's fresh admission not only of having seen the add-subtract mechanism demonstrated, but of having understood it as an electronic device and having been convinced that it did indeed work.

Four years earlier, in his October 1967 deposition for the so-called Regenerative Memory case (*Sperry Rand* v. *Control Data*), Mauchly had responded quite differently to a question by Control Data attorney Allen Kirkpatrick about tests he had seen in Atanasoff's laboratory.[3]

> First of all, let me say I saw no tests performed. This device [the computer] was covered up in the basement and the cover—that is the tarpaulin or cloth had to be a dust cover of flexible material, as I remember it; had to be removed from it in order for me to see it, and there was no evidence to me at the time that anybody was doing any work on it.
>
> Now, I was told that tests had been made, but I was not told what the results of those tests were, except the general indication that these tests gave Dr. Atanasoff confidence that when it was completed he thought it would work.

In testifying in this earlier case, Mauchly did refer to the Atanasoff-Berry Computer's "electronic circuitry" and to its task of "perform[ing] the necessary arithmetic operations . . . as a kind of binary adder."[4]

The present writer's husband, Arthur Burks, recalls sitting with Mauchly at a meeting of the Association for Computing Machinery in August 1967, six weeks before the deposition just quoted, and being told by Mauchly that he had had trouble getting Atanasoff even to remove the cover from his computer so that he could get a look at it. In general, Mauchly's memory of his experience in Ames in 1941 did grow stronger over time. This might be entirely natural, since his interrogators were constantly refreshing his memory with copies of letters he had written and other reminders. On the other hand, it is hard to account for the certainty with which he professed, in the earlier sessions, not to have seen or understood things that he later acknowledged seeing and understanding perfectly well.

Now the chief relevance of Atanasoff's add-subtract mechanism, or binary serial adder, to the ENIAC patent case is that it was the first electronic switching circuit of any complexity ever invented; and that, while the ENIAC did not use serial adders, it did use electronic switching circuits throughout.

This adder had constituted an electronic breakthrough because it was the first circuit to interconnect vacuum tubes and resistors to produce desired arithmetic results—in this case, logical results that represented the binary addition or subtraction of two numbers simultaneously entering the adder, digit pair by digit pair, from a rotating drum memory. Atanasoff had taken the traditionally *analog* vacuum tube of radio technology and, for the first time, successfully adapted it to complex *digital* tasks.

Before this breakthrough, there had been so-called scaling circuits or scale-

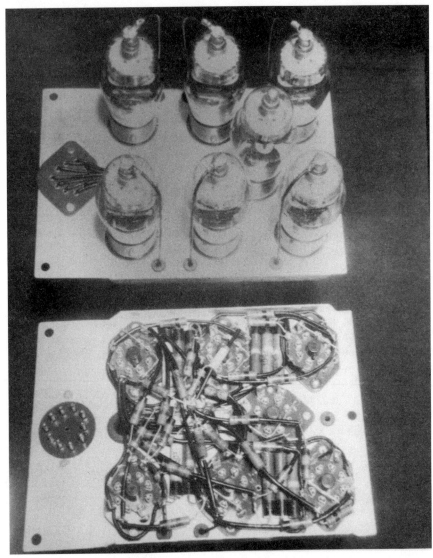

Figure 2. Add-subtract mechanism. These photographs from Atanasoff's 1940 manuscript are top and bottom views of his binary serial adder, the basic component of the ABC's arithmetic unit. The seven vacuum tubes were double triodes, or envelopes, containing fourteen triodes, of which thirteen were active in the circuitry. The add-subtract mechanisms were modular, easily plugged into terminals on the computer and unplugged for inspection, repair, or replacement. Each one measured only five by seven inches.

of-two counters, vacuum-tube devices that *counted* pulses emitted by cosmic-ray detectors, but never any electronic instrument that could receive more than one stream of pulses simultaneously and *add* or *subtract* those streams.

Eckert and Mauchly were to achieve this same goal for the decimal ENIAC; not, however, by adopting Atanasoff's concept of a logical adder but by extending the counting principle. They invented an electronic accumulator based on decimal counters, that is, a unit that added and subtracted decimal numbers by *counting* them one onto another, with the total continually registered. But in so doing they used Atanasoff's principle of interconnecting vacuum tubes and resistors to build switching circuits. Moreover, they used that principle throughout the ENIAC for both arithmetic and control operations.

Atanasoff's bank of thirty binary serial adders, while not the only electronic aspect of his machine, was central to its function and critical to its being deemed an electronic computer at the ENIAC patent trial. Both the *priority* of Atanasoff's electronic computer and the *derivation* of the ENIAC from its electronic principles were cited by Judge Larson as cause for declaring the Eckert-Mauchly patent on the ENIAC invalid (Finding 3).[5]

A secondary but more immediately striking relevance of Atanasoff's adders to the ENIAC patent case is that Eckert and Mauchly, in the design of the EDVAC (Electronic Discrete Variable Computer), abandoned decimal counters for a binary serial adder interacting, not with a separate drum memory as in the ABC, but with another, novel, form of memory, the mercury delay line. And they went on to take out several patents on binary serial adders without reference to Atanasoff's prior invention. These patents, issued in the early 1950s, were discussed at the ENIAC trial as items in a large package of patents that Sperry Rand had acquired in addition to the ENIAC patent. Judge Larson declared all of these Eckert-Mauchly patents unenforceable on a number of serious grounds (Finding 14).[6]

Mauchly's sudden acknowledgment to Halladay of his familiarity with Atanasoff's electronic add-subtract mechanisms long before he and Eckert set about designing the ENIAC was a great concession. As to the rest of the testimony quoted so far, his recall was correct in large part, but incomplete—sometimes surprisingly incomplete in light of the true situation.

Mauchly was right in noting the frequent occurrence of problems entailing the solution of systems of simultaneous linear algebraic equations. Atanasoff, in his August 1940 proposal for the ABC, listed nine broad categories of such problems "in the applied fields of statistics, physics, and technology."[7] For six of these, the problems were expressible directly as sets of linear algebraic equations, which have exact solutions. For the other three categories, the problems took the form of sets of partial differential equations—which could, however, be converted to sets of linear algebraic equations and then solved to an acceptable approximation. Actually, it was large sets of these partial differential equations that Atanasoff and other scientists encountered most often in their research and that, once converted, required working with large sets of linear algebraic equations—*very* large for that day before computers, when sets of even ten were rarely attempted because they were too time-consuming and too susceptible to human error.

Mauchly did see a rotating drum studded with contacts on the surface, those contacts in turn connected to condensers, or capacitors, on the inside. More precisely, he saw *two* such (identical) drums, mounted on the same axle and turning together at the same speed. The contacts were arranged in parallel rings around the drums, each drum having thirty rings and each ring fifty contacts. Each contact represented one binary digit, or *bit*, ("0" or "1"), so that each ring stored one fifty-place, or fifty-bit, serial number and each drum stored up to thirty such numbers.

These two memory drums had different functions, in accord with the computer's purpose, which was, as Mauchly testified, to solve sets of simultaneous linear equations. The ABC was designed to solve sets of up to twenty-nine equations in twenty-nine variables, or unknowns, using a novel variant of the common Gaussian elimination procedure of high school algebra. The binary numbers on the rings of fifty contact studs circling each drum were the coefficients and constant term of an equation in up to twenty-nine variables, so that the two drums together held two complete equations of up to thirty terms (twenty-nine coefficients and one constant term) in a given set, or, for elimination purposes, one pair that could be made to interact arithmetically.

The two drums' functions were controlled from the separate arithmetic unit, which received two streams of pulses representing one pair of equations—thirty binary serial numbers in parallel from each drum—into its thirty add-subtract mechanisms, processed them, and returned results to the drums. Atanasoff's variant on Gauss retained Gauss's overall procedure, or algorithm, consisting in a *forward* part and a *backward* part. For the forward part, repeatedly pair off equations in the original set and operate on those pairs in such a way as to eliminate a designated variable from one equation of each pair, thus creating a new set of equations in one fewer variables; then repeatedly pair off equations in that new set and eliminate another designated variable; and so on, until a "set" of just one equation in one variable is achieved. For the backward part, work back up from this single-variable equation through equations in two, then three, then four variables, and so on until a complete set of single-variable equations is achieved. In short, the goal of the forward part was to achieve a single equation in a single variable, and the goal of the backward part was to achieve such a single-variable equation for each of the variables in the original set.

Now the critical difference is that Gauss's algorithm entailed all four arith-

Figure 3. Rear view of the ABC as of August 1940. This close-up shows the two main storage drums in place on their axle, the "counter" drum on the left and the "keyboard" drum on the right. Between and beyond them can be seen the backs of three add-subtract mechanisms, and above these the three terminal blocks to which the plug-in sockets of the add-subtract mechanisms were connected.

---

metic operations, whereas Atanasoff's entailed only addition and subtraction. And it *was* a critical difference, because multiplying and dividing automatically would have been much harder to accomplish. Atanasoff turned to the idea that multiplication can be achieved by a series of additions, division by a series of subtractions. See table 1 for a quick comparison of the two algorithms, as applied to a set of just two equations in two variables, written in the decimal mode and involving whole numbers only.

Atanasoff's treatment of the forward part of the procedure, as depicted in the table, paralleled Gauss's, as each treatment eliminated the same variable from the pair of equations and arrived at the same single-variable equation. This parallelism would also prevail for a larger set of equations as, again, each treatment eliminated designated variables from successive pairs of equations until the desired single-variable equation emerged. The general elimination rule for Gauss was: divide the designated variable's coefficient in the first equation by its coef-

	(1) 2x + 3y − 7 = 0
	(2) x + y − 3 = 0

Gauss	Atanasoff
Forward:	Forward:
Divide the x-coefficient of (1) by the x-coefficient of (2) and multiply (2) through by the quotient 2, getting a new but equivalent equation: (2′) 2x + 2y − 6 = 0	Subtract (2) from (1) twice: (1) 2x + 3y − 7 = 0 (2) x + y − 3 = 0 (3) x + 2y − 4 = 0 (2) x + y − 3 = 0 (4) y − 1 = 0
Subtract (2′) from (1): (1) 2x + 3y − 7 = 0 (2′) 2x + 2y − 6 = 0 (3) y − 1 = 0	Backward:
	Subtract (4) from (1) three times: (1) 2x + 3y − 7 = 0 (4) y − 1 = 0 (5) 2x + 2y − 6 = 0 (4) y − 1 = 0 (6) 2x + y − 5 = 0 (4) y − 1 = 0 (7) 2x − 4 = 0
Backward:	
Solve (3) for y, getting y = 1	
Substitute 1 for y in (2): (4) x + 1 − 3 = 0	
Solve for x, getting x = 2.	Solve (4) for y (no division necessary since y-coefficient is 1), getting y = 1
	Solve (7) for x (dividing constant term 4 by x-coefficient 2), getting x = 2.

Table 1. Atanasoff's Variant of Gauss's Algorithm

---

ficient in the second equation, multiply the second equation through by the quotient, and subtract this new equation from the first equation. Since the designated variable's coefficients in the two equations were now identical, the subtraction eliminated that variable and achieved a new equation in one fewer variables. The general rule for Atanasoff was: subtract [or add] the two equations repeatedly until the coefficient of the designated variable is eliminated, thereby also achieving a new equation in one fewer variables.

The two algorithms diverged drastically, however, for the backward part.

Here Gauss immediately solved for the variable in his ultimate single-variable equation by dividing the constant term by the variable's coefficient; substituted that solution in an equation with that variable and one other to solve for this second variable; substituted his two solutions in an equation in three variables to solve for the third variable; and so on, successively achieving equations in one variable, solving for each in turn with a division of constant term by coefficient, and executing further substitutions until all variables were solved.

Instead of Gauss's back-substitutions, Atanasoff continued to apply his pairing operation as in the forward part. He paired his ultimate single-variable equation with an equation in two variables and added or subtracted them enough times to eliminate the first variable and achieve an equation in the second variable. He then paired each of these two single-variable equations in turn with an equation in three variables, adding or subtracting enough times to achieve a third equation in a single variable; and so on until he had a complete set of single-variable equations. Note that one *division* for each variable did now become necessary, that is, a division of each single-variable equation's constant term by its coefficient. Atanasoff decided to perform those divisions off-line, on the standard desk calculator of his day. Note also that he had been working with binary numbers, made possible by an initial conversion of the coefficients and constant terms of a set of decimal equations to binary, and now he had to convert his solution coefficients and constant terms back to decimal in order to do these divisions; but, of course, he required his final solutions in decimal form anyway.

Obviously, in the practical application both Gauss's and Atanasoff's algorithms would be considerably more complex than is evident from our two-equation example; Atanasoff's in particular as he worked with fifty-bit serial additions and subtractions and executed these operations simultaneously on up to twenty-nine equations of thirty terms each. For Gauss, his divisions and multiplications would inevitably produce fractions (or decimals) to manipulate. For Atanasoff, the fact that his binary numbers would not work out evenly, either, meant that he had to introduce means of sign detection and shifting; that is, his computer had to recognize when a subtraction or addition of coefficients of his designated variable passed zero, then shift one place and proceed with the opposite operation (a process called non-restoring division, because an alternative would have been to restore the last operation that had caused the calculation to pass zero and then shift).[8]

<<<>>>

We return now to the ABC as Mauchly experienced it in Ames, Iowa, that mid-June of 1941. As we have said, there were two identical memory drums with different functions, although Mauchly spoke mistakenly at trial of just one. The function of one of Atanasoff's drums was to store the numbers to be subtracted from or added to those on the other drum, and the function of that other drum was to store the accruing differences or sums. Atanasoff named the drum that held the numbers to be repeatedly subtracted or added the *keyboard* drum and the one that continually held the results the *counter* drum, after similarities he saw, respectively, to the keyboard and the counting registers of the mechanical adding machines of his day. The analogy is quite loose, however. The numbers entered onto both the keyboard drum and the counter drum at the start of each elimination procedure came from punched cards, not from a keyboard, and totals accrued on the counter drum came from the logical adders of the arithmetic unit, not from counters.

This procedure of simultaneously adding or subtracting thirty pairs of numbers, or *words*, would today be called vector processing. In view of Mauchly's claim that he rejected the ABC because it was to solve only this one "very special class of problems," we might observe that the first supercomputers were built explicitly for the rapid execution of such parallel operations on vectors. Note here that it was because this basic procedure was a vector procedure that Atanasoff required thirty (identical) serial binary adders, working in parallel, each processing the bits of one equation coefficient as received serially from the two drums and returning the result to one of those drums.

The two equations on the memory drums at the start of each elimination procedure were entered from $8\frac{1}{2}$"-by-11" binary cards, one card per equation. After a designated variable was eliminated from this pair, the resulting equation in one fewer variables was read out onto another, blank, binary card. Once a complete set of equations in one fewer variables had been calculated and collected on binary cards, this new set was ready to be subjected to the same elimination procedure, pair by pair. Entering numbers on and reading numbers from the drums was done via the add-subtract mechanisms.

Communication back and forth between the memory drums and the arithmetic unit was over two sets of insulated electric wires with brushes at the drum end. As the drums rotated, numbers were read from the surface contacts by these brushes and sent to the add-subtract mechanisms over one set of wires. Similarly, numbers were returned to the two drums over the other set of wires and written on the contacts from brushes.

Although Mauchly could not recall how many add-subtract mechanisms he had seen, he did recall that there were to be thirty of them. Actually, Atanasoff had written in his August 1940 proposal that all thirty add-subtract mechanisms were finished, so that the set was complete long before Mauchly's visit.

As indicated earlier, because the original equations to be solved were in decimal form, any elimination procedure had to be preceded by the conversion of the original equations to binary form. This entailed converting fifteen-place decimal numbers to their fifty-place binary counterparts; it was done from standard (IBM) cards punched with the decimal coefficients and placed on a nonstandard decimal-card reader designed by Atanasoff. The decimal numbers were converted, via a base-conversion drum and the add-subtract mechanisms, onto the counter drum, then read off onto binary cards. (Atanasoff reversed this procedure, at the end of a problem run, to read his binary solutions out onto decimal dials.)

The decimal-binary conversion system had been constructed well before Mauchly's visit. Also completed by then and constituting part of its arithmetic unit was another set of thirty vacuum-tube devices, the computer's restore-shift mechanisms, which were clustered in a single module. Atanasoff had decided to use capacitors as memory elements only after realizing that their charges could be restored—refreshed, recharged, or regenerated—with each drum rotation, by vacuum tubes in the arithmetic unit. He also realized that the sums or differences being sent to the counter drum would be restored automatically as they were produced by the vacuum tubes of the add-subtract mechanisms. But he had to provide a further set of vacuum-tube mechanisms to refresh the numbers to be returned to the keyboard drum. He then gave these mechanisms a second function, that of shifting the keyboard numbers as required by his variant of Gauss's elimination algorithm.

Mauchly did not mention the restore-shift mechanisms explicitly, but he must have seen them. And we know that he also understood them just as well as he understood the add-subtract mechanisms, because he cited them in his deposition for the 1967 Regenerative Memory case.[9]

As to Mauchly's testimony that he could not recall the nature of demonstrations he had seen in June 1941—or whether he had seen them on the machine or on separate test equipment—the court had already heard Atanasoff's detailed accounts of demonstrations he had given select visitors as early as January of that year.[10]

Atanasoff, too, had distinguished static testing of components on bench equipment from dynamic testing on the computer itself. Individual add-subtract mechanisms were tested on the bench, he said, with results read out on voltmeters, one binary digit per meter. A number of other tests were run on the computer, with one entire binary number, forty-nine digits and sign, displayed on an oscilloscope as a row of hills and valleys. One such test demonstrated the refreshing of rings of capacitors on the keyboard drum; another, the addition and subtraction of two numbers on corresponding rings of capacitors on the counter and keyboard drums; a third, the borrow step of a subtraction; and a fourth, the shifting of a number on the keyboard drum.

Mauchly was correct in recalling that numbers were entered on the memory drums manually during his visit, that is, by touching the external contacts with a battery-driven probe. Atanasoff had testified, however, that Mauchly also saw numbers entered from decimal cards, as in the very beginning of an elimination procedure.[11] The ABC was capable at that time of reading numbers from the decimal-card reader and entering them in binary form on the two memory drums. But

Figure 4. Clifford Berry holding restore-shift mechanisms. This photograph accompanied an article in the January 15, 1941, edition of the *Des Moines Tribune* that told of the "giant computing machine" being built at Iowa State College. It shows Berry holding a module containing all thirty of the ABC's restore-shift mechanisms, three vacuum tubes per mechanism or ninety in all (forty-five envelopes). The picture was captioned "Machine Remembers," and its legend referred to the computer's separate "memory."

Two triodes of each restore-shift mechanism served to restore, or regenerate, the charges on its associated ring of capacitors on the keyboard drum. (Two were needed because the triodes reversed their signals—changed high voltages to low and low voltages to high—as they passed through.) The third triodes of all the mechanisms served to shift the vector represented by all the rings of the keyboard drum as required by Atanasoff's variant of the Gaussian algorithm.

(By permission of the *Des Moines Register.*)

it was not capable of reading the intermediate binary solutions out onto binary cards and returning them from these cards for further processing. Thus the initial decimal data could be read in automatically, but the intermediate binary results had to be taken out or entered manually, with a probe.

In any case, Mauchly surely understood, both from what Atanasoff and Berry told him and from the written proposal, that automatic methods of entering and removing binary data had already been designed and were being built at that time. This procedure, in fact, was the topic of Berry's master's thesis, which had a deadline of July 1, 1941, just two weeks from Mauchly's visit. He also surely understood that the several internal procedures of the computer were to consist of sequences of automatic steps.

Mauchly was far from the mark in stating that Atanasoff's August 1940 proposal was limited to "just describing the utility of wanting to solve certain classes of problems . . . and then some detail—but not very much—as to how you would do it." That document was detailed enough and thorough enough that, on the basis of testimony from expert witnesses, Judge Larson declared it "adequate to enable one of ordinary skill in electronics at that time to make and use an ABC computer" (Finding 3).[12] Because it was so comprehensive, Halladay in his cross-examination pressed Mauchly hard on just how carefully he had read Atanasoff's proposal.[13] He got nowhere for a time, but then was rewarded with another of Mauchly's sudden self-defeating admissions.

When Halladay first broached the subject, Mauchly repeatedly challenged the authenticity of a photocopy of Atanasoff's 1940 manuscript, a Plaintiff's Exhibit that he was handed.[14] He did acknowledge that he had probably read *the one he was given in Iowa* "very carefully," but then backed away from a suggestion that he had read it "with professional care." It was in this rather testy exchange that Mauchly made his surprising admission, one that seemed to reverse his fundamental position on his own inventive aims.

> *Halladay:* Do you want the Court to understand, Dr. Mauchly, that you spent from Friday evening, June 13, 1941, until Wednesday morning of the following week and did not read the Atanasoff manuscript with professional care?
>
> *Mauchly:* It's that phrase "with professional care," I guess, that is the hooker here. I read whatever I read with sufficient care to satisfy myself as to what it was that seemed to be described there, but not—I wasn't interested then in all the details of what was described there, so why should I read details? Now, what you call "professional care," of course, I haven't learned yet.
>
> *Halladay:* Well, I was assuming that you had your own standard of professional care.
>
> *Mauchly:* I did indeed, yes.

Halladay: And it was asked in that sense. Now, if you didn't use your usual standard of professional care in reading the Atanasoff manuscript, then tell us that you didn't.

Mr. DeLone: Well, I object to the form of the question. It's a play on words. The witness wants to know what Mr. Halladay means by professional care, and the term is undefined.

The Court: (To the witness) You may answer.

Mauchly: It may be a little hard for anyone to understand at this late date just what my attitude was and why I did what I did in those days, but I was searching for ideas which might be useful to help me in computing. *I wasn't even thinking about inventing computing machines.* I was just thinking about: Could I build something, for instance, which would help me. But I was looking in various places for better ways of implementing computational jobs, many of which I had in front of me if I wanted to do research work, on weather, and such things.

   I came to Iowa with much the same attitude that I went to the World's Fair and other places. Is there something here which would be useful to aid my computations or anyone else's computations? Once there I found out rather quickly the general nature of what Dr. Atanasoff's machine was intended to do and how he was intending to do this. I no longer became interested in the details. . . . [italics added]

. . .

Halladay: [Do you mean] that all you were interested in in the manuscript was the highlights?

Mauchly: Well, I won't say I wasn't interested in the way he described the various applications that this machine was good for. It's always interesting to see how somebody else puts in words things that you already know and you want to see how they treated them, but when it comes down to what today we would call the nitty gritty details of how he implemented or intended to implement something, this was not something that I was particularly interested in. In fact, it's something I probably wouldn't retain very well by memory. And he told me I couldn't take anything home with me. So I was more interested, as I say, in general discussions with Dr. Atanasoff than I was in trying to photographically memorize a book, which I did not do.

Halladay: I didn't suggest that and I still don't know whether you read the manuscript . . . with any kind of care. . . .

Atanasoff, on the other hand, had testified in his pretrial deposition that Mauchly not only read the booklet but discussed it at length with him.[15]

We discussed it in the evening. We discussed it during the day. We discussed it, as far as I could see, in detail. I know of no part of it that was not covered in discussion at this time.

More recently, in the July 1984 *Annals of the History of Computing*, Atanasoff has written of providing Mauchly "white bond paper" on which to take notes from his manuscript.[16] Berry, too, mentioned Mauchly's notes in a March 1963 letter to R. K. Richards cited by Control Data in its 1967 deposition of Mauchly.[17] Mauchly himself, in that same deposition, stated that so far as he knew he "never made any notes whatsoever" on what he learned of Atanasoff's computer.[18] On the other hand, Lura, Atanasoff's wife at the time, mentioned in her deposition for that earlier case that Mauchly had "even" jotted down a note at the dinner table as her husband talked about his machine.[19]

Unfortunately, what would have been invaluable testimony by Clifford Berry on this and many other aspects of Mauchly's visit was precluded by his untimely death, by suicide, in October 1963. (His widow, Jean R. Berry, gives a fine account of his career, including his work on the Atanasoff-Berry Computer, in the October 1986 issue of the *Annals of the History of Computing*.[20] She could not accept that her husband took his own life; she—like Atanasoff, she writes—suspects foul play.)

On the one point, then, of how carefully Mauchly studied Atanasoff's 1940 proposal, it did in the end come down to one man's word against the other's. The thoroughness of Atanasoff's recall of details as contrasted with Mauchly's sketchy recall, however, and the impressions the two men made on the stand, led Judge Larson to find for Atanasoff's version. He ruled, first, "Mauchly . . . did read, but was not permitted to take with him, a copy of the comprehensive manuscript," and, second, "The Court has heard the testimony of both Atanasoff and Mauchly, and finds the testimony of Atanasoff with respect to the knowledge and information derived by Mauchly credible" (Finding 3).[21]

Finally, Mauchly's emphasis on not being permitted to take home a copy of the proposal is curious. In those days before photocopying, it was no easy matter to provide a copy of any unpublished work. Atanasoff had just one original and two or three carbon copies of his paper, typed by a secretary. But what is curious is that Mauchly seems to imply that because he did not carry away a copy, Atanasoff was assured that the contents would not be circulated. Yet Mauchly had testified, in the Regenerative Memory case, to freely telling Eckert and others at the University of Pennsylvania's Moore School of Electrical Engineering about Atanasoff's machine and discussing with them its pros and cons for his own purposes.[22]

Mauchly departed drastically from the truth in his long response to the questions defense attorney DeLone asked about Atanasoff's cost estimate for the ABC. He told of his great puzzlement over the figure, "$2.00 per digit," mentioned by Atanasoff during their first meeting on December 28, 1940, at the University of Pennsylvania. But he claimed not to have pursued an explanation in Iowa, because of his great disappointment in the computer itself. Its rotating drum memory, he said, rendered it not fully electronic, not a good basis for the all-electronic general-purpose computer he himself had in mind.

It is true that Mauchly was puzzled by Atanasoff's startlingly low estimate. Back at Ursinus College in nearby Collegeville, he grappled with this figure throughout the spring of 1941, and it was indeed a factor in his driving to Iowa in June to see the computer. But it is not true that the ABC's mechanically rotated memory came as a surprise to Mauchly. His own papers, produced under subpoena, showed that Atanasoff had told him of it when they first met. A drawing made just three days later, on January 1, 1941, depicted a drum or a disk with radial contacts receiving signals from and sending signals to vacuum tubes.[23] Mauchly had written "At. machine" in the lower left-hand corner of this note!

Nor is it true that Mauchly was surprised to find a special-purpose computer when he visited Atanasoff, or even that he had any plan—or intention or hope—of building a general-purpose computer himself. Atanasoff testified in his pretrial deposition that he had mentioned the ABC's purpose in Philadelphia.[24] And at trial he identified a sketch he had drawn on one of the notes Mauchly was making during their discussion of his computer as a layout of coefficients for a system of simultaneous equations.[25]

Atanasoff also testified that "[Mauchly] seemed to be a very nice and likable person, and we seemed to strike up a very warm and cordial relation."[26] This impression led him to go well beyond his usual "stock in trade" of design features to be revealed freely.[27] Yet he did reserve five items that he deemed absolutely essential to his computer's patentability. Atanasoff did not tell Mauchly that the ABC would use capacitors for memory elements; that those capacitors would be regenerated, or refreshed, periodically from the separate arithmetic unit; that it would compute in the binary, not the decimal, system; that it would, accordingly, have base conversion; and that it would perform its arithmetic functions on a logical rather than a counting basis.

For his part, Mauchly recalled his own version of Atanasoff's omissions in their Philadelphia talk with some bitterness. He said that "the most" Atanasoff did was to make him "very curious" by representing his computer as the sort of "very low cost device" he himself was seeking.[28] He remembered that Atanasoff had told him his machine used vacuum tubes, but the matter of *how* it used them "was exactly the point where he was saying if I wanted to know anything more about this, I would have to go to Iowa."[29] He thought the computer's purpose, other than doing arithmetic, may have been withheld as "part of what I had to go to Iowa to learn."[30] He called the ABC's regenerative memory "the secret teaser which he was reserving to lure me to Iowa."[31]

Mauchly did agree that Atanasoff had promised to tell him "all about" his computer if he came to Iowa.[32] From his point of view, though, his testimony indicated that he could have been spared a lot of pondering, a long trip, and ultimate disappointment if Atanasoff had simply told him all about his computer in their first meeting.

<<<>>>

Even though Mauchly knew of the separate drum memory before he actually saw the ABC, it was not memory elements that concerned him in the spring of 1941. Instead, he concentrated on counters, simply assuming that Atanasoff's digital electronic arithmetic devices had to be counters—or, rather, registers made up of counters.

Among the many features of Atanasoff's computer that attracted Mauchly to Iowa, then, perhaps the most enticing was his own expectation of learning how to build vacuum-tube counters to perform arithmetic operations. Atanasoff, however, had already explored that route and rejected it! For he had discovered a simpler and cheaper way to add and subtract with vacuum tubes, in the process interlocking two remarkably novel and enduring concepts of electronic computation: the concept of separate but cooperating memory and arithmetic unit, the former holding the working data at any given moment, the latter performing the required arithmetic operations; and the concept of periodic memory regeneration.

As Atanasoff explained in his 1940 manuscript, he conceived the large memory first, with very cheap (capacitor) elements to be recharged by separate vacuum-tube devices. His decision to use the Gaussian pairing algorithm to solve the large sets of equations he constantly encountered in his research had led him to seek a memory with a capacity for two very long equations. His need to communicate with separate electronic devices had further inspired the concept of mounting the capacitors on a rotating drum, as an economical way of accessing the information they held.

With this storage idea rather firmly fixed, Atanasoff set about constructing an electronic device to perform the required additions and subtractions of paired binary numbers. Like Mauchly, he first assumed that this would be a counter, the standard mechanism of the day for digital computation, found (in decimal form) in both the mechanical desk calculators and the electromechanical punched-card tabulators. But he had difficulty in designing a counter to add numbers serially, rather than in parallel as those machines did.

Then, suddenly, he realized that a counter encompasses both arithmetic and storage. It adds (counts upward) or subtracts (counts downward) *and* it continually stores (registers) the total. Atanasoff now saw that he had already provided for just such storage of successive totals on one of his two memory drums (the one that he called the counter drum). With this storage aspect taken care of, all that remained was the arithmetic aspect: the addition or subtraction of the successive digits of a pair of numbers as they entered an arithmetic mechanism from the two drums, so as to return the sum or difference to that total-storing drum. For these operations, he did not have to count! He could use binary logic!

He drew up what logicians would call a truth table, giving the four possible combinations of two binary digits that would enter one of his arithmetic devices and, corresponding to these combinations, the appropriate sum or difference. Then he designed a thirteen-tube device, his add-subtract mechanism, to execute these functions.

It was not as simple or straightforward as this presentation makes it sound, of course. Atanasoff had to design a third drum, on which carry and borrow digits could be remembered momentarily and returned to the add-subtract mechanisms simultaneously with the paired digits arriving from the main memory drums. And he had to take these carry-borrow digits into account in his truth table.

He had to design resistor networks to interconnect the vacuum tubes of the add-subtract mechanism so that these complex logical functions would be executed. And he had to arrange for communication between the capacitors of the rotating memory and the vacuum tubes of the stationary arithmetic unit, as numbers flowed back and forth between them—taking account, as well, of the differing voltage levels of the tubes and the capacitors.

Lastly, he had to design the restore-shift mechanisms to work with the add-subtract mechanisms in refreshing the capacitors of the keyboard and the counter drums and in shifting the numbers of the keyboard drum as needed.

Mauchly must have been amazed when he first viewed those thirty add-subtract mechanisms, together with the thirty restore-shift mechanisms, mounted on the computer in lieu of the counters he was expecting. He must have been surprised at the size of that sixty-word memory, to and from which data were transmitted. And he must have been fascinated by the descriptions of both the regenerative memory system and the electronic arithmetic devices laid out in Atanasoff's 1940 manuscript.

He must have been amazed by Atanasoff's use of the binary number system for all internal computation, and by his further arrangements for base conversion at the start and finish of a problem run. He had to be impressed with the ingenious algorithm by which Atanasoff was able to avoid the complexities of multiplication and division and to perform all his procedures, including base conversions, through the repeated interaction of his main memory and his arithmetic unit.

Finally, Mauchly had to be impressed with that $2.00-per-digit estimate, which was right on target. The 1,500 binary digits stored on each drum meant a total of 3,000 digits in action at any given moment in the calculations, and 3,000 times $2.00 is $6,000, just slightly below the final cost of the entire project!

But Mauchly, at trial, dismissed all these features, and the entire computer, out of hand. He had been led to expect a fully electronic computer, because—so far as he could recall—he had not been told that it was *not* fully electronic. Here, in his judgment, was "a mechanical gadget which uses some electronic tubes," but was not at all "what I was interested in from the point of view of electronic speed gadgets." Moreover, he said, while it was clearly Atanasoff's "privilege" to construct a machine to solve simultaneous linear equations, he, Mauchly, wanted to construct "general purpose machines"—retaining the stricture, of course, that they be both all electronic and very cheap.

Figure 5. Top view of finished ABC, May 1942. The "keyboard" storage drum is exposed in this photograph, while the "counter" storage drum is covered by its casing. To the left of the keyboard drum is the smaller base-conversion drum, with bundles of wires to carry its signals to other parts of the computer. The large tray in the front left corner received blank binary cards, one at a time, to be passed through a recording mechanism at the extreme left, and the large tray next to it received the recorded cards to be read back into the computer by a similar mechanism. A keyboard of manual controls is partly visible at the top right. Between it and the binary-card recording tray is the somewhat elevated decimal-card reader, by which the initial decimal data were entered for base conversion and recording on the storage drums.

Visible on the face of the computer are, to the left, thyratrons (gas tubes) used in recording on and reading from the binary cards and, to the right, triodes (vacuum tubes) of a few of the add-subtract mechanisms. The restore-shift mechanisms are out of sight, just to the left of the thyratrons. Also out of sight, on the extreme top right, is the carry-borrow drum. The Atanasoff-Berry Computer was about the size of an office desk, but taller.

And so it was that Mauchly testified in the ENIAC trial that Atanasoff's computer, this remarkably integrated, completely novel electronic computer—the first ever invented—was beneath his consideration in 1941. And so it was that he defended this position with a number of claims as to what he himself had aspired to before seeing the ABC, what he had learned of it before seeing it, and what he learned of it once he did see it.

What Mauchly was doing in this testimony was anticipating features of the ENIAC that he first formulated, in the broadest terms, more than a year after his exposure to Atanasoff's computer.[33] Eckert and Mauchly did reject Atanasoff's slow drum memory and opt instead for counters for the ENIAC. And they did make it a general-purpose computer. On the other hand, the ENIAC could hardly have been said to be all electronic, with its time-consuming manual setup. Nor was it exactly cheap, at a cost of over $400,000 and a limitation of just twenty words of read-write (as distinguished from read-only) memory, in its twenty accumulators, as against Atanasoff's sixty words, on his two drums.

Mauchly was also overlooking the use that he and Eckert made, in both the ENIAC and the ensuing EDVAC, of Atanasoff's startling breakthrough in electronic technology, his successful adaptation of vacuum tubes to complex digital tasks. And—at least as importantly—he was completely bypassing the further use that he and Eckert made of Atanasoff's ideas in their basic conception of the EDVAC, where they abandoned counters for an adder to be used in conjunction with a separate memory. They could not have made this shift without Atanasoff's concept of such arithmetic devices separate from but working in conjunction with a large electronically regenerated read-write memory. Only when Eckert later conceived the mercury-delay-line memory, continually refreshed by vacuum-tube circuits, did they decide to abandon the old counting principle. Note here that the EDVAC was not a vector computer, and so required only one adder (still binary serial and still based on Atanasoff's logic principle), whereas the ABC required its bank of thirty adders.

The overriding factor, of course, in Mauchly and Eckert's choice both of counters for the ENIAC and of an adder for the EDVAC, was one of speed. Eckert's counter, operating at 100,000 pulses per second, could far outdo Atanasoff's combination of electronic adders and mechanically rotated drum memory. In this regard, it should be noted that whereas the ABC's adders were limited to an operating speed of just sixty pulses per second, they were of course capable of much greater speed; they were limited by the memory drums' rotation rate of once per second, which in turn was dictated by the slow rate at which the binary cards could be written on.

The mercury delay line, on the other hand, could keep up with an electronic adder. In the dimension of speed alone, then—and speed is the key to many other advances—the EDVAC was superior to the ENIAC and the ENIAC was superior to the ABC. Yet both owed the ABC a fundamental debt for their basic electronics, and the EDVAC owed a further debt for the concept of a separate regenerative memory interacting with a binary serial adder.

Just as Eckert and Mauchly took out the ENIAC patent and several binary serial adder patents without reference to Atanasoff's work or their acquaintance with it, so they also took out the Regenerative Memory patent as entirely their own. And just as Judge Larson found their ENIAC patent invalid and their adder patents unenforceable, so he found their Regenerative Memory patent unenforceable—because of derivation from Atanasoff (Finding 14).[34]

Atanasoff's rotating drum memory, which Mauchly claimed to see as rendering the ABC primarily "a mechanical gadget," established three firsts that remain critical features of electronic computers to this day. Virtually all computers make fundamental use of *memory regeneration*. The Dynamic Random Access Memory (DRAM) chips of both personal computers and mainframes make fundamental use of *capacitor memory* elements—for the same reason Atanasoff did: economy. And, yes, personal computers and mainframes make fundamental use of *mechanically rotating memories*, in the form of hard disks and floppies—again, for Atanasoff's reason: accessibility.

In the end, the inescapable truth is that Mauchly took many basic electronic computing principles from Atanasoff's Iowa State laboratory to the Moore School of Electrical Engineering, some that he and Eckert used in the ENIAC and more that they used in the EDVAC, the BINAC (Binary Automatic Computer), and the UNIVAC (Universal Automatic Computer).

Mauchly, however, was unwilling to acknowledge his debt to Atanasoff, either in the patenting process from 1947 to 1964, or in court in 1971. He testified, again and again, to his disappointment in the ABC, once he had seen it, because it was not at all what he had had in mind. This disappointment was so keen, he said, as to shut off all interest in what he saw and heard and read, either as a visitor to Atanasoff's laboratory or as a guest in his home.

But was Mauchly disappointed at the time, for whatever reason? Was he not interested? Did he see no use he himself might make of Atanasoff's ideas for electronic computation? The examination of these questions—and the pertinent evidence and testimony—first became a matter of record in the 1967 Regenerative Memory patent case.

TWO

MAUCHLY
IN DEPOSITION

I t was Wednesday, October 11, 1967, four years prior to Mauchly's appearance before Judge Larson in the ENIAC patent trial. Again, the dispute involved Sperry Rand, but now Sperry Rand was the plaintiff, suing Control Data for infringement of the Regenerative Memory patent—that is, for use of the concept of memory regeneration in their computers. Like the ENIAC patent, the Regenerative Memory patent had been taken out by J. Presper Eckert and John W. Mauchly and passed along to Sperry Rand via Remington Rand. And, like Honeywell in the ENIAC case, Control Data was challenging the patent's validity, charging derivation from John V. Atanasoff.

This time the place was not the United States District Courthouse in Baltimore, where the suit had been filed, but the Land Title Building in Philadelphia. And the witness, Mauchly, though still under oath, was not on the stand but in pretrial deposition. Indeed, no courtroom testimony was ever taken in this case, probably because the pretrial depositions were themselves so revealing. The suit broke off after a few weeks of actual trial in 1972, to be settled secretly nine years later. An odd twist is that in the meantime, in 1973, Judge Larson went beyond his finding of invalidity for the ENIAC patent and found the Regenerative Memory patent unenforceable, on that very ground of derivation from Atanasoff.

Mauchly was deposed by attorney Allen Kirkpatrick, who had subpoenaed him on behalf of Control Data. Attorney Laurence B. Dodds represented Sperry Rand and Mauchly. Dodds chose not to cross-examine Mauchly, partly because in that pretrial setting it was both risky and unnecessary to press a witness who was on his own side, but also because he was as confounded as Mauchly by the documents Kirkpatrick set before them, one after another. Dodds did interrupt, frequently, to object to questions and to instruct Mauchly not to answer.

Kirkpatrick began by reading into the record the conditions under which Mauchly had been subpoenaed, namely, that he was to bring in *all* his documents relating to any design of, plan for, or activity concerning computers prior to October 31, 1947, the date of the Regenerative Memory patent application.[1] (The patent was issued in 1953.) Mauchly replied somewhat tentatively that he had brought in "a collection" from his filing cabinets, and Kirkpatrick said that he would be referring to that collection later.

This exchange makes clear that Kirkpatrick had not seen these Mauchly papers before, and—strangely enough—Dodds made clear later that he had not seen them either.[2] Mauchly, in fact, testified that Sperry Rand had never previously requested *any* such papers from him.[3] And—even more strangely—Mauchly himself had not reviewed what he now brought in, but had just pulled out file folders, "first by tab and second by cursory inspection of the contents."[4] Dodds did take the opportunity to examine the papers overnight.[5]

After quizzing Mauchly at length on his education and his teaching, research, and business pursuits, Kirkpatrick zeroed in on his Ursinus College period, 1933 to 1941. He then turned to Mauchly's transition to the Moore School of Electrical Engineering in June of 1941—there to enroll in an electronics course for which master's candidate Eckert was the lab instructor.[6] Atanasoff's name entered the picture on the second day. Mauchly cited him as the one person of possible significance outside the Moore School with whom he had discussed computers before August 1942, when he first proposed, in writing, an electronic digital computer.[7]

He told of meeting Atanasoff in Philadelphia, at a session of the American Association for the Advancement of Science, in which he himself gave a paper "on some of my meteorological work having to do with periodicities in precipitation." But he placed that meeting in December *1939* instead of *1940*, an error that Kirkpatrick did not correct—and of which Dodds hadn't a clue—as Mauchly fumbled through the many pieces of surprise evidence the Control Data attorney presented.

Mauchly went on to tell of his trip to Iowa.[8]

> I apparently had indicated in my paper . . . that I had been devising electronic and electrical computing devices in order to aid me in my work.
>
> We talked for a short while and I found him somewhat reluctant to say more about what he was doing other than in very general terms, but he gave me an invitation to come to Ames and talk further about their plans, and offered that if I did so he would show me the calculator they were building.
>
> I had no opportunity to do that for more than a year [*sic*] thereafter, but made arrangements in the spring of 1941 to drive to Ames immediately at the

close of my teaching duties at Ursinus, and I did so.

. . .

> My companion on this drive to Ames was my six-year-old son.

Mauchly noted that he and his son "were cordially welcomed by Dr. Atanasoff and I believe stayed at his house for the period of my visit." After telling of a talk he gave in the Physics Building, on the use of his (electrical) harmonic analyzer to analyze weather data, he turned to his experience of Atanasoff's computer.[9]

> With regard to the digital computing device which he had told me about in 1939 [sic], it was evident that there was a hesitation on their part to disclose a great deal about it, and this was in fact explained to me as a conscious, deliberate hesitation because they believed their device novel and patentable and they were apparently fearful that certain large corporations might try to take advantage of them. They were not free with their disclosures.
>
> . . .
>
> Since my first knowledge of this came from Dr. Atanasoff's meeting with me in 1939 [sic], the device had already been at least in the planning stage since 1939, and at this point, a year and a half later, although there was equipment to show there was, so far as I could tell, not yet an operable machine.

But now, as if warming to his subject, Mauchly launched into a long description of the Atanasoff-Berry Computer—actually, one of several—that belied his protest of a limited exposure.[10] This description was surprising both in its detail and in its insight into some of the computer's more ingenious features. Mauchly noted that the decimal-card reader for entering initial data was "by no means a conventional card reader," as it utilized the capacitors of the main memory drums to compute and store the newly converted binary results. He continued:

> All of these capacitors were mounted in a single, revolving cylinder, with every capacitor having one of its terminals connected in common with all others to a slip ring insulated from the main frame of the machine.
>
> The other terminal of each capacitor was connected to a metal contact imbedded in the exterior cylindrical surface of the rotating cylinder, and thus that end of the capacitor was normally open circuit.
>
> Wire brushes similar to those used in IBM equipment for electrical sensing of holes in cards were then mounted in the stationary frame of the machine such that as the cylinder rotated these terminals on the exterior surface of the cylinder would successively make contact with the wire brushes.
>
> I believe the rotational speed of the cylinder was chosen to have some simple relationship with the speed of a synchronous motor from the sixty-cycle supply line.
>
> The drum might then—although I am not sure of this—rotate, say, once per second, or possibly some multiple of this.

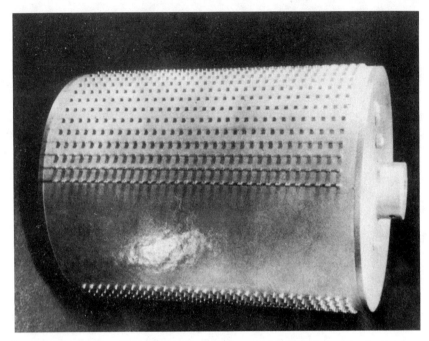

Figure 6. Memory drum. This 1940 photograph of one of the ABC's two main storage drums shows the arrangement of thirty rings of brass contact studs, fifty per ring, around its circumference. Each ring stored one of the thirty binary coefficients of one of a pair of equations from which—as the basic step in Atanasoff's algorithm—a coefficient was to be eliminated. Inside the drum, arranged radially to correspond with the 1,500 studs, were thirty rings of capacitors, with their outer wires connected to the studs, and their inner wires joined and connected to the power supply system through an end mounting plate.

As can be seen here, the rings of studs did not completely encircle the drum. A sixty-degree blank stretch was left to allow one-sixth of a second per rotation for the computer's control circuits to make decisions and order succeeding steps in the solution process. The controls might, for example, determine that it was time to shift the vector on the keyboard drum, or that the designated coefficient had been completely eliminated and it was time to stop adding or subtracting and read the resulting equation out onto a binary card.

Each of the two drums was eight inches in diameter and eleven inches long. Their cylindrical shells were made of a compound similar to Bakelite, and the removable end plates were made of aluminum.

The stationary brushes were then connected to some electronic circuitry which performed two functions.

One function was to regenerate the charges on the condensers [capacitors] so that numbers once stored as charges on those elements could be maintained despite the inevitable leakage due to imperfect insulation.

To make this possible there were, I believe, two brushes in each track of the cylinder, so that a charge sensed by the first brush as the cylinder rotated could then be amplified and restored to the same capacitor an instant later, as that capacitor passed the second brush.

The second function of the electronic circuitry was to perform the necessary arithmetic operations and, therefore, this circuitry essentially functioned as a kind of binary adder.

The precise circuits whereby this was accomplished were not communicated to me, but this much was made evident to me of the general principles by which they hoped this machine would perform its computations successively, adding or subtracting numbers from certain tracks on the drum and putting the results of such arithmetic operations on other tracks of the drum, under a program control which would eventually result in the values representing the solution set of the simultaneous equations whose coefficients had been entered.

Mauchly then addressed the ABC's binary-card input-output system.

The output device was again a novel one in that the binary numbers were recorded on punch cards, not by punching but by using a higher voltage spark to rupture the dielectric paper of the punch paper card and create what you might describe as a minute pinhole in the card.

It was claimed that such cards could then be read in again because of the fact that a smaller voltage spark would penetrate a position already so ruptured but would not penetrate those positions of the card which had not been ruptured by the spark.

Mauchly here showed a remarkable recollection of the ABC, some twenty-six years after his visit to Atanasoff's laboratory. His sole technical error was that of recalling a single memory drum instead of two. He was even right about the rotation rate of once per second for this main memory and its timing by a synchronous motor from the [building's] sixty-cycle supply line. Later he was to comment that the "[binary] card movement had to be synchronized with the rotation of the drum," and, indeed, these two had to be further synchronized with the firing of sparks to punch and read cards as Mauchly described that process.[11]

Despite this impressive overview, Mauchly continued to claim very little exposure to the ABC.[12] He recalled spending "perhaps a half hour in the presence of this incomplete device," about which "there was no great enthusiasm on anyone's part to make a full disclosure." Pressed by Kirkpatrick, he allowed that he "might have spent an hour or an hour and a half." But, here again, he went on to furnish further details of the ABC, this time of its physical appearance at the time of his visit.

Mauchly did stress, however, throughout his Regenerative Memory deposition, that no matter how much he had learned in his brief time with the computer, he had learned only *what* it was supposed to do, not *how* or even *whether* its var-

Figure 7. Binary-card trays and rollers. Atanasoff departed from the traditional method of "writing" on and "reading" from cards, namely, punching them mechanically at certain points on a grid and later detecting the punched holes, again mechanically. He invented a novel electronic sparking method of writing on cards by arcing through them from one set of electrodes to another. Each such arc left a small burn, or char, at some particular point on the card's grid. It may also have left a tiny pinhole, but this was incidental to the char: a card was read by detecting the charred spots, this time by arcing between sets of electrodes at voltages too low to char an uncharred spot but high enough to pass through a charred one.

In representing the binary digits of coefficients of equations on cards, Atanasoff chose to let each charred spot signify a "1," each uncharred spot a "0." He found that he could safely fit an entire binary equation (of thirty terms) on the grid of an $8^1/_2$"-by-11" card, that is, on a grid with thirty rows by fifty columns of "spots" corresponding to the thirty rings of fifty binary digits on each of his main memory drums. He could then transfer each equation, whether writing it from a drum onto a card or reading it from a card onto a drum, in one one-second drum rotation.

The photograph shows the writing tray on the left and the reading tray on the right. Each had two small hooks at the front to pass a card into the rollers at the back. As a blank card passed through the rollers of the writing tray, 5,000-volt arcs burned points on the card's grid where "1s" were relayed from a memory drum via the add-subtract mechanisms. Later in the solution process, as that same card passed through the rollers of the reading tray, 1,600-volt arcs penetrated the card only at points already charred, relaying these "1s" to a memory drum, also via the add-subtract mechanisms. This sparking process was controlled by both vacuum tubes and thyratrons (gas tubes).

ious systems worked.[13] In particular, he denied seeing the electronic adding and restoring circuits in action or having their design disclosed to him.[14] Not until the ENIAC trial did he finally admit both his understanding of the add-subtract mechanisms and his conviction that they worked as intended.

Mauchly also insisted in his Regenerative Memory deposition—as he would later in the ENIAC trial—that he had learned nothing to suit his own aspirations from his contact with Atanasoff. He cited, in particular, the ABC's mechanically rotated drum memory and the feeling he shared with Eckert at the Moore School that relying on such a memory "in what was otherwise an electronic machine, was a poor way to start out."[15]

The counterargument here is the same as in the later lawsuit. Mauchly was ignoring the fact that he and Eckert did use electronic switching circuits—first invented by Atanasoff—throughout the ENIAC, and did also use electronic memory regeneration and an electronic binary serial adder—both first invented by Atanasoff—as the central concept of the EDVAC.

Now Control Data attorney Kirkpatrick was primarily interested in the EDVAC and its regenerative mercury-delay-line memory as patented by Eckert and Mauchly. He seemed surprised by Mauchly's ready admission that the ABC also had a regenerative memory, electronically refreshed.[16] What Mauchly would not concede, again to Kirkpatrick's apparent surprise, was that he had first learned of such a memory from Atanasoff.[17] He suggested that he might have conceived of regeneration on his own, at some point, although he really did not know when or how he had first learned of it. This was a question, he said, that he "had not thought much about before."

Kirkpatrick responded by reading him a paragraph from an article Eckert had published in October 1953, in *Proceedings of the Institute of Radio Engineers*.[18] The paragraph opened with the sentence, "Probably the first example of what might generally be termed regenerative memory was developed earlier than 1942 by Atanasoff in Iowa," and it went on to describe (and praise) Atanasoff's form of regenerative memory.

Mauchly then shifted from the issue of priority of invention to the position that priority was irrelevant to the invention of the EDVAC's regenerative memory! Kirkpatrick, he said, was "separating the idea of the regenerative aspects of a storage system from whether they are all electronic or not" and so was "asking questions about the mere idea of regeneration of storage," whereas he and Eckert had been "considering practical and economic means for getting electronic regenerative storage."

If Mauchly was in trouble with his admission that the ABC's memory was regenerative, he was in deeper trouble with this attempt to explain it away. For he and Eckert were not entitled to appropriate Atanasoff's prior idea of a regenerative memory simply because their application of it was more advanced. Furthermore, their mercury-delay-line memory was *not* all electronic, since it, too, relied on mechanical motion, the vibration of mercury in a tube. Its great advantage over Atanasoff's rotating-drum version was its speed, equal to that of the EDVAC's electronic circuitry. Basically, both forms of memory could be considered electronic only in that they were integral parts of *memory systems* that "remembered" through the good graces of external vacuum-tube circuits.

Mauchly did not entirely abandon his denial of Atanasoff's priority, however, but restated his "feeling" that "it would be possible to find earlier examples of regenerative systems" than Atanasoff's if one went looking for them "in mechanical or . . . fluid or other systems, and perhaps even part electronic systems."

With Mauchly unable to produce any documentation of the existence of the concept before Atanasoff's work, Kirkpatrick decided to let the priority issue rest there. He stipulated only that Sperry Rand attorney Dodds provide him with copies of any newfound documents—whether Mauchly's own or someone else's—showing an earlier regenerative memory than Atanasoff's. No such evidence was ever found, for this case or the ENIAC case.

Kirkpatrick next raised a startling question about Mauchly's intent in taking out this patent: Was the patent meant to prevent Atanasoff "from making that machine that he had out there [in Iowa]?"[19] Mauchly protested indignantly, on this and several later occasions, that he had no such intention. He seemed, though, not to recall just what forms of memory the patent actually covered, other than its main "embodiment of an electronic device which also employed a sonic delay line for storage." Kirkpatrick did not point out to Mauchly what forms were covered, but did hand him a copy of the patent.

Because it is not the purpose of pretrial depositions to prove a case but only to gather material on which to build one, Kirkpatrick never said why he had made such an inquiry. The question did arise again, as an arguing point in the ENIAC trial, where the case *was* being made. There the Honeywell side demonstrated not only that the ABC's memory system was the original regenerative memory, but that Eckert and Mauchly, in their patent, had actually included an electrostatic (capacitor) rotating store—clearly Atanasoff's invention, Mauchly acknowledged—as their own! They included it both as an "embodiment" of their concept and as a "claim" to patent protection.[20]

This fact, then, was what Kirkpatrick was aiming at, with his seemingly impertinent question. Under the Eckert-Mauchly Regenerative Memory patent, Atanasoff would indeed have had to get their permission to build a computer with the ABC's memory system!

As to Mauchly's other argument against Kirkpatrick's separation of the "mere idea" of regeneration from the form of a particular memory, in their patent he and Eckert made that same separation themselves. They began with a general definition of the regeneration "principle," next described two delay-line systems as "preferred," and then described several mechanically rotating systems as "equivalent to" the delay-line systems because of their common feature of regeneration.[21] In short, they patented not just a number of forms of regenerative memory, including Atanasoff's, but the very concept of regeneration itself, learned, in fact, from him.

<<<>>>

On that second day of his deposition, Mauchly could not recall corresponding with Atanasoff before or after his Ames visit, but thought he must have written to set up that visit.[22] Nor was there, in the eight folders he had collected in response to his subpoena, any correspondence concerning Atanasoff and his computer, either with Atanasoff himself or with anyone else. When, on the third and last day, it became apparent that Kirkpatrick had one such letter, Mauchly explained that he had probably filed it "in a miscellaneous correspondence file" for situations "where I would only have one letter or two."[23]

But the parade of letters to and from Atanasoff went on and on, for a total of eight before the June 1941 visit and three thereafter.[24] Inspecting them one by one, Mauchly tried to cast them as mere preliminaries to his Iowa trip. As this stance grew increasingly strained, he took to citing particular passages to show, for example, "how reluctant the group at Iowa were to make disclosures" (instead of how eager *he* was to learn more), or how long it took him to decide to visit Atanasoff's laboratory, "in that I met him in 1939 [and] he extended an invitation to me, which I did not accept immediately, nor for some time" (whereas he had really met him in 1940).

Even though Kirkpatrick had eleven letters, supplied by Atanasoff, he lacked three others, located later by Mauchly for the ENIAC trial: a letter written by Mauchly on January 19, 1941, three weeks after the Philadelphia meeting; a letter written by Atanasoff on January 23, in reply; and a letter written by Mauchly on June 22, four days after he left Ames. Mauchly also brought to the ENIAC trial a letter he had written on June 28 to a meteorologist friend, H. Helm Clayton, about Atanasoff's computer. Here are the relevant passages of these fifteen letters, in chronological order.

Mauchly to Atanasoff, January 19, 1941:

I am wondering how your plans with regard to computing devices are working out. Need I say again that I await with some suspense the time when you will be able to let me have more information? . . . less than $2 per digit sounds next to impossible, and yet that is what I understood you to say, approximately.

Your suggestion about visiting Iowa seemed rather fantastic when first made, but the idea grows on me. I've gone so far as to note that our Spring

Recess is March 21 to 31, whereas the meetings in Washington are about May 1. . . .

If you aren't too busy, perhaps you can drop a few hints as to your progress.[25]

Atanasoff to Mauchly, January 23, 1941:

Your letter came as a pleasant surprise. . . .

As you know, we have been in active construction on the computing machine for more than a year, and now our plans have assumed rather definite form, and progress is good without too much attention on my part. I am expecting shortly to hear whether or not I will receive a grant-in-aid from an outside source to help in completing the machine. All in all progress is very satisfactory to me, and I expect that our plans will commence to mature in about a year.

. . . Just after my return we had a visit from Dr. S. H. Caldwell of M.I.T. who gave me a rather complete picture of calculating machine activities in the country. . . .

By all means arrange to pay us a visit in Ames during your spring recess. . . . I can think of many things that I would like to talk to you about. . . . I will be glad to have you as my guest while you are in Ames. As an additional inducement I will explain the two dollar per digit business.[26]

Mauchly to Atanasoff, February 24, 1941:

Your invitation and the promised explanation are indeed powerful inducements, and I hope that I shall be able to take advantage of them.

. . .

My crew of N.Y.A. [National Youth Administration] people has been augmented, but perhaps not for the better. The new members are fit only for adding machine work. . . .

We recently had to take the back off of the harmonic analyzer for a few minor adjustments. Some of the IRC 50,000 ohm resistors had aged to the point where they were not within the one percent that we desire. Someday we'll put wire-wounds in and forget them, I hope.

So far we have turned out about 1400 harmonic analyses—each one for eight Fourier coefficients. At 3 minutes per, this has taken just 70 hours. The tabular method that we would otherwise use takes about 5 times as long (but does yield more accurate values, which we do not need for this work). Hence we figure we have saved 280 hours . . . [Mauchly's ellipsis] which is about the amount of time it took to design and build the device. It wouldn't take that long to build another, of course, especially if one purchased precision wire-wound resistors to assemble.

Here's hoping that you have made progress in Iowa, and that I'll get out to see it all.[27]

Atanasoff to Mauchly, March 7, 1941:

> By all means pay us a visit. . . .
>
> Several of the projects which I told you about are progressing satisfactorily. Pieces for the computing machine are coming off the production line, and I have developed a theory of how graininess in photographic material should be described, and have also devised and constructed a machine which directly makes estimates of graininess according to these principles. We will try to have something to interest you when you arrive, if nothing more than a speech which you make.[28]

[Telegram, Mauchly to Atanasoff, March 22, 1941, canceling spring visit]

Mauchly to Atanasoff, March 31, 1941:

> . . . I hope to see you in Washington when you come to the meetings, and you can let me know then how things shape up for a June visit.
>
> I haven't been able to do more than just paper-work for a computing machine here, so I haven't yet found out how practical my ideas are. We've been very busy running barometric pressures through the harmonic analyzer in order to get some more information on the 12-hour tidal oscillation.
>
> It's good to hear that your "production line" is producing. Is there any chance that you can now disclose more information?[29]

Atanasoff to Mauchly, April 22, 1941:

> Please excuse my delay in writing. I am undertaking some of that activity that is taking the country by storm; as a result everything else that I should do suffers.
>
> I shall be at the Washington meeting and am looking forward to seeing you.[30]

Atanasoff to Mauchly, May 21, 1941:

> . . . It was one of my keen disappointments not to be able to see you while in the East. . . . Several matters connected with the defense project which I have undertaken made my visit in the East a very strenuous one. I am looking forward to seeing you in some way or another in the near future.[31]

Mauchly to Atanasoff, May 27, 1941:

> It was a disappointment to me, too, not to get in touch with you while in Washington. . . .
>
> Well, anyway, there is more than a little prospect of my making the trip, starting from here about the tenth of June. I have a passenger who will very likely pay for the gas, and that will help.

From your letters I have gathered that your national defense work is unconnected with the computing machine. This puzzles me, for as I understand it, rapid computation devices are involved in N.D. [National Defense]. In a recent talk with [Professor Irven] Travis, of the E. E. School at U. of Pa. I asked him about this, and the matter seemed the same way to him. But if Caldwell has looked over your plans (I think you said that he was out there) and hasn't seen any N.D. possibilities, I suppose that that means your computer is not considered adaptable to fire control devices, or that they have something even better. Travis (who goes into active duty with Navy this week) pointed out the advantages of lightness and mass-production for electronic computing methods, but said that when he was consulting with General Electric over plans for the G.E. differential integraph [differential analyzer] they figured it would take about one-half million dollars to do the job electronically, and they would only spend 1/5 of that, so they built the mechanical type with polaroid torque-amplifiers.[32]

Atanasoff to Mauchly, May 31, 1941:

I think that it is an excellent idea for you to come west during the month of June. . . . We have plenty of room and will be delighted to have you stay with us while here.

As you may surmise, I am somewhat out of the beaten track of computing machine gossip, and so I am always interested in any details you can give me. The figures on the electronic differential integraph seem absolutely startling. During Dr. Caldwell's last visit here [January 6], I suddenly obtained an idea as to how the computing machine which we are building can be converted into an integraph. Its action would be analogous to numerical integration and not like that of the Bush integraph which is, of course, an analogue machine, but it would be very rapid, and the steps in the numerical integration could be made arbitrarily small. It should therefore equal the Bush machine in speed and excell [sic] it in accuracy.

Progress on the construction of the machine is excellent in spite of the amount of time that defense work is taking, and I am still in a high state of enthusiasm about its ultimate success. I hope to see you within two or three weeks.[33]

Mauchly to Atanasoff, June 7, 1941:

At present I can't say when I shall arrive. . . .

. . . you might expect to hear from me that Friday or Saturday [June 13 or 14], or perhaps find me on your doorstep at some late or early hour.

Enclosed is an announcement that you might find interesting as an example of what goes on around here. I suppose there are similar enterprises all over the country. Pennsylvania is going in for a defense training course for high school graduates, too. I thought I might be teaching in that program, but they haven't notified me of any need for my abilities—and they have hired our chemistry men. One hears, all around, that physicists are in so much demand, but it doesn't seem so in the neighborhood of Collegeville.

I'll finish this letter when I see you.[34]

Mauchly to Atanasoff, June 22, 1941:

The trip back here was uneventful, except for the fact that I was carrying on a mental debate with myself on the question of whether to teach [a defense course for high-school graduates] at Hazleton [Pa.], or to learn something at U. of Pa. My natural avarice for knowledge vied with that for money, and won out, so after obtaining assurance . . . that some one else [could] take the Hazleton work, I dropped that and prepared to become a student again.

I drove to Southbridge, Mass., Friday evening [June 20], and looked through the American Optical plant on Saturday morning. They seemed quite serious in their intentions toward me, but no decision was to be made for several weeks.

On the way back east a lot of ideas came barging into my consciousness, but I haven't had time to sift them or organize them. They were on the subject of computing devices, of course. If any look promising, you may hear more later.

. . . The tubes that I ordered two weeks ago aren't here yet, so I couldn't try anything here even if I had time.

I forgot to ask what happens to Clif Berry after he gets a master's degree— does he stay on for Ph.D. work?

Please give the enclosed note to your wife. We enjoyed our trip very much, and hope you can stop here sometime.[35]

Mauchly to Clayton, June 28, 1941:

Up to a few days ago I was in hope of making a trip to Massachusetts this June with the possibility of returning the Sundstrand machine which you so kindly lent us. Now it appears that I can't do that, and within the week I shall properly pack the machine and forward it by express.

I know this must have inconvenienced you already, and I feel that we owe you a great deal for the loan.

Immediately after commencement here, I went out to Iowa State University to see the computing device which a friend of mine is constructing there. His machine, now nearing completion, is electronic in operation, and will solve within a very few minutes any system of linear equations involving no more than thirty variables. It can be adapted to do the job of the Bush differential analyzer more rapidly than the Bush machine does, and it costs a lot less.

My own computing devices use a different principle, more likely to fit small computing jobs.

While at Iowa, I talked on the construction of harmonic analyzers. . . .

All of my time since coming back from Iowa has been taken up with an Emergency Defense Training Course at the Univ. of Pa. I had a chance to teach for the summer in a defense course given to high school graduates, but turned that down in order to become a student myself. I am working in electrical engineering and electronics. Whether or not I am given a defense job involving electronics later on, the training will be helpful in connection with electronic computing devices.

I haven't had any chance to work on weather problems recently. . . . Let's hope your own work is getting along well.[36]

Mauchly to Atanasoff, September 30, 1941:

This is to let you know that I still have the same living quarters, but a different job. During the summer I looked around a bit while sounding out the Ursinus people as to promotions and assistance; I finally gave up the idea of taking an industrial job (or a navy job) and stayed in the ranks of teaching.

The Moore School of Electrical Engineering is what I have joined up with, and they have me teaching circuit theory and measurements and machinery— but only 11 hours a week instead of the 33 that Ursinus had developed into.

As time goes on, I expect to get a first-hand knowledge of the operation of the differential analyzer—I have already spent a bit of time watching the process of setting up and operating the thing—and with this background I hope to outdo the analyzer electronically.

A number of different ideas have come to me recently anent computing circuits—some of which are more or less hybrids, combining your methods with other things, and some of which are nothing like your machine. The question in my mind is this: is there any objection, from your point of view, to my building some sort of computer which incorporates some of the features of your machine? For the time being, of course, I shall be lucky to find time and material to do more than make exploratory tests of some of my different ideas, with the hope of getting something very speedy, not too costly, etc.

Ultimately a second question might come up, of course, and that is, in the event that your present design were to hold the field against all challengers, and I got the Moore School interested in having something of the sort, would the way be open for us to build an *"Atanasoff Calculator"* (a la *Bush* analyzer) here? [Mauchly's italics]

I am occupying the office of Travis, the man who designed the analyzer here (duplicated at Aberdeen); I think I told you that he is now in the Navy, so I have no opportunity of benefiting by his rich experience.

I hope your defense efforts have been successful, but not so time-consuming as to stop progress on the computer. When you are East, arrange to see us. Perhaps you would like to look over the diff. analyzer, etc.

Convey my best regards to your family, and Clif Berry and all the gang.[37]

Atanasoff to Mauchly, October 7, 1941:

I am delighted to hear that you are teaching in the Department of Electrical Engineering at the University of Pennsylvania, and I will be sure to get in touch with you the next time I come east which should be in the very near future.

At that time we can discuss our mutual interest in calculators.

Our attorney has emphasized the need of being careful about the dissemination of information about our device until a patent application is filed. This
should not require too long, and, of course, I have no qualms about having
informed you about our device, but it does require that we refrain from making
public any details for the time being. It is, as a matter of fact, preventing me
from making an invited address to the American Statistical Association.[38]

[Three notes back and forth, October 18, 19, and 20, hoping to arrange an Atanasoff stop-over in Philadelphia]

Atanasoff to Mauchly, October 30, 1941:

I am so sorry that our visit did not materialize. What actually happened was that
items were piled on my itinerary and agenda until a stop in Philadelphia long enough
to visit you was impossible. I regard the last two weeks as among the most strenuous
of my life. I expect, however, to be east again in not too many months and of course
I will do everything I can to make possible a visit with you at that time.

I took about an hour off (with some misgivings) while in Cambridge to visit
the new integraph. Everyone was very enthusiastic about it and it certainly is a most
pretentious structure. I understand its total cost is nearing a half a million dollars.

Let me hear all about your plans when you have time.

[Handwritten postscript] Lura sends regards.[39]

Perhaps most striking about these Mauchly-Atanasoff letters is the warmth and
cordiality of their relationship from the very start. Two physicists of about the
same age, after a half-hour conversation at a gathering of their peers, looked forward to meeting again and exploring a common interest in automatic computation. Both were engaged in research requiring the manipulation of large quantities of numerical data. Neither had found other scientists who shared their vision
of inexpensive computing machines to reduce the tedium and hasten the results
of such research.

But one was to give, the other to receive. Atanasoff had already invented and
was well along in building an electronic digital computer; Mauchly had a strong
appreciation of the potential of electronics for computing, yet only a vague hope
of building anything himself. Mauchly saw Atanasoff as someone whose ideas
might be useful; Atanasoff saw Mauchly as someone who would share his own
enthusiasm for, but not misuse, his ideas. Here Atanasoff was mistaken. For,
though Mauchly did not go to Iowa with the intention of using Atanasoff's ideas
without permission, he did in the end—when that permission was denied or at
least deferred—so use them. And he claimed them as his own.

In both the Regenerative Memory and the ENIAC patent suits, Mauchly's

Figure 8. Front view of the ABC as of fall 1941. The add-subtract mechanisms are all in place in this photograph, with fifteen visible on the front right face. To their left is the bank of vacuum tubes of the restore-shift mechanisms, and just above and behind these are the thyratrons (gas tubes) of the binary-card processing circuits. Above the add-subtract mechanisms is the keyboard of manual controls, to its left is the decimal-card processing mechanism, and farther to the left are the trays of the binary-card system. Finally, in the top rear from left to right, the base-conversion drum, the keyboard drum, the timing drum, and the counter drum are covered with casings.

---

letters leading up to and following his five-day stay with Atanasoff were vital to weighing his claims to invention. They confirmed Atanasoff's story that he had, at their first brief meeting, revealed a number of key features of his computer and offered to reveal the rest if Mauchly came to Iowa. They made a mockery of Mauchly's protestations that critical information was withheld in Iowa and that, in any case, he was disappointed in the Atanasoff-Berry Computer and lost all interest once he had seen it and its rotating drum memory.

Mauchly's own remarks on his state of mind after seeing the ABC suggested not just an enlightened observer, but one excited and inspired—almost over-whelmed—by the flood of new ideas. He did not see the drum as slowing the arithmetic processing of equations unduly. He called the computer electronic. He did not object to its special purpose of solving sets of up to twenty-nine equations in twenty-nine variables. He did not say that he himself was intent on a general-purpose computer but rather that he had in mind devices suited to small com-puting jobs—certainly smaller, less general than the ABC's.

Atanasoff's letters were in sharp contrast to Mauchly's. He was not seeking help. He had supreme confidence in the computer he was building and complete satisfaction with its progress, despite the growing pressure of his national defense projects. He was even nurturing an idea for the next computer he would build, an extension of the principles of the ABC to an electronic digital equivalent of the differential analyzer. This idea, too, he freely disclosed to Mauchly in his May 31 letter and discussed with him in person during his June visit: it was one more item that struck a strong responsive chord in Mauchly.

It also impressed the judge in the ENIAC case. In his decision, Larson quoted both Mauchly's June 28 letter to Clayton, where he praised the idea, and his September 30 letter to Atanasoff, where he expressed a possible interest in using it (Finding 13).[40]

It is a second striking aspect of this Atanasoff-Mauchly correspondence that the differential analyzer was mentioned so many times. Why was this huge electrically powered mechanical device for the analog solution of differential equations of such interest to Mauchly and Atanasoff? The answer is that, in terms of power and generality, differential analyzers were the best computing instruments of the day. Vannevar Bush had built the original version at MIT in 1931, and a half dozen or so upgraded versions had followed in the United States and Europe. They were the crowning achievement of analog computing, and both Mauchly and Atanasoff recognized the enormous potential for an electronic digital machine that could solve the same problems faster and more accurately.

The ENIAC trial established that the ENIAC was, in fact, conceived as an electronic digital version of the mechanical analog differential analyzer. This connection was implicit in the Mauchly 1942 memorandum and was made explicit in the Eckert-Mauchly 1943 proposal to Army Ordnance.[41]

Mauchly had learned of the analyzer primarily through Irven Travis, the Moore School professor who had directed the building of two analyzers in 1934: one for the Moore School, the other for the Army's Ballistic Research Laboratory at Aberdeen Proving Ground, Aberdeen, Maryland. For several years before taking the 1941 defense training course, Mauchly had dropped in periodically to talk with Travis. They had discussed the new, highly sophisticated differential analyzer being built at MIT by Bush and his colleague, Samuel Caldwell. They had also discussed the consulting work Travis did for General Electric throughout 1939 and 1940, in which he suggested and explored ideas for an electronic differential analyzer. As Mauchly noted in his May 27, 1941, letter to Atanasoff, cost considerations led General Electric to build yet another mechanical analog machine.

The Bush-Caldwell analyzer had an electronic aspect, in that it replaced the original manual setup with an automatic setup based on paper tapes and on elec-

Figure 9. Differential analyzer. The differential analyzer shown here was built in the basement of the Moore School of Electrical Engineering, University of Pennsylvania, under the direction of Irven Travis. Travis also directed the construction of a differential analyzer at Aberdeen Proving Ground, as the other half of a mutual arrangement between the university and the U.S. Army Ordnance Department. Both machines were built in 1934, and both were used to compute artillery firing tables during World War II.

The integrators were the basic computing components. The Moore School analyzer had fourteen integrators, ranged in a row on the left, each with its motor-driven torque amplifier to turn the appropriate shaft in the center bay. The four input and output plotting tables are seen on the right. Six banks of five counter wheels, similar to odometers, are in front, along with a tray for the paper on which they printed the machine's numerical output.

The center bay had placements for shafts running both crosswise and lengthwise. To set up a problem, the operators interconnected these shafts so as to establish intercommunication among the integrators, the plotting tables, the independent variable motor, and the output counters as required by the problem. Fixed gears, for multiplication and division by constants, and differential gears, for addition and subtraction, were placed in the bay. The cupboards on the left wall held the required assortment of shafts and gears for problem setup.

(Photo Courtesy of Arthur W. Burks.)

---

trical, electromagnetic, and electronic *control and communication* techniques. It still *computed*, however, by means of mechanical analog integrators and gears.

The integrator was the basic unit of the differential analyzer: to be solved on this machine, differential equations had first to be converted to integral equations. That is why the analyzer was often called an integraph, as by Atanasoff and Mauchly in their letters. The number of integrators in the mechanical versions ranged from six in the original MIT analyzer to fourteen in the Moore School analyzer.

Travis recognized that to compute electronically a differential analyzer had to have electronic integrators. He wrote two reports for General Electric, both of which included suggestions of electronic numerical integrators.[42]

Travis's second report spelled out in some detail the idea of replacing the integrators of the mechanical differential analyzer with accumulators that would integrate in small discrete steps. The equations to be solved by this analyzer would be difference equations, as converted from the original differential equations—the standard procedure for solving differential equations on a desk calculator. The report spoke first of accumulators in the form of the existing adding machines, but later recommended "electronic adding machines" for a very short (and competitive) solution time.

By the fall of 1940, this concept had gotten so far in the Moore School as to prompt a group of six professors, including Travis, to request funds from the National Defense Research Council for developing an electronic integrator. Although the proposal was directed to the use of such integrators in antiaircraft fire-control equipment, it was clearly an outgrowth of Travis's consulting work, which was directed to their use in differential analyzers. Travis himself testified in court that the proposal came from discussions of possibilities "based to a fair extent upon the ideas that were in the two GE reports."[43]

Atanasoff had learned of analyzers in a study he made of all current computing devices before he decided to build his own computer. He was also reminded of them regularly during Caldwell's site visits to his defense projects. Atanasoff clearly did not think much of the mechanical differential analyzers, including the MIT version that Caldwell described with such pride. He once told the present writer and Arthur Burks that it was actually Caldwell's spirited descriptions that inspired—or provoked—him to consider how he might create an electronic digital computer to solve differential equations!

Atanasoff also planned to convert the differential equations into difference equations. But instead of modeling his machine on the mechanical differential analyzer, he meant to model it on his own computer, the electronic digital machine he was now building to solve linear equations. He would adapt the design of the ABC to solve difference equations.

Atanasoff did not work out this modified design, or even begin to work it out, but both his May 31 letter to Mauchly and his ENIAC trial testimony indicated an intention to stay with his basic computing apparatus: logical adders interacting with rotating capacitor memories.[44]

Mauchly testified before Judge Larson that Atanasoff's May 31 suggestion that the ABC could be "converted into an integraph" had been meaningful to him and had further excited his interest and his desire to learn more in Iowa.[45] His June 28 letter to Clayton affirmed his satisfaction, from what he did learn there, that the ABC could be "adapted to do the job" of the differential analyzer. Finally, his September 30 letter to Atanasoff noted his own hope of outdoing the analyzer electronically and expressed his continued consideration of Atanasoff's idea. It even went so far as to request permission to build "an '*Atanasoff Calculator*' (a la *Bush* analyzer)," in the event Atanasoff's "present design were to hold the field against all challengers."

But that last Mauchly letter had another, alternative, request. He referred to some of his own ideas as "hybrids, combining your methods with other things," and he asked if Atanasoff would object to his building "some sort of computer which incorporates some of the features of your machine." Thus Mauchly, as of late September 1941, was weighing two options for the electronic digital solution of differential equations—both of which he recognized would use Atanasoff's technology to some degree.

One of these options, the one *not* chosen, was clearly the conversion, or adaptation, of the ABC. The other option, which *was* chosen and evolved into the ENIAC, was not spelled out in Mauchly's letter, but in all probability arose from Irven Travis's idea for an electronic digital version of the differential analyzer.

Architecturally, then, the two options were very different. Atanasoff envisioned only a *functional* replacement of the differential analyzer. He meant to retain the centralized architecture of his ABC, organized around separate store and arithmetic unit. Travis, on the other hand, envisioned a *structural* as well as *functional* replacement of the differential analyzer. He meant to retain the distributive architecture of the differential analyzer, organized around a set of accumulators functioning as integrators.

Eckert and Mauchly did just that with the ENIAC. Indeed, there is no other way to account for the odd architecture of the ENIAC than to see its parallel in the differential analyzer's architecture. Moreover, once they had conceived the mercury-delay-line memory, which could be used with a separate adder, they themselves turned to a centralized architecture for the EDVAC.

The link between their conception of the ENIAC and Travis's idea of electronic integrators, whether for a differential analyzer or for fire-control devices, is further fortified by Travis's ENIAC trial testimony about the Moore School proposal. He said that "with an integrator one can couple two together and . . . get sines and cosines, and by two integrators one can multiply."[46]

Figure 1 of the 1943 Eckert-Mauchly proposal depicts a setup for producing sines and cosines.[47] And the "small ENIAC" built a year later to "prove" the ENIAC was a two-accumulator model that generated sines and cosines.

The "feature" of Atanasoff's computer that Mauchly was requesting permission to use in his September 30 letter was its basic technology of vacuum-tube switching. For while Travis was confident that he could construct vacuum-tube circuits for digital computing, he had never tried to do so, because neither General Electric nor the National Defense Research Council was receptive to his proposals. Atanasoff, though, had actually constructed complex digital electronic circuits, and he had proven their feasibility for computing by designing and building a machine that made fundamental and critical use of them.

Between September 1941 and August 1942, when Mauchly wrote his first, very sketchy, proposal for an electronic digital "calculator" or "computor" [*sic*], he had had a full academic year in which to familiarize himself with the Moore School's differential analyzer *and* to discuss computers with Eckert, who was fast acquiring a reputation as an electronics expert.

Also by August 1942, Mauchly had had the added stimulus of the school's recent commitment to calculating firing tables for the army, as the nation shifted from a defense posture to all-out war. The differential analyzers at both the Moore School and Aberdeen's Ballistic Research Laboratory were now being used exclusively to compute artillery trajectories for firing tables. And a large contingent of human "computers" was already being recruited and trained to compute them by the numerical method on desk machines.

But the need was clear for faster devices. Preparing just one firing table, for firing a given shell from a given gun under varying conditions, required the calculation of three to four thousand trajectories from a system of differential equations. Each trajectory required fifteen to thirty minutes on the analyzer and many hours on a desk calculator.

Mauchly, with Eckert's assurance that he could design an electronic counter to operate reliably at 100,000 pulses per second, opted for the counting, or accumulating, principle as against Atanasoff's logical adder principle. A machine based on accumulators would be many times faster than one based on adders that could not realize their electronic speed potential because of a slowly operating memory. The architectural parallel to the existing differential analyzer was also appealing in light of the wartime urgency.

At the same time, Mauchly and Eckert did see, almost from the start, ways to make the new electronic computer more general than the analyzer. Mauchly included mention of a "programming device" in his 1942 proposal, and by the time he and Eckert wrote their formal proposal eight months later, they were thinking of a programmable, general-purpose computer with capabilities far beyond those of the analyzer. Again, however, as we noted in chapter 1, program entry was to be done manually, by plugging in jumper cables and setting switches, not automatically, as via paper tape.

It was, in fact, these joint ideas of Mauchly and Eckert that led them to insist on adding the words "and Computer" to the words "Electronic Numerical Integrator" in the ENIAC's title. And it was these same ideas that Mauchly, in his trial testimony, backdated to the spring before his visit to Atanasoff's laboratory, so as to claim that what he learned there was of no interest to him. If this were the case, of course, he would not have been entertaining Atanasoff's ideas as late as the following fall, and asking permission to use them!

Atanasoff, in his letter of October 7, 1941, declined Mauchly's requests, citing his patent lawyer's concerns. Judge Larson made reference to this letter, too, in his decision (Finding 13).[48]

In sum, although Eckert and Mauchly did not build the ENIAC as an extension of Atanasoff's computer, his idea for doing so inspired them to explore alternatives for an electronic digital differential analyzer. And, in all probability, his more basic electronic computing technology enabled them to extend Travis's ideas for such a machine. In any case, they did employ that technology—without his permission and without acknowledgment—in their design of the ENIAC.

Besides the Mauchly-Atanasoff correspondence, Control Data attorney Kirkpatrick introduced two other critical documents on that final day of the deposition. The first was the 1963 letter from Clifford Berry to R. K. Richards mentioned in chapter 1.[49] Richards was an old Ames friend of Berry's who had seen Atanasoff's computer in 1941 and was now researching his third book on digital computing devices. It was this book, in fact, that drew the attention of attorneys in both the Honeywell-Sperry Rand and the Sperry Rand-Control Data cases to the ABC's priority over the ENIAC.[50] (It was in this book, too, that the Atanasoff-Berry Computer was first so designated in print; Atanasoff also so named it after Berry's death, to honor his graduate assistant's inventive contributions to it.)

Berry, director of engineering at Consolidated Electrodynamics when he received Richards's inquiry, responded with suggestions on sources of information, a succinct description of the computer, and the following paragraph about Mauchly's visit:

> An interesting sidelight is that in 1940 or 1941 we had a visit from Dr. John Mauchly who spent a week learning all of the details of our computer and the philosophy of its design. He was the only person outside of the Research Corporation [which funded the machine] and the patent counsel who was given this opportunity, and he may still have notes of what he learned from us.

Kirkpatrick and Mauchly had this exchange:

> *Kirkpatrick:* Now, the paragraph you just read . . . states that you spent the time learning all the details of the computer they had there. Now, does this refresh you as to the extent of the disclosure that was provided to you . . . ?
>
> *Mauchly:* . . . I would regard what Mr. Berry says in his letter as being to the best of his general recollection but not necessarily any more accurate than what I said, and my testimony was to the effect that I learned something about the "philosophy" of the proposed machine but that I did not learn the details of it, in the sense of having enough information to reproduce it or to understand whether or not it would actually if built perform reliably.

Kirkpatrick: As to the willingness of Atanasoff and Berry to disclose details to you during your visit, wouldn't it be more the case that they did have an apprehension about widely disseminating the details prior to their patenting but they took you into their confidence and did give you the details rather than withhold the details from you?

Mauchly: That seems to involve two points. I have already discussed my impression of their reluctance to discuss this machine and their open statements that they did not want to widely disseminate information or disclose what they were doing.

On the second point, it was my impression that they were giving me more information than others, but since they seemed to be giving no one else any information then anything I received was more than others.

I stand by my statement yesterday that the amount of information which they were giving me was by no means complete.

For one thing, they never disclosed to me that the Research Corporation that is named in this paragraph was involved in this.[51]

Here, of course, Mauchly was confusing disclosure of the "involvement" of a foundation with disclosure of details of the computer.

The second critical document introduced by the Control Data attorney on that last day of Mauchly's deposition was Atanasoff's 1940 manuscript, a full description of the computer written with the dual purpose of applying for support and applying for a patent. Kirkpatrick began by showing Mauchly a series of photographs dated August 7, 1940, and a circuit diagram, all of which had in fact been used to illustrate the manuscript.[52] But he got nowhere in his effort to "bring back more recollection of the individual logic circuits," the add-subtract mechanisms. Mauchly would admit only that "a vacuum tube device" was depicted in each of two pictures, one by itself, the other on the machine. There was "no way of being sure," he said, that they were photographs of the same device. Nor could he recall whether this was a "plug-in" module.

There was then this curious exchange:

Kirkpatrick: Is your memory refreshed to any extent that while you were there at Ames with Dr. Atanasoff concerning his computer, you were given a written description to read?

Mauchly: I don't remember being given such a written description, but on the other hand, I cannot be sure that I was not given one to read. I can say very definitely I was not given one to—

Kirkpatrick: To take home?

Mauchly: To take home.

Had Kirkpatrick, after three days, become so familiar with Mauchly's style that he could anticipate his response? Or had he learned from Atanasoff what both he and Mauchly would testify later at the ENIAC trial, namely, that Mauchly had read the document and had requested but been denied a copy? In either case, it was one more item, besides the modular add-subtract mechanism, on which Mauchly's memory improved significantly over the next four years.

Kirkpatrick went on to introduce the manuscript, "Computing Machine for the Solution of Large Systems of Linear Algebraic Equations, John V. Atanasoff," which he described as "a booklet in a spiral binder sort of thing with a blue cover," having thirty pages of text and diagrams plus a few pages of photographs.[53] But, again, Mauchly's examination of it did not "refresh" his recollection. "Looking at it now," he said, "doesn't suggest to me that it was something that I had seen and did read." Indeed he added, "In particular, I note that there is no date on this document, so I don't even know whether it was in existence when I was there." Kirkpatrick assured him that the date would "be established by other evidence."

Kirkpatrick pointed to the place in the manuscript where Atanasoff listed, among possible alternative elements for binary storage, "3. A small piece of retentive ferromagnetic material, the two states being the directions of magnetization of the material."

> *Kirkpatrick:* Does that bring back a recollection of discussing the use of retentive ferromagnetic material as a storage device with Dr. Atanasoff?
> *Mauchly:* No, I don't remember whether that was discussed or not. It could have been.
>   So far as persons such as Dr. Atanasoff and myself and many others who were interested in the development of calculating elements, the desirability of having physical phenomena which could be put in either one of the two discrete states was quite evident, and the phenomenon of ferromagnetism and the retention of magnetism by ferroelectric elements was one phenomenon which probably everyone considered.
> . . .
> *Kirkpatrick:* Well, do any of the documents that you have brought with you in response to the subpoena deal in any way with the use of magnetic material in digital computers?
> *Mauchly:* I don't believe so. It is rather ironic that after all the discussions which Eckert and I and others had at the Moore School with respect to ferromagnetic elements, core storage devices, and so forth, that we thought these were so obvious that we did not anticipate by documentation what has now been patented by others.

Once more, as with electronic switching and electronic memory regeneration, Mauchly was denying Atanasoff an original computer concept by claiming for himself a degree of expertise he had yet to acquire—through extended discussions with Eckert over the next several years.

And, again, Kirkpatrick's inquiry reflected his study of the Regenerative Memory patent that he was interested in overturning. For the true irony of Mauchly's testimony is that, just as he and Eckert had included Atanasoff's rotating capacitor memory in their patent, so, too, they had included his idea for a rotating memory based on "magnetized spots," as they called them.[54] So far as this "obvious" form of magnetic memory was concerned, they themselves were the "others" who had patented it!

(Magnetic memories, of course, do not require regeneration; this patent, usually referred to as the Eckert-Mauchly Regenerative Memory patent, was actually titled "Memory System," and was not limited to forms that require regeneration.)

Finally, in the course of this deposition Kirkpatrick drew from Mauchly two admissions of a surprisingly lax attitude toward appropriating the ideas of others.

The first arose from his explanation of contacts he had had with Atanasoff at the Naval Ordnance Laboratory (NOL) in Washington, D.C., during the latter stages of the ENIAC project.[55] Atanasoff had left Iowa State College in the fall of 1942 to join NOL as chief of acoustical mine testing, and Mauchly had dropped in on him there a few times when he happened to be in Washington. When, in the spring of 1944, Mauchly found his Moore School teaching income cut off—the army had terminated its special training courses—he appealed to Atanasoff for a consulting job. Atanasoff responded by arranging for his appointment as a statistical consultant in his own section of the Laboratory; Mauchly worked there, for a day or so a week, from the fall of 1944 until early 1946.

Mauchly told Kirkpatrick of his observations during this period, with regard both to any current interest Atanasoff might have in computing and to the status of the computer he had left behind. His impression was that Atanasoff now "felt committed to administrative duties, and so far as I could tell had no interest in the design of computers," and that "the computer had never been finished at Iowa." Mauchly then brought these observations to bear on his state of mind as he applied for the Regenerative Memory patent in 1947:

> I already understood that the Atanasoff machine had never been completed and this, too, rightly or wrongly, made me feel that I was signing an application which had nothing to do with any machine on which a patent would ever be applied for.

In short, Mauchly felt *safe*, "rightly or wrongly," in patenting concepts of the earlier machine.

Mauchly's second admission of this lax attitude came late in the last day of the deposition and actually seemed to occasion a loss of temper by Kirkpatrick—the attorney who had, earlier that day, so coolly surprised the witness with one after another long-forgotten letter. Kirkpatrick had been inquiring about a 1967 meeting of the Association for Computing Machinery in Washington. Mauchly, who was to give a paper, had been asked at the last minute to tell of his 1941 visit to Atanasoff's Iowa laboratory. There was this exchange:

Kirkpatrick: Did it occur to you to [invite Atanasoff to come, too, and tell about his machine]? Of course, maybe there wasn't time.

Mauchly: At that point there wasn't time. Or at least I can't say for sure there wasn't time, because I understand that Atanasoff was somewhere in the vicinity of Washington.

But of course, as I testified earlier, I was rather amazed at the fact that once he became imbedded in the administrative duties at Naval Ordnance Laboratory he did not actually seem to want to talk about his machine or to have much to do with the technical features of computers, and he has never as to my knowledge ever appeared at any Association for Computing Machinery meetings or any of the related society meetings relating to computers, so I thought that this was a case where he was sort of out of the field, but I recognize, of course, that that does not—should not prejudice exposure of his ideas.

Kirkpatrick: In other words, if a scientist describes something and is run over by a truck the next day, that is no reason for the rest of the world to move in and appropriate what they might have learned from him; you would agree with that?

Mr. Dodds: I object to that question. I think the witness should not answer it.

Kirkpatrick: You are not going to answer?

Mauchly: It is an irrelevant question, as far as I am concerned.

Kirkpatrick: Well, we will see what the Court thinks about that.[56]

Here again was Mauchly's feeling that it was *safe* to ignore the part Atanasoff's ideas played in inventions he and Eckert were claiming as their own, because Atanasoff was showing no interest.

It should be noted that Atanasoff, in his *Annals of the History of Computing* article, "Advent of Electronic Digital Computing," gave a different version of this period of his life.[57] In this version, it was Mauchly who would not discuss computers and who would characterize the ENIAC only as "a new way to compute," explaining that he could not say more because the project was "classified." Atanasoff realized sometime later, he wrote, that "JWM could have arranged to tell me about his discovery." He went on to quote his NOL superior, Royal Weller, as believing that Mauchly was using his visits there to "watch" Atanasoff, presumably to make the very observations he mentioned to Kirkpatrick with regard to his own patent interests.

As to Mauchly's impression that Atanasoff had become "imbedded" in administration at NOL, this was simply not the case. Atanasoff was deeply involved in acoustical mine testing throughout the war, and after the war he led his staff in two further testing projects, as he also reported in his *Annals* article: "studying the sound generated by the atomic blast in the water and in the air" during atomic testing on Bikini Atoll in 1946; and "monitor[ing] the explosive wave through the earth (earthquake)" created when the British blew up a German depository of ammunition on the island of Helgoland in 1947.

Of the second of these undertakings, the measurements for which stretched from northern Germany to northern Italy, Atanasoff concluded: "This laid the groundwork for long-range detection of atomic explosions. The chief of Ordnance gave me a citation for this work." So did the Seismological Society of America, for whom he and his staff presented a paper that "created a certain sensation," he wrote.

Mauchly persisted in claiming, throughout both the Regenerative Memory and the ENIAC patent cases—and, indeed, for the rest of his life—that he had been disappointed in the Atanasoff-Berry Computer, that he had lost interest in it on first sight, and that he himself had envisaged no use he might make of any of Atanasoff's ideas about electronic computing. Yet his own testimony in the two cases, his own correspondence with Atanasoff and others, and the similarities of Atanasoff's ideas to those embodied in the Eckert-Mauchly patents make it very hard to countenance these repeated protestations.

And what of the other side of the story? What sort of case could be made for the opposite position—that Atanasoff was the inventor of the first electronic computer and that Mauchly and Eckert derived crucial concepts from him? The testimony of Atanasoff and of several other witnesses spoke eloquently to this question.

THREE

ATANASOFF
AS WITNESS

On Tuesday, June 15, 1971, exactly two weeks into the ENIAC patent trial and exactly thirty years after John W. Mauchly's visit to his physics laboratory in Ames, Iowa, John V. Atanasoff took the witness stand. He faced direct examination by Honeywell attorney Henry Halladay and cross-examination by Sperry Rand attorney Thomas M. Ferrill, Jr. The issue was twofold: What was the state of Atanasoff's computer at the time of Mauchly's visit, and what was Mauchly's experience of it at the hands of Atanasoff and Berry?

Atanasoff was plaintiff Honeywell's key witness, just as Mauchly would be defendant Sperry Rand's in November—but with one critical difference. The burden of proof rested squarely on Honeywell. The Sperry side did not have to prove that Mauchly and Eckert had proceeded independently of Atanasoff; the Honeywell side had to prove that they had not.

In this sense, the case would turn on the testimony Atanasoff gave and the documents, props, and artifacts he exhibited. It would also turn on his performance as a witness: his credibility as revealed in his memory for details, his consistency, his apparent competence, his very demeanor.

Halladay was concerned enough about these "critical questions of credibility" that, on the opening day, he asked Atanasoff to explain differential, partial differential, and linear equations without resorting to a blackboard. He said that he wanted the court to be able to "appraise this witness live from the stand as he gives testimony on both pragmatic and esoteric subjects." At the same time, he said, such a presentation would serve to clarify the mathematics for laypersons like himself, because without a blackboard Atanasoff would have "to teach or attempt to teach" in terms closer to everyday experience. Atanasoff attacked this assignment for some ten transcript pages, only once appealing to Halladay for use of the courtroom blackboard—and being denied.[1]

The central point, of course, was that Atanasoff had created his electronic computer to solve large sets of simultaneous linear algebraic equations, as converted from the sets of partial differential equations he so frequently encountered in his research. It was not at all critical that the judge understand any but those relatively simple equations of high school algebra, which we have explained in chapter 1 and which are further elaborated (by the witness) in the current chapter, in order to understand the mathematics of the Atanasoff-Berry Computer. As Halladay himself had indicated, he wanted to impress the court with the erudition of this witness, as well as to explicate the mathematics at the lay level. Judge Larson, who had received tutorial instruction prior to the trial, did follow attentively, even on one occasion requesting elaboration.

Of the six days given to direct examination of Atanasoff, the Honeywell attorney spent the first four quizzing him on a series of topics designed to set the stage for his exploration of Mauchly's visit. These topics ranged from Atanasoff's childhood and education, through his teaching and research, and on to his need for and conception of the ABC, the construction of a preliminary model, and the chief features of the machine itself.

Atanasoff's responses to questions about his childhood and education quickly established both a precocious competence and a long and keen memory. He told of his growing interest in mathematics and science at the age of nine, when his family lived in the town of Brewster, Florida. His father, he explained, was an electrical engineer in a phosphate-mining company and had a good stock of textbooks from his university and correspondence school studies. Atanasoff recalled his fascination with his father's slide rule and with logarithms, and he remembered three particular physics books.[2]

> *Atanasoff:* . . . My father had an elementary book in physics and I know I was disturbed when he loaned it to somebody else to read but the other man didn't take much interest in it and returned it after a month, after which I devoured the book. . . .
>
> *Halladay:* Do you remember the name of that text?
>
> *Atanasoff:* No. I remember it had a brown cover but I cannot remember the author of this book. Then there were two other books in physics there, a two volume set of physics by an author, and my memory tells me that the author is Chute, C-h-u-t-e. . . .
>
> As my interest in the slide rule grew, I had a book of instructions that I commenced to study on its use and there was a short introduction to the theory of logarithms and I began the study of logarithms in the year 1913.
> . . .
>
> *Halladay:* Dr. Atanasoff, can you tell the Court in words that I would understand, you hope, what is a logarithm?

That done, Halladay returned to his witness's "pursuit of subjects mathematical and scientific."[3] Atanasoff continued:

As soon as I grasped the principle behind logarithms, I commenced to look for other books about [them], and I commenced to wonder how such things were calculated. I soon found out that this is a very advanced subject and this subject I looked at from my position at that time, of course, and this subject occupied my attention for three or four years.

Later, during Ferrill's cross-examination, Atanasoff mentioned his mother's role in his investigation of logarithms and number bases at such an early age.[4] She had taught mathematics in a country school after finishing high school, and she had a book called *Robinson's Arithmetic*, he said, that covered other bases than ten and that he read "assiduously." He once told my husband, Arthur, and me of his fruitless search for that book, which he remembered fondly. He also remembered his mother's love of algebra. Well into her nineties, he said, she practiced solving algebraic equations just to keep her mind sharp!

In court, Atanasoff allowed that he did play baseball "part of the time" and of course attended school. He explained that he was permitted "to roam in mathematics" in the Brewster schools and that he began the study of algebra in sixth grade and completed the first and second years of high school algebra in seventh grade.

He recalled his father's instructing him in the elementary principles of electricity and taking him to visit "the generating plants, and the transmission lines, and the motor installations" of the phosphate-mining company.[5]

I remember that this phosphate mine had been initiated two or three years before, and a complete group of houses for the employees were constructed there. When the magic of electricity came to our home—and this was the first time I had encountered electricity in the home, perhaps in the year 1913—every light worked except one, and this particular light refused to go on. I plagued my father to secure the repair of this installation, and he was too busy. Things were going very fast—he wouldn't do it himself and he wouldn't send one of his men to do it, and finally I ascended to the attic, with poor illumination—I remember distinctly the illumination was in the form of a kerosene lamp—and "jockeyed" across the joists and felt the connections until I discovered why the light would not work. I repaired this point. . . .

I did not make a solder joint, I remember that distinctly, but knowing something of the dangers of electricity, I was careful to tape the wire well. It was . . . tube and knob wiring, I think it is called.

He also recalled—again from that prophetic tenth year—"two small books of English origin" that his father owned on the subjects of radio, telegraphy and telephony."[6] He added:

> Of course, you cannot say that I had a good grasp of these subjects at that time,
> but I commenced to understand the first principles and theory of eletromagnetic
> radiation.

He could not remember the authors of these books, but he did remember "that they
had a faint green color and that they had the price . . . in sterling on the cover."

Lastly, Atanasoff told of an experiment-gone-awry from his high school days in
Mulberry, Florida, where he had been given his own key to the science laboratory.

> I had a curiosity in regard to nitroglycerin, and the materials for constructing it
> were at hand, and I tried it. I had read the account of the production of nitroglyc-
> erin very carefully, and the account stated—although I was producing it in very
> small amounts in a test tube in a rack, a large test tube in a rack—I was
> instructed that if the temperature rose too fast, there was danger in store, and I
> had mixed the glycerin with a mixture of concentrated nitric and sulfuric acids,
> the sulfuric acid being used largely as a drying agent, as I remember it from
> those days. Well, when the temperature rose, I pitched the whole thing out the
> window and it descended upon some students below, but it didn't blow up. They
> felt the effects of the nitric acid and so they ran and washed themselves off pretty
> quickly, and there was an investigation of this, and I was rather mildly, in
> consideration of the occasion, admonished to be more careful in the future.[7]

The sixty-seven-year-old witness's memory proved exceptional throughout
Halladay's long direct examination. In addition to these far-off childhood recollections, he provided details of many events from his days at Iowa State College.
One such was a meeting he attended in 1941 at the Bureau of Standards in Washington. He particularly remembered "meeting with Dr. W. G. Cady" of "the New
England Wesleyan College," and having "a very good discussion about vibrating
crystals," a subject on which some of his students were working.[8]

Atanasoff's teaching ability was evident from a number of extemporaneous discourses he gave at Halladay's request: for example, on his master's thesis topic,
the virial of Clausius; on his quartz research, for which he published two papers
jointly with postdoctoral students in the January 1, 1941, issue of *The Physical
Review* (one with Philip J. Hart and one with Erwin Kammer); and on the parallel, as he saw it, between physical research and artistic pursuits.[9]

Halladay also submitted, for the record, a long string of theses written by
Atanasoff's graduate students from 1932 to 1940. When Sperry attorney Ferrill
objected that these were irrelevant to the issue of Atanasoff's computer, Halladay
countered that they showed the depth of his immersion in physics and mathematics.

Judge Larson turned to Atanasoff.

Judge Larson: As to each of these theses, Dr. Atanasoff, did you have personal knowledge of each thesis?

Atanasoff: Yes, sir.

Judge Larson: Did you review each one?

Atanasoff: I reviewed each one and initiated each one and I counseled with the student as he was writing each one, and I participated in laboratory experimentation in regard to each of these theses, if it required laboratory experimentation. The subject matter was a matter of my own conception, and this matter motivated me strongly in these years.

. . .

Judge Larson: The exhibits will be received.[10]

Halladay turned next to two efforts Atanasoff had made, between 1935 and 1937, to adapt existing machines for the solution of simultaneous linear equations. In each instance he meant to employ the variant of the Gaussian elimination procedure he had already formulated and would, shortly, make the centerpiece of an electronic computer of his own design.

For the first of these efforts, Atanasoff said, he had worked out a scheme to modify an IBM punched-card tabulator through the addition of a piece of "auxiliary apparatus."[11] He had already succeeded with a similar modification for the analysis of spectra, he explained, but ultimately abandoned it for solving his sets of thirty or so equations "because of the limited memory and computational capacity of the IBM tabulator."

For his second attempt to make do with the current technology, he conceived of hooking together, or "ganging," a series of desk calculators.[12] Halladay introduced and read from a September 1937 letter in which Atanasoff asked a Washington law firm to make a preliminary patent search for this idea. In the stark style of scientists writing for scientists, Atanasoff first noted that the carriages and dials of the successive machines would be so interconnected as to permit simultaneous addition or subtraction throughout the series, with results for each machine entered onto its dials. The whole arrangement, he said, would be so controlled as to permit the reduction to zero of the dial readings of one of the machines, as required by his algorithm.

He then explained, in one long, lean sentence, the process of eliminating a designated variable from a pair of equations—the basic step in his algorithm, the repetition of which, he wrote, "enables the solution of a system of equations."

Now if the successive coefficients and constant term of one equation are set up on the successive sets of dials of the sequence of mechanisms [machines] and if successive coefficients and constant term of another equation are set up on the successive keyboards of the sequence of mechanisms the results of reduction of the dial readings of one mechanism to zero will be that the readings of the dials of the other mechanisms will represent the coefficients and constant term of an equation with one less unknown variable.

In court, Atanasoff concluded that this contemplated array of some thirty desk machines was "getting to be a mechanical monster," and that he had accordingly abandoned this project, as well.

The patent search turned up no other inventor's scheme for ganging calculators. By odd coincidence, however, the Moore School's Irven Travis wrote up a similar idea for General Electric in 1940, with the added suggestion that it might be made practical by using *electronic* rather than mechanical calculators (see chap. 2). Mauchly, too, in his 1942 memorandum, likened his proposed computer—what was to be the ENIAC—to such a series of interconnected calculators.[13]

Both Travis and Mauchly, of course, wanted machines to solve full, not partial, differential equations, as digital replacements for the differential analyzer. Travis saw the calculators as replacements for the integrators of the analyzer, while Mauchly saw them as a way to visualize what were to be the electronic accumulators of the ENIAC, which in turn were also replacements for the analyzer's integrators.

Halladay further illustrated Atanasoff's expertise as a researcher at Iowa State by examining him about a National Defense project he had conducted simultaneously with his computer project.[14] It was this antiaircraft fire-control project that occasioned periodic visits by Samuel Caldwell of MIT. Atanasoff said he spent "a good deal of time" on that "sharply classified" project, working with Sam Legvold, another graduate assistant who, like Berry, had joined him in the fall of 1939.

In antiaircraft fire at the time Atanasoff was given the problem, a tracker had the task of keeping the crosshairs of a telescope trained on an enemy plane until that plane's trajectory was established and the gunner could fire with some assurance of a hit. The tracker, with an eye at the telescope, moved the instrument along with the plane by turning two wheels—one with each hand—the first to track the plane's horizontal movement, the second to track its vertical movement. This was an extremely difficult task, demanding total concentration and excellent coordination, even when the plane did not engage in evasive maneuvers.

Atanasoff and Legvold conceived a small analog, nonelectronic computer to assist the tracker and maximize his success in keeping the crosshairs on the target. As Atanasoff explained in court:

> . . . It is better if when you turn the wheel, it does two things, it moves the telescope but it simultaneously cranks in at an automatic rate of motion of the telescope so that you don't have to worry about turning the wheel [as] the whole burden to making the telescope follow the device.

Finally, Halladay took Atanasoff through the wide range of computing applications he had anticipated for his computer in his proposal of August 1940 (see chap. 1).[15] Here, too, Halladay pressed his witness to relate his explanations to "the real world." Atanasoff came closest to this requirement in his account of "curve fitting," for which he used the "growth phase of bacteria" as an example. This portion of his testimony was impressive for its obvious erudition, whether or not it was entirely comprehensible to the ever-attentive judge.

Atanasoff gave a complete description of the preliminary model of his computer that he and Berry had begun to build in September of 1939, as soon as Berry joined him, and finished a month or two later.[16] He first explained his rationale for building this model:

> I was continually worried about whether a vacuum tube could be made into a machine that would calculate, and so our first effort was in that direction. Before Mr. Berry came to work, I had developed diagrams for a logic circuit, and immediately upon Mr. Berry's starting work, we commenced throwing together a test prototype to help us evaluate the problems and to convince us that vacuum tubes in a computing machine was not a pipedream.

Atanasoff then gave over forty pages of testimony on this "prototype," referring often to a large drawing made under his direction and that of Charles G. Call, chief investigative attorney for Honeywell (in the firm of Allegretti, Newitt, Witcoff & McAndrews, Ltd.) and himself an electrical engineer. Every detail was examined as the operations of addition and subtraction of vectors were explained.

The model was a thin slice of the central apparatus of the projected computer. Representing the arithmetic unit were one add-subtract mechanism, an associated carry-borrow capacitor mounted on a small rotating disk, and one restore mechanism. Representing the main memory were two bands of capacitors mounted on either side of a large rotating disk, one band for the counter drum and one for the keyboard drum.

The courtroom exploration of this model served as a preview of the ABC itself. Atanasoff described the serial transmission of binary numbers into the add-subtract mechanism from the counter and keyboard bands via wires and brushes, the transmission of numbers back to the two bands via other wires and brushes, the simultaneous regeneration of the capacitors of those bands, and the role of the separate carry-borrow capacitor.

He also went into several finer features: the synchronization of operations, the momentary "boosting" of the capacitor voltages to accommodate the amplification aspect of vacuum tubes, the faster rotation of the carry-borrow memory to minimize hardware, and (for test purposes) the installation of a one-cycle switch and of means to read out "1s" and "0s" on a voltmeter or an oscilloscope.

The drawing and Atanasoff's testimony—together with that of witnesses who had seen the model demonstrated—led Judge Larson to rule that "this bread-

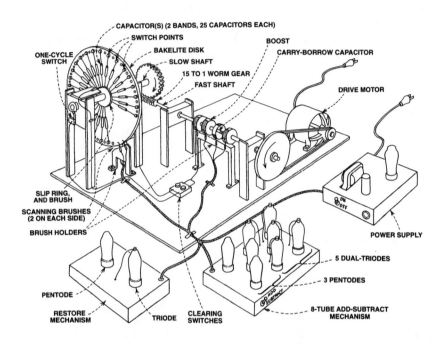

Figure 10. Drawing of 1939 model. This drawing (now slightly modified) was made for use in court about thirty years after the model had been tested and then dismantled.

The model had two storage rings, each with twenty-five capacitors, on the outer faces of a large disk. These rings represented one pair of corresponding rings on the counter and keyboard drums of the planned computer, each holding a binary coefficient of one term of an equation. It had an add-subtract mechanism, served by a single carry-borrow capacitor, to add or subtract the two coefficients. It also had a mechanism to restore the charges on the keyboard capacitors during the arithmetic operations, but not to shift the keyboard coefficient as would be required for a complete execution of Atanasoff's elimination algorithm.

The model established the feasibility of Atanasoff's principles of electronic computation. On the basis of this success and the manuscript he finished in August 1940, the nonprofit Research Corporation, of New York City, gave him a grant of $5,000 to build the computer.

(Drawing modified by David Oliver.)

---

board model . . . permitted the various components of the machine to be tested under actual operating conditions [and] established the soundness of the basic principles of design" (Finding 3).[17] These considerations have also led some to pronounce this test model the world's first electronic computer, setting 1939 as the date of that historic invention instead of the ABC's completion date of 1942. Either way, the inventor is the same!

<<<>>>

Atanasoff's testimony on the finished computer was proportionately longer than on the model—nearly 300 pages.[18] It began with identification of his 1940 descriptive manuscript and of the accompanying tables, diagrams, and photographs.[19] It went on to trace the course of construction from January 1940 until Mauchly's visit eighteen months later. Not only were full descriptions given of the components completed as of that visit, but all sorts of documents kept by Atanasoff all those years—letters, orders, bills, receipts, grants, payroll vouchers, and dated photographs—were presented to validate his version of the state of the machine at each point along the way.

Halladay made clear from the outset that he had no "nicely tailored and prepared script" worked out with his witness for this direct examination on some 1,300 documents; that Atanasoff was speaking extemporaneously about each and every one.[20]

The Honeywell attorney delved into a wide variety of activities affecting Atanasoff's realization of the invention: efforts at funding, steps toward a patent, trips taken, and names of parties with whom the computer was discussed. He introduced Berry's master's thesis on the binary input-output system, but postponed questions about a difficulty with that system that was to emerge later. He brought out that demonstrations were given to certain visitors as early as March 1940, barely two months into construction, and he elicited details of those demonstrations and names of those visitors. It turned out that Mauchly was the only one who was neither a close associate of Atanasoff nor a representative of some private or governmental agency from whom he was seeking support.

The highlight of this examination on the ABC was a live demonstration of the add-subtract mechanism, for which Atanasoff used newly constructed duplicates of both the mechanism itself and a special laboratory test set.[21] This test set had been designed to send the input pulses to the mechanism and receive the output pulses from it. On one end were three pushbuttons for entering bits as if from the counter, keyboard, and carry-borrow drums—pushed for "1," not pushed for "0"—and on the top were two terminal lights for indicating the resulting sum and carry bits or difference and borrow bits—lighted for "1," not lighted for "0." It also had a switch for selecting addition or subtraction.

Atanasoff preceded this demonstration of the add-subtract mechanism with a lengthy review of the binary number system, for which Halladay did permit him to use the blackboard. He began by translating numbers back and forth between decimal and binary, and he ended by performing the basic step of his add-subtract mechanism, adding and subtracting all possible combinations of three input bits.

The demonstration itself consisted of setting the switch for addition or subtraction, entering various combinations of three bits with the pushbuttons, and pointing to the bit solutions on the two lights. Atanasoff conducted it in the pres-

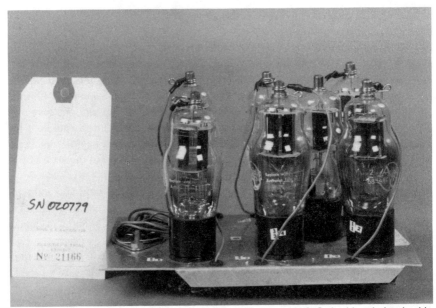

Figure 11. Courtroom add-subtract mechanism. The seven 6C8G double triodes in this reconstructed add-subtract mechanism were from the original computer, salvaged when it was dismantled in 1948. Each of the two tubes in one glass "envelope" had a cylindrical metal plate, a cylindrical wire-coil grid within the plate, and a cylindrical metal cathode within the grid. Input was to the grid, output from the plate, with the cathode held at a fixed voltage as a reference.

A heating wire inside the cathode made it so hot that it boiled off electrons. These electrons were attracted to the plate, but the grid voltage controlled whether or not they would pass through the grid to the plate. The vacuum allowed the electrons to move freely. In the 1950s, the transistor, a solid-state device that performs an equivalent function, replaced the vacuum tube.

Interconnections among the triodes were accomplished in the circuitry on the underside of the add-subtract mechanism. These consisted of resistor networks designed to allow the mechanism to execute a number of logical operations, such as, most basically, "NOT," "AND," and "OR," as the three streams of pulses (bits) passed through.

(Exhibit 21166.5 from the *Honeywell v. Sperry Rand* Records, Charles Babbage Institute, University of Minnesota, Minneapolis.)

---

ence of a greatly enlarged copy of the table of bit values from his original manuscript—essentially a logical truth table—to which he referred repeatedly to show that the mechanism was indeed producing the correct answers.

Then, in the presence of a second blown-up chart from that 1940 proposal, the circuit diagram of the add-subtract mechanism, Atanasoff traced the changing voltages of all the vacuum tubes (or triodes) of the mechanism, again, for both bit-addition and bit-subtraction. For this rather arduous feat, he adopted the con-

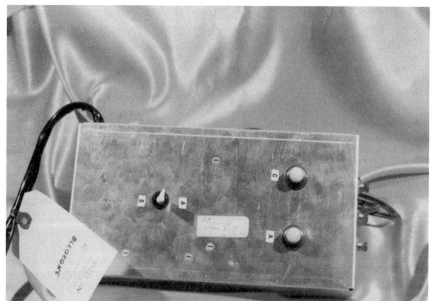

Figure 12. Courtroom test set. The original of this set was used by Atanasoff and Berry to test individual add-subtract mechanisms as they were built. At the right end in this photograph are the three input pushbuttons for entering "1s" or "0s" (pushed for "1," not for "0"), as though from the computer's counter, keyboard, and carry-borrow drums. The two output lights, indicating the solutions as though destined for the keyboard and carry-borrow drums (on for "1" and off for "0"), are on the right top. The cable at the right end transmitted the input signals to the demonstration add-subtract mechanism, and the cable at the left end transmitted the solution signals back from that mechanism. The switch on the left top, now off, could be turned to "A" for addition or "S" for subtraction.

(Exhibit 21165.3 from the *Honeywell v. Sperry Rand* Records, Charles Babbage Institute, University of Minnesota, Minneapolis.)

---

vention of placing a green sticker on the (incoming) grid of each tube receiving a low voltage, representing "1," and a red sticker on the grid of each tube receiving a high voltage, representing "0." But, because in his use of these tubes their signals changed direction as they passed through (high voltages to low and low to high), he had to remember to place the colored stickers in reverse order on the (outgoing) plates! Moreover, a tube grid could receive up to three (high or low) voltages, and a tube plate could relay its (high or low) voltages to as many as four grids!

The courtroom was in a state of some agitation throughout these complex presentations. The judge was concerned that everyone be able to see the "live" exhibits and the mounted charts, and especially that the court reporter be able to hear the testimony when the witness necessarily had his back to her. Honeywell

Addition					Subtraction				
Bits In			Bits Out		Bits In			Bits Out	
Counter	Keyboard	Carry	Sum	Carry	Counter	Keyboard	Borrow	Difference	Borrow
0	0	0	0	0	0	0	0	0	0
0	0	1	1	0	0	0	1	1	1
0	1	0	1	0	0	1	0	1	1
0	1	1	0	1	0	1	1	0	1
1	0	0	1	0	1	0	0	1	0
1	0	1	0	1	1	0	1	0	0
1	1	0	0	1	1	1	0	0	0
1	1	1	1	1	1	1	1	1	1

Table 2. Truth table for binary addition and subtraction. This table is adapted from the 1940 original, in which the "0s" and "1s" shown here were shown instead in terms of high and low input and output voltages, or "H's" and "L's." Addition is given on the left half, subtraction on the right.

In his courtroom demonstration, Atanasoff put his add-subtract mechanism through a number of these bit (binary digit) operations, tracing the entries and solutions on an enlargement of this table.

He illustrated the last row in addition, for example, by setting the switch to add and entering three "1s" at the pushbuttons: a "1" from a ring of the counter drum, a "1" to be added to it from the corresponding ring of the keyboard drum, and a further "1" from the carry-borrow drum as carried from the previous bit addition. He then showed that his add-subtract mechanism, in accordance with the table, had caused the two output lights to come on, indicating a "1" to be recorded and a "1" to be carried to the next bit addition. That is, "1" plus "1" plus "1" equals "11" in the binary system, and so the mechanism returned a "1" to the counter drum and a "1" to the carry-borrow drum.

The essence of Atanasoff's logical add-subtract mechanism, of course, was that it did not add or subtract by counting but produced the answers required by this table. Rather than add "1" plus "1" plus "1" by counting from 01 to 10 to 11, it so interconnected its vacuum tubes that when three "1s" (low voltages) were entered, two "1s" (low voltages) came out. Similarly, in adding two "0s" (high voltages) and a "1" (low voltage), it produced a "1" (low voltage) and a "0" (high voltage), in accord with the table's second row for addition.

---

attorney Halladay injected a note of humor by instructing his obviously excited witness that "the most important person in the courtroom" was the reporter.[22] "She counts more than the judge or anybody," he said, "so speak up, will you please?"

Sperry attorney Ferrill had the task of seeing that the reporter did not miss any weaknesses in Atanasoff's performance. Indeed, he discharged this task so assiduously that Atanasoff finally fell to inserting his own "let the record show"! Typical of the thirteen pages of transcript on the tortuous circuitry of the add-subtract mechanism was this excerpt:

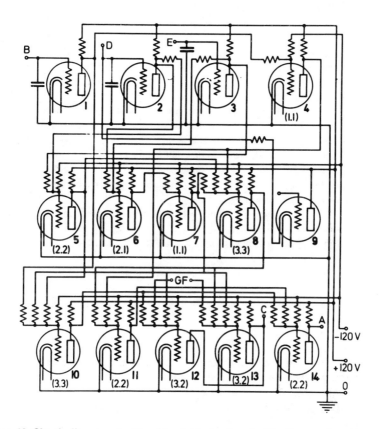

Figure 13. Circuit diagram of add-subtract mechanism. In this diagram from Atanasoff's 1940 manuscript, the triodes, numbers 1 to 14, are shown individually rather than paired in double envelopes. *B, D,* and *E* on the upper left represent the input points for the reception of bits from the counter, keyboard, and carry-borrow drums, respectively, to the first three triodes. The three long "equal signs" indicate capacitors, one per input triode, to keep the incoming signals alive through the 1/60th second procedure. *A* and *C,* at the lower right, represent the two output points, *A* the sum or difference emitted from triode 14—recall that the sums and differences in the truth table were the same—*C* the carry or borrow bit from paired triodes 12 and 13.

Each triode has a cathode (a hook) on the left, a plate (a rectangle) on the right, and a grid (a zigzag) in between. Interconnections among triodes, as well as connections to ground (0 volts) and the +120 and -120 voltage supplies on the lower right, are shown by straight lines, with zigzag interruptions indicating resistors. The *(p,q)* notations, (1,1), (2,2), etc., stand for the logical operations identified with each triode beyond the input triodes, except for the inactive extra triode 9.

The complexity of Atanasoff's add-subtract mechanism must have been evident as he described and labeled the enlarged copy of this diagram in the courtroom. But so must its elegance—its efficiency and it accomplishment—given the technology of the time.

Atanasoff: Now let's go to triode number 3 [input tube for the carry-borrow stream of pulses]. . . . There's one connection that comes down this way (indicating). It's red, meaning high, and one connection comes down this way (indicating) and is one high connection to the grid of tube 5. There are two high connections to the grid of tube 5, as a matter of fact, and that's all there are to tube 5.

　　So we reassemble here and we say the tube will not be cut off. This tube will not be cut off because the voltages are high, so the tube is wide open, so the voltage of the plate is low, and low is a green sticker, meaning "1." All I have to do is keep this up and keep everything straight and we will be all right.

Ferrill: Let the record show the witness is going back to his papers at the stand.

Judge Larson: Very well.

Atanasoff: I have got a page here which seems to be lost. I want to look at a page a moment.

Judge Larson: It's about time to recess. We will take about a 10-minute recess.

(Recess taken)

Halladay: Dr. Atanasoff, just at the point of recess you were looking for some notes. Did you find them?

Atanasoff: I found them, yes.

Halladay: All right.

Atanasoff: It was just a crutch, as you call it, to keep me from going wrong, but I appear to be right as far as I am wrong.

. . .

Atanasoff: From triode 5, the green sticker goes on the grid of triode 10 and on the grid of triode 8. (Stickers placed thereon.)

. . .

Atanasoff: Triode 8 has a "3,3" symbol, and this means that there must be three low voltages, or green voltages, in order to cause that tube to cut off, but there are only two, so the tube is not cut off, and the tube not being cut off will have a low voltage upon its plate. (Green sticker placed thereon.)

Ferrill: Let the record show the witness checking again his papers at the stand.

Atanasoff: Now, the low voltage from triode 8, the plate of triode 8, is transmitted to the grid of triode 13 and to the grid of triode 11.

　　The low voltage from . . . the plate of triode 5 is transmitted to the grid of triode 10, and a green sticker is placed there. Triode 10 has a "3,3" symbol on it and it means. . . .

　　. . . The plate of triode 10, . . . the low voltage on the plate of triode 10 also transmits . . . to the grid of triode 13—no, it doesn't, I am sorry. I am messing up my convention. . . .

Judge Larson: What was that last, Dr. Atanasoff?

Atanasoff: I will try to speak louder, yes, sir. The plate of triode 10 transmits a low voltage to the grid of triode 12 and to the grid of triode 14. The plate of triode 7 transmits a high voltage to the grid of triode 10, which was incorrectly marked.

Ferrill: Let the record show the removal of the green sticker from tube number 10 on one of the grids and the placing of a red sticker in place of it.

Atanasoff: . . . We are talking about a transmission from 7 to the grid of triode 10 to the grid of triode 12 and to the grid of triode 13. . . .

. . .

Atanasoff: Now the triode 13—let the record show that I am referring to my notes to check my work so far. . . .[23]

Atanasoff told my husband and me how happy and relieved he was, at the end of that day's testimony, to have gotten through those meticulous presentations, especially the one on the circuitry of the add-subtract mechanism, and to have made just that one slip.

<<<>>>

As chief witness for the plaintiff, Atanasoff gave perhaps his most engaging courtroom soliloquy when he told of the two dramatic breakthroughs he had experienced in a single winter's night, as his many preliminary ideas coalesced:

. . . I remember that the winter of 1937 was a desperate one for me because I had this problem and I had outlined my objectives but nothing was happening, and as winter deepened, my despair grew and I have told you about the kind of items that were rattling around in my mind and we come to a day in the middle of winter when I went out to the office intending to spend the evening trying to resolve some of these questions and I was in such a mental state that no resolution was possible. I was just unhappy to an extreme, and at that time I did something that I had done on such occasions—I don't do it anymore—I went out to my automobile, got in and started driving over the good highways of Iowa in those years at a high rate of speed.

I remember the pavement was clean and dry, and I was forced to give attention to my driving, and as a consequence of that, I was less nervous, and I drove that way for several hours. Then I sort of became aware of my surroundings. I had, of course, been aware of the road before, but I then became aware of where I was and I had reached the Mississippi River, starting from Ames and was crossing the Mississippi River at a place where there are three cities there, one of which is Rock Island.

I drove into Illinois and turned off the good highway into a little road, and went into a roadhouse there which had bright lights. It was extremely cold and I took off my overcoat. I had a very heavy coat, and hung it up, and sat down and ordered a drink, and as the delivery of the drink was made, I realized that I was no longer so nervous and my thoughts turned again to computing machines.

Now, I don't know why my mind worked then when it had not worked previously, but things seemed to be good and cool and quiet. There were not many people in the tavern, and the waitress didn't bother me particularly with repetitious offers of drinks. I would suspect that I drank two drinks perhaps, and then I realized that thoughts were coming good and I had some positive results.

During this evening in the tavern, I generated within my mind the possibility of the regenerative memory. I called it "jogging" at that time. I'm thinking about the condensers [capacitors] for memory units, and the fact that the condensers would regenerate their own state, so their state would not change with time. If they were in the plus state, for instance, they would stay in the plus state; or, if they were in the negative state, they would stay in the negative state. They would not blink off to zero. . . .

During that same evening, I gained an initial concept of what is called today the "logic circuits." That is a non-racheting approach to the interaction between two memory units, or, as I called them in those days, "abaci," . . . two abaci units . . . , and I visualized a black box at that time but not the inner workings. There would be a black box, and a state of abacus 1 would pass into the box and the state of abacus 2 would pass into the box, and the box would yield the correct results on output terminals. And somewhere late in the evening I got in my car and drove home at a slower rate.[24]

These "abaci" were, of course, the bands of capacitors in the two drums of the main memory of his projected computer; the "non-racheting approach" was the substitution of logical circuitry for the conventional counters; and the "black box" was an add-subtract mechanism that received streams of pulses from the two drums, one stream from an "abacus" of the counter drum and one from an "abacus" of the keyboard drum, added or subtracted the two streams, and emitted sums or differences.

Under questioning from Halladay, Atanasoff explained the concept of a black box:

Halladay: You say you envisioned these two abaci and a black box in between?
Atanasoff: I did, yes.
Halladay: Did you say you envisioned the black box that night?
Atanasoff: I envisioned the black box, but you know a black box has unknown contents.
Halladay: Yes.
Atanasoff: I did not envision the contents of the box that night. I just envisioned that it might be possible to construct such a box. The "black box" is kind of a conventional term, and it's called "black" because you can't see inside, and it's used in science—when we just have an input-output question before us, we are likely to use a black box with input terminals and output terminals.[25]

What Atanasoff had firmed up, then, at the end of his long, calming drive—with an assist from a "good and cool and quiet" tavern and a few shots of whiskey—were his two major contributions to electronic computing: *memory regeneration* and *logical arithmetic devices*. He saw, on the one hand, that he could make the cheap and accessible capacitors into reliable memory elements by continually restoring their charges from the electronic arithmetic unit, and, on the other hand, that he could bypass the troublesome counters in favor of logical add-subtract mechanisms.

The black-box concept was the key to the logic insight. It reduced the role of each mechanism to that of *intermediary* between the "input" of three streams of bits (including the carry-borrow stream, once that was taken into account) and the "output" of two other streams. Within the box, each arriving trio of input bits had to be combined in accord with the truth table for addition and subtraction to produce the correct duo of output bits.

This sudden triumph—the culmination, actually, of many months of thinking and exploring—was the sweeter because all of Atanasoff's other earlier concepts now fell into place: a rotating-drum memory, vacuum tubes computing in the digital mode, binary as the preferred digital mode, and a novel algorithm for solving the large sets of linear algebraic equations he and so many other scientists needed to solve.

<<<>>>

In his cross-examination of Atanasoff, Sperry Rand attorney Ferrill challenged him on the date of his roadhouse trip and the jelling of his plan for an electronic computer.[26] Atanasoff had testified that he took the drive into Illinois in late 1937, or possibly early 1938, but Ferrill tried to shift it forward to late 1938 or early 1939, on two grounds.

First, he reasoned, Atanasoff had been busy until the fall of 1937 considering such measures as the ganging of desk calculators and the modification of IBM tabulating machines for the solution of his large systems of equations. There was too little time for him to conceive the several schemes for an electronic computer that were in the mix he untangled at the tavern that late winter's night. Second, Atanasoff did not begin work on the model for his computer until the fall of 1939, and this, Ferrill thought, was too much time at the other end, too much time before actuation of the plan.

Atanasoff was unshakable on this point. He said he had begun to think of building an electronic computer as early as 1935, even as he explored mechanical and electromechanical possibilities. And, he explained, he could not start building the model until he had worked out the logic circuits for the add-subtract mechanism and secured a grant from Iowa State College. He said he spent about ten months—most of 1938—on the logic, applied for the grant, and received it in the spring of 1939. Only then did he hire Berry, a senior in engineering, to join him in the fall as his graduate assistant.

But Ferrill persisted, only to be rewarded with an eloquent recital of the economic constraints on scientists in the 1930s.

> *Ferrill:* Do you know for certain that it was not near the end of 1938 when you made the trip to Illinois to the roadhouse?

> *Atanasoff:* I am very convinced in my own mind, sir. It has to do with my state of mind and the state of mind of other men of that day. It has to do with my feeling of uncertainty about this whole process of development of a machine in which there's a radical change in elements thereof. . . . I knew that when I went—when I requested funds I would be under severe cross-examination and I delayed asking for funds until I had worked out the details and felt quite certain [about them]. And I remember the pressures of that time and the fact that I several times went back over my calculations and the methods of approach to this problem to insure that I could answer the assistant dean's questions. . . . He was a good friend of mine, but he was also known to be a very severe man in regard to the disbursement of funds and I hated to go up and ask him for funds and I wouldn't do it until I was quite certain that I had a logic system worked out and the methods pretty well in detail. . . .
>
> . . .
>
> *Ferrill:* Wasn't it actually your practice to sort of try to work things out as you go, first starting with kind of a framework and then fitting things in?
>
> *Atanasoff:* It certainly was my standard practice, yes, sir.
>
> *Ferrill:* To do it that way?
>
> *Atanasoff:* Yes. I mixed everything in together but that doesn't mean—that doesn't mean that I didn't feel the pressures of this professor of genetics who had become the disburser of funds there, that I didn't feel very uncertain about my quest for funds from him, and, you know, the quest for, what was it, $450 looked like a mountain to me in those days.

Ferrill continued to disparage Atanasoff's version of these events, suggesting that he would not really have had to "spell out details" of his computer to the college's disburser of funds and that his account was just "an expression of what you consider a strong belief of yours."

Honeywell attorney Halladay had the last word, however, in redirect examination, when he read from a letter that Atanasoff had written in 1940 requesting further financing from the Research Corporation.[27] There he set "seven years ago" (1933) for the start of his efforts and "three years ago" (1937) for the succession of design ideas.

Ferrill, in his cross-examination, challenged another date in Atanasoff's testimony, that of the completion of the test model of the ABC—this time by only a month or two! Atanasoff had placed his demonstrations of this "prototype" in late 1939, "November and December."[28] And he had already been supported on this point by the testimony of his graduate assistant on the antiaircraft fire-control project, Sam Legvold, who recalled the model's successful operation in "either October or November of 1939."[29] Yet Ferrill proposed January 1940 as the correct date, and he seemed, this time, to be right.[30] He savored the moment.

> *Ferrill:* Dr. Atanasoff, if I suggest to you the proving out with your tests with this prototype occurred rather in January, 1940, would you say that that by your memory is wrong?

Atanasoff: I wouldn't say there wasn't one chance in a million but I would say there wasn't much more than that that that occurred.

Ferrill: Let me ask you to refer, please, to your manuscript [of 1940] . . . Page 31. Do you have a copy of it before you?

Atanasoff: Yes.

Ferrill: Would you read the next to the last paragraph, Dr. Atanasoff?

. . .

Atanasoff: "A test setup of an abacus and add-subtract mechanism and converter was made in January of 1940. The arrangement performed perfectly and allowed actual tests under working conditions to be given to various components."

Ferrill: Now, this was your own writing, something you wrote in August of 1940—

Atanasoff: Yes.

Ferrill:—wasn't it?

Atanasoff: Yes, sir.

Ferrill: And that was about seven months after January, 1940?

Atanasoff: Yes, sir.

Ferrill: Is my arithmetic right?

Atanasoff: Yes, sir.

Ferrill: And you were reporting on the prototype, here?

Atanasoff: I was reporting on the prototype, yes, sir.

Ferrill: Well, would this be the correct time of the test?

Atanasoff: Well, this is a sentence that convinces me that it was January.

Ferrill: 1940?

Atanasoff: Yes, sir. I would believe this before I would believe my own memory.

Ferrill then placed a large time chart on the courtroom easel, running from 1937 to 1942, and asked Atanasoff to write "Testing of prototype" in the January 1940 slot.

Unfortunately for Ferrill, Halladay in his redirect examination again proved him mistaken.[31] The key word in the manuscript statement, he explained, was "converter." Only a converter, a device Atanasoff now described as an "additional gadget of Mr. Berry's" for "sticking numbers in the machine while it was rotating," was added in January. The successful demonstrations of the model had, indeed, been conducted in the last months of 1939.

Of course, as Ferrill conducted his cross-examination, he could not anticipate Halladay's later refutation of these attempts of his to impugn the witness's memory—for such had to be his main objective in challenging Atanasoff's account of his steps along the way to a finished computer. There was no question of either the start of work on the model in the fall of 1939 or the completion of work on the ABC itself in the spring of 1942. But doubt might be cast on the witness's memory, or even his truthfulness, at a number of these intermediate steps.

And so Ferrill pushed on, bringing one last case in which his *sole* objective seemed to be the impugning of Atanasoff's memory, this time not only of dates but of materials. At issue was the metal used in the rings of contact studs embedded in the surfaces of the ABC's two large storage drums.[32] In the presence of one of those original drums, Atanasoff testified that the studs had been cut from brass rod stock, or spelter, with the ends flattened in a die. He commented that he thought "a procurement document from the instrument shop" was among the records he had produced for this trial. But Ferrill was convinced the studs were made of brass tubing.

> *Ferrill:* Do you know for sure that these contacts were made of rod stock and were not made of a small tubing?
> *Atanasoff:* Yes, I think I do.
> *Ferrill:* You are not certain of that?
> *Atanasoff:* Well, my memory is pretty strong again. I just can't imagine tubing being used in those things. This is the kind of memory I have and I could be wrong. You could pull one of those out and look at it and tell if it's tubing. . . .

Ferrill then handed the witness an invoice from his own records and had him read off its notation of "53 feet of hard drawn seamless brass tubing" and also the inner and outer dimensions specified there. He continued:

> *Ferrill:* . . . What were you getting 53 feet of this hard drawn seamless brass tubing for?
> *Atanasoff:* Let me think—may I think on this a while?
> *Ferrill:* Certainly. I want you to take your time, Dr. Atanasoff.
> *Atanasoff:* Thank you sir. My memory persists that those [contacts] are made of spelter, and spelter is not hollow. . . . My memory persists strongly that that was true. Now, let's see as to the tubing. Well, I have got a thought about the tubing. You know, the tubing was used for brush holders, I believe. The brush holders—let's reach for, if you please, sir, the exhibit containing the brushes [used to read from and write on the drum contacts].
> . . .
> *Atanasoff [holding a brush from the exhibit]:* . . . The brass tubing was used for the brush holders. The brushes went through the center of the brass tubing and it furnished an additional support for these [wire] brushes and we soldered the outside of the brass tubing and this way made contact with the brushes.

At this point in a morning session of the court, Ferrill seemed to drop the issue of the contact studs, going on to other matters. Yet he returned to it after the lunch break.[33] Noting that the Sperry team had been inspecting the drum, he asked Atanasoff to take one more look at the studs, particularly at one now encircled by a tiny rubber band. Didn't he see "hollow spaces in the middle of these flattened ends?" Didn't he see, in the one with the rubber band, "a little opening . . . where it wasn't flattened down completely?"

Atanasoff: Well—

Ferrill: What I want you to do is inspect that and then tell me whether after careful inspection this was made with pieces of brass tubing there and flattened down and inserted?

Atanasoff: Well, the way of a witness is hard. My memory is very clear that the pins were made of rod, . . . of a form of rod which is used for brazing called spelter.

Now, I am faced with a rubber band upon certain pins here and . . . a slight hollow and I myself am unable to ascertain. . . .

Now, I want to say a word about metals. Now, when you take a metal and squeeze it flat certain distortions and disturbances occur in the fibers and the working ratio is pretty high in these fibers. I suspect that the hollows which counsel has so assiduously discovered in the center of these terminals is due to the working thereof. I don't know, and I may be wrong. Goodness knows, I may be wrong. As far as I am concerned, counsel can take a pin out. . . .

Atanasoff paused here to explain that actually he did not know who had the property rights to this drum, although he believed it had been secured as a trial exhibit from Iowa State University. In 1948, Sam Legvold, by then an associate professor of physics, had rescued it and a few smaller parts as the ABC was being dismantled.

Atanasoff: . . . It was discovered by Sam . . . and taken to his office and put there, and various people seized upon it and contemporaneously had custody of it, and who has custody of it and who has property rights must be ascertained by a process best known to counsel.

Ferrill: Well, are you indicating that there may be some obstacle to our opening up one of the pins?

Atanasoff: I will make none. I will make none. . . .

Ferrill: You don't think, do you, that anyone is about to use it to make a computing apparatus or try to?

Atanasoff: I have strong doubt, sir.

It is a mystery why Ferrill persisted in this increasingly insulting line, in the face of the detailed responses of this witness, who was, after all, not only an expert in the technology of the period but the very inventor of the devices under question—*and* in the face of the witness's remark that there existed a "procurement document" for the rod stock. Perhaps Ferrill thought the Sperry team's experts were better. Perhaps he thought the document Atanasoff recalled was not, in fact, for the rod stock but for the tubing.

Whatever Ferrill's reason, persist he did, turning now to the tubing invoice itself and challenging Atanasoff about *it* and how it had come into his hands at this late date. He succeeded, finally, in provoking Atanasoff to a rare show of annoyance on the stand.

Ferrill: Well, are you saying that you have been keeping a copy of this and the
hundreds of other papers in Plaintiff's Exhibit 266 in your file at home for
some years prior to 1967?
Atanasoff: Many years prior. I would say thirty years prior.
Ferrill: And it is still your testimony, is it, Dr. Atanasoff, that you are convinced
that the pins in this Exhibit 21408 are rod stock and not flattened tubing?
Atanasoff: It is my best belief, sir, that they are rod stock.
Ferrill: But you are not certain?
Atanasoff: Well, goodness, I don't have x-ray eyes. My memory tells me it was
rod stock. My memory tells me the alloy which was used. I know this alloy
to be hard, I know it will work. If it is worked severely, it will fragment
inside. I know these things, so it seems rational and proper and also
according to the tenets of my memory to state that those are rod stock.

Atanasoff's wife, Alice, told Arthur and me that from the time of their mar-
riage in 1949 until August 1967, when attorneys for Honeywell met with them in
their home, she and "JV" had moved a number of sealed cartons from one
dwelling to another, always keeping them stored in some safe place. Her husband
never revealed what was in them, she said, but she knew they were special to him;
and, indeed, they held his records of the ABC. Atanasoff himself told us of the
delight with which the Honeywell lawyers greeted each scrap of paper as they
went through the hundreds of items together in his living room.

Among those records was the instrument shop's bill for the rod stock! Halladay produced it in his redirect examination, noting that it was dated some five
months prior to the invoice for the brass tubing and that it showed a charge not
only for the rod stock but for the dies to form the ends of the contacts![34]

Not all of Ferrill's cross-examination was so contentious. He did, once more,
bring Atanasoff to the point of annoyance, as he put him through a half day's
exercise in describing how the ABC would have solved a set of five equations in
five variables.[35] But in the end that exchange became more amicable.

Ferrill had again set up a series of charts on which the witness was to enter
the steps of the solution procedure, one by one. About midway through this
demanding task, Atanasoff explained how the coefficients on the keyboard drum
were shifted during the elimination of a variable.

Ferrill: What is the apparatus that causes these things you have just recited to
occur, Dr. Atanasoff?
Atanasoff: I don't know—a machine of some kind, I suppose. It's a machine
which is built into the thing.
Well, I could build one easily enough. I could build one easier than I
could—not easier, because it would take me a week, perhaps.
Ferrill: Easier than you can describe it? Was that what you were going to say?
Atanasoff: Well, easier than I can describe it if each time I utter three words, I
have to stop and write what I have said down, and then I have to reform

what I have said into a kind of grammar, and which is peculiar to the written word, and do a hundred and one other things that I'm pursuing at the moment. But I'll do my best.

Now, this is just a temporary complaint—no problem here. (Laughter) I'm having a hard time, and you know it. (Laughter) I don't mind, and I can take this quite a while. . . .

Ferrill: I want to tell you, quite sincerely, Dr. Atanasoff, that I'm not really intending to make a hard time for you—

Atanasoff: No, and doggone it, I know you could be much worse. That's one of the things that plagues me currently. (Laughter) You're not doing so badly, no.

Pardon me, Your Honor, for giving such remarks.

With that release, Atanasoff was able to describe the mechanism in question very well and to complete the exercise with an enthusiasm that proved contagious. Even Ferrill became so absorbed in Atanasoff's exposition that he slipped from inquisitor to pupil at times, welcoming, for example, an offer to explain the elimination process in the more familiar decimal system. And, at least for the moment, he dropped his prosecutorial manner, raising an admiring comment from the judge on this note of harmony in his courtroom.

Ferrill: I think the record ought to show, Dr. Atanasoff, that you did that string of computations on this new sheet . . . in about seven minutes even with my interruptions to ask you questions about it.

Atanasoff: Good.

Ferrill: I can see you have been in mathematics a long time.

Atanasoff: Thank you, sir.

Judge Larson: With all these compliments going around the room, we will take our afternoon recess.

Nor were all of Ferrill's challenges so misguided as the ones cited above. Returning from that afternoon recess to quiz Atanasoff on the time the ABC would have required to solve the set of five equations worked out on the charts, he quickly refuted Atanasoff's estimate that, in general, the machine time would have been "a hundred fold faster" than that of a desk calculator.[36] Atanasoff acknowledged his error, but he also pointed out that the hour or two required to solve a set of five equations was not to be taken as typical. The ABC, he explained, would have been much more efficient in solving the very large sets— up to twenty-nine equations—for which it had been designed, sets beyond human solution, even on a calculator, for all practical purposes.

Ferrill then turned to the operating speed of the electronic add-subtract mechanism, questioning an estimate Atanasoff had made, in direct examination, as to how much of the time required for a single bit addition or subtraction was taken up by the add-subtract mechanism.[37] Atanasoff had estimated that, of each such sixtieth-of-a-second cycle—from counter drum through add-subtract mechanism and back to counter drum—the electronics consumed only "a few millionths of a second or one-millionth of a second or a half a millionth of a second."[38]

Ferrill now proposed 100 microseconds (millionths of a second) as a more likely figure, and Atanasoff, confessing that he had not made a circuit analysis when he testified earlier, proceeded to do so there in court, arriving, some twenty transcript pages later, at a revised figure of twenty-five microseconds.[39]

From Atanasoff's point of view, this focus on the operating speed of a single add-subtract mechanism was as wide of the mark as Ferrill's earlier focus on the solution time for a small set of equations. The very essence of the ABC's design as a vector processor had been that, in solving large sets of equations, it would add or subtract up to thirty pairs of numbers *simultaneously*, whereas an operator of a desk calculator would have to add or subtract each pair individually. In the ABC, the operating speed of *all* thirty add-subtract mechanisms together was the same as the operating speed of a single add-subtract mechanism! In both of his lines of inquiry here, Ferrill was bypassing the computer's basic rationale.

Atanasoff did make this point briefly, noting that the speed of the machine "was enhanced" by the fact that it had "thirty parallel channels of calculation."[40] At the same time, he testified that he had not been concerned about the precise speed of the add-subtract mechanisms because he was sure it was more than adequate when compared to the speed of "the mechanical switching which is associated with the rotation of the drum in question."

All in all, Ferrill's cross-examination on the first four days of Atanasoff's testimony served to confirm what Halladay had tried to establish: that the witness's memory was sharp and accurate, that his technical competence was of a high order, that he was straightforward on the stand and not evasive, and that his version of events was consistent and credible. The Sperry team is not to be faulted, however, for their unsuccessful attempts to discredit this witness's story. *They did what they could with what they had.* It simply turned out that almost all of their counterarguments were without substance.

Or were irrelevant. How fast or slow Atanasoff's add-subtract mechanism was, for example, was irrelevant to the fact that, at the time Mauchly saw it in action, it was an entirely novel electronic computing device *with enormous potential*, one whose technology he and Eckert then exploited to their own advantage.

<<<>>>

On Monday, June 21, 1971, the fifth day of Atanasoff's direct testimony, Halladay came to the heart of the Honeywell case: Mauchly's experience of the computer during his visit to Iowa State College in mid-June 1941. He prefaced this inquiry with a review of the Mauchly-Atanasoff correspondence that spring (see chap. 2).[41] In so doing, he established: on the one hand, Mauchly's absorption in the analysis of weather data on his harmonic analyzer, his great curiosity about Atanasoff's computer, and his lack of progress toward his own electronic computing goals; on the other hand, Atanasoff's enthusiasm for his computer, his thoughts about converting it into an *electronic digital* differential analyzer, and his concurrent handling of several other research projects.

Atanasoff gave a detailed description of Mauchly's visit.[42] He said that Mauchly arrived at dusk on Friday, June 13, with his son, "a boy of six or seven," and that "some supper was prepared" because they had not eaten. The two men discussed the machine at that time, he said, together with "a variety of other things and such gossip as he could bring me of computing machines from the east." He continued:

> During the weekend, accompanied by Dr. Mauchly and the children, we went over and we entered the computing room where the computing machine was and [it] was shown to him in some detail and there were discussions during the weekend of the theory of the machine and the method of its operation.

He explained that the computer had been "all torn up" prior to Mauchly's visit and that he had had Berry mount all completed units on the framework.

> Now, I remember Monday morning, I took Dr. Mauchly and we went over the first thing in the morning and went in to see the machine. Clifford Berry was there and there may have been one or two other people . . . , and Clifford Berry and Mauchly immediately went into discussion of the various details of the machine and during the morning, I took pains to show him . . . a copy of a document which I have here before me [the August 1940 descriptive manuscript].
> . . .
> He had a copy of this document while he was visiting me but at the end of the visit, he asked me if he could take it back to the east with him and I told him that I preferred that he did not.

Atanasoff told of a lecture Mauchly gave about "his analysis of meteorological phenomena" on "his Fourier analyzer" to the twenty or twenty-five graduate students Atanasoff was able to assemble from throughout the Physics Building. This was, he said, the one activity not directly connected to the ABC that he could recall Mauchly engaged in during his visit. As for the balance of Mauchly's time on campus:

> . . . he was around the machine on frequent occasions with Mr. Clifford Berry and . . . with me and . . . with Mr. Sam Legvold, and he participated frequently with Clifford Berry in various discussions and even manipulation of the parts of the machine and during this period, the machine was demonstrated for him in detail. . . . He seemed to follow in detail our explanations and expressed joy at the results, at the fact that these vacuum tubes would actually compute.

Atanasoff testified that he and Berry demonstrated various aspects of the ABC to Mauchly. Numbers on decimal cards were automatically read, converted to binary, and entered onto the memory drums, with the results verified on an oscilloscope. Then arithmetic operations, including shifting, were carried out on these binary numbers, also automatically, with the results again verified on an oscilloscope. Such demonstrations required the participation of many key components: the add-subtract mechanisms, the restore-shift mechanisms, the keyboard and counter drums, the carry-borrow drum, the decimal-card reader, and the base-conversion drum.

Atanasoff made clear that certain portions of the computer were incomplete at the time of Mauchly's visit. The binary-card writing and reading system was such that he could demonstrate the writing of a number (charring or burning) on a card, but could not yet demonstrate the reading portion. As we saw in chapter 2, however, Mauchly learned enough about this system to describe it accurately in his Control Data deposition. Also, the brushes for writing on and reading from drums were represented by just a few sets, and the carry-borrow drum had only two bands. Finally, the general controls of the computer were still in the planning stage. Because of all these limitations, the overall solution process could not be demonstrated.

The add-subtract mechanisms were demonstrated not only on the computer but on the separate test set, similar to the one shown in court, and their results checked on meters. Atanasoff referred to this last demonstration as a way of explaining "the logic system" of the add-subtract mechanisms. He further recalled a session in which he and Berry "discussed the logic element in considerable detail with Dr. Mauchly."

At Halladay's bidding, Atanasoff estimated that he spent a total of "25 to 30 hours" with Mauchly during his visit. He could not say how many hours Mauchly was "in the presence of the machine," but he commented that Mauchly "certainly had free access" to it and "spent most of his time while visiting us either sleeping, or eating, or in the presence of the machine," whether with him or with Berry or with both. Asked if he had declined to answer any of Mauchly's questions or had limited Berry in this regard, he replied in the negative.

Atanasoff thought that, as promised, he had talked to Mauchly about his plan to adapt the ABC for the solution of differential equations. He was certain that he had discussed the distinction between analog and digital computers, although the term *digital* had not yet come into use. He observed that his own "very clumsy term" for digital machines had been "computing machines proper," by which he meant that they did arithmetic calculations directly rather than by analogy to some physical property—length, for example, in the slide rule, or shaft rotation in the differential analyzer. He seems to have been the first person to apply the term *analog* to computers, in his 1940 manuscript, where he rejected that approach for his own purposes.

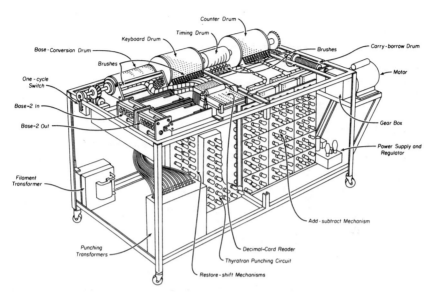

Counter Drum
Timing Drum
Keyboard Drum
Base-Conversion Drum
Brushes
One-cycle Switch
Base-2 In
Base-2 Out
Filament Transformer
Punching Transformers
Brushes
Carry-borrow Drum
Motor
Gear Box
Power Supply and Regulator
Add-subtract Mechanism
Decimal-Card Reader
Thyratron Punching Circuit
Restore-shift Mechanisms

Figure 14. Drawing of the ABC. Like Figure 17, this drawing (now slightly modified) was drafted for use in court. Atanasoff spoke from it extensively, both to explain the computer's operation and to detail and defend its state during Mauchly's June 1941 visit.
(Drawing modified by David Oliver.)

As to what, if any, parts of that manuscript he had discussed with Mauchly, Atanasoff said, somewhat indignantly:

> I remember an occasion in my home—he had the copy in his possession, he took it to my home and read it evenings and I remember us in my own study at home, in my home, reading and discussing the manuscript. I remember that one subject discussed at that time was the carry mechanism.

He also remembered explaining to Mauchly how to "follow through for himself" the circuit diagram for the add-subtract mechanism and how to interpret the truth table for addition and subtraction. Finally, he recalled Mauchly's "surprise that the base 2 number system was advantageous for computing." His recollection, he said, was that Mauchly "was not proficient in base 2 calculations" at the time of his visit, and that they had worked through some problems together.

In his cross-examination of Atanasoff on Mauchly's June 1941 visit, Sperry Rand attorney Ferrill elicited the state of the Atanasoff-Berry Computer at that time in considerable detail, including the approximate completion date of each part.[43] Later, he questioned one discrepancy between the witness's courtroom version and that of his earlier deposition.[44] This discrepancy concerned the decimal-card reader, along with the brushes and wiring for communicating with the base-conversion drum as decimal equations were converted to binary form. Atanasoff had recalled in deposition that this system was not in place for the Mauchly visit, but in court he recalled that it was in place.[45]

When Atanasoff reaffirmed this revised position, Ferrill queried him as to how his memory could be *better* three years *later*. He came down hard on this point, forcing Atanasoff to agree repeatedly as to what his deposition testimony had been and to admit that it had been "not correct" or "not true" on this particular matter. He also took him through a list of persons he may have contacted after the 1968 deposition, implying that he had altered his position on the basis of their recollections rather than his own. In each instance, Atanasoff remembered some contact *before* the deposition, but none *after* it, and never any contact, either in deposition or at trial, that influenced his testimony on the decimal-card reader.

Ferrill went so far as to refer broadly to Atanasoff's "testimony at trial" as "inconsistent with and contrary to your deposition testimony," rather than just to this one item of discrepancy. He concluded this interrogation with the question: "Actually, Dr. Atanasoff, do you know what the machine had on it and didn't have on it when Dr. Mauchly was there in June, 1941?"

Atanasoff replied that he did know, "subject to the vagaries of memory."

Of course, as in his earlier unsuccessful challenges to Atanasoff's testimony on the brass rod stock and on the dates for the roadhouse trip and the computer model, it was Atanasoff's very memory that Ferrill was impugning. He went on to grill him about his firm recollection that Mauchly had arrived at his home on Friday, June 13, and his less-than-firm recollection that he had left the following Thursday morning.[46] Ferrill himself, citing Mauchly's testimony of "a very few days" in Ames, suggested first Saturday and then Friday for the arrival, Tuesday for the departure. Atanasoff was sure Mauchly had not left on Tuesday. There was this final exchange:

> *Ferrill:* Do you think maybe . . . that Dr. Mauchly was perhaps there from sometime, like, Friday evening until Tuesday and left on Tuesday?
> *Atanasoff:* My memory gives me no such results, no, sir.
> *Ferrill:* Well, is your memory really reliable on this point, would you think?
> *Atanasoff:* I imagine you better test my memory, sir. I will let it stand on the results thereof. I can't give answers to things like that.

On the basis of Mauchly's June 22 letter to Atanasoff, saying that he drove to Stockton, Massachusetts (from Collegeville, Pennsylvania) on Friday evening, June 20, it is probable that he left Ames on Wednesday. In her *Annals of the History of Computing* article, Kathleen R. Mauchly, whom he married in 1948 after the death of his first wife, also gives "Friday evening" for his arrival and "early

Wednesday morning" for his departure.[47] Ferrill's suggestion of Tuesday as the departure day was no better than Atanasoff's of Thursday.

It would seem that, for all his hammering away at the one shift in Atanasoff's testimony from deposition to trial, Ferrill did not succeed here, either, in denting the courtroom impression of a witness possessed of a remarkable long-term memory. Nor, it would seem, did he tarnish the image of a witness struggling to respond candidly to the severest challenges to his integrity without sacrificing his dignity and self-respect.

Atanasoff's performance as a witness was in sharp contrast to Mauchly's. Mauchly on numerous occasions claimed no recall at all. And he revealed, not just one, but many shifts over the four years stretching from his deposition in the Regenerative Memory case, through his deposition in the ENIAC case, and on to the ENIAC trial. As for what he saw during his Iowa visit, he shifted from a flat denial, in the earlier case, that he saw any tests performed, to an open admission, in the later case, that he saw both tests on laboratory equipment and demonstrations on the computer. As for the ABC's exact state, he neither confirmed not disputed Atanasoff's version. He pleaded a lack of detailed recall, chiefly out of a loss of interest once he had had a superficial look.

It was mid-afternoon on June 21, 1971—still the fifth day of his direct examination of Atanasoff—when Halladay broached the matter of a problem with the binary-card input-output system that turned up only as the computer neared completion in the spring of 1942.[48] Atanasoff and Berry had had to leave this rather vexing flaw unresolved to take war-research positions elsewhere not long after it was discovered.

Atanasoff explained in court that his algorithm called for the writing out of a new equation onto a large binary card after each elimination of a variable from a pair of equations, to be followed later by the reading back in of that new equation as one of a new set of one fewer equations in one fewer variables. Halladay was at pains to make the difficulty with this card-writing and -reading system clear to the judge.

> *Halladay:* Do I understand, Dr. Atanasoff, that the machine as designed was supposed to give you a punched card output and you take those punched cards and somehow feed them back to the machine?
> *Atanasoff:* Exactly that.
> *Halladay:* And do it again, again, and again?
> *Atanasoff:* In a certain order and then the complete solution would eventuate.

Asked whether there was ever a time when the ABC "actually went through the total process of solving a large set of linear algebraic equations," Atanasoff said there was not, because of a problem with this binary input-output system—

specifically, a problem with the card material, or dielectric. In 1940, when he first worked out his novel, nonmechanical method of punching cards and reading from them, he and Berry ran satisfactory laboratory tests on several different card materials. But when the computer was finished and they could test the entire complement of writing and reading units, only one such sample proved consistently satisfactory. And they could not locate the source of that one sample! Atanasoff recalled that they made a rather extensive search, but the United States was now at war and "the industrial supply situation was getting more and more difficult."

Halladay had not examined Atanasoff in court about his binary-card system, although detailed descriptions were to be found in Berry's master's thesis and in Atanasoff's 1940 manuscript, both of which became part of the trial record. Mauchly had characterized it very well in his Regenerative Memory deposition, as a method of burning a spot on a card (for a "1") with a certain *high-voltage* spark, then later reading that burned spot (as a "1") with a *low-voltage* spark— just high enough to pass through wherever there was a burn, but not high enough to create a burn where there was none.

Under questioning by Halladay, Atanasoff explained that the card material had to function within the constraints of the desired writing and reading voltages, which he had determined to be in a ratio of about three to one. More recently, he told my husband and me that of course he and Berry had experimented with different writing and reading voltages, as well as with different card materials, but had failed to find a combination of all three factors that gave satisfactory results.

Atanasoff testified further that it was not the writing function but the reading function—detecting all charred spots—that was unreliable.

> . . . I believe the reliability was about 95 percent, and, of course, that . . . meant that 5 percent of the time the readback would not duplicate the printout.

He rejected the possibility, sometimes suggested, that moisture could have caused the problem with the paper, concluding instead that "if a proper dielectric had been found, the method would have been successful."

At the end of June, Atanasoff's brilliant graduate assistant left for a draft-deferred job in Pasadena, California. Clifford Berry took with him his new bride, Jean Reed, whom he had earlier steered to the position of secretary to his boss. Atanasoff had been able to secure deferments for Sam Legvold and others on his antiaircraft project, but not for Berry on the computer project. Then he, too, he testified, "was importuned to take a position at the Naval Ordnance Laboratory" and left for Washington in mid-September.

Ferrill, in cross-examination, explored the difficulty with the binary cards during Atanasoff's extended testimony on the solution of a set of five linear equations, presented earlier. He also read an April 9, 1942, report to the Research Corporation in which Atanasoff mentioned this difficulty with the binary-card "apparatus," and he went on to suggest that Atanasoff did not know how to make the apparatus work.[49]

Of course, the failure of the ABC's binary-card input-output system had no bearing on the central, fourfold issue before the judge: Did Atanasoff originate useful electronic computing principles? Did Mauchly learn of such principles from Atanasoff? Were these principles new to Mauchly? Was the invention of the ENIAC (accordingly) derived from Atanasoff? Judge Larson devoted his entire Finding 3 to these questions.[50]

As to Atanasoff's accomplishments, he ruled, first:

> 3.1.4 Between 1937 and 1942, Atanasoff, then a professor of physics and mathematics at Iowa State College, Ames, Iowa, developed and built an automatic electronic digital computer for solving large systems of simultaneous linear algebraic equations.

He went on to say that the 1939 model itself established "the basic principles of design," and that Atanasoff's 1940 manuscript was not only adequate for construction and use of "an ABC computer" but was also the basis for funding recommendations by "experts in the art." He commented further that at the time of Mauchly's visit construction of the machine was "sufficiently well advanced [that] the principles of its operation, including detail design features," could be (and were) "explained and demonstrated to Mauchly."

As to what Mauchly learned from Atanasoff, he ruled:

> 3.1.16 The discussions Mauchly had with both Atanasoff and Berry while at Ames were free and open and no significant information concerning the machine's theory, design, construction, use or operation was withheld.

As to the state of Mauchly's own expertise, he ruled:

> 3.1.17 Prior to his visit to Ames, Iowa, Mauchly had been broadly interested in electrical analog calculating devices, but had not conceived an automatic electronic digital computer.

As to derivation of the ENIAC from Atanasoff, he ruled:

> 3.1.18 As a result of this visit, the discussions of Mauchly with Atanasoff and Berry, the demonstrations, and the review of the manuscript, Mauchly derived from the ABC "the invention of the automatic electronic digital computer" claimed in the ENIAC patent.

In addition to these rulings on the central issue before him, Judge Larson also addressed the fact that Atanasoff had been unable to make the ABC completely operable before he joined the war effort, and that after the war he effectively abandoned it (Finding 12).[51] Here he cited patent law:

> 12.2.5.4 The utilization of ideas in a device prior to the time of the alleged invention, whether or not the device was subsequently abandoned, is evidence that when those ideas are incorporated in a later development along the same line, they do not amount to invention.

From all these arguments, Judge Larson concluded:

> 12.2.5 Eckert and Mauchly did not themselves first invent "the automatic electronic digital computer," which SR and ISD [Sperry Rand and its subsidiary, Illinois Scientific Developments] contend to be the subject matter of the ENIAC patent, but instead derived that broad subject matter from Dr. John V. Atanasoff, and the ENIAC patent is thereby invalid.

As we have said, the testimony of Clifford Berry concerning Mauchly's experience of the ABC would have been invaluable had he lived. But two other eyewitnesses to these events of June 1941 did give compelling accounts, in both the ENIAC and the Regenerative Memory cases. One was Sam Legvold, who worked with Atanasoff during the war and who later received his doctorate from Columbia University and joined the physics faculty at Iowa State.[52] The other was Atanasoff's first wife, Lura Atanasoff, from whom he was divorced in 1949.[53]

These two witnesses gave particularly poignant testimony in their depositions for the Regenerative Memory case, under questioning by Allen Kirkpatrick, attorney for the defendant, Control Data, and by Laurence B. Dodds, attorney for the plaintiff, Sperry Rand. Both were called on behalf of Control Data and were deposed in December 1967, Legvold in Ames, Lura Atanasoff in Denver.

Legvold testified, in direct examination, that he was a doctoral student in 1939 when he started to work for Atanasoff on the secret antiaircraft fire-control project. He said that he often walked the short distance from his sealed-off project to Atanasoff's computer project to see the machine, but also to consult with "electronics expert" Berry.

Legvold described both the model, which he had seen being built and demonstrated that first fall, and the computer as he remembered it during Mauchly's 1941 visit. He said he had witnessed many tests and demonstrations of the computer in May and June, just prior to that visit, and he also identified details of photographs taken of the ABC, again, prior to that visit.

He recalled Berry's writing his master's thesis on the binary input-output system, which he characterized favorably as "a whole new realm of trying to get information in and out of the machine." He also recalled that the decimal-card reader and the conversion drum were "operable early in 1941."

Of Mauchly's visit, he told Kirkpatrick:

> My most vivid recollection . . . is of Mauchly in shirt-sleeves helping Clifford and the other people working on the computer, doing things with the computer and on the computer. This, I think, indicates something of the spirit of the meeting that he had with these people. They were deeply interested in computers and were exchanging freely all ideas that they had about computers, and Clifford would detail for him all of the operations, as I recall it now.
>
> I would have a tough time picking any particular part of the machine and saying that I know he saw this and that. All I know is that . . . Clifford Berry and J. V. Atanasoff and Mauchly all together were mutually stimulating people relative to work on computers, and this is typical of people who, I think, carry out research projects, and the whole spirit of this meeting of Mauchly with Berry and Atanasoff was one where ideas were freely exchanged.

Asked how long "this sort of exchange" went on, Legvold replied, "My recollection indicates he was there three working days, but I know it was two for sure [Monday and Tuesday]." Told that Mauchly had said in his own deposition that he did not recall spending "more than perhaps a half hour" with the computer, Legvold estimated that it was "more like 12 to sixteen hours with the machine," plus more hours "discussing this with Atanasoff in periods outside of the [computer] room."

Dodds, in cross-examination, drew from Legvold an admission that he could not testify to any specific topics discussed by Mauchly, Atanasoff, and Berry, so that he could have no real basis for thinking their exchanges were full and frank. Legvold, however, defended his impression:

> Well, you understand I was very close to Clifford Berry. I always was, you see. Also to Atanasoff, you understand. So that I was around enough . . . all the time that Mauchly was there, so that my knowledge that the exchange was free and open I think is substantial. . . . There was no reason that I know of . . . why [since they] encouraged him to visit, why they should not discuss computers to the hilt and I think this is what they did.

He added:

> I don't recall any specific conversation, but I recall the tenor of the encounter. I do recall this right, and I think this is in agreement with what disclosure Clifford Berry would make if he were here actually.

Kirkpatrick, in redirect, examined the witness further on his recall of the "tenor of the encounter" Mauchly had with Atanasoff and Berry and their computer.

> *Kirkpatrick:* Dr. Legvold, referring back to the occasions when you saw Dr. Mauchly in the computer room in the physics building with Berry and/or Atanasoff, were they talking about the computer or were they just passing the time of day about something else?
> *Legvold:* Their conversations were about computers.
> *Kirkpatrick:* About the computer in the room?
> *Legvold:* About the computer in the room and how to make computers in general.
> *Kirkpatrick:* Would you say that that predominated over small talk or other talk?
> *Legvold:* Oh, yes, yes. . . .

The examination on this subject ended with this exchange:

> *Kirkpatrick:* What was your impression of Dr. Mauchly during the visit in 1941 that he made out here as to his ability to absorb and understand what he was told about technical matters?
> *Legvold:* Anyone who knows Dr. Mauchly knows he is a sharp cookie, bright fellow, and that he has a high understanding of electronics and computer technology, and he had, I think, a high interest in it at the time he paid the visit here and . . . it was perhaps a big stimulus to him in his subsequent work on computers himself.

Finally, under recross by Dodds, Legvold acknowledged that the subject of "one of the many conversations" about computers that he overheard could have concerned Mauchly's analog device, the subject of his lecture in the Physics Building.

Lura Meeks met her future husband on Thanksgiving Day, 1925. She had been working her way through Iowa State College in home economics and the arts by leaving periodically to teach school. He was a newly arrived master's student in mathematics. They were married the following June, a few days after he received his degree. Lura and Vincent, as she called him, had three children, two daughters and a son. In her 1967 Regenerative Memory deposition, she gave her occupation as "artist"—she was a painter.

Under direct examination by Control Data attorney Kirkpatrick, she spoke at length of her husband's involvement with his computer and of Mauchly's visit to Ames. This testimony is best presented as a series of excerpts. Their original order is preserved.

[My husband] spent every spare minute working on his computer. He had always been dreaming about this. . . . He was always working on it, and then when he got actively producing it . . . and enough means to go ahead and construct it, well, then he put more and more time, everytime he had a minute, his weekends, and everything. Well, of course, that affects a family, you know, you know it.

And sometimes the children and I would go over to see his progress, what he was doing, because that was just his life.

. . . when I would go with the children, you know, they could run up and down the [basement] halls, kind of deserted. And this place had been fixed up where he could build and experiment and work.

[Berry] was helping him build it because it took him a tremendous amount of work. . . . And he was an unusual graduate student. . . . [My husband] was always attracted to students with intellect.

Well, when I was really aware [of Mauchly] is when he appeared at my home late one hot afternoon and was to—I learned he was to spend a few days with us.

Yes, with his little boy. I was surprised. I didn't have the guest room ready, and I had to fly around, go to the attic, get extra pillows, and everything. And . . . immediately I thought he was kind of an odd, quiet fellow, didn't say a word. The only thing he said was, "I thought my wife needed a vacation," that was his only apology for bringing the little boy along, and I thought, "Oh."

And the morning came and breakfast was over, so here they go with their briefcases, they go over to the college and no one says, "Will you babysit with my little boy," who was six or seven. You know, I have my family, my house, and everything, and [they] just go off, there I have another child. And he spends all his time with my husband, and when they come back for lunch they are talking.

And I like guests, I enjoy them, but I was so completely ignored that I, you know, you get kind of critical. So I kind of noticed him. . . . Even at the table there was—there seemed to be no polite conversation . . . , and even once he took a note—he took a little card or something out of his pocket and jotted down, "Now, that's interesting," and so on.

Oh, they were talking about some little technical part of the computer. . . . And he kept asking, he asked, always asking questions.

And my husband was so full of enthusiasm . . . because this was his brainchild, this thing was supposed to do even more than a human brain . . . and he was very proud of it. And . . . I [told him privately], "You must be careful until this is patented."

Because he talked so much, you know, like a little boy with something grand that he has built. . . . And he thought I was suspicious. . . . "Oh, this is a fine, honorable man, you don't have to worry about him," [he said]. So I felt kind of mean. [But when] you are doing something nice for someone and they don't even notice . . . you are a little bit critical. So I always noticed, and I kind of resented him. I was ashamed of it.

When my son called me . . . two or three months ago, he said, "There is some litigation . . . about daddy's computing machine." And I said, "Who? That old Mauchly?" Immediately I thought of that man, because I thought of his questions.

Well, it seemed that Mauchly had kind of struck a stump . . . , and at this meeting in the East . . . these learned men get together . . . and talk. So Mauchly was trying to do something that my husband was doing, and this had gone along, so he came—here he drives clear out to Iowa to see about it, not my husband going out to where he was. And then he spends all his time with us and he really spent it, he never patted a child, he never paid any attention to the children, he came in and left his little boy and he went on about his business.

Well, it seemed like longer than it was. It was probably four or five days. I'm sure it was at least four. I'm surprised, I—well, you know, you remember disagreeable things, and maybe that's why I remember him so well.

Never did we go out. I always cooked the meals, and here we had the four children and three grown-ups, we had a big table, we always had the meals together, it was just a homey affair. He came to our home and shared our home.

Well, I'm sure they went back to the college at least an evening or so. Then they would sit around and talk, or go to my husband's study and talk. And it seemed to be always the same thing. Even at the table . . . nothing but computer . . . and the little kids around, and everybody was kind of overawed. It was just entertaining Mr. Mauchly.

Well, this little boy was six or seven, a little older than my Johnny, so that made a little bit of problem there, you know, because the older one is a little more aggressive. And my daughters, they were four or five years older, but they made things go nicely.

Jimmy, this little boy, they made him fit in pretty well. . . . Mr. Mauchly was daddy's guest and it was our business to make things as pleasant as we could. That's the way we always did. But you have your kind of secret feelings about it when you are being imposed on.

Well, they always appeared together talking, and . . . several times they mentioned they had just left the physics building . . . where [my husband] had been showing off his brainchild, his computing machine. My husband, I think, is really kind. . . . just a few weeks ago . . . he said to me . . . , "Lura, I don't think Mauchly really intended to use any of my ideas at first." You see, he had some loyalty to the man, he had liked him, he hated to be deceived. . . . [He was] kind of apologizing, which I thought was very kindhearted, because he could just hate the man.

They would go into the study, and if I happened to have to call someone to the telephone . . . , it seemed like they were deep in conversation about [the computer].

And . . . when I was saying, "Now, Vincent, do be careful, don't talk too much," he said, "Now, you don't need to worry . . . , I don't think his [machine] will work." And I said, "Well, then you should be more careful. . . . If he is doing a machine, you should be extra careful."

Well, you know, my husband would be showing [a drawing], and they would be talking [about] all those little connections and those little funny things. . . . And then I would go back to my duties . . . , but I would hear little snatches of conversation like that. So there couldn't be any doubt in my mind that that was what it was.

And I was always proud of this because I thought my husband would be famous some day, and I would be very proud of it for my children's sake, too. So that's why I was really suspicious and watching.

It was Sperry attorney Dodds who, while cross-examining the witness, brought out that she and the children had gone to the computer room with her husband and his guest on Saturday or Sunday afternoon. She said they "had all the children and it was kind of unsatisfactory, but we all went to the basement where the computer was and it was shown off."

It was also Dodds who, in this deposition, quoted Mauchly's testimony that he did not recall spending "more than perhaps a half hour" with the computer, and then his concession, when pressed, that it might have been "an hour or an hour and a half." A long argument—essentially on the issue of hearsay—ended with the witness yielding, sort of.

Dodds: So actually you don't have any basis for indicating how much time Dr. Mauchly was actually at the machine because you weren't there, isn't that right?
Lura Atanasoff: Well, I was there the time we visited.
Dodds: And how long were you there [then]?
Lura Atanasoff: Oh, perhaps an hour before we got the kids—I got the kids gathered up and away, and—
Dodds: You say perhaps—
Lura Atanasoff: And he and Mr. Mauchly stayed around and we went outside. That was a pretty long visit.

Dodds: You say perhaps an hour, could it have been a half hour?

Lura Atanasoff: Oh, no. You can't get kids in and out of a building in half an hour, four kids running every direction.

Dodds: But you don't actually know how much time Dr. Mauchly spent at the machine?

Lura Atanasoff: I couldn't put it down in minutes. . . .

Dodds: You don't have any personal knowledge except at the time when you and the children were all there with them, is that correct?

Lura Atanasoff: Well, sitting at the table, "After seeing your machine," and so on, I know he had been there.

Dodds: Yes, but that is information you got from hearing somebody say something, you don't have—

Lura Atanasoff: Those two, Mr. Mauchly and John Atanasoff.

Dodds: Yes, from what they said, but you, yourself, weren't there or don't know exactly how much time they spent at the machine, is that correct?

Lura Atanasoff: I couldn't put it down in actual time. . . .

Dodds: Actually, since you weren't there, you couldn't measure the time, keep track of the time that they may have actually been at the machine?

Lura Atanasoff: No. But if he is—he's a doctor of physics and mathematics, it might not take such a long time for him to gain knowledge, have you thought of that?

Here is how this deposition of Lura Atanasoff in the Regenerative Memory case came to a close:

Dodds: Can you tell me, Mrs. Atanasoff, are you being compensated for coming and appearing for taking your testimony this morning?

Lura Atanasoff: Slightly.

Kirkpatrick: Let the record show Mrs. Atanasoff has been subpoenaed, and I believe the fee has been tendered to Mrs. Atanasoff.

Dodds: I am not speaking about the statutory subpoena fee. I am talking about compensation for her time, and she said she had been compensated.

Lura Atanasoff: Well, just that $9.47 [for bus fare] or something like that, for my total compensation.

Dodds: Have you any arrangement with Mr. Kirkpatrick or his client for compensation for your time later?

Lura Atanasoff: No.

Dodds: I think that's all.

Lura Atanasoff: I didn't expect any compensation.

<<<>>>

John V. Atanasoff, too, was deposed for the Regenerative Memory case, in February 1968.[54] Subpoenaed by Sperry Rand, he submitted his 1940 proposal and other documents, but was questioned only briefly. The chief topic of inquiry concerned steps taken by him and Berry and by Iowa State College toward applying for a patent on the computer. (Atanasoff and Iowa State had agreed to share the profits equally; Atanasoff had arranged for Berry to receive 10 percent of his half.) The Regenerative Memory suit barely saw the light of a courtroom before it was informally dropped, to be settled privately nearly a decade later through a small payment by Sperry Rand to Control Data.

<<<>>>

Despite the overwhelming evidence to the contrary—especially his own letters before and after his Iowa visit—Mauchly never gave up the one position he had clung to throughout both lawsuits: whatever his experience of Atanasoff's computer, he learned nothing new that he could use to build the electronic digital computer he already had in mind. Judge Larson, he held, had erred in finding that Mauchly "had not conceived an automatic electronic digital computer" before his Ames visit; Larson had erred, he held, in finding that the ENIAC and other devices patented by Eckert and Mauchly were derived from Atanasoff.

So Mauchly argued, repeatedly, after the trial. And so his widow, Kathleen Mauchly (now Antonelli), and other supporters have argued since his death in 1980. So, too, has Eckert argued, with his own twist to the effect that Atanasoff had nothing worth stealing anyway!

What testimony, what evidence of pre-Atanasoff accomplishments did Mauchly bring to the ENIAC trial for Larson to weigh? What case did he make for such accomplishments in his earlier Regenerative Memory deposition? Were there sources outside these two lawsuits that his supporters could cite on his behalf?

These questions take us to a further exploration of the court transcripts and, among other items, to a look at Kathleen R. Mauchly's 1984 article in the *Annals of the History of Computing*, "John Mauchly's Early Years."

FOUR

MAUCHLY BEFORE ATANASOFF

"Now why did we happen to do it?" John W. Mauchly asked his audience in Rome in 1973.[1] "Well," he said, "somebody else might have someday. All I can tell you is how it happened in the actual case. So I'd like to begin that story way back, *way back*, when I was a struggling graduate student." The "we" who happened to do it was Mauchly and J. Presper Eckert, and the "it" was invent the electronic computer.

In this speech, billed as "An Informal After-Dinner Talk by the Co-Inventor of the First Electronic Digital Computer," Mauchly told of the "little calculating machines, mechanical types" he used in his doctoral work at Johns Hopkins and of his growing frustration over both the machines' slowness and the amount of hand copying required. "That was 1930," he said. "Would you believe that it took until 1941 before I was anywhere near a place where we could cure that problem of having to wait so long and do all that nasty work by hand?"

He went on to his prewar years at Ursinus College, where, he explained, he generated enough weather data to convince himself of his hypothesis (that weather phenomena were correlated to solar activity) but would need "a hundred or a thousand times as much work" to convince other meteorologists, none of whom "had any faith in what I was doing." And so he turned to the literature, devoted at that time to "the big fad of nuclear physics," and learned that "the nuclear physicists had vacuum tubes all over their laboratories . . . measuring cosmic rays or other nuclear matters at rates like up to a million counts a second."

"Well," he continued, "if they could use little vacuum tubes for a million counts a second, as far as I was concerned, let's forget about the cosmic rays and let's get those counts counting whatever I wanted to count." He proceeded to buy vacuum tubes (out of his own pocket) and to put things together in the laboratory showing "you could generate counts and use these counting devices with vacuum tubes in them." He moved on from Ursinus College to the University of Pennsylvania, "the authorities in the computing field," he said, only to find that their calculators, too, were all mechanical: ". . . clever, some very complicated. . . . But so far as I could see they were slow, slow, *slow*! Compared with what you could do with a vacuum tube if you just put it in a circuit and let it go!"

Mauchly next related his long struggle at Penn's Moore School of Electrical Engineering, in the pre-ENIAC years when a major project was the computation of firing tables for Army Ordnance. There, he said, the faculty were of one mind: "You could never do anything with vacuum tubes." Only a young graduate student—"wouldn't you just know"—believed it was possible to design a circuit to count. "'It'll count,'" he quoted Eckert. "'And you can design circuits that will also switch—they'll select which of two routes the next part of the calculation is going to take.'"

With the powerful faculty opposed to his ideas on electronic computation, Mauchly said, he turned to "a secret weapon," one Joseph Chapline, a former student from Ursinus College whom he had gotten hired "to sit down in the [differential] analyzer room and keep it calibrated and adjusted properly." He had prompted Chapline to tell everyone who came in from Army Ordnance about "that professor upstairs who thinks you could do all this with vacuum tubes."

Mauchly explained that it was the army's liaison officer, Lt. Herman H. Goldstine, who listened to Chapline, talked to Mauchly, and got the ball rolling toward a proposal for the ENIAC.

The timing of all these events is crucial, of course, to Mauchly's claims to invention. He had taught physics at Ursinus College from 1933 to 1941. In June 1941, without resigning his associate professorship at Ursinus, he had entered the Moore School as a student in a crash summer course in electrical engineering, one of many prewar national defense courses being given throughout the country. That summer he discussed electronic digital computing with Eckert, his lab instructor, and at the end of the course accepted a Moore School instructorship himself. He had further discussions with Eckert throughout the 1941–42 school year.

Mauchly wrote his first brief proposal for an electronic computer in August 1942; he was approached by Goldstine in March 1943; and he and Eckert wrote up the technical side of the official proposal—still quite preliminary—in early April 1943, with nontechnical input from John G. Brainerd, who was to become the ENIAC project director.

But in his Rome talk, the dates Mauchly assigned for the critical early events of this sequence were curiously off by a year—in his favor! He gave his Ursinus years as 1932 to 1940, instead of 1933 to 1941, and he said he joined the Moore

School faculty in the fall of 1940, instead of the fall of 1941. Such a shift conveniently allowed him to bypass Atanasoff's influence entirely, since he had first met Atanasoff in late 1940 and visited him in Iowa in June 1941. It would appear that he had already discussed the prospective ENIAC with Eckert before he ever encountered Atanasoff! This shift is all the more curious—and more suspect—given that Mauchly, speaking in November 1973, had been through the ENIAC patent trial, where the timing of these events had been thoroughly aired. The year's shift also made it possible, even necessary, to bypass the summer engineering course, since no emergency defense courses were offered in 1940.

So it was that Mauchly, in this "Fireside Chat" given in the Villa Les Aigles at the Sperry Univac International Executive Centre near Rome, failed to mention his exposure to vacuum-tube switching at the hands of Atanasoff. So it was that he failed to mention his need to learn more electronics when he enrolled in that summer course at the Moore School, just after his visit to Atanasoff, thus enhancing his own status as an electronics expert. And, to top off these lapses, Mauchly made one other vital omission in this speech to an international gathering of senior managers from government, industry, and academia: he failed to mention that a federal court, scarcely three weeks earlier, had declared the ENIAC patent invalid!

Carl Hammer, who taped the speech, wrote an introduction for its appearance in the July 1982 *Annals of the History of Computing*. There he noted the setting in "the villa's plush drawing room before a six-by-eight-foot modern Italian Majolika fireplace mantle, with Persian carpets and Roman artifacts in glass vitrines, in a mellow atmosphere brought about by much good food and spirits." He wrote that though it had been almost a decade ago he could "still conjure up John's image, the focal point of an excited audience," as they all shared the vision of "this great inventor and innovator whose role . . . would be remembered for centuries." Like Mauchly, Hammer, director of computer science at this Univac Division of Sperry Rand, mentioned neither Atanasoff nor the ENIAC patent case.

Hammer made a point, in his introduction, of relating how Mauchly finished his talk "almost on the dot with the tape's end." One wonders whether some bold soul in that distinguished audience may have raised an embarrassing question or two that Hammer, regrettably, was unable to record!

Mauchly did not say, at Les Aigles in 1973, what "things" he had constructed in his Ursinus years to show that electronic computation was possible. As we have seen, he had made broad claims for such activity in both his 1967 Regenerative Memory deposition and his 1971 ENIAC trial testimony: his statement, in the former, that before meeting Atanasoff he "had been devising electronic and electrical computing devices" to aid in his statistical analysis of weather data (chap. 2); and his statement, in the latter, that before traveling to Iowa he had been contemplating a cheap, fast, all-electronic, general-purpose computer—a goal so firm, he said, that he not only rejected Atanasoff's computer at first sight but went on to make suggestions of his own, "Why don't you do this and why didn't you do that?" (chap. 1).

Attorneys in the two lawsuits had probed for details of these claims. Control Data's Allen Kirkpatrick opened his inquiry into them with a question about the mechanical desk calculator Mauchly had bought soon after his arrival in Collegeville.[2] The witness's response drove home the stark reality of the computing art as most researchers knew it in the 1930s.

> *Mauchly*: It was an old Marchant which had an electric motor and [was] identified quite often by saying it had a Lima bean handle which caused the— with your thumb you caused the carriage to shift to the right or the left, and it had the first suggestion of automatic division. It did not have automatic division, as such, as I remember it, but it would stop subtracting on an overdraft so that all you had to do was to push the subtraction bar and hold it down until an overdraft occurred, when the machine would stop, and then you could proceed with a division by coordinating your thumb shift with the storing overdraft and proceeding to the next place in the division.
>
> *Kirkpatrick*: So it would, of course, add but it would also subtract?
>
> *Mauchly*: Well, it would add, subtract and multiply. The multiplication is directly controlled by multiplier buttons in the Marchant machines.
>
> This was not just an adding machine but a machine which was provided with buttons so that when you pushed an 8 on the multiplier panel it would add 8 times without your having to count the times yourself. By a combination of pushing multiplier buttons and coordinating the shift with your thumb, why, you could rather quickly produce a product of, say, a ten-digit number by a ten-digit number.
>
> You could also, of course, do short multiplications by multiplying by 9, by actually multiplying by 10 and then shifting and subtracting 1. In other words, it left a lot of freedom to the person operating it to do things as he saw fit.
>
> *Kirkpatrick*: Did you tinker with it? . . .
>
> *Mauchly*: Only to repair malfunctions and deficiencies which sometimes occurred.
>
> . . .
>
> *Mauchly*: I would certainly dig into it, and if I found that I couldn't fix it I would call the repairman, but usually the malfunctions were simple jams of interlock mechanisms. . . .
>
> *Kirkpatrick*: What did the machine basically have inside? Is this a gear and cam and lever type assembly?
>
> *Mauchly*: Yes, it is a rotary machine with a carryover mechanism which was peculiar to the Marchant people. Not quite the same as the ones in other makes.

Mauchly went on to explain that he also bought an adding machine in the early 1930s, to be used by student assistants under a plan known as the National Youth Administration, or NYA.

> . . . while other departments in the college had students raking leaves and rolling the [athletic] track the college administration seemed to appreciate my being able to provide mathematically and scientifically minded students with a different form of employment whereby they earned a subsidy under [the NYA], and so I had students assisting me in taking data from weather maps and making totals and statistical analyses. For the pure totaling, an adding machine was obviously sufficient, so I was able to increase the productivity of this group by buying out of my own pocket an adding machine as well as a calculating device.

Kirkpatrick then moved forward to Mauchly's first thoughts about replacing these mechanical—though electrically driven—devices with electronic ones. Mauchly explained:

> Well, at some period in there, and I can't place it exactly, I became interested in the possibility of doing computations electronically. I was interested in this from several points of view.
> One was to speed up the calculations, purely because a vacuum tube device should be capable of accomplishing the process of arithmetic faster.
> I was also interested in the fact that in the kind of statistical analysis I was doing, such as correlations, progressions, and so on, it was necessary to enter the data into the customary desk calculator many times. There was no facility, of course, in such machines for storing the data so that you could use it over and over again having entered it once.
> And I was thirdly interested in storing the sequence of operations because some of these operations could be both complex and tedious, and therefore, having to be sure that you carried out the operations correctly each time that you undertook to do the same type of operation, seemed to me was an added burden which could be relieved. If you had proper storage of the operations the machine could be controlled so that once you devised operations in the sequence you wanted them, you only had to give that information to the machine once in detail and thereafter you could call for that operation, complex though it be, to be executed again and again on different data.

As to what he hoped to accomplish with some such electronic device, he testified:

> The results that I had been able to obtain on statistical analysis of weather data indicated that millions of numbers would have to be handled to obtain significant results, and I could even begin to guess that one person or two would not in their lifetime complete all the things that I had in mind doing.

Mauchly placed this thinking "around 1935." He then responded to Kirkpatrick's request for "the next event . . . in connection with calculators."

> *Mauchly*: Well, one of the things which bothered me was budget. I couldn't with my own limited facilities do this all out of my own pocket and so having been trained up in a laboratory [at Johns Hopkins] where such physicists as R. W. Wood and A. H. Pfund believed you could do practically everything with sealing wax and deKhotinsky cement, with a little glass blowing, perhaps, the first thing that I tried to do was to see if there were any ingenious ways in which I could throw together at low cost something that I could use myself without expending a lot of money.
>
> At some period in there, then, I saw a new device on the market known as an indicator fuse . . . which contained a small two-element gas tube known as a neon light.
>
> I merely went out and bought a large carton of these and dissected the fuses and threw the fuses away and kept the neon lamps, which I conceived of as being useful lamps, working on low power and fairly cheap to obtain, as visual output devices for a computer.
>
> I further became interested in the so-called nonlinear characteristics of such a lamp and its ability, then, to store information by the fact that its keep-alive current, or its keep-alive voltage, rather, was lower than its starting voltage.
>
> I then began constructing small experimental devices utilizing both neon bulbs and vacuum tubes to see what I could make with such equipment.

Mauchly placed this construction in "the years like 1935, '36, '37." He went on to tell of conceiving and building a cipher machine, or cryptographic device, for encoding and decoding messages, and of putting the tiny (3/4") neon lamps to work in it.

> And so somewhere in that era I got an idea for a cryptographic device . . . which would utilize the properties I mentioned of the . . . neon bulbs, and a combination of switching circuits which I had devised to produce what seemed to me a rather sophisticated ciphering result.

He told of his unsuccessful effort to interest the U.S. Army Security Agency in this device, which used neon bulbs in the readout capacity he first mentioned, that is, as external indicator lights for the message within. Although he also mentioned experimenting with these lamps in conjunction with vacuum tubes, which might have facilitated their use in a storage capacity, his cipher machine had no vacuum tubes.

Mauchly placed this machine "prior to 1939," because by 1939 he was designing another machine, the harmonic analyzer that occasioned his first meeting with Atanasoff in Philadelphia and that was the subject of his talk to Atanasoff's physics students and colleagues in Ames. He responded to Kirk-

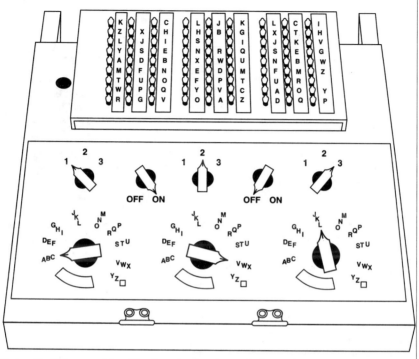

Figure 15. Cipher machine. The three banks of neon indicator lamps, twenty-seven lamps per bank, can be seen in this drawing of Mauchly's electrical cipher machine. The characters corresponding to these readout lamps—for each bank, the twenty-six alphabet letters and a space—were marked on strips of paper along the columns. One of two possible codes for a given message was selected by turning on one of two switches on the face of the machine.

The message to be coded was then entered, three characters at a time, by setting a nine-position switch and a three-position switch for each character: an "A" might be entered at the first bank, for example, by setting that bank's nine-position knob at "ABC" and its three-position knob at "1." The coded message would now be displayed by the indicator lamps and could be read out from the strips of paper along the columns.

(Drawing by artist David Oliver.)

---

patrick's question as to the general nature of his harmonic analyzer.

> *Mauchly:* . . . This was an analog device to facilitate the calculations of Fourier coefficients . . . to represent a time series such as barometric pressure in terms of components of various frequencies and amplitudes.
>
> . . .
>
> Specifically, this required the input of twelve equally spaced values and the read-out from a meter of the harmonic coefficients, including a con-

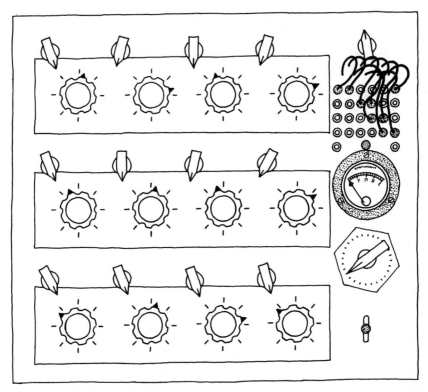

Figure 16. Harmonic analyzer. The harmonic analyzer Mauchly built in 1939 and early 1940—and used at Ursinus College through the spring of 1941—was designed to analyze weather data along such variables as precipitation and barometric pressure. He thought his analyses would reveal periodicities in these variables corresponding to the appearance of solar flares as the Sun rotated, so that these flares could be shown to have a causal effect on Earth's weather, just as they had been shown to have on Earth's magnetic field.

This artist's sketch shows the twelve large potentiometer knobs on which ordinate values were entered and the twelve smaller associated switches on which their signs were set. The resulting Fourier coefficients were read, each in turn, from the meter on the right, the particular coefficient having been selected by the switch below this meter. The plug board above was used to change the scale of the reading on the meter dial.

(Drawing by artist Leslie R. Thurston.)

---

stant term and the coefficients for the first four harmonics.

Kirkpatrick: And you say this machine you actually—you completed the construction of it?

Mauchly: This machine was completed and used by students under my direction.

On the basis of a letter he had written to International Resistance Company inquiring about parts for it, Mauchly thought 1940 was an appropriate date for the completion of his harmonic analyzer. He summed up the period of Kirkpatrick's inquiry.

> Well, the main thing which was going on during this period '35 to '40, aside from these two instances of completed devices, was a continuing experimentation with electronic circuits and a continued study of literature available to me, including the Review of Scientific Instruments, which contained a lot of electronic instrumentation used in cosmic ray work, and I was extremely interested in the scaling circuits or counters as they were using them and their gating circuits or coincidence circuits, as they call them, and their applicability to the general process of digital computing.

He concluded that he had built "various kinds of ring counters [and] pulse generators to activate them," but as for documents to date such experimentation he could point only to "a set of notes taken from articles in the Review of Scientific Instruments." Mauchly's exchange with Kirkpatrick on his Ursinus period ended with his agreement that he "did make some fairly extensive literature searches for pertinent material."

Kirkpatrick's inquiry, then, netted descriptions of two devices built by Mauchly before his first encounter with Atanasoff, both of them electrical but not electronic: a digital cryptographic machine that he meant to sell to the government and an analog harmonic analyzer that he used intensively in his own research. Although he expounded on the *rationale* for computing with vacuum tubes—as envisaged by him at the time, he said—and spoke of studying the literature and experimenting with vacuum-tube circuits, *Mauchly failed to cite a single electronic computing device for his entire Ursinus period.*

Nor did Mauchly produce any documentation of ideas or plans for such a device, let alone the full-fledged general-purpose computer he would claim, at the ENIAC trial, to have aspired to during this period. Even his earliest drawings of circuits combining vacuum tubes with neons, as produced for the later trial, were dated 1941, *after* his discussion of both these elements with Atanasoff in Philadelphia, not "1935, '36, '37."[3]

At the ENIAC trial, Sperry Rand's H. Francis DeLone delved much more deeply into the cipher machine and the harmonic analyzer, then turned to a third, *electronic* device not mentioned in the Regenerative Memory deposition. This neon device was, in fact, the only Mauchly contrivance of any kind actually shown and demonstrated in either patent case.

Of his cipher machine, represented in court by photographs, Mauchly explained to DeLone that it was not ready for regular use but was "a sort of pilot model to show the principles," one that ideally would have had means of typing in and typing out messages.[4] He said that it handled twenty-seven values, entered by setting a three-position and a nine-position switch, with the "almost accidental property" that tweny-seven values could represent the English alphabet of twenty-six letters, plus, say, a space or a punctuation mark. On this basis he stated several times that his cipher machine worked on "a base 3 number system," since "27 happens to be 3 times 3 times 3."

> It's the only device I know of in the digital field which turned out to—the base 3 system was the most appropriate for it and where something actually got built and was working on a base 3 system.

But, he acknowledged:

> If I had had a 27 point switch, I probably would have used it, but these were radio surplus parts which were available to me at a low price, and so the simplest way of getting a selection of any one of 27 values here was to use a nine times three combination of these two switches.

The sixty-four-year-old witness testified at length and with mounting enthusiasm about his harmonic analyzer—again, in the presence of photographs—and about the meteorological research it was designed to facilitate.[5] He explained that his aim had been to find periodicities in weather phenomena corresponding to the Sun's twenty-seven-day rotation period and to relate these to the occurrence of solar flares.

His father, he said, had been head of the Section of Terrestrial Electricity and Magnetism at the Carnegie Institution in Washington, and he himself had worked there in the summers of 1936, '37, and '38, trying to correlate events in Earth's magnetic field with observable solar activities. Others at the Carnegie Institution, he testified,

> had already found . . . that the magnetic field of the earth had a little pulse in it coincident with these solar flares. This was a big discovery for them, too, because it was the first time that they had seen anything in their magnetic data which was absolutely simultaneous with something that was seen on the sun.

Now, at Ursinus College, Mauchly hoped to demonstrate a similar, causal relationship between solar activity and variations in Earth's weather by drawing on the more sophisticated statistical procedures of the psychologists and mathematicians. He told DeLone that the "magneticians" of the Carnegie Institution tried to discourage him, arguing that the study of magnetism was "an exact science," whereas the study of the highly elusive weather phenomena "never would be a science." Even though they had not used the modern statistical methods themselves, they did not believe that his using them could bear out his hypothesis.

Their attitude, he said, only steeled his resolve.

There you meet the positive psychological spur, you might say, of all, and that
is that as soon as somebody told me that I had better quit, stay out of this, "You
are not going to get anywhere, you know, this is not scientific, . . . we just know
it's no good," well . . . that spurred me on.

Despite their doubts—and the doubts of U.S. Weather Bureau experts—the
Carnegie scientists allowed Mauchly to take away, free of charge, the last twenty
years of daily weather maps from 200 stations throughout the North American
continent. They also let him have meteorological publications from around the
world.

Mauchly explained that because his was a twelve-ordinate harmonic analyzer, he could insert only twelve values of a given weather phenomenon at a time
and so had "to devise a way of going from the twenty-seven days of a solar rotation down to twelve values." This he and his NYA students did, presumably, by
interpolation. They started with daily rainfall readings from the weather station
charts, attacking this huge store of data first on the desk machines, then on the
new machine.

Mauchly expressed his satisfaction with the harmonic analyzer.

It was a pleasure to find out after we had gone through building this thing that
one of the students could set new data into this and read off the three or four harmonics we wanted in, I think, about two minutes per set of data, where it took
us about 20 minutes to do this when we were just tabulating the results and using
a desk calculator to aid us in doing multiplications. So it was about 10 to 1 speed
up here and we succeeded in getting just sufficient accuracy to be adequate for
the purpose we needed. An analog device like this cannot be capable of any
accuracy you desire, but here we were about one per cent, which is what we
desired, and that's about what the design is.

Mauchly's extended testimony on his harmonic analyzer made clear that his
weather project dominated his research time through December 1940, when he
reported on it to the AAAS session attended by Atanasoff. By that time, as he
wrote his meteorologist friend H. Helm Clayton on November 15, he was even
well along in the design of a second, better-suited twenty-seven-ordinate harmonic analyzer. (Mauchly did not produce this letter for trial; see our reference
to it later in this chapter.) His 1941 letters to Atanasoff also indicated a continuing commitment to this project, as his group moved on from rainfall to barometric pressure readings (see chap. 2).

After his June visit to Iowa—and his summer course in electronics—
Mauchly abandoned his meteorological research. He never went back to it. But
he never lost faith in it, either, as he declared in Rome in 1973:

I'll conclude with the fact that the U.S. Weather Bureau finally got a big computer some years later. It wasn't one that I had anything to do with, but it was a big one, and they promptly went off solving the equations of weather their way; nobody's ever done it my way. I'm still of the belief that if it's done properly, we can make long-range forecasts better, as well as short-range. And now that I've sort of reached that happy old age where you've got to do something useful in this world, I've decided the most useful thing I could do is maybe to get that weather job started again.

<<<>>>

For all his pride in his harmonic analyzer, as depicted to DeLone at the ENIAC trial, Mauchly ran into serious difficulty over it during cross-examination.[6] Henry Halladay did not challenge the merits of the machine itself, nor its application to Mauchly's research, but instead zeroed in on his originality in creating it. And Mauchly responded, in the end, by suddenly blurting out *more* than was being sought. We saw two other such surprising admissions to Halladay in chapter 1: first, that Mauchly had been "perfectly convinced" in Iowa that Atanasoff's add-subtract mechanism worked as intended; second, that he himself when he went to Iowa "wasn't even thinking about inventing computing machines." This third one was just as surprising.

It was also just as damaging to the Sperry Rand case. For the issue of Mauchly's originality, even with respect to a nonelectronic, nondigital computing device, was highly relevant in this lawsuit charging derivation of the ENIAC from Atanasoff. Equally relevant was Mauchly's concern—or lack of concern—for prior art.

There had been no mention, in direct examination, of earlier electrical harmonic analyzers. (Mechanical versions date back to a tidal harmonic analyzer built by William Thomson, Lord Kelvin around 1875.) Yet the implication was strong that Mauchly had devised this electrical analog instrument without benefit of any earlier models, and when the Honeywell attorney broached the issue directly, Mauchly did indeed claim to have conceived it entirely on his own.

Halladay: Well, had you modeled this [harmonic analyzer] on the work of someone else?

Mauchly: No.

Halladay: Had you read about it somewhere else?

Mauchly: I don't believe that I had read about anything electrical of this sort. I read about the differential analyzers and tide calculators which worked by mechanical means—some with pulleys, ropes, and others with friction disks, and things of that sort.

Halladay: Well, do you mean to say, then, that this harmonic analyzer . . . was built by you entirely of your own conception?

Mauchly: So far as I recall, it was. My children weren't old enough to help.

Halladay: Your children weren't old enough to help?

Mauchly: No, they weren't at that time.

Halladay: Let me read you something, Dr. Mauchly.

It says: "Possibly you might be able to offer some advice in connection with a research project which we are now undertaking—namely, the construction of a network for the purpose of performing Fourier analyses. The circuit is already worked out (a modification of one used at M.I.T. some years ago) and a 12-ordinate analyzer, of perhaps $1\frac{1}{2}$ percent accuracy has been built, using G.R. voltage dividers."

Now, does that reading refresh your memory as to a source of information upon which you had drawn in building your 12-part harmonic analyzer?

Mauchly: I would like to hear it again, or see it—

Halladay: All right. I will read it again. I am referring to Plaintiff's Exhibit 22,522, part of the file which you produced, Dr. Mauchly, or had produced in response to one or another of the subpoenas that you have referred to before. It's a letter dated November 2, 1940, addressed to General Radio Co., Cambridge, Massachusetts.

And the part I read is as follows. . . .

Now my question was, does that not refresh your memory that the 12-ordinate harmonic analyzer which is depicted in these photographs . . . stem[s] from the work of somebody besides yourself?

Mauchly: It refreshes my memory that I apparently wrote down something like that in a letter to General Radio seeking some more information or advice from them with regard to how to use their equipment. It does not really refresh my memory as to what had been done earlier at MIT and how much of a modification there was from that. I just don't remember.

Halladay: Would you now agree, however, that the harmonic analyzer which is depicted in the exhibits before you—

Mauchly: Could I see the letter that we are talking about?

Halladay:—was not entirely of your design, but in fact was a modification of one used at MIT some years prior to 1940 and which had come to your attention in one way or another?

Mauchly: I will stand by what I said in my letter. I am not sure that your question applies to the same thing or not.

Halladay: Well, then, I would like you to answer the question, if you would, please.

Mauchly: Well—

Halladay: Shall I put it again?

Mauchly: Would you show me the material from which I drew this design? I don't recall it.

Charles Call, chief out-of-house investigator for the Honeywell side, once commented to Arthur Burks that this courtroom scene epitomized Mauchly's performance as a witness—and Halladay's as an examining attorney. Mauchly had a pattern not only of searching his files superficially but also of failing to study the documents he did locate and submit. So now Halladay, with the dramatic streak of many a courtroom attorney, took advantage of the witness's unfamiliarity with his own letter to dangle it before him, just out of arm's reach, as he questioned him about its meaning. He was not obligated to show Mauchly the letter, which he *had* identified for him, and he did not intend to do so.

> *Halladay:* All I am trying to do is to get you to answer the question. If the question isn't plain, tell me it is not plain and I will try to rephrase it. The question is simply this, Dr. Mauchly: Will you not agree that the harmonic analyzer which is depicted in these photographs before you . . . was not entirely of your design, but was a modification of a design used at MIT some years prior to 1940?
>
> *Mauchly:* Well, the answer has to be qualified because I don't know and cannot now recall what the other design was, and I have no reference at the present moment to help me. I can't even see what I wrote in the letter, apparently.
>
> *Halladay:* Is the—
>
> *Mauchly:* So I have to give a qualified answer.
>
> *Halladay:* Is the question unclear? Let me try it once more.
>
> *Mauchly:* Yes.
>
> *Halladay:* If it is not clear, I will try to rephrase it.
>
> *DeLone:* I do object to the interruption. The witness went on and endeavored to give a qualified answer and there was an interruption.
>
> *Judge Larson:* The question has been stated several times, Dr. Mauchly. Please answer it.
>
> *Mauchly:* I stand by my letter which says that I had received some kind of a suggestion from some prior work, which I do not now recall, but which is referred to in the letter and which apparently no one else can find right now. So that this was not a flash from heaven, a full-blown device without any prior suggestion as to how anybody could do anything, but neither was any other calculating machine, as far as I know, and neither were the mechanical type calculators and harmonic analyzers, so far as I know. Each one was building on somebody else's work.
>
> *Halladay:* Then do you agree, Dr. Mauchly—
>
> *Mauchly:* I agree I did not do this in a vacuum.
>
> *Judge Larson (to the witness):* Will you wait for the question, please?
>
> *Halladay:* You agree that you didn't do it in a vacuum, that it was not entirely your own design, and that it was in fact a modification of one used at MIT some years prior to 1940. Will you not agree that that is a suitable and correct statement?
>
> *Mauchly:* I will agree if that's what my letter says.
>
> *Halladay:* "The circuit is already worked out"—
>
> *Mauchly:* My circuit is.
>
> *Halladay:*—"a modification of one used at MIT some years ago, and a 12-ordinate analyzer of perhaps one and a half per cent accuracy has been built, using G.R. voltage dividers."
>
> *Mauchly:* Yes. What I am trying to get across in my answer by way of qualifica-

tion is that the pronoun "one," as I understand the reading now, which occurs in that circuit [sentence] with respect to something that was built at MIT earlier, its antecedent may be circuit. I don't know whether what I did adapt was a different kind of a circuit which came for a different purpose to a harmonic analyzer or whether MIT had already published and I had read about a differential analyzer—I mean, a harmonic analyzer. Excuse me—but, in any case, let me say that I did not build this thing in a vacuum. I have never built anything in a vacuum. *I have always used prior art* where it seemed proper, and useful, appropriate. You don't do these things without having a few people ahead of you who have worked out something before. I used Ohm's law, for instance. Mr. Ohm published that quite a while ago. [italics added]
Halladay: Does that end the qualification you wanted—
Mauchly: I will say that is the end of the question.

Mauchly was not entirely clear here, as to the possible interpretations of his letter to General Radio. What was clear to him, and surely to the court, was that he could no longer claim to have built his harmonic analyzer "entirely of [his] own conception." Realizing that, and being flustered by the realization, he hastened to defend his use of prior art in this instance. But then, somehow needing to reinforce his increasingly defiant stance, he rushed on to the generalization that he had *always* used prior art—didn't everyone?

Halladay accepted Mauchly's closing of that discussion and turned to another document, again from Mauchly's own files: "Bibliography of Literature on Calculating Machines."[7] This bibliography had been compiled in 1938 by the Moore School's computer expert, Irven Travis (see chaps. 2 and 3). It included a listing of "Harmonic analysers," with twenty-five entries, which Halladay used to press Mauchly to retreat from his initial claim not to have read about "anything electrical of this sort."

Halladay: As a matter of fact, by the time you had built the harmonic analyzer there had been a substantial volume of literature on the subject, had there not?
Mauchly: I would believe so.
Halladay: And you had done research in that literature to educate yourself on how to build such a device, had you not?
Mauchly: I had read the literature. I really hadn't done something I would dignify by calling research.

Mauchly's carelessness in submitting documents is hard to understand, not only because he risked being trapped by his own trial exhibits, but also because Sperry Rand was paying him handsomely for his time. His initial attitude on the stand suggests overconfidence. He clearly expected to outwit the Honeywell attorneys. But how much was he deceiving himself? Did he also want to believe there could be nothing damaging in those files?

In any case, Mauchly did himself—and Sperry Rand—a disservice, as his lack of preparation shifted the focus from a positive impression of notable achievement to a negative one of dissembling under oath. His harmonic analyzer should have come off as a novel and original application of the current analog technology. Instead, it came off as a device "borrowed" from that technology, with credit to its predecessors yielded only grudgingly.

Halladay chose not to cross-examine Mauchly about the cipher machine with neon indicator lamps, but came down hard on a small device that made essential electronic use of those lamps. Somehow forgotten in the earlier Regenerative Memory case, it was now on display in court. Here Halladay was not so concerned with Mauchly's originality in creating the device as with his presentation of it as a *binary counter*.

Under direct examination by DeLone, Mauchly had said that his impetus for building this two-state, two-neon device had come from reading the growing body of literature on the physicists' scaling circuits.[8] These vacuum-tube circuits, used to count cosmic rays, had inspired him to try to do the same job with neon bulbs.

> And if I had had all the means I wanted, . . . why, I would have been constructing vacuum tube counters of the sort that I saw described in literature as my main extra occupation after teaching. What I did instead was to try to use some of these cheaper components to see whether I could make them do the same job perhaps a little more slowly, but much more cheaply, and that I could not find in literature. I had to do that on my own. There wasn't anything in the literature, so far as I know, for instance, which showed how to make a binary counter out of these little neon bulbs, which, incidentally, I first got by buying fuses, taking out a piece of the fuse, which was an indicator lamp.

Mauchly described this device in the presence of two large photographs with the sign, "RR Stop," posted above them. He did not explain that sign to DeLone, but stuck to his "counter" version.

> This I referred to as a binary counter and it's one of very simple construction. All the parts to it are in the base of a cardboard cover for an ice cream half-pint container, or something, and the—a couple of resistors and a condenser in the base and then the two neon lamps which are shown at the top of the glass rod.

He went on to assert that just one of these devices, connected to a battery of proper voltage, "could be used as a counter." What it counted, he explained, was "interruptions in the power supplied to it." That is, when first connected to the battery, the device would have one lamp on and one lamp off, but this situation would be reversed if the voltage was interrupted ever so briefly—for, "say, a hun-

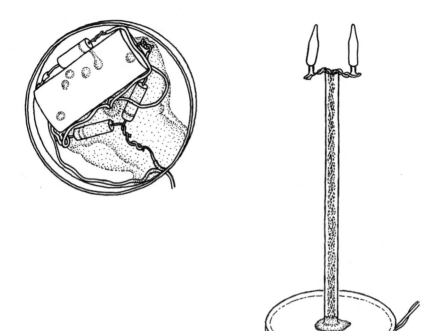

Figure 17. Front and underside views of two-neon device. This is a drawing of the device Mauchly built to employ small gas indicator lamps in what he testified was alternatively a counting capacity and an oscillating (or flashing) capacity. He said he built it in about 1939. It was the only specific electronic "computing" component he claimed to have originated in his pre-Atanasoff period, and the only Mauchly invention presented physically in court.

The hollow glass rod carried wires from the base to the two neon bulbs at the top. In the cardboard box-top base were three resistors and a capacitor set in wax. The two emerging wires went to a battery or other power source. Mauchly explained that this instrument, when connected to a battery of appropriate voltage, could count manually administered power interruptions of very short duration (about a hundredth of a second). When permanently connected to a different battery, again of appropriate voltage, it functioned as a toy railroad crossing light, with the two lamps flashing back and forth indefinitely.

(Drawing by artist Leslie R. Thurston.)

---

dredth of a second or less." This was such a short period of time, he added, that a special switch might be required rather than relying on manually administered interruptions.

> Now, if you were a little clumsy about this and you just scratched a wire across the terminal, you might have made a dozen interruptions in that process and you

might see the same lamp on that you saw before you did this. Now, all that means is that you interrupted the circuit an even number of times.

But if you have a switch which you carefully controlled so that you know that you were interrupting just once, then the lamp will alternate back and forth for each interruption, and you could see it do that if you do it slowly enough.

He continued:

> If you wished to put on other apparatus such as pulse generators, then you could test how fast this thing would respond to such interruptions and how fast it will count.
>
> But in all cases what it is doing is counting in the binary system; that is, it has only two possible indications: either the left lamp is on or the right lamp is on. Never both, but one is on.

Mauchly told DeLone that he had built this "binary counter" in his laboratory at Ursinus College and had used it there, sometimes with a battery and sometimes with another power source. He said, in fact, that he had built "several more of the same kind." He did not claim, however, to have connected a switch or a pulse generator or any other "apparatus" to one of these devices. Nor did he claim to have connected two or more such devices in series.

Honeywell's Halladay attacked the very essence of Mauchly's "binary counter."[9] How did it count, in any meaningful way? Didn't it have to have something added to it in order to count? Wasn't it really just a toy, a flashing "stop" signal for a toy railroad, as the sign over the photographs indicated?

Halladay began by reviewing Mauchly's earlier testimony and asking whether there was any way in which this two-neon "counter" could be made to "flash on left, and off left, and on right, off right, and on left alternately" while permanently connected to its power supply. Mauchly responded that, yes, with a battery of different, appropriately chosen, voltage the device would "flash back and forth without interruption of the battery circuits." This exchange followed:

> *Halladay:* And you did in fact do that before you ever met Dr. Atanasoff?
> *Mauchly:* Yes.
> . . .
> *Halladay:* [But] going on and off would not be counting in a binary sense, would it?
> *Mauchly:* No. . . . That is called a relaxation oscillator, or in the vernacular I used it was a railroad crossing light. . . . It flashes, which could be used with a toy railroad train, for instance.
> *Halladay:* And as a matter of fact that's what the sign says at the top of the exhibit we took the picture of, doesn't it?
> *Mauchly:* Yes.
> *Halladay:* "RR Stop"?
> *Mauchly:* Yes.

Halladay went on to press Mauchly for his definition of a counter, and of a binary counter in particular. He soon found himself engaged in a heated "war of words"—again, with a defiant and self-assured witness.

> *Halladay:* When you say "counter," Dr. Mauchly, as of December 1940 what does your term "counter" mean?
>
> *Mauchly:* Well, broadly it would mean anything that counts, if you are asking how you would specifically apply it to a circuit.
>
> *Halladay:* No, I am not. . . . I am asking for a meaning of a word, and it doesn't give us a meaning to simply repeat the word.
>
> *Mauchly:* All right. A counter is something that counts.
>
> *Halladay:* Again that simply repeats the word. Do you mean it enumerates successively?
>
> *Mauchly:* It seems that saying a counter is something that counts is too simple, maybe saying it is something that enumerates successively is maybe a little too simple, too.
>
> *Halladay:* Well, I am trying to find out your use of the term and what it means and to what it applies. In order for a device to be called a counter, would it not have to enumerate successively and do more than just register on or off or 0 and 1, and particularly to count in a binary mode?
>
> *Mauchly:* If I had a count—well, I shouldn't be asking questions, I guess. I should ask you to clarify your question.

Mauchly may have been about to offer a clarification himself, when he thought better of it. What was needed in this inquiry, but never provided, was the distinction between *counter* as a single element in a set of like elements, comparable to one dial in the set of dials in an odometer, and *counter* as a complete set of such elements. Mauchly could defend his device only as the former, one element meant to be connected to others in series, whereas Halladay was clearly alluding to the latter, popular version of the term. Mauchly could, in fact, hardly even defend his device as one in a series, because he had provided no means of connecting it to others: his "counter" had no input, no output—just a power source.

From Mauchly's perspective, then, it was safer to spar with Halladay over the definition than to invite exposure of this problem with his device. Halladay, for his part, was as aware as Mauchly of the double meaning of the term under question. But, while he would give Mauchly plenty of opportunity to clarify his usage, he himself was better off sticking to what was surely the judge's notion of a counter—one that would "enumerate successively."

A long and testy exchange ensued, with witness setting examiner straight as to the two different "modes" of his device. What Mauchly called the "railroad flasher" mode, in which the two neons flashed back and forth spontaneously, was *not* what he called the "counting" mode, in which one neon remained on until the operator caused a shift to the other. "So let's not confuse things," he said, "by referring to it as a railroad flasher when we are talking about it as a counter."

Then at last Mauchly ventured a definition, Halladay challenged its utility if nothing were added, and Mauchly jousted a bit more before settling for a lone device with two states, "0" and "1"—in short, a device that "won't count over one."

> *Mauchly:* . . . Now, a two-state device which maintains one state until it receives a signal which causes it to change state and always, on perceiving that signal, changes from one state to the other is to my way of using the word a binary counter.
>
> *Halladay:* You agree, do you not, that it would be impossible to use that device in that condition with nothing added to count in the binary mode, do you not?
>
> *Mauchly:* I do not agree.
>
> *Halladay:* Well, what would you do with the device when it got over 2?
>
> *Mauchly:* This device won't count over one.
>
> . . .
>
> *Halladay:* . . . we were talking about [a device] that wouldn't count over 1, which if it won't count over 1 does not permit of successive enumeration. Is that right?
>
> *Mauchly:* I am not answering your question about successive enumeration. I am answering your question about whether this is a binary counter, as I understand it, and I say it is a binary counter.
>
> *Halladay:* Even though it won't count over 1?
>
> *Mauchly:* That is right.
>
> *Halladay:* All right.
>
> *Mauchly:* It has two stable states.
>
> *Halladay:* Well, that then we will take as your definition of a binary counter,—
>
> *Mauchly:* Well, the fact that—
>
> *Halladay:*—a device which has two stable states and will count to 1? Is that acceptable?
>
> *Mauchly:* Yes.

Just as Mauchly had seemed to take satisfaction in explaining to DeLone that *his* binary counter counted power interruptions, he may have taken satisfaction here in giving such a bare-bones definition of the term. Any engineer in 1940, however, would have thought it fantastic to call this device a counter, particularly a neon counter equivalent to the vacuum-tube counter of the cosmic physicists. Not only did it have no provision for interconnection with like elements in series, but its very reliance on neons was fundamentally flawed. Neons are diodes—weak diodes, at that—and diodes do not amplify as triodes do. They do not provide enough power either to operate a further device or to permit other circuits to read their states.

In the courtroom, what Mauchly was reduced to was this: a "binary counter" with the wholly fruitless function of counting power interruptions, these to be created by a human operator who, admittedly, could not do so reliably without the addition of a special switch, which was, in fact, never added—a "binary counter" that could signal "0" and "1" alternately, but that (supposedly, though not actually) could have gone beyond "1" with the addition of other "binary counters," which were, in fact, never added. Judge Larson must have seen its presentation as a desperate ploy incredibly attempted by a man of Mauchly's expertise as evidence of his progress toward the invention of the electronic computer.

It is natural to ask why Mauchly chose to bring this device into court at all. The answer, first and foremost, is that it was the only electronic invention he could claim for his pre-Atanasoff period. But, as in other instances, this intellectually aggressive witness was also relying too heavily on his own considerable cleverness and discounting too heavily the knowledge and resourcefulness of the opposing legal team.

Halladay, still obviously irked despite his apparent victory, went on to challenge Mauchly's testimony that he had built this little device before he ever met Atanasoff. Mauchly claimed to have drawn circuit diagrams for it, but all he could point to among his subpoenaed papers was a sketch that he had drawn for Atanasoff during their first meeting in Philadelphia! This sketch included a battery, but not its voltage, so that he had to admit in court that even this one rendition was nondescript as to whether it portrayed a "counter" or a "relaxation oscillator."

There is little reason to doubt Mauchly's estimate as to when he first built his two-neon device. What is doubtful is that he conceived it as a binary counter, rather than simply a relaxation oscillator or, in his own words, a toy railroad flasher. Just the form it took, mounted high on a post in an ice-cream box top, suggests that it was a toy, not a computer component. What is even more doubtful is that he "used" it as a counter at Ursinus College, given his failure to equip it as such.

Nevertheless, Mauchly could well have been *considering* neons as counting elements before he met Atanasoff and discussed them with him. He certainly was pursuing this idea soon after that. He showed Halladay a whole file of papers with diagrams of neon counters interspersed with vacuum tubes—all dated 1941, from New Year's Day, just three days after the AAAS meeting, until mid-August.[10]

A more cynical interpretation of all this is that Mauchly thought of his two-neon device as a possible binary counter only as he was preparing for the ENIAC trial, perhaps under pressure from the Sperry team to come up with something. It certainly is strange that he failed to mention it in his Regenerative Memory deposition, when asked by Kirkpatrick about his moves toward electronic computing in his Ursinus period, yet made so much of it in the later suit.

In any event, Mauchly was clearly fascinated by these tiny gas diodes. He had built the toy railroad signal of them. He had used them as indicator lights in his cipher machine. He was still trying to use them in counting circuits two months after seeing Atanasoff's vacuum-tube computer. And when he joined the Moore School faculty in September 1941, he put his two-neon device on display in his office, permanently flashing back and forth in its "toy" mode. Atanasoff, too, testified that the only digital concept of his own that Mauchly had ever volunteered to him was his experimentation with these "neon glow lamps."[11]

<<<>>>

Mauchly had barely mentioned his experiments with electronic ring counters to Control Data's Kirkpatrick, and now under direct examination by DeLone he again passed over them lightly.[12] As in the earlier case, he indicated that he was trying to duplicate the physicists' scaling circuits described so often in the literature. But he also mentioned his goal of using "gas tubes rather than vacuum tubes," and it came out, ultimately, that this experimentation involved gas *triodes* as well as gas *diodes*.[13]

DeLone asked explicitly about a photograph of circuit boards with gas triodes plugged into them. Mauchly could not say "exactly what these boards are wired up for," but said he had used such boards to test ring counters, "primarily with gas trigger tubes of a cold cathode type," as in the photograph. The attorney also showed him a photograph that Mauchly identified as "a pulse generating device" used in his experiments with the ring counters. Finally, DeLone asked the purpose of this experimentation.

> Well, the purpose was to find out for myself whether I had any hope of designing and building a rather low cost digital device which would make the work that I was doing easier. These weather statistics and things of that sort required so much computation that I had the feeling that I needed some better computing equipment than what was available to me at the time, or even what I might procure if I had had some money just to buy what was on the market.

Halladay did not cross-examine Mauchly about the ring counters but did inquire about the pulse generator, which Mauchly now termed a "pulse former."[14] He explained that this was "essentially a test device" for use with an oscilloscope, and that his was a simple one for which "the change in shape or the variety of shape [of incoming pulses] was not great." Actually, *pulse generator* is the broader term, comprising both a *pulse former* and an *oscillator*. Mauchly's device did include an oscillator, which provided a basic saw-tooth wave (as he testified), and a pulse former, which reshaped this saw-tooth wave into a succession of "somewhat distinct" pulses (as he also testified).

Although Mauchly had no papers to verify his claim that he had built his ring counters at Ursinus College, he surely had done so. Kathleen Mauchly, in her *Annals* article, "John Mauchly's Early Years," dated the counters 1937–41, keeping them in the Ursinus period but taking them beyond the first Mauchly-Atanasoff meeting of December 28, 1940.[15] It is doubtful, however, that that meeting did more than assure Mauchly that vacuum tubes could be made to compute. His ring counters remained what he said they were, attempts to duplicate the scaling circuits of the literature, to see if he "had any hope of designing and building a rather low cost digital device." His pulse generator, too, was only what he said it was, an instrument to test his counters by observing the shapes of their pulses at various points.

<<<>>>

As it has turned out, there was documentation of this *hope* of Mauchly's in his pre-Atanasoff Ursinus period. It took the form of two letters he wrote in late 1940. He did not bring these letters into court, but Mrs. Mauchly found them in a sealed file shortly after his death in 1980. The first, written on November 15, 1940, to meteorologist H. Helm Clayton, was published in the same *Annals* article as the Rome address presented earlier.[16] The relevant paragraph had also appeared in the November 1980 *Datamation*, as quoted in a letter from Mauchly's son-in-law, James McNulty:

> In a week or two my academic work will not be quite so heavy, and I shall begin to give some time to the construction of computing devices. We have further simplified the design of our proposed twenty-seven-ordinate analyser. In addition, we are now considering the construction of an electrical computing machine to obtain sums of squares and cross-products as rapidly as the numbers can be punched into the machine. The machine would perform its operations in about 1/200 second, using vacuum tube relays, and yielding mathematically exact, not approximate, results. That is, its accuracy would not be limited to the accuracy with which one can read a meter scale, but could be carried to any number of places if one cared to construct the machine with that many parts. With conventional tubes, it would be rather bulky, but special tubes could be designed to make it very compact.[17]

McNulty quoted a paragraph from the second long-lost letter, as well. Dated December 4, 1940, it was to former Ursinus student John DeWire:

> For your own private information, I expect to have, in a year or so, when I get the stuff and put it together, an electronic computing machine, which will have the answer as fast as the buttons can be depressed. The secret lies in "scaling circuits," of course. Keep this dark, since I haven't the equipment this year to carry it out and I want to be the first.

<<<>>>

Now Kathleen Mauchly, in her 1984 *Annals* article, found the "seeds of an ENIAC" in her late husband's Ursinus creations, and she took his two 1940 letters as fortification for her argument. She introduced this argument in two summary statements.

> The development of the ENIAC (Electronic Numerical Integrator and Computer) flows in a simple, logical, natural way from the work of John William Mauchly while he was at Ursinus College in Collegeville, Pennsylvania, and from the genius, inventiveness, and experience of his partner, J. Presper Eckert, Jr. Mauchly's background and work prepared him for his part in the conception, design, and construction of the first electronic digital computer.
>
> . . . we have the physical components of the electronic computer that Mauchly was building during the time he was teaching at Ursinus College. These components alone are evidence that Mauchly's concept of an electronic "computer-calculator" predated any association with John V. Atanasoff and led directly to the design of the ENIAC.

Mrs. Mauchly set 1936 as the year in which Mauchly first aspired to an electronic "desk calculator with storage facilities." Although she began by envisioning the Ursinus devices examined at trial as the basic components of this projected calculator, she soon expanded them further to encompass the basic features of the ENIAC.

She saw the two-neon device not only as the "binary counters" of a desk calculator, but also as its "flip-flops" and its "control switches." Later, it became one of the four ENIAC "seeds," taking the form of "vacuum tubes for control and circuit switching" as results were transferred "from one register to another."

She saw the gas-triode ring counters as the desk calculator's "decade counters" (under the control of the two-neon device). Later, they also became a "seed" of the ENIAC, its "basic building blocks," in the form of accumulating counters or "registers" that "perform the arithmetic and store the numbers."

Claiming further that these counters "would advance in response to pulses [in a calculator] just as the ENIAC ultimately advanced to pulses using vacuum tubes," Mrs. Mauchly moved on to the pulse generator. Though this was actually a piece of laboratory equipment built by Mauchly at a time when scientists often built their own equipment, and though he had testified that it was merely a test device of very limited capacity, she saw it in an ever-expanding light.

In Mrs. Mauchly's eyes, this instrument was first a "pulse former" for the calculator, but "similar," she said, "to what was later used in the ENIAC to precede the counter" and ensure its reliability. Later, it became the third and fourth "seeds" of that machine: "pulse formers with controls on amplitude and duration to precede each ring-counter circuit" and "a low-frequency oscillator type source for pulses."

She turned to Mauchly's two 1940 letters to establish his "intentions" to build a machine featuring "a keyboard input for the data and operations" and a design "based on the standard mechanical desk calculator, with electronic ring counters taking the place of the mechanical counters." Then, completely overlooking Mauchly's explicit statement to Clayton that his projected calculator was "to obtain sums of squares and cross-products," Mrs. Mauchly managed to conclude:

> In his careful, methodical way, Mauchly had thought out, built, and tested the components of an automatic electronic *general-purpose* calculator. [italics added]

"John Mauchly's Early Years" continued in similar vein with the author's interpretation of the Mauchly-Atanasoff interaction, then returned to these computer "components" for Eckert's assessment of them at the Moore School.

> As often as he could, Mauchly discussed his computer ideas with Eckert. Eckert suggested that Mauchly bring in the ring counters and other components of his computer that were still in the Physics Lab at Ursinus. Eckert tested these gas-tube cicuits on a bench at the Moore School. He concluded that although gas tubes were cheap and would work for this purpose, hard vacuum tubes offered the most promise. . . . The most important result of this testing was the boost it gave to Mauchly's hopes. Eckert had convinced Mauchly that it was entirely possible to build a computer having only electronic elements. There was no reason why these elements could not be used in decade ring counters as Mauchly was proposing.

She closed her presentation on this light note:

> Mauchly packed up his biquinary ring counters, his pulse former, and his neon flip-flops and took them home. But on his desk at the Moore School he kept one neon flip-flop, mounted in a coffee-container lid, blinking at him.

What is most striking about this article, of course, is the *author's* "inventiveness" in finding the ENIAC in Mauchly's rudimentary devices. Striking, too, is the contrast between her claims for them and his own claims at trial. Under her nurturing, they grew from desk calculator components, to forerunners of ENIAC components, to actual general-purpose computer components (built and tested). Mauchly, on the other hand, never called any of them components of any actual computing device. The most he claimed was that his two-neon device and his gas-triode ring counters were attempts to duplicate the physicists' scaling circuits. He did not even claim to have succeeded in those attempts.

It is true that Mauchly, in direct examination by DeLone, testified that he rejected Atanasoff's computer once he had seen it, because "my general interest was in trying to get computers which would be versatile and not restricted to some one class of problems" (see chap. 1). This statement may have been Mrs.

Mauchly's grounds for applying the "general-purpose" label to his Ursinus efforts; she did quote it, much later, without comment. Yet Mauchly never suggested, on the stand, that he was *working on* a general-purpose computer at Ursinus
College. Even in his Rome talk in 1973, he cited his Ursinus devices only as satisfying him that electronic computation was possible.

Finally, we need to recall Mauchly's testimony to Halladay that he "wasn't
even thinking about inventing computing machines" when he visited Atanasoff
(see chap. 1). Mrs. Mauchly, in her article, did not acknowledge this testimony.
Yet—oddly enough—she herself, in her own pretrial deposition, had given an
account of the state of her husband's mind that was remarkably similar to his testimony.[18] Halladay had asked her whether she had ever heard of Atanasoff.

> [Mauchly's] original desire was to find a computer, not to have to build one. Any
> time he heard of anyone who might have a computer he was going to build, John
> tried to get by to see how and find out when the person would have something
> that he could use or if they would.
>   . . . He indicated that he went to see Atanasoff, but Atanasoff didn't have
> what he wanted.

Thus far, we have seen that Judge Larson's 1973 ruling in the ENIAC trial struck
down both the ENIAC and the Regenerative Memory patents because of derivation from Atanasoff. But it went even further with regard to Atanasoff, tying his
work to the EDVAC and so, by implication, to the Eckert-Mauchly BINAC and
UNIVAC.

It also declared the ENIAC patent invalid on three counts of late filing, and
unenforceable on two counts of misconduct before the United States Patent
Office.

How sound was this very broad decision? Was Larson wise and fair in
sewing up the case in such a way as to preclude an appeal by either side? Or was
he just a "nutty judge," as Eckert characterized him some years later in an interview by Pamela L. Eblen in the Autumn 1984 issue of *ICP Data Processing
Management?*[19]

The answers to these questions lie in the ruling itself, where Larson not only
traced the entire history, from the creative activities of Atanasoff and Mauchly in
the late 1930s to the securing of the ENIAC patent by Eckert and Mauchly in
1964, but also addressed many controversial issues as they affected his findings:
Atanasoff's apparent abandonment of the ABC and his failure to file for a patent
on it; possible coinventors on the ENIAC team at the Moore School; various
"derelictions" of Mauchly and Eckert and their lawyers in the patenting process;
and the relevance of documents and testimony provided by the principals and
other witnesses.

FIVE

LARSON FROM THE BENCH

It was Friday, October 19, 1973, judgment day for the *Honeywell Inc. v. Sperry Rand Corporation et al.* suit over ENIAC patent 3,120,606, and also over the so-called 30A package of further Eckert-Mauchly patents owned by Sperry Rand. The trial had run almost continuously for nine and one-half months, from June 1, 1971, through March 13, 1972, and Judge Earl R. Larson had taken another nineteen months to prepare his 420-page decision.

The *et al.* in the suit title was Illinois Scientific Developments (ISD), a subsidiary created by Sperry Rand in 1964 to hold and market the rights to the newly issued ENIAC patent. ISD set about demanding royalties from General Electric, Control Data, RCA, Burroughs, National Cash Register, Philco-Ford, and Honeywell, claiming that the ENIAC patent alone covered all the electronic data processing equipment these companies would produce over the seventeen-year life of the patent.

Absent from this list was giant IBM, which had entered a cross-licensing agreement with Sperry Rand back in 1956. Absent also were Western Electric and Bell Telephone Laboratories, production and research arms of American Telephone and Telegraph, because of their 1961 cross-licensing agreement with Sperry Rand.

ISD sought royalties from many peripheral equipment manufacturers, as well. But only Honeywell ended up in court over the ENIAC patent (though, as we have seen, Control Data was sued over the Regenerative Memory patent). In fact, none of the others approached by ISD ever paid a cent in royalties or entered any agreement concerning the ENIAC patent. ISD had begun by demanding royalties of $250 million from Honeywell! This compared to just under $150 million being asked of all the other six larger firms together, and to just $11.1 million paid by IBM in 1956. Even though the figure of $250 million was drastically reduced, finally, to $20 million, Honeywell found that amount, too, excessive.

So it was that ISD brought suit in Washington, D.C., on May 26, 1967, charging Honeywell with infringement of the ENIAC patent—and that Honeywell brought suit in Minneapolis that same day, charging Sperry Rand with antitrust behavior for monopolizing the computer industry by fraudulently procuring an invalid patent. Through a series of steps, the two cases were consolidated into one, encompassing both the ENIAC patent and the 30A package, and were assigned to Larson's U.S. District Court in Minneapolis. Honeywell was now the plaintiff, charging infirmities in all of these patents, and Sperry Rand and ISD were the defendants, countercharging patent infringement.

We have seen that Judge Larson ruled the ENIAC patent invalid, on grounds of derivation from Atanasoff. We have also seen that he ruled the 30A package, including the Regenerative Memory patent and several binary serial adder patents, unenforceable—he was not asked to rule on the package's validity—and that he ruled the Regenerative Memory patent, in particular, derived from Atanasoff.

Larson made his major decision on the ENIAC's derivation from Atanasoff in his Finding 3, titled "Atanasoff."[1] In twenty brief paragraphs he gave his decision, argued it, traced the history behind it, reaffirmed it, and closed with a comment on the relative veracity of the two principals, Atanasoff and Mauchly. Here is that finding in its entirety:

> 3.1 The subject matter of one or more claims of the ENIAC was derived from Atanasoff, and the invention claimed in the ENIAC was derived from Atanasoff.
>
> 3.1.1 SR and ISD are bound by their representation in support of the counterclaim herein that the invention claimed in the ENIAC patent is broadly "the invention of the Automatic Electronic Digital Computer."
>
> 3.1.2 Eckert and Mauchly did not themselves first invent the automatic electronic digital computer, but instead derived that subject matter from one Dr. John Vincent Atanasoff.
>
> 3.1.3 Although not necessary to the finding of derivation of "the invention" of the ENIAC patent, Honeywell has proved that the claimed subject matter of the ENIAC patent relied on in support of the counterclaim herein is not patentable over the subject matter derived by Mauchly from Atanasoff. As a representative example, Honeywell has shown that the subject matter of detailed claims 88 and 89 of the ENIAC patent corresponds to the work of Atanasoff which was known to Mauchly before any effort pertinent to the ENIAC machine or patent began.

3.1.4 Between 1937 and 1942, Atanasoff, then a professor of physics and mathematics at Iowa State College, Ames, Iowa, developed and built an automatic electronic digital computer for solving large systems of simultaneous linear algebraic equations.

3.1.5 In December, 1939, Atanasoff completed and reduced to practice his basic conception in the form of an operating breadboard model of a computing machine.

3.1.6 This breadboard model machine, constructed with the assistance of a graduate student, Clifford Berry, permitted the various components of the machine to be tested under actual operating conditions.

3.1.7 The breadboard model established the soundness of the basic principles of design, and Atanasoff and Berry began the construction of a prototype or pilot model, capable of solving with a high degree of accuracy a system of as many as 29 simultaneous equations having 29 unknowns.

3.1.8 By August, 1940, in connection with efforts at further funding, Atanasoff prepared a comprehensive manuscript which fully described the principles of his machine, including detail design features.

3.1.9 By the time the manuscript was prepared in August, 1940, construction of the machine, destined to be termed in this litigation the Atanasoff-Berry computer or "ABC," was already far advanced.

3.1.10 The description contained in the manuscript was adequate to enable one of ordinary skill in electronics at that time to make and use an ABC computer.

3.1.11 The manuscript was studied by experts in the art of aids to mathematical computation, who recommended its financial support, and these recommendations resulted in a grant of funds by Research Corporation for the ABC's continued construction.

3.1.12 In December, 1940, Atanasoff first met Mauchly while attending a meeting of the American Association for the Advancement of Science in Philadelphia, and generally informed Mauchly about the computing machine which was under construction at Iowa State College. Because of Mauchly's expression of interest in the machine and its principles, Atanasoff invited Mauchly to come to Ames, Iowa, to learn more about the computer.

3.1.13 After correspondence on the subject with Atanasoff, Mauchly went to Ames, Iowa, as a houseguest of Atanasoff for several days, where he discussed the ABC as well as other ideas of Atanasoff's relating to the computing art.

3.1.14 Mauchly was given an opportunity to read, and did read, but was not permitted to take with him, a copy of the comprehensive manuscript which Atanasoff had prepared in August, 1940.

3.1.15 At the time of Mauchly's visit, although the ABC was not entirely complete, its construction was sufficiently well advanced so that the principles of its operation, including detail design features, were explained and demonstrated to Mauchly.

3.1.16 The discussions Mauchly had with both Atanasoff and Berry while at Ames were free and open and no significant information concerning the machine's theory, design, construction, use or operation was withheld.

3.1.17 Prior to his visit to Ames, Iowa, Mauchly had been broadly interested in electrical analog calculating devices, but had not conceived an automatic electronic digital computer.

3.1.18 As a result of this visit, the discussions of Mauchly with Atanasoff and Berry, the demonstrations, and the review of the manuscript, Mauchly derived from the ABC "the invention of the automatic electronic digital computer" claimed in the ENIAC patent.

3.1.19 The Court has heard the testimony at trial of both Atanasoff and Mauchly, and finds the testimony of Atanasoff with respect to the knowledge and information derived by Mauchly to be credible.

Larson's repeated reference to "the automatic electronic digital computer" as "the claimed subject matter of the ENIAC patent" lies at the heart of his finding of derivation from Atanasoff. To collect royalties on all electronic data processing equipment for the life of the ENIAC patent, Sperry Rand and Illinois Scientific Developments thought it best to have the ENIAC acknowledged as the original, seminal machine, *the first automatic electronic digital computer.* This meant, though, that Honeywell could have the entire patent invalidated if it could prove derivation of this broad subject matter from an earlier automatic electronic digital computer. It did not have to prove derivation of any particular ENIAC patent claim. Judge Larson, in finding that Honeywell did establish two such claims (88 and 89), observed that this was "not necessary."

The question arises as to whether Sperry Rand might have been more successful here had it not framed its case in terms of the patent's subject matter, but rather in terms of its formal list of some 148 claims. That approach would have allowed only those claims shown to "read on" Atanasoff's work to be declared invalid, perhaps twenty in all. A still-valuable patent would have remained.

Indeed, had the preliminary negotiations between Sperry Rand and Honeywell been conducted in terms of the individual claims, it is possible that Honeywell, in order to avoid a more difficult and less favorable suit, might have agreed to the $20 million settlement. And then Atanasoff's work might not have entered the picture, in any public way. Such speculation becomes quite convoluted when taken in its broader context. For example, might some other computer company have refused to settle with Sperry Rand, citing Atanasoff's influence on the ENIAC? Or might the Regenerative Memory patent suit, between Sperry Rand and Control Data, have brought Atanasoff's work to public attention anyway?

A third possible scenario arises. What if Mauchly and Eckert had claimed only their own contributions in the first place, excluding from the ENIAC patent all ideas derived from Atanasoff? As it happens they did, on the very first page of the patent, call the ENIAC "the first general-purpose automatic electronic digital computing machine known to us," which would seem to distinguish it from Atanasoff's first *special-purpose* electronic computer known to them. If they had held to that distinction throughout, they would have had a valuable patent. And, again, Atanasoff's work would probably not have gained widespread recognition!

The Sperry attorneys, as they prepared for trial, clearly expected to ward off the Honeywell charge of derivation from Atanasoff. In assuming this stance, they had relied to a large extent on the presumably informed opinions of both Eckert and Mauchly, who, however, seem to have increasingly discounted Atanasoff's original ideas as they carried them to greater and greater heights in their own machines. The Sperry attorneys had also relied on Mauchly alone for his accounts both of his firsthand experience of the Atanasoff-Berry Computer in Iowa and of his own early accomplishments. Apparently they saw in him a good prospective witness, as well. On all these scores, they must have been severely disappointed. They may even have felt deceived.

Judge Larson's recounting of the history in his Finding 3 not only established a series of crucial dates, some of which had been contested by Sperry Rand in court, but resolved a number of other disputed matters. Atanasoff's 1940 manuscript did describe the ABC comprehensively, and Mauchly did read that manuscript during his Iowa visit.[2] Mauchly did see the ABC at a point when even "detail design features" could be demonstrated and explained. Both Atanasoff and Berry were completely forthcoming to Mauchly about the ABC's "theory, design, construction, use [and] operation."

As to Mauchly's own interest in calculating devices before his visit, Larson noted that this had centered on analog devices (harmonic analyzers). And though it has been argued that the judge did not credit Mauchly's digital *intentions* as expressed in two personal letters before he met Atanasoff (because Mauchly failed to produce these late 1940 letters from his files), the fact remains that, as Larson went on to rule, he had not conceived any "automatic electronic digital computer."

The judge's recognition that the model built by Atanasoff and Berry "reduced to practice his basic conception . . . of a computing machine" established December 1939 as a milestone date in the history, if not the date of the invention of the first electronic computer. His reference to the ABC as a "prototype or pilot model" acknowledged Atanasoff's plan to move on to more advanced machines, including an electronic integraph, or differential analyzer. His reference to "other ideas of Atanasoff's relating to the computing art" discussed with Mauchly in Iowa was further acknowledgment of that same plan.

Lastly, with regard to the conflicting stories of the two men as to what Mauchly derived from Atanasoff, the judge's finding of credibility for Atanasoff's testimony would seem also to mean that he did not believe Mauchly's testimony!

Judge Larson referred to Atanasoff again in Finding 4, "Inventors," in which he declared Mauchly and Eckert "the inventors" of the ENIAC, "the true and actual inventors" as named in their patent.[3] This section has been cited by critics as evidence of flawed reasoning on the part of the judge because, it is argued, it contradicts the preceding finding that the ENIAC was derived from Atanasoff. How, the argument goes, could Mauchly and Eckert be "the inventors" if their invention was derived from a prior inventor?

The answer is that this finding was not addressing the issue of *prior inventors* but of *coinventors on the ENIAC team*, and Larson was merely responding to a Honeywell charge that Eckert and Mauchly had wrongfully omitted the names of other Moore School inventors from the ENIAC patent. Moreover, he was careful to emphasize the distinction of these team members from prior inventor Atanasoff by repeating that the ENIAC remained "barred from patentability" because of its derivation from Atanasoff.

He continued:

> 4.1.5 . . . Although Eckert and Mauchly were therefore not entitled to patent that claimed invention, they have not been shown to have incorrectly excluded as named co-inventors, other members of the Moore School team.

What Honeywell had failed to do, the judge explained, was prove coinvention by other team members "on a claim-by-claim basis." For while, by patent law, it could prove *prior invention* without citing specific claims, it could prove *coinvention* only by attributing specific patent claims to specific inventors. In fact, however, Honeywell had no wish to establish other inventors of the ENIAC! It wished only to establish the team aspect of the ENIAC project and the heavy reliance of Eckert and Mauchly on their fellow engineers—with an implication of coinvention. And so, rather than citing particular patent claims, it chose to cite "inventive contributions" by certain individuals.

Here Honeywell did not fail. Larson upheld its case for inventive contributions by those "other members of the Moore School team."

> 4.2 I am inclined to be of the view that the work on the ENIAC was a group or team effort and that inventive contributions were made by Sharpless, Burks, Shaw, and others.

4.2.1 Arthur W. Burks made major contributions to the design of the accumulator and the multiplier of ENIAC and signed at least 77 drawings.

4.2.2 T. K. Sharpless made major contributions to the design of the high-speed multiplier, the initiating and cycling units, and the accumulator of ENIAC and signed at least 83 drawings.

4.2.3 Robert F. Shaw contributed to the design of the function table, the accumulator, the master programmer, the initiating unit, the constant transmitter and the printer of ENIAC and signed at least 103 drawings.

Larson went on to name three more, John H. Davis, Frank Mural, and Chuan Chu, for their contributions to design and their signings of drawings.

One further distinction needs to be made between Atanasoff and the ENIAC team members. As we have seen, the question before the court in the case of Atanasoff was whether he had invented *an earlier electronic computer* from which the ENIAC was derived, whereas the question in the case of the team members was whether they were actually inventors of the *ENIAC*, along with Eckert and Mauchly. Larson ruled the first case proven, the second not. But he never ruled that Atanasoff was an inventor of the ENIAC, as some critics have claimed he did—and have then wondered at his doing so, given the tremendous difference between the two machines! Larson even alluded to that difference at a later point in his decision. (Finding 13).[4]

In addition to derivation from Atanasoff, the judge found the ENIAC patent, or certain of its 148 formal claims, invalid on five other grounds. He invalidated the entire patent on three technical grounds having nothing to do with the invention itself, but rather with the amount of time that Mauchly and Eckert allowed to elapse between their public disclosure of it and their application for a patent on it. These grounds of premature disclosure were the computer's *public use*, its placement *on sale*, and *publication* of its key features; the judge addressed them in Findings 1, 2, and 7, respectively.

He also invalidated three particular claims of the patent that he found anticipated by a second prior inventor, Byron E. Phelps, of IBM; he addressed this ground in Finding 6.

He further invalidated some fourteen claims that used the concept of a "pulse" as redefined in an eleventh-hour amendment to the original application; he addressed this ground in Finding 10.

Finally, Judge Larson ruled the entire patent unenforceable, but not invalid, on two grounds: *delay* before the U.S. Patent Office, addressed in Finding 11; and *fraud* on the U.S. Patent Office, addressed in Finding 13.

The three patent-invalidating technical counts bearing on public disclosure of the ENIAC fell under one broad patent-filing requirement, as the judge explained. A patent on an invention can be denied by the Patent Office, or invalidated by a court, if the subject matter of that invention was made public more than one year prior to the patent application date. Conversely, the inventor is allowed one year, but only one year, to file for a patent following public disclosure of the invention. The rationale behind this rule rests on the basic purpose of the patent system: to promote the public good by encouraging invention, on the one hand, and by making inventive advances generally available, on the other. *And it holds no matter who has made the public disclosure.*

The filing date for the ENIAC patent was June 26, 1947, so that its so-called *critical date* was June 26, 1946. That is, any public disclosure prior to June 26, 1946, would render the patent invalid.

In Finding 1, "Public Use," Larson cited numerous "statutorily barring" instances of use of the finished computer by outsiders.[5] The earliest was the running of a hydrogen bomb problem, between December 1945 and February 1946, by Nicholas Metropolis and Stanley P. Frankel of the Los Alamos National Laboratory. Other scientists also ran problems on the ENIAC in the spring of 1946, most notably Douglas R. Hartree of Cambridge University. Perhaps even more damaging was a series of events that February, when the ENIAC was formally unveiled: a press demonstration, a newsreel, a Moore School open house, and dedication ceremonies.

At trial, Eckert and Mauchly called all of these instances experimental, part of the process of completing the invention, and so permissible. Judge Larson, however, found that both the solution of problems on the computer and the publicity for it constituted "non-experimental public use . . . prior to the critical date." He found all uses of the computer after December 1, 1945, when it came under the control of "the customer, Army Ordnance," to be "for its intended practical purpose," rather than "for the purpose of completing . . . the ENIAC machine." All changes to it, as recorded in a Service Log, he wrote, were "minor and routine refinements or adjustments of a non-inventive nature."

He pointed out that construction of the ENIAC was finished in November 1945 and that the Los Alamos problem, which "employed 99 percent of its capacity" and yielded positive expectations for the bomb, marked December 1945 as the date of "full-scale operating use." Eckert and Mauchly themselves, he said, had advertised the ENIAC as operating by January 1946 and had so maintained to the Patent Office. He ruled further that the ensuing public displays were intended "to show to all the world the developments in computing which had been proved operational." Moreover, he observed, "Eckert and Mauchly as participants therein had been warned [by Army Ordnance] that the display of the machine would foreclose any of their private patent rights if not promptly pursued."

Larson drew special attention to the strong participation of the two inventors in these efforts "to achieve saturation publicity for the completion of the ENIAC": in planning the problem runs for the press demonstration; in giving speeches, granting interviews, and distributing computer printouts at that demonstration; in editing the Army Ordnance press releases for the dedication ceremony "to insure specific recognition" for themselves; and in influencing the guest list and seating chart for the dedication banquet to advance their own "business enterprise plans."

The judge then expanded on what he saw as the "private interest" of Mauchly and Eckert in these public uses of the ENIAC: "their own commercial gain." In fact, he wrote, their attempts to exploit the ENIAC commercially had begun "at least as early as the fall of 1944," when they described and demonstrated the machine-in-progress to "their intended customers." There were meetings with the U.S. Weather Bureau "as early as April, 1945, . . . to discuss the ENIAC and future work with them" and, later that same year, with "about a dozen Census Bureau officials" to describe the ENIAC and seek "a contract to develop a similar but more advanced machine" for them.

These contacts intensified with the public ceremonies of February 1946, and with follow-up demonstrations and sales talks by Eckert and Mauchly. What is more, their commercial efforts paid off. The Census Bureau, Larson found, relied almost entirely on their presentation of the ENIAC in deciding to award a contract for the development of a more advanced computer, known ultimately as the UNIVAC.

Larson also noted that, as part and parcel of their private business pursuits, Eckert and Mauchly in March 1945 had effectively forced the University of Pennsylvania to give them "the commercial rights to any patents" on the ENIAC, and in March 1946 had resigned from the university rather than "subjugate their personal commercial interest to the interests of the University."

Judge Larson wound up this lengthy finding on public use by crediting the "heavy weight of evidence" provided by the "thousands of documents" he had received and the "22 live witnesses" he had heard. He also credited the February 1946 newsreel film in which he had been able to view the ENIAC "actually being used for its intended purpose in a clearly publicly intended setting."

Finding 2, "On Sale," addressed the second public disclosure violation for which Larson invalidated the ENIAC patent.[6] It, too, had to do with commercialization of the ENIAC. But whereas Finding 1 had dealt with efforts to sell *an improved version* of the computer by exploiting its various public uses, Finding 2 now dealt with the sale of *the ENIAC itself*, by the Moore School to Army Ordnance, before the critical date of June 26, 1946.

Development and construction of the ENIAC were "financed by the United States Government," the judge observed, through a series of "fixed price" contractual arrangements, beginning with the original June 5, 1943, contract. These arrangements ultimately set December 31, 1945, for delivery of the finished ENIAC to the army (f.o.b. the Moore School). In mid-June 1946, the army both affirmed that delivery date, after the fact, and formally accepted the final

Figure 18. The ENIAC. The decimal ENIAC consisted of thirty semiautonomous units arranged in an eighty-foot U along three walls of a room. Transmission of numbers among units was over a plug-board trunk system. The operators entered a program by setting switches on the front panels of the units, then interconnecting those panels with jumper cables for the required sequencing of instructions throughout the computer.

Here two people can be seen entering arbitrary functions on free-standing read-only panels within the U (left front, right rear), and two others checking switches and cable connections (left rear, right front). The IBM punched-card reader, for input, and the IBM card punch, for output, are also free-standing, on the right.

(Photo courtesy of Arthur W. Burks.)

Report on the ENIAC. The claimed invention, then, was "barred from valid patentability," Larson ruled, because it was "on sale prior to the critical date."

Larson used this same issue to locate the sole test-model of the ENIAC in the historical sequence. This two-accumulator system was operated successfully by July 1944, he found, and so was both "on sale and sold to Army Ordnance" as of that date. This system, he held, was itself "an automatic electronic digital computer," the essence of the invention claimed in the ENIAC patent; indeed, it was also "an electronic numerical integrator and computer," for which the acronym "ENIAC" stood. Finally, he noted, the 1944 model had been represented to the Patent Office "by the applicants, Eckert and Mauchly, to embody fully and constitute an actual reduction to practice of the invention claimed in the ENIAC patent application."

Judge Larson went on to address explicitly this recurring conflict between the trial testimony of the two witnesses and their representations to the Patent Office in the early 1950s. He cited eight affidavits, submitted in response to Patent Office interferences by other inventors, in which Mauchly and Eckert swore that the ENIAC had been reduced to practice by December 10, 1945, the starting date for the Los Alamos problem. These affidavits were in sharp contrast to their trial testimony, in which they maintained that the purpose of this and all other uses of the ENIAC before the critical date had been to perfect and complete the computer.

In balancing these conflicting positions, the judge held that statements the two men made to the Patent Office "many years nearer to the events and prior to the emergence of public use and on sale as substantial issues" were to be credited over their trial testimony. Their earlier stance, of course, was directed toward establishing priority for their invention, their later stance toward denying the proscribed public disclosures.

<<<>>>

The third violation of the public disclosure rule was that of publication of the subject matter of the invention before the critical date, addressed in Finding 7.[7] Oddly enough, the publication cited here concerned, not the ENIAC, but the EDVAC. Larson ruled that this document, mathematician John von Neumann's "First Draft of a Report on the EDVAC," distributed by Army Ordnance's Herman Goldstine in June 1945, was not only a publication under the law but also an enabling disclosure of *both* the EDVAC *and* the ENIAC.[8]

The report in question had followed a series of meetings at the Moore School that spring, called to discuss the computer that would succeed the ENIAC. The major improvement of the EDVAC over the ENIAC anticipated at that time was the move away from counters, which, as they computed, also stored the latest results. Now there would be two distinct units: first, a regenerative main store based on Eckert's concept of a mercury-delay-line memory; second, a binary serial adder separate from but interacting with that memory.

This form of memory had arisen from Eckert's earlier adaptation, for the MIT Radiation Laboratory, of William B. Shockley's acoustic-delay-line tube for use in timing radar signals. With critical help from Kite Sharpless, Eckert had successfully replaced Shockley's particular acoustic medium, ethylene glycol, with the superior mercury. He had then thought of a further adaptation to create a computer memory: instead of the radar device's single crystal and movable reflecting metal plate, he conceived of using two stationary crystals, one at each end of a tube of mercury.

As we explained in chapters 1 and 2, such a system would be structurally and, to some extent, substantively similar to Atanasoff's computer, with its regen-

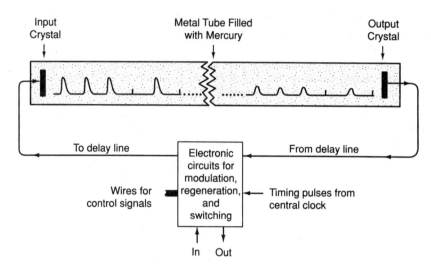

Figure 19. Diagram of mercury-delay-line memory. Depicted here schematically is the sequence of acoustic pulses and blanks traveling down a mercury-delay-line tube from the input crystal on the left to the output crystal on the right, with a pulse representing "1" and the absence of a pulse "0." The electronic circuits associated with each memory tube (and controlled by the computer) had two functions: on each cycle they regenerated the binary digits, which otherwise would have weakened when stored without access over a long period; and they read instructions and numbers in and out during a problem run.

The EDVAC's memory had thirty-two mercury-delay-line tubes, each holding thirty-two words (numbers) of thirty-two bits (binary digits) each. Each word represented either a thirty-one-bit signed binary number or a thirty-one-bit coded instruction, together with an initial bit to identify it as a number or an instruction.

The metal mercury-delay-line tubes of the EDVAC and other EDVAC-type computers were about four feet long and were arranged lengthwise in several layers in a slightly longer tank, also metal, with a medium that preserved a constant temperature.

---

erative drum memory and binary serial adders (or add-subtract mechanisms, as he called them). But it would have the advantage of a memory that could keep pace with the machine's adder—also greatly enhanced over the ABC's.

Thus, just as Eckert's 100,000-pulses-per-second electronic counter (for the ENIAC) would be dramatically faster than Atanasoff's combination of electronic adders and slowly rotating memory, so his mercury-delay-line memory in combination with a 1,000,000-pulses-per-second adder (for the EDVAC) would be dramatically faster than that ENIAC counter.

The mercury-delay-line memory would have the additional great advantage over the ENIAC that such a large memory could store the program, or instructions for a given problem, as well as the arithmetic data, those instructions to be expressed in numerical code. Moreover, with the contemplation of this giant step forward in storage technology, a second giant step was now contemplated in the problem-entry technology.

In the ENIAC (still under construction), the arithmetic data were to be entered automatically from IBM punched cards, but the program was to be entered manually through hours, even days, of setting switches on the various units and plugging in jumper cables between units. Now, because the mercury-delay-line memory would be *erasable*, a program could be replaced very simply between problem runs.

Participants in the four March and April 1945 meetings were Eckert, Mauchly, Burks, Goldstine (Army Ordnance liaison to the Moore School, now a captain), S. Reid Warren (newly appointed director of the EDVAC project), and John von Neumann (Army Ordnance consultant to the Moore School). Von Neumann, who had first visited the ENIAC project the previous summer, was excited by the prospect of applying the new electronic technology to the nuclear weapons problems of the Los Alamos National Laboratory, where he also served as a scientific advisor. Indeed, he was the link that brought the hydrogen bomb problem to the ENIAC in late 1945.

Von Neumann's "First Draft of a Report on the EDVAC" resulted from his offer, at the end of the second meeting, to summarize and organize the discussions. The offer had been received enthusiastically, but in fact his report both fell short of summarizing the discussions and went well beyond their subject matter. Consequently, the report itself, its distribution, and, much later, the judge's rulings on it caused considerable bitterness.

Judge Larson noted in Finding 7 that the First Draft Report was incomplete—with gaps to be filled in later—but declared it still "a substantial and major part" of the intended total. Its fifteen chapters dealt in detail, he said, "with the logical organization and makeup" of the computer it disclosed, to the exclusion of "the specific hardware to mechanize" that computer. He found further, on the basis of expert witness testimony, that this report, despite its lack of hardware detail, was "sufficient to enable persons skilled in the art to make and use the computer set forth."

As to the report's applicability to the ENIAC patent, Larson ruled that it included certain features of the ENIAC, even though it did not address those features as such; that, indeed, it anticipated nine particular claims in the ENIAC patent. The judge's finding that this publication was an "enabling disclosure" of the *ENIAC* rests upon these ENIAC features and ENIAC patent claims. He did not find that "persons skilled in the art" could construct an ENIAC; he found only that they could construct "the computer set forth," or, in another passage, simply "a computer." The fact, then, that this document with these disclosures was published more than a year before Eckert and Mauchly applied for the ENIAC patent rendered that patent invalid.

Just as seriously, Judge Larson ruled that the computer described in the von Neumann report was an "automatic electronic digital computer"! So here again was the issue of *that* entity, which the Sperry side had chosen to designate "the claimed subject matter" of the ENIAC patent. This Sperry strategy had misfired in the matter of *priority of invention*, as Atanasoff's earlier invention was found to be such a computer. And now it misfired in the matter of *prior publication*, as the von Neumann report was found to disclose such a computer before the critical date.

As to whether that report really was a publication, despite its informal distribution, Larson ruled that it was "a printed publication, within the meaning of 35 U.S.C. #102." He noted that Goldstine, with von Neumann's approval, had sent out "a large number of mimeographed copies of the First Draft Report for the express purpose of making the knowledge therein publicly available to advance the state of the computer art . . . as widely and as early as feasible." He said that this report had been distributed first within the Moore School and then to persons representing various institutions in the United States and England. Lastly, he said that this distribution "had an important influence on the continuing development of electronic computers."

Judge Larson concluded this Finding 7 by citing an April 8, 1947, meeting at the Moore School, in which it was "clearly and unequivocally established," in the presence of Eckert and Mauchly and their patent lawyers from Army Ordnance, that the First Draft Report was an enabling and barring publication.[9] He quoted a statement made to von Neumann, who was there as well, by the presiding Ordnance lawyer, Joseph P. Church:

> It is our firm belief from the facts that we have now that this report of yours dated 30 June 1945 is a publication and will prohibit you or anyone else from obtaining a patent on anything it discloses because it has been published more than a year.

The judge also quoted Church's opinion on the extent of the report's disclosure:

> I think the broad conception is there and to one skilled in the art it is sufficient to put them on the road of accomplishing a development.

Now, the participants in that 1947 meeting were addressing only the patentability of the *EDVAC*. The Army Ordnance attorneys did not consider that the von Neumann report affected the *ENIAC* patent, as Larson would later. Accordingly, they told Eckert and Mauchly that they remained free to pursue the ENIAC patent and would have Ordnance's continuing help in doing so.

Because of this publication barrier, however, the Ordnance attorneys would no longer assist in patenting the EDVAC itself or any feature of it disclosed in the report. Moreover, they declared, they would assist with undisclosed features only if Eckert and Mauchly could reach agreement with von Neumann as to who did what. All three, of course, could still apply for patents through their private attorneys. Von Neumann, while he wanted to protect his ideas, had no interest in pursuing monetary gain. Eckert and Mauchly preferred to proceed on their own; ultimately, as we have seen, they did not try to patent the entire EDVAC, but applied for and secured patents on certain hardware features not disclosed in the von Neumann report.

The judge added one last blow, observing that Mauchly was to have given a copy of this report to the Army Ordnance Patent Department when it was issued, but had not done so, and that it came to that department's attention only when von Neumann submitted it the following year.

Von Neumann's 1945 EDVAC report—its publication and its content—bear some scrutiny. The bitterness on the part of Mauchly and Eckert over its publication had several aspects. First and foremost, of course, was the fact that the report was distributed widely enough to constitute a publication in the legal sense. As we have just seen, this fact alone cost them (in 1947) the army's help in securing patents on the EDVAC and related concepts; and it led ultimately (in 1973) to invalidation of the ENIAC patent, which the army *had* helped them secure.

A closely related aspect was the further fact that the von Neumann report went out as an "unclassified" document, so that its disclosures were not protected in the way that the Moore School's "classified" reports on the ENIAC and the EDVAC projects were. A collection of Sperry Rand papers at the Hagley Museum and Library Archives, Greenville, Delaware, has EDVAC project director Reid Warren's explanation of this failure to classify. In an April 2, 1947, statement prepared for the April 8 Moore School meeting, Warren recalled being assured by Goldstine that "no classification was necessary," since the report "was for use only within the group working on the EDVAC." It was certainly unfortunate for Eckert and Mauchly that Goldstine did send it to other interested parties and, further, that they apparently did not learn of its barring implications until after the one-year allowance for patent application had expired.

(When Goldstine sent out the von Neumann report in June 1945, he may have supposed that both the EDVAC and the ENIAC patent applications were well along, because for some eight months Mauchly's main job at the Moore School had been to work on these. Also, there is no indication that Goldstine viewed his distribution of the report as a publication, much less a barring one— and certainly not a barring one for the *ENIAC*, as Larson would find.)

A third aspect of the bitterness over publication of the First Draft Report, and the one most immediately felt, was the fact that it bore only von Neumann's name as author, whereas it had had its impetus in joint discussions centering on Eckert's memory concept. Goldstine had received a handwritten version from von Neumann with neither title nor author. He had had this typed, with carbon copies for Mauchly, Eckert, and Burks, and then a slightly edited version prepared for mimeographing, together with a cover page giving the title, "First Draft of a Report on the EDVAC," and author, John von Neumann. The acronym EDVAC appeared only in that title, not in von Neumann's text; nor did the cover disclose the full name, Electronic Discrete Variable Computer.

Von Neumann also omitted any reference to the Moore School team or the four planning meetings. Moreover, despite his focus on logical design, he mentioned hardware items invented by Eckert without citing him. Chief among these was a delay-line memory, although in that case, as he made clear in the 1947 Moore School meeting with the Army Ordnance lawyers, he deliberately used the broader term *acoustic*-delay-line memory, rather than Eckert's particular contribution, the *mercury*-delay-line memory, so as, he said, to leave Eckert free to claim that invention.

<<<>>>

The distribution of this report, then, framed as it was, gave several knowledgeable scientists not only the liberty to share its contents with others, but also the impression that von Neumann was the principal inventor of the EDVAC. Together with later reports, it led to his worldwide recognition as inventor of what came to be called the *stored-program concept*, which had in fact had a twofold development: the first part, Eckert's; the second, von Neumann's.

In brief, von Neumann had depended upon Eckert's advances over the ENIAC to move on to his own equally ingenious concept. As we saw, on Eckert's conception the speed of computation would be markedly enhanced, both by the combination of a large, fast regenerative memory with an electronic serial adder and by the much faster entry of arithmetic data, and especially of coded instructions, at the start of a given problem. This last also meant that the EDVAC would be practical for many more types of problems than the ENIAC, which was best suited to problems of a repetitive nature (such as computing artillery firing tables) that ran for long periods of time from an initial program entry.

What von Neumann did was take further advantage of the *erasable* feature of the mercury-delay-line memory, which Eckert had seen as allowing for easy replacement of an old program by a new one at the end of one problem run and the start of the next. Von Neumann saw that such a feature would not only expedite entry of a *preset* program, as in the case of the ENIAC, but would also allow that program to *change* automatically as the problem ran.

Although the terms "read-only" and "read-write" were yet to be coined, this is the relevant distinction here. There had been a growing awareness of the greater utility that a read-write memory such as the mercury delay line would provide: a memory in which digital sequences could be written, erased, and replaced, all under the control of the machine. Atanasoff's ABC had its two large read-write storage drums, and the ENIAC its twenty read-write accumulators. Atanasoff had also mentioned, in his 1940 proposal, the possibility of using read-write magnetic drums; and Perry Crawford had, in 1942, written his MIT master's thesis proposing a read-write magnetic disk memory. Neither Atanasoff nor Crawford, however, had conceived of programming an electronic computer, whereas Eckert and Mauchly had—for the ENIAC.

Moreover, Eckert had come to realize, even before he conceived his mercury-delay-line memory, that *any* form of erasable memory would permit the replacement, *between problem runs*, not just of arithmetic data as in the ENIAC accumulators, but of programs. In January 1944, having read Crawford's thesis, he wrote a very brief "disclosure" of his own concept of a rotating magnetic memory, in disk or drum form, and there included what he termed "temporary" (read-write) programming as well as "permanent" (read-only) programming.[10]

He gave no indication, however, that such a "temporary" store could allow automatic modification of a program within a problem run: not in that early 1944 memorandum, not a few months later when he conceived the mercury-delay-line memory, not even a year later at the time of the Moore School meetings with von Neumann. This, as we have said, was the further step that von Neumann took in his "First Draft of a Report on the EDVAC."

For Eckert had continued to think in terms of the ENIAC's *read-only* program, a preset entity that remained unchanged in a problem run. Von Neumann, on the other hand, saw that the program itself would be *read-write*, and that a *program language* could be devised to allow the program for a given problem to modify itself as the problem ran. Stated more technically, von Neumann, in contemplating automatic program modification, was applying the distinction, later formulated by Burks, between the read-only *constant-address* program of the ENIAC and a read-write *variable-address* program that could change its own addresses.[11]

In his EDVAC report, von Neumann presented a variable-address program language, including a substitution instruction for altering another instruction by changing its address. This substitution instruction was contained in a table and remarked upon—with an exclamation point—in the final paragraph of this unfinished document. It would of course be applicable not just to instructions in its own program, but to those in other programs stored in the same memory. And this possibility, in turn, would open the way for programs to alter instructions in programs in other memories, as in assembling and compiling.

Von Neumann also revealed in this report his new idea for a cathode-ray-tube memory, which, as it turned out, would allow *random access* of data and instructions, a great architectural improvement over the *serial access* of the delay-line tubes and one that became standard for main memories.

<<<>>>

Serious ill feeling on both sides over von Neumann's June 1945 report seems not to have erupted until March 1946, shortly before Eckert and Mauchly left the Moore School because of its demand that they subjugate their future commercial ventures to the interests of the university. At that point von Neumann told Burks, who was about to join him at his home base, the Institute for Advanced Study, Princeton, New Jersey, that he had learned Eckert and Mauchly were trying to steal his ideas—to patent them—and that Burks was not to tell them about the computer being planned for the Institute.

How von Neumann came to this belief is not clear, but he was right. The Hagley archives have two lists of ideas drawn up by Mauchly and Eckert as their own, the earlier of which, "Main outline of material suggested for patent application," was dated February 5, 1945. These lists included what was clearly an original von Neumann concept for computer storage, the cathode ray tube. Goldstine has, in his 1972 book, *The Computer from Pascal to von Neumann*, provided documentation for pursuit of this concept by von Neumann, working with RCA, as early as September 1944.[12] It is the form of memory, in fact, that von Neumann went on to use in the Institute machine, rather than Eckert's mercury-delay-line memory. Indeed, the Hagley papers reveal that the Army Ordnance attorneys, to whom these suggestions for patent application were addressed, responded by citing a difficulty that Eckert and Mauchly could not resolve and that, in the end, precluded their making any application for a patent on the cathode-ray-tube memory in their names.

For their part, Eckert and Mauchly were not only incensed that von Neumann, in this far-ranging disclosure of the stored-program concept, failed to credit their contributions. They also claimed that the First Draft Report amounted to a mere recording of the group discussions held at the Moore School. Eckert, in a 1976 paper for a computer history conference at the Los Alamos Scientific Laboratory (actually delivered in his absence by Mauchly), puts the matter this way:

> It is our opinion that von Neumann adopted many of our ideas and rewrote them with the "neuron notation" of McCullough [*sic*] and Pitts. It has always upset me (and John, too) that von Neumann gave talks on the work we had done on the Moore School ENIAC/EDVAC project, rarely if ever giving any credit to the University or to the people who had actually produced the ideas.[13]

He also refers to von Neumann's activity as "translating from electronic circuit terms into neural notation." This "neural notation," published by Warren S. McCulloch and Walter H. Pitts in 1943, was a logical symbolism for depicting the elementary thinking and memory processes of neurons (and neuron networks) without having to describe their much more complex physiology and chemistry.[14] Von Neumann converted this logical symbolism into one for depicting the corresponding operations of vacuum-tube and delay-line circuits without having to work out their electronics.

Von Neumann did not "rewrite" or "translate" electronics into logic. His whole aim was to start with the logical representation, as the simpler way of conceiving and portraying the desired processes; their electronic realizations were to follow. Moreover, there were actually only two instances of discussion of electronic circuitry in those spring 1945 meetings that could possibly have been so reconstrued in von Neumann's report.

One instance concerned the design of a binary serial adder. And here it was von Neumann who first presented designs he had already worked out in his *logical symbolism*. Then Mauchly proceeded to show some *electronic* designs that he and Eckert had worked out.

The other instance concerned the question, raised by Eckert, of whether to have two switches or one for use in transmitting signals to or from the mercury-delay-line store(s): two if data and instructions were to be in separate memories, one if in the same memory. Partial electronic designs for each option were discussed, but no determination was made as to which would be better. Later, in his report, von Neumann gave his own complete conception of his preference, a single switch, again in the simpler logical notation.

Eckert is equally disingenuous in claiming for the Moore School group other ideas first committed to writing in that EDVAC report. It was there that von Neumann proposed a preliminary form of what would become known as the von Neumann architecture, with its three main units—memory, arithmetic unit, and control—together with communications among them. He then worked out much of the detailed logical design of the EDVAC (for the memory and the arithmetic unit, but not for the control). He also specified, in that report, the program language mentioned above, for the efficient solution of problems in accord with his logical design.

These were true von Neumann innovations, all of which, as it turned out, were to have far-reaching influence on computer design. The logical symbolism he developed was later used for transistor circuits and is used today to describe the details of computer chips. His procedure of working out the logic first, rather than going directly to the electronics as in the ENIAC, also became standard. His program language, or some variant of it, was immediately adopted by others and opened the way to modern programming with all its intricacies. And, of course, the von Neumann architecture has persisted as the basis for nearly all modern computers.

In short, while Eckert had a perfect right to complain that von Neumann did not credit the Moore School discussions, he was wrong in his broad claim that von Neumann was merely documenting ideas developed earlier by the Moore School group; and he was wrong in his specific claim that von Neumann merely converted that group's electronics into logic.

In that same Los Alamos paper, "The ENIAC," Eckert cites his January 1944 disclosure as a proposal to "use magnetic disks either erasable or permanently for
the storage of information both alterable or unchangeable." And he adds, overlooking the fact that Atanasoff's computer had both a read-only drum (for base
conversion) and two read-write drums (for computing): "The concept of general
internal storage started in this memo."

As we have seen, that disclosure of Eckert's, published for the first time
within this Los Alamos paper, did not reveal the possible advantages of "temporary" storage. Nevertheless, he goes on to lay claim to the idea that a program
could be modified from within as a problem ran:

> My best computer idea, today briefly called "stored program," became to us an
> "obvious idea," and one that we started to take for granted. It was obvious that
> computer instructions could be conveyed in numerical code, and that whatever
> machines we might build after the ENIAC would want to avoid the setup prob-
> lems that our hastily built first try ENIAC made evident. It was also obvious that
> the functions supplied by the Master Programmer [of the ENIAC] in controlling
> loops and counting iterations, etc., *would be achieved very naturally by allowing
> instructions to be subject to alterations within the calculator.* [italics added]

Here Eckert's first observation, that the ENIAC's setup problems could be
avoided in future computers, was indeed recognized early on—given his concept
of a read-write memory large enough to store an entire program internally. His
second claim to the "obvious," however, is highly misleading in two respects.
One, "allowing instructions to be subject to alterations" would have been an
*un*natural, highly impractical way of achieving these Master Programmer functions in the EDVAC; and, in fact, like the ENIAC, the EDVAC—and all machines
of its type—controlled loops and counted iterations at the hardware level, without
employing the facility to alter instructions.

Two, there is no evidence that Eckert or any of the Moore School group recognized the possibility of altering instructions before von Neumann formulated
his substitution instruction in his June 1945 report. It must also be noted, in this
regard, that von Neumann's insight, once he learned of Eckert's mercury-delay-
line memory, went far beyond the "obvious" or "very natural" implications of
that read-write memory.

It is of interest that Mauchly, in his own paper for the 1976 Los Alamos conference, outdoes Eckert in distorting history to claim for themselves both stages
of the stored-program concept.[15] In a single amazing paragraph, he declares that
the ENIAC's Master Programmer "provided program storage that could be
altered by the program itself"! The ENIAC did *not* have, *could not* have had the
facility to alter its instructions from within, because of the read-only nature of its

program memory, whether as centralized in the Master Programmer or as distributed over the various units. Like Eckert, Mauchly puts his claim in terms of the ENIAC's branching capability, but branching merely allows a choice of paths through the computer's read-only program, not a change in the program itself.

A further, more technical argument is relevant here. As mentioned above, a discussion of electronic circuitry in early 1945 dealt with the question of whether to have one switch or two for transmitting signals to or from the storage devices. The question was complicated, because (in either case) the stored instructions were to be moved to the control unit for execution and the stored data were to be moved to the arithmetic unit for processing. If two switches were used, data and instructions would be in separate memories, to be accessed and transmitted in parallel; if one switch was used, data and instructions would be mixed in the same memory, with successive transmission to or from either the arithmetic unit or the control. The discussion centered on the issue of speed of operation.

It was as he opted for the single switch in his First Draft Report that von Neumann realized the new programming possibility that we have been attributing to him, the possibility of incorporating a substitution instruction to modify the program. For, with instructions commingled with data, the arithmetic unit could operate on instructions as well as data to suit the needs of the problem as they arose. The single switch option, with von Neumann's elaboration of it, also became and remains standard to this day.

Finally, just as von Neumann could not have "translated" his logical circuitry from electronic circuitry disclosed at the 1945 Moore School meetings, so he could not have "recorded" his ideas for programming the new computer from that source, either. There was no attempt to develop a program language in those meetings, let alone the specific idea of an instruction to modify other instructions! The Moore School group first encountered such a development in the von Neumann report.

The content of these discussions as to both circuitry and programming is strongly attested to by Arthur Burks, who was a participant in all four meetings. But we have much more than his recollection to go on. He took notes on each occasion, and though he turned these in for typing and official use, he did later obtain the typed versions of the first two sets at the time of the ENIAC trial. Still later, the present writer found the last two sets, in typed form with editing notations in Arthur Burks's hand, at the Hagley archives in Delaware. They confirm his memory of these events.

<<<>>>

Lastly, and most devastatingly for the claims of Eckert and Mauchly in Los Alamos in 1976, we have their own official EDVAC report of September 30, 1945, "Automatic High-Speed Computing, A Progress Report on the EDVAC," in which they explicitly recognize von Neumann's contributions to programming the new computer.[16] As early as page 3 of the introduction and summary, they write:

> During the latter part of 1944, and continuing to the present time, Dr. John von Neumann, consultant to the Ballistic Research Laboratory, has fortunately been available for consultation. He has contributed to many discussions on the logical controls of the EDVAC, has proposed certain instruction codes, and has tested those proposed systems by writing out the coded instructions for specific problems.

Now those "certain instruction codes" are, in the terminology of the day, von Neumann's program language, as worked out in his First Draft Report. The reference to testing that language "by writing out the coded instructions for specific problems" is to his creation of a computer program—just one, in fact, that of sorting and merging, which he submitted soon after his report. He undertook this problem of alphabetizing files as one that was difficult enough to be challenging, at the same time that its solution could be compared to the procedure of alphabetizing punched cards on an IBM machine. It was later rewritten in symbolic assembler language by Donald E. Knuth as "Von Neumann's First Computer Program."[17]

On pages 5–6 of their progress report, Eckert and Mauchly call "coding the problem" one of many topics concerning which the Moore School group "has benefited greatly from conferences with and work done by Dr. John von Neumann." On page 9, they say that in part 6 they will present "some desiderata for coding," including "an instruction code suggested by von Neumann." And in that part 6, on page 75, they introduce a "plan for orders [that is] essentially that which von Neumann has proposed after trying out various coding methods on typical problems."

Perhaps most striking of all in this regard is their recognition, in this September 1945 report on the EDVAC project, of von Neumann's idea for program modification—a prime feature of his program language. On page 77, in section 6.3, they write:

> Von Neumann has specified that some order symbols be capable of modification by deleting a given part of the order and inserting something else in place of this part. This allows for the substitution referred to in Section 2.9.4, so that function tables may be used, subroutines called in, etc.

In that section 2.9.4, pages 39–40, they address "the way in which repetitive and iterative processes are ordered" in terms of cost. "Essentially," they explain, "the machine must be made to perform 'substitutions,'" as, for example, in function-table lookup:

> Hunting through the table for a certain argument can be avoided by having the argument specify the place in the memory at which the desired value is to be

found. But to do this, the order code must be made with provision for substi-
tuting a number (obtained from that part of the memory which holds the argument) into an order, so as to specify where the function is to be found.

We have emphasized that all of these programming ideas, so forthrightly recognized in this Eckert-Mauchly progress report, were first committed to writing
in von Neumann's earlier EDVAC report, and that none of them had been
explored in the discussions at the Moore School that spring of 1945. Yet the
Eckert-Mauchly report did also contain one passage that seems to contradict the
others. It occurs on page 3 of the introductory section, as the conclusion of the
passage quoted above on instruction codes:

> Dr. von Neumann has also written a preliminary report [First Draft of a Report
> on the EDVAC: June 30, 1945] in which most of the results of earlier discus-
> sions are summarized. In his report, the physical structures and devices proposed
> by Eckert and Mauchly are replaced by idealized elements to avoid raising engi-
> neering problems which might distract attention from the logical considerations
> under discussion.

It is this assessment of von Neumann's report that is repeated by Eckert at
Los Alamos some thirty years later, and that we have already argued against.
Clearly, it is a purposely misleading characterization of the First Draft Report,
and must be seen as such in light of the detailed presentation of von Neumann's
contributions in the rest of this same document: his formulation of a program language, his provision of a problem to illustrate that language, and his inclusion of
a substitution instruction in that language (and in that problem).

Finally, Eckert and Mauchly also presented the fundamentals of von Neumann's architecture in this same progress report—but as their own, without attribution to him. In part 5, pages 66–70, they give a "general structure" of the
EDVAC featuring the same three major components as those proposed by von
Neumann three months earlier (memory, arithmetic unit, and control). They introduce these on page 66:

> [The EDVAC] should have a large memory capacity, any part of which can be
> used for the storage of program information or numbers, including function
> tables. A central computing device must have immediate or almost immediate
> access to any part of the memory. Control circuits to direct the computing
> process must have similar access to the memory.

Again, just as there had been no attempt to develop a program language in the
spring 1945 meetings, neither had there been any consideration of a computer
architecture. Both concepts were clearly taken from von Neumann, with the
former recognized, the latter not, in their September 1945 report.

Just how soon did Mauchly and Eckert start to claim program modifiability—the major advance they so candidly attributed to von Neumann in that official EDVAC report? Both did so within a year. The occasion was the Moore School's famous lecture series of the summer of 1946, first published in mimeographed form in 1947–1948 and distributed freely by the Moore School, then republished in 1985 by the Charles Babbage Institute.[18] Quotations here are taken from the Babbage collection.

In Lecture 9, "The Use of Function Tables with Computing Machines," Mauchly works out examples of function-table lookup of the sort credited to von Neumann in the EDVAC progress report; ultimately, on page 104, he comes to the observation: "We then use the ability of the machine to modify its own instructions."

More generally, on page 455 in Lecture 37, "Code and Control II: Machine Design and Instruction Codes," Mauchly elaborates what was actually von Neumann's decision to commingle data and instructions in a single memory. He notes particularly the advantage that under such an arrangement the instructions can be modified from within:

> A general requirement for the form of the instructions is that they must be such as can be conveniently stored in the same internal memory devices as are used for numerical information or other data to be operated upon by the machine. This requirement is in part dictated by the desire to simplify the design and construction of the machine, making it unnecessary to have different kinds of equipment for different kinds of storage, and also making it unnecessary to decide in advance what proportion of the storage capacity shall be used for instructions and what proportion for data [as would be necessary if they were stored in two separate memories]. *A much more fundamental reason for this requirement is that the instructions themselves can then be operated upon by the use of other instructions.* It should be possible to carry out such operations upon instructions by the use of the same instructions as would be utilized when operating upon numbers. [italics added]

Eckert, in Table 1, Code "A," on pages 122–23 in Lecture 10, "A Preview of a Digital Computing Machine," also has a version of the substitution instruction. It is described on page 125:

> The next order, symbolized by an "e," is called the extraction order. This specifies that certain digits are to be extracted from the register alpha and used to replace the corresponding digits in register beta.

<<<>>>

We indicated earlier that von Neumann broke with Mauchly and Eckert because he thought they were trying to steal his ideas. His own—and Goldstine's—lack of concern for Eckert and Mauchly's historical credit in the issuance of his First Draft Report must be called into question, of course. On the other hand, *patenting* the inventions of another—as they were trying to do, with respect to Atanasoff as well as von Neumann—would seem much more objectionable.

Moreover, von Neumann did recognize explicitly, at the April 1947 meeting with the Ordnance lawyers, that the mercury-delay-line memory (among other features of the EDVAC) was Eckert's. Since von Neumann's death in 1957, Goldstine and others on his side of this dispute, including Arthur Burks, have done so as well in the published literature. The Eckert-Mauchly side, however, has persisted in denying that it was von Neumann who took the second major step to what became known as the stored-program concept, that of program modifiability. Nor has it recognized the two stellar inventive achievements of the von Neumann report: the architecture for a stored-program computer, together with the detailed logical design of its memory and its arithmetic unit; and the first modern program language (in which program modifiability was a feature).

There is one further point, nearly always overlooked in analyses of this controversy: other inventors made significant contributions. As we saw, Eckert conceived the mercury-delay-line memory for a computer only after he had, with help from the Moore School's Sharpless, developed an improvement over an acoustic delay line invented by Bell Laboratories' Shockley. And the concepts of both an electronically regenerated memory and an electronic serial adder came from Atanasoff directly to the EDVAC project via Mauchly.

As we noted earlier, in addition to invalidating the entire ENIAC patent on the three technical grounds of premature public disclosure, Judge Larson also invalidated particular claims of that patent. He devoted Finding 6, "Claims Anticipated," to examining IBM engineer Byron Phelps's invention of an electronic multiplier, which, he said, had been successfully tested in 1942, "before the ENIAC project work had even begun."[19] He pronounced three ENIAC patent claims "readable" on the Phelps patent and so "barred from patentability." He made no finding of derivation here, however, because Phelps did not file his patent application until late 1945 and Mauchly and Eckert had not known of his invention. Moreover, this invalidation applied only to the three individual claims, not the entire ENIAC patent, because Phelps's invention was not an automatic electronic digital computer, but just an electronic multiplier.

Judge Larson devoted Finding 10, "Pulse," to the second instance in which the validity of certain claims had been challenged by Honeywell.[20] He observed that both the ENIAC patent application of 1947 and the patent as issued in 1964 had claims in which the term "pulse" was "of material importance to the determination of their patentability." He also observed that the term was used extensively in the descriptive portion of both those documents, that is, in the presentation of the invention's features that normally precedes the list of claims to original ideas stemming from the invention. Naturally, inventors and their attorneys make these claims as extensive and as general as possible—we saw in chapter 2 how far Eckert and Mauchly reached, and overreached, in their list of claims for their Regenerative Memory patent. But they committed a serious error with regard to the concept of a pulse in the case of the ENIAC patent, and they corrected it only nine months before the patent was issued.

It seems that the descriptive portion of the 1947 application gave a number of definitions, including the term "pulse," definitions that would carry over to the claims portion of the document. Larson noted that in both this explicit definition and the numerous usages of the term throughout the descriptive portion, a pulse was consistently said to have a duration time of *at least* two microseconds (as "two to five microseconds" or "two microseconds or longer"). Now the use of that lower limit of two microseconds for describing the ENIAC was appropriate, given that machine's operating speed of 100,000 pulses per second. But Eckert and Mauchly were already planning the EDVAC-type machines, which would operate at 1,000,000 pulses per second, so that for the purpose of their patent's *claims* they should have defined "pulse" as having a duration of only one-tenth that of the ENIAC. Indeed, their safest course would have been to omit any lower limit at all!

The odd thing is that it was not until the early 1960s that they and/or the Sperry Rand attorneys came to this realization. In May 1963, those attorneys filed an amendment to the ENIAC patent application, with the effect that in the patent as issued a second sentence was added to the original single-sentence definition of "pulse." The term was now defined in these two sentences in section 1.2.1:

> A pulse is a positive or negative change in potential which has a duration of about two to five microseconds (m sec.). Within the meaning of the appended claims "pulse" will be construed to mean a change or excursion in potential or current which has a duration time not exceeding about five microseconds.

The judge, however, agreed with the Honeywell attorneys that such a late amendment was, as he put it, not only "unreasonably delayed" but also "an exigent afterthought to capture the subsequent contributions of others already in the public domain." He cited Honeywell's own 11-800 computer of 1960, which, he said, "used pulses having a duration of less than 0.25 microseconds." He accordingly invalidated fourteen particular claims containing the words "pulse" or the equivalent "impulse" or "signal" that he found dependent on the redefinition of that concept.

Let us turn now to the two grounds on which Judge Larson declared the entire ENIAC patent *unenforceable, but not invalid*: delay before and fraud on the U.S. Patent Office.

On the issue of delay, patent law requires expeditious pursuit of a patent. The temptation to circumvent the law lies in a desire to have the seventeen-year period of patent protection commence as late as possible. The judge explained that there is a fine line between "unnecessary and unreasonable delay," which can render a patent unenforceable, and "undue delay," which can render it invalid.

In Finding 11, "Delay," Larson recounted many instances of unnecessary and unreasonable delay in Sperry Rand's pursuit of the patent, but concluded "with reluctance" that undue delay had not been proven.[21] He said that Sperry Rand had both availed itself of and stayed within the patent laws, and that Honeywell had not established "any improper conduct on the part of SR or its counsel which caused undue delay." He also observed that the pendency of the ENIAC patent (1947–1964) was not unusually long, given that pioneering achievements such as the ENIAC typically involved more time-consuming patent interferences than other inventions.

In Finding 13, "Fraud on Patent Office," Judge Larson drew another fine line, here noting that certain "derelictions" before the Patent Office can render a patent unenforceable, but only in the presence of "willful and intentional fraud" can they render it invalid.[22] He then recounted "the various derelictions of Eckert and Mauchly and their counsel before the Patent Office," but concluded that Honeywell had not proven willful and intentional fraud. He pointed out that "proof of fraud must be by clear, unequivocal and convincing evidence: a mere preponderance of evidence is not enough," and that "good faith or an honest mistake is a complete defense."

On this basis he found, for example, that Eckert and Mauchly may have "acted in good faith in that they did not know what on sale meant," and that while they knew of the problem Douglas Hartree ran on the ENIAC in early 1946, they "were possibly unaware of the results obtained and may then have acted in good faith."

The judge gave considerable space to the role of Atanasoff in Mauchly's initial conception of the ENIAC, citing the evidence but here, too, stopping short of finding fraud. He first referred to his earlier Finding 3, on Atanasoff, then made several points not made there.

He began with quotations from two of Mauchly's letters: his June 29, 1941, letter to H. Helm Clayton in which he praised the electronic computer he had just seen in Iowa, remarking that "it can be adapted to do the job of the Bush differential analyzer more rapidly . . . and costs a lot less"; and his September 30, 1941, letter to Atanasoff in which he asked permission either to use "some of the features" of the ABC in a computer he himself might build or to have the Moore School build "an 'Atanasoff Calculator' (a la Bush analyzer)."[23]

Larson went on to comment that the ENIAC proposal of April 1943 "referred to the Atanasoff work, but did not identify it."[24] He also observed that Eckert and Mauchly had visited Atanasoff's Naval Ordnance Laboratory in August 1944 to ask his help with the EDVAC's mercury-delay-line memory—on the very same day that they visited Army Ordnance lawyers to make plans for patenting the ENIAC and several other inventions, including that EDVAC memory!

Finally, he noted that "neither Eckert nor Mauchly disclosed Atanasoff's work to their attorneys in filing the ENIAC patent application." On the other hand, he added, neither had Atanasoff and Berry made their work known to the Patent Office by following through on their early efforts to patent the ABC.

Judge Larson then concluded that, while complete candor before the Patent Office is required, what should be disclosed about prior art and derivation "must in some degree be left to the judgment and conscience of the applicant." And so Mauchly "may in good faith have believed that the monstrous machine he helped create had no relationship to the ABC or Atanasoff" and "may in good faith have believed that he did not derive the subject matter claimed in the ENIAC patent from Atanasoff." Moreover, he said, Atanasoff, though he had seen the ENIAC in October 1945 and though there had been extensive publicity in early 1946, "did not assert that the ENIAC included anything of his until two decades later."

The "various derelictions" Larson cited in this finding on fraud included, among others: suppressing documents, withholding information, securing misleading affidavits, reversing legal positions in response to new evidence, blocking efforts of competitors to secure documents from the government, and proceeding with patent applications despite warnings of infirmities. He marshaled detailed instances of these offenses, often in strong language, yet concluded again and again that the party or parties "may have acted in good faith" due to some circumstance or other. The ENIAC patent, accordingly, was rendered unenforceable but not invalid by such derelictions.

The judge devoted Finding 12, "Validity," to summarizing his rulings on the ENIAC patent.[25] As we have seen, he found the entire patent both invalid and unenforceable on four grounds, the first of which was derivation of the subject matter (the automatic electronic digital computer) from Atanasoff. The other three were acts of public disclosure undertaken more than a year before the patent application was filed: the computer's public use (by Los Alamos scientists and others); its placement on sale (by the Moore School to Army Ordnance); and its anticipation in a publication (von Neumann's EDVAC report).

Larson also here recounted his invalidation of three particular ENIAC patent claims on grounds of anticipation by Phelps, and of fourteen claims on grounds of unreasonably delayed redefinition of the term "pulse."

He closed Finding 12 with remarks on the issues of delay before and fraud on the U.S. Patent Office. In particular, he spelled out the meaning of unenforceability for the patent holder. Whereas "inequitable conduct on the part of an applicant in obtaining a patent" may be insufficient to invalidate the patent, he wrote, it is sufficient "to dissuade a court of equity from rendering aid in enforcing it."

This distinction between invalidity and unenforceability may seem insignificant, since on either score the patent lost all value. In the case of fraud, however, the distinction was critical to the final outcome of the ENIAC trial. That is, it was critical to the Sperry side that the ENIAC patent not be invalidated on this ground, for the commission of fraud in securing a patent is a criminal offense. Mauchly or Eckert or one or more of their counsel could have been subject to prosecution.

Moreover, violation of the antitrust laws was at stake: Honeywell had charged Sperry Rand with violating the Sherman Antitrust Act by fraudulently procuring the ENIAC patent—and proceeding to monopolize the computer industry. Had Judge Larson gone so far, Honeywell would have been entitled to triple damages from Sperry Rand.

As to these broader charges, Judge Larson did rule that Sperry Rand had attempted to monopolize the electronic data processing industry, in violation of the Sherman Act, and also that Honeywell had suffered injury and probable damage. He based this finding, however, *not* on the procurement of the ENIAC patent, but on the cross-licensing agreement Sperry Rand had signed with IBM in 1956! He found the two companies coconspirators in this effort to monopolize the industry. He found further that IBM, but not Sperry Rand, had actually succeeded in creating such a monopoly—another violation of the Sherman Act.

Larson did not arrive at these two rulings on conspiracy and monopoly lightly. He devoted the longest section of his entire decision, Finding 15, "SR-IBM August 21, 1956 Agreement," to an exploration of the ramifications of this liaison as various competitors struggled to gain a foothold in the new field of electronic computing.[26] He noted, for example, that in 1956 IBM held about 85 percent of the market, and Sperry Rand about 10 percent, and that their agreement to share know-how—to the deliberate exclusion of others—was designed to give both a competitive advantage. This information access did ensure IBM's continuing predominant role, he added, because of a tremendous customer base already in existence. Sperry Rand, with no such base, lost market share as others made inroads.

Despite his ruling that Sperry Rand had participated in a conspiracy, with adverse consequences for Honeywell, Larson awarded no monetary damages. He found, again after thorough analysis, that Honeywell had failed to protect its interests in the market and had itself stalled as it tried to improve its own portfolio for licensing purposes. IBM, although found in violation of the Sherman Act on two scores, was not subject to damages because it was not a defendant in the case!

In Finding 23, "Infringement of ENIAC," Larson ruled that Honeywell had infringed, but he awarded no damages here, either, since the infringed patent was invalid.[27]

Judge Larson left open the possibility that the ENIAC patent might, in an appeal, be found either to be valid, on the one hand, or to have been fraudulently procured, on the other. Neither side, however, did appeal his decision. Atanasoff, in his *Annals* article, "Advent of Electronic Digital Computing," commented:

Everyone expected that Larson's decision would be appealed, but it was quickly set-tled by the payment of money and an agreement between the parties that each would support the judge's decision of 1973. I have been told that SR paid $3.5 million—sufficient to reimburse H for the cost of the trial. Thus ended this important case.[28]

Clearly, of the four grounds on which Larson ruled the entire ENIAC patent invalid, his finding of derivation from Atanasoff has the greatest historical significance. The issues of premature public use, sale, and publication, while they raise serious ques-tions of impropriety as well as ineptitude on the Sperry Rand side, nevertheless are quite apart from the central concern of originality in the invention of the ENIAC.

Several aspects of Larson's finding of derivation of the ENIAC from Atana-soff deserve further comment. One is the judge's treatment of Eckert with regard to it. In tracing the history of that derivation (Finding 3), Larson concluded that *Mauchly*, as a result of his Iowa visit, "derived from the ABC 'the invention of the automatic electronic digital computer' claimed in the ENIAC patent." But he also ruled, there and elsewhere, that *Eckert and Mauchly* made this derivation, without saying just what had transpired between the two.

Mauchly testified in the ENIAC trial that he could not recall telling Eckert about Atanasoff's computer, though he might have mentioned it.[29] Eckert, in his trial testimony, acknowledged some discussion of the Atanasoff-Berry Computer, but claimed to recall very little beyond the rotating capacitor memory and the sys-tem of burning holes in punch cards.[30] When reminded by Honeywell attorney Henry Halladay of the computer's electronic features, Eckert said he could nei-ther confirm nor deny hearing of these from Mauchly, even though it would seem that they above all else would have caught the interest of an electronics expert exploring ideas for an electronic computer.[31]

Now Mauchly, in his earlier Regenerative Memory deposition, had testified that "of course" he had told Eckert and others at the Moore School about "this device at Ames" and that he had discussed with Eckert in particular "what ideas we had in relationship to possible calculators in light of what I had seen out there."[32] Whether or not Judge Larson relied on this earlier testimony—he *had* studied the Regenerative Memory case in order to rule on that patent—he did become convinced that Eckert derived critical concepts for both the ENIAC and the EDVAC from Atanasoff through Mauchly.

As to Larson's rather stern observation (Finding 13) that Mauchly and Eckert had asked Atanasoff's help with the mercury-delay-line memory "on the same day"—August 30, 1944—that they consulted lawyers about patenting that memory, Larson may have been especially piqued by a further circumstance: Atanasoff had by that time agreed to take Mauchly on as a consultant in his sec-tion of the Naval Ordnance Laboratory (see chap. 2)!

(The expertise Eckert and Mauchly were seeking stemmed from Atanasoff's research on quartz crystals at Iowa State. As we saw earlier, the new form of memory was to have a transmitting crystal at one end, a receiving crystal at the other, and a tube of mercury between them; and there was a problem in making the crystals interact properly with the mercury as electrical pulses were fed into and removed from the line.)

Another interesting aspect of Judge Larson's decision on Atanasoff is his comment (again, Finding 13) that Atanasoff and Berry themselves had not made the ABC known to the Patent Office by filing a patent application. Actually, considerable groundwork was laid for an application, as Larson went on to note: not only the "definitive manuscript" but also "a draft application specification which was prepared by Clifford Berry but . . . never filed."

Atanasoff has explained this situation from his point of view in his *Annals* article.[33] In August 1940, when he finished his manuscript describing his computer, he sent a copy to Richard R. Trexler, the Chicago attorney he had chosen to prepare a patent application.[34] Atanasoff and Berry then went to Chicago a few times to see Trexler, and Trexler visited them once in Ames. At the lawyer's request, Berry, with some help from Atanasoff, wrote up "an extensive specification"; and they both worked with a draftsman to produce drawings beyond those in the original manuscript. This latter packet went out in August 1942, by which time Berry had moved to California and Atanasoff was preparing to move to Washington.

Meanwhile, in March 1941, the Research Corporation had notified Iowa State College president Charles E. Friley of its approval of a grant for Atanasoff's computer project. Friley then insisted on a patent agreement with Atanasoff, starting with an offer of 10 percent as the inventor's share and ending up, after some unpleasantness, with an agreement to 50 percent. Atanasoff, concerned about Berry, contracted to give his graduate assistant 10 percent of his own share, again with some resistance from the college.

After July 1941, when he signed the two contracts, Atanasoff's communications concerning the patent application were with both Trexler and the Iowa State College Research Foundation. One can surmise from Atanasoff's courtroom testimony, as well as from his written account, that there was hard feeling all around.[35] The attorney kept requesting more material; Atanasoff obliged, up to a point, but felt that more than enough had been provided; and the College Research Foundation dragged its feet after making its agreement with the inventor. One highly complicating factor was the loss of a group of patent drawings as Atanasoff, in Washington, tried to have them sent from Ames to Chicago.

In any event, no patent application was ever filed on this most profound and influential invention, the electronic computer. All parties, of course, have been greatly embarrassed, the more so as the emergence of a "computer age" became ever more apparent, *and* as, ultimately, the priority and influence of Atanasoff's original version were formally recognized in federal court. Clearly, however, a number of extraneous circumstances played critical roles in this drama.

Foremost among these was World War II, which first caused Atanasoff and Berry to leave their machine, then diverted their energies from the patenting process. Iowa State College was similarly affected, as Atanasoff came to understand on his visits home from Washington: "I realized that everything at the college was on a war footing," he wrote in his 1984 *Annals* article. A compelling case can also be made that without the army's urgent need for faster computation of artillery firing tables—because of the war—there would have been no funding and very little motivation to create the ENIAC!

Second, the invention itself was so novel that the patent attorney, hardly an electronics expert, must have had great difficulty in comprehending it, let alone making it comprehensible to the Patent Office.

Lastly, there was undoubtedly a clash of perspectives, if not personalities, at work in this whole process, by the very nature of the cooperative effort required. The Iowa State people surely regarded Atanasoff's machine in terms of a limited utility, not as constituting a revolutionary breakthrough that could reap huge dividends. Trexler, for his part, seems to have been a conscientious attorney trying to do a good job but in over his depth. And Atanasoff, the brilliant physicist whose invention had been his primary focus for so many years, was too impatient with others who failed to grasp, or took too long to grasp, his sufficient but sparse descriptions.

A further point in Larson's decision is his comment that Atanasoff, once the ENIAC became known, let two decades pass before claiming that it "included anything of his." Atanasoff did not address this finding in his 1984 article, except to say that Mauchly had told him at NOL that he and Eckert "had found a new way to compute, different from mine, and I believed him despite the fact he did not tell me about it, on the ground that it was classified."

Atanasoff also told Arthur Burks and me that he simply accepted Mauchly's claim of a computer based on principles different from the ABC's. This was, after all, the man he had so intuitively trusted in 1941—even against his wife's contrary judgment—that he had happily revealed his invention to him. And he still trusted him a few years later at NOL, when he said, in effect, that the machine he and Eckert were building at the University of Pennsylvania derived nothing from the one Atanasoff and Berry had built at Iowa State College.

Judge Larson's comment that he had waited too long to step forward once the ENIAC was unveiled must have been a particularly bitter pill for Atanasoff. While the judge's point was perfectly sound, it would seem that all the publicity about the ENIAC, rather than stimulating his concern for possible derivation, merely convinced him that he had been outdone, defeated, in this, the greatest endeavor of his career.

At the same time, he had become deeply involved in exciting and challenging research in a different area of physics, one that continued to demand his close attention. He may have found it relatively easy, then, to stay thus involved when this enormous government-sponsored machine, capable of solving problems far beyond the ABC's, was presented to the world as the first electronic computer.

A further explanation of Atanasoff's two-decade silence is that this was the same two decades before the ENIAC patent was issued—that is, before he could study its claims and compare them with features of his own invention. There is considerable merit to this argument, especially as it reflects the patent system itself. Presumably, an inventor would not be expected to claim misappropriation of his or her ideas by another inventor until that other inventor's patent had been made public; and, indeed, the ENIAC patent was overturned for misappropriation from Atanasoff. Yet, in this case, the invention had been so widely publicized that the same judge who overturned the patent faulted the original inventor for not having spoken up sooner—and so excused the misappropriators to a degree.

At any rate, the judge was correct in finding that Atanasoff could have learned about the ENIAC long before the patent was granted, so that, again, it is hard to explain his shutting this matter from his mind except by saying it *was* his state of mind that turned him off—that and his enduring trust in Mauchly.

It was in Finding 14 that Judge Larson declared the Eckert-Mauchly Regenerative Memory patent 2,629,827 (either '827 or EM-1 to the Court) unenforceable because of derivation from Atanasoff.[36] (See chap. 2 for Control Data attorney Allen Kirkpatrick's examination of Mauchly on this issue in response to Sperry Rand's charge of patent infringement.) Larson first explained how the EDVAC version of regenerative memory, as claimed in this patent, paralleled the ABC version, then observed that the ABC version itself was claimed! He also observed that Eckert had—in his 1953 Institute of Radio Engineers article (again, see chap. 2)—credited Atanasoff with "probably" the first regenerative memory.[37] Lastly, Larson explicitly noted the passage of technical information from Atanasoff to Mauchly and on to Eckert.

Here are the pertinent paragraphs from the finding:

14.11.3 Subject matter claimed in the EM-1 patent was derived from Atanasoff.

. . .

14.11.3.2 Subject matter claimed in the EM-1 application as the joint invention of Eckert and Mauchly was disclosed to Mauchly by Atanasoff in June of 1941.

14.11.3.3 In one embodiment of the EM-1 application, information is stored in a coded sequence of pulses, the pulses being temporarily recorded on a rotating carrier as electrostatic charges, carried by rotation to another station where they give rise to electrical potential pulses which are handled through an external feedback circuit for replacement or reinforcement of the pulses on the carrier.

14.11.3.4 This subject matter as claimed in the '827 patent was anticipated by the disclosure contained in the Atanasoff manuscript disclosed to Mauchly.

14.11.3.5 Atanasoff's concept of the recirculating or regenerative memory was used in the EDVAC program, with Atanasoff's rotating electrostatic charge carrier being replaced by the recirculation of pulses through an electrical delay line; this delay line version of a recirculating memory was disclosed in the EM-1 application as yet another embodiment of Eckert's and Mauchly's invention.

14.11.3.6 The Atanasoff electrostatic charge version of a recirculating memory was also disclosed in the EM-1 application as yet another embodiment of Eckert's and Mauchly's alleged invention.

14.11.3.7 In October 1953, after the '827 patent was granted on the EM-1 application, Eckert stated that prior to 1942, Atanasoff had developed what was probably the first example of what could generally be termed regenerative memory; Eckert's knowledge of Atanasoff's prior work was based on what Mauchly had earlier told him.

I remarked at the start of chapter 2 that it was by an odd twist that Judge Larson ruled on the Regenerative Memory patent as well as the ENIAC patent in his 1973 decision. He did so because the *Sperry Rand* v. *Control Data Corp.* suit had broken off in 1972, and the Honeywell attorneys wanted a court finding on this important electronic computing concept. In fact, Honeywell asked Judge Larson to declare an entire package of some twenty-five patents—of which the Regenerative Memory patent was but one—unenforceable, arguing that they were all subject to the same kinds of infirmities as the ENIAC patent. The rationale for gathering them under one head was twofold: first, they all dealt with hardware features of the EDVAC-type computers; second, they had all been applied for by Eckert and Mauchly and then, as in the case of the ENIAC patent, passed along to Sperry Rand. The rationale for introducing them at the ENIAC trial was that Sperry Rand had used these patents as bargaining chips in its negotiations with a number of computer firms, including Honeywell, prior to the lawsuit.

This so-called 30A package included already granted patents on the regenerative memory and several binary adders; it also included still pending patents on the BINAC (Binary Automatic Computer) and the UNIVAC (Universal Automatic Computer). Judge Larson examined each of the 25, and he ruled them all unenforceable, both as a collection and severally, for a variety of infirmities. His primary focus, though, was on Honeywell's complaint of premature public disclosure. In the case of the binary adder patents, for example, which were surely as traceable to Atanasoff as the regenerative memory patent, he found these unenforceable because of prior publication, of both the official EDVAC Report of June 30, 1946, and the Moore School lectures of July and August 1946. Most important to Honeywell, of course, were the pending BINAC and UNIVAC patents, both of which Larson ruled unenforceable because of prior publication of the official UNIVAC Report to the Bureau of the Census, among other grounds.

<<<>>>

When Eckert and Mauchly left the Moore School in early 1946, Eckert's leadership in the design and construction of the EDVAC fell to Kite Sharpless; its "team" shifted many times, and the machine was not completed until 1952.

Eckert and Mauchly formed the Eckert-Mauchly Computer Corp. (initially the Electronic Control Co.) and built both the BINAC and the UNIVAC utilizing basic EDVAC principles. The UNIVAC was the first electronic computer to be marketed in this country. Successive corporate owners Remington Rand and Sperry Rand sold forty-six of the original UNIVACs, starting with its contracted sale to the Census Bureau on March 31, 1951. A number of other computers, both in the United States and abroad, were also modeled on the EDVAC.

As to a worldwide "first" for commercialization, S. H. Lavington, of Manchester University in England, writes that "a production version" of the Manchester MARK I built by Ferranti Ltd. and called the Ferranti MARK I "was delivered in February 1951 [to Manchester University]"; this machine, with a cathode-ray-tube memory, is therefore "believed to be the first commercially available stored-program computer."[38]

Von Neumann, with Burks and Goldstine, proceeded to work out the general design of the Institute for Advanced Study Computer in the monograph, *Preliminary Discussion of the Logical Design of an Electronic Computing Instrument.*[39] This document provided the paradigmatic form of the "von Neumann architecture."

The von Neumann architecture, it should be noted, was made possible by the earlier work of both Atanasoff and Eckert: Atanasoff for his invention of electronic binary adders separate from and interacting with his read-write drum memory; Eckert for his invention of a large and fast read-write memory. For the Institute computer, however, von Neumann turned to his own concept of a random-access cathode-ray-tube memory as a step beyond Eckert's serial mercury-delay-line memory.

Von Neumann never tried to patent any of his computing ideas. Instead, he changed the patent policy for the Institute project from one assigning rights to specific individuals to one placing all ideas in the public domain.

As with the EDVAC, a number of computers in this country and abroad were modeled on the IAS (Institute for Advanced Study) Computer. Here the IBM 701, formally dedicated in early 1953, was the commercial version; nineteen IBM 701s were installed, as rental machines, chiefly for military and aerospace applications.

Figures 20–23 depict the respective architectures of the ABC, the ENIAC, the EDVAC, and the IAS Computer. Figure 24 charts the sequence of development of the electronic digital computer.

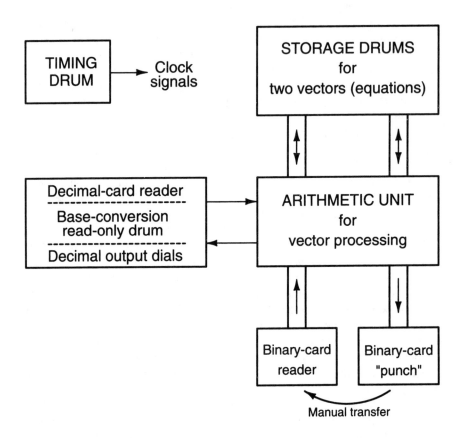

Figure 20. ABC architecture. This diagram depicts the centralized architecture of Atanasoff's machine, the first electronic computer. It was designed and built for the special purpose of solving large sets of simultaneous linear equations, doing so through a variant of the Gaussian method of eliminating a designated variable from successive pairs of equations until a single equation in a single variable is obtained. Atanasoff's algorithm called for performing each elimination by repeated subtractions (or additions) of one equation from (or to) the other, with shifting, until the designated variable was eliminated from one of the two equations. He thus simplified his hardware considerably by avoiding Gauss's divisions and multiplications throughout this *forward* part of the procedure. And, having reached a single-variable equation, he again avoided the Gaussian multiplications and divisions of successive substitutions in the *backward* part by applying the same pairing method to obtain a full set of single-variable equations. Here, for the solution to each such equation, he did resort to offline division, one such operation for each of his original variables.

During this basic elimination procedure, input and output signals flowed over sets of wires to and from the arithmetic unit, which calculated by interacting, again via wires, with the other major unit, the two-drum rotating memory. That is, with the read-write storage drums initially holding the coefficients of a given pair of equations, the arithmetic unit repeatedly combined those of the keyboard drum with those of the counter drum until the designated variable was eliminated from the equation on the counter drum.

These additions and subtractions were done, not on the counting principle of accumulation, but on the logic principle of solutions from a truth table. And they were done in the *binary* mode, with equations read off of and onto the two drums via a binary-card "punch" and a binary-card reader, respectively. The punched cards were removed from the card-punch tray by hand and assembled into the appropriate pairs for hand entry from the card-reader tray onto the memory drums.

The initial decimal data were converted to binary and entered into that memory from the decimal-card reader through the interaction of the arithmetic unit and the read-only base-conversion drum. Similarly, the solution equations in binary were converted to decimal and entered on dials through the interaction of the arithmetic unit and the base-conversion drum. The final divisions, then, were done in decimal on a desk calculator of that day.

The elements of the arithmetic unit were vacuum tubes. Those of the memory were capacitors, regularly regenerated by vacuum tubes in the arithmetic unit. The arithmetic operations were coordinated by a timing drum located between and driven by the same synchronous motor as the main storage drums.

(Drawn by artist Eugene G. Leppanen.)

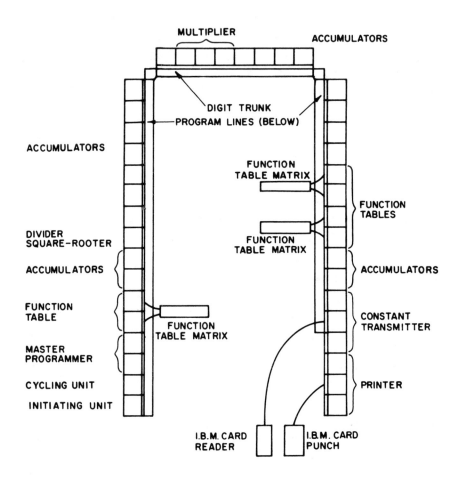

Figure 21. ENIAC architecture. Unlike the ABC, the ENIAC computed in the decimal mode and on the counting, or accumulating, principle. Its architecture was also distributive, rather than centralized, so that it is best depicted in its U-shaped floor plan. The ENIAC was conceived to create artillery firing tables for the U.S. Army by solving systems of differential equations; that is, by solving, for a single table for a given shell to be fired from a given gun under varying conditions, several thousand trajectories from the system of differential equations for that shell and gun To achieve this objective, Eckert and Mauchly built in programmability, and this programmability, albeit manual, rendered the ENIAC the first *general-purpose* electronic computer.

The thirty separate units occupied forty panels of equal size. The twenty read-write accumulators, occupying one panel each, computed in the manner of the registers of a desk calculator, performing both the arithmetic and the storage functions. The other arithmetic units were the three-panel high-speed multiplier and the one-panel divider/square-rooter, both of which used accumulators in their operations. The three read-only function tables, each connected to a free-standing matrix of one hundred ten-digit signed numbers, occupied two panels each; a function table received a number from an accumulator, looked up the function value for that number on its associated matrix, and transmitted that value to a different accumulator. The constant transmitter, which received numbers from the IBM card reader, and the so-called printer, which sent numbers to the IBM card punch, occupied three panels each. The two-panel master programmer coordinated the noncyclic local programs as preset on all of these units in advance and as itself programmed in advance. The one-panel cycling unit provided synchronized timing for all of the units. And the one-panel initiating unit started the problem run after the machine had been checked and the complete program entered.

A program for a particular problem was first written up and then entered by hand on the panels' protruding "front panels" of switches. Running above these front panels and transmitting decimal numbers was the numerical part of the multichannel trunk system of electrical cables and trays; running below them and transmitting program pulses was the programming part of that system. Communication among the units was over this trunk system, which was interconnected by jumper cables that were plugged into sockets on the front panels, also during problem setup. The switches on the function-table matrices were set by hand, as well.

The computing elements of the ENIAC were some 18,000 vacuum tubes, interconnected with resistors and capacitors to form complex switching circuits.

Although the accumulators did arithmetic on the counting principle of the digital desk calculator, the ENIAC's architecture followed closely that of the analog differential analyzer, with electronic accumulators replacing the analyzer's mechanical integrators and with the numerical part of the trunk system replacing the analyzer's interconnecting gear and shaft system.

(Drawn by artist Eugene G. Leppanen.)

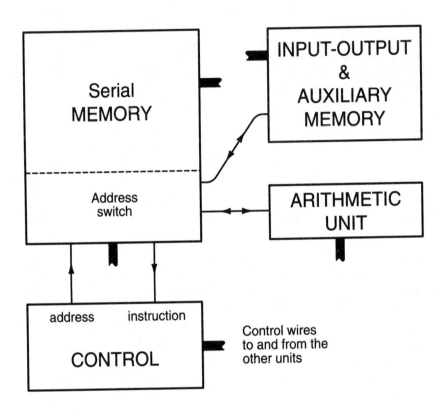

Figure 22. EDVAC architecture. When Eckert and Mauchly abandoned the counters of the ENIAC—and the decimal system—for a binary serial adder and a separate regenerative memory in the EDVAC, they were following Atanasoff in an even more fundamental way. Moreover, their organization could now be centralized, like his. The computing elements of the EDVAC remained vacuum tubes, except for the interspersing of solid-state diodes for switching. The "elements" of the main memory were mercury delay lines, and input-output was via paper tape. An auxiliary memory of magnetic wire or tape was contemplated initially, but only later was such a memory inserted, in the form of a magnetic drum.

Whereas the ABC had a read-write memory of sixty words and the ENIAC one of twenty words, the EDVAC's was over one thousand words. What is more, in contrast to the ABC's rotating capacitor memory, its mercury-delay-line memory matched the electronic speed of the adder of its arithmetic unit. Eckert and Mauchly had also increased the EDVAC's adder speed to 1,000,000 pulses per second, as compared to the 100,000 pulse-per-second speed of the ENIAC's counters.

The EDVAC's centralized architecture, worked out by von Neumann after the spring 1945 meetings at the Moore School, allowed for a separate control unit. This was a great improvement over the ENIAC's combination of local controls on the individual units and a master programmer to coordinate these. The program could be entered in the computer's memory automatically, via tape, rather than manually, at the start of a problem run; *and* the program could change itself automatically to suit the needs of a problem in the course of the problem run. This "stored-program" concept evolved in two stages: first, the automatic entry stage, contributed by Eckert's conception of the mercury-delay-line memory; second, the automatic modification stage, contributed by von Neumann's conception of the substitution instruction.

Each of the EDVAC's thirty-two mercury-delay-line tubes held thirty-two words of thirty-two bits each, representing either coded instructions or signed binary numbers. One instruction was required for each signed number being accessed. An instruction was transferred serially to the control unit, which contained a thirty-two-bit register, and a signed number was transferred serially to the arithmetic unit, with its binary serial adder. For either process, a given mercury-delay-line tube was selected and its thirty-two-bit streams of pulses were circulated, so that in each case the required sequence had to be awaited.

Computation in the binary mode did require base conversion, but this was easily accomplished by programming for it.

The EDVAC was the first stored-program computer to be conceived, though others of the EDVAC and IAS types were completed before it was.

(Drawn by artist Eugene G. Leppanen.)

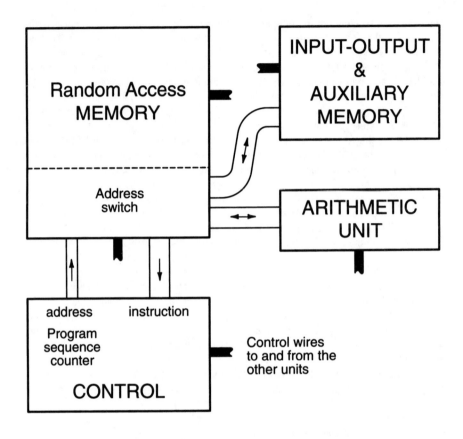

Figure 23. IAS Computer (von Neumann) architecture. Von Neumann developed his IAS Computer architecture starting from that of the EDVAC, to which he had contributed substantially. A fundamental difference between the two lay in a new parallelism in the storage and processing of the bits of a word representing either coded instructions or signed numbers. And this parallelism was different from that of the ABC, as well.

The memory of the IAS Computer consisted in a span of forty cathode ray tubes, each with a capacity for 1,024 bits as in the EDVAC. But an arithmetic word was represented by a horizontal array of bits across the forty tubes, one bit per tube. Thus the bits of a signed number were accessed in parallel, all from the same location on the grid of every tube, and each word was trasmitted to a parallel accumulator with forty adders that received one bit each to be added or subtracted, with time allowance for carry-over in each place.

The case was slightly different for instructions. These were only twenty bits long, rather than forty, so that two instructions could be stored in any forty-bit array across the cathode ray tubes. They were designated by the programmer as left-hand and right-hand instructions.

A second great difference between the IAS Computer and the EDVAC was the random-access feature of the cathode-ray-tube memory. The EDVAC's having to stream all of its thirty-two instructions or signed binary numbers from a given mercury-delay-line tube to select the required word was very time-consuming. The IAS Computer could access a word with no such waiting.

Thus while the IAS Computer had the same word storage capacity as the EDVAC and a slightly larger word length, this random access, together with the parallelism of access to and processing of bits, meant a computer over five times as fast as the EDVAC.

Both the parallelism feature and the random-access feature of the IAS Computer were to become standard for all future generations of computers.

(Drawn by artist Eugene G. Leppanen.)

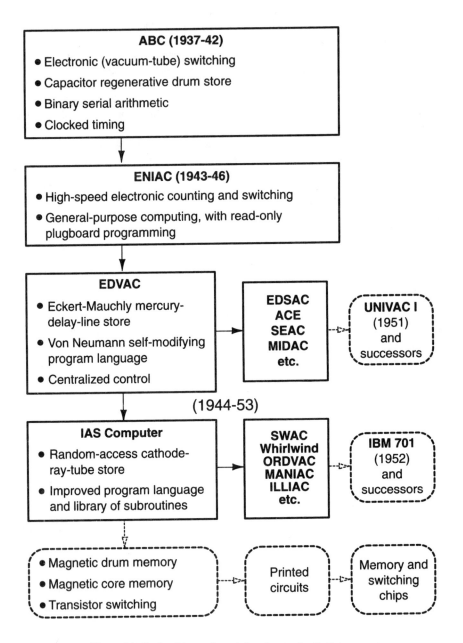

Figure 24. Chain of invention of the electronic digital computer.
(Drawn by artist Eugene G. Leppanen.)

In my own considered judgment, U.S. District Judge Earl R. Larson rendered a thorough, responsible, and equitable decision in the *Honeywell Inc. v. Sperry Rand Corporation et al.* patent suit. It was a finely balanced instrument, undoubtedly written with a view to forestalling an appeal by either side. Honeywell could hardly risk losing its gains, the invalidation of the ENIAC patent and also this judge's scathing recital of misconduct charges against Eckert, Mauchly, and the Sperry attorneys. And Sperry Rand could ill afford to challenge the invalidation, given the finding of no fraud for that misconduct; indeed, in the end it seems to have made a substantial settlement with Honeywell, together with an agreement to support Larson's decision.

Almost incomprehensibly, however, what should have been greeted as a landmark decision was largely ignored, first by the media and then, over the years, by the scholarly community. Admittedly, when the decision was announced on October 19, 1973, media attention was focused on the Watergate scandal. The so-called Saturday night massacre, in which three central figures of the Nixon administration abruptly resigned, occurred the very next day. Admittedly, also, by the time of this decision the computing community's belief in the ENIAC as the first electronic computer, and in Eckert and Mauchly as its inventors, was quite firmly set.

Still, it would seem that this story to the contrary—of an invention, after all, of immeasurable impact the world over—this story of a lone scientist doggedly creating his own prior computer only to have its principles usurped by those same celebrated inventors, this story of an extended federal courtroom drama and its unappealed decision, should have caught the public imagination.

B.

THE COURT OF PUBLIC OPINION

SIX

BREAKING INTO PRINT

O f the two institutions, the media and the scholars, that have to a large extent slighted Judge Earl Larson's decision in the ENIAC patent suit, the more surprising—and much more disappointing—are the many respected members of academia engaged in researching and writing this history. The Honeywell-Sperry Rand lawsuit created a vast reservoir of detailed material on the genesis of the electronic computer, one that could not have been created outside the justice system. No researcher could have gained access to the subpoenaed documents and sworn testimony assembled for this trial—especially the internal corporate papers harvested by the antitrust issue—much less had the benefit of close scrutiny by lawyers from both sides and careful item-by-item analysis and argument by a judge at the federal level. Yet the scant attention of computer historians has centered largely on a few sections of the tightly wrought decision itself, with hardly any serious consideration of the proceedings that led to it.

Most disturbing of all is the fact that what should be seen as a triumph of the United States justice system has been discredited and its judge maligned as incompetent and/or biased. John Atanasoff has been disparaged, as well, his work misrepresented and incorrectly interpreted with respect to that of his predecessors and his successors. Logic has been defied by critics who credit John Mauchly's *posttrial* word that he had already thought of the many new concepts he was exposed to in Atanasoff's laboratory, against both his *courtroom* characterizations of those concepts as novel and the total absence of evidence for his later story. Indeed, the issue is often presented as just a matter of one man's word against the other's, with no examination of what those words were, both in the correspondence of the two at the time and in their sworn court testimony.

Finally, arguments against Larson's findings have often taken on an *ad hominem* aspect that borders on the reckless. And this has been so not only for the principals in the case but for those few who have tried to present the facts of this history and argue for their relevance. In my introduction to this work, I alerted readers that both my husband, Arthur Burks, and I were to become players in certain aspects of this drama, particularly in its recording. We were first drawn in because of Arthur's having lived the history, beginning with his role as a designer of the ENIAC during World War II and his postwar work on the logical design of the Institute for Advanced Study Computer; continuing with his teaching of both computer science and computer history at the University of Michigan. Ultimately, I became absorbed in the issues of the ENIAC patent trial and its aftermath, with mounting dismay over the failure of the professional historians to confront the readily available facts. Little did we realize that entering the fray would lead to *our* being given the *ad hominem* treatment, as well.

I also indicated in my introduction that I meant this book to constitute something of a trial in itself. Thus, while Arthur and I are far from being Exhibit A in this case, I beg the indulgence of my readers—the *judges* of this work—as I from time to time report on our efforts and their consequences. I further remarked that in the course of presenting this history I would step on some toes. I hope that my doing so will be taken in the spirit in which it is done—as unavoidable if the history of one of the most far-reaching inventions of the past century is to be clarified.

The story I am attempting to unravel has become increasingly an unhappy tangle of opinions and emotions. Its telling has also become an increasingly cynical experience for publishers, producers, and others who take it on. Too often these parties start out with a genuine concern for the truth—and an eagerness to present it—only to end up yielding, in whole or in part, to behind-the-scenes proponents of a counter-version of "the truth." In this sense, the story of the invention of the electronic computer will be seen by some as a reflection of today's society, attested to by the steady stream of complaints about encroachment by vested interests on our decision-making processes. In my view, the exertion of pressure by such interests to record a false history, often through subtle threats to funding and even to career advancement, is the saddest twist of all.

Arthur and I had our first glimmering of what lay ahead for us when Bernard Galler phoned to say that Presper Eckert was threatening to sue—Arthur, me, him, and the *Annals of the History of Computing*—if that journal published our article on the ENIAC. We had finished this very long paper, "The ENIAC: First General-Purpose Electronic Computer," in January of 1981, and it was scheduled for publication in the October 1981 issue of the *Annals* (though the journal was running some months late in actual publication).

Bernie Galler, editor in chief of *the* premier periodical in this history and a colleague of Art's at Michigan, had asked him to write a paper describing the ENIAC and its creation at the Moore School. This was the first work for which I had moved beyond the role of editor/critic, citable in a footnote, to that of researcher into various aspects of the history, worthy of a "with," and finally on to full coauthor.

It was early March of that year when Pres phoned Bernie and Bernie in turn phoned Art about Pres's threat. In late January Bernie had sent copies of our paper to all parties mentioned in it, so far as these could be located, and to several others from the ENIAC era. This was in accord with a suggestion made by Art, as a member of the editorial board of the recently launched quarterly, that in the interest of historical accuracy *all* possibly controversial articles be so distributed for comment prior to publication. It seemed appropriate to take such a precaution not only because of the importance of the topic but also because of the time that had elapsed since the occurrence of the key events.

Bernie, in his covering letter for that mailing, had referred to "established *Annals* policy," though it was now being exercised for the first time. He had promised everyone an appropriate response: revisions or acknowledgments within the paper or, possibly, publication of differing views in the same issue. Coincidentally, Bernie had written Art to thank him for the manuscript, praising it as "a beautiful paper, very well-written and clearly and effectively organized" and thanking both of us for "this magnificent contribution to the *Annals*."

Pres Eckert had received a copy and so had Kathleen Mauchly, as John Mauchly's widow and a keenly interested party. (John had died a year earlier, on January 8, 1980.) Bernie told Art of an hour-long talk with Pres, in which Pres expressed his anger over our paper and threatened a lawsuit. Bernie said that he had managed to calm Pres down, ultimately, and had gotten him to agree to submit his criticisms in writing. Bernie followed up on March 11 with two letters, one to Pres and one to Art.

He wrote Pres that he had enjoyed their conversation of the other day and would look forward to receiving his comments on our paper. Acknowledging that Pres had expressed a need for two months in which to respond, he set a deadline of May 15. He then promised to make "as complete an accommodation" to Pres's views as possible. In closing, he thanked him for calling. He did not mention the threat.

Bernie wrote Art that he had discussed Pres's phone call with *Annals* assistant editor in chief Nancy Stern, and that she had recommended both encouraging Pres to respond and holding him to the deadline. Bernie's main purpose in writing Art, though, was to enclose the responses he had received so far, most of which were gratifyingly positive. John V. Atanasoff was pleased with "an admirable paper in this very difficult subject"—not surprisingly, since it went into the ENIAC trial and spelled out in considerable detail the linkage from Atanasoff and the ABC to John Mauchly and the ENIAC.

One respondent found the article "most absorbing" and expressed happiness "that we are to have a first-hand description of ENIAC." Another, sending congratulations for "this natural description," found it "so well done that one felt personally" the difficulties in the computer's development. Yet another said it was "so enjoyable that I have already managed to complete reading it and provide . . . comments." Humboldt State University professor Henry Tropp, the journal's editor for both Anecdotes and Reviews, wrote directly to congratulate Art, calling the paper "of epic proportions" and saying he was "delighted that we are going to have the privilege of publishing it in the Annals."

Kay Mauchly's response came in a letter to Bernie dated March 22, 1981, which she termed "a personal letter and not for publication." Whereas Bernie had sent us the originals of the other responses, he sent us a photocopy of this one— and then only after learning, a few weeks later, that both Pres and Kay had voiced strong objections to the publication of our paper during a thirtieth-anniversary celebration of UNIVAC I at the Blue Bell, Pennsylvania, headquarters of Sperry Rand's Univac Division.

Kay wrote Bernie that, in her opinion, the Burks article "goes beyond simply not telling the truth, which is readily available, but actually amounts to defamation of John Mauchly's character and the whole ENIAC project"; moreover, that *"there are many others who agree with me that some drastic steps should be taken to correct this defamation"* [italics added].

She objected strongly to our position that Mauchly had derived ideas for a computer from Atanasoff and, in particular, to our claim that he had worked on the machine in Iowa and had taken notes on Atanasoff's manuscript describing it.[1] "Mauchly," she said, "never laid a hand on the incomplete machine" and "took no notes on a machine in which he had absolutely no interest because it was computing mechanically instead of electronically."

She objected just as strongly to our position that Mauchly, in his 1942 proposal for what came to be the ENIAC, was aiming at an *electronic digital* version of the Moore School's *mechanical analog* differential analyzer.[2] She felt we were ignoring his background in digital devices, especially in electronic counters, even though our argument was that he meant to use electronic counting devices to replace the mechanical integrators of the differential analyzer.

Another of the earlier respondents had also expressed surprise at our "tying the ENIAC design back to the DA's." We replied to him that we had treated the subject in some detail because the differential analyzer really had played a central role in the invention of the ENIAC. There were marked architectural parallels between the ENIAC and the differential analyzer; indeed, there is no other way to explain the ENIAC's distributive architecture than to see it as modeled on the differential analyzer (see chap. 2). The two court cases also pointed up the ENIAC's conception as a replacement for the analyzer, to solve electronically the very ballistics problems the analyzer was then solving mechanically for the U.S.

Army. We felt it necessary to spell out this connection in our ENIAC paper, not only because it was a crucial part of the history but because neither Pres nor John had ever accepted it.

Bernie Galler's initial alarm over Pres's threat to sue was rekindled by Kay's letter, particularly by her charge of "defamation" and her allusion to "drastic steps." He proceeded to seek the advice of the *Annals'* publisher, the American Federation of Information Processing Societies (AFIPS). He set up a five-way teleconference that included the executive director of AFIPS; an attorney for AFIPS; Bernie himself as editor in chief of the journal; and Art and me as authors of the article in question. The discussion focused on the likelihood of a lawsuit if our article was published, and on *Annals* policy—or lack thereof—for the protection of authors and editors.

Several critical points emerged in this May 12, 1981, conference. First, from the AFIPS attorney: In his view, threats of libel suits should not in themselves cause a journal not to publish. If we were sued, it would be for libel with a claim of defamation, but, he said, truth is an absolute defense against libel. Any suit would probably be directed against all parties, who could then countersue and request damages. He thought the chance of success of a suit in this instance was minimal. Finally, corporate interests might be involved because of recent Sperry Univac advertisements calling the ENIAC the first electronic computer, and these interests might either increase or decrease the likelihood of a suit—depending, he said.

Second, from the AFIPS executive director: The fact was that the publisher had no money to support a lawsuit on behalf of any individuals. Indeed, AFIPS had *no policy* with regard to such suits, but, he thought, should establish one. Finally, he advised Bernie and Art to take up the possibility of legal protection for themselves, as professors, by the University of Michigan.

In a May 23 phone call to us, J. V. Atanasoff confirmed, from his own memory, that John Mauchly, contrary to Kay's assertion, had both worked on the ABC and taken notes on the written description of it during his visit to Ames (positions we had drawn from ENIAC trial documents and testimony of witnesses other than J. V.). He called again on May 26 to give us his understanding of the views of D. Dennis Allegretti, head of Honeywell's outside counsel in that trial, as to Sperry Univac's June 5, 1979, *Wall Street Journal* ad.[3]

Allegretti considered this ad, a two-page spread introducing the Sperry Univac 1100/60 computer, a violation of a mutual contract reached in the ENIAC case that both sides would abide by Judge Larson's decision. It features Pres Eckert posing with the new machine against a backdrop photo of the ENIAC. A large-print heading asks: "WHO WOULD HAVE THOUGHT THAT THE

FATHER OF GOLIATH WOULD BE INTRODUCING DAVID?" Eckert is the father, Goliath is the ENIAC, David is the 1100/60, and the stone in David's sling is the computer's microprocessor, a single one of which "is in many ways more powerful than an entire 1946 ENIAC."

The particular violation of the Sperry Rand-Honeywell contract is the ad's claim that the ENIAC was "the first electronic digital computer," but other wording is also misleading. Eckert is identified only as "vice-president of Sperry Univac"; the creation of the ENIAC at the University of Pennsylvania, under army sponsorship, is not credited. And while Eckert is said to be "co-inventor" of the ENIAC, he is its "father" and it becomes "his giant computer"; not even Mauchly is named in this ad.

In Allegretti's opinion, J. V. told us, Honeywell could sue Sperry Rand over this ad, and, in fact, the ad violated Atanasoff's personal rights as well. Moreover, Allegretti ventured, Eckert would not dare sue over our ENIAC article. Nor would Sperry Rand sue.

We had our revisions of the article ready by late May, responding to some of our critics by incorporating their suggestions in the new draft, to others by rewriting or expanding on the text, and to still others by holding to our original versions. In each case, I prepared a detailed, point-by-point argument for our position. Bernie Galler sent this second draft, together with the individual arguments, to all who had received the first draft, plus one or two others whose names had arisen.

Bernie made clear in this mailing that we would consider further comments, but that we expected to make very few changes for the third and final draft. He invited any and all to submit their criticisms for inclusion in the October issue along with our article, to be followed by any replies we cared to make in turn. At about this time, Bernie told Art by phone that he had seen Pres Eckert in Chicago, at another UNIVAC I celebration, and that Pres did still plan to write, presumably for publication. (His May 15 deadline for a response to the first draft had passed, but he could now respond to the new draft along with everyone else.)

Bernie next set up a June 4 meeting with University of Michigan general counsel Roderick Daane, to get his opinion on university legal support. Art happened to be away at that time, but Bernie thought the matter urgent enough that he and I should go ahead without him. I called Art (in Los Alamos) and he agreed.

At Bernie's behest, I explained to Daane that the ENIAC was not the first electronic computer as was commonly thought. Rather, I said, that distinction fell to Atanasoff's ABC. Because the ABC was a *special-purpose* electronic computer, however, the ENIAC remained the first *general-purpose* electronic computer—hence the title of our paper. I told Daane of the ENIAC patent trial, in which Judge Larson found not only that the ABC was a prior electronic computer, but also that basic concepts for the ENIAC had been taken directly from the ABC. In response to a question from Daane, I said that while Art and I had used the trial proceedings to spell out this derivation, we did give our own analysis of Atanasoff's work and influence, as well.

Daane then asked if the purpose of the article was primarily to establish Atanasoff. Bernie and I explained that this was a long (60,000-word) historical exposition of the ENIAC, the major thrust of which was the ENIAC itself: its design, development, and significance. I said that Pres Eckert and Kay Mauchly objected to the part near the beginning where we traced it back to Atanasoff and his computer. I added that they also objected to our finding of architectural parallels to the differential analyzer.

Daane was very reassuring about Art and Bernie. He thought it improbable that the article was libelous, and since they were performing their professorial functions in producing it, the university's insurance would cover them, not only for defense expenses at trial but for damages if they lost.

As to any protection for me—not a faculty member—Daane phoned the university's insurance office and explained the situation very much as I had to him. The university's insurer, he learned, might refuse to pay my (prorated) costs, but then the university itself would probably pick these up—because, he said, slipping into his ready legal jargon, "You are in bed with Art"! He hastened to rephrase, explaining that my interests were tied up with Art's and would be inseparable at trial. He estimated the extra cost to the university, in such an event, at about $5,000.

The question then arose as to whether I might better withdraw as coauthor—something I was of course reluctant to do. Daane explained, though, that my liability would be the same whether or not I was listed as coauthor. Either way I was a collaborator!

I also asked if the court would consider Eckert and Mauchly public figures. Daane responded, "Absolutely—this is the computer!" As public figures, the plaintiffs would have to make a much stronger case for *intent* to falsify than they would as private figures. Errors of fact in our article would be considered innocent if we could show a great effort to be accurate.

Daane said, too, that Kay Mauchly's letter of March 22 to Bernie was to be taken much more seriously than Eckert's earlier telephoned threat, simply because she had put a charge of defamation in writing. Finally, Daane cautioned that everything he had told us in this meeting was to be considered only probable, since he had not studied the whole situation.

Bernie and I were both reassured by the general counsel's opinion, even if it was only probable, to the effect that there was little to fear so long as our historical account was honest and scholarly. I recall Bernie's laughing response to some comment of Daane's as we were leaving: "Yes, we're the good guys—we're with the judge!"

The very next day, June 5, Bernie had a call from Kay that took an amazingly different tack. He immediately phoned me to report on this very friendly, nonthreatening overture. She agreed, he said, that the matters in dispute should be aired and discussed professionally. She said she would send him a number of documents substantiating her position on Atanasoff as opposed to ours, adding that anything she sent him was to be shared with the Burkses.

Although she again voiced her objection to our tying the ENIAC to the differential analyzer, she went on to say that the technical part of our article (still the first draft) was "superb," Bernie told me.

He also said that Kay had a lot of nice things to say about Art in this phone conversation. One was that the ENIAC would not have worked if Art had not worked out the details, as she put it. Another was that it was Art who had sat down with her (Kay McNulty at that time) and taught her how to program the ENIAC when things were chaotic at the Moore School. (As the machine was being finished in the last half of 1945, Kay and other young women at the Moore School were shifted from calculating artillery firing tables on desk calculators and the differential analyzer to programming the new computer for this job. At Kay's request, Art assisted a number of these women on several occasions.)

But then, just three weeks later, Kay again wrote to Bernie expressing strong displeasure, this time with the revised paper: "I still maintain that the Burks' interpretation of the chain of events leading to the development of ENIAC is false and misleading and a defamation of John Mauchly."

She referred again to John's work with electronic counters, some of which she said she had in her house. To substantiate her complaint, she sent along copies of two of his letters. The first was a 1940 letter to a friend, meteorologist H. Helm Clayton, from which she quoted his mention of "using vacuum tubes for computing before John had met Atanasoff" (see chap. 4). The second was a 1978 letter to Henry Tropp, which she said "almost seems as if John were anticipating the Burks' attack." Kay closed this June 25, 1981, letter to Bernie with a promise of a response to our paper *by Pres and her jointly* "in the very near future."

Although we were all somewhat alarmed, once more, by Kay's reference to "defamation," we soon received three reassuring opinions as to any lawsuit. The AFIPS attorney, having studied our article, advised Bernie that it was not libelous. Charles G. Call, a member of Allegretti's law firm and its chief investigator in the ENIAC case, told us that we need not be concerned, our paper was not libelous, the second draft even "safer" than the first because we now quoted the court more often.

Finally, on July 30, Roderick Daane wrote Bernie to confirm that the university's insurance carrier would, in his opinion, cover both defense and damages for Art and Bernie. He thought it would also cover my defense, which would very probably prove "incapable of isolation" from Art's. The carrier could not, however, be expected to cover any damages I might incur, and the university could not either.

On August 3, Call also put in writing his assessment of our ENIAC paper as expressed on the phone a week earlier. He wrote:

> I read your description of the Atanasoff-Berry Computer (and of John Mauchly's contact with that machine) with particular care. In my view you have said nothing which is not borne out by the record and the Court's findings in <u>Honey-well v. Sperry Rand</u>.

and:

> You are both to be congratulated for completing this important historical record of the origins of electronic computation. My own investigations in the <u>Honey-well v. Sperry Rand</u> litigation made it clear that much of what has been written concerning those early days has often been little more than fantasy proliferated through plagiarism. Your work gives authoritative insight into the complex combination of influences which led to the ENIAC and its successors.

Call's words, "fantasy proliferated through plagiarism," were to echo over the years as reviews and other articles appeared concerning both this paper on the ENIAC and our later book, *The First Electronic Computer: The Atanasoff Story*.[4]

Bernie Galler had also been reassured by assistant editor in chief Nancy Stern's comments on the second draft of our article. In a June 16 letter, she wrote, "I regard the paper . . . of singular importance in the history of computing, not only because it was written by two participants but because it represents a well researched, well documented and on the whole balanced account of one of the most important developments in modern history." She did, somewhat ominously, express her belief that there would be "no consensus" on "who was the <u>real</u> inventor of the first electronic digital computer—Atanasoff or Eckert-Mauchly," but still felt that Art and I had presented "an articulate version, one which is unquestionably important."

In early September of 1981, Bernie informed Art of his seemingly firm expectations from the Eckert-Mauchly side. Pres and Kay would send just a short response to accompany our final version of the paper in the October 1981 issue of the *Annals*, but would write a full response for the following January 1982 issue. Along with this latter piece, Bernie hoped to publish the 1978 Mauchly letter to Tropp that Kay had sent him in June and also the "Fireside Chat" given by Mauchly at the Sperry Univac conference in Rome in late 1973 (again, see chap. 4).

Bernie said Kay understood that Art and I would be permitted to reply, in that same January issue, to their article and the two Mauchly items. He added that both Kay and Pres were friendly when he last talked to them and neither mentioned suing.

Bernie, in his role as the journal's editor in chief, continued to wax enthusiastic about this public airing of the dispute over invention of the electronic computer. He was looking forward to publication of our article and the exchanges between us and our respondents. He was also looking forward to publication of the longer response by Pres and Kay, *and* he was now encouraging Atanasoff to write his side of this history. On September 9, he sent us the responses to our article—five in all, from John V. Atanasoff, John Grist Brainerd, Kathleen R. Mauchly and J. Presper Eckert, Brian Randell, and Konrad Zuse—and formally invited us to comment on each one.

"This has certainly been a most interesting sequence of events," Bernie concluded. "The publication of your paper has turned out to be a historical event itself. I am sure that the October, 1981 issue of the Annals will be well regarded by all who see it." As always, he sent copies of his letter to concerned parties, in this case to *Annals* assistant editor in chief Nancy Stern, Anecdotes and Reviews editor Henry Tropp, and, in the New York City editorial offices, managing editor Rosamond Dana.

Bernie, however, had reached this happy state only after weathering a behind-the-scenes dispute over the publication of John Mauchly's Univac speech—its timing, that is, relative to our ENIAC article. Managing editor Mondy Dana had informed Art and me, quite suddenly by telephone, that this Mauchly talk was to be published on its own, as a separate article *with no connection to ours and so no reply from us.* Indeed, Mondy said, it was being readied not for the issue *after* ours but for the July 1981 issue, the one *before* ours! (Recall that the quarterly *Annals* at this time was running about five months late—the October 1981 issue was not to appear until March 1982—so that the July 1981 issue was still being prepared in July 1981!)

Now we felt that our article had instigated this whole debate, and to be preempted by an opposing Mauchly version in the preceding issue would be unfair. Besides, what of the "established *Annals* policy"—applied in the case of our article—of getting reactions from the involved parties and including these in the same issue, in the name of historical accuracy? And what of concerns over libel and editorial responsibility? We appealed to Bernie, who ultimately decided to revert to the original plan, namely, to run the Univac speech in the issue after ours and, as he wrote to Kay on August 13, allow us to comment—and her to reply if she wished—"out of fairness to everyone."

Our tiff with managing editor Dana over Mauchly's Univac speech was just one of several occasions on which she was the conduit for news of *Annals* plans that seemed to us to contradict the policies of editor in chief Galler. Art, as a member of the journal's board, received her monthly publication schedules, and she also spoke to us often by phone, especially as copyeditor of our forthcoming article. Since she had no inherent interest in the dispute over that article, we could only infer that pressure was being brought to bear in the *Annals* editorial offices by outside parties, presumably those "many others" Kay had mentioned in her March 22 letter, who agreed with her that "drastic steps should be taken to correct [the ENIAC article's] defamation" of Mauchly and the ENIAC project.

One further such scrape with Mondy Dana occurred as the time drew near for our paper and our exchanges with respondents to appear. Again by phone, she remarked offhandedly that of course she would be showing all these respondents our replies to them in advance of publication—even allowing them to change their responses in light of our replies! Once more our quick appeal to Bernie brought a firm admonition to Mondy against that procedure.

Our paper, "The ENIAC: First General-Purpose Electronic Computer," did appear as originally scheduled in the October 1981 issue.[5] In their brief response, Kay and Pres charged us with "inaccuracies of fact, supposition, and conclusion which should not have been present had a reasonable research effort been made"; with taking "excerpts from Mauchly's letters out of context"; with "hiding behind the conclusions of the court . . . without examining the evidence"; and with failing to consult Eckert before "concocting" our story of Atanasoff's influence on Mauchly. They concluded with their promise of a paper for the *Annals* to "correct at least some of the inaccuracies set forth by the Burkses" and to "mitigate the discredit that Burks insists on directing to John W. Mauchly." The word *defamation* was not used.

We replied at some length, arguing against each of these charges in turn and noting the lack of any specific instance, let alone any documentation, for a single one of them. As to our not consulting Eckert, we pointed out that he had been given the opportunity to offer his criticisms as each draft of our paper was finished but had chosen not to do so. We added that we did take into account Mrs. Mauchly's responses to the successive drafts, though primarily by expanding and clarifying our arguments. We closed with our own promise to reply to any specific criticisms they cared to make in their more comprehensive paper.

Our situation at this juncture, we felt, was quite positive. We could assume, by the very fact of this published response from Pres and Kay, that there would be no lawsuit over our ENIAC article. We could also look forward to a continuing debate in the public forum. Not only would a longer critique by Pres and Kay be published in the *Annals*, but other items from John Mauchly that were said to counter our arguments would also be published, *and* Bernie had explicitly invited us to reply to each and every one.

We remained somewhat apprehensive, however, because of our several negative encounters with the *Annals* editorial offices—in the person of the managing editor, but, we sensed, under the direction of undisclosed parties making policy changes that at times even bypassed the editor in chief. We felt the journal's attempt to publish Mauchly's Rome talk in the issue before ours was especially ominous, so that, while reminding ourselves not to be paranoid, we remained alert to further shifts.

And shifts there were, in rapid succession, particularly with regard to the promised longer response of Pres and Kay to our ENIAC article; indeed, shifts that would ultimately squeeze Art and me out of *our* promised right to reply. Mondy had told us, over the phone from time to time, of their paper's progress. A Sperry Rand attorney was working with them, she said. Next, Kay had finished her part and cleared it with the Sperry attorneys. Finally, Pres was expected to finish his part for publication in the July 1982 issue. But then, in the June 1982 *Annals* schedule, even as the publication date slipped to January 1983, Kay Mauchly's name suddenly stood alone! Pres Eckert had withdrawn as coauthor! By September of that year, Kay had submitted a work under her name only, with publication now advancing to April 1983. *And* it had metamorphosed into a biography of John Mauchly, assigned to *Annals* biographies editor Eric Weiss and subject to the regular editorial review process. Mondy Dana told us over the phone that it "just came in" as an article by itself, *not as a response to ours.*

In his dealings with us about Kay Mauchly's submission, Eric Weiss started out candidly enough, as others had done, only to beat a fast retreat. "I think it may be at least part of the response to your article in the October [1981] <u>Annals</u>," he wrote on September 10, 1982, and he offered to send us a copy for our "informal or formal comment." But in the week's time that it took that copy to reach us, he had switched to what was by now a familiar pattern of off-putting. An attached note mentioned only the informal, or refereeing, part of our comment and asked us to "shoot for October 1," less than two weeks away. When we wrote back on September 25, recommending publication of Kay's paper as an important contribution, but reminding Eric of the *Annals'* long-standing commitment to carry our response in the same issue— and requesting two months in which to prepare it—he was indignant.

Any formal reply from us, he now wrote, "would have to be refereed as all formal <u>Annals</u> papers are," and he was "unwilling to delay publication of the Mauchly paper in order to get both papers into the same issue." If we held to our two-month requirement, he said, "the soonest that it could be published would be in the issue following the one containing the Mauchly paper." If, on the other hand, we could get our formal reply to him by October 15, he would "make every effort" to have it in the issue with Kay's—*if* he and his reviewers should "decide that this coincidence contributes to an understanding of the events described." He added a warning that he was neither promising to publish our reply nor guaranteeing a particular issue for its appearance.

How far we had come from the journal's published policy! And how far we had come from the initial pronouncements by key *Annals* people on our article and its preservation of the history! Eric now wrote that he knew his position did not satisfy our requirements "or even what you believe you have been promised." But, he said, "it satisfies, as best I can manage, my personal requirements as an editor that Annals be as good a publication as we can make it." He closed with: "I understand your distress about the controversy, but I am unwilling to let my sympathy for your feelings influence my concern for excellence in Annals, an excellence which includes content and timeliness in publishing submitted manuscripts."

Eric's hurry for our response was prompted by that April 1983 publication date Mondy had set for Kay's article. But our hurry to meet his October 15 deadline with a brief comment for publication proved to no avail. Our last word from him on the matter came in a December 16, 1982, letter. Kay Mauchly's paper, though now in final form, was not expected to "make print until 1984," because, he said, Mondy's schedule was full. And the final touch: *it had been decided that no reply by us—or anyone else—would be published with it*!

At long last, Eric gave the reason:

> We have had some very pointed, even barbed, comments from thoughtful senior members of the computing community to the effect that the Annals is encouraging controversy. The case at point was your article and the accompanying comments and counter comments. Consequently, I have recommended to Bernie, and he has tentatively accepted my recommendation, that we not follow the model of your article but instead publish Mrs. Mauchly's paper . . . without comments but solicit, review, and publish comments and criticisms that meet our standards in later issues. This will preserve for the historical record the several views and interpretations of the events, and will avoid any appearance of the attempt to aid, abet, and encourage unedifying controversy.

As "John Mauchly's Early Years" by Kathleen R. Mauchly finally appeared in the April 1984 *Annals of the History of Computing*, it avoided any outward semblance of a response to our paper, setting forth instead her own parallel version of Mauchly's achievements apart from any Atanasoff influence.[6] *Annals* policy, as originally suggested by Art and enthusiastically embraced by the editor in chief, had collapsed with regard to what was surely Kay Mauchly's response to us.

So it was that, slowly but steadily, in both time and form, the long-promised Pres Eckert/Kay Mauchly response to our ENIAC article had been distanced from it—shifting from an original projected date of January 1982 to its actual publication date some twenty-seven months later, in the process losing coauthor Pres Eckert entirely and becoming simply a "biography" of John Mauchly, with no connection to our article.

Bernie Galler had communicated with us several times over the course of Eric's handling of Kay's paper. He first phoned on October 3, 1982, just as Eric was responding so indignantly to our request for two months in which to reply to Kay. He now echoed Mondy Dana's declaration that this paper was *not* the long-awaited response to ours but had come in as an "article" and would be handled accordingly. He did admit, when pressed, that Kay, having written this article, would very likely never write the promised "response"—nor would Pres. As for the *Annals* policy of seeking responses to be published with any given controversial article, he observed simply that the journal was having to "rethink" that policy.

What happened to Bernie, it seems to us, is what also appears to have happened to a number of other individuals and institutions in the face of this controversy. They first saw the dispute, naively perhaps, as simply a contest between Atanasoff, on the one hand, and Mauchly and Eckert, on the other, for recognition as originator(s) of an instrument of profound—*revolutionary*—technological influence.

Ultimately, however, they heard from the large contingent of Mauchly-Eckert champions with a great deal of emotional, if not also professional and financial, investment in the outcome of this contest—people with tremendous clout in the computing community, those "thoughtful senior members" of that community who had sent Eric Weiss their "very pointed, even barbed, comments" about the journal's policy of "encouraging controversy." Our paper, bringing to light the thus-far largely ignored court case with its huge store of documentation and its invalidation of the ENIAC patent, raised a lot of blood pressures. The idea of inviting further debate in this controversy raised them even further.

As Art and I watched and endeavored to uphold our end of the matter, we saw the debate evolve into an eerie "controversy over controversy" within the *Annals* editorial board. And it was the editor in chief who sought to have it resolved. Bernie Galler, having viewed historical controversy as healthy—supporting it for two years despite the threat of a lawsuit and a number of rather transparent attempts in the New York offices to undercut his position—and finally having had his announced "established *Annals* policy" withdrawn, devised a "Hypothetical Situation" to pose to members of that editorial board.

Suppose, he wrote in the Agenda for their October 26, 1982, meeting, the *Annals* had decided to publish a special issue of articles on an important past event. An official of the main company involved was asked to host, and did host, a taped discussion among some of the original participants, together with some *Annals* representatives, with the intention of including this discussion in the special issue.

Now this official had deliberately excluded several of the original participants from the taped discussion, and the journal's editor in chief had expressed
his wish to get comments from those absent parties. The official objected, however, saying that he was concerned over possible bad publicity for his company
because of what the excluded participants might say. When told that he would be
given an opportunity to comment in return [in the same issue], he still objected,
and when told that those parties would probably respond in later issues, anyway,
he simply hoped that they would not.

Bernie, in this "Hypothetical Situation," had the editor in chief cite, as an
example of his procedure, "the treatment of the ENIAC article by Arthur and
Alice Burks"! And he closed this "Item 7" of his Agenda for the October meeting
with three questions for the editorial board: "Does the *Annals* have the right to
pursue this course of action? Does it have an obligation to the company not to?
Are these the right questions?"

He gave the answers of the board members in the minutes of the meeting.
They were aware, he wrote, that they "could lose the future (or even present)
cooperation of the company involved," and they questioned whether they wanted
"to encourage controversy or simply accept it when it arises." They felt that their
"objective is to present history, and that this implies automatically accepting controversy, but only as much as necessary to present the history well."

Bernie explained that the journal had had "clear ground rules" in previous
controversial cases, and he again cited our manuscript and spelled out those rules.
In the hypothetical situation under consideration, however, he said, the ground
rules were not clear. For it, the board decided, the journal "should seek responses
and comments [from the excluded individuals] as part of compiling the complete
history."

Apparently still mindful of the journal's need to avoid "losing the cooperation of the company involved," even as it went about "compiling the complete history," the board recommended a more circuitous approach than that of
the current policy—one that could hardly be declared publicly: *first* publish the
taped discussion, *then* "send a published issue . . . to all participants and the
people mentioned [in the issue], subtly suggesting that they have an opportunity
to comment, or even to write an article."

As the board noted, there would now be "no possibility of commenting in the
same issue as the original document." On the other hand, it also noted that such
comments would not be "subjected to the normal refereeing process that applied
to articles"—a favorable pronouncement that had been upheld earlier by Bernie
but was not being honored with regard to our comments on Kay's article.

Two things were brought home to Art and me by this "Hypothetical Situation" and its resolution. One was that the *Annals* policy of encouraging debate in
the name of historical truth was under serious attack; the other was that commercial interests were deeply involved in that attack. The handling of our article was

the centerpiece of the issues before the editorial board; and a company's cooperation with the journal was at stake.

A third thing sank in more gradually. Although we continued to feel let down
as Eric Weiss backed away from the commitments that had been made to us over
a long period, we saw that a new policy was emerging, and we came to see its
inevitability. Our fears were slowly verified that the "word" being fed to us in
small doses by Mondy Dana had a behind-the-scenes life of its own, and that its
purposes were being brought to bear, however clandestinely, upon the persons
running this journal. The time had passed when we could appeal to Bernie as the
editor in chief and have that "word" reversed.

As we saw in chapter 4, the *Annals* did publish all three posthumous Mauchly
items in its July 1982 issue (his 1940 letter to Clayton, his 1973 talk to the Sperry
Univac convention, and his 1978 letter to Tropp). They appeared as "Mauchly:
Unpublished Remarks," with a foreword by Tropp, an introduction to the "Fireside Chat" by Univac's Carl Hammer, and an afterword by Art and me.[7] Even
though we were not allowed to respond to Kay's article, we could take considerable satisfaction in responding to those three pieces, as of course we had taken
satisfaction in the very publication of our article, together with responses, in the
October 1981 issue.

As for Atanasoff's reaction to Kay's article—Eric Weiss had also sent him a
copy for comment—if we were somewhat upset, J. V. was truly distressed, so
much so that he had difficulty speaking when he phoned us about it. He was
working hard on his own *Annals* article, and because of this and other matters he
could not write an adequate critique of her work at this time. He calmed down
when we assured him that we had been studying the manuscript ourselves and
would be responding in one form or another. As we have said, this turned out to
be an appendix in our 1988 book on Atanasoff and the ABC. J. V. then decided
to make do with a short letter for Eric to publish in the same issue.

In this letter, dated October 16, 1982, he said he feared that Kay's paper
would "tend to give your readers an incorrect opinion of an important element in
the history of computing." He continued:

> At first I had in mind to give a complete reply to this paper. When the short
> period of time was announced, I found that imminent and pressing duties pre-
> vented a proper response. However, I remind your readers that I have in prepara-
> tion a manuscript, "Advent of Digital Electronic Computers," which I expect to
> submit to the Annals in the near future. This paper will cover, in part, much of
> the same material and I have decided to let my paper act as a reply to the paper
> by K. Mauchly.

Of course, just two months later Eric wrote of the journal's decision not to include any such comments because of the strong objections from outsiders. The *Annals* did publish J. V.'s article, however, having made Art its editor, in the July 1984 issue.[8] It marked the final "catching up" of the journal's time schedule.

An interesting footnote is that, although Pres never wrote his promised response to our article, he did express his opinion of *us*, as supporters of Atanasoff and Judge Larson, in an interview at the time. Marshall Ledger quotes him in his article, "The E.N.I.A.C.'s Muddled History," for the November 1982 *University of Pennsylvania Gazette*.[9] Citing Art (and me as coauthor) for our *Annals* article, he writes that John Mauchly in his last years had tried to correct some of the historical errors but that Pres Eckert despaired of the attempt.

> Eckert, widely read in the history of technology, doubts that history is correctable, especially when he sees what those associated with the E.N.I.A.C. have said. "If the world is full of people like this, why are we worried about setting the record straight?" he exclaims. "Let's just live our lives and forget these liars."

SEVEN

OTHER VOICES

Nancy Stern, assistant editor in chief of the *Annals* and chair of the Department of Administrative Computer Systems at Hofstra University, soon emerged as a principal advocate for the Eckert-Mauchly claims to inventive recognition, as against the Atanasoff claims. Her book, *From ENIAC to UNIVAC: An Appraisal of the Eckert-Mauchly Computers*, appeared the same year as our ENIAC article.[1] Combined with her academic status and her position on the *Annals*, this book made her name as an authority on this subject.

A rather close look at this work is warranted, both for its substance and for its caliber as a scholarly production, but also for its largely favorable reception by several other highly respected historians of science. Moreover, it seems to be the source, though not always credited as such, of condemnations of Judge Earl Larson's decision in the ENIAC patent trial, condemnations based on misconceptions of his findings and of the nature and intent of patent law.

Stern opens her book with a statement of her three major purposes, each centered on the roles of Pres Eckert and John Mauchly in the "burgeoning computer field" of their era: first, a study of the process of development; second, an analysis of the social forces (academic, governmental, and commercial) influencing this process; and third, an attempt to place the achievements of these two men "in the appropriate historical context," given the considerable controversy surrounding their work. For this last purpose—our chief concern here—she would try to remain "as objective as possible," to base her position "firmly on the evidence," and to maintain "a consistent point of view."

She enlarges on this third purpose in her introduction, telling of the ENIAC patent trial, noting that Sperry Rand had not appealed the Court's invalidation of the patent, and promising, as "a major objective of this book," to analyze and assess this historic verdict. She adds: "The relationship between John Mauchly and John Vincent Atanasoff is considered in an effort to shed some light on the ideas that were exchanged between the two men."

How well does Nancy Stern live up to her promise of an objective, factual, consistent analysis of this controversy over the invention of the electronic computer? On that same page 4 of her introduction, she has already quoted Judge Larson's ruling: "Eckert and Mauchly did not themselves first invent the automatic electronic digital computer, but instead derived that subject matter from one Dr. John Vincent Atanasoff" (Finding 3).[2] She has gone on, however, to term this opinion "somewhat contradictory since the judge also stated that Eckert and Mauchly were the inventors of the ENIAC and the ENIAC patent claims did not rest on Atanasoff's work."

This argument is simply false. In the first place, it is not contradictory to find someone an inventor of a given device and at the same time to find that device derived from a prior invention. Judge Larson based his finding of derivation from the ABC on the ENIAC's use of both broad and particular aspects of that prior computer. At the same time, and even as he recognized Atanasoff as the inventor of the ABC, he declared Eckert and Mauchly the sole inventors of the more advanced ENIAC (Finding 4).[3] Moreover, as we saw in chapter 5, he made this latter ruling in the context of possible coinvention, *not by Atanasoff*, but by other members of the Moore School team. Larson himself tried to forestall this very misinterpretation of his decision by stating in Finding 4 that Finding 3 still held, despite his naming Eckert and Mauchly inventors of the ENIAC. Their invention remained "barred from patentability," he repeated, because of its derivation from Atanasoff.

In the second place, the judge *did not say* that ENIAC patent claims did not rest on Atanasoff's work. Indeed, he explicitly ruled in Finding 3: "The subject matter of one or more claims of the ENIAC was derived from Atanasoff"; and he cited claims 88 and 89 as representative. Nowhere did he reverse that ruling.

These errors in Stern's introduction are especially lamentable in that she provides no reference other than an endnote citing the entire decision. I find it also lamentable, and rather odd, that she does not once name Judge Larson in the course of this, her initial presentation of him and the *Honeywell v. Sperry Rand* patent case, merely calling him "the judge" or "the presiding judge." Indeed, so far as I can determine, his name does not appear at all in the main text of this book, despite many references to the case! Certainly, and perhaps accordingly, it is not listed in the index. (I find just three occurrences of "E. R. Larson" or "Larson," as author of the decision, in two endnotes and the bibliography.)

It is difficult not to sense bias in Nancy Stern's treatment of this controversy over priority—and derivation—through just such distortion of the evidence. In many instances, straight statements of fact are interlaced with unsubstantiated assumptions, yielding misleading or plainly incorrect impressions that are then carried forward as established fact.

Early in her first chapter, Stern complains that the judge's finding of derivation of ideas from Atanasoff "minimized the significance of Mauchly's early work" because, with no papers describing his "proposed invention," Mauchly "had no way of proving that he had conceived the idea of an electronic digital computer prior to his [1940] meeting with Atanasoff." For Stern, there *was* significant "early work" and there *was* a "proposed invention" before any contact with Atanasoff, despite the lack of evidence.

Stern concludes this paragraph with a still more troubling sentence: "Although Joseph Chapline, one of Mauchly's students at Ursinus and later a contributor to the ENIAC, knew of Mauchly's early work in vacuum-tube computers, the judge in *Honeywell v. Sperry Rand*, in the absence of documentation or an actual device, was not convinced of Mauchly's pioneering efforts." She does not go on to say that Chapline did testify at the trial as a defense witness, but failed to connect any of Mauchly's early work to any electronic computer.[4]

Again, for Stern, that early work has become "pioneering efforts," and she is convinced even if the judge is not. Beyond her claim of what Chapline "knew," she offers only quotations from Mauchly himself, made in the years after the trial: assertions of his accomplishments in the 1930s and denials of any benefit whatsoever from his contacts with Atanasoff. For the most part, and throughout, Stern simply proceeds on the assumption that Mauchly, before meeting Atanasoff, had at least conceived of an electronic digital computer in sufficient detail to have learned nothing new from him.

She does acknowledge, in her second chapter, that Mauchly "had prior knowledge of Atanasoff's work," having learned of it at their December 1940 meeting in Philadelphia and having seen it firsthand in Iowa in 1941. She even quotes from his January 19, 1941, letter to Atanasoff, seeking more information about this computer-in-progress. In allowing a slight influence, however, she also augments her fanciful store of original Mauchly concepts with that of the general-purpose computer: "In that year [1941]," she writes, "Mauchly brought his own ideas of a general-purpose computer, combined with his knowledge of Atanasoff's work on a small, special-purpose device, to the Moore School."

Stern does not characterize this "knowledge" further, either here or as she alludes to it again in her final, summary chapter. There she goes so far as to cite Mauchly's "adaptation of Atanasoff's work, combined with his own work in the field"; but in reviewing the history of the two men, she tells only of their initial meeting and is somehow able to conclude: "The influence of Atanasoff on Mauchly seems to have ended at that point"! Mauchly's visit to Iowa and his firsthand experience of the ABC, noted by her earlier, have fallen by the wayside.

As for Stern's attribution of the general-purpose concept to Mauchly, independently of Atanasoff, she simply overlooks the evidence. For, in contrast to the absence of documentation of Mauchly's claims prior to his meeting Atanasoff, there was plenty of documentation of his thinking immediately thereafter and on through much of 1941—all to the contrary of Stern's view. Letters from that period reveal not only that Mauchly had not envisioned a general-purpose electronic computer on his own, but that it was *Atanasoff* who provided his initial impetus to build an electronic differential analyzer, his first big step toward the general-purpose machine.

As we saw in chapter 2, Atanasoff wrote Mauchly on May 31 about his idea for converting the ABC into an electronic digital differential analyzer; and on June 28 Mauchly, fresh from his Iowa visit, wrote his friend Helm Clayton about the ABC, adding his own conviction that it could be adapted to do the work of the differential analyzer. Mauchly then remarked: "My own computing devices use a different principle, more likely to fit small computing jobs." And again, on September 30, Mauchly wrote to Atanasoff asking permission for the Moore School "to build an '*Atanasoff Calculator*' (a la *Bush* analyzer)" [Mauchly's italics].

Stern chose to ignore these letters, relying instead on the fact that the *eventual outcome* of Mauchly's thinking—together with Eckert's—was the general-purpose ENIAC. She cites this aspect of the ENIAC often in her book, in the context of its superiority over the special-purpose ABC. And she faults Larson for finding the ENIAC derived from the ABC despite this and other differences between the two machines.

Here Stern fails to realize that such differences do not detract from the pioneering character of the ABC, any more than the limitations of the ENIAC detract from its own pioneering character. The ENIAC filled a large room and used 18,000 vacuum tubes to do what could, not so many years later, be done with a single chip the size of a thumbnail. Historians and others do not cite this fact to denigrate the ENIAC but rather to marvel at the pace of technology.

Stern also introduces the element of expediency to bolster her case, arguing, again, in her second chapter, that "Mauchly had taken advantage of the urgency of wartime to spur development of the high-speed, general-purpose ENIAC," whereas "Atanasoff had put his low-speed, special-purpose computer aside during the war." She then pursues this new theme, that Atanasoff failed while Mauchly succeeded, through a long discourse on the distinction between *invention* and *innovation*. Innovation, she claims, is the "application or adaptation of an idea, even an existing one, in such a manner that the resulting technology is rendered practical and useful"; invention seems to be the creation of the idea itself. Stern sees "Mauchly as the innovator and Eckert as the inventor" of the ENIAC and their later computers—with the unfortunate result, she writes, that Mauchly has been accorded less acclaim because of a popular misconception that inventors are more important than innovators.

Stern applies this dichotomy to the Mauchly-Atanasoff situation: "It was this innovative component in the Eckert-Mauchly organization that enabled it to succeed where Atanasoff failed, that is, in producing fully operational computers." And so, for her, the concept of technological advancement has come to supersede the concept of invention itself. In such a view, though, she leaves her reader pondering what the "innovator," Mauchly, could have accomplished without the contributions of the "inventors," Atanasoff and Eckert.

More seriously, Stern also misconstrues patent law. The government protects inventors' rights in order to *encourage* invention, for the good of society. Would a prospective inventor be encouraged by a system that granted a patent to the first "innovator" who succeeded in making the inventor's ideas "fully operational"? Moreover, the law does also encourage innovation by providing ways to use the ideas of prior inventors through payment of royalties and other forms of mutual accommodation.

I would note, further, that inventors are often innovators as well, that they are in fact driven by their expectations of becoming innovators. In creating the ABC, for example, Atanasoff was as concerned as Mauchly with applicability and had every expectation of being able to capitalize on his invention.

Stern does admit in her closing chapter that "the question of priority . . . is an issue." She grants Atanasoff priority over Mauchly and Eckert for what she calls his "model of an electronic digital computer," but only as the last in a long string of others who "scooped" all three, clear back to Charles Babbage. In the same breath, she again praises Mauchly and Eckert for showing "applicability as well as creativity," for bringing "their ideas to fruition," and for being able "to convince the government of the applicability of [their] machine . . . for wartime use"—all factors, she finds, in their resultant, deserved recognition.

For Stern, then, the priority of an invention counts for little as against its development, by the inventor or by others. Indeed, for her the very concept is suspect: "The question of priority . . . is frequently given too much consideration by some historians. Such a question serves no real purpose in understanding the dynamics of technological development."

Finally, Stern disparages the Atanasoff-Berry Computer by repeatedly referring to it as a "model" (or "only a model"), as "never completed," and as seemingly willfully "abandoned." There was, of course, a *model* built in 1939 to test out the basic electronic computing principles of the prospective machine, which was then built between 1940 and 1942. But the ABC itself was never meant to be a model, even though Atanasoff came to see that it could be the basis for a much more general electronic computer—long before he had finished building it, in fact, just as Eckert and Mauchly came to see that the ENIAC could be the basis for the EDVAC long before they had finished building it.

As to Atanasoff's "abandonment" of his computer, left behind, actually, with heavy heart in the interest of serving the war effort, Judge Larson dismissed this as irrelevant to the status of the ENIAC patent. He explained that ideas taken from an earlier device, "whether or not the device was subsequently abandoned . . . do not amount to invention" (Finding 12).[5]

And as to Stern's view that Atanasoff's computer was "never completed," Judge Larson's very finding that the ABC was an "automatic electronic digital computer" implies that he considered it completed. What is more important, though, for his finding of derivation, is the fact that completion in itself is not essential to invention; reduction to practice of novel concepts is.

Larson ruled, in Finding 3, that even for his 1939 model Atanasoff had "completed and reduced to practice his basic conception" of a computing machine. Still more tellingly, he ruled that it was from the ABC *as it existed in June 1941* that Mauchly derived the invention claimed in the ENIAC patent: not a finished machine, but one "sufficiently well advanced so that the principles of its operation, including detail design features," could be and were disclosed to and demonstrated for Mauchly. (See chap. 5.)

At one point in her second chapter, Stern herself acknowledges a significant degree of completion, as she quotes Brian Randell from p. 288 of his 1973 collection of papers: "The electronic part of the computer was operational . . . when in 1942 Atanasoff left Iowa State."[6] But she does not recognize that this was the crucial state of completion: that it was the machine's proven electronic computing principles that Mauchly appropriated for the ENIAC—and even more so for the EDVAC.

Indeed, this same reduction-to-practice argument applies to all of Stern's concerns about the final state of Atanasoff's computer, so far as the judge's finding of derivation goes. Regardless of its limitation as a special-purpose device, regardless of whether it was fully realized, regardless of its ultimate abandonment, Mauchly was able to observe the ABC in the "practice" of basic novel concepts that he then used in his own devices.

Stern seems to feel that patent law is too harsh, or too narrow—or that Judge Larson was. But the ENIAC patent would have survived the law—and the judge—in this regard if it had claimed only what was novel to the ENIAC.

Stern's central concern in presenting the Mauchly-Atanasoff controversy is, of course, the patent trial. Most striking is how very scant her depiction of that trial turns out to be, in terms of the relevant evidence it actually produced. As we saw earlier, she is highly selective with regard to Mauchly's correspondence. She omits a number of letters that are harmful to the case she is making, and she gives the impression that the single Mauchly letter she quotes was the only one of any significance.

Her presentation of Mauchly's courtroom testimony, on pages 37–38, is limited to two brief excerpts (both actually condensed from much longer passages). In one he admitted to Honeywell attorney Halladay that he had "always used prior art"; in the other he maintained, also to Halladay, that a computer with the ABC's purpose would represent "no advance really at all" unless its "cost, utility, availability" were taken into account. Stern cites the first excerpt to support her view of Mauchly as "the innovator" on the Eckert-Mauchly team, the second to note that "application, adaptation, and economics" are essential aspects of innovation.

Omitted are Mauchly's more damaging admissions concerning his achievements and his aspirations before his visit to Atanasoff, as, for example, his ultimate, heated protest that he "wasn't even thinking of inventing computing machines" when he set out for Iowa; and his concessions on what he learned while there, as that he was "perfectly convinced . . . that [Atanasoff's] add-subtract mechanism did in fact work" (see chap. 1).

Stern's assessment of Judge Larson's decision, "a major objective" of her book, misses the mark entirely. As we explained in chapter 5, the validity of the ENIAC patent rested broadly, but critically, on Sperry Rand's own representation that the invention claimed in the patent was "the invention of the Automatic Electronic Digital Computer": the subject matter of the ENIAC patent, as argued by Sperry Rand, *was* the electronic computer, the original, ground-breaking version. And the judge found, on the reams of evidence and testimony, first, that the ABC was a prior "automatic electronic digital computer," and, second, that the ENIAC was derived from it.

In her book, Stern quotes Larson's two similarly worded rulings on this derivation, in Findings 3 and 12, that "Eckert and Mauchly did not themselves first invent the automatic electronic digital computer" but derived that "subject matter" from Atanasoff. In each case, however, she omits his accompanying explanation that it was Sperry Rand's own position, in its counterclaim against Honeywell, that he was addressing.

All these errors of fact, of interpretation, and of omission in Stern's presentation of this controversy are both perplexing and disturbing. Perhaps the most disturbing aspect of all, however, is her failure to address the issue of ethics in building her case for innovation over invention.

One senses that Stern is highly conflicted, as she moves from accepting Mauchly's claim that he did not use Atanasoff's ideas to defending his role as the adapter of those ideas. But once having arrived at that point, she does not differentiate between the Atanasoff-to-Mauchly transfer, on the one hand, and the Mauchly-to-Eckert transfer (and collaboration), on the other, so long as the inventor-innovator roles served the "technological process."

She may feel that her final downgrading of priority as an overrated principle allows her to excuse Mauchly's use of Atanasoff's prior ideas. How, though, does she excuse his claiming those ideas—and their priority—for himself?

It hardly seems necessary to conclude that Nancy Stern fell far short of the broad scholarly goals—objectivity, factuality, and consistency—that she set herself for the presentation of this controversy. More specifically, her promised analysis and assessment of Judge Larson's verdict are limited to a very few charges that misconstrue either what he wrote or what his task was. And her promised consideration of the relationship between Mauchly and Atanasoff, meant to illuminate their exchange of ideas, is woefully inadequate, completely bypassing Atanasoff's 1940 write-up of the ABC, most of his correspondence with Mauchly, and his courtroom testimony and demonstrations.

Nevertheless, the publication of her book sealed Stern's reputation in the computing community as an expert on the *Honeywell v. Sperry Rand* case, as well as on the larger topic of the Eckert-Mauchly enterprises.

From ENIAC to UNIVAC received strong reviews in the *Annals of the History of Computing* and in *Science*. In the October 1981 issue of *Science*, Paul E. Ceruzzi, at that time a historian at Clemson University, picks up on Stern's inventor-innovator distinction, praising her for stressing "Eckert's and Mauchly's crucial importance as innovators—men who made the computer a commercial product," and for showing "how questions of marketing and funding were just as important as more technical matters in pointing the way toward the modern computer."[7]

He also credits her with taking care "to sort out and assess the controversies" over both the invention of the ENIAC and the origin of the stored-program concept. Here he writes:

> On these and other issues, Stern generally supports Eckert and Mauchly, but she is fair to all sides and always carefully documents her arguments. One wishes at times that questions like "Who really invented the computer?" were never asked, since they obviously admit of no simple answers, but since they have been brought up elsewhere Stern has no choice but to deal with them, and she does a good job. In particular, she has examined the suit filed by Honeywell, Inc., against Sperry Rand . . . , in which the question whether Eckert and Mauchly really were the inventors of the first electronic computer was put before a court of law. . . . [She] has made good use of the thousands of pages of transcripts from the trial . . . [to] shed much light on how the ENIAC came into being.

Strangely, Ceruzzi mentions Atanasoff as a primary figure in the controversy over the ENIAC but does not associate him with the court case. Nor does he disclose the outcome of that case. Clearly, I do not agree with this reviewer that Stern "does a good job" of dealing with the question of the invention of the computer, nor do I agree that she "has made good use" of the trial transcripts.

Ceruzzi concludes of Stern's book:

It deserves a wide readership, both among historians of science and technology and among computer professionals, for whom the breathtaking pace of innovation and impact of computing have overshadowed the remarkable personal story of its beginnings.

Annals editor Henry Tropp, in a July 1981 "Capsule Review" of Stern's book, lauds the breadth of her research and her "emphasis on people and environment, with the proper balance of technology"; he finds her final summary chapter "an incisive retrospective essay."[8] And he concludes:

> I strongly recommend the book to anyone interested in the origins of information processing. It should be required reading for students in courses on the history of computing or twentieth-century technology.

Then, in a full review in the January 1983 issue of *Annals*, Harvard historian of science I. Bernard Cohen also has high praise for this, "the first historical book [in the field] by a talented scholar of whom we shall be hearing more in the years to come."[9] Like Ceruzzi, he commends Stern's delineation of innovations that advance the existing technology, citing in particular her assertion that the verdict in the ENIAC patent case "failed to recognize a significant 'facet of the technological process.'"

He finds it a shortcoming, at least for his own purposes, that "there is almost no technical information concerning the design, operation, and actual use of the machines to which the book is devoted." Overall, however, he writes:

> *From ENIAC to UNIVAC* is, without question, a major addition to the literature of early computer history. It is a pioneering work, one that will serve for a long time as a model of careful research in a wide variety of primary sources.

It is interesting that both Ceruzzi and Cohen see Stern's treatment of the ENIAC trial as a desirable distancing of the work of the historian from that of the courts. Stern herself, as quoted in an earlier *Annals* item, had made this distinction still more explicitly:

> As for the Honeywell-Sperry verdict, the basis for a legal decision is not necessarily relevant or appropriate for historians, economists, sociologists, and others who assess technological development in different ways.[10]

In the past, Arthur and I have responded to this argument—as made by others, as well—by pointing out that while a court's judgment cannot be accepted blindly *the possibility that it is correct* must be entertained. Where large quantities of data are available, as through a trial, the researcher should make an independent study and reach an independent assessment of the case.

Although Stern claims to have done this for her book, her assessment is not only sparse but selectively biased against Atanasoff, as to both what he accomplished and what Mauchly learned from him. And, as we have noted, her conclusion overlooks both the ethical considerations and the rationale of patent law.

All three of these historians (Stern, Ceruzzi, and Cohen) are right, then, in asserting a distinction between legal and historical judgments. But all three are also bound by Stern's formulation—in her book—of this particular court's body of evidence, a formulation that is fraught with error.

The end result of this work by Stern, so far as the Atanasoff vs. Eckert-Mauchly dispute is concerned, is, of course, the discounting of both the ABC's priority and its influence on subsequent computers, together with the enhancing of the ENIAC's contribution. I would respond that, however important the ENIAC was as a great step forward in electronic technology and as itself a great invention, or even as a machine that launched a succession of great machines, the broad claims for it must stop there. The importance of the ENIAC can neither logically nor morally be used to deny the ABC its role as the true starting point for that succession of great electronic machines.

We should note in passing that Stern had taken a still bolder stance on Mauchly's early, independent progress toward an electronic computer in two *Annals* items published prior to her 1981 book. The first was an excerpt from the doctoral thesis on which that book was based; the second was a Mauchly obituary.[11] Whereas on the very first page of her book she qualifies her depiction of the ENIAC, calling it "the first fully operational large-scale electronic digital computer," in both earlier items she depicts it without qualification as "the first electronic digital computer." And she credits Mauchly with its conception long before the evidence allows.

In her thesis excerpt, Stern states: "The idea for this computer originated with John William Mauchly in the 1930s" and "By 1940 Mauchly had developed the idea for a totally new electronic digital computer which could operate with vacuum tubes." In her Mauchly obituary, she credits him both with conceiving the idea for the ENIAC and with envisioning "how it might be applied to problems in ballistics as well as meteorology [his focus in his Ursinus College years]." In neither case does she offer any specifics. And in both cases she completely bypasses Mauchly's 1940–1941 contacts with Atanasoff, moving directly from his Ursinus tenure to his enrollment in the Moore School's wartime training course in the summer of 1941, to his discussions with Eckert, and on to his 1942 memorandum and the early 1943 securing of the army contract for the ENIAC project.

Taken together, Stern's book and these two earlier works are of considerable historical significance. In fact, they constitute a meta-history of their own, in that Stern's arguments on this issue of the first electronic computer, as against the Court's arguments, have been put forth ever since by supporters of the Eckert-Mauchly side—with little discernible evidence of any independent examination of the trial records. (See Charles Call's comment, as quoted in chap. 6.)

<<<>>>

The ENIAC patent trial had ended on March 13, 1972, and Judge Larson had issued his decision on October 19, 1973. As we have noted, this momentous, unappealed decision from a U.S. District Court captured very little media attention and failed to sway a large portion of the computing community from its firm commitment to the Eckert-Mauchly formulation of the matter.

Over the nearly twenty-eight years from the dedication of the ENIAC to the verdict that invalidated its patent, the press version of the invention of the electronic computer is typified by a 1971 *New York Times* editorial. On this version, the ENIAC was the world's first electronic computer, its inventors were Eckert and Mauchly, and both of these facts were all but unknown to the general public.[12]

This *Times* editorial of August 9 was actually occasioned by the celebration of the 25th anniversary of the ENIAC in Chicago during the previous week. It begins with an eloquent lament that the celebration "was confined virtually entirely to the industry itself.

> President Nixon was not moved to declare a national holiday; no brass bands marched through the streets, and the average American citizen remained completely unaware of the anniversary.

It continues with the comment that the names of Eckert and Mauchly were "not likely ever to become household words," adding that there was "gross injustice in all this," since the computer was "certainly one of the most important inventions in all history." It cites space exploration, the issuance of paychecks and bills, nationwide reservation systems, even dating services, among the computer's conquests.

The editorial does address the great invention's "mixed blessings": "the wounds of unpleasant confrontation so many have experienced since this omnipresent tool entered their lives"! With references to depersonalization, loss of privacy, and commonly felt exasperation, it signs off on this cautionary note: "In short, as the computer begins its second quarter-century, many remain unsure whether this Janus machine will eventually prove more friend than foe."

This editorial was preceded by an article on the same topic in the Business/Finance section of the August 4 editorial.[13] The formal ENIAC celebration, a black-tie cocktail party and banquet held in Chicago's Museum of Science and Industry, had been sponsored by the Univac Division of Sperry Rand Corporation as the main event of a meeting of the Association for Computing Machinery, ACM '71. The author of this article, William D. Smith, chose, however, to focus on the "shirtsleeve self-criticism" voiced by speakers at an ACM seminar in the afternoon before the evening's events.

The complaints of these speakers at the twenty-five-year mark offer some perspective as we pass the fifty-year mark, as to how far we have yet to go and, perhaps more so, how far we have already come. They were enough to leave the moderator, Harvard's Anthony Oettinger, wondering at "the hair shirt being thrust upon the industry."

Smith relayed these "faults": "the computer had as yet failed to give companies a competitive edge in business," it "had done little to change management styles or reorganize corporate structures despite early predictions," and it "often had created restraints."

More broadly, Smith said, one speaker asserted that the computer was "neither as useful as some of its supporters had supposed nor anywhere near as harmful as its detractors would have people believe," and another objected that the emphasis had been on "advancement of the state of the art at all costs and change just for the sake of change."

Finally, there was a very specific gripe: "Why can't we just write English to get solutions out of problems? Why do we still need programmers?"

Of the banquet, Smith wrote:

> The black-tie dinner at the Museum of Science and Industry was given in honor of the pioneers of the computer industry, specifically Dr. J. Presper Eckert and Dr. John W. Mauchly, who invented the world's first electronic computer in 1946 at the Moore School of Electrical Engineering at the University of Pennsylvania.

Indeed, the event *was* billed as a celebration of the industry pioneers and, indeed, it *was* specifically directed to Eckert and Mauchly. Art was one of those in attendance at the banquet. He recalls being approached at the earlier cocktail party by IBM's Walter Carlson, president of the ACM, who said that he had tried to have Art and others recognized in the program, without success, but that in opening the celebration in his role as president he would ask all members of the ENIAC team to rise for applause. This he did, and there proved to be a goodly number present.

In that same year, Mauchly and Eckert's own story of the invention of "an electronic marvel which is having a revolutionary impact on the world" was published in the December issue of *Nation's Business*.[14] In his "The Little Known Creators of the Computer," written from personal interviews, John Costello calls the ENIAC "granddaddy of the electronic computers of today" and the "very first one." Although it was published in the seventh month of the ENIAC patent trial, shortly after Mauchly had testified, no mention was made of the trial or of Atanasoff.

As its title indicates, a major theme of this story is that "their accomplishment brought Mauchly and Eckert neither fame nor fortune." Mauchly is quoted as saying, "All told we each made about $200,000 to $250,000 out of our invention." Costello adds that neither man was in *Who's Who*, "an inexplicable omission," but here he is mistaken. Eckert was in *Who's Who in America* from 1956 through 1977, with the single exception of the 1968–69 volume; Mauchly, from 1960 to 1979, except for 1970–71 and 1972–73.

Another theme of Costello's story is that there was very little support for the ENIAC project in the scientific community, with even Enrico Fermi among the serious doubters. He closes his article with this dispirited—and dispiriting—exchange with Mauchly:

> Did they ever despair of success?
>
> "Well," Dr. Mauchly replies, "it was discouraging to find there was no great enthusiasm over the idea. There were all kinds of wet blankets thrown over it—lots of reasons advanced why it couldn't be done.
>
> "So these were discouraging. But, on the other hand, I didn't have any reason to think that life would be otherwise.
>
> "I hoped it would be—but I didn't have any real reason to think so."

Mauchly's appraisal here contrasts sharply with Art's and mine, as to both the atmosphere at the Moore School during the project and Mauchly's own state of mind at the time. We recall an air of excitement, of intense engagement, as the ENIAC was being designed and built, the EDVAC anticipated. We recall the surge of confidence in the summer of 1944, just one year into the project, when the two-accumulator model proved that the ENIAC system would work reliably at the intended rate of 100,000 pulses per second. And we recall Mauchly as one of the cheeriest, in his droll way, one of the most upbeat, members of the team. There were doubters, even within the school, but there was no hovering cloud of ridicule or disparagement or even discouragement to contend with as the work progressed smoothly and rapidly.

This *Nation's Business* article is actually the only one concerning the ENIAC or Eckert or Mauchly that I found through the *Reader's Guide to Periodical Literature* for the years 1971 to 1981, when both our *Annals* article on the ENIAC and Stern's book on the Eckert-Mauchly enterprises appeared. But while neither the twenty-fifth anniversary of the ENIAC nor the issuance of the trial verdict created much of a stir in the popular press during this decade, there was one trade magazine with broad appeal that did follow the court case, starting even before it was concluded.

In its June 1973 issue, *Datamation* ran an article by Richard A. McLaughlin, "ENIAC in Court: What Might Have Happened," that begins with a reference to Eckert and Mauchly as inventors of "the first electronic digital computer—the ENIAC—in 1946," but ends with the possibility that "other scientists and inventors—heretofore unheralded—will receive some of the credit for the invention of the computer."[15]

The author reports that Judge Larson in April 1973—six months prior to his official verdict and with no release of the trial proceedings—notified both sides in the suit of his forthcoming decision: first, in Honeywell's favor, to invalidate the ENIAC patent; and second, in Sperry Rand's favor, to award no antitrust damages. McLaughlin provides a summary of the issues, with the comment that had the decision been otherwise "the ramifications would have been virtually earth shattering for the industry."

> A decision that the ENIAC patent was valid, for instance, could have enabled Sperry Rand's Univac division to lay claim to patent infringements by scores— perhaps hundreds—of computer firms.

McLaughlin also provides a fairly detailed descriptive history of the ENIAC over its nine-year life at Aberdeen Proving Ground. And he finds it ironic that "the case presented to knock down the patent [for the first electronic digital computer] was prepared in large part by an electronic digital computer." This was, in fact, the first court case in which one side, Honeywell, made advantageous use of a computer to index its documents for immediate location (in filing cabinets, still).

Then, shortly after the decision was handed down, *Datamation* published two successive articles by W. David Gardner, in January and February 1974. The first, "How the Judge Looked at the IBM-Sperry Rand ENIAC Pact," concentrates on the antitrust issue, particularly on what Gardner calls Judge Larson's finding of "collusion between two industrial giants."[16] Here are his opening paragraphs:

> It's not so much that the computer business won't be the same after Federal District Court Judge Earl R. Larson took a long hard look at the industry, it's just that we didn't know what it was really like until he examined it.
>
> The judge found a big surprise: IBM and Sperry Rand, two companies which between them controlled 95 percent of the edp [electronic data processing] industry in 1956, entered into a secret "technological merger" that year. The impact on the remainder of the then-emerging edp industry was "stifling," the judge has stated in a virtually unnoticed case he completed last year.

Gardner writes that although Larson found Honeywell damaged by up to $575 million in the years 1958 to 1967, when it filed its suit against Sperry Rand, he did not award those damages. Gardner explains that even though "the details of the agreement [to share computer know-how] were so carefully guarded that it would have been virtually impossible" for competitors to learn them, the judge ruled that Honeywell and other affected newcomers to the market should have sued Sperry Rand and IBM at the time (see chap. 5). "Honeywell did collect a $3 million settlement from Sperry Rand for unspecified reasons," Gardner adds.

The author traces Judge Larson's journey "through an amazingly tangled trail" of conspiracy and intrigue by the two parties, who pressed on to this cross-licensing agreement despite the warnings of their own attorneys—but somehow with the acquiescence of the Justice Department, which agreed to keep the matter confidential. He spells out the details of the deal and the judge's scathing denunciation of both firms for failing to offer equal access to the competition.

Gardner notes that the 1956 "merger" included the payment of $10 million by IBM to Sperry Rand to dismiss an antitrust suit against IBM. It was from this sum that Eckert and Mauchly received the disappointingly small half-million or so that Mauchly mentioned to *Nation's Business* interviewer Costello.

A decade later Pamela L. Eblen quoted Pres Eckert in the Autumn 1984 issue of *ICP Data Processing Management* as to why his side had not appealed the ENIAC patent trial decision:

> . . . there was a nutty judge who threatened to turn the whole thing into an antitrust case against Sperry and we didn't want to get into that. It had nothing to do with the case.[17]

In fact, it was a major component of the case. Honeywell's original reason to sue was Sperry's demand for excessive royalties. Its investigations revealed not only that the ENIAC had been derived from Atanasoff's earlier electronic computer, but also that Sperry had formed a secret liaison with IBM in an effort to monopolize the industry. Sperry, having already been found in violation of the Sherman Antitrust Act, could not risk the possibility that a higher court might assess damages as well. It would seem that the settlement Sperry made on Honeywell was to forestall *its* appealing on this count.

Gardner's second *Datamation* article, "Will the Inventor of the First Digital Computer Please Stand Up?" begins with the decision's *Eckert and Mauchly did not themselves first invent the automatic electronic digital computer, but instead derived that subject matter from one Dr. John Vincent Atanasoff.*[18] He then declares:

> With those words, Judge Larson defrocked Dr. J. Presper Eckert and Dr. John W. Mauchly as the high priests of electronic digital computer invention and, at the same time, proclaimed a new Alexander Graham Bell of the industry: "One Dr. John Vincent Atanasoff."

He continues:

> The Minnesota judge ruled that Sperry's ENIAC patent was invalid, largely because the basic ideas embodied in the ENIAC were derived from Atanasoff's machine.

Gardner says Mauchly "was amazed that the judge did not uphold the ENIAC patent" and quotes Mauchly's reference to Atanasoff's computer as a "little gismo" that was "not automatic."

Gardner now traces the history of the ABC, quoting from a recent interview of its inventor to explain its novelty and its concepts. Concerning the successful completion of his 1939 model, Atanasoff spoke of his vision for the future of electronic computing:

> ... when I looked at that little breadboard model—it fit on a desk—I realized I could compute Pi to a thousand places easily enough.

Gardner goes on to tell of the first meeting between Atanasoff and Mauchly in December 1940, of Mauchly's letters of inquiry before his June 1941 visit to Iowa, and of the visit itself. He quotes Larson's rulings on what Mauchly learned from Atanasoff as contrasted with what he had accomplished at Ursinus College: Mauchly had not "conceived an automatic electronic digital computer" by the time of his visit to Iowa, and while there he "derived from the ABC the invention of the automatic electronic digital computer claimed in the ENIAC patent." Gardner also quotes Mauchly's September 1941 letter asking permission to incorporate some of Atanasoff's ideas in a computer he might build at the Moore School.

He tells of the other counts on which Judge Larson ruled the ENIAC patent invalid, there explaining how the commercial interests of Eckert and Mauchly conflicted with those of the University of Pennsylvania. He quotes Larson's ruling in Finding 1 that the two men pressured Penn to give them the patent rights it wished to claim for itself as their employer:

> Facing the fact that it would require the cooperation of Eckert and Mauchly to fulfill its contractual obligations to the U.S. Government, the University yielded the commercial rights to any patents they might obtain based on the work of the contract.[19]

The university had contracted to grant the government a royalty-free license under the ENIAC patent, but because it had no patent agreement with the actual inventors its ownership of the patent was unclear.

The author tells of Penn's unhappiness with this outcome and of its ultimatum to Mauchly and Eckert that led to their leaving the Moore School in March 1946, the month after the ENIAC was dedicated (see chap. 5). Some writers are of the impression that they were asked to sign away rights to their earlier inventions for the EDVAC, and even for the ENIAC, in order to stay at Penn; in fact, they were to retain rights for "all work" up until March 31, and even beyond for any further work on the ENIAC.[20]

In this article, Gardner also has a "boxed" profile of Atanasoff that reveals the more human aspects of his makeup. He cites as "indicative of the way Atanasoff's inventive mind works" the story of how he experienced his breakthrough into electronic computing in an Illinois roadhouse after taking to the highway to relieve his mounting frustration (see chap. 3). Atanasoff told Gardner:

I have always filled myself up with a subject until I've exhausted everything I can get. And then I worry and worry and worry. These things just torment me. Then, one day, I get an idea.

Gardner finds Atanasoff, at age seventy, "vigorous and intellectually dynamic," and possessed of "a remarkably clear memory." He writes of Atanasoff's high praise for Clifford Berry as "an extraordinarily able man as well as a good friend," and of his "suspicions that Berry may not have committed suicide," but rather came to a "foul end." He tells of Atanasoff's adaptability, as he moved from science into business in 1952: "When he started his firm he allowed himself three days to study accounting and three weeks to study corporate law," and then he drew up his own corporate papers.

And he writes of Atanasoff's feelings about Mauchly:

In spite of the fact that Atanasoff made no money from his computer inventions and that Eckert and Mauchly were enriched by the ENIAC patent, which Judge Earl Larson has decreed to be invalid and derived from Atanasoff's work, Atanasoff holds no ill will against anybody in the whole matter. "John Mauchly and I are still pretty good friends," says Atanasoff.

Gardner adds that Mauchly, too, has said that a recent meeting with Atanasoff was "affable."

There followed in the aftermath of the ENIAC trial two scholarly books that recognized Atanasoff's role in this story, the first by an economist, the second by a computer scientist. Both provide considerable historical background, including the trial and its verdict, and both also conclude that had the ENIAC patent not been overturned it would have had profound and far-reaching consequences for the industry.

In his book, *The U.S. Computer Industry*, University of Arizona economist Gerald W. Brock focuses primarily on the corporate struggles for commercial advantage.[21] Terming Atanasoff's commercial influence "indirect," he describes Mauchly's Iowa visit and his "detailed" exposure to the ABC, and he quotes, on page 10, from Mauchly's September 1941 letter of inquiry to Atanasoff. From there, he moves on to the Eckert-Mauchly design of the ENIAC and their ensuing commercial pursuits. On page 64, Brock calls the ENIAC patent the "most important patent in the industry," which, if its broad claims had endured, would have covered "most general purpose computers" built thereafter.

University of Illinois computer scientist David J. Kuck, in his 1978 book, *The Structure of Computers and Computations,* volume 1, writes on pages 60–61:

Four men ushered in the modern digital computer era in the 1930s. They were Howard H. Aiken of Harvard University, John V. Atanasoff of Iowa State College (now University), George R. Stibitz of Bell Telephone Laboratories, and Konrad Zuse of the Technische Hochschule in Berlin. Aiken, Stibitz, and Zuse designed and built a number of relay machines and by the 1940s, each had completed a general-purpose programmable digital computer. They all apparently worked independently of one another, although Aiken used the engineering talent of IBM to build his machine [the Mark I]. . . . Atanasoff began work on digital electronic circuits in the late 1930s and by 1939 had produced a breadboard model of a special-purpose digital computer.[22]

He comments that Atanasoff's "role as a computer pioneer was all but lost in the shadows of [Aiken, Stibitz, and Zuse] and the ENIAC designers at the University of Pennsylvania (the group traditionally credited with the building of the first electronic computer)." He adds that that group's computer "was more successful than Atanasoff's, but they owed a direct debt to him," and he notes of the trial verdict that "the legal and financial implications that would have followed a reverse decision are interesting to contemplate!"

The year 1980 saw a further spate of *Datamation* articles occasioned both by Mauchly's death and by an honor conferred on Atanasoff in the name of "righting a wrong." The March issue ran four tributes to Mauchly, under the caption, "In the Beginning, there was Mauchly." The first of these, "He was an Idea Sparker," by Becky Barna, terms him "coinventor of the world's first electronic digital computer."[23] The second *Datamation* tribute, "Mauchly was His Own Man," by Anne Dewees, associate editor of *Sperry Univac News*, very briefly traces Mauchly's life goals and successes from his—and Sperry's—perspective.[24] She differentiates the contributions of Eckert and Mauchly to the ENIAC: Mauchly provides "the theory, the specifications on what their creation would do, and how it would work from the user's point of view"; Eckert is "the specialist in building a reliable machine to do the job."

The third tribute, "Interview with John Mauchly," also by Dewees, quotes from "perhaps [his] last formal interview" in late 1979.[25] Mauchly, an inveterate punster, owns that "a pun is the highest form of humor"—"almost a mathematical kind of humor as opposed to situation humor." He ventures that he had been happiest as a teacher—"leaving out how much money you need to live on."

Mauchly explains his weather prediction theories to Dewees and his impatience with "what the weather bureau is still doing"—making more and more observations of "smaller and smaller pieces of the earth." Here, though, he is concerned not with the effect of *solar* activity on our rainfall, as in his trial testimony, but with that of *lunar* activity. He says:

What I wanted to do was take a larger view, standing off from the earth . . . and asking what's happening on the large scale. That enabled me in 1952 to prove (I proved it to myself) that the moon does affect our weather, whereas the meteorologists thought they'd proved the opposite.

He goes on to say that a 1963 investigation showed he was right, but that meteorologists still do not use this fact because "they don't know why it happens."

Mauchly takes in stride the question "What are the difficulties in raising a family of seven and being a creative genius?" He responds that he has been "ultrapermissive . . . , trying not to swamp my family with my problems and my job," and that the result has been a diversity of interests.

He makes two other points. He believes history will change its view of him and Eckert for the better: "It will gradually lose its emphasis on thinking that big mathematicians or logicians were the people who played the important part." This seems to be a reference to the widespread view of von Neumann as chief inventor of the stored-program computer.

And, contrary to Stern, when asked to name his "biggest deficiency," Mauchly responds, "I'm not a good salesman"! He calls the selling of the ENIAC to Army Ordnance "a purely fortuitous thing" owing to the war and his luck in being in "the right place at the right time." He concludes: "It's a big game of chance. That time I happened to win, and the world happened to win."

Datamation's fourth tribute to Mauchly, "A Man Not Bound by Tradition," is an excerpt of Eckert's eulogy at the funeral service.[26] Deeming his association with Mauchly "the high point of my entire life, professionally speaking," Eckert says that it was Mauchly's freedom from inhibitions, his ability to see things as they really were, that lay at the heart of his ability to invent; and that Mauchly imparted this spirit to those around him, enabling them also "to break with tradition and to advance tradition, rather than to be held back by tradition."

Datamation's pendulum swung back to Atanasoff with an article by Linda F. Runyan, "A Master of Understatement," in the May issue.[27] The master understater was, in the author's view, the "self-effacing, low-key" Atanasoff, speaking at an Interface '80 conference luncheon hosted in his honor by DPF Inc. of Hartsdale, New York. This tribute was aimed at "giving the inventor long-overdue recognition" as creator of the first electronic computer. Runyan writes:

Atanasoff himself doesn't seem at all bothered or bitter about the past—a past which saw the plaudits going to Dr. J. Presper Eckert and Dr. John W. Mauchly of ENIAC and UNIVAC I fame.

She adds that Atanasoff made only passing mention of the lawsuit that established him and Berry as the original inventors, proceeding rather to retrace his steps to the 1942 machine. She does report on the case and on Mauchly's familiarity with Atanasoff's work prior to the building of the ENIAC. And she describes the ABC and its novel features. In closing, she points to Atanasoff's pride of achievement despite his inclination to understate:

> In an oblique reference to Mauchly and Eckert, he boldly proclaims of his and Berry's work: "We did it. And after that, it's easier for the next man who comes along."

Datamation had also carried a letter in June 1980 arguing against Mauchly's lunar theory. Alan J. Robinson tells of his own investigation in the mid-1960s of "someone's" claim that rainfall varied with the phases of the moon.[28] He explains:

> The problem is that the phases of the moon do not correspond to equal intervals of time, owing to perturbations in the moon's orbit. In particular, there is one perturbation, discovered by Ptolemy, whose period is exactly one-half the fundamental period of 28 days, so that averaging over a number of periods, the various phases of the moon will not be of equal duration.

Robinson adds a comment on the lack of support in the scientific community for Mauchly's theory that the moon affects the Earth's weather.

Datamation followed in September 1982 with a third article by Gardner on Atanasoff. In "The Independent Inventor," he tells of a man "so stubborn that some who knew him thought him downright bullheaded."[29] His theme is that "John V. Atanasoff, creator of the automatic digital computer, did it his own way." He recounts the inventor's frustrations, both in securing industry support and in securing a patent for his machine. And he describes his level-headed, almost sanguine performance before, during, and after the trial.

Gardner offers this overall assessment:

> His thinking on the logic structure and architecture of computing machines was years ahead of his time. But he was years advanced on the practical side, too; while the lords of the calculating and tabulating field in industry and academia would remain convinced for years that electronic components were unreliable, Atanasoff challenged that rigid gospel from the start. Thus, the importance of Atanasoff's work was in his unique blend of mathematician and theoretical physicist on his abstract side and laboratory and machine shop handyman on his practical side.

Finally, one other piece portraying Atanasoff favorably in this period came from a less likely source, *Car and Driver* magazine. In its June 1984 issue, writer Patrick Bedard zeroes in on "The Midnight Ride of John Vincent Atanasoff" with the comment that "if John Vincent Atanasoff had had to take a horse for his flight across Iowa in the winter of 1937, we might still be living in the abacus age"!³⁰ Bedard recounts the history of the ABC accurately, together with Atanasoff's story of that drive to the Illinois "honky-tonk" where all the ideas he had been struggling with fell into place.

Of Atanasoff's recognition in court and lack of recognition in the media, he writes:

> John Vincent Atanasoff, as everyone knows (you didn't?), is the guy who invented the electronic digital computer. This was officially decided in federal court after a few years of corporate wrangling and announced on October 19, 1973. Atanasoff didn't get nearly the credit due him because the decision was issued just one day before the Watergate-inspired "Saturday Night Massacre" and it lacked the combination of inconsequentiality and putrescence necessary to compete for media attention.

This author is naturally almost as interested in overcoming the obscurity of "the role of the automobile in the computer's inception" as he is in overcoming the obscurity of the man behind that inception. He quotes Atanasoff's recollection of the car he drove to Illinois, "a Ford V-8, 'a full-powered Ford,' as he says, 'not the V-8 60,'" with "a Southwind gasoline heater made by Stewart-Warner." He tells of Atanasoff's learning to drive at age eleven, in a 1914 Model-T that his father had bought new for $614. And he concludes with the observation that today it would be illegal for "our computer inventor" to drive 190 miles at a speed of 80 or 90 miles an hour late at night in order to get his mind off "'that damn computer'" so that he could invent it over a drink or two.

Patrick Bedard's cynical remark on the story's lack of "inconsequentiality and putrescence" aside, it remains a mystery why the decision in the ENIAC trial was accorded such meager public notice. In our book, *The First Electronic Computer: The Atanasoff Story*, Art and I do embrace the Watergate explanation set forth by Bedard and others. On page 195, we write:

> It is a historical quirk that news of the decision on the invention of the electronic computer received very little media attention because it came at the height of the Watergate scandal. October 19, 1973, was just nine days after the resignation of Vice-President Agnew, and just one day before the so-called Saturday night massacre that saw the departures from the Nixon administration of Archibald Cox, Elliot Richardson, and William D. Ruckelshaus.³¹

A recent search through the *New York Times*, *Newsweek*, and *Time*, however, has led me to temper this view. It is true that for the balance of 1973, pages and pages were devoted to Watergate and to the Middle Eastern war going on then as well. But there was still plenty of space for stories on other court cases, on computers and electronics, and even on other news from Minneapolis (the mayoral race).

A partial answer seems to be that the media had not been following this particular case—*Reader's Guide* lists many articles on other cases, especially
antitrust suits against IBM, from 1972 to 1982. The question then is: Why had
they *not* been following it?

A further partial answer is that the decision, for the most part, maintained the
status quo. But, again, no one could have foreseen that outcome, and a different
one would have turned the whole industry on its head. There was, at the least,
cause for celebration by all the companies that would have had to pay royalties
to Sperry Rand had it won. And Sperry, even as it grieved its loss of those royalties, could still celebrate its escape from antitrust damages arising from its cross-
licensing deal with IBM,.

Only IBM was left with little to celebrate—other than not having been on
trial itself for antitrust in this instance, since its offense was found to be much
greater than Sperry's. Indeed, IBM's market position would have been *stronger*
had the ENIAC patent been upheld, because its competitors would be paying
Sperry royalties and it would not, by virtue of its deal with Sperry.

As for the computing community, it reacted for the most part as blithely as
Mauchly did in his "Fireside Chat" in Italy, with nary a murmur about the outcome of this historic case.

We can conclude, I believe, that while "fortune" for the invention of the ENIAC
did elude Mauchly and Eckert, "fame" did not if we distinguish the general public
from the smaller yet still large computing community. The 1971 *Times* editorial
was right, Eckert and Mauchly were not to become household names, although
their UNIVAC had already come close, and the ENIAC has, too, after many years
of sporadic mention. But to the computing community Eckert and Mauchly
became heroes: the "high priests" of the invention of the electronic computer, as
Gardner put it in 1974, immediately after the ENIAC trial—though not so readily
"defrocked" by the court ruling as Gardner expected.

By the end of the 1970s, and with the death of John Mauchly in early 1980,
this heroism was to become emotionally charged. Virginia Walker, for example,
in an article in the April 1981 *Annals*, reports on the ACM '80 meeting in
Nashville the previous October:

> Notable among these sessions was the Special Awards Luncheon honoring J.
> Presper Eckert, Jr., and the late John W. Mauchly for "extending the frontiers of
> technology for the good of mankind by designing and building the first electron-
> ic computer, ENIAC, in 1945, and the first commercial electronic computer,
> UNIVAC, in 1951." In honor of the occasion a bronze medallion, struck from
> photographs of Eckert and Mauchly, was given to all conference registrants,
> courtesy of Sperry Univac.[32]

She continues:

> The banquet room was filled with emotion as W. Buell Evans, conference awards chairman, presented Mauchly's award to his wife, Kay Mauchly, a computer pioneer in her own right [as a programmer of the ENIAC].

To the credit of the *Annals*, it also ran—in this same April 1981 issue—a story of a contrasting hue: James Rogers's report on Atanasoff's November 11, 1980, lecture at the Digital Computer Museum (later renamed the Computer Museum).[33] Rogers remarks on "Atanasoff's steadfast conviction that he, in fact, invented the first electronic computer," yet detects "no hint of rancor or ill will toward anyone [he] might feel had unduly profited from his invention."

The author concludes with a comment on the irony of Atanasoff's situation:

> The overall tone of Atanasoff's presentation was that of good-humored exuberance. The only departure from this tone occurred near the end of his talk, when Atanasoff mentioned the fact that the People's Republic of Bulgaria, in recognition of his invention, presented him with that nation's highest award for scientific achievement, during a visit to his ancestral homeland in 1970. Atanasoff described these events with very obvious pride, but some listeners detected a note of sadness. They wondered if Atanasoff finds it ironic that he had to leave the United States and travel over 5000 miles in order to receive some official recognition of his achievement.

Before leaving this period—the 1970s and early 1980s—I want to acknowledge two books that have enjoyed a wide readership and that have been invaluable for addressing the issues of concern to us here. Both are edited collections of papers in the history.

In *The Origins of Digital Computers: Selected Papers*, Brian Randell runs the full gamut of mechanical, electrical, electromechanical, and electronic digital devices, from analytical engines through the first stored-program computers.[34] Here are published for the first time both Atanasoff's 1940 exposition of his computer-in-progress and Mauchly's 1942 proposal for an electronic version of the differential analyzer. These are followed by a paper on the ENIAC by Herman Goldstine and his wife Adele.[35]

In the stored-program category are excerpts from "First Draft of a Report on the EDVAC" and from *Preliminary Discussion of the Logical Design of an Electronic Computing Instrument*, on which the Institute for Advanced Study Computer was based.[36] Also reprinted in this collection is a 1947 Mauchly paper, "Preparation of Problems for EDVAC-type Machines," in which he takes a stance similar to that of his 1946 lectures at the Moore School.[37]

Editor Brian Randell, professor of computing science at the University of

Newcastle upon Tyne, introduces each of his eight sets of essays with his own insightful survey of the events they portray. And, to top off this most valuable contribution to the literature, he provides a large bibliography that includes brief notes on all its entries. He extended this listing, which ran from 1785 to 1972 in the book, on through June 1979 for publication in the October 1979 issue of the *Annals of the History of Computing*.[38]

The second book I want to acknowledge is a collection of papers the original versions of which were presented at the International Research Conference on the History of Computing, at the Los Alamos Scientific Research Laboratory in June 1976. Titled *A History of Computing in the Twentieth Century*, it is edited by Nicholas Metropolis, Jack Howlett, and Gian-Carlo Rota.[39]

Major funding for the conference—and for the book—came from the National Science Foundation, through the good offices of John R. Pasta, who wished to preserve firsthand accounts of the history (till about 1960, actually) by participants and other witnesses while those accounts were still available. The papers describe developments in the United States, Britain, Germany, Austria, Holland, Czechoslovakia, the USSR, and Japan in university-, industry-, and government-sponsored projects.

There are papers on the history of the ENIAC by John Mauchly, Pres Eckert (as read by Mauchly at the conference in Eckert's absence), and Arthur Burks, though each goes beyond that machine to the ensuing stored-program machines. Eckert's and Mauchly's are both titled simply "The ENIAC." In chapter 5, we looked at Eckert's rather expansive treatment of his differences with von Neumann over the stored-program concept, as he claims not only the idea of storing problem instructions internally, but the further idea of having these instructions modified from within during the course of solution.[40] We also cited Mauchly's quite amazing claim that the *ENIAC* also had this latter facility, despite its preset, read-only program.[41]

Eckert does not mention Atanasoff in his Los Alamos paper, but Mauchly takes on both Atanasoff and Judge Larson—again, in amazing fashion. He tells of experimenting with digital circuits at Ursinus College and adds:

> All of this predates a visit I made to Ames, Iowa, where I found it impossible to persuade Dr. Atanasoff that his projected machine did not realize the potential speeds of electronic calculation that I had in mind.

And, later:

> It is unfortunate that the ABC machine was not completed, and that Atanasoff never gave the patent attorneys the information that they requested so that a patent application could be filed. When I joined the Moore School in 1941, I wrote to him suggesting that he might join us and possibly have a better chance of developing his ideas, but he chose not to do this.

Mauchly is here construing as an invitation to the Moore School his September 30, 1941, letter to Atanasoff asking permission to use his ideas at the Moore School! Atanasoff's response of October 7 certainly gave no hint that he took it as such. (See chap. 2.)

Of the ENIAC trial outcome, Mauchly writes:

> Because I visited J.V. Atanasoff for just two or three days in 1941, the 1974 [*sic*] decision of Judge Larsen [*sic*] was that I had derived all my notions about building electronic computers from Atanasoff.

Hardly what the judge said.

Art's paper, "From ENIAC to the Stored-Program Computer: Two Revolutions in Computers," addresses both the ENIAC's antecedents and its successors.[42] He begins by delineating the "two revolutions":

> The first was the employment of vacuum tubes to make a fast, reliable, powerful, general-purpose computer. This development began with John Atanasoff's slow, special-purpose electronic computer. It culminated in ENIAC, . . . developed, designed, and built by a group of engineers, including myself, under the direction of Pres Eckert and John Mauchly. ENIAC was revolutionary: it was the first electronic, digital, general-purpose, scientific computer, and it computed 1,000 times as fast as its electromechanical competitors.
>
> The second revolution was the stored-program computer. It too had important antecedents, which I shall explain in due course. There were two main steps. Pres and John invented the circulating mercury delay line store, with enough capacity to store program information as well as data. Von Neumann created the first modern order code and worked out the logical design of an electronic computer to execute it.

Art explains the ENIAC's roots in mechanical and electromechanical computing, with many of its electronic circuits modeled on counterparts in both of these earlier technologies and with its architecture modeled on the mechanical differential analyzer. He tells of Atanasoff's pioneering in the use of vacuum-tube circuits for computing at a time when vacuum tubes were still used mainly in analog, or continuous, fashion. He describes the ABC briefly and notes that in the spring of 1941 Atanasoff conveyed to Mauchly his idea for a digital electronic version of the differential analyzer. He moves on to a quite detailed description of the ENIAC—actually the heart of the paper—and concludes with its stored-program aftermath, the EDVAC and the Institute for Advanced Study Computer and the many "copies" those two machines inspired. The article encompasses a large number of individual inventors and individual devices contributing to the two "revolutions."

To the best of my knowledge, this paper of Art's is the first after the ENIAC patent trial to cite Atanasoff's contributions, both of a special-purpose electronic computer and of the concept of its adaptation for broader application. I believe it is also the first paper not only to sort out the two stages of the invention of the stored-program computer but to argue for the attribution of the first stage to Eckert and Mauchly, the second to von Neumann.

This Los Alamos paper, delivered in 1976 and published in 1980, marks the beginning of considerable negative speculation as to Art's motivation in advocating for Atanasoff's—and Judge Larson's—side of the dispute over the invention of the electronic computer. Such speculation, together with the honest concerns it raised, gained momentum with the publication of the joint article by Art and me in the 1981 *Annals*, and further intensified with the 1988 publication of our joint book. It seems appropriate, then, to close the present chapter with a clarification of this bit of the history.

Judge Larson's full decision became available to the general public with the issuance of the March 25, 1974, *U.S. Patent Quarterly*.[43] Here the 420-page courtroom typescript was reduced to 100 two-column journal pages.

Art began immediately to study it, not just for its treatment of Atanasoff but for its treatment of himself and two of his fellow ENIAC designers, T. Kite Sharpless and Robert F. Shaw. Indeed, it had been through the interest of this trio in the patent case that Art had learned of Atanasoff's role. Shortly after the ENIAC patent was issued in early 1964, a New York attorney named Seymour Yuter had contacted him with startling news: in his opinion, Art could legitimately claim coinvention of the ENIAC, along with Pres Eckert and John Mauchly, as also could Bob Shaw and Kite Sharpless, clients of Sy Yuter's in connection with their more recent inventions.

This patent attorney explained that the original designs the three had contributed constituted invention. Moreover, if their names could be attached to the ENIAC patent, they, too, could sell licenses for its use. They could, as patentees, undercut the excessive royalty demands being made by Sperry Rand. Sy wanted Art to join Bob and Kite in claiming coinvention. He would then try to persuade computer companies to take licenses from these three coinventors, for a fair royalty rate, *but at the same time* to agree to carry the burden of any lawsuit by Sperry Rand.

In particular, Sy had learned that Honeywell, which Sperry had selected as its "target" corporation, was resisting the high royalty demands and was weighing its legal options. So he invited several attorneys from the Honeywell side to meet with him and Art at his home, and he suggested to them that their best strategy would be to take a license from his three clients and risk having to defend their claims to coinvention. The Honeywell attorneys, however, had a different strategy in mind!

To Art, the idea that he was a coinventor of the ENIAC had come as a surprise; he had always believed that Mauchly and Eckert, as originators of the initial broad concept, were the computer's sole inventors. But it came as more shock than surprise to hear the Honeywell lawyers say that they had learned of a man outside the ENIAC team who had invented a prior electronic computer, a man whose novel ideas had been misappropriated by Mauchly and Eckert for the ENIAC. On this basis, these lawyers said, they hoped to break the ENIAC patent rather than add new names to it.

Art did recognize the name John Atanasoff. He remembered that, as the ENIAC project was getting started in 1943, Mauchly had mentioned seeing Atanasoff's machine two years earlier, and that although Mauchly had alluded to vacuum tubes he had focused on the slow rotating memory. The overall impression had been dismissive.

Sy wanted to proceed with his approach and Art agreed to help, despite some misgivings. Many hours of work would be required: reviewing old records, studying the ENIAC patent, recalling who had done what, writing reports. Bob Shaw lived on Long Island and was available for discussions, but Kite Sharpless, in Haverford, Pennsylvania, was too ill to participate much beyond agreeing to Sy's plan. And while the rewards for success would be great, Art felt the chances were rather slim.

Of course, his skepticism was compounded by the entrance of Atanasoff into the picture. For, if Honeywell could have the ENIAC patent invalidated because of a prior inventor's work, the market value of coinvention would be nil.

Art drew up two reports, dated August 11 and November 27, 1964, respectively, and Bob drew up one dated October 31, 1964. These together spelled out their contributions—and Kite's—to the ENIAC on the basis of their study of the patent claims and with Sy's definition of "joint inventor" in mind. Art remembers poring over a copy of this inch-thick patent in a hotel room in Istanbul that August, en route from his brother's home in Munich to a conference in Israel.

On February 1, 1972, as the ENIAC trial was winding down, Sy filed a large bundle of documents with Judge Larson, asking him to order the commissioner of patents "to issue a certificate adding as a joint inventor, at least Professor Burks, and also Sharpless and Shaw, so that the ENIAC patent will not be invalid because of nonjoinder." He had been unsuccessful in selling licenses for the patent up to this point, and so, with the courtroom phase of the ENIAC trial ending, he decided to file amicus curiae papers in that case. Meanwhile, Kite had died of his illness, and Bob had also died as the result of an auto accident. (Their estates, of course, would have benefited from a favorable response by the judge.)

We have seen that Judge Larson addressed this issue in Finding 4, acknowledging "inventive contributions" by these three and others on the Moore School team, but declining to find coinvention because Honeywell had failed to establish it "on a claim-by-claim basis"—something Honeywell had no real interest in doing (see chap. 5). Larson ruled further that none of these others had "identified or asserted any inventive contribution to the inventive subject matter claimed in the ENIAC patent [for] some twenty years," so that their "assertions are not sustainable." As we have also seen, this issue became moot with the invalidation of the ENIAC patent.

It has been suggested that Art agrees with every one of Judge Larson's rulings, except, *of course*, the one against himself. The truth is that he was pleased with Larson's confirmation of his "inventive" role in the design of the ENIAC, and he could accept the finding that his petition was too late.

It has also been suggested that Art supports Atanasoff's claim to invention of the electronic computer because of disappointment over his own lack of recognition by Eckert and Mauchly. Nancy Stern, for example, in an article in the Fall 1983 edition of the new magazine *Abacus*, reformulates her book's arguments on the Atanasoff-Mauchly controversy and takes on Art as a major Atanasoff proponent.[44] She finds that "Burks ignores the facts"—her facts, not the judge's—as to the ABC's final state and its influence on Mauchly. Offering her own (undocumented) assessment that there is "some tangible evidence that Mauchly did, indeed, conceive of an electronic digital computer prior to his meeting with Atanasoff," she remarks:

> In fairness to the Mauchlys, however, it should be noted that Arthur Burks has always believed that he did not receive appropriate credit for his own contributions; and it is possible that this opinion has clouded his perception of Mauchly and prodded the attempt to discredit him.

The truth is that Art has promoted Atanasoff's cause because he believes in it, not for want of personal recognition; indeed, people have been perplexed when we have confirmed Art's work on the ENIAC but added that it was not, however, the first electronic computer—there was this man in Iowa!

Finally, it has been suggested that Art owed some allegiance to Honeywell in its suit against Sperry Rand. One reviewer of our book on Atanasoff, very favorable overall, cautions that "a strong economic motivation taints ever so slightly Burks's role in telling the story," that "while he worked with Eckert and Mauchly to build the ENIAC, he had no qualms about encouraging his later employer, Honeywell, to challenge his old comrades' patent claims."[45]

Art was never an employee of Honeywell. He had no economic interest in its winning the lawsuit. He was happy for Atanasoff, he felt Mauchly and Eckert got their due—and were lucky to escape a finding of fraud before the Patent Office—and he thought Larson was wise to balance the outcomes for both Honeywell and Sperry Rand so as to forestall any appeal.

This notion that Art was in Honeywell's employ may have arisen from the fact that, prior to the trial's commencement in 1971, he had consulted for parties to the ENIAC patent controversy, including both Honeywell and Sperry Rand

(and also IBM). In each case, he provided information about the ENIAC project: the machine's stages of completion in the months leading up to its February 1946 dedication, for example. At no time was he under any pressure—or "economic motivation"—to tell anything but the truth.

John V. Atanasoff, in 1925, upon graduation from the University of Florida.
Courtesy of Alice C. Atanasoff.

John V. Atanasoff at Iowa State College in 1939, the year his computer model was built. Courtesy of Alice C. Atanasoff.

Clifford E. Berry at Iowa State College in 1942, upon completion of the Atanasoff-Berry Computer.

John W. Mauchly, principal consultant on the Moore School's ENIAC project, in 1946, the year the ENIAC was dedicated and the Eckert-Mauchly Computing Corporation was formed. Sketch done by artist David Oliver.

J. Presper Eckert, chief engineer on the ENIAC project, in 1946, the year the computer was dedicated and the Eckert-Mauchly Computing Corporation was formed. Sketch done by artist David Oliver.

Arthur W. Burks, a principal designer of the ENIAC, in 1946, when the computer was dedicated and he left the Moore School to join von Neumann at the Institute for Advanced Study. Courtesy of Arthur W. Burks.

T. Kite Sharpless, a principal designer of the ENIAC and briefly head of the EDVAC project, in 1948 in his office at the newly formed Technitrol Company. Courtesy of Thomas K. Sharpless.

EIGHT

LINES IN THE SAND

B ernie Galler, who served as editor in chief of the *Annals of the History of Computing* until 1987, told us recently that our 1981 article, "The ENIAC: First General-Purpose Electronic Computer," had generated more response than any other. This response was chiefly to our support of the Atanasoff side, as against the Eckert-Mauchly side, in the controversy over invention of the electronic computer. It included comments published with the article by the people who had received advance copies, together with our replies; further articles and letters on particular aspects of it; the three posthumous Mauchly pieces submitted by Kay Mauchly, one of which she felt actually anticipated our "attack" on her late husband; Kay's own article on his behalf; and Atanasoff's autobiographical article.[1]

Response outside the *Annals* was also appreciable, not only to our article but to Nancy Stern's writings in the same time frame. We often found ourselves, viewed as champions of the Atanasoff cause, cast against her, champion of the Eckert-Mauchly cause.

A major obstacle to a resolution of this dispute has been a misunderstanding of the two basic issues, priority of invention and derivation from a prior invention. As to priority, the issue is that of the first *electronic computer*—or, as Judge Larson put it, the first *automatic electronic digital computer*. Yet critics frequently confuse this issue of priority by injecting the qualifier *general-purpose*. *Computerworld*, for example, in July of 1984 presented parallel condensations of the *Annals* articles by Kay Mauchly and Atanasoff, fairly selected, I think, but titled, "Who invented the electronic general-purpose digital computer?"[2] The

247

qualifier, *general-purpose*, of course, gave the prize to Eckert and Mauchly as inventors of the ENIAC.

Art and I have always recognized the ENIAC as the first *general-purpose* electronic computer, even as we have designated the *special-purpose* ABC the first electronic computer. We have also recognized the British Colossus code-breaking machine—the first model operated in late 1943—as a *special-purpose* electronic computer predating the ENIAC but postdating the ABC.

As to the second misunderstood issue, that of derivation, many influential writers on this history contend that Judge Larson is inconsistent in finding the ENIAC derived from the ABC and then declaring Eckert and Mauchly its sole inventors (overlooking the fact that this latter was in the context of possible coin-ventors on the Moore School team). Some writers have even gone so far as to say that in finding the ENIAC derived from the ABC the judge found Atanasoff a *coinventor* of the ENIAC. He, of course, found fundamental concepts of the ENIAC taken from Atanasoff, but at no point did he find Atanasoff an ENIAC coinventor.

As we saw in chapter 7, Stern was perhaps the first to allege such an inconsistency in the ENIAC patent trial decision. Joel Shurkin follows suit in his widely quoted book, *Engines of the Mind: A History of the Computer*.[3] Others merely pick up on that stance, remarking that the decision was "inconsistent," or "apparently inconsistent," without saying how.

In addition to this first major obstacle, the misunderstanding of the issues of priority and derivation, I want in the present chapter to critique three other major obstacles to resolving this controversy. These are: a challenge to the *fact* of derivation, that is, did Mauchly really derive the ENIAC from Atanasoff and his ABC; a challenge to Atanasoff's accomplishments before he and Mauchly met, that is, did Atanasoff really have anything for Mauchly to derive; and a challenge to a definition of *computer* that includes the ABC, that is, was the ABC a computer or just a calculator?

Judge Larson's finding of derivation of the ENIAC from the ABC has been questioned by many, even by some who accept the ABC as the first electronic computer and the ENIAC as the first general-purpose electronic computer. For, with the implication of theft of inventive concepts, derivation is by far the more sensitive issue.

The argument here has always rested heavily on John Mauchly's own claims to ideas he had independently of Atanasoff, claims that include the goal of a general-purpose electronic computer as early as the 1930s. Lately, an even stronger factor has been the claim that artifacts from Mauchly's Ursinus College days *prove* that he had conceived, if not actually invented, the ENIAC before he met Atanasoff.

In chapter 2 we saw Mauchly, in his 1967 Regenerative Memory deposition, allude to building electronic computing devices. But he cited nothing more specific than "small experimental devices utilizing both neon bulbs and vacuum tubes to see what I could make with such equipment."

In chapter 4 we saw him, in other settings, address his early progress toward an electronic computer. In his 1971 ENIAC trial testimony, he exhibited and defended his two-neon toy railroad crossing signal as a "binary counter," which, however, could "not count over one" and had no means of input or output. This was, in fact, the only electronic artifact—actually, the only artifact at all—that Mauchly chose to display as a witness in either case.

In his 1973 "Fireside Chat" in Rome, he cited "things" he had put together to show that "you could generate counts and use these counting devices with vacuum tubes in them." But these were clearly, by his own testimony, the ring counters he had copied from the literature to show that they could be made to work when he replaced the standard vacuum tubes with the cheaper gas tubes, or thyratrons.

Finally, both at trial and in subsequent statements, Mauchly made broad assertions as to his pre-Atanasoff ideas for a general-purpose electronic computer. At the same time, however, he did not, could not produce a shred of evidence for these claims. On the contrary, his notes from his Ursinus period placed his earliest attempts at electronic circuitry (combining neons with vacuum tubes) in the spring of 1941, after he had met Atanasoff. And even the two letters he wrote just before meeting Atanasoff in late 1940, the one to H. Helm Clayton, the other to John DeWire, disclosed only a hope of devising, in the next year or so, a very limited desk machine.

While Nancy Stern, in her 1981 book, credits these claims of Mauchly's, she does not try to associate any specific Ursinus creation with any specific aspect of the ENIAC. Rather, it was Kay Mauchly, in her later *Annals* article, who first committed to print the notion that Mauchly's Ursinus devices were actually the "physical components of [an] electronic computer Mauchly was building"; indeed, they were the "seeds of an ENIAC," with the two-neon device, for example, now serving the function of "vacuum tubes for control and circuit switching" (again, see chap. 4).

Kay complains that these items were not adequately presented at the ENIAC trial, and she blames the Sperry team on two scores:

> Mauchly had repeatedly stressed to the Sperry lawyers the importance of bringing in some witnesses from the Ursinus period, but they disregarded any such suggestions. Consequently, although *pictures* of nearly all the devices Mauchly had built at Ursinus were introduced, and Mauchly described them for the court, no testimony was given to relate these devices to the ENIAC that was built later at the Moore School. The devices themselves were never brought into the courtroom and, of course, were never demonstrated.

As to omitted witnesses, she names Mauchly's Ursinus student, John DeWire, and quotes a letter he wrote to her in 1982. DeWire recalls "a Geiger counter and some kind of counting circuit" and, especially, "John's interest in flip-flops." But he does not go beyond saying that everyone around John was "fully aware that the motivation behind this work was to develop a device to do arithmetic calculations electronically using binary digits." Moreover, what better witness could the attorneys have had to relate Mauchly's Ursinus College efforts to specific aspects of the ENIAC than Mauchly himself? Yet he did no such thing, despite extended probing by both sides.

As to courtroom demonstrations, it is hard to imagine that lawyers who let Mauchly demonstrate the two-neon device would not have seized upon *any* other truly original, truly electronic computing device he might have proposed to them. The fact is that it has been Kay Mauchly, not John Mauchly, who has seen these artifacts as nascent ENIAC components.

Yet Kay's claims have enjoyed strong support. A 1984 notice in the journal of the Association for Computing Machinery is one example:

> In the April 1984 issue of the *Annals* . . . , Kathleen R. Mauchly published her story of how long-hidden devices and documents were found in her house and barn after her husband's death. Her article shows pictures of components from Mauchly's electronic experiments in the 1930s, along with contemporary letters and diary notes. Kathleen Mauchly concludes: "Mauchly's concept of an electronic 'computer-calculator' predated any association with John V. Atanasoff and led directly to the design of the ENIAC."[4]

It should be noted that Kay's article cites only long-lost *documents*, "a letter file"; the *devices* she cites were never missing (chap. 4).

Kay's published claims for Mauchly's Ursinus inventions had actually been anticipated—to a degree—by an article in the October 1982 *University of Pennsylvania Gazette* that cited these "machines."[5] Penn, of course, has had a deep interest in fostering its own major role in the computer revolution. In "The Case of the E.N.I.A.C.," for which he interviewed Kay, Marshall Ledger says that she is "upset about the omission" of these pieces of evidence by the Sperry defense. He mentions Mauchly's cipher machine, his two-neon device, and his gas-tube ring counters (on all of which Mauchly did testify). But he stops short of associating these items directly with the ENIAC. Rather, he writes: "So he inched his way to the principles computers would eventually use."

The history by Joel Shurkin, a science writer and lecturer in communication at Stanford University, came out the same year as Kay Mauchly's *Annals* article. Shurkin wrote Art at the time that he had earlier been science editor of the

Philadelphia Inquirer, hence his interest in the ENIAC. Although he too refrains from portraying Kay's Ursinus "components" as ENIAC counterparts, he does accept them as significant steps toward electronic computation—more by declaration, however, than by substantiation.

On page 292 of his book, Shurkin offers this summary:

> We have seen in great detail the work Mauchly had done at Ursinus College experimenting with flip-flops and vacuum tubes. Mauchly had spent a considerable amount of time in cosmic-ray research labs, with his father or his father's friends, and seen them count electronically. He had observed researchers at the Bartol Research Foundation at Swarthmore using scaling circuits. He had constructed several devices, all of which are still in his house in Ambler, Pennsylvania. He had signed up for courses at the University of Pennsylvania specifically to learn how to build a computer with these tubes. What Atanasoff had accomplished may have confirmed in his own mind that he was right in assuming vacuum tubes could count and compute, but it is doubtful that he needed much confirmation.

Shurkin, like Stern, has had considerable influence, both in the computing community and in the popular media. The problem with his argument, clearly not checked out by those who rely on him, is that his "great detail" is neither great nor even correct so far as it goes. Back on pages 112–13, for example, he quotes Mauchly for a description of his ring counters. But then he represents these "tubes in little boxes" as elements of Mauchly's harmonic analyzer, of which he says Mauchly "actually built several."

Of course, as we saw in chapter 4, Mauchly's harmonic analyzer was not electronic, having no tubes at all; and *actually* he built only one, the twelve-ordinate version about which he testified at length in the ENIAC trial. Shurkin also represents Mauchly's two-neon "railroad signal" device as having the neons "in wooden blocks," whereas in fact they were mounted on the top of a hollow glass rod, with their mechanism assembled on the underside of an ice-cream box top.

A footnote here observes that Mauchly's "work on electronic circuits at Ursinus was ignored by the court . . . because the lawyers thought it unimportant." Shurkin, however, finds this work "vital" to understanding ensuing events and Atanasoff's "true role" in this story. Later, he speculates that even if Mauchly had recorded his Ursinus endeavors, "the Sperry lawyers would probably not have had this evidence admitted," because they took this aspect of the trial less seriously than other aspects. Shurkin does not realize that Mauchly had been subpoenaed to turn in all such records for perusal by both sides, nor that every scrap he did turn in for this period was scrutinized in court.

In the last analysis, Shurkin finds Atanasoff's creation a near-miss with no creditable influence. On page 298, he writes, of both the trial judge and Art, whom he has ordained the chief Atanasoff advocate:

The evidence is unmistakable that Judge Larson and Arthur Burks are wrong. Atanasoff was a brilliant innovator who came very close to building the first electronic computer, but did not contribute anything but enthusiasm to the invention that won. He demonstrated that what Mauchly wanted to do was feasible.

Shurkin feels it comes down to "the semantic argument over the word *invention*." He quotes "the dictionary" definition of *invent* as "originate by experiment; devise for the first time," but somehow does not see its application to the ABC. Instead, he turns to Stern's book for her invocation of the requirement to "demonstrate applicability as well as creativity" in order to merit recognition.

Shurkin, in fact, cites Stern liberally throughout *Engines of the Mind* to sustain his story line, so much so, in fact, that she registers an objection in her review for the October 1984 *Annals*.[6] She first faults Shurkin's failure to prove his points with verifiable source material—a well-taken criticism—and then expresses irritation that Shurkin has drawn "most of his conclusions" on "the Eckert and Mauchly affair" from *her* book! It is not surprising, she concludes, "that I agree with every major conclusion Shurkin states."

Nevertheless, despite also charging him with oversimplification, exaggeration, and even sensationalism, Stern finally pronounces Shurkin's work an "excellent popularist account" and commends it to readers who are "willing to accept a secondary historical account without benefit of knowing what sources were used to arrive at specific conclusions."

Fred Hapgood, in his review for *Science 84*, while very critical of Shurkin as "an indifferent writer," also ultimately finds merit in what he sees as the book's overall lesson.[7] By showing that "the computer was created by our civilization as a whole" rather than by "a single human intelligence, imagination, personality," he writes, "Shurkin's book may just turn out to fill an important gap in our national mythology."

As for that "single human," Atanasoff, Hapgood goes beyond Shurkin to state flatly that it was an "ignorant judge" who invalidated the ENIAC patent, and he faults Shurkin for giving so much space to Atanasoff's claims only to conclude that what he did "was really not that significant."

In her 1984 *Annals* article, Kay Mauchly had said that the Ursinus artifacts were destined for the van Pelt Library of the University of Pennsylvania, to join the documentary material already deposited there. Ultimately, we learned that they were, at least temporarily, on display at Ursinus College. In March of 1985, an Ursinus College publication took the strongest position I have seen with regard to her claim that these items were actual computer components; it even concurred in declaring them "rudimentary pieces of what was to become ENIAC."[8]

This article simply hews to Kay's line: her allegations about Mauchly's life-long devotion to his ill-received weather hypothesis, about the logical equivalence of neons to vacuum tubes, about Mauchly's aspirations to a general-purpose computer before he ever met Atanasoff, about Mauchly's disappointment in the ABC, about Sperry Rand's mismanagement of the ENIAC patent trial, about the judge's inconsistency as to who invented the ENIAC, and, finally, about the injustice of the decision as to both the priority of the ABC and derivation of the ENIAC from it.

The Ursinus article quotes Kay:

> Everyone who knows anything about computers says that the judge was wrong. This judge didn't understand the difference between digital and analogue computers, and he apparently didn't understand the expert testimony of Mauchly and Atanasoff as to what they had done. This just proves that the Patent Office should hear cases of patent infringement, and not just an ordinary circuit judge [*sic*]. It was so unfair, and so unreal. It was such a blow to John, because it was such a challenge to his integrity.

This completely unfounded assessment is followed by an assertion from John DeWire that Mauchly "was an easy mark for some who saw the opportunity to take credit from him" because he "loved to talk about his work and plans." There is also a remark by former Ursinus student Joseph Chapline that the trial outcome "was one of the things that really killed John Mauchly."

The main burden of this overwrought Ursinus *Bulletin* article is that the decision of a misguided judge has influenced some historians, and that it is only to be hoped that Mauchly's "Ursinus-era 'boxes'" on exhibit in his old Pfahler Hall will set the record straight. Unfortunately, this message rests unquestioningly on the one that Kay Mauchly had been spreading, very effectively, over a long period of time: "[She] now spends much of her time," it reports, "talking, writing, and speaking about her husband. . . . 'It's my favorite subject,' she said."

Of course, one can discount the influence of a small college newsletter seeking recognition, quite naturally, as the birthplace of the ENIAC, indeed of the electronic computer. As it happened, however, this Ursinus College article found its way into the editorial offices of *Physics Today*, the highly reputable journal of the American Institute of Physics.

In the early 1980s, *Physics Today* carried a number of letters debating the origins of the electronic computer, including one from noted physicist Allan R. Mackintosh, professor at the University of Copenhagen and director of NORDITA (*Nordisk Institut for Teoretisk Atomfysik*), Copenhagen. Mackintosh entered the fray in April 1984, with the comment that he found it "remarkable that the physicist who invented the electronic digital computer, J. V. Atanasoff, has not been mentioned."[9]

He summarizes the history, including Mauchly's Iowa visit and the Atanasoff-Mauchly correspondence on both the ABC and ideas for an electronic differential analyzer. He describes the ABC briefly, noting principles that carried over to the ENIAC. And he quotes from the trial proceedings.

Physics Today then invited Mackintosh to write a much fuller account of Atanasoff's work, and he obliged with an article, "The First Electronic Computer," published in the March 1987 issue.[10] As a European, Mackintosh's main goal was to supplant the European view of the British Colossus's primacy, as well as the American view of the ENIAC's primacy, with the historical truth of Atanasoff's original electronic computer. He very carefully sorts out the "firsts" of Atanasoff's machine, noting even the "astonishing similarity between ABC and a modern vector processor for solving linear equations."

Mackintosh traces the history, from Atanasoff's need for such a computer to the 1939 model and on to the final product, in the process quoting extensively from the 1941 correspondence and from Judge Larson's decision. He observes that the ABC is customarily described as "an uncompleted machine," but in his opinion is perhaps more accurately characterized as "a functioning but fallible computer." In any case, he observes, "the electronic computing part . . . was a brilliant success." Although he finds that "ENIAC was much faster and larger than ABC, with thousands rather than hundreds of vacuum tubes," and was programmable as well, he also finds that Eckert and Mauchly "inherited the basic ideas of electronic digital computing from Atanasoff."

Mackintosh offers his own analysis of the "extraordinary delay of over 40 years" in Atanasoff's recognition. Among other circumstances, he cites Iowa State's isolation from the major centers of academic influence, even though it is "an excellent university, with, for example, one of the first and best materials science centers in the world." "Had Atanasoff done his work at Berkeley or Harvard, or indeed Cambridge or Copenhagen," Mackintosh suggests, "he would have been recognized as the inventor of the electronic computer long ago."

Finally, Mackintosh analyzes Atanasoff's conception of the ABC as "a classic example of the creative process . . . familiar to most research scientists":

> He started with the long and frequently frustrating process of immersing himself in all aspects of the problem, without making much obvious progress. But when he had absorbed all this information, and his mind had time to work on it, largely unconsciously, the perfect solution became apparent to him while he was engaged in a completely different activity.

He writes that "Atanasoff knew perfectly well what he was doing" when he took that long drive through dry Iowa to a tavern in wet Illinois—not just as "a particularly inefficient way" of getting a drink but as a way of giving his mind the required "variety and relaxation to perform its creative mysteries."

This distinguished physicist, who had clearly studied the ABC in depth, concludes that the design Atanasoff attained through this process "was so perfect that it is difficult, even in hindsight, to see how it could be improved upon with the resources that were available to him." He cites Atanasoff's 1940 description of his invention as "a major milestone in the history of computing" and lauds what some would consider "eccentric behavior for a theoretical physicist" as he and Clifford Berry went on to build the computer with their own hands.

Mackintosh closes with an obvious reflection of his own pride in Atanasoff's opinion that "'theoretical physics is a uniquely effective discipline'" for the innovator, adding a conviction that "the frontiers of science and technology are inextricably intertwined."

Now it happens that Mackintosh first learned of Atanasoff's role in this history indirectly through Art and me—amazingly enough, he writes, since he had spent six years at Iowa State in the early 1960s, often having coffee in the very basement where the ABC had been built, without ever hearing a word about it or its inventor. Rather, it was twenty years later, while he was again doing research there, that an associate remarked on Atanasoff's achievement and handed him a copy of our 1981 *Annals* article. Mackintosh praises our efforts in his *Physics Today* article, commenting that Atanasoff had only really been recognized in the 1980s, largely due to "the investigations and writings of the Burkses."

Mackintosh's article drew a response from Evan S. Snyder, chairman of physics at Ursinus College. In the December 1987 issue, Snyder objects to what he sees as Mackintosh's heavy reliance on the ENIAC trial decision and on our article.[11] For the former, he lays the usual blame on the judge and the defense attorneys, concluding that "a competent scholar would not place so much trust in the results of an adversarial court proceeding." For the latter, he falls back on Art's imagined bitterness over not being recognized as a coinventor of the ENIAC, concluding that "the Burkses' . . . objectivity may well be questionable."

Of greatest interest to me is that Snyder now turns to the Mauchly artifacts: "Here at Ursinus College we proudly display early prototype components of what was to become ENIAC, built by Mauchly during the years that he taught physics here (1933–41)." Without further explanation, Snyder refers the reader to the *Ursinus College Bulletin* article and encloses a copy for *Physics Today*. (*Physics Today* then sent copies of the *Bulletin* article, and of Snyder's letter, to Mackintosh and to Art and me for our responses—which we supplied in due course.)

I am not sure why, but somehow I expected a physicist, especially a physicist challenging another physicist's scholarship, to fill in the blanks left in that earlier publication. Perhaps I felt disillusioned because of Mackintosh's remarks on a physicist's discipline. Snyder's response here is that "[physicists] have read of Larson's decision and been unable to find any logic in it," and, further, "one does not need to be a scientist to see the huge contradictions in Larson's findings." He offers no examples.

In a way, I think, the Atanasoff side of this dispute can be glad the so-called

Ursinus boxes have been preserved, for they are admittedly the only "evidence" that ever existed to support the other side's case for Mauchly's pre-Atanasoff achievements.

<<<>>>

Lastly, I want to cite two particularly flagrant instances of arguments against Judge Larson's finding of derivation of the ENIAC from the ABC, beyond Mauchly's broad claims for independent invention and beyond the evidence of his work at Ursinus College.

The first is from Kay Mauchly, as quoted by Joel Shurkin on pages 292–93 of his book. The reason Atanasoff had loomed so large in the ENIAC patent trial was—in the view of the Sperry lawyers, she says—that "Atanasoff was a 'red herring' thrown in there [by the Honeywell side] to distract the judge." The Sperry lawyers, Kay explains, "never dreamt that he would buy the whole thing."

Well—as we pointed out in chapter 5—the Sperry lawyers were caught completely unawares by the Atanasoff issue because Mauchly had misled them about his experience in Iowa. Certainly the Honeywell lawyers saw the ABC and the Atanasoff-Mauchly connection, not as a means of distracting the judge, but as central to their argument for invalidation of the ENIAC patent. And certainly Judge Larson was not one to be deceived by red herrings.

My second example takes us back to Nancy Stern, this time to her Fall 1983 *Abacus* article, "Who Invented the Electronic Digital Computer?" Despite her title, Stern's real concern is not priority but influence. After a lengthy presentation of the trial issues, with large pieces borrowed from her 1981 book, she offers her historian's refutation of Larson's finding on derivation of the ENIAC from the ABC:

> In an historical sense, one aspect remains critical: the fact that the computer pioneers in the 1940s and 1950s were unaware of Atanasoff's early work and instead drew heavily on the Eckert-Mauchly inventions. Even if Atanasoff had been first, he had no direct impact at all on his contemporaries in the 1940s.

Never mind that those Eckert-Mauchly inventions had in turn drawn heavily on the Atanasoff invention. *No one knew!*

Philip H. Dorn, reviewing Stern's *Abacus* article for the April 1984 *Annals*, is not entirely happy with her, although firmly in her corner on the controversy.[12] Calling it her "*n*th revision of her 1978 Ph.D. dissertation," he writes:

> This article is yet another rehash of the seemingly endless Atanasoff versus Eckert-Mauchly squabble. The unbiased observer, if any such person remains, has long since recognized the silliness of the argument.

Dorn is, however, happy with her disposition of Atanasoff on the ground that the computer designers of the 1940s and 1950s had never heard of him. He concludes defiantly:

> Consequently, their work proceeded from the Eckert and Mauchly base. And that, Judge Larson, really settles the matter once and for all.

Dorn blames the *Abacus* editors for two flaws he sees in Stern's work. The first is more than a flaw: it is a photograph labeled "The ABC Computer" that is not the ABC but the small 1939 model as rebuilt for demonstration in the Control Data and ENIAC patent cases.

His second "flaw" is the magazine's emphasis on middle names: "John *Vincent* Atanasoff," "John *William* Mauchly," "John *Grist* Brainerd." As it happens, Atanasoff was Vincent as a child; Mauchly was Bill or Billy; and Brainerd remained Grist as an adult. Dorn does not remark on it, but others have noted that all the principals in this story are named *John*: Eckert is John Presper and von Neumann is John Louis. One wag was even moved to scatological verse about these "Johns," defiling Atanasoff in a long poem that he mailed out to a number of people, including Atanasoff.

<<<>>>

So much for our first and second major obstacles to a resolution of this dispute: the first obstacle, a misconstruing of the dispute itself through a failure to sort out its two basic issues—the ABC's priority as the first (*special-purpose*) electronic computer and the ENIAC's derivation from the ABC as the first *general-purpose* electronic computer; the second obstacle, a challenge to the *fact* of derivation on a variety of misunderstandings and fabrications about the history. Our third major obstacle takes the form of denying Atanasoff's prior accomplishments: not only did Mauchly derive nothing from Atanasoff, it is argued, but—the other side of the coin—Atanasoff had nothing for him to derive. It then follows that his ABC could not have been the first electronic computer, let alone have influenced the ENIAC.

Stern espoused this position following publication of her book and her several articles, ever more carelessly overlooking what Mauchly derived both for the ENIAC and for the EDVAC. The *New York Times*, for example, in a March 22, 1983, article titled "Who Should Get the Glory For Inventing the Computer?" calls on Stern for her opinion of Judge Larson's invalidation of the ENIAC patent.[13]

The author, William J. Broad, begins with a fine brief description, complete with photographs, of both the ENIAC and the ABC, terming the latter an earlier "machine (though a more limited one) that also performed complex calculations." The issue for scholars, Broad explains, is whether the ABC is, as some now contend, "the true inspiration for all computers to come" or, as others argue, "merely a sophisticated toy." He tells of the lawsuit and cites the influence of Mauchly's own correspondence on the judge's decision, but notes that computer scholars in the Eckert-Mauchly camp remain unconvinced.

He now turns to "Dr. Nancy Stern, a historian and computer expert at Hofstra University . . . [and author of] a recent book on the controversy," for her view that "the court ignored the critical facts" concerning Atanasoff's machine. He quotes her usual litany of the never-used, only-a-prototype, special-purpose ABC, together now with this boldest yet attempt to squelch it: "Just because you have a pile of tubes and that kind of stuff, doesn't mean you have a working computer"! Broad also grants an "unperturbed" Dr. Atanasoff his say:

> It's true that my machine wasn't used much, but that's not the point. I introduced seven or eight fundamental things for which other people have taken credit.

Fundamentals, Broad adds, that Atanasoff maintains "are the foundation for every computer in the world today."

Broad closes with some neutral thoughts on the future of the debate:

> In all likelihood, if the past is an indication, the controversy over who invented the computer will continue for years to come. Such arguments often run on until the principals have passed away, and judgment is left to posterity. And when the verdict is finally in, of course, everyone will wonder what all the fuss was about in the first place.

This move toward writing off Atanasoff is reflected in other books and articles, often by simple omission, often by a single glancing blow. In October 1985, *American History Illustrated* ran an article by Simon J. Langlais, "ENIAC: Revisiting the Legend," that sings the praises of "the world's premier electronic computer."[14] It traces the story from Mauchly's original "dream" to his partnership with Eckert in planning and creating "this electronic marvel," and it goes on to describe the ENIAC's work at Aberdeen Proving Ground. It does not mention Atanasoff or the court case.

Time magazine marked the fortieth anniversary celebration of the ENIAC, held on February 13, 1986, at the Computer Museum in Boston, with a story by Philip Elmer-DeWitt.[15] Titled "A Birthday Party for ENIAC," it alludes to Atanasoff in the negative context of a court decision that constituted "the final insult" to Eckert and Mauchly after their business reverses:

> Honeywell convinced a federal judge that Mauchly had based his ideas for ENIAC on the work of a computer pioneer named John Atanasoff. The patent was dismissed, and Mauchly and Eckert lost legal claim to one of the great inventions of the 20th century.

Elsie Atanasoff Whistler had a letter in the March 24 issue objecting to *Time*'s making her father "the villain of the piece."[16] She describes the trial as a "lengthy and thorough process" that accrued a "transcript of 20,667 pages," and she quotes from Larson's decision.

And Eric Weiss, in a January 1987 *Annals* book review, merely scoffs at "Atanasoff's ABC monstrosity."[17]

By far, the most strident denigrator of Atanasoff's achievement was Pres Eckert. Unfortunately, he was often mistaken not just in his arguments but in his underlying facts. Pamela L. Eblen in her 1984 article, "Who Really Invented the Computer?" quotes Eckert's notion of Mauchly's 1941 visit to Ames:

> Atanasoff didn't even have a computer. He had a couple of counting circuits and a description of what he was going to build. And it didn't work. Actually, Mauchly saw what Atanasoff had in an hour's time.[18]

He seems to have forgotten that the ABC was, like the EDVAC, based on adders, not, like the ENIAC, on counters; moreover, that there *was* a machine in an advanced state of completion.

Eckert also gave Eblen his version of why Atanasoff never got a patent on the ABC:

> He tried to get a patent on it and the patent office said that "What you have isn't adequate—there isn't enough information or details even to apply for a patent."

Actually, it was patent attorney Richard Trexler who requested additional information, owing more to his own unfamiliarity with the technology than to any inadequacy of descriptive detail provided by Atanasoff (and Berry). Atanasoff never applied to the Patent Office for this invention; indeed, it was entirely up to Iowa State College to apply. (See chap. 5.)

As to Atanasoff's claim to have invented the electronic computer, Eblen quotes Eckert:

> It's such an outlandish exaggeration to consider that he did it—it's a complete joke. He doesn't tell the truth—that's all. He did some little thing which he never finished and which wouldn't have worked if he had finished it.

Again, it is Eckert who is being outlandish.

Like Broad of the *New York Times*, Eblen has described the court case fairly and has given space to Atanasoff's views. She quotes his remark on the verdict: "I was sure the court would reach that conclusion, and when it did I thought that would end it, but it's gone on for ten years since then."

And on the Eckert-Mauchly claims for the priority of the ENIAC: "I don't think I ever got very angry at them, but I'm sort of irritated with the fact that they continued to pursue the idea that they had invented it first."

Eblen also maintains her neutrality throughout, opining in the end: "So who *really* invented the computer? The verdict might well be: They both did."

A year or so later, Eckert was less disparaging on this issue, yet no closer to reality. As keynoter for the ENIAC's "Big Birthday Bash" at the Computer Museum, he acknowledged the ABC's existence as a "machine"—but not an "invention":

> The best way to dismiss Atanasoff is to say the machine really never worked and he didn't have a system. That's the big thing about an invention: it's that you have a whole system that works. . . . The ENIAC was built as a system that has led directly to today's computers.[19]

And so a new error has been introduced. For one of the truly impressive aspects of the Atanasoff-Berry Computer was that it had a system *par excellence*: tightly integrated, economical of material and design, organized into complex interacting major units. The centralized architecture of the ABC finds its counterpart in the modern computer's separation of arithmetic, memory, and control in a way that the distributive architecture of the ENIAC simply does not. Moreover, as we have seen and as is widely acknowledged, the ABC's *system* did work.

On November 3 of that same year, *Computerworld* published its own special fortieth anniversary issue, *Celebrating the Computer Age*.[20] This volume of 191 oversize pages of charts, photos, articles, and industry ads opens with an interview of Eckert in which editor George Harrar asks him about the "earlier computers." Eckert responds:

> Well, Atanasoff claimed to have built something. Number one, if you examine his circuits and things, you find it wouldn't have worked. Number two, he applied for a patent and was told he didn't have sufficient information to apply. Number three, he had no method of program control—he didn't have the concept of subroutines.
>
> It was a rudimentary attempt that was never carried through; it was a complete failure. Why some judge inferred otherwise is hard to say. The legal system's nuts—we know this from many things.

Art and I have always credited Eckert and Mauchly with the first programmable computer—and added that if they had claimed *that*, among other innovations (including subroutines), but not Atanasoff's prior inventions, they would have had an extremely valuable patent.

Asked now if he had seen the ABC, as Mauchly had, Eckert replies:

> I don't even know if he saw it. I know that he heard about it from Atanasoff and saw something there, a few tubes hooked up.

It might be equivalent to saying that Atanasoff had some ideas for storage which were never fully instrumented, and he had an idea for building an adder which he had instrumented and said worked. But nobody else knew whether it worked or not.

Eckert seems to be unaware—or to have forgotten—that Mauchly himself testified to having seen the adders and to having been "perfectly convinced" that they did indeed work as intended (see chap. 1). He seems to be unaware—or to have forgotten—that not only did Mauchly testify to Atanasoff's electronically refreshed regenerative memory but that he himself, in 1953, published an article crediting Atanasoff with "probably the first example of what might be termed regenerative memory" (see chap. 2).[21]

In response to a question on the ENIAC's place in history, Eckert makes the further rash claim that it was "the first execution of reliable electronic circuits," which was, in fact, the ENIAC's greatest debt to the ABC! And, lastly, asked whether he would tell a layman that it was Eckert and Mauchly who invented the computer, he says that he would.

As to Eckert's condemnation, here and elsewhere, of our legal system, on the basis of a suit his side lost, I am intrigued that he should do so without concern for the specifics of the case. His hallmark as a brilliant design engineer was the caution and attention to detail that he brought to his creative vision, as Art and I explain at some length in our ENIAC article. One suspects that, for both Eckert and Mauchly, the many years of adulation prior to the court decision encouraged a degree of reckless abandon on their part—abandon that has worked in their favor, with their dissenting "verdicts" widely credited.

This lengthy special issue of the highly respected *Computerworld* supports Eckert's dismissal of Atanasoff from the outset by taking the 1946 unveiling of the ENIAC as the starting point for its "Computer Age." Editor Harrar does acknowledge several earlier "worthy attempts at computing," including Charles Babbage's analytical engine of the 1830s, Howard Aiken's Mark I of 1943, and:

> John Atanasoff's prototype ABC, a model that led to a judge's decision in 1973 stating that it was Atanasoff who invented the concept of the "automatic digital computer."

So here again is the prototype-model limitation. And of course Judge Larson did not say that Atanasoff invented the *concept of* the computer, nor did he neglect to include the word *electronic*: he said that Atanasoff invented the *automatic electronic digital computer*. Harrar, by setting 1946 as the starting point and by identifying the ABC with the ENIAC's mechanical and electromechanical predecessors, has simply eliminated Atanasoff from the running.

The magazine proceeds accordingly to "A time line, 1946 A.D. to 2000 A.D." with Atanasoff now cited under 1973, for the year when he won the court decision. Only toward the end of the issue, in a second "time line" for the *Precomputer Age* "500 B.C. to 1946 A.D." does *Computerworld* recognize Atanasoff's invention, in 1939, of what "is said to be the first working model of the electronic digital computer." Incidentally, the Colossus is also listed, under 1943, as "an electronic computer" of this "precomputer age."

The last section of the magazine, on milestones in the history, has pieces on Atanasoff and on Mauchly and Eckert. The one on Atanasoff contains the publication's only hint of a possible connection between these parties, with the comment that Atanasoff is "said by some to have directly inspired John Mauchly's work on the ENIAC computer." Even here, though, Mauchly's counter-opinion is interjected: that the ABC was "just a crude little machine that wouldn't really do anything," whereas the ENIAC was "a highly sophisticated and operational machine." The piece on Mauchly and Eckert does not mention Atanasoff at all.

So it is that *Computerworld*, in this landmark publication—actually its 1,000th issue—excludes Atanasoff from his rightful place, first, by arbitrarily defining "the computer age" (and a "precomputer age" that includes "electronic computers") and, second, by withholding critical facts as to both his achievement and his immediate and profound influence. There is also here, as we have seen in other accounts, a *semblance* of providing the full story by including, in disparate and very spare fashion, all the relevant topics but not all the relevant data.

In light of all this support for Eckert and Mauchly in the years *after* Judge Larson's 1973 decision—and the abandon with which they condemned that decision—the question arises as to just how early this pattern of misappropriating Atanasoff's ideas started. The answer is, for Mauchly at least, *very early!* One example is outstanding. It concerns the ABC's add-subtract mechanism, or binary serial adder, as adapted for the EDVAC.

Once the Moore School team had opted for the counter/accumulator core of the ENIAC, it did not explore the concept of an electronic adder working with a separate memory until Eckert conceived his delay-line memory. As this possibility was now being discussed, in late 1944 or early 1945, Mauchly invited Art into his office to look at a plan for a binary serial adder. Art was greatly impressed; it was years before he realized that the source of this idea, of which Mauchly was so proud, was Atanasoff and the ABC.

Eckert and Mauchly applied for their first Serial Binary Adder patent in late 1950 and received it in mid-1952. As to their Regenerative Memory patent, which actually included Atanasoff's version of an electrostatic store, they applied for it in late 1947 and received it in February 1953.

We saw in chapter 5 that Mauchly said in his deposition for the Regenerative Memory case that on his return from Iowa he had told Eckert and others at the

Moore School about Atanasoff's computer. In particular, he and Eckert had discussed their ideas for "possible calculators in light of what I'd seen out there." It is inconceivable that electronics expert Eckert, in filing for these patents, was unaware of the source of their "invention," not only of the regenerative memory but of the binary serial adder, as well.

Before leaving this third post in our obstacle course, the discrediting of Atanasoff, I want to mention one influential writer on this period who casts him in a much more positive light than do most others. This is Michael R. Williams, who was to succeed J. A. N. Lee as editor in chief of the *Annals* in 1996.

In his 1985 survey, *A History of Computing Technology*, this University of Calgary computer scientist acknowledges the ABC's priority as "the world's first working electronic digital calculator," and he credits both its influence on the ENIAC, through Mauchly, and its subsequent "huge influence on the rapid development of electronic computing machines."[22] Indeed, he finds the ABC, along with the ENIAC and the Colossus, one of the "three penultimate steps" that were "the seed bed from which the modern electronic [stored-program] computer sprang just after the end of the Second World War."

Williams is one of the few writers to draw a clear distinction between Atanasoff's "working prototype machine" of 1939 and his "full-scale machine" of 1942. He is also one of the few to cite the ABC's electronic regenerative memory and its 300-tube arithmetic unit as original and influential features. Oddly, I think, Williams completely bypasses the ENIAC patent trial and its outcome, both in his presentation of the ABC and in his presentation of the ENIAC and the subsequent Eckert-Mauchly commercial enterprises.

This seems also an appropriate spot in which to relate the story of my own experience in bringing the message of priority and derivation to children. On January 24, 1984, the editor of *Cobblestone*, "the history magazine for young people," wrote to tell me of plans for an issue devoted to the history of computers, scheduled for June. She said that she had assigned the task of writing about the ENIAC to a woman in Massachusetts, who had responded that I would be a better choice, since I was a children's writer as well as a writer on the subject of the ENIAC controversy over Atanasoff.

Like any good editor, this *Cobblestone* editor seized upon the theme of a controversy and asked me to tell about it, still including, however, a detailed description of the ENIAC. She also said that *Annals* editor Bernard Galler and assistant editor Nancy Stern were serving as consultants for this issue, and that

Galler had already helped with its overall plan. I held to the prescribed limit of 750 words for a story about the ABC as the first electronic computer, together with its linkage to the much larger, more powerful, more general ENIAC and the federal court's invalidation of the patent on that later, wartime, creation. I then wrote a separate description of the ENIAC for the editor to use or not as she chose. She did like this idea of two articles, with the ENIAC featured on its own even as it was toppled from its historic pedestal.

She now returned both manuscripts for my approval, with only minor editorial modifications of the ENIAC piece, but with revisions of the ABC piece that all but destroyed its major thrust. The changes were both shocking and familiar, as they reflected oft-repeated arguments against Atanasoff's achievement. In my account of the trial, for example, my characterization of the ABC as "finished" in May 1942 was changed to "partially built" as of that date, and the stark sentence inserted, "Professor Atanasoff's computer was never finished, and it only partly worked." My comment on the state of Atanasoff's machine at the time of Mauchly's visit to Iowa State was also weakened, from "when his computer was well along" to "while his computer was being built."

I wrote back that, as the author responsible for the substance of the article, I could not accept such changes, but that the matter was easily resolved by letting Judge Larson, instead of the author, make these assertions. That is, Larson had ruled that the computer had been "developed and built" by 1942 and was "well advanced" when Mauchly visited, and that even his 1939 model had been "reduced to practice" as a computing machine (see chap. 7). I revised my original version to reflect this shift in authority from myself to Larson.

I also objected to other changes that detracted from Atanasoff's success; for example, the removal of my evaluation of the ABC as "an ingenious pioneering effort." I said that it seemed odd not to express any opinion at all of his machine, given my presentation of its primacy and its influence.

Of course, I was well aware of the *Cobblestone* editor's predicament, caught as she was between an author's account and her consultants' attack on that account. I reminded her, though, that I had the judge on my side, and that if she published the consultant's version she would be telling children, parents, and librarians—without explanation—that an unappealed federal court decision in a matter of great historical significance was wrong.

The published versions followed my recommendations, with this editor's note: "The story of the first electronic computer is a complicated one, and individuals tend to disagree whether the first electronic computer was the ENIAC or the ABC. Alice Burks supports the court decision in favor of the ABC."[23]

I was happy with that.

<<<>>>

The fourth and last major obstacle to resolving this dispute over invention of the electronic computer—and one completely unanticipated by the Atanasoff side—is a redefinition of the word *computer* that excludes the ABC. Although the argument has taken many forms, it has usually entailed a distinction between *calculator* and *computer*. A *computer*, it is said by some, must be a *general-purpose* device, so that the ABC, as a *special-purpose* machine and so a *calculator*, is ruled out as "first electronic computer," with that honor going to the general-purpose ENIAC. For others, a *computer* must be a *stored-program* device, so that even the ENIAC is excluded!

Many who stipulate the stored-program facility, however, insert exceptions that allow the ENIAC—though not the ABC—to remain a computer. IBM historian Charles J. Bashe, for example, draws a distinction between *computer* and *calculator* that he traces to the early 1950s, when the term computer "came to be understood to denote a stored-program, electronic digital machine."[24] But he excuses certain inconsistencies in his, and in IBM's, application of this distinction. IBM, he notes, referred to its (early 1950s) 701 and 650 as calculators, despite their being "general-purpose, stored-program, electronic, and digital." As to the ENIAC:

> While it is probably no more appropriate to call the ENIAC (with its manually plugged program) a computer than to call [the IBM 650 and 701] calculators, the term *computer* is used here [for the ENIAC] because it is part of the full name given to the machine—Electronic Numerical Integrator and Computer.

Another prominent computer historian, William Aspray, makes the computer-calculator distinction much more insistently than Bashe, but then falls into some inconsistencies of his own. He opens an October 1986 *Annals* article with this bold assertion:

> At the end of the war in 1945, no computers existed, if we mean by *computer* what we mean today: a general-purpose, digital, electronic, stored-program calculating system. Two electronic digital calculators built near the end of the war represented the furthest advances in computing technology: the Colossus . . . and the ENIAC.[25]

It is striking that in this definition, comput*ing* is distinguished from the activities of a comput*er*, and calculat*ing* from the activities of a calculat*or*. A computer is a "calculating system," and calculators do "computing." Aspray carries this distinction throughout his writings, perhaps out of some common-sense appeal, as, for example, in the book *Computing Before Computers* that he edited and to which he contributed essays.[26]

That issue aside, Aspray's four specifications for the term *computer* also suffer considerable slippage as he proceeds in his *Annals* article. He calls differential analyzers "analog computers," though they were in fact not general-purpose, not digital, not electronic, and not stored-program. And he counts the electromechanical "Harvard University Mark I" among the British and U.S. "computers" that received the most international attention in the seminal 1945–1955 period. Aspray explicitly excuses the Mark I, along with other relay machines, from his requirement that computers be electronic, on the ground that they were "used effectively in large-scale computation." Yet he makes no such exception for the ENIAC, which is universally recognized as having been both large-scale and used effectively during that same decade. And it was electronic! And it certainly received international attention!

Other arguments on definition of terms have arisen. Brian Randell, for example, while allowing the ENIAC—and the ABC—to be called computers, classifies both as special-purpose, asserting that to be *general-purpose* a machine must also be *stored-program*.[27] He accordingly reserves the accolade "first general-purpose computer" for the EDVAC.

Like Bashe and Aspray, Randell appeals to "what we would now regard" as appropriate usage. Another writer who makes this same appeal is Fred Gruenberger, who in fact believes he was the first to distinguish between *calculator* and *computer*, with the requirement that the latter have the stored-program facility.[28] But he also is troubled as the issue becomes "quite fuzzy" with the arrival of those "sophisticated pocket programmable machines."

A readily apparent objection to these attempts to define critical terms on the basis of "current" usage is that "current" is constantly changing. But the chief objection that Art and I have is that such definitions miss the opportunity to present the history of the modern computer as an evolving process. Historians of science do not ordinarily deny invention to the pioneers on the basis of later advances, but cite the succession of advances from the very first "light bulb" of inspiration that culminated in its reduction to practice, at however rudimentary a level.

Accordingly, I will close out this chapter with a brief summary of what is primarily Art's delineation of the stage-by-stage calculator/computer development, as reached by him in his teaching and writing on the subject—a delineation that embraces the mechanical, electromechanical, and electronic technologies and gives deserved credit to each of the successive inventors and their machines along the way. (Not that these necessarily formed a neat chronological or causal sequence!)

First, as to the terms *calculator* and *computer*: on pages 267–68 of our 1988 book, *The First Electronic Computer: The Atanasoff Story*, we formulate this distinction in terms of degree of automaticity.[29] On this criterion, we distinguish Atanasoff's computer from the calculators of its day—and also compare it favorably with the ENIAC. We define an *automatic operation* as "one that, once started, carries out a sequence of steps independently of further external command." And we argue that the ABC had three basic automatic operations "complex enough to qualify the ABC as an *automatic computer*."

We contrast the ABC's operation of eliminating a variable between two equations, for example, with the operations of "bank accounting machines and the IBM 601 cross-footing multiplier," both of which "executed formulas of a few straightforward arithmetic steps." Several other preelectronic machines, however, do qualify as computers rather than calculators on our degree-of-automaticity criterion. The Mark I of Harvard (and IBM) and the Bell Labs Model V, both relay machines of the electromechanical technology, are clear-cut examples of digital *computers*, while even the mechanical differential analyzer qualifies as an analog *computer*.

Second, as to the terms *special-purpose* and *general-purpose*: Art's definition of *general-purpose* for our 1981 *Annals* article requires programmability, with specifications for particular capabilities, such as branching (on either a constant or a variable), that substantially enhance the range of problems a machine can solve. On this view, the electronic ENIAC is a general-purpose computer, while the ABC is a special-purpose computer (as also are the electronic Colossi of World War II that became known only many years later, about which more in chaps. 10 and 11).

But, again, as with the distinction between *calculator* and *computer*, this distinction between *general-purpose* and *special-purpose* can also be applied to computers of the earlier technologies, not just the electronic. The electromechanical Model V and Mark I (the latter as supplemented after the war) are seen not just as computers but as *general-purpose* computers, while the mechanical differential analyzer is a *special-purpose* computer.

Art responds to Randell's requirement that to be general-purpose a computer must have the stored-program facility by arguing instead that, from an historical perspective, it is helpful to divide general-purpose digital computers into two categories, those without and those with that facility. The ENIAC, with its preset read-only program, falls in the first category, whereas the EDVAC, with its read-write stored program capable of self-modification, falls in the second category (see chap. 5). Such a division clearly elucidates the transition from the ENIAC to the EDVAC even as the ENIAC was still under construction. At the same time, it assigns the preelectronic computers mentioned above their special place in history for achieving the degree of generality that they did, even though they were not stored-program machines.

Finally, I would just note that at a basic level no definition—or redefinition—of terms should affect either the issue of priority of invention or that of derivation of an invention from an earlier invention, *so long as original and enduring principles are entailed*. To exclude Atanasoff's computer from consideration on the basis of definition, especially in the matter of priority, seems to me inappropriate, given the list of "firsts" the ABC encompassed, "firsts" that persist in the most sophisticated computers to this day. Yet this practice has continued to hold broad sway, through the writings of the initial respected historians cited here and of others, both individuals and institutions, who have picked up on it.

There have, of course, been writers who have taken a more independent view of the history from the start. Economist Gerald Brock, for example, with his focus on the computer industry, had no difficulty in 1975 in calling the ABC a *computer* or the ENIAC a *general-purpose computer*. Likewise, computer scientist David Kuck in 1978 called the ABC a *special-purpose computer* and the ENIAC a *general-purpose computer*. Kuck then placed the stored-program concept among those "improvements introduced in the next wave of machines," along with "large internal memories, . . . index registers, and magnetic tape and drum secondary storage." (See chap. 7 on Brock and Kuck.)

NINE

THE MATTER OF
VON NEUMANN

In the preceding chapter, I spelled out and argued against what I see as the major obstacles to resolving the dispute over invention of the electronic compter—a dispute concerned largely with the issues of priority and derivation and mainly pitting John Atanasoff, on the one hand, against John Mauchly and Pres Eckert, on the other. In responding to the last obstacle, the imposition of highly restrictive definitions of the term *computer* itself, I offered a definition that spanned the three computer technologies: mechanical, electromechanical, and electronic. This endeavor once again highlighted the progression within the electronic technology from the *special-purpose* ABC to the *general-purpose* ENIAC to the *stored-program* EDVAC and Institute for Advanced Study Computer.

Now, there is a second dispute over the issue of *who invented the stored-program concept*, this one pitting Eckert and Mauchly against John von Neumann. Just one major obstacle has stood in the way of resolving this dispute, marked though it has been by even greater bitterness among the parties, perhaps because they had actually worked together in a common effort to improve upon the ENIAC. The obstacle here is an unwillingness to recognize, or a failure to realize, that the invention of the stored-program concept entailed two distinct steps, the first taken by Eckert, the second by von Neumann.

In chapter 5, we saw in some detail just what constituted these two steps toward the binary EDVAC as the decimal ENIAC's successor. Eckert's part evolved as a solution to the serious bottleneck caused by the ENIAC's time-consuming manual program entry at the start of each new problem. He envisaged a computer with memory large enough for internal storage of the binary-coded program as well as the binary arithmetic data, together with some form of automatic entry (probably, originally, paper tape or magnetic wire).

In his January 1944 disclosure of a magnetic drum or disk form of memory, Eckert mentions "automatic programming" that could be either "temporary" or "permanent," so that presumably—he does not say—a program could be erased at the end of a problem run and a new program entered.[1] Several months later, he was envisaging his mercury-delay-line memory, again a store large enough for both instructions and data and with some form of automatic entry (now probably magnetic wire, but, possibly, magnetic tape).

Von Neumann's part, which evolved from Eckert's idea for this large computer memory, was to put its read-write aspect to further use. He saw that a *program language* could be devised so that a problem's program, as well as its arithmetic data, could change during the solution process. That is, the computer's program could be made to modify itself, depending upon the requirements of the problem at any given juncture. In his June 1945 "First Draft of a Report on the EDVAC," von Neumann presented such a program language, having first provided the detailed logical design of his proposed arithmetic unit and memory.[2]

Again as we saw in chapter 5, the role of each of these two highly creative men is clear from what occurred—and what did not occur—at the Moore School meetings in the spring of 1945. Eckert's (and Mauchly's) thinking for the EDVAC was concerned solely with overcoming the ENIAC's program-entry difficulty. Just as in the ENIAC, once a program was entered, that program was to remain unchanged throughout the problem run. Only with von Neumann's report two months later did Eckert and Mauchly grasp the further potential of a read-write program within the solution process.

The purveyors of this history have provided a variety of interpretations of both the stored-program concept and its origins. These run the full gamut from viewing it in its simplest form—easily credited to Eckert and Mauchly—to including the automatic internal modification of programs as an essential second aspect—seldom, however, clearly credited to von Neumann.

University of Calgary computer scientist Michael R. Williams, whom we met in chapter 8 with regard to Atanasoff, is in the first category. In his survey, *A History of Computing Technology*, he assigns von Neumann an auxiliary role in helping to refine Eckert's basic storage idea.[3] As Mauchly and Eckert had done over the years, he presents von Neumann as a reporter or summarizer of design discussions—to which he was, nevertheless, a major contributor. Of von Neumann's "active part in the discussions concerning the design of the EDVAC," he writes on page 302:

> It is undoubtedly the case that he made many major contributions to these discussions but it is also true to say that the germ of the stored program idea existed

before von Neumann became involved with the project, and, even after he was a regular participant in the design discussions, they also involved all the other members of the ENIAC team. Eventually it was von Neumann's genius for organizing material and his penchant for producing reports which led him to write down the results of all these design meetings in a document which . . . first described, in detail, the concept of the stored program digital computer.

But Williams, in characterizing the stored-program facility of the EDVAC, says only that it "was capable of storing its instruction tape internally within its memory and issuing its instructions at electronic speeds which were comparable with those available in the rest of the machine." He does not attribute the idea of program self-modification to either von Neumann or the Moore School group—or raise it as an issue at all. (Incidentally, by no means did "all the members of the ENIAC team" participate in those spring 1945 meetings; only team members Mauchly, Eckert, and Burks participated, together with von Neumann and Goldstine from Aberdeen and the school's EDVAC project director Warren.)

Williams, then, has captured the essence of the improvement over the ENIAC envisioned by Eckert and Mauchly long before that computer's completion. But he has failed to recognize von Neumann's realization of the further potential of their vision first set forth in his EDVAC report and developed in subsequent documents coauthored with Burks and Goldstine. Surprisingly, he has also missed the fact that it was von Neumann who, quite explicitly in that report, first proposed the cathode-ray-tube form of computer memory. Rather, he cites Eckert's mention of it in a Moore School lecture, over a year later, as evidence that "the initial idea," though made into "a working reality" by F. C. Williams of Manchester University in England, may well have been Eckert's.

Computer pioneer Harry D. Huskey likewise limits the concept to the Eckert portion in his memoir, "Harry D. Huskey: The Early Days," published in the October 1991 *Annals*.[4] He writes that in the spring of 1945, about a year after he had joined the ENIAC team, Eckert explained to him how a mercury-delay-line memory would constitute a great improvement over the ENIAC's accumulators for the storage of numbers. He describes his reaction:

> My first question to Eckert: thinking about the pluggable connections to control the ENIAC, "How do you control the operations?" "Instructions are stored in the mercury lines just like numbers," he said. Of course! Once he said it, it was so obvious, and the *only* way that instructions could come available at rates comparable to the data rates. That was the *stored program computer*—the first to be designed was the EDVAC. . . . The stored program concept gave another tremendous step in flexibility, making it possible to process programs.

Huskey tells of von Neumann's role as a consultant and of his First Draft Report, which he found "of little help" to designers of computer hardware, but

"of immeasurable value in supporting the development of automatic computers."
As to credit, he writes:

> The question has been asked, "Who was responsible for the concept of the stored
> program computer?" John Mauchly had been interested in computing in mete-
> orological applications. He joined with Eckert, who had the hardware experi-
> ence, and they developed the proposal for Aberdeen Proving Ground which led
> to the ENIAC. The limited memory of the ENIAC was an obvious shortcoming.
> Thus, it was natural that Eckert, using his experience with mercury delay lines
> for radar ranging purposes, would suggest the use of delay lines. The suggestion
> would, of course, immediately lead to the question of how to control the com-
> putational process. I feel that Eckert and Mauchly jointly deserve credit for the
> stored program idea—certainly, von Neumann does not.

And so, even while recognizing that the concept "gave another tremendous
step in flexibility, making it possible to process programs," Huskey does not recognize that it was von Neumann's contribution of program modifiability that
made that surge possible—or that this idea was in the von Neumann report.

British computer pioneer Stanley Gill, writing in the third edition of the
Encyclopedia of Computer Science, recognizes both the initial storage aspect and
the program modification aspect of the stored-program concept, but he depicts
the former as definitive, with the latter *an advantage that accrued from it*.[5] Gill
terms the concept the "key design feature of modern computers, which allows
instructions to be held in the internal store while they are awaiting execution." He
goes on to note as a significant advantage the fact that "the instructions held in
the internal store were accessible to be operated upon the same way as the data
during the execution of the program."

As to assigning credits for either the initial storage aspect or the ensuing
modification aspect, Gill chooses not to sort them out. He writes, quite correctly
of course, that "the stored program concept emerged . . . from discussions that
took place at the Moore School," the participants including Eckert, Mauchly, and
von Neumann, and that "the concept was first documented in a Moore School
report drafted by von Neumann."

And now, in this same issue of the *Encyclopedia of Computer Science*,
Robert F. Rosin, of Enhanced Service Providers, Inc., does cite as definitive what
Arthur and I consider the two essentials of the stored-program concept.[6] But, like
Gill, he opts for the group approach to their source or sources. His topic is the von
Neumann machine:

> The most influential paper in the history of computer science, whether or not
> anyone else expressed similar ideas earlier, was written in 1946 by John von
> Neumann, then on the staff of the Institute for Advanced Study . . . , in
> collaboration with Arthur W. Burks and Herman H. Goldstine. Its title is "Pre-
> liminary Discussion of the Logical Design of an Electronic Computing Instru-

ment," and the ideas it contains, collectively known as *the von Neumann machine*, have provided the foundation for essentially all computer system development since that date.

Central to the von Neumann machine is the concept of the stored program—the principle that instructions and data are to be stored together in a single, uniform storage medium rather than separately, as was previously the case.... One exploitation of this [arrangement] results in the technique of instruction modification.

Nicholas Metropolis and J. Worlton, both of the Los Alamos Scientific Research Laboratory, also recognize the two aspects of the stored-program concept in their oft-quoted article, "A Trilogy on Errors in the History of Computing."[7] In this work, however, published in the January 1980 *Annals* but actually presented eight years earlier at the first U.S.A.-Japan Computer Conference in Tokyo, their explicit goal is to counter what they see as a widespread misconception that von Neumann alone conceived the stored-program computer. And then they go to the other extreme of assigning the entire concept to Eckert and Mauchly!

Metropolis and Worlton are careful to lay out "the stages through which program control in scientific computers evolved during the 1940's," ending in stage 5, "*Read-write* memories for stored programs . . . based on the design of the EDVAC (1945)." And they explicitly recognize that the EDVAC's stored-program feature included "a *dynamically modifiable* stored program." As to originators of the concept, they write:

Another point concerning the stored-program history which needs clarification is the unwarranted assumption that J. von Neumann alone deserves the credit for the stored-program concept.

But to support this wholly warranted statement, they cite Maurice V. Wilkes's 1967 Turing lecture—with its inaccurate rendition of this issue.[8] Wilkes credits Eckert and Mauchly with proposing *both* the delay-line store *and* the mixing of instructions and numbers "in the same memory." As we explained in chapter 5, Eckert and Mauchly did not propose the commingling of program and data in the *same* memory; rather, it was von Neumann who resolved what had been left open at the Moore School meetings—in favor of the single-memory concept, which he realized would permit the automatic modification of instructions (among other advantages over separate storage).

Wilkes says that "the computing field owes a very great debt to von Neumann": first, for appreciating at once "the potentialities implicit in the stored program principle"; second, for bringing "his great prestige and influence to bear" against "powerful voices" who argued "that the ultrasonic memory would not be reliable enough, and that to mix instructions and numbers in the same memory was going against nature"! He concludes that "subsequent developments have provided a decisive vindication of the principles taught by Eckert and Mauchly."

In their *Annals* article, Metropolis and Worlton turn from Wilkes's lecture to what they consider "the historical document which is crucial to this discussion." This is the September 1945 official report on the EDVAC written by Eckert and Mauchly those three months *after* the issuance of von Neumann's report on that machine (and discussed at some length in chapter 5).[9] Metropolis and Worlton first quote a passage from this report that quite rightly cites Eckert's January 1944 "Disclosure of Magnetic Calculating Machine," where he stipulates that "operating instructions and function tables would be stored in exactly the *same sort of* memory device as that used for numbers" [italics added]; and another passage from this report that also rightly cites "the invention of the acoustic delay line memory device" in early 1944.

Metropolis and Worlton then quote from that progress report's introductory comment on von Neumann's role:

> During the latter part of 1944, and continuing to the present time, Dr. John von Neumann, consultant to the Ballistic Research Laboratory, has fortunately been available for consultation. He has contributed to many discussions on the logical controls of the EDVAC, has prepared certain instruction codes, and has tested these proposed systems by writing out the coded instructions for specific problems. Dr. von Neumann has also written a preliminary report in which most of the results of earlier discussions are summarized.

They follow with their own acceptance of this view of von Neumann's Draft Report as a summary of the Moore School meetings:

> From this it is clear that the stored-program concept predates von Neumann's participation in the EDVAC design. That von Neumann is often given credit for this fundamental concept is likely due to the fact that he wrote a preliminary report which summarized the earlier work on the EDVAC design, including the stored-program concept. Von Neumann contributed to the *development* of this concept, but to credit him with its invention is an historical error.

In short, these writers, while they recognize the two definitive aspects of the concept as realized in the EDVAC, do not recognize that von Neumann's "*development*" of the concept included the second aspect, namely, what they have termed "a *dynamically modifiable* stored program." They do not realize that Eckert and Mauchly themselves credited von Neumann with that idea in this same progress report (see chap. 5)! Their finding of "an historical error" is correct, but their shifting of all the credit from von Neumann to Eckert and Mauchly is not.

As to Wilkes's position, he has come down on the side of Eckert and Mauchly in other contexts. One was in his function of presiding over Arthur Burks's Digital Computer Museum lecture of February 16, 1982, in which Art distinguished the role of von Neumann from that of Eckert in the creation of the stored-program concept. Afterwards, Wilkes stepped forward to make clear to the audience that Art's depiction of events was merely his personal "recollection"— others had differing "recollections." Art responded that, in fact, it was not just a recollection: it was borne out by the still-existing official notes he took at the design meetings.

On June 9 of that same year, at a session of the National Computer Conference held in Houston, Wilkes expressed a very strong view of the role played by electronic design engineers in the creation of the stored-program concept, as against that played by von Neumann. As reported by William Aspray in the October 1982 *Annals*, Wilkes downgraded what he termed von Neumann's "formalization of the concept" in his 1945 EDVAC report, saying that it "merely restated in biological terminology simple ideas well understood by engineers."[10] Aspray continues:

> [For Wilkes] the formalization was at a trivial level for engineers; it presented the 10 percent of the stored-program concept of interest to mathematicians without addressing the difficult 90 percent of the engineering problems. Accordingly, claimed Wilkes, more credit should be given to the engineers who solved the concomitant engineering problems and less credit to von Neumann.

But, as we saw in chapter 5, von Neumann did not "formalize" in neural symbolism "simple ideas" already familiar to others; rather, he adapted neural symbolism to the design of circuitry at a simpler level than the electronic—a purely logical level. And he moved on, not only to settle issues left open in the spring 1945 Moore School meetings but also to formulate new ideas, including a preliminary architecture and a program language that allowed program modification.

While it is true, as Wilkes claims, that a logical specification of an electronic circuit was not found useful by most of the people who designed those first EDVAC-type machines, including the EDSAC with which his name is associated, it later became and remained standard to work from logical-net symbolism and diagrams.

It is also true, as we recognized in chapter 5, that the electronic design was more complex, perhaps more difficult. But doing the electronics without a prior logical design had of necessity to eventuate in a logical construct, which included a program language and an architecture. Moreover, the designers of the EDSAC did use a variant of von Neumann's instruction set. They also used the architecture that he originated for the EDVAC (memory, arithmetic unit, and control interconnected by a single switch), as did the designers of all EDVAC-type machines.

I want now to look at the arguments of several other highly regarded writers in this history—all of whom we have met earlier in a variety of contexts—writers who have treated the stored-program issue more extensively than those cited above. Their views are worth examining, not only because they constitute different positions along the broad spectrum of this controversy, but also because they shed further light upon the concept of program modification, its ramifications, and von Neumann's role throughout. These writers are, in turn, Paul Ceruzzi, Nancy Stern, William Aspray, and Herman Goldstine.

Ceruzzi, over a number of years, moves the full length of the spectrum, from defining the stored-program concept merely as that of storing both program and numerical data in a computer's memory to acknowledging its perhaps most profound aspect of all as that of program modifiability. In his 1983 book, *Reckoners: The Prehistory of the Digital Computer from Relays to the Stored Program Concept, 1935-1945*, he allows this latter aspect to emerge only gradually over the years.[11] Indeed, he approaches the subject by allotting the entire ten-year post-ENIAC period, 1945–1955, to this emergence!

Ceruzzi starts by stating that the pioneers in this decade came to two realizations: first, that the computer could do more than numerical operations; second, that instructions "should be kept internally in its memory alongside the data . . . because they were not really different entities, and it would be artificial to keep them separate." Later, he calls this equivalency fundamental, "the essence of the stored program principle." Not until his penultimate chapter does he get to the idea of program modification—and then only in connection with the compiler programs that appeared in the 1950s. Although he makes very clear that this capability resulted from the stored-program concept, in his view it took years to evolve from the original idea of storing the instructions along with the data.

It would seem, in fact, that the pioneers themselves (including von Neumann) failed to grasp what Ceruzzi terms "the logical basis" of their own inventions! He writes on page 132:

> An understanding of the true nature of computing emerged [after the war] from discussions among the computer pioneers about their machines, and especially about a feature they were considering for future computers. That feature was of course the stored-program concept, which, *when finally understood*, revealed the logical basis of what they had invented. [italics added]

He repeats several times, in this 1983 work, that the concept took a long time to be understood—and had yet to be fully understood at the time of his writing.

As to Eckert's role, Ceruzzi cites his invention of the mercury-delay-line memory to store both instructions and data, noting that it was conceived not only as a way to increase storage capacity and speed of operation but also as a way to make the EDVAC much easier to program. As to von Neumann's role, though he goes so far as to term him "the central figure in the transition of computing from machines like the ENIAC to the modern stored-program computer," he does not recognize either the particular advance that he brought to Eckert's original idea or his suggestion of the cathode-ray-tube memory that was used in the Institute for Advanced Study (IAS) family of stored-program computers.

Another decade later, however, Ceruzzi (now curator of aerospace computing and electronics at the Smithsonian's National Air and Space Museum) at last expands the stored-program concept to include, rather than just make possible, program self-modification through the substitution instruction. Indeed, he even finds that facility at its earliest appearance, in von Neumann's 1945 report. He comes to this revised view of the history in an article for the *Encyclopedia of Computer Science*.[12]

Like Gill and Rosin in this same volume, Ceruzzi has now settled on perceiving "the so-called von Neumann machine model of computer architecture" as a single, Moore School package, "originally conceived by J. Presper Eckert, John Mauchly, and John von Neumann in the mid-1940's." The First Draft Report, which becomes the main focus of this article, is accordingly cast as a summary of the joint ideas of these three men.

Ceruzzi here provides a clear and perceptive characterization of the stored-program concept, as formulated in that report:

> What is most remembered about the EDVAC Report is its description of the stored program principle. . . . As initially conceived, it had three features. First, storing programs in high-speed memory meant that the processor could fetch instructions at the same high speeds as data. Second, by not having a fixed barrier between data and program storage, a computer could solve a variety of problems in which the ratio of instructions to data might vary. Third, by storing instructions in the same memory unit as data, the processor could operate on and modify those instructions, especially by computing new addresses for operands required by an instruction.

Without recognizing (or realizing) that the last of his three listed features was von Neumann's alone, he goes on to praise it in particular as "the most profound innovation" of "the EDVAC group"—one "as much responsible for the present-day 'computer age' as is the invention of the integrated circuit." Oddly enough, though—and as he did in his first venture onto this turf—Ceruzzi continues to deny that Moore School group, or anyone else, much insight into the implications of their innovation before the mid-1950s! Rather, he finds it "testimony to the originality of the team's thinking that their original concept has proved so adaptable and seminal."

<<<>>>

Stern's treatment of this controversy in her 1981 book takes a different tack entirely, centering on a broad speculative view of the roles played by the two sides.[13] As to the stored-program concept itself, although she offers no explicit definition, it is for her just the original idea of automatic program storage in a large read-write memory as proposed by Eckert. At no point does she mention, or even allude to, von Neumann's further idea of automatic program modification as an aspect of that concept.

Stern begins with the suggestion that the stored-program concept arose from a recognition by the Moore School engineers of a need to achieve "automatic control" in the machine that would succeed the ENIAC; a need that would, in turn, she writes on page 28, require a suitable memory:

> The stored-program concept that became the basis for automatic control in all subsequent computers required the invention of a computer memory, a technological achievement that proved exceedingly difficult for postwar engineers.

As to credit for the concept, she cites Eckert's January 1944 disclosure of a magnetic drum or disk form of memory as "broadly indicating a stored-program device" well before von Neumann's arrival on the scene. At the same time, however, she credits von Neumann with assisting in the concept's development once he joined the Moore School group. She also cites Eckert's conception of the mercury-delay-line store for the EDVAC and von Neumann's conception of the cathode-ray-tube store for the IAS Computer, both designed to facilitate the stored-program concept.

Stern devotes her chapter 3 to von Neumann and his First Draft Report, the distribution of which, she notes, "formed the basis for computer and stored programming design in the late 1940s."[14] And here she offers her own (flawed) differentiation between Eckert and Mauchly on the one hand, and von Neumann on the other, that is reminiscent of her elaborate (likewise flawed) designation of Atanasoff as "inventor" and Mauchly as "innovator" elsewhere in that same book (see chap. 7).

Eckert and Mauchly are seen as primarily practical engineers or applied scientists, von Neumann as primarily a theorist or pure scientist. She writes, on page 79:

> Whereas Eckert and Mauchly were predominantly concerned with technical feasibility and with the actual construction of an operational product, von Neumann's primary interest was in providing a theoretical construct for electronic digital computers.

Of von Neumann's report (actually published for the first time in full as an appendix to her book), Stern states that its objective was to develop a "logical structure" that was "machine-independent and hence could be universally applied"; for him, then, "the technical aspects of any specific high-speed computer were not of major significance."

Her problem here is that von Neumann did care, very much, about the potential practical outcome of his formulations. His goal was a *computer*, first the projected EDVAC of the Moore School, then his own Institute for Advanced Study Computer. In the EDVAC report, he created logical constructs as a step toward particular electronic applications, always with an eye to the practical limitations of the current technology.

Stern herself reveals this concern in a quote from section 5.7 of that report, where von Neumann is addressing the serious problem of vacuum-tube failure. He proposes using as few tubes as possible to build a device (such as a multiplier), rather than using many more tubes in order to speed up its operation. But he recognizes the need to take careful account of the state of tube technology in reaching any decision:

> The point to which the application of this principle can be profitably pushed will, of course, depend on the actual physical characteristics of the available vacuum tube elements. It may be, that the optimum is not at a 100 percent application of this principle and that some compromise will be found to be optimal. However, this will always depend on the momentary state of the vacuum tube technique.

Stern takes this passage to indicate that while "von Neumann recognized that technological considerations might, in the end, impose constraints on his structure," nevertheless "their import, in terms of overall design, was minimal." I take the passage, rather, to indicate an ever-present regard for such considerations.

In a later passage, not quoted by Stern, von Neumann makes this practical goal even more explicit in explaining why he resorts to neural elements for the logical constructs of his machine design. He writes in section 6.1:

> The ideal procedure would be to treat the elements as what they are intended to be: as vacuum tubes. However, this would necessitate a detailed analysis of specific radio engineering questions at this early stage of the discussion, when too many alternatives are still open, to be treated all exhaustively and in detail. Also, the numerous alternative possibilities for arranging arithmetical procedures, logical control, etc., would superpose on the equally numerous possibilities for the choice of types and sizes of vacuum tubes and other circuit elements from the point of view of practical performance, etc. All this would produce an involved and opaque situation in which the preliminary orientation which we are now attempting would be hardly possible.
>
> In order to avoid this we will base our considerations on a hypothetical element, which functions essentially like a vacuum tube. . . . We re-emphasize: This simplification is only temporary, only a transient standpoint, to make the present preliminary discussion possible. After the conclusions of the preliminary discussion *the elements will have to be reconsidered in their true electromagnetic nature*. [italics added]

He adds that the "analogs of human neurons [as adapted from the McCulloch-Pitts notation] seem to provide elements of just the kind postulated [here]."

Finally, the degree of von Neumann's regard for the practical should also be apparent from his suggestion, in that same Draft Report, of cathode-ray-tube storage as an alternative to Eckert's mercury-delay-line storage.

I find William Aspray's treatment of this controversy especially perplexing. In chapter 8, we saw him assert, in both a 1986 *Annals* article and a 1990 coauthored book, that a machine must be stored program to merit the designation *computer*— difficult as such a stricture became for him. In neither instance, however, does he address the question of credit for the concept. Now, in a book devoted entirely to one of the contending parties, *John von Neumann and the Origins of Modern Computing*, also published in 1990, Aspray delves into the issue.[15] Yet, in the course of providing extended (valuable) documentation of the claims of the two sides, he neither renders a judgment of his own nor defines the debated concept, even implicitly.

Instead, his procedure, as given on pages 37–39, is first to let the concept arise from the Moore School's spring 1945 meetings, which by their very nature make assessment of individual contributions "difficult," he feels; then to let the concept find expression in von Neumann's June report. Like Stern (and others), however, in his portrayal of that report, "the focal point of the controversy over von Neumann's role in the development of the stored-program computer," he makes no allusion to the aspect of internal program modification.

Only some thirty pages later, long after he has left the stored-program concept, does Aspray come upon that second aspect in a Goldstine-von Neumann document of April 1947, *Planning and Coding of Problems for an Electronic Computing Instrument*, Volume 1.[16] Here he writes:

> The authors pointed out that in the execution of orders, the computer does not simply pass through them a single time in a linear fashion. To gain its full flexibility, the computer must be able to execute transfer orders (which allow it to jump backward or forward to some specified place in the instruction sequence) and substitution sequences (which allow the coded sequence of instructions to be modified in the course of the computation), and these changes may be conditioned on the results obtained earlier in the computation.

Aspray seems not only to have separated this aspect from the essence of the stored-program concept, but also to have failed to realize that the substitution instruction was included in the 1945 Draft Report; moreover, that it was fully and explicitly depicted in the 1946 *Preliminary Discussion of the Logical Design of an Electronic Computing Instrument*, which he has, in fact, just presented.[17]

It should be noted that Aspray, in a different context in a different book, also from that same year 1990, has included this vital von Neumann contribution in his presentation of the stored-program concept—*without reference*, however, to the role of either Eckert or von Neumann. In his epilog to *Computers Before Computing*, he both defines the concept fully and acknowledges its enhancement of computer technology:

> The use of stored programming (i.e., instructing the machine through the use of programs which the machine stores internally and modifies and executes automatically) makes practical the computer's general-purpose capability.[18]

Finally, Aspray's failure, in his book on von Neumann, to delineate these two men's contributions shortchanges Eckert. Although he quotes Eckert and Mauchly from various sources as to what von Neumann did and did not do, and presents them as vital members of the Moore School discussions, he never clearly credits Eckert with the original *idea* for a large read-write memory to store both instructions and data. Rather, he credits him with the *invention* of such a memory, but, at least by implication, credits Goldstine, among others at Aberdeen's Ballistic Research Laboratory, with providing its rationale—after its invention!

On page 36 of that von Neumann volume Aspray has Eckert, in his January 1944 disclosure of a magnetic calculating machine, proposing to include automatic programming but making "no suggestions about the implementation." He also has him, "several months later," conceiving his mercury-delay-line memory as "a register to store numbers" and proposing its use "for the internal memory in the new computing device."

But now he writes:

> By late summer the BRL representatives, especially Goldstine and [Leland E.] Cunningham, had decided they wanted to improve on the ENIAC's clumsy setup procedures and small number (twenty) of internal storage registers [accumulators]. On 11 August Goldstine wrote to Colonel [Leslie E.] Simon [BRL Director] suggesting a new research and development contract for a computing machine that would improve ENIAC's programming and memory facilities.

Of course, it was Eckert's desire to improve on the ENIAC in just this way that had motivated him, months earlier, to invent his delay-line store and to propose automatic data and program entry!

Aspray appears, to a certain extent, to be following Goldstine here. In his book, *The Computer from Pascal to von Neumann*, Goldstine presents "the idea of the stored program" as evolving only in that "late summer" of 1944, with himself a key figure in this evolution.[19] On pages 198–200, he quotes two letters he wrote to Colonel Paul N. Gillon, BRL Assistant Director, one on August 21, the other on September 2, 1944. Both of these letters, like that of his August 11 memorandum to Colonel Simon cited by Aspray, were reports to his superiors by Captain Goldstine, written in his capacity as Army Ordnance liaison officer to the Moore School.

These letters explained the ENIAC's already recognized shortcomings in some detail, together with "the improvements I wish to realize" in a new machine. The second one in particular suggested storage of "the program routine . . . in coded form in the same type storage devices" as the data. This letter also noted that "von Neumann, Eckert, and I have formulated quite definite ideas along these lines," while the first had noted that von Neumann was "displaying great interest in the ENIAC" and that Eckert had "some excellent ideas on a very cheap device" to replace the ENIAC's accumulator for the storage of data.

Goldstine explains in his text that von Neumann "had only just become acquainted with the project" (having first visited on or about August 7) and cites his immediate engagement as "an excellent example of the speed of his mind." He then writes:

> Notice that in the fortnight between the two letters the idea of the stored program seems to have evolved. Indeed, in the September letter the concept already appears in quite modern guise, whereas in the August one the author [Goldstine] was trying to evolve an emendation of the ENIAC's controls to make it a little more useful.

He adds:

> All this must make clear that the fall of 1944 was perhaps the most eventful time in the intellectual history of the computer. All evidence from the correspondence of the period certainly bears this out.

This general assessment, along with other more specific assertions, effectively limits Eckert to the invention of a memory device that suited the vision of others. These other assertions include what can only be seen as a manipulation of the dates involved. For Goldstine, unlike Aspray (and Stern, and Metropolis and Worlton), recognizes neither the January 1944 date of Eckert's proposal of magnetic storage, with automatic programming, nor the early 1944 date of his invention of the mercury-delay-line memory. He manages to postdate both—to his own advantage, it seems.

On page 208 of his book, Goldstine credits Eckert and Mauchly with the idea for "a rotating magnetic device" only as of their EDVAC project report of September 1945, a year and nine months late. He quotes most of the sentence on page 2 of that report in which they describe this rotating magnetic device, but he simply passes over their reference, *in the very same sentence*, to Eckert's "January, 1944" disclosure—and their further comment on the storage of "operating instructions and function tables."

Similarly, Goldstine overlooks, *in the very next paragraph* on this same page 2, their claim of "the invention of the acoustic delay line memory device by Eckert and Mauchly early in 1944." Instead, he places this invention as late as August of that year, on the basis of the date when *he* first learned of it. Goldstine writes, on page 185:

> It is evident that by mid-August . . . new technological ideas had emerged. In fact there is an undated report by Eckert and Mauchly, written that summer prior to 31 August, when it was sent by Brainerd to me, describing a device, called a delay line, for increasing the storage capacity of the machine. This device, discussed at length below, was to be crucial to the next phase of development.

So it is that, much as he praises this new memory device—even as integral to the great strides being made—Goldstine denies Eckert both the true date of its invention and the original insight into its rationale.

Goldstine is, I fear, resorting to selective editing that promotes his own involvement in the origin of critical concepts in the invention of the EDVAC. He is also inferring too much from his own army documents, to the exclusion of other evidence and other firsthand witnesses. Art recalls sitting with Harry Huskey at the 1976 Los Alamos conference, for example, listening as Mauchly delivered Eckert's paper in his absence. Mauchly paused to comment that Huskey had told him of hearing "about storing programs in the same storage used for computer data" back in April of 1944, when he first joined the ENIAC team.[20]

In a whispered conversation, Harry assured Art that this was his recollection. Art himself is certain that he had heard not only of the idea for automatic program storage but of the idea for the mercury-delay-line memory that same spring of 1944.

At Los Alamos, Mauchly also objected to Goldstine's presentation of this period in his book, attributing his misunderstanding, possibly, to a long absence due to illness. As Goldstine notes in his book, he was hospitalized with infectious hepatitis some time in May of 1944 and was not back on duty until July 24. It seems that he may well have missed out on critical developments in that interim. This hardly excuses his editorial oversights, though, in recording the history.

I find curious, too, Goldstine's claim that "the fall of 1944 was perhaps the most eventful time in the intellectual history of the computer," given that the EDVAC design discussions took place only the following spring, and that von Neumann's Draft Report setting forth his further contributions appeared later yet. Indeed, Goldstine does not present the four 1945 meetings as the distinct events that they were. Nor does he refer to the official notes from those March and April meetings, taken by Art. As we have seen, Art's notes provide the historically crucial delineation of the considerations, as of that spring, for a computer based on the mercury-delay-line memory; they also serve to distinguish the advances in architecture and programming made by von Neumann in his June report (see chap. 5).

This omission does allow Goldstine to attribute much more to the summer and fall of 1944 than was really the case. To that end, he even goes so far as to say, on page 186, that the group formed to explore this "new idea" actually started meeting regularly with von Neumann as of that August. The fact is, though discussions did take place during von Neumann's earliest visits, they were of an impromptu nature, in impromptu groupings, as von Neumann was being introduced to the ENIAC and to its evolving successor.

Art recalls quite vividly von Neumann's first visit, in early August, when Mauchly demonstrated the recently finished two-accumulator model for him, and when Art showed him the ENIAC. He also recalls the second visit, in September, when, in the morning, he (Art) stood at a blackboard with a theoretical mathematician von Neumann had brought along from the Institute, discussing this guest's concerns about the stability of flip-flops; and Eckert stood nearby with von Neumann, discussing the differential equation of the vacuum tube. (Eckert had raised the question of whether working out this equation would be useful for his purposes, von Neumann had responded that it would not.)

Art recalls further that on that same September day, he, Eckert, Mauchly, Goldstine, von Neumann, and von Neumann's guest all met together in the afternoon. He does not recall any other meetings that fall or winter, although there may have been one or more. The point here is, however, that the particular group that would tackle EDVAC design problems was assembled in a more formal way—with EDVAC project director S. Reid Warren present—to meet in a particular room on just those four occasions in March and April of 1945. This group was formed, and these meetings held, at von Neumann's instigation to suit his calendar that spring, because he wanted to discuss questions he had been considering with regard to the EDVAC.

In a recent trip to my public library, I was quite amazed to discover the extent to which this wishful hindsight of Goldstine's has led him to shift the timing of events so central to the development of the stored-program concept. The 1996 *Encyclopedia Americana* has a very long entry, "Computers and Computer Science," which in turn has a long article, "History of the Computer," coauthored by Herman Goldstine and Harwood Kolsky. Here all the developments, from those of Eckert in early 1944 to those of von Neumann in mid-1945—and beyond—are encapsulated in a grand three-week spell in August 1944:

> **EDVAC.** In August 1944 Goldstine introduced the mathematician John von Neumann to the ENIAC staff. Von Neumann was captivated by the ENIAC and by the electronic computer in general. A study group consisting of A. W. Burks, J. Presper Eckert, A. K. Goldstine, H. H. Goldstine, Mauchly, von Neumann, and several others was formed, and discussions of a successor to the ENIAC began. In late August 1944 these discussions gave birth to the stored-program

concept and other basic ideas that were to govern computer development for the next two decades. Among these ideas were separation of storage, arithmetic, and control; random-access memory; stored program; arithmetic modification of instructions; conditional branching; binary number and decimal number representations, and consideration of serial and parallel operation. . . .

Von Neumann wrote up the results of this activity in a report entitled "First Draft of a Report on the EDVAC" in 1945.

The authors apparently elected to buy into the Eckert-Mauchly claim that von Neumann's report was no more than a summary of the group discussions—even as they also chose to backdate those discussions from the spring of 1945 to the summer of 1944. In so doing, they sacrifice, as specifically von Neumann's, his idea for program self-modification suggested in that report, and also his post-report realization of the random-access capability of the cathode-ray-tube memory. This depiction also fails to credit Eckert's prior idea for automatic program entry and his conception of the mercury-delay-line store to make that idea feasible. Moreover, at least by implication, von Neumann has become the impetus for all this rapid-fire creativity, at a time when he was just becoming acquainted with electronic computing.

I suppose it might be argued that an article for an encyclopedia requires such condensation of ideas. In that case, however, it could just as easily have been assigned the correct span of time: a year and a half, not three weeks! The purpose served by this move is, apparently, the same as Goldstine proclaims in his 1972 book. He wants to illustrate, more forcefully still, "the speed of [von Neumann's] mind." I cannot think that von Neumann himself would have relished this diminution of the seminal ideas of Eckert, ideas that he credited explicitly in the Moore School meeting of 1947. Nor does the quickness of von Neumann's mind need exaggeration!

Goldstine does, in both his encyclopedia article and his book, credit the von Neumann report with tremendous influence. And he does also, in his book, extol von Neumann's "elucidation of the now famous stored program concept" in that report. Here, in fact, he goes so far as to find him preeminent in the whole process, even as he does recognize the delay-line memory as Eckert's. On pages 197–98, he writes:

To recapitulate: It is obvious that von Neumann, by writing this report, crystallized thinking in the field of computers as no other person ever did. He was, among all members of the group at the Moore School, *the* indispensable one. Everyone there was indispensable as regards some part of the project—Eckert, for example, was unique in his invention of the delay line as a memory device—but only von Neumann was essential to the entire task.

As to associating the feature of program self-modification with the stored-program concept, Goldstine does this in his book also, on pages 259 and 265–66, but only in the context of the Burks-Goldstine-von Neumann *Preliminary Discussion* of June 1946 and the Goldstine-von Neumann *Planning and Coding* report (Vol. 1) of April 1947 (both written at the Institute for Advanced Study).

Let me make clear in passing that my comments on Goldstine's presentation of this history are not meant in any way to discount his major role in the launching of both the ENIAC and the EDVAC projects. Without his appreciation of the potential for each machine in succession, it is doubtful that they would have been funded by the army and built by the Moore School.

I want to close out this presentation of the various positions taken by prominent computer scientists and historians on the definition of, and credit for, the stored-program concept with a computer scientist who extends the concept beyond the two facets we have been addressing. Allan G. Bromley of the University of Sydney, Australia, in an article for the July 1983 *Annals*, delineates *three* "stages" of development for the stored-program concept.[21] Writing in response to our 1981 *Annals* article on the ENIAC, he accepts the two features Art and I put forward, and also, at least tentatively, our crediting the earlier one to Eckert, the later to von Neumann. But he believes the concept should include a third stage, the idea that "programs could be used to build other programs."

Now this is the idea of a library of subroutines (predecessor to the compiler and the assembler), from which a special *combining routine* could make selections to form a new program for the purposes of each particular problem. These library items might be stored in separate auxiliary memories or grouped in an auxiliary memory system. Bromley, again offering a "guess, though only a guess" as to the source of this third stage, suggests that it was reached "with the EDSAC [Electronic Delay Storage Automatic Calculator] before mid-1949" by Wilkes and David J. Wheeler, at the University of Cambridge.

Aside from whether Bromley's third stage is properly a definitive element in the stored-program concept, it is an interesting one to contemplate, and one not easily pinned down as to credit. We know that von Neumann had thought of a library of subroutines by the spring or early summer of 1946. Art recalls hearing of it from Goldstine not long after he joined the Institute that spring; and he recalls working on it himself while commuting by train between Philadelphia and Princeton, then giving Goldstine a substantial writeup of it before he left for the University of Michigan that fall. We know, too, that the idea was first worked out and written up fully and precisely, with examples, between April 1947 and August 1948, in the Goldstine-von Neumann *Planning and Coding* report.[22] (Art's contribution to *Planning and Coding* is acknowledged in Vol. 1 of that three-volume work.)

Art also published a paper in 1950, "The Logic of Programming Electronic

Digital Computers," giving a detailed analysis of the relation of logic to programming.[23] There he describes the substitution instruction, or command, as a *logical command*, to be distinguished from an *arithmetic command*:

> The substitution command S(x,y,i,z) orders the control to modify the command at y by substituting in its i'th argument place (i = 1,2,3, or 4) the number at address x, and then to go to z for the next command.

He also explains the concept of a library of subroutines, or subprograms, and its rationale in a way that clearly "dates" the thinking of that era as these basic ideas were evolving:

> Most problems solved on a computer can be broken down into a number of sub-problems. . . . When a specific problem is to be solved it is not programmed as if it were unique but is dealt with in the following way. First, the program functions corresponding to the fundamental processes involved in solving the problem are selected from a library of programs. Second, a statement is made in the machine language of the unique features of the problem. . . . Finally, a <u>combining program</u> which will bind all of the free variables (including the addresses) of the sub-programs is added to these programs to give the desired definite program.
>
> There is a very practical reason for employing this method of instructing a computer. An electronic digital computer is extremely fast. . . . It is important that the increased speed of computation provided by electronic machines be matched by a corresponding increase in the speed of programming. This is possible if programs are constructed by combining already prepared program functions. It should be noted that the specification of program functions into definite programs is not accomplished by rewriting the programs by hand outside of the machine, but is done by the machine under the direction of the combining program. This is significant, for since most of the addresses in the program are represented by free variables the task of specification is a substantial one. Thus a large part of the work of program composition is done by the machine.

Art then "briefly suggests" the idea of an intermediate program language for data processing. Of this, he concludes:

> Thus we can teach the machine to make the translation from the programmer's language to the machine language, and once this is done the more convenient programmer's language can be used for instructing the machine to solve problems.

He went on to develop this idea in a report to the Burroughs Adding Machine Co., where he was consulting. Donald E. Knuth and Luis Trabb Pardo summarize this Burroughs report in their Los Alamos paper, "The Early Development of Programming Languages."[24] They comment that "Burks took portions of two machine programs . . . and showed how they could be expressed at a higher level of abstraction."

In their 1951 book, *The Preparation of Programs for an Electronic Digital Computer*, Wilkes and coauthors Wheeler and Stanley Gill present a version of a library of subroutines that differs from the Goldstine-von Neumann version of 1947–1948 in two important respects.[25] First, the earlier work uses the code of the IAS Computer, with its random-access cathode-ray-tube main memory; the later work uses the code of the EDSAC, with its EDVAC-type serial-access mercury-delay-line main memory. Second, the earlier work details a potential library to be stored on magnetic tape or wire; the later work details an actual punched-paper-tape library of subroutines already built or anticipated for the performance of particular tasks on the EDSAC.

It is relevant here that no library of subroutines was developed for the IAS Computer, and that even its input-output was via punched paper tape and then punched cards, not magnetic wire or tape. Thus Wilkes and his colleagues describe the *actual*, whereas Goldstine and von Neumann describe the *possible*. It is also relevant that the later authors acknowledge in their preface a debt "to Dr. H. H. Goldstine and to Dr. J. von Neumann . . . , whose privately circulated reports we have been privileged to use."

Regardless of who first had the idea for a library of subroutines, it was Mauchly who first went public with it, in his paper on "EDVAC-type machines" given at Harvard University in January 1947.[26] There he presents it as a natural by-product of the basic substitution instruction:

> Even greater powers are conferred by the ability to use one instruction to modify another. An unlimited number of different instructions may be generated within the machine by this process. One can, therefore, modify not only the numbers which are substituted into the process, but the process itself, in any desired systematic way.

Although he does not work out its implementation, he goes on to introduce the idea of building new programs from other programs:

> In order that such subroutines, as they can well be called, be truly general, the machine must be endowed with the ability to modify instructions, such as placing specific quantities into general subroutines. Thus is created a new set of operations which might be said to form a calculus of instructions.

Mauchly concludes with a number of questions that remain to be explored for the establishment of "a library" and the means of integrating withdrawals from it.

As to Bromley's stipulation of this idea as a "stage 3" in the stored-program concept, Art and I do not consider it a defining feature of that concept. Bromley justifies his position on the ground of its further advancement of the programming technology:

> This is the essential idea of the assemblers and compilers that give modern computers so much of their power and has extended the concept of what is naturally and easily programmable far beyond the obvious capabilities of the machine itself.

We argue for a cutoff at "stage 2" in what is essentially a hierarchical development of ideas that could go on, in fact, to the present day. We point out that while von Neumann thought of internal program modification only after Eckert had thought of storing instructions, like arithmetic data, in read-write memory devices, the two ideas together were both necessary to and sufficient for the ensuing developments of which Bromley writes, and beyond.

There is the further technological argument that what Eckert and von Neumann provided was *hardware* and *software* design for the EDVAC, whereas the library of subroutines was software design alone. To trace the steps: Eckert's idea for automatic programmability was a software idea that depended on the hardware design of a large, fast read-write memory; von Neumann's idea of including a substitution instruction in his program language was a software idea that depended on the design of new control hardware; the idea of a library of subroutines was a software idea that required no further hardware design of the basic machine. Indeed, the Wilkes-Wheeler-Gill library was not developed until *after* the EDSAC was completed in mid-1949—the date Bromley cites for that library.

In short, the original hardware and software design of Eckert and von Neumann showed the way for a multitude of programming possibilities. Bromley himself recognizes as much in his comment that the ability to build new programs "has extended the concept of what is naturally programmable far beyond the obvious capabilities *of the machine itself*" [italics added here]. Of course, phenomenal hardware developments also ensued, but they supplanted and augmented the original conceptions rather than basically altering them.

Moreover, Wilkes and his coauthors, like Mauchly in his Harvard paper, present libraries of subroutines, not as integral to the EDVAC concept but as evolving from a computer's facility to modify its program—a facility they characterize on page 9 as "of great importance [and] perhaps the feature most characteristic of program design for machines like the EDSAC." As we saw earlier, Wilkes in his 1982 talk in Houston—for reasons best known to him—was to omit from consideration von Neumann's original inventive idea of program modifiability, which Wilkes and his coauthors in 1951 had considered so central to their computer's program design.

Clearly, as with the definitions of *computer* and *general-purpose*, the definition of *stored-program* has its arbitrary element. Art and I espouse our view of a two-stage (Eckert-von Neumann) process in the hope of establishing a reasoned standard. For, not only is there disagreement among those who define the term, but there is widespread usage of it with no indication at all of its meaning.

We think the historical context supports our definition, even though the term itself did not come into currency until long after the concept was invented. It had a clear antecedent in the expression *EDVAC-type machine*, which had arisen from the June 1945 von Neumann report on the EDVAC and the September 1945 Eckert-Mauchly progress report on the EDVAC, both of which included the two aspects. The expression "stored-program computer" was then used by early designers, and it continues in use to this day by historians as they recognize the EDVAC-type machines and the IAS-type machines as the two earliest families of stored-program computers.

I hasten to add that we are not nearly so concerned about definition as we are about the assignment of credit that often accompanies references to the concept. Most writers—I have cited several—attribute the concept to Eckert and Mauchly, or the Moore School group, usually with the implication, at least, that the term covers only the initial aspect. Some do sort out the two aspects but assign both to Eckert and Mauchly. Still others assign them to all three parties as one unified concept. No one, of course, assigns both aspects to von Neumann, who himself disavowed any part in the invention of the mercury-delay-line memory as early as 1947, in a meeting called by Dean Harold Pender at the Moore School.

We hope that in the long run writers will come to treat both aspects of the concept as definitive, with credit apportioned separately. Short of that, we hope that writers who see the program modification aspect only as derivative from the automatic program storage aspect also will apportion credit. And we do acknowledge a great step forward by those who recognize that von Neumann did much more than "summarize" the thinking of Eckert and Mauchly, even as they elect to attribute both aspects to both sides of the controversy.

It seems fitting to conclude this chapter on the major obstacle to a resolution of the dispute over invention of the stored-program concept (or computer) with one of the most engaging *Annals* pieces on this topic. In its April 1985 issue, that journal reproduced the minutes of the April 8, 1947, meeting called by Dean Harold Pender of the Moore School to try to iron out differences between Eckert and Mauchly, on the one hand, and von Neumann, on the other, as to their respective contributions to the EDVAC.[27] It is fascinating just to have these three back together in one room grappling with a document whose import not one of them had fully realized earlier.

As we saw in chapter 5, ENIAC trial Judge Larson was to declare this document, von Neumann's "First Draft of a Report on the EDVAC," a publication barring patent claims on any of its inventive content, no matter whose ideas were at stake. He applied this "bar" to the ENIAC as well as to the EDVAC because, he explained, the Draft Report disclosed not just the EDVAC but, more broadly, an "automatic electronic digital computer," the entity for which Sperry Rand was claiming absolute priority for Mauchly and Eckert.

Larson said that as a publication the report was barring because it had been circulated in June of 1945, more than a year before the ENIAC patent was applied for (and even longer with regard to EDVAC patents). Indeed, the ENIAC application had yet to be filed at the time of the Moore School conference.

We also saw that Army Ordnance, as contractors for both the ENIAC and the EDVAC, had been supplying the legal work for the procurement of patents in the names of Eckert and Mauchly. Now three Ordnance attorneys from Washington and two Aberdeen Proving Ground scientists were in attendance. The Moore School was represented by two faculty members in addition to Pender, and the University of Pennsylvania by an administrative officer. Von Neumann was accompanied by Goldstine, who by then had joined him on a permanent basis at the Institute for Advanced Study.

In his 1973 decision, Larson cited this 1947 conference as the point at which it had been "clearly and unequivocally established" that the von Neumann report was a barring publication. The entire focus at the conference, however, was on aspects of the EDVAC, not at all on the ENIAC. Ordnance had every intention of proceeding with the ENIAC patent, but was deeply concerned both with the patentability of the EDVAC because of the report and with possible contention over inventorship.

Ordnance attorney Joseph P. Church, serving as chairman, voiced his department's interest in securing an agreement among the three principals as to who invented what. He stated emphatically, a number of times, that if they could not agree, Ordnance would no longer participate in the patenting process for any aspect of the EDVAC. He also stated emphatically, and a number of times, that Ordnance considered the Draft Report a barring publication. The principals were free, of course, to pursue patents on their own, with their private attorneys. But, regardless of who applied for patents on the EDVAC, his department would send a copy of the report to the U.S. Patent Office, together with an opinion that it was a publication.

> In other words, if the parties left here not agreed on a course of action, each would be free to file applications to the Patent Office and each would be confronted with this publication.

After all, he said, Ordnance was a part of the U.S. government. Mauchly and Eckert had disclosed to Ordnance their own inventive claims for the EDVAC, and now Church urged them to reveal these "embodiments" to von Neumann in the hope that either he would accede to them or the three could argue them out. Neither Church nor his colleagues really expected the present gathering to sift through the many detailed Eckert-Mauchly disclosures; all parties soon agreed instead to identify and discuss only major patentable features of the EDVAC. The hope was really for agreement on a procedure so that Ordnance could move forward—or not.

The minutes of this meeting reflect considerable confusion—it was von Neumann who more than once declared his own confusion—over patent law and

Patent Office procedure. There were also frequent shifts in subject as the parties tried to clarify the issues affecting themselves. One fact, however, became clear fairly early and was accepted by all. *If* this Draft Report was a publication, the EDVAC as portrayed therein could not be patented!

As Church explained, the report embraced the "broad conception" sufficiently for persons skilled in electronics to "work up an embodiment of the thing"—*some* embodiment, that is. And, again, *if* the report was a publication, only specific inventions not disclosed in it could now be patented. "You have got the publication which might just as well be a patent," he said.

Eckert, Mauchly, and von Neumann all seemed genuinely surprised by this characterization of the report. Eckert was particularly dismayed, feeling that the report should have been classified and should not have been distributed, but having to face the fact that the law cared only *whether* it had been distributed. Ultimately, he agreed to proceed as though it were a barring publication, reserving the right to consult his private attorney, a Mr. Smith, later.

Von Neumann had stated that he had no financial interest in his own contributions to the EDVAC and no intention of filing for any patents. Yet the invention had been a joint endeavor, so that it was "a matter to consider to the interest of anyone concerned." Whatever rights he had, he said, would probably be turned over to the Institute for Advanced Study. As to the status of his report:

> This report was not written as a document but as a report to clarify my own ideas
> or for discussion with others in the group and was certainly not written to stake
> out claims. However, I don't think it makes discussion superfluous.

He now found it "very difficult" that the Draft Report should be considered a barring publication. In the end, though, as Church pressed the matter, he agreed to its being so presented for purposes of patent application.

Mauchly held out most strongly for the possibility that the Patent Office might not find the report a publication. Asked by Goldstine if he would "go along and accept this as a publication and agree to limit any claims accordingly," he said:

> I'm not sure it's strictly the right thing to do. Seems that inasmuch as we didn't
> publish it or distribute it we should try to claim whatever we can. We may find
> it not allowed.

All three did explore at some length which items they would claim if the Draft Report was indeed a publication. Von Neumann volunteered that the acoustic-delay-line memory, mentioned in the report, was Eckert's idea. He also clarified his deliberate omission of any reference to the *mercury*-delay-line memory (which, in fact, was classified at the time), leaving Eckert free to file on that specific version. Pender here brought up Sharpless's claim to coinvention—

his crucial suggestion of polishing the tube's end crystals for the reliable transmission of signals in mercury—but Eckert claimed that this had been his idea and Sharpless had merely done the polishing.

It was Eckert who volunteered that the Draft Report mentioned the broader principle of memory regeneration, wondering whether "general means" could be claimed. Church responded with Ordnance's opinion that "that report would prevent you from getting any dominating claim" on such a device.

On the issue of binary serial adders, Eckert said that these had been discussed before von Neumann entered the picture; Goldstine said that later forms were essentially von Neumann's; and, in the end, von Neumann said that his side would very probably "have nothing to say" if Eckert and Mauchly applied for patents on particular adders.

As this meeting drew to a close, the Ordnance lawyers felt quite secure about filing for the mercury-delay-line memory and several adders, at least, but they were still unwilling to proceed without explicit acquiescence by von Neumann on other aspects of the EDVAC. Church now urged Eckert and Mauchly to agree to show von Neumann their patent applications before they submitted them. He also again urged them to agree to reveal the disclosures they had already submitted to Ordnance, so as to address any von Neumann objections as early as possible in the application process.

Ultimately, Church reached a satisfactory settlement. Subject to the advice of private counsel, each side agreed to reveal its disclosures and then its patent applications. Ordnance was assured a minimum of effort—and strain—in filing for EDVAC features on behalf of Eckert and Mauchly, even as it moved forward with the ENIAC application (filed on June 26). Eckert and Mauchly remained free to reject Church's view of the von Neumann Draft Report as a barring publication if they were so advised, but would lose Ordnance's help with EDVAC items if they did.

Actually, as we have seen, they did something in between. They applied for patents through their own attorneys, not revealing any information to von Neumann. And, despite Church's prediction, they were granted a patent not just on the mercury-delay-line memory but also on the broad concept of a regenerative memory. They obtained various adder patents, as well. Then, years later, Judge Larson found the Regenerative Memory patent unenforceable because of derivation from Atanasoff, and the adder patents, also really derived from Atanasoff, unenforceable on other, equally serious, grounds. (See chaps. 1, 2, and 5.)

At the same time, while they did not concede that the Draft Report was a publication, Eckert and Mauchly were apparently sufficiently convinced that it was—or that the Patent Office would think it was—to refrain from trying to patent the EDVAC as a complete entity.

It is striking that at the April 1947 conference, von Neumann not only acknowledged the delay-line memory as Eckert's and let the adders rest with him and Mauchly, but also declared that "certainly" not all of the material in his Draft Report was his; whereas Mauchly and Eckert avoided an outright admission that any EDVAC concepts originated with von Neumann. The closest they came was Mauchly's concession that not all of the material was "necessarily" theirs. In later years, they were to claim it all. Von Neumann has often been charged with never admitting Eckert's contribution to items in his report, which went out under his name only, but he clearly did so, and freely, at this meeting.

The atmosphere of the meeting—given that we have only the spoken word to go by, not facial expression or tone of voice—was on the whole civil if not always courteous. There were frequent attempts, by the four contenders themselves, to find fruitful avenues for discussion, followed by some progress toward mutual understanding. The greatest discord was over the issuance of the report, with the sharpest exchanges between Eckert and Goldstine, who pressed von Neumann's case rather more aggressively than von Neumann himself did.

Goldstine saw his distribution of this "paper" as an act within an academic setting that happened to "[bar] several persons involved without any particular attempt to." Eckert objected that "some ideas which [he and Mauchly] suggested" were included without their knowing it. Eckert said that he felt on the defensive—as well he might, with Goldstine suggesting it was enough that they knew of the report at the time it was issued, and with Samuel Lubkin of Aberdeen reminding them that they had had a year in which to apply for patents on anything in the report that was theirs.

Eckert did, in the course of summing up progress toward the EDVAC before von Neumann's arrival at the Moore School, make a comment that belied his later claims concerning the stored-program concept. Noting that "what we needed was a large memory," he said that the first proposal (of 1944) was to use magnetized disks that could be either permanent or nonpermanent, the latter "essentially established for setting up a given problem."

Here then was Eckert's explicit acknowledgment that he *had* seen the read-write feature of a large memory as a way to overcome the ENIAC's manual setup difficulty. Apparently, in 1947 he was still allowing von Neumann the further idea of program modifiability, as he and Mauchly had done in their September 1945 report on the EDVAC.

On the other hand, Eckert overreached the EDVAC concepts under discussion when he staked a claim in undisputable von Neumann territory. He had gone on from the magnetized disk form of memory to his idea for the mercury-delay-line form, but then he mentioned another "alternative," also prior to von Neumann's arrival: "obviously use a cathode ray tube." We have seen all along that the mercury-delay-line memory *was* Eckert's idea. But the cathode-ray-tube memory, with its potential for random access, was definitely von Neumann's (see chap. 5).

Neither von Neumann nor Goldstine said a word at this conference when Eckert laid claim to von Neumann's invention as "obvious." This may have been partly because Dean Pender (who had already been reminded by Ordnance lawyer Max Libman that he could have avoided "all this difficulty" if he had "tied Mauchly and Eckert up in the first place") jumped in once more to grill Eckert on the issue of coinvention by others on the Moore School team. As we saw in chapter 5, von Neumann based the Institute for Advanced Study Computer on the cathode-ray-tube memory, and Mauchly and Eckert were not able to develop it sufficiently to apply for a patent.

In her introduction to this *Annals* presentation of the conference minutes, Nancy Stern finds more open discord than I do, commenting, for example, that Eckert and Mauchly "only barely masked their fury toward von Neumann and Goldstine." While Eckert was obviously frustrated over the status of the Draft Report, he used no stronger language than "I object that" or "I don't agree" or "We are worried about." When told that the report would prevent the patenting of a broad regenerative memory device, he said, "That is actually pretty serious." And as the bad news truly sank in that he and Mauchly were blocked from claims on anything in the report, however original and valuable, he responded, "We might just as well face it philosophically."

Stern also surmises that the Ordnance lawyers "were so respectful of, or even awed by, von Neumann's abilities and prestige that they were unable or unwilling to make any accusations." She makes this charge with regard to "the apparent breach of confidentiality" in his report's distribution, a breach that she claims "was given short shrift by the government attorneys." But here, as in her book's criticism of Judge Larson, she fails to see that, like Larson, these lawyers had no choice but to follow patent law: they had to recognize that, rightly or wrongly, the report *had been distributed.* She fails to see the proper function of the people she is criticizing.

At the same time, Stern also surmises that even though Church in his role as chairman "claimed complete objectivity," his "sympathies rested squarely with Eckert and Mauchly"! I would say that he was not only firm but downright blunt in breaking the bad news to them.

TEN

A HAPPY CONVERGENCE

On May 7, 1988, Arthur and I were in Ames, Iowa, for the formal unveiling of Clark R. Mollenhoff's book, *Atanasoff: Forgotten Father of the Computer*, by the Iowa State University Press.[1] Since our book, *The First Electronic Computer: The Atanasoff Story*, was being issued at this same time by the University of Michigan Press, the folks at Iowa were gracious enough not only to invite us to Clark's presentation but to present our book to their large audience as well.[2] Although we and Clark had written our books independently, we had become acquainted by telephone and had agreed that we were not competitors, but pursuers of a common goal: to establish John Atanasoff as both the inventor and the progenitor of the electronic computer.

As a lawyer and a Pulitzer Prize–winning journalist, Clark had written a cross between a biography and a detailed unfolding of the ENIAC court case. *Atanasoff: Forgotten Father of the Computer* was the last of his eleven books, the culmination of a career devoted to exposing corruption in a wide range of arenas. Clark had taught journalism for twelve years at Washington and Lee University in Lexington, Virginia. For nearly thirty years prior to that, he had worked almost continuously as an investigative reporter for Cowles Publications, in Washington, D.C., writing columns for the *Des Moines Register and Tribune*, the *Minneapolis Star and Tribune*, and *Look Magazine*. He died on March 2, 1991.

Of his career in journalism, Robert D. McFadden writes in the *New York Times* obituary of March 4, 1991:

> Mr. Mollenhoff, whose reporting exposed labor rackets, influence peddling and wrongdoing in government, won the 1958 Pulitzer Prize for national reporting

for his inquiries into corrupt labor practices, including those that sent James R. Hoffa, the president of the teamsters' union, to jail.

He also won many other awards for his reporting, which exposed influence-peddling by Robert G. Baker, an aide to Lyndon B. Johnson when he was Senate majority leader, and the improper acceptance of gifts by Sherman Adams, an aide to President Dwight D. Eisenhower.[3]

Others heap praise upon him as a demanding but inspiring teacher, a fearless investigative reporter, and an impartial critic of presidents.

Fellow journalist George S. Mills, in his Foreword to Mollenhoff's book on Atanasoff, calls him "a legend in Washington" and cites his "courage in confronting formidable officials with unpleasant facts about illegal activities. He is big in size, big in energy, and big in use of the printed word to fight graft and corruption."

As to the legal arm of his professional makeup, I find in *Who's Who in America* that Clark Mollenhoff was admitted to the bar not just in his native Iowa but also in Washington, D.C., in the Supreme Courts of Iowa and of the United States, and in the federal courts.

Clearly, he brought to his Atanasoff venture a remarkable combination of talents and expertise. He also had a kindred interest in the role of his home state in the invention of the computer and, as it happened, an unexpected connection to the man to whose cause he was to devote his last years. For, as he explains in his book, it was J. V.'s wife, Alice, who first called his attention to the ENIAC trial and its outcome, after two months of fruitless waiting for any significant press coverage.

On pages 215–16, he tells of Alice's phone call in mid-December 1973, and of his surprise not only to hear from a woman he had known back in high school in Webster City, Iowa, as the younger sister of his classmate Victor Crosby, but also to hear her claims about her husband's inventive exploits.

Although Alice Atanasoff was approaching Mollenhoff in his capacity as Washington bureau chief for the *Des Moines Register*, she explained that she was not asking him to do a story but to advise her. Mollenhoff tells how, in speaking of her husband, Alice converted his own initial skepticism into a serious involvement:

> When she stated that he was "the inventor of the computer" and that he was having difficulty getting proper public credit for his invention, I was not immediately impressed. However, she was a friend from high school days, and it would not be too much trouble to lend a sympathetic ear to her problem.
>
> John Atanasoff was her husband and she probably had an exaggerated view of his achievements and was unduly upset that her spouse had not been accorded the honor she believed was due him. When she mentioned that he had been a professor of mathematics and physics at Iowa State College, I believed it plausible that he might have some legitimate computer invention claim that would be worth exploring for a story in the *Des Moines Register*.

It was not until Alice made mention of a U.S. District Court decision that established he was the legal father of the electronic digital computer that I became deeply interested, but still with some caution. I asked her several questions about the contents of the decision, and after she read me several paragraphs from that decision, I was convinced. It could be a great story for Iowa and Iowa State University, as well as for the Atanasoffs.

At this point in his book Mollenhoff has already told, in his customarily direct and spirited style, most of the story of the Atanasoff-Berry Computer, the Mauchly connection, the ENIAC project, the approaches to Atanasoff by various corporations leading up to the trial, and the trial itself. He continues with an account of his visit to the Atanasoffs, where he was able to examine the key documents, including Judge Earl Larson's opinion and the Atanasoff-Mauchly correspondence.[4] He also reports on his telephone interviews of both John Mauchly, for his Des Moines article, and, much later, Pres Eckert, for his book.

From my perspective, one of the most fruitful of Mollenhoff's investigative pursuits is his recounting of a series of circumstances that taken together shed considerable light on Mauchly's poor performance at trial and in deposition: his marked failure to prepare and his frequently cavalier attitude.

The first such circumstance, of course, was the impression Atanasoff himself gave Mauchly when he so freely disclosed details of his computer—and even suggestions for converting it into an electronic digital differential analyzer—during Mauchly's visit in 1941. Mauchly's feeling that he was welcome to use Atanasoff's ideas is borne out by his letter, a few months later, simply requesting permission to build, on his own, "some sort of computer which incorporates some of the features of your machine," or, failing such a hybrid, to join with others at the Moore School to build "an '*Atanasoff Calculator*' (a la *Bush* analyzer)."

As we saw in chapter 2, Atanasoff replied that they could discuss their "mutual interests in calculators" at a meeting "in the very near future," but advised him of the need to be "careful about the dissemination of information about our device until a patent application is filed." No such later discussion took place, however, and Mauchly and Eckert proceeded with plans for the ENIAC without further inquiry of Atanasoff. (No such patent application was filed, either.)

Next came Mauchly's part-time employment, from September of 1944 till early 1946, in the Naval Ordnance Laboratory where Atanasoff was engaged in war research. There, as he told Control Data's Allen Kirkpatrick in his 1967 deposition, he not only learned that "the computer had never been finished at Iowa" but also observed that Atanasoff "so far as I could tell had no interest in the design of computers" (see chap. 2). He explained that for these reasons, "rightly or wrongly," he felt free to apply, along with Eckert, for the Regenerative Memory patent.

It became clear in that same deposition that Mauchly—and Sperry Rand attorney Laurence B. Dodds—were caught completely off guard by Kirkpatrick's revelation of one letter after another from the 1941 correspondence, as provided by Atanasoff from his files. It turned out that Mauchly, too, had saved copies of these letters, so crucial in both the Honeywell suit against Sperry Rand and the Sperry Rand suit against Control Data, but had not bothered to find them, whether or not he recalled writing and receiving them.

Mollenhoff's account suggests why Mauchly continued to feel safe as he ignored the subpoena to bring whatever papers he could find to this deposition. Only a few years earlier, Richard K. Richards—Iowa State graduate, boyhood friend of Clifford Berry, and IBM engineer turned full-time writer—had contacted Mauchly about the ABC, in the process revealing an apparent dearth of documentation. As quoted by Mollenhoff on page 98 of his book, Richards said in his March 19, 1963, letter to Mauchly:

> I am writing a new book on digital computers, and I would like to include a bit about Dr. Atanasoff's computer in the historical section. As yet, however, I have been unable to locate any written material describing it. Although a number of people here in Ames saw the computer, none of them seems to know much about how it worked or even what it did. Even Dr. Atanasoff, whom I talked to on the telephone recently, has not come up with anything written.

It had been Atanasoff, in that telephone call, who had prompted Richards to write to Mauchly. But Richards had also contacted Berry, who responded with a March 22 letter telling of Mauchly's Ames visit and suggesting that Mauchly "may still have notes of what he learned from us" (see chaps. 1 and 2).

Mollenhoff states on page 102 that Berry, in this letter and in another dated July 12, also described the ABC from memory in such detail that Richards felt secure in crowning it the first electronic digital computer. Richards was encouraged as well by Berry's comment that copies might still exist of the large number of reports and patent drafts written by himself and Atanasoff. Finally, Mollenhoff states that Richards, with the question of priority out of the way, began to entertain the equally critical possibility of derivation of the ENIAC from the Atanasoff-Berry Computer—as he had begun to call it—via John Mauchly.

With new reason to track down Mauchly, who had not responded to his March letter, Richards finally reached him by phone late in the summer. Told of Berry's recollections of his visit, Mauchly admitted only to having spent several days with Atanasoff in the summer of 1940 (!) or 1941, during which he did see the machine and discuss its operation with Atanasoff—but to a much lesser extent than Berry maintained. In fact, although he remembered Atanasoff, he could not really remember Berry, he said. Nor could he remember having learned anything of consequence on that visit to Iowa.

In chapter 1 of his book, Richards does cite Mauchly's visit to Iowa—"for the specific purpose of studying the computer"—as an "interesting link between the machine and later work."[5] As we saw earlier, it was Richards's 1966 book that first alerted Control Data's Kirkpatrick and the Honeywell lawyers—in that order, as the two firms agreed to share information—to Atanasoff's work and to possible improper claiming in both the Regenerative Memory and the ENIAC patents. Mollenhoff also notes, on pages 131–32 of his book, that while Richards was "a generally reluctant witness," the letters from Berry that he had generated did provide invaluable "testimony from the grave" for trial purposes.

But Mauchly, unaware of such "testimony" and reassured by Richards's 1963 letter to him on the apparent paucity of "written material," still felt quite safe in October 1967, as he approached his deposition in the Regenerative Memory patent case being brought by Sperry Rand against Control Data. Evidently, neither Atanasoff nor anyone else possessed documentation of Atanasoff's machine or of Mauchly's acquaintance with it. With Atanasoff himself still showing no interest, it seemed to have come down to Mauchly's word against Berry's. And, by the time of this deposition, he surely knew that Berry was lost as a witness, having died in October of 1963, just months after being drawn back into this decades-old business by Richards.

But Atanasoff did possess documentation, stacks of it. And the Honeywell and Control Data lawyers, following Richards's lead, had won Atanasoff's confidence to the extent that, on August 29, 1967, he turned over a veritable bonanza of records about his machine and about his contacts with Mauchly. On pages 115–16 of his book, Mollenhoff points up the irony for Honeywell's Charles Call as, the very next day, he attended Mauchly's talk to the Association for Computing Machinery (ACM) in Washington, where moderator Isaac Auerbach suddenly asked Mauchly to comment on Richards's recent claims for the Atanasoff-Berry Computer and any connection to the ENIAC.

Mollenhoff tells of Mauchly's deprecation of the ABC as an incomplete device "that wouldn't do anything" and of his claim to have learned nothing in Iowa; he then writes:

> To Call, who only a few hours earlier had read the text of Mauchly's 1941 letters to Atanasoff, it was an amazing performance. Mauchly had either forgotten what he had written to Atanasoff or believed that those 1941 letters had been lost or destroyed. Call knew then that if Mauchly told the same story under oath in pretrial depositions and during the trial, he would lose his credibility.

So it was that Mauchly, just six weeks later, was taken completely by surprise when Kirkpatrick exhibited all those revealing letters he had written to Atanasoff before and after his fateful Iowa visit. Yet the question remains: Why, after his experience in the Regenerative Memory case, did Mauchly still not prepare for the ENIAC case? He knew now that Atanasoff had indeed saved their correspondence and other papers, including his 1940 detailed description of the

ABC. And he had now been exposed to an opposition attorney's sharp challenges to his originality, even his integrity.

For, Mollenhoff reports on pages 135 and 138, Mauchly appeared at the first three-day session of his ENIAC trial deposition in October 1968 with a very scanty collection of papers—all he could find, he said. Only after stern warning by the Honeywell side as to the meaning of his subpoena did Mauchly produce a trunkful of records and letters for the second three-day session in April 1969. (There was a third, four-day, session in May.) What is striking here is that Mauchly still did not review, much less study, the documents he himself supplied, so that he was repeatedly tripped up on the witness stand by his own evidence (see, especially, chap. 4).

We have come very close, I think, to some sort of psychological denial, fueled in Mauchly by several factors: twenty years of widespread acceptance of his claims, even hero-worship for his supposed inventive achievements; a growing belief in his own story as it went unchallenged; and confidence that his considerable cleverness, together with his technical expertise, would prevail in a courtroom. But I think a third factor persisted in his mind with regard to the major figure on the other side, John Atanasoff. Mauchly continued to trust in his original impression of this man whose ideas he had so gradually "borrowed," then appropriated as his own.

Mauchly was persuaded that Atanasoff posed no serious threat. It was this conviction that enabled him to discount Atanasoff's work to the Sperry Rand attorneys so that they never entertained a realistic picture of what to expect in either lawsuit: indeed, so that they were emboldened in the Honeywell suit not only to deny derivation of the ENIAC from the ABC but, more fundamentally, to declare the ENIAC the original electronic computer, due untold millions in royalties.

It was this same conviction that enabled Mauchly and Sperry attorney Dodds to visit Atanasoff just two months after their embarrassing experience at the Control Data deposition. Dodds wanted to learn what Atanasoff intended to say at his own deposition in that case. Atanasoff recorded the story of this December 16, 1967, visit—his first contact with Mauchly in twenty-two years—in his *Annals of the History of Computing* article, from notes that he and Alice made immediately afterwards.[6] If his two guests were seeking reassurance, Atanasoff did not furnish it.

On the issue of derivation, for example, Atanasoff stated that Mauchly had, while in Ames, gained a full and detailed understanding of the computer: "If you don't like it, that is just too bad because those are the facts. The courts must decide if this was derivation." When Mauchly asked whether Atanasoff contended that he had read the machine description while in Ames, Atanasoff said that yes, he did so contend. And when Dodds asked if he would "treat us as well as our opponents," Atanasoff writes that he replied:

> "I do not see why I should place you and your opponents on exactly the same footing. It is obviously to your advantage to prove that there was no development of a computing machine at Ames, Iowa. Your opponents contend the opposite, and my interests must lie in that direction."

Dodds, though primarily concerned at this point with the Regenerative Memory patent case, was also anticipating the ENIAC patent case, and he pressed Atanasoff on both. When Dodds insisted that the Regenerative Memory patent may have described the ABC's capacitor memory system but did not *claim* it, Atanasoff read out that patent's very first claim and asked how it differed from his own invention as seen by Mauchly in Iowa. Neither Dodds nor Mauchly attempted a response. When Dodds next asked Atanasoff if he also contended that his work bore upon the ENIAC patent, noting that the ENIAC had no regenerative memory, Atanasoff countered that the ENIAC did have "interaction of logic circuits in the computing elements, and that is an item which is derived from my work." Dodds now agreed that indeed there were logic circuits in the ENIAC patent.

Atanasoff writes that Mauchly participated very little in these discussions, often pleading poor memory—but also making the excuse that he had been instructed by counsel not to try to recall this period of his life! Atanasoff himself, apparently, grew a little playful, irritating Dodds by asking him how he expected to win at trial and suggesting a small wager. Dodds retorted, Atanasoff writes, that federal judges sometimes decide questions "upon their own impulses instead of on fact, law, or reason"; but then he thought better of it and said that this was not so of Judge Watkins in the Regenerative Memory case, in Baltimore.

Dodds chided that there was no testimony except Atanasoff's, a strange comment since he had just represented Sperry Rand in the Control Data depositions of Lura Atanasoff, on December 5, and Sam Legvold, on December 6, both of whom gave very strong testimony.[7] As we saw in chapter 3, that case got nowhere and was finally disposed of in 1981 with a small settlement actually paid by plaintiff Sperry Rand to defendant Control Data.

Whether Laurence Dodds was disheartened, first by the documentation presented at Mauchly's deposition and then by Atanasoff's unexpected toughness in person, or Sperry Rand was dissatisfied with Dodds's handling of this Regenerative Memory case, a new legal team was brought in for the ENIAC case. And, with both Mauchly and Eckert still downgrading Atanasoff's achievements, Sperry retained its goal of establishing the ENIAC as the world's premier electronic computer.

As for Mauchly, surely also disappointed that Atanasoff was not the complacent, even helpful, figure he had hoped to find that mid-December day in 1967, it would seem that denial won out over reason: twenty-year-old fables die hard.

He pressed forward, in deposition, at trial, and for the rest of his life, with his story of invention of the ENIAC independently of his association with Atanasoff. Or, perhaps, it was his best course, if not Sperry Rand's.

Mollenhoff, in reporting from this same Atanasoff article, concludes on a more positive note, "All in all, it was not an unpleasant afternoon and dinner hour," as Mauchly lingered after Dodds's 3:00 o'clock departure. He even refers to the "gentle sparring" between Dodds and Atanasoff. Perhaps this reading by Mollenhoff does resonate better with Atanasoff's denial, in interviews, of any ill feeling toward Mauchly.

A major contribution of Mollenhoff's book is his exploration of corporate activities prior to the initiation of the Regenerative Memory (*Sperry Rand v. Control Data*) and ENIAC (*Honeywell v. Sperry Rand*) patent suits. For, though both Control Data and Honeywell had been alerted to the ABC by Richards's 1966 book, they were not the first to "discover" Atanasoff and bring his computer to bear on patent issues. Indeed, that same Regenerative Memory patent, granted in early 1953, eleven years before the ENIAC patent, had caught the eye—and the concern—of several corporations developing computers with rotating magnetic drum memories. And here, too, by an odd twist, Berry had played a vital role.

One of those corporations was Consolidated Electrodynamics, a Bell and Howell subsidiary located in Pasadena, California, which Berry had joined when he left Iowa in 1942. Consolidated Electrodynamics was working with IBM in an effort to limit the scope of what was generally referred to as the Eckert-Mauchly *revolver* patent, after its broad general principle of signal recirculation. Not long after that patent was issued, Berry, director of engineering, informed his firm's patent counsel, James B. Christie, of his work at Iowa State on a computer that used that same principle.

As Mollenhoff explains in his chapter 9, Christie and IBM's A. Robert Noll decided to pursue this lead with an interview of Berry. But even before that could be arranged, there came another pleasant surprise, an inexplicable gift from Eckert: his article in the *Proceedings of the IRE* citing Atanasoff's drum form of computer memory as "probably the first example of what might generally be termed regenerative memory" (see chap. 2).[8] He goes on to describe this especially economical "capacitor memory" and its "reading-in, reading-out and regenerating" features, seeming to have forgotten that he himself, together with Mauchly, had obtained a patent covering just such an electrostatic regenerative memory only eight months earlier!

(Mollenhoff reports later, on pages 227–28, that Eckert told him in his 1987 telephone interview that he himself had conceived the regenerative memory, independently, in 1943. Whereas in his article he credited Atanasoff with the idea "earlier than 1942," he now claimed that Mauchly did not tell him of this aspect of the ABC until late 1943. Of course, Mauchly in his Regenerative Memory deposition freely acknowledged debating its merits with Eckert in the summer of 1941 [see chap. 2]. When Mollenhoff asked why he had cited Atanasoff in his 1953 article, Eckert said simply that he had wanted to credit the development of "a comparable concept at Iowa.")

Consolidated Electrodynamics's Christie, armed with a list of questions from IBM's Noll as well as his own, interviewed Berry in May of 1954 and sent a full report to Noll. Then, in June, A. J. Etienne of IBM visited Atanasoff in his recently formed Ordnance Engineering Corporation in Rockville, Maryland, seeking his cooperation in proving that concepts in the Eckert-Mauchly Regenerative Memory patent had been derived from him. Atanasoff writes in his 1984 *Annals* article:

> I was, of course, pleased that [Etienne] had found my efforts in computing to have merit, but I had to tell him that we were a small corporation with little reserve, and that I and my friends had our "all" invested in [this corporation].

Later in June, Etienne sent him a copy of that patent, which had been unknown to him, and again asked his help. Atanasoff continues:

> He hoped I would turn my files over to him, and I searched briefly for them, without success. My memory is that I wrote him of my intention to search further, but pleaded lack of immediate time for work on this case. I heard nothing more from Etienne.

Mollenhoff suggests, on page 112, that IBM used Atanasoff—used the fact of his prior concepts—to negotiate its 1956 cross-licensing agreement with Sperry Rand, which included not just the Regenerative Memory patent concepts but those of the still-pending ENIAC patent (see chaps. 5 and 7). In fact, he attributes Atanasoff's later caution and skepticism about working with big corporate lawyers to his feeling that Etienne had used him.

Sperry Rand itself approached Atanasoff in April of 1959. At the close of Chapter 9, Mollenhoff tells of a luncheon at the Cosmos Club in Washington, where R. H. Sorenson, assistant to the Sperry vice president for engineering, quizzed Atanasoff about his Iowa State project. And he quotes from Sorenson's memorandum on that interview, in which he listed a number of assuredly critical concepts claimed by Atanasoff, but also reported his sense of Atanasoff's apparent reluctance to get involved:

> For personal reasons, Atanasoff seems anxious not to become embroiled in any legal entanglements on behalf of ourselves or others. . . . [He was] cordial to us, but resisted any further discussion which might require the review or copying of his own records.

Meanwhile, Sorenson had discovered, through letters and a visit, that Iowa State University had almost no record of this history. That information, together with Sorenson's impression of Atanasoff himself, must also have been a factor in Sperry Rand's discounting of Atanasoff as an effective witness even after he did, some years later, produce his considerable documentation.

Atanasoff's prolonged resistance to revisiting this period of his life, only ultimately to delve into it so wholeheartedly, *is* something of an enigma. It is explained in part, of course, by his aversion to thinking ill of Mauchly, and in part by his aversion to opening up old feelings of failure. But it is also the case that the Regenerative Memory patent entailed only one aspect of his machine, whereas the ENIAC patent entailed the entire computer. When patent lawyers Call and Allegretti and trial lawyer Halladay approached him on behalf of Honeywell, Atanasoff realized that he now had a great deal to gain in terms of meaningful recognition.

It also happens that these Honeywell lawyers—and Control Data's Kirkpatrick, with whom they were sharing data and strategy—had a stronger personal appeal to Atanasoff than any who had approached him earlier. They truly understood what he had accomplished. Moreover, they were seriously litigating: they were prepared to produce models of his devices to exhibit at trial, and they were prepared to employ him in a consulting capacity with a generous, though standard, stipend. Atanasoff writes in his *Annals* article:

> I conclude this introduction by saying that I did not realize how long a period of study, analysis, and training lay ahead, before the preparatory process was finished and the trials began. Nor have I ever had associates and co-workers of such skill and ability as those who represented Control Data Corporation and Honeywell Incorporated throughout the whole procedure, and in the trials themselves. Our sojourn was arduous to the extreme, and counsel often had good cause to be irritated with me—and the reverse—but these men were gentlemen of the first order.

Finally, it seems probable that Atanasoff was moved by the death of Berry to help create a lasting recognition for him as well as for himself.

Mollenhoff's early 1974 phone interview of Mauchly for his *Des Moines Register* story, recounted on pages 220–21 of his book, was not a pleasant encounter. Mauchly's main pitch was that Judge Larson had been wrong, had simply not understood "some very important technical evidence" in the case. At the same time, Mollenhoff writes, "Mauchly rejected my repeated efforts to gain an explanation of this technical evidence." He then evaded several pointed questions by claiming that he had spent his time in Iowa just "trying to help the guy" get financing for his machine.

As for that machine, however, Mauchly was "thoroughly derogatory," calling it "just a little piece of junk" and "a crude little machine that wouldn't do anything," as contrasted to the ENIAC, a "highly sophisticated and operational machine." Mauchly also said, Mollenhoff notes, that the Sperry attorneys "never explained to his satisfaction why they did not appeal" Larson's decision as he suggested they should.

The interview ended when Mollenhoff inquired about Mauchly's December 1967 visit to Atanasoff's home. Mauchly, declining to answer any more questions, hung up the telephone.

It is significant that Mollenhoff's story in the Des Moines newspaper marked Iowa State University's first notice of the historic October 1973 federal court decision. With his journalist's satisfaction in scoring a scoop, Mollenhoff writes, on page 221, about the appearance of his article:

> My story on the front page of the *Des Moines Sunday Register* on 27 January 1974 was the first information the Iowa State University public affairs office had that a federal court had ruled that the first electronic digital computer had been invented at Iowa State. I had avoided any calls to Iowa State before my story appeared to reduce the possibility that somehow it might be leaked to Iowa newspapers before I was fully prepared to publish.

Mollenhoff adds that Carl Hamilton, Iowa State vice president for publicity, "was elated," and that he commenced "a series of events . . . over a period of years" to honor the university's own Professor John Atanasoff and graduate assistant Clifford Berry.

Mollenhoff's later telephone interview of Eckert for his book was no less contentious than the one with Mauchly. He writes, on page 226:

> At the time of my conversation with Eckert in April 1987, he was a bitter man and still unwilling to accept Judge Larson's decision as the final word on JV's pioneering role in electronic digital computing concepts.
> . . . He trashed the Atanasoff Berry Computer, attacked Atanasoff's credibility, and criticized Judge Larson's decision. Eckert was equally caustic as he spoke of Sperry Rand's lawyers and their handling of the investigation and trial, and of the Sperry Rand management of the decision not to appeal.

Eckert called the trial "a farce," Larson "a nutty judge" who was "too egotistical" to take help from technical experts. And, of the ABC:

> "Atanasoff's machine was a joke," Eckert continued. "It was simply a mathematical device of very limited ability. It had defective circuits, and it wasn't even patentable. . . ."
> "Atanasoff was a liar about what he said Mauchly saw, and he was paid a lot of money for the testimony he gave at the trial," Eckert charged.

Eckert also charged the Sperry defense team with incompetence, declaring: "I have a lot of material, material that was not used at the trial, and the Mauchly family has a lot of material that will prove what a farce the trial was." Like Mauchly in his interview, Eckert declined to let Mollenhoff examine his "material" for possible use in his book, saying that he was not yet ready "to zap the critics." But, he said, "we will bring it out at the right time—after everyone else has had his say about the matter."

Much of what Eckert told Mollenhoff is reminiscent of what he had told Pamela Eblen in 1984. but then toned down appreciably in his 1986 address at the Computer Museum (see chap. 8). Clearly, Mollenhoff caught him in a very negative state of mind with respect to this history. And, just as clearly, he had his "facts" wrong.

It is not true, for example, that Judge Larson refused expert guidance. In the Introduction to his decision, he tells of the "extensive tutorial testimony" from which he benefited in his conduct of this trial (Finding 0).[9] And, as Mollenhoff observes on pages 147–48:

> Judge Larson acknowledged his lack of technical expertise to lawyers for Honeywell and Sperry Rand, and for that reason he placed upon them the burden and the responsibility of providing expert witnesses, charts, and devices to clarify technical matters not only for the court but also to make certain that the witnesses understood and agreed on the meaning of words and concepts and the importance of certain specific dates.

Mollenhoff also notes that by the time Larson took jurisdiction of this case, at age fifty-eight, he "had earned a reputation as a hardworking and serious judge," experienced in "complex investigations" and "rarely reversed on appeal."

As for blaming the defense team for the trial's outcome, the truth is that the Sperry Rand attorneys eked every last drop of advantage from what little they had to work with. As for the oft-promised disclosure of untapped—and mysteriously secret—evidence, the truth is that there is no such evidence. All efforts to "zap the critics" and prove the trial "a farce" amount to mere words: the careless distortions and empty promises of persons confident in the steadfastness of the prevailing impression that the electronic computing age began with the ENIAC.

Mollenhoff speculates briefly on the bravado with which both Eckert and Mauchly pressed on with their original stories in the wake of this federal court decision. On pages 217–18, he tells in particular of Mauchly's 1982 "Fireside Chat" at Sperry Univac's Rome villa, just three weeks after the decision was handed down.[10] As we saw in chapter 4, Mauchly's version of events entailed a shifting of dates to preclude Atanasoff's influence—omitted, in fact, any reference to Atanasoff, his own Iowa State visit, or the trial.

Mollenhoff writes that the very lack of media attention itself served to make Mauchly "bold and arrogant." And he attributes that lack not just to the coincidence of the decision's announcement with President Nixon's "midnight massacre" but to the length and complexity of the decision:

> Few newspaper reporters had the patience to plow through the complicated 200-page opinion, much less comb through the thousands of pages of depositions and trial transcripts upon which Judge Larson's opinion was based.

I would add that few historians have had such patience, either, but also that the decision was up against a quarter century of contrary propaganda.

Mollenhoff closes his book with a commentary on the regrets of Iowa State University, expressed some forty-five years after the event, for failing to reap the rewards of Atanasoff's invention. President Gordon P. Eaton, in his inaugural address in early 1987, acknowledged Allan R. Mackintosh's criticism of Iowa State in his recently published article on Atanasoff in *Physics Today* (see chap. 8).[11] On page 239, Mollenhoff writes:

> Eaton noted that Mackintosh had said, "Iowa State deserves credit for supporting [Atanasoff's] project at its inception," but that "the officials concerned clearly had no concept of its significance, and their obtuseness cost the university dearly when they failed to apply for a patent."

Eaton admitted to this "lost opportunity for enormous economic growth in Iowa," but also found solace in Mackintosh's account of how IBM, too, had passed over Atanasoff's attempt to convince that huge corporation of "the potentialities of electronic computation" in the early 1940s. Eaton pronounced Mackintosh's analysis of the failure of both Iowa State and IBM with regard to Atanasoff a classic example of hindsight, on the one hand, and a lesson for the future, on the other. He hoped, Mollenhoff writes, that past failures would serve as a warning so that "the genius of the John Atanasoffs and the Cliff Berrys of the future would be recognized, encouraged, and given administrative support."

Iowa State has made a great effort to right the wrong to Atanasoff. Mollenhoff remarks that President Eaton gave some sixty speeches in his first few months in office and "mentioned John Atanasoff in nearly every one." He tells of a number of campus-wide affairs, the most notable perhaps the October 1983 celebration, under President William R. Parks, marking both the tenth anniversary of the ENIAC trial decision and Atanasoff's eightieth birthday. He also tells of a May 1987 celebration, under Eaton, a highlight of which was a trip to Des Moines to show the Atanasoffs the new Iowa Historical Building and Museum where a room was to be devoted to his work. Also in 1987, the university created an annual J. V. Atanasoff Fellowship in Computer Science and announced plans for an Atanasoff Hall of Computer Science.

The May 1988 celebration of Mollenhoff's book carried on in this same spirit; indeed, it included the formal dedication of that building. It was held in conjunction with the annual Veishea festivities, named for the land-grant university's original schools (Veterinary Medicine, Industrial Science, Home Economics, and Agriculture), and it was attended by over a quarter million people. As grand marshal of the Veishea Parade, Atanasoff rode with Alice in a Cadillac convertible sandwiched between two vintage Packards, a 1953 Caribbean at the head and a 1952 "300" sedan to their rear.

The press conference opened with a talk by Arthur Oldehoeft, chairman of computer science, who demonstrated the replica of Atanasoff's 1939 model built in 1968 for trial purposes. Clark Mollenhoff then told of his book and Art's and mine. Calling our two books complementary, he said he hoped they would be reviewed jointly. Mollenhoff also acknowledged publicly a debt he had mentioned to us privately by telephone, one that reflected his admitted lack of expertise in the engineering aspect of his subject. He had not so much presented our technical material as relied on it, he said, for his thesis: while he felt sure of the soundness of Judge Larson's decision, he would not have felt comfortable in the technical area without our *Annals* article to fall back on.

For Art, a highlight of an afternoon reception was his discussion with Judge Larson, who had driven down from Minneapolis with his wife and who had agreed by phone to an interview. On the matter of the technical nature of the trial, Larson said that he had decided to conduct it more in the manner of a jury trial: to require that issues be explained clearly and plainly enough that the average person could grasp them, certainly so that the lawyers and witnesses could. He also commented—although Art did not raise the matter—that he had regretted having to reject the petition of Burks, Sharpless, and Shaw for coinvention of the ENIAC because it was so late (see chap. 7). Art assured the judge that he had understood his action and accepted it as fair.

There was a final banquet in which Clark and Art spoke from their different perspectives, and J. V. himself spoke. It was a very warm occasion, attended by J. V.'s three children and their spouses and the grandchildren. We had met Elsie (Whistler) earlier, at the Atanasoffs' home, but not Joanne (Gathers) or John V. II. They all expressed their thanks to us for our efforts on their father's behalf. Also present were Clifford Berry's mother, Grace Berry, and his two brothers, Dean and Keith.

<<<>>>

Our book *is* very different from Mollenhoff's. It starts with a complete description of the Atanasoff-Berry Computer, with the components presented in the order of their conception so as to convey a sense of the inventive process—live, as it were. We derived this chronology chiefly from Atanasoff's 1940 memorandum. For the machine's details, however, we went beyond that document's bare-bones depictions to his testimony in court and to extended phone calls to him. These phone interviews occurred on an almost weekly basis, with Art posing questions one Sunday and Atanasoff reporting what "my memory tells me" the next.

Of course, Art's own expertise in vacuum-tube computing technology enabled him both to ask the right questions and to confirm the soundness, the engineering fit, of the answers. And I, as first author, contributed my *inexpertise* to the cause by insisting on explanations that I could understand and translate into lay English.

This seventy-page stretch of the book, titled "A Computer in the Making," was certainly the most arduous for me, with many a trip down the hall to my main source's study. I recall spending days on a few paragraphs of a certain manuscript page 39, feeling both frustrated at the slow progress and exhilarated at each step forward. I also recall that part of my difficulty derived from the fact that scientists often have two or three terms for a single element or phenomenon. I determined that once I had revealed the alternate names for a given item, I would thereafter use only that one that Art could settle on as the preferred one.

My training in mathematics, on the other hand, allowed me a measure of excitement over *what* the computer was doing. If the *how* of vacuum tubes and capacitors was new territory for me, Atanasoff's processing of equations through his ingeniously integrated set of components yielded a series of "Aha's" as I pored over his minimal descriptions.

The high point of all this was my coming to understand his basic algorithm for eliminating a variable from a pair of linear equations, starting with an arbitrary pair from an original set of twenty-nine equations in twenty-nine variables (see chap. 1). To this day, many writers explain Atanasoff's procedure as the standard Gaussian method, one that requires division, multiplication, and, for the final solution process, back-substitution.

Using his variant of that method, Atanasoff was able to limit his arithmetic operations to repeated subtractions and additions (with shifting) of a pair of equations (vectors), as the machine reduced to zero the coefficient of one designated variable in one of the equations. This still seems to me a rather critical aspect of his computer design and function, for not only did he create a computer of very much simpler design than the standard algorithm would have required, but he also created the world's first vector computer.

The next major topic of our book was Mauchly's pursuit of electronic computation. Using trial transcript copies of his testimony, notes, and correspondence, we examined in detail: his achievements prior to his first meeting with Atanasoff, that meeting itself (December 1940), his efforts during his last term at Ursinus College (spring 1941), his Iowa visit (June 1941), his brief pro-

posal for an electronic digital computer (August 1942), and his joining with
Eckert for a preliminary design of what was to be the ENIAC (April 1943). This
presentation constituted two long chapters, "Mauchly's Pre-Atanasoff Years" and
"The ENIAC Connection."

We followed with a similar presentation of Atanasoff's pursuit of electronic
computation, again using court records to scrutinize his testimony and his extensive documentation. We called this chapter "Atanasoff's Day in Court."
Researching these three chapters, making fresh discoveries, and figuring out the
timing of events and the interactions of the central characters in the drama
proved, again, both taxing and fulfilling. We felt that we had, on the basis of an
extremely well conducted legal investigation, made the Atanasoff case for the
computing community, and beyond.

We called our fifth and last chapter "Atanasoff's Place in History." This is
Art's analysis of the technological revolution, in the context of a "causal chain of
invention" worked out in his years of teaching computer history at Michigan.
Here we wrote:

> In this final chapter we build on the four preceding chapters to elucidate the
> causal chain of invention from Atanasoff through the ENIAC and the stored-pro-
> gram EDVAC and IAS (Institute for Advanced Study) machine, and on to the
> computers of today, thus establishing unequivocally that it was he who started
> the computer revolution. We will show that Mauchly and Eckert began where
> Atanasoff left off.

There are two appendixes. The first is a professedly technical treatise on the
logic of electronic switching written by Art for readers interested in this logic.
The second is a response to Kathleen Mauchly's 1984 *Annals* article on
Mauchly's supposedly independent journey to the invention of the ENIAC,
which I wrote for readers who may (or may not) have been persuaded by her
arguments.[12]

We agree with Mollenhoff that our two books are complementary treatments of a
single phenomenon, the long-postponed and strongly resisted recognition of the
creator of one of history's most influential inventions, the electronic computer. In
an afterword to Mollenhoff's book, Allan Mackintosh, to whom we had sent a
manuscript copy of our book for his comment, also remarks on the fortunate concurrence of these two works. The fact is, though, that he himself supplied a third
major thrust in this convergence of efforts to establish Atanasoff, as interest in his
1987 *Physics Today* article led to a more general article in the August 1988
Scientific American (again, see chap. 8).[13]

Mackintosh was putting the finishing touches on this new paper when we visited him and his institutions, the University of Copenhagen and NORDITA (*Nordish Institut for Teoretisk Atomfysik*), in September of 1987. The editor, he said, had asked him to write a semipopular presentation, bearing in mind three objectives: to convey the fundamentals of electronic computing in lay terminology, to demonstrate that the path from invention to recognition could be rough, and to give due credit for one of the most important inventions of our time.

Mackintosh's article, "Dr. Atanasoff's Computer," met these specifications brilliantly. We are all indebted to this distinguished British scientist for taking time from his own research in solid-state physics to help set the record straight on the invention of the computer—especially since, as he makes clear, without Atanasoff's invention the British Colossus would stand as the world's first electronic computer.

While all three of these works appeared within a three-month span in 1988, the article by Mackintosh surely had an immediate worldwide impact that the two book-length treatments would not enjoy for years to come. Friends in Japan, for example, told us that they had seen—and read, in English—this *Scientific American* article.

Incidentally, there has been extraordinary interest in Japan in this whole matter. Several writers have contacted Art and me with regard to articles they were writing, and we ourselves were invited by the Japanese journal *Bosei* to recount the story of our efforts to preserve this history. Like Mackintosh, we were asked to write for the general public as well as for scholars. This article, with our names and our title, "Working in the History of Computers: A Husband-Wife Memoir," given in English as well as Japanese, appeared in the February and March 1996 issues.[14] (We were astonished to learn that *Bosei* has a circulation of some 50,000!) A slightly expanded English version of our article was published in the *Michigan Quarterly Review* of Spring 1997.[15]

Most recently, both Mollenhoff's and our book have been translated into Japanese.

Fortunately for us, William Aspray, reviews editor for *Annals of the History of Computing*, decided to invite Mackintosh to write that journal's review of our book. Mackintosh had already studied the manuscript rather thoroughly, and he wrote a most favorable appraisal.[16] After giving a brief summary of Atanasoff's computer and its influence on the ENIAC through Mauchly, against the backdrop of the court proceedings, Mackintosh remarks on the current state of the controversy over these issues:

> [Mauchly's] supporters have managed to reverse the burden of proof with great skill. It is no longer denied that he was shown and himself examined the ABC, held extensive discussions with Atanasoff, and had every opportunity to read the

latter's great article of 1940, in which a remarkably high proportion of the principles of modern computing were enunciated, but it is asserted that there is no proof that he was influenced by what he learned. The Burkses give in fact many very clear examples of such influence, either conscious or unconscious, on the design of the ENIAC. . . .

. . . [They] have changed the paradigm about the invention of the electronic computer. They are critical, in my view justifiably, of those historians who have clung to the fashionable view that the ENIAC was the first electronic computer. . . . In future those who wish to maintain this viewpoint will have to argue for it.

Saul Rosen, computer scientist at Purdue University, wrote a response for the April 1989 *Annals* that was as negative as Mackintosh's review was positive.[17] His piece rang with the all-too-familiar inaccuracies and irrelevancies: the ABC was unfinished, he said, it was abandoned, it was vastly different from the ENIAC; Atanasoff could have helped matters by publishing his 1940 descriptive paper and patenting his computer; Mauchly was not allowed to take away a copy of that paper; Atanasoff made no further contribution to electronic computation and is remembered for his work in computing "only because of the great work of Eckert and Mauchly"; finally, he noted, *Eckert himself* has stated that Atanasoff's "circuits and things" would not have worked.

Rosen's response to Mackintosh also has many erroneous interpretations. He states that Judge Larson ruled the ENIAC patent invalid on the ground that Mauchly learned of "the possibility of automatic electronic computing" from Atanasoff; that among other "fantasies of Arthur Burks" is the idea that major parts of the ENIAC and the EDVAC were derived directly from Atanasoff; that our book is best understood as "another phase in Arthur Burks's ongoing vendetta against John Mauchly"; and that we are party to "what appears to be a concerted attempt to deprive [Eckert] of credit for his most outstanding achievements."

Art and I replied to Rosen in the January 1990 issue.[18] On the matter of Art's "fantasies," we point out that in fact "major parts" of the ENIAC and the EDVAC were not the issue, but computing concepts, including basic circuitry, were—and that Eckert and Mauchly specifically claimed such critical concepts in their various patents.

On the matter of Art's "vendetta" against Mauchly, we note that *it* is fantasy, since Art became critical of Mauchly only after the ENIAC trial revealed his misappropriation of Atanasoff's ideas. And, on the matter of our deprivation of credit to Eckert, we note that in our book we describe the ENIAC in considerable detail, citing its advances over the ABC; we also remind Rosen that our earlier ninety-page article on the ENIAC is the fullest exposition of that machine to appear in the literature. We could have added that in both works, we praise Eckert as an ingenious electronics engineer in a number of challenging situations.

There were other favorable reviews, some of which also drew responses from the readership. One such was a long review by G. Michael Vose in the September 1988 issue of *Byte*.[19] Vose tells very neatly of Atanasoff's steps toward a computer in the context of the algorithm he wanted to solve; indeed, he commends us for so presenting it. He also commends us for presenting the history in the context of the court case. Here he writes:

> They quote the trial transcript on many occasions to reveal how the Honeywell attorneys extracted from Mauchly testimony revealing that much of his ENIAC knowledge had come from letters exchanged with Atanasoff and from a 1941 visit to Iowa to see the ABC machine.
>
> . . .
>   . . . the trial finally established who invented what. The authors' use of the trial as a device to frame the historical narrative makes an otherwise dry read much more exciting.

It was heartening to have a reviewer understand the structure of Atanasoff's computer in terms of the minimal algorithm that was its focus, and to see that it was really Mauchly who "convicted" himself in that trial.

As we noted in chapter 7, Vose did have the impression that Art had been an employee of Honeywell and so had a "strong economic motivation" in writing of the trial. *Byte* published Art's letter correcting this misconception—while also expressing appreciation for Vose's "perceptive account"—in the December 1988 issue.[20]

That letter was followed by one from a Mauchly family member, John William, Jr., in the July 1989 issue.[21] It begins by chastising Vose for failing to recognize our "story" as "a concerted attempt to discredit my father" and for not questioning its two "huge" and "false" claims: that Atanasoff "invented the first electronic computer" and that Mauchly "stole the idea of the computer from him."

The younger Mauchly marshals his own definitions to argue that the ABC was not first ("never ran"), was not electronic (had a rotating memory that rendered it partly "electromechanical"), and was not a computer ("was not general-purpose"). He then states that what "bothers me the most, however," is what he sees as our effort to prove that his father got the very idea of electronic computation from Atanasoff, whereas "John Mauchly worked and experimented on electronic computing for years before meeting Atanasoff."

Our reply was published in the December 1989 issue of *Byte*.[22] We remark particularly on his complete omission of any reference to the ENIAC trial on which we, and Vose, base our arguments as to what both Atanasoff and Mauchly did or did not achieve. We quote a few items from that trial, such as Mauchly's comment that he "wasn't even thinking about inventing computing machines" when he went to Iowa in 1941. On the other hand, we say, we never claimed that Mauchly got *the idea* for electronic computing from Atanasoff and in our book actually cite Mauchly's aspiration, in late 1940, to build an electronic keyboard-operated desk calculator. (See chap. 4.)

We also counter his arguments against the designation "first electronic computer." With regard to the ABC's rotating electrostatic memory, for example, we point out that it had three novel principles universally employed to this day: "electronic regeneration of memory elements, rotation as a means of memory access, and the use of capacitors as memory elements." (On the younger Mauchly's criteria, the IBM 650, with its main memory in the form of a rotating magnetic drum, would not be electronic, either.)

John Mauchly, Jr.'s, letter to *Byte* elicited two other replies, one from George Wright of Lutherville, Maryland, in the October 1989 issue, the other from Donald Michie of Glasgow, Scotland, in the January 1990 issue.[23] Wright is highly indignant that Mauchly's son could "write an 800-word letter on the Atanasoff/Mauchly controversy . . . without acknowledging the court decision." He remarks on the actual paucity of purportedly "ample evidence" cited by the son on the father's behalf, and he refers readers to Mollenhoff's book on Atanasoff for an unbiased presentation.

Donald Michie writes as chief scientist, The Turing Institute. He apparently accepts John Mauchly Jr.'s "correcting" of Vose's claim that the ABC was the world's first electronic computer, but challenges his awarding of that accolade to the ENIAC. Instead, Michie advances "the Colossus machines, of which about 10 were operating on a 24-hour duty cycle by the end of the war." He explains his position:

> [The Colossi] were like the ENIAC in being plug-programmable only, not stored-program, universal machines in the modern sense.
>
> The fact that those of us who worked with the Colossus range were inhibited until the 1970s by wartime secrecy from mentioning their existence explains the widespread persistence, especially in the U.S., of the false belief that the ENIAC was the first electronic computer.

So here is one British scientist who, unlike Mackintosh, does not yield to Eckert-Mauchly *or* Atanasoff!

Another very positive review of our book appeared in the *Minneapolis Star Tribune*, on July 2, 1989.[24] Computer technology writer Jane Pejsa starts with high praise for Judge Larson's 1973 "landmark decision" in a trial "involving two giant corporations, both with strong roots in Minnesota." After reciting the history—one that for her is "a wonderful story of justice triumphant"—she turns to our book, noting especially our suitability for the task: Arthur's as an associate of Eckert and Mauchly in the development of the ENIAC, and mine as a writer she feels brings "highly sophisticated concepts to the reader" in such a way as to make the book "an adventure."

Pejsa sees our work as an effort, fifteen years after the ENIAC trial, both to correct ingrained misconceptions about Eckert and Mauchly and to counter the widespread second-guessing of Larson's decision still being made "without reference to the overwhelming evidence" from that trial.

A strongly favorable review of our book together with Mollenhoff's also appeared in *Jurimetrics: Journal of Law, Science and Technology*, published by the Section of Science and Technology of the American Bar Association (ABA).[25] (Judge Larson sent us a copy.) Washington attorney Lee Loevinger, one of the founders of that journal and past chair of that section of the ABA, provides a comprehensive overview of the history. Indeed, he recounts not only the particulars of the legal dispute and the outcome of the ENIAC trial, but also the mathematical and engineering challenges of that early era and the efforts of the principal figures to meet them. He concludes:

> This bare outline of the story that is told in detail in each of these books cannot begin to convey the human interest of the drama involved or of the absolutely compelling force of the evidence which is summarized and analyzed in each book. . . . The Mollenhoff book is much more personal in its focus on the individuals involved and the narrative account. The Burks' book is far more analytical and not only summarizes the evidence available from the court records, but also analyzes the elements of the Atanasoff computer, the ENIAC, and successor computers to demonstrate the degree to which the ENIAC and its successors were derived from and dependent upon the inventive genius of Atanasoff.

We were pleasantly surprised to have lawyer Loevinger recommend Art's technical appendix to those "truly interested in the technique of electronic computing" for its explanation of "both the logic and the circuitry not only of the Atanasoff and ENIAC computers, but of computers generally from the earliest mechanical models to the modern."

As to the trial itself, and our legal system, Loevinger writes:

> In addition to telling the story of the origin of modern computers, these two books, each in its own way, present a comprehensive account of the trial of one of the most massive and complex cases in federal court history. It is a tribute to the legal system (as well as to Judge Larson) that this arcane segment of modern history was unearthed and put on the public record. The authors of both books have performed a public service by making the massive documentation of this litigation available to all who are interested in history, computers, or the ability of the judicial system to handle large complex cases.

Two historians of computers wrote reviews of our book that were a mix of plusses and minuses. These are Paul Ceruzzi in *Science* and Martin Campbell-Kelly, of the University of Warwich, England, in *ISIS*.[26]

There is little new in either of these accounts, except, unfortunately, for several new errors of fact and misunderstandings of both the ENIAC patent trial and our support of its outcome. Ceruzzi, for example, praises our presentation of the trial documents, but adds that we have also supplemented these with our own *posttrial* "extensive correspondence" with Atanasoff himself. Of course, there is no such correspondence: the letters we quote were those of Atanasoff and Mauchly, mostly with each other, back in 1941.

To our dismay, Ceruzzi also has us accusing Mauchly of "unethical, unpatriotic, and unprofessional behavior." Art and I take very seriously calling anyone *unpatriotic*, and we never applied this term to Mauchly—or even considered him so in any context. Neither, for that matter, have we called him unprofessional, though we certainly have brought into question his ethics with regard to both Atanasoff and von Neumann.

Finally, Ceruzzi charges us with being "unwilling to accept" that Atanasoff did not start the computer revolution directly but only through the ENIAC. Yet we do in fact credit Atanasoff with starting that revolution *because of* his prior computer's influence on the ENIAC and the ensuing EDVAC and IAS Computer. Ceruzzi closes out this charge with his observation that our not being historians by training is a "serious problem, as their treatment of this theme makes evident"!

Campbell-Kelly finds our book an "excellent" work—especially valuable for its description of "one of the most important trials testing a patent to be heard in recent years." But he effectively rejects our conclusions, chiefly by passing over the major elements of our arguments, and of Judge Larson's. For example, he finds "the most crucial event in the [ABC-to-ENIAC] connection" the initial meeting between Atanasoff and Mauchly in December 1940. Completely overlooking their 1941 correspondence and Mauchly's visit to Iowa in June of that year, he notes that "it was well after this meeting that [Mauchly in August 1942] proposed the building of the electronic computer that was to become the ENIAC," as though, accordingly, the linkage, if any, would have been very weak.

Finally, on the issue of priority of invention, Campbell-Kelly falls back on the fact that Eckert and Mauchly "are still considered by some to be *the* inventors of the electronic computer." And again, on the issue of derivation, he pronounces it sufficient for Atanasoff to be designated the inventor *if* posterity should so recognize him.

By far, our most negative reviewer was *Annals* biographies editor Eric Weiss, writing in the April 1989 issue of *Computing Reviews*.[27] Curiously, for the first time since our encounter with him in connection with our ENIAC article and the responses to it (see chap. 6), Weiss now presents a history that affirms our basic arguments regarding the ABC's priority, derivation of the ENIAC from the ABC via Mauchly, and Judge Larson's decision to invalidate the ENIAC patent. At the same time, however, he attacks our work as an "angry and often vicious book," as he cites what he considers our "unnecessarily fierce and vindictive antagonism and hatred for Mauchly, which casts a dark and sorry shadow over what is otherwise a splendid work." He sees our treatment of Atanasoff and Mauchly in terms of "certain carefully selected personality traits" that have the effect of pinning a "halo" on Atanasoff and a "forked tail" on Mauchly.

In the rebuttal we were allowed by *Computing Reviews* in that same issue, we objected that our book was "not a study of personalities, but an analytical history of the invention of the electronic computer," observing further that his criticisms employed "stronger terms than any we use," and noting that he offered "not a single substantiating quotation" for his charges.

Weiss also wrote a review of both our book and Mollenhoff's for the July-August 1989 issue of *American Scientist*.[28] Here, too, he accepts the history as both of us have presented it, each from our own perspective, but now also sees two "angry books" that tell the story of the first electronic computer with a common purpose: "to destroy John W. Mauchly's reputation as its inventor and establish John V. Atanasoff in that heroic position."

In stunning contrast to these Weiss reviews is a review of Mollenhoff's book alone, by David E. Ross, of Agoura, California, that also appeared in that same April 1989 issue of *Computing Reviews*.[29] Computer analyst Ross begins by commending the U.S. legal system for permitting "facts about past human actions [to be] formally and conclusively decided in a court of law." He finds that the verdict in the ENIAC trial gave Atanasoff "the right to claim the electronic digital computer as his own invention," while Eckert and Mauchly, "long hailed as the inventors . . . because of their development of ENIAC and EDVAC, were recast by this decision into the roles of opportunistic extenders of Atanasoff's original concept."

Ross then summarizes Mollenhoff's book, adding his own explanation of the trial issues and noting the novel concepts of Atanasoff's computer, which, he writes, when "appropriated" by Mauchly "led to the development of the ENIAC and subsequent computers and prevail today in both personal computers and supercomputers."

Ross comments on Mollenhoff's portrayal of Mauchly:

> Throughout the book, Mollenhoff characterizes Mauchly as a rogue who intentionally defrauded Atanasoff, the US Patent Office, and the world in general (he admits that Judge Larson characterized Mauchly much less severely).

And on Mollenhoff's portrayal of corporate involvement in the patent struggle:

> He describes related actions by Sperry and IBM as exemplifications of institutional knavery; the section that presents Sperry's pretrial attempts to strengthen the bases for their patents reads almost like a spy novel.

(Ross's use here of *rogue* and *defraud* and *knavery* does accurately reflect Mollenhoff's own language in this book.)

Finally, Ross offers a brief note on counterarguments from the Mauchly-Eckert side—from writer Joel Shurkin, in particular:

> Some recent authors, however, question the broad applicability of Judge Larson's decision. Shurkin, for example, would narrow the decision's scope to the technical legality of the patent; speculating about their undocumented thoughts, he would also uphold Mauchly and Eckert's "paternity" of the computer. Taking a legalistic attitude, I agree with Mollenhoff in concluding that Larson's decision—based on unimpeachable evidence—was both broad and conclusive.

<<<>>>

I want to close out this "review of reviews" by citing one last one that raises a question not addressed by any other: that of *academic integrity*. In his review of Clark Mollenhoff's book, in the May 1990 issue of *Mathematical Reviews*, Albert A. Mullin, of Huntsville, Alabama, accepts the author's version of what he himself calls "the sordid story of many people, all too human, caught up in the emotional fury of a great technological invention, the electronic digital computer."[30] He then asks: "How can a network of fraud and deception infiltrate an intellectual environment?"

His answer is more a plea than an explanation of the phenomenon:

> In summary, this book leads inexorably to the conclusion that ethical behavior is *not* optional in engineering or science. Yet, today, there are documented cases of serious wrongdoing in engineering, science, philosophy and even poetry! I cannot believe that engineers are either unconcerned or unashamed about ethical problems in their profession. Engineers must be *first* to confront the misconduct of the "fraud culture" wherever it is found, be it in fabrication, falsification, plagiarism or deception. For these reasons, I highly recommend this well-written book to students and teachers of computer engineering and science as well as to the general reader.

As we have seen, most reviewers have come a long way toward accepting the basic elements of the Atanasoff story. They have acknowledged the ABC's priority, at least as an electronic arithmetic device, and they have granted it some influence, at least on the ENIAC through Mauchly. But all except Mullin have seen the ethical issue in terms of *Mauchly's* conduct alone—whether he was, and whether he should be called, *unethical*. Colonel Mullin, of the U.S. Army Strategic Defense Command, not only finds Mauchly unethical; he pushes the issue further, into academia as the environment for Mauchly's conduct.

For Mullin, the academic community bears a responsibility to denounce such conduct, certainly not to accept or turn a blind eye to it. This further issue, involving the accuracy of recorded history as well as the public recognition of a stellar achievement, is, of course, a major focus of the present book.

Art and I have very much appreciated being associated with both Clark Mollen-hoff and Allan Mackintosh in the effort to establish John Atanasoff in his rightful place in the history of computing. Unfortunately, in addition to losing Clark to cancer in early 1991, the cause lost Allan to an automobile accident in December 1995. While Allan had returned to his physics research in Copenhagen after publishing his *Scientific American* article in 1988, Clark, as journalist and lawyer, carried on in this effort until his death—working in particular to have Atanasoff's true role recognized by the Smithsonian Institution, as we shall see in the next chapter.

U.S. District Judge Earl R. Larson, in 1972 as he presided over the
Honeywell v. Sperry Rand patent trial in Minneapolis. Courtesy of Cecill Larson.

Charles G. Call, attorney and chief investigator for Honeywell, in 1972. Sketch done by artist David Oliver.

Henry Halladay, attorney and chief courtroom examiner for Honeywell, in 1959. Sketch done by artist David Oliver.

Allen Kirkpatrick, attorney and chief examiner for Control Data Corporation in *Sperry Rand v. CDC*, in 1967. Sketch done by artist David Oliver.

John von Neumann, mathematician/physicist, consultant to the Moore School team, and critical design contributor to the EDVAC and the Institute for Advanced Study Computer, in 1950. Courtesy of Marina von Neumann Whitman.

Clark R. Mollenhoff, attorney/author instrumental in bringing recognition to
Atanasoff, in 1980. Courtesy of Raymond Mollenhoff.

John V. Atanasoff and Alice C. Atanasoff, at Iowa State University celebration in 1988. Courtesy of Alice C. Atanasoff.

ELEVEN

THE PUBLIC EYE

For Arthur and me, the odd unfolding of events at the Smithsonian began in the fall of 1988. Someone phoned from that institution's National Museum of American History to tell Art of the exhibition on computer history being developed there, and to ask if he would like to receive progress bulletins. Of course he would! Soon the Spring 1988 issue arrived, announcing the as-yet-unnamed "permanent display on the history of information technologies and services and their social and cultural significance (1837–present) . . . scheduled to open in March 1990, on the first floor of the Museum."

We assumed that one of the historians associated with this project had suggested Art's name for the mailing list: Henry Tropp, principal investigator; Martin Campbell-Kelly or Michael Williams, who had each put in three months as consultants; or Paul Ceruzzi, the computer history expert for the institution's Air and Space Museum. Art was not, however, consulted on this history.

He received just two publications. The Spring 1988 one, titled *News of the Information Exhibition, A Quarterly Bulletin*, was actually No. 2 of Vol. 2, so that it had perhaps five predecessors.[1] The second one bore no date or number but arrived in the spring of 1989 under the exhibition's newly chosen name, *Information Age: People, Information, & Technology*.[2]

We had first read of plans for this exhibition in an article, "Why AFIPS Invested in History," written two years earlier by Walter M. Carlson for a special AFIPS issue of the *Annals of the* History of Computing.[3] Carlson, introduced in my chapter 7 as president of the ACM at the time of the ENIAC's twenty-fifth anniversary celebration, had been one of the founders of the American Federation of Information Processing Societies in 1961. He was chairman of the history of computing committee of that "Society of Societies," now celebrating its own twenty-fifth anniversary.

Carlson tells of AFIPS's first collaboration with the Smithsonian, from 1967 to 1973, during which nearly 250 oral histories were taped, "supplemented by the collection of the appropriate bibliographic, pictorial, and video materials, along with some artifacts." Attempts to raise funds from industry, however, failed, except for a positive response from IBM—a response that Carlson discounts because he himself was working for IBM at the time. And now, new management in both AFIPS and the Smithsonian cut off their support, as well, on the argument that "the project seemed to be all input and no output." For his part, Carlson felt that the input phase had to come first: that "reliable history products depend mainly on the building of a solid, comprehensive resource base."

There ensued a hiatus of twelve years before the Smithsonian's National Museum of American History returned to an active role in computer history, as "driven by two forces," Carlson writes, "one intellectual and the other financial." First, museum director Roger G. Kennedy recognized the need to represent computer technology along with others already represented, and new Smithsonian secretary Robert McCormick Adams saw the value of portraying the impact of information systems, both past and present, on society. Second, IBM entered into discussions with the Smithsonian to organize an industrywide effort to support a permanent Information Revolution Exhibition. IBM committed to $1 million, provided that an additional $3.3 million could be raised from other companies.

Carlson writes that in the hiatus after the first Smithsonian project, a stronger concern for preserving the history arose in industry, in government agencies, and in academic settings. He credits AFIPS—through its publication of the *Annals* and through conferences, video presentations, and advertising—with a vital role in this movement. And he now feels that the "input processes" for a second project are ensured; the prospective "output market," on the other hand, in the form of "an enlarged exhibit area, scholarly publications, and education programs," will depend upon how much money the museum can raise.

The Spring 1988 bulletin announced that $3 million had been raised. A year later, the goal of $4.3 million was topped at $4.5 million, even as a still greater need was seen, chiefly to take advantage of "some of the most exciting ideas" being suggested by the various donors.

Four items in the earlier bulletin caught our eye. First, Unisys, the new corporation born of the merger of Sperry and Burroughs, had signed on as a sponsor in the $300,000–$999,999 category. Second, a videotaped talk by J. Presper Eckert "on the development of the ENIAC" would be a feature of the ENIAC display. Third, Atanasoff was not mentioned for any of the six sections of the exhibition's layout—not for Section 2, covering 1837–1939, and not for Section 3, covering

World War II. Fourth, a highlight of the World War II section would be "a walk through the ENIAC," which was said to be "the first electronic digital computer."

We expressed our alarm in an October 3 letter to David Lendt, the Iowa State University director of university relations. We noted in particular our fear that the corporate donors financing the exhibition could be exerting an undue degree of bias:

> Atanasoff has always suffered from having no corporate entity behind his inven-tion, except in the 1971–73 court case where Honeywell's interest coincided with his. But he has emerged from that unappealed Federal court case as the inventor of an "automatic electronic digital computer" prior to the ENIAC, one from which the ENIAC was found to have been "derived. . . ."
>
> It would be outrageous if the Smithsonian Institution should go against this Federal court ruling and allow private parties to perpetuate their own false claims to invention in the National Museum of American History, itself a Fed-eral entity. It is deeply disturbing to imagine that the Museum, with all its authority and credibility, could present an incorrect version of history to the mil-lions who will stream through this exhibit. Our task of getting out the correct version would be set back enormously, if not made impossible.

Lendt had apparently not seen the Spring 1988 bulletin prior to receiving our letter with a copy enclosed. He had been alerted by a number of ISU alumni to the plans for an exhibition, however, and had already written a precautionary letter, hoping but not assuming, he said, that Atanasoff's contribution would be "properly represented." This June 15 letter to Marie Mattson, one of the planners, traced the history, referred her to the 1988 Mollenhoff and Burks books, and enclosed a copy of Mackintosh's 1987 *Physics Today* article. Lendt concluded:

> Atanasoff has been ignored far too long. The injustices of happenstance and human frailty should be corrected while the 84-year-old Atanasoff is alive. No institution is better qualified to set the record straight than is the Smithsonian.

Our October 3 letter to David Lendt prompted him to realize that he had not had a reply from Marie Mattson, and so he wrote her once more, on October 13 (again sending us a copy). This time he expressed his concern—and that of the ISU com-munity and other Atanasoff supporters—much more strongly, putting it in terms of a "growing uneasiness," indeed "a growing, and understandable, suspicion that the Smithsonian may be planning an exhibit that is biased in favor of a major financial supporter of the exhibit and the supporter's view of the history of computing."

Lendt told me later, over the phone, that a reply had come from David Allison, chief planner of the exhibition. Allison, he said, had protested Lendt's suggestion of monetary influence: the Smithsonian had never been bought and Lendt was the first to suggest the possibility. Moreover, Atanasoff *would* be rep-resented in a display immediately prior to the ENIAC display, along with Stibitz, Bush, Turing, Aiken, and other pioneers. Lendt wrote back to Allison on

December 7, saying that this "lumping" of Atanasoff with those other predecessors of the ENIAC sidestepped Lendt's "major point," namely, that Atanasoff should be singled out as *the* inventor of the electronic computer.

Meanwhile, Art and I had decided to write to the Smithsonian ourselves. In an October 14 letter to Museum Director Roger G. Kennedy, we focused on the Spring 1988 bulletin's omission of Atanasoff and its designation of the ENIAC as "the first electronic digital computer." With regard to Judge Larson's decision and the usual argument that court findings are different from historical findings, we referred Kennedy to our book as the first and only work to examine the materials on which the judge based his findings. We said that in it we show the actual coincidence of historical and courtroom fact in this particular case: Atanasoff *did* invent the first electronic computer; basic concepts of the ENIAC, the EDVAC, and the UNIVAC *were* derived from it. We concluded:

> Thus we do firmly believe that Atanasoff's contribution, both his computer and its influence, belong in any official history of the electronic computer. We also believe that, for a complete presentation, the Federal Court case itself, which figured so prominently in the determination of that history, belongs in such a presentation. It represents, after all, a triumph of justice in the matter of an invention of enormous import, something in which we as Americans can take pride. Moreover, plenty of glory remains for the creators of the ENIAC, the world's first general-purpose and first programmable electronic computer.

At Director Kennedy's request, David Allison replied to our letter, as well, under his official title, Curator of Computers, Information, & Society. In this October 25 letter, Allison said that the phrase in the bulletin "that gave you pause" (their calling the ENIAC first) was "shorthand"; it was "not a good indication of how we will treat the origin of the digital computer." He now acknowledged that the ENIAC would be "a major artifact," but assured us of their plan to "touch on" Atanasoff in a prior display, Birth of the Digital Computer, together with those others "whose pioneering helped lead the way to the establishment of a computer industry after World War II."

The museum was, in fact, adopting the view—first pressed by Nancy Stern—that the ENIAC was the significant milestone in computer history, since it had served as the impetus for the postwar computer industry. Allison wrote:

> Our presentation of the ENIAC in the exhibition will be as a culmination of many previous developments and a major transition from World War II to the post-war development of stored-program computers.

And, as to the issue of priority:

> In general, our goal is not to document or recognize "firsts" as such. We find that most major innovations are the products of many minds and a variety of social forces, not just one person.

In brief, the museum seemed to be retracting its initial, erroneous designation of the ENIAC as such a "first" by electing to declare no "first" at all. This stance, however, would allow the ENIAC to enter history free and clear of the influence of a prior electronic computer. Indeed, featuring the ENIAC as a major artifact in a separate display, with emphasis on its role in postwar developments, while placing the ABC in a prior display with the electromechanical giants, would surely leave visitors with the *impression* that the ENIAC was the first electronic computer—especially since this was the prevailing view anyway, the very one that needed correction. By implication, then, the original designation remained intact!

We wrote back on November 5, expressing our continuing concern over both the museum's denial of this critical "first" to Atanasoff and its plan only to "touch on" his work in a prior grouping. We agreed with Allison that major innovations often have many sources. But we reminded him that Atanasoff's computer "marked a distinct departure" from the technology of his day. The ABC, we said, "stands alone at the start of the computer revolution."

We also pointed out the consequences of his current plan:

> Not featuring the ABC as the first electronic computer would be a grave injustice to the man. But it would also be a grave injustice to the country, for which our National Museum can rightfully claim the invention of *the* first electronic computer. If the United States Government downgrades Atanasoff's machine from its rightful place, that distinction will fall to the British for their wartime Colossus, which postdated the ABC but preceded the ENIAC.

We now marshaled our arguments for the ABC's status as *first*, as *electronic*, and as *computer*; wondered "why the National Museum is reluctant to promote this tremendous American achievement"; and urged Allison to reconsider.

We received no reply to this second letter. Since we had copied it to Director Kennedy, who had turned our original letter over to Allison, Kennedy must have concurred in the decision not to answer. As we shall see, Roger Kennedy did prefer to leave such decisions, together with details of the exhibit plans, to his subordinates. Only parties with more clout than ours could ultimately reach him.

When the Smithsonian declined to answer our serious concerns about its treatment of Atanasoff beyond its initial, unsatisfactory reassurances, we again thought of Iowa State and its stake in this matter. On January 23, I phoned Dave Lendt again. I was beginning to feel a bit like a gadfly, but he was always cordial and willing to explore my ideas. This time I asked if he had thought of going to the press. Indeed he had, and the person to do that, he felt, was Clark Mollenhoff, with his many media contacts.

On January 26, Lendt wrote to Mollenhoff, stating two circumstances that had "frustrated and saddened" him. One, he said, was news from Alice Atanasoff of "a dramatic decline in JV's condition and his prospects." The other was his exchange of correspondence with the Smithsonian, so unsatisfactory that he had "thought long and hard about paying a visit to the principals in the company of members of Iowa's Congressional delegation":

> . . . but I am wondering whether that might not be just the wrong way to go.
>   Earlier this week, I talked with Alice Burks. . . . As you probably know, she and Arthur were the first to call the Institution's hand on this issue. . . .
>   She made a suggestion that had also occurred to me. Why not take the story to the media? . . .
>   It seems to me that you, as a professional journalist and the biographer of JVA, would be in a better position [than I] to bring the situation to the attention of the appropriate people. And you know the appropriate people better than I, as well.

He concluded:

> I would certainly appreciate your guidance. I have a feeling time is running out. I also have a feeling that this [exhibition] is a watershed development in the effort to bring to JVA the recognition owed him by his country.

Lendt enclosed copies of his correspondence with the Smithsonian.

We heard of no further developments for some months. But in March we learned that Mollenhoff had lost his elder daughter to a prolonged illness in late December. Knowing that Lendt had prodded him and not wanting to disturb him further, we decided to bide our time. Meanwhile, in that spring of 1989, Art received his second—and last—museum bulletin. It started out very disturbingly, emphasizing even more strongly than the earlier one the museum's dependence on industry, for money *and* for planning. It opened with a "Thanks!" followed by:

> When we began this project several years ago, Smithsonian Secretary Robert McCormick Adams told us, "Be bold!" We have been. But an exhibit as ambitious as ours would have been unthinkable if we had tried to do it alone. Fortunately, you in the information industry have given generously of your money, time, and talents. . . . Equally important have been your ideas and advice. This is truly a cooperative endeavor.

Next came a plea for additional supporters and a chart showing the donors to date, with the total standing at $4.5 million. Unisys was now one of six corporations in the $300,000–$1,000,000 (Sponsors) category; IBM was joined in the >$1,000,000 (Founders) category by a consortium of seven corporations.

Although Atanasoff was not mentioned in this bulletin, either, the display where presumably his work would be placed was mentioned. This display was within the third section, World War II: The Information War, 1940–1945, and it was said to show "early experimentation with digital computers."

The characterization *experimentation* was blatantly unjust, of course, not only to Atanasoff but to two other pre-ENIAC digital pioneers destined for this same display. Bell Laboratories' George Stibitz and Harvard's Howard Aiken (with IBM engineers) conceived and built electromechanical (relay) computers that did useful work for a number of years. In no way were their machines experimental.

The next display in that third section, the ENIAC, was presented as the real thing, essentially the starting point of the computer revolution:

> Turn the corner and you are standing inside ENIAC, the largest, most powerful early computer. Built to compute ballistics tables for the Army, ENIAC set the stage for further computer development after the war. You will not only see the artifact, but also listen in on an interview with Pres Eckert, ENIAC's chief engineer.

Emerging very clearly from this 1989 *Information Age* bulletin was the fact that the Smithsonian was determined not to present the ABC as the first electronic computer, much less cite the ENIAC patent trial or note the ABC's influence on later computers. The ENIAC, *by implication*, would be cast in both those roles.

We phoned Mollenhoff on June 7, raising the matter of taking this story to the media. We asked if he could suggest someone to us or if he would prefer to do something himself. He responded very warmly, saying that we had caught him at a good time: with the spring term just finished, he expected to go to Washington at least once a week for all but one of the next six. He said that he planned to see Congressman Neal Smith of Iowa, a ranking member of the House Appropriations Committee, and others in the Iowa Delegation. He then asked us to write up the issues for him to show to people—he wanted us to do this, he said, because he was afraid he would not get the technical part right.

We drew up four short summary statements: "Museum Plans"; "Arguments: Technical, and Otherwise"; "History: The ABC and the ENIAC"; and "Trial Excerpts." I mailed these to Mollenhoff on June 16, together with copies of relevant documents. In a covering letter to him, we emphasized our main point: the Smithsonian, if it decides to go against a Federal Court ruling, should have to give explicit reasons, not simply brush that ruling aside as controversial "even as it accepts hundreds of thousands of dollars from the corporation in whose interests it is deciding."

Apparently, Mollenhoff ran off copies and gave packets not just to members of the Iowa Congressional Delegation but to several newspaper reporters and columnists. For we soon began to receive phone calls from writers and then copies of articles from friends around the country. Alice Atanasoff wrote on June 29 that Mollenhoff had called to ask her to send us a copy of his covering letter for these packets. She had started with the observation that Clark was "off and

running again, doing what he does best: exposing wrongdoers and the misinformed." But she went on to this shocking piece of news:

> And in passing he mentioned that he was entering U of Va hospital yesterday for
> 5 radiation treatments and removal of an eye at the end of next week (cancer).

Alice marveled that he sounded so cheerful and was working so hard with
this on his mind. The fact is that he was to devote the next, and last, twenty
months of his life largely to the Atanasoff cause. Alice's letter closed on a
cheerier note: "JV is improving all the time and is happy about his first great
grandson."

As to Mollenhoff's covering letter aimed at enlisting help from the press and
from prominent Iowans, Alice commented that Clark expressed admiration for
our approach, but felt "it was past time for diplomacy." His letter certainly reflected this feeling, as it expressed fears for "the credibility of the Smithsonian
Institution," which he charged with planning an exhibit "that includes half-truths,
falsehoods and misleading impressions about the genesis of electronic digital
computing."

Mollenhoff referred to our book on Atanasoff, as well as his own, and also
to the fact that our correspondence with the director of the National Museum of
American History had had "no significant impact." He especially lamented the
Smithsonian's lack of attention to the "unchallenged decision of a federal court,"
as detailed in both books:

> The Smithsonian's errors might be understandable if it was not for the seven
> years of litigation that invalidated the ENIAC patent and the unappealed find-
> ings that Dr. Mauchly stole the basic electronic digital computing ideas from Dr.
> Atanasoff in his visit to Ames, Iowa, in June, 1941.

Finally, he cited what he considered the Smithsonian's outrageous offense to
Iowans and Iowa institutions for this "falsification of history" regarding "one of
the greatest inventions of this century"; and he speculated as to its motivation,
given its financial dependence on its corporate sponsors.

Two people responded immediately to Mollenhoff's urging. One was Congressman Neal Smith, the other was reporter Norm Brewer of the *Des Moines
Register*'s Washington Bureau. Dave Lendt wrote us on June 30 that Smith's top
assistant had just read him the congressman's "very hard-hitting letter" to museum
director Roger Kennedy over the phone. Lendt, now in university relations at the
University of Missouri but still actively engaged in the struggle with the Smithsonian, enclosed a copy of his own letter to Museum Curator Allison; like Mollen-

hoff, he expressed his fear that unless Allison reconsidered, "a serious and irreparable disservice will be done to history by the foremost institution of its kind."

That same day, Norm Brewer called to say that he was writing an article on the museum's handling of Atanasoff. He had many questions, about the history and about particulars of both the ABC and the ENIAC. Several people, including Judge Larson, sent us copies of this article, which appeared on the front page of the Sunday, July 2, edition of the *Register*.[4] Brewer's very good summary of the whole situation opened arrestingly:

> Just as Dr. John V. Atanasoff is gaining belated recognition as the "father" of the first electronic computer, the Smithsonian Institution is preparing an exhibit that could snatch that honor away.
>
> At the same time, the Smithsonian—by not acknowledging that Atanasoff constructed the first computer while he was a physics professor at Iowa State College—is rapidly finding itself in a controversy of international reach.

He went on to tell of Great Britain's Colossus, of the ENIAC trial, and of the risk to "the Smithsonian's reputation for historical integrity" posed by its financial dependence on "major computer companies," including Unisys. He quoted from Mollenhoff, from Mackintosh, and from Art and me, but most extensively from David Allison as to the museum's position.

Most striking for us was Brewer's inability to pin Allison down on the matter of inventive priority. Allison asserted that the museum was not to be a "hall of fame of firsts," that even Alexander Graham Bell was "apt to be described not as the inventor of the telephone, but as an inventor who obtained the first patent on a telephone"! As to the museum's initial reference to the ENIAC as "the first electronic digital computer," Brewer writes that the museum seemed to be "backing away" from that characterization but that Allison "did not flatly say it won't be used." He just said, "I don't anticipate using that."

Brewer writes that Allison said the Smithsonian would not be drawn into the debate over who invented the computer, because that depended on the definition of *computer*. Allison himself considered the ABC to be not a computer but a calculator, even calling it, in his interview with Brewer, "an effort to try to make an electronic calculator." As we saw in chapter 8, William Aspray went to great lengths to foster this distinction a few years earlier. Allison added that it was fine if historians wanted to debate who invented what, but he himself, as a historian, thought that "that kind of thinking really misrepresents how things get developed in our society."

He denied any corporate influence on the exhibition. "We don't horse-trade space for money," he told Brewer.

Norm Brewer followed this article with another, dated July 4, 1989, reporting sharp reactions by Representative Smith and by Iowa Senator Charles Grassley to the museum's plans for its Information Age exhibition.[5] He quotes Smith's June 30 letter to Kennedy as citing not only the court finding for Atanasoff but also Mauchly's courtroom acknowledgment that he had examined both "the Atanasoff computer and the 35-page booklet explaining its theories and operation." He then quotes Grassley as saying that he, too, would write, for he considered the museum's handling of Atanasoff's invention "a breach of one of the basic laws of scholarship." In a third article dated July 11, Brewer quotes a further (July 5) letter from Smith to Kennedy as suggesting "the strong possibility of a conflict of interest leading to this revision of established historical fact."[6]

Alice Atanasoff, who was in contact with both Smith and Grassley, sent us copies of Roger Kennedy's two responses to Smith. The first, dated July 10, assured Smith of appropriate treatment of Atanasoff's contributions and, for the first time, stated flatly that the museum would "not be presenting the ENIAC as the 'original' or 'first' computer." Kennedy then echoed Allison's assurances to us and to Dave Lendt that, instead, the exhibit would show that "there were many early developments that led to the emergence of the computer industry and its effects on Society after World War II," including Atanasoff's work, the development of the ENIAC, and also the work of Aiken and Stibitz.

Kennedy's second letter, dated July 17, assured Smith that no conditions were attached to the financial contributions to the exhibition. He added:

> I can assure you that we will urge the scholars working on this exhibition to take very seriously the evidence with respect to Dr. Atanasoff's contribution. We will, as you request, "review the documented facts of record." We will do so as scrupulously as you might expect we would.
>
> Thank you for your interest in the matter and for your continued support of the quest for truth which underlies the role of the Smithsonian Institution in American society.

This reference to support, of course, was an allusion to Smith's position on the House Appropriations Committee.

That same July 17, *USA Today* carried a report of this correspondence, calling it "a war of letters."[7] This piece has a still dissatisfied Smith suggesting that the Smithsonian "show the Iowa machine as first electronic digital computer; the ENIAC, as first programmable one." It closes with a comment by John Wise of Unisys, ENIAC's "corporate descendant," that encyclopedias generally list the ENIAC as the "first electronic digital computer."

Alice Atanasoff sent us a copy of the *Washington Times*'s Associated Press article, also of July 17.[8] It tells the same story but with emphasis on the Smithsonian's effort to "duck trouble" by deciding "to spread the credit among several computer pioneers," rather than call the ENIAC first.

Again on that same day, David Allison visited the Atanasoffs' home to explain the museum's plans for presenting the ABC. The following day he sent Alice Atanasoff the latest floor plan of the area in which the display case, Birth of the Computer, would be located—just prior to the ENIAC room. This display would still be composed of Stibitz, Aiken, and Atanasoff, but would now have a transitional note about the ENIAC. In an accompanying letter, Allison wrote that the "general intent in that [display] case is to introduce the idea of 'instantaneous,' or electronic processing" by "comparing a 10 position relay from the Mark I and an electronic tube similar to what was used in the ABC computer":

> Then we will show photographs and components of the ABC computer (if artifacts are available) and its inventors and introduce the notion of electronic digital computing.

Thus Atanasoff's machine had acquired the modifier *electronic* and was also being called a *computer*—at least in Allison's letter. But it was still not called the *first electronic computer*. And its placement after the two electromechanical computers—first clarified in this letter to Alice Atanasoff—was out of chronological order: the ABC was completed two years before the Harvard-IBM Mark I and four years before the Bell Laboratories Model V.

Charles Grassley carried his theme of "scholarship" to the floor of the Senate in a speech recorded in the *Congressional Record* of July 25, 1989.[9] Like so many other critics, he opened his argument by citing the Smithsonian's reference to the ENIAC as "the first electronic digital computer" in its Spring 1988 bulletin—which no one seemed to believe was just some kind of "shorthand," as Allison alleged.

After recounting the story of the ENIAC patent trial, noting the forfeiture to England's earlier Colossus if the ABC was not declared "first," and recommending Mollenhoff's book to his Senate colleagues, Grassley closed with a promise to return to this matter unless a satisfactory resolution was forthcoming. Norm Brewer, in yet another, July 27, article in the *Des Moines Register*, presents this last as a threat "to seek legislation, if necessary," to assure Atanasoff his "rightful place in history."[10]

We next received, from a variety of sources, copies of an August 11 "Washington Merry-Go-Round" article by Jack Anderson and Dale Van Atta.[11] Art and I had been interviewed for this piece on July 13 by Anderson assistant Ken Rogerson. Rogerson said that Mollenhoff had supplied a copy of our four write-ups of this history, and Anderson needed permission to quote from these. He asked a lot of questions, particularly as related to the other interviews he had conducted.

For us, the most interesting aspect of this Merry-Go-Round article was its reporting of remarks by Paul Ceruzzi, as well as David Allison. It begins with this charge:

> At the Smithsonian Institution, the title, "Father of the Computer" has become more a matter of politics than paternity. A Smithsonian exhibit ... will give short shrift to a man many people believe invented the first electronic computer—John Vincent Atanasoff.

Instead, the exhibit focuses on John W. Mauchly, an early computer pioneer who worked for Sperry Rand Corp., now a part of Unisys Corp., which, just by coincidence, is underwriting the Smithsonian exhibit.

And it asks:

Is the Smithsonian dabbling in revisionist history to satisfy a patron? "No," says David Allison. . . . He told our reporter Ken Rogerson, "We haven't discussed with any of our sponsors what will be in the exhibit."
Paul Ceruzzi, a Smithsonian historian, said IBM gave $1 million to the exhibit, and the company doesn't believe either Atanasoff or Mauchly created the first computer. IBM believes it did, Ceruzzi said.

The article also has Ceruzzi taking a position that originated with Nancy Stern—embraced by Ceruzzi in his review of her book (see chap. 7)—even as he does credit Atanasoff:

Ceruzzi admits that Atanasoff was the inventor of the computer, but says that Mauchly and Eckert were the "effective" inventors because they patented it and made something that was useful. "We always felt like (Atanasoff) belonged in the exhibit," Ceruzzi said.

But then this Jack Anderson article casts the recurring doubt:

Well, maybe not "always." In the spring of 1988, a Smithsonian bulletin about the exhibit in the planning stages referred to ENIAC as the "first" computer. Then, after Atanasoff's supporters came out of the woodwork, Smithsonian literature started calling ENIAC the "largest, most powerful early computer."

It concludes by returning to the issue of paternity: "As the exhibit progresses, the Smithsonian says knowing who the father was isn't as important as the computer itself."

Meanwhile, two other prominent figures were urging the Smithsonian to bow to Judge Earl R. Larson's findings in the ENIAC patent trial. On August 8, Iowa Representative Fred Grandy wrote a very strong letter to Museum Director Kennedy. He focused on points in Larson's opinion that explain why that opinion "was not appealed by Sperry Rand despite the fact that it invalidated patent rights worth hundreds of millions of dollars and perhaps billions." He then noted the trial's value for computer history:

Historians, in searching for the truth on the first electronic digital computer, could never dig deeper than the seven-year record of the litigation that invalidated the ENIAC patent.

Grandy felt that the unchallenged decision of a United States District Court "should carry a great deal of weight" with the Smithsonian unless its own historians could produce "solid evidence that Judge Larson was wrong."

President Gordon P. Eaton of Iowa State University wrote to Kennedy on August 14, 1989. Noting that the decision on the ENIAC, "which had been patented mistakenly as the first electronic digital computer," had never been challenged, he expressed puzzlement:

> There is no litigation active or, to my knowledge, pending, involving the ENIAC, the Atanasoff-Berry Computer, the families of those involved in the development of either machine, or the computer industries originally involved in the litigation. The debate continues, however, due primarily to a strange and puzzling unwillingness on the part of established authors and institutions, such as the Smithsonian, to accept the legal record facts and findings.

Calling Larson's decision "a seminal landmark in the history of computing technology," he referred Kennedy to Art and me and to Mackintosh for our "independent findings" on the matter.

President Eaton said of his university's efforts:

> Since 1973, the year Judge Larson issued his ruling, Iowa State University has been engaged in an educational campaign to clarify this clouded and unfortunate aspect of technological history. It has been an uphill battle, but one that is finally starting to see results. Increasingly, new editions of textbooks and resource books are acknowledging Atanasoff's significant contributions and role in the development of the computer.
>
> No one, myself included, is trying to diminish the role and significance of the ENIAC. As the Burkses note, the ENIAC was a "tremendous machine" and it was the first "general-purpose" electronic digital computer. However, the ABC deserves the place in history as the very first electronic digital computer.

It was now late summer of 1989, just six months before the scheduled opening of the Information Age exhibition. Despite the press exposure and the efforts of the various concerned parties, little had changed—at least in effect—since the Spring 1988 museum bulletin that had so alarmed the Atanasoff advocates. David Allison had answered critics of the bulletin's allusion to the ENIAC as "the first electronic digital computer" by saying that the exhibition would not *feature* "firsts." But this seemed to reflect more a reluctance to bestow that title on the ABC than a willingness to drop the designation for the ENIAC. It took Roger Kennedy in his July 10, 1989, letter to Representative Neal Smith actually to say, at last, that the ENIAC would not be called "first."

The Smithsonian had given no indication that it would mention the ENIAC patent trial, which effectively shifted that "first" from the ENIAC to the ABC. Nor had it given any indication that it would note the influence of the ABC on the ENIAC, through the Mauchly contacts with Atanasoff, as also exposed in that trial. Indeed, for lack of such information and because of the size and placement of the several displays, the impression would remain that the ENIAC, not the ABC, was the first electronic computer.

The Smithsonian seemed unwilling even to accept the compromise language of ISU President Gordon Eaton (or, earlier, of Congressman Smith): call the ABC the *first* electronic computer and the ENIAC the *first general-purpose* (or *programmable*) electronic computer.

We had a long phone conversation with Clark Mollenhoff on the first of September. As always, at the same time that he had strong words for the opposition we were facing, he remained somewhat optimistic. First, he thought our side was doing the best it could. Second, he thought we had a good case, which the museum could not ignore. Third, he thought the museum knew that the Iowa Congressional Delegation would follow through on this issue. Fourth, he thought the favorable review of both our books by Lee Loevinger, a highly respected lawyer, would help (see chap. 10). And fifth, he had learned from John Anderson, David Lendt's replacement in the ISU public relations office, that the Smithsonian had requested the university's input on the Atanasoff presentation—apparently both materials and ideas.

Of course, dearest to Mollenhoff's heart was the court case, the burden of his book on Atanasoff. He told us that he had been discussing a possible display about that case with Kennedy, who, he said, happened to be in his circle of lawyer friends.

Then, on September 18, he wrote Kennedy a three-page letter, a copy of which Alice Atanasoff sent us at his request. Here he laid out his argument for including Judge Larson's decision in the ABC-ENIAC portion of the exhibition. He began by remarking on the "hard fact of life" that the "revolution in communication that created the Information Age" had been stimulated by the invention of the electronic computer—as recognized, he said, "in every Mass Communication text book that I am aware of . . . and in every aspect of university life today."

Mollenhoff then referred to the ENIAC trial in cautioning Kennedy not to "avoid, dodge or minimize the role of the Atanasoff Berry Computer":

> Unless you and the people you have working on the Information Age show are able to produce evidence to overcome the overwhelming evidence supporting Judge Earl R. Larson's decision, you must accept the hard fact that an unchallenged federal court decision has found that Dr. Mauchly and Presper Eckert "derived" the basic electronic digital computer concepts from Dr. John V. Atanasoff.

He said that Museum Curator Allison should either produce his evidence against Larson's finding or accept its "hard clear truth," lest the Smithsonian's reputation be soiled.

Mollenhoff now repeated the suggestion that Kennedy present the ENIAC as the first *general-purpose* electronic computer—though with a proviso:

> However, having said that, it is only fair and accurate to make clear reference to the Atanasoff Berry Computer and simply quote in a manner that cannot be missed that the ENIAC patents were invalidated by a United States District Court decision that was not challenged. The exhibit should state: "Eckert and Mauchly did not themselves first invent the automatic electronic digital computer, but instead derived that subject matter from one Dr. John Vincent Atanasoff."

Mollenhoff felt that such a presentation could be made without necessarily endorsing Judge Larson's decision. It was only necessary, he said, that the museum "acknowledge its existence."

On the other hand, he observed:

> It would seem to me that you and others involved in the decision-making on the Information Age show would find the Atanasoff story a fascinating and thoroughly documented story for an enlightened public to know and enjoy the triumph of right over deception.

Indeed, he argued for the trial's particular relevance to this exhibition (surely with amusement at the irony):

> If the development of ENIAC is important, and I believe it is, then one of the most important "information transfers" in an Information Age show would be the "information transfer" that took place in Dr. John Mauchly's five day visit as a house guest of Dr. Atanasoff in June, 1941.

One further attraction for this story, he added (and one further irony), would be the fact that "the Honeywell-Sperry Rand litigation lasting more than six years was the first complicated trial record that was managed by computers":

> Honeywell's lawyers used the system they called ELF (for Electronic Legal File) to keep on top of the information management of a court record that included 25,686 plaintiff exhibits, 6,968 defendant exhibits, the testimony of 77 court witnesses, and 80 deposition witnesses.
>
> This was, as far as I know, the first use of electronic computers to manage the record in a major litigation, and it is interesting that the litigation dealt with a fight over the computer patent rights held by Sperry Rand through Mauchly and Eckert.

Mollenhoff concluded by inviting Kennedy to inform him of his "precise points of disagreement," if any, with "the theses in my book or in this letter," so that "those points can be discussed."

A few days later, Mollenhoff sent Kennedy a write-up of the ELF system used in the ENIAC trial, as requested by Kennedy. This document had been prepared for Mollenhoff by attorney Charles Call, who had played such a key role for the Honeywell side. It details how ELF kept track of the huge volume of trial data, *and* made its listings available to Judge Larson as well as to the Honeywell counsel.

(Call's document is interesting in itself. He comments that ELF's aid to the judge became essential because "the Court's minute clerk was unable to cope with the volume using traditional manual methods." At one point, for example, "ELF revealed that Judge Larson had a backlog of more than 15,000 exhibits which had been offered in evidence over objection—and he had not yet ruled on their admissibility." Its great value for Honeywell, of course, was its ability to locate decades-old papers needed to verify or refute the recollections of witnesses on an overnight basis. "Testimony based on 'wishful thinking' was dramatically curtailed," Call writes, "and many witnesses commented that the lawyers seemed to know more about their activities than they themselves could hope to recall.")

Now, it is not hard to see the dilemma for the Smithsonian in presenting the court case along with its room-size display of the ENIAC. Doing so, even without endorsing the decision as Mollenhoff suggests, would cast a cloud not just over the ENIAC as any kind of "first" but over Mauchly and Eckert as its chief inventors. Doing so in a way that would celebrate "the triumph of right over deception" by featuring this "fascinating and thoroughly documented" story would shift the entire emphasis from the ENIAC to the ABC—going against the long-standing conventional wisdom and, more relevantly, the "wisdom" of the exhibition's sponsors. The museum was committed, from the start, to building this section of its presentation around the ENIAC, together with Eckert's video about it.

The other horn of the Smithsonian's dilemma, of course, was its need, its *function*, to give an honest historical accounting.

Mollenhoff's letter of September 18 set off an exchange of letters that culminated in a most astonishing admission by the museum director. Kennedy's "Dear Clark" of September 22, slightly tinged with irritability at Mollenhoff's persistence and insistence with regard to Atanasoff's role in the history, compared his job as director to that of a university president who would not "tell scholars what the results of their research should be." He said that the museum was currently producing "between 25 and 30 major, permanent exhibitions," that he was "not a historian of the origin of the computer," and that his staff was "much better qualified" than he to produce this history exhibition.

Kennedy said he was "delighted" to pass on to his staff letters with "new information," but as for himself, he concluded:

> I have enormous respect for your past and present services to the nation, but I must withdraw from "the loop" to pursue my own responsibilities to that nation.

He penned an appreciative, but still door-closing postscript: "I *do* thank you immensely for your help. We'll do the best we can—RK." And with that he turned Mollenhoff's September 18 letter over to Allison.

Allison responded on October 2 with yet another explanation of the museum's plan to place Atanasoff among the World War II "pioneers" whose work helped set the stage for the *postwar* "development of the computer, and the information age of which it is a part." He simply ignored Mollenhoff's challenge to produce his evidence against Judge Larson's findings.

Allison did now cite two books to bolster his position, both survey texts with only brief treatments of Atanasoff and no mention at all of the court case:

> Our presentation is fully in tune with recent scholarly works that put Atanasoff's work in broad historical context, such as Stan Augarten's *Bit by Bit* and Michael R. Williams' *A History of Computing Technology*.[12]

Meanwhile, Mollenhoff was not to be put off by his friend Kennedy's attempt to leave all decisions to his staff. On September 29, he dispatched a second three-page "Dear Roger," this one a carefully reasoned exposition of the dangers of such a policy—especially in a situation where Kennedy, as the ultimately responsible party, had been made aware of sound arguments against that staff's plans. Subordinates may err, he said, whether through "laxity, misjudgments, frauds or willful sell-outs."

With Cassandra-like frustration, Mollenhoff recounted his own efforts, in his newspaper columns or in person, to caution every president from Truman to Reagan—and "a list of cabinet officers as long as your arm"—against blind reliance on the advice of those around them, however expert or brilliant they were. Yet, he said:

> On a few occasions, presidents and cabinet officers have examined the evidence and taken some corrective action. More frequently, they have failed to recognize the problem or unwittingly relied upon a careless or treacherous subordinate when a close examination of the hard evidence would have disclosed serious errors or willful deceptions.

All he was suggesting, he continued, was that Kennedy ask his historians to explain why they were ignoring the federal court decision. He followed with this personal appeal:

> While you modestly declare that the historians in the history of science and technology are "much better qualified than" you are to make decisions, I would beg to differ with you. You are a good lawyer with common sense, and from our conversations you understand the hard evidence of documentation, the difference between corroborated and uncorroborated testimony of witnesses, and the importance of the chronological development of that evidence. You also under-

stand the value of direct examination and cross-examination of key witnesses to get to the truth.

Mollenhoff went on to recite in detail the major points of "hard evidence" elicited in the ENIAC patent trial, from which he concluded:

> It seems to me that this court record puts the burden of proof on the historians . . . to come up with some evidence or convincing explanation as to why they are willing to ignore, deprecate or deride an unchallenged federal court decision.

He did not like to be "a pest." He only wanted to enable Kennedy "to ask the right questions" of his staff and "to make a few sound suggestions" in order to improve this exhibition and to preserve the Smithsonian's "long-time image." He did understand Kennedy's wish "to withdraw from 'the loop' of responsibility" because of his "other important responsibilities to the nation." But he "would point out that maintaining the reputation of the Smithsonian Institution for depth research and integrity is probably the most important part of that responsibility."

Mollenhoff declared that his own research on the court case had made him "more confident than I have ever been on any investigation in my entire life." But he also indicated a willingness to reexamine his position in the face of new information. He closed, "I know I will be pleased if you do the best you can as a conscientious administrator and as a good lawyer."

Several days later, after he had received Allison's response to his first letter to Kennedy, but not Kennedy's own response to his second letter, Mollenhoff phoned Art and me. He was clearly still perturbed by Kennedy's attempt to withdraw from "the loop." He was also perturbed by Allison's response, with its "nice, don't-trouble-yourself tone" and its apparent refusal to consider Judge Larson's arguments. He said that he was studying the Augarten and Williams books cited by Allison.

On October 9, Mollenhoff wrote Allison that he was "generally satisfied" that both freelance writer Augarten's and historian Williams's books acknowledged the ABC's influence on the ENIAC (which the museum's plans still omitted). But he was "deeply troubled," he said, by the failure of these books to acknowledge the court case and by their errors of fact that contradicted the "overwhelming evidence" of that case. He attributed these and other errors to the nature of such broad historical texts, and he again urged the inclusion of "the court record and findings" in the museum's presentation.

Kennedy's response to Mollenhoff's plea that he return to "the loop" was dated October 5, 1989. Far from resenting Mollenhoff's somewhat preachy tone, he took his letter as it was intended—an urgent, caring message from a friend who also had a personal involvement in the issues. He began:

> You have my personal assurance and my assurance as the Director of this Museum that I will do exactly what you have asked me to do in your helpful

letter of September 29—the best I can as a conscientious administrator and as someone who tries to be a good lawyer.

While he was sure "nobody here will be guilty of 'fraud' or 'willful sellout,'" and he would guard against "laxity or misjudgment," Kennedy was "delighted" this time that Mollenhoff would be "out there being sure that we are even more unlikely to lapse."

He then thanked Mollenhoff for a letter of September 25, in which he had apparently commented that he might write a book about the ELF system and its usefulness, and also about LEXIS (an ensuing legal research system that was by 1989 the most widely used database for this purpose).

Now Kennedy made this startling statement:

> Furthermore, though I may be out of my gourd in making such a suggestion, I think you might find it intriguing to include in such a book some reflections of your own on the resistance of the corporate and scholarly communities to what you would feel to be the full recognition of Atanasoff's role. It's easy enough to understand why certain computer manufacturers and their close allies would have an interest in one outcome of scholarly inquiry. It's more interesting, in a way, to wonder what forces in scholarship, external to the case itself, may have militated against full recognition of the Atanasoff kind of achievement. Aside from "why doesn't Atanasoff get his due?" there is a broader inquiry into what's going on in the view of invention and inventors that is characteristic of the 1970s and 1980s, different from the view of inventors and invention of let us say the 1940s to say nothing of the 1920s.

He went on to elaborate and to speculate on this new view:

> As you can imagine, one of the reasons for my desire to avoid setting myself up as an expert in this field is the volume of input. What I get from you represents a relatively small proportion of my mail on this subject, some of it from people who feel more vehemently than you but come at it from what should be described as "the other" point of view. That other point of view can be very honestly held by people who have no connection to the computer companies who have a pecuniary interest in the matter. And that point of view, so far as I now understand it, holds that nothing is really "invented" unless it comes fully into existence, and that, so it goes, large and complex machines only come into existence in a large and complex institutional environment.

He added:

> Let me stress that I am not presenting that point of view as though it's "true," but merely that it does exert a powerful influence upon this controversy, quite independent of one's view of Dr. Atanasoff's specific achievements.

Kennedy closed by reassuring Mollenhoff that his purpose here was to encourage him to proceed with his inquiry, but also to broaden that inquiry to reflect on "the nature of contemporary scholarship and its political and industrial ambience."

This highly revealing transition, from out-of-the-loop to out-of-his-gourd at Mollenhoff's prodding, gave credence, at last, to the strong suspicions of Atanasoff advocates with regard to the Information Age exhibition. All of us had long been aware of an undercurrent of pressure on the historians of computers. Art and I had experienced it in our relations with the preeminent journal in the field, *Annals of the History of Computing*, when we were finally told why, despite earlier promises, we could not respond to Kay Mauchly's article: the editors had received "some very pointed, even barbed comments" from the computing community, objecting not to our position, of course, but to the journal's fostering of "controversy" (see chap. 6).

As to the perfect honesty of those who were simply, though vehemently, urging a redefinition of the key term *invention* "quite independent" of Atanasoff's achievements, it is only prudent to take a close look at what those innocent protestations would mean for those achievements. Just as a redefinition of *computer* would make the ABC—and, for some, even the ENIAC—*not a computer* but *a calculator* (see chaps. 7 and 8), so this redefinition of *invention* would make the ABC *not an invention*, whatever else it might be. In both cases, it becomes convenient to brush aside the fact that this machine encompassed—and reduced to practice—a remarkable assemblage of original and enduring electronic computing concepts. On this argument, Judge Larson's findings need not be addressed, either: his definitions were antiquated.

This revised view of *invention* also served to promote a relatively recent notion from which all industry could profit: we have industry to thank for our great new products. Even the lone scientist who happens to create a novel device has not *invented* anything unless he or she manages to "develop" it into a useful, and marketable, product. As Mollenhoff put it to us in an October 13 phone conversation, "Industry is saying that no invention is really an invention until industry promotes it." What is more, if others accomplish this development instead, well, they are the true *inventors*. (Compare Stern's distinction between invention and innovation, a forerunner of this argument, in chapter 7.)

Kennedy, in accepting the detachment of the "scholarly community," seemed puzzled as to its motivation. He did point the way, however, when he suggested that Mollenhoff reflect on "the nature of contemporary scholarship and its political and industrial ambience." The extent to which the pecuniary interests of academia have become linked to the pecuniary interests of industry is widely attested and regularly protested—and as widely denied.

We need to realize, too, that the scholars who petitioned the *Annals* or the Smithsonian against Atanasoff, though far more numerous than those who felt "vehemently" enough to petition for him, were not necessarily representative of the scholarly community. In 1985, when EDUCOM, the Inter-university Communications Council, gave Atanasoff its Computing Appreciation Award, the membership was divided about fifty-fifty over how to credit him. A member of the nominating committee told Art and me that the adverse feeling was so strong that, in the end, the committee decided to honor him not as "inventor" but as "pioneer."

<<<>>>

Whatever their reasons, the Smithsonian's own scholars were among those opposed to any serious recognition of Atanasoff. Museum director Kennedy, on the other hand, had to have doubts about resorting to the ploy of redefinition of a well-established term in order to escape the verdict of a federal court—and to evade the position of the U.S. Patent Office, with its definition of *invention* and its rationale of encouraging the *inventor* to *invent*. Then there was the Iowa Congressional Delegation to contend with. Finally, there was the matter of claiming this world-shaking invention for the United States, rather than letting it slip away to Britain's Colossus.

There had to be some "give." And it had to appear that there was no "give": that the museum had planned all along to recognize Atanasoff appropriately. This situation is summed up very nicely by Norm Brewer in a November 15, 1989, article distributed by *Gannett News Service*.[13] Here Brewer tells of the new rapprochement between the Smithsonian and Iowa State University. He reports that curator David Allison has found the university "reasonable and cooperative" in their discussions. His museum now expects to borrow and display the original memory drum, together with a few vacuum tubes, and also an add-subtract mechanism reconstructed for the ENIAC trial.

Brewer then reports that ISU spokesman John Anderson is now satisfied, having been reassured "that Atanasoff's role will be portrayed accurately and that a 'major segment' of the exhibit on World War II computers will be devoted to Atanasoff." But, he adds, "Allison said the Smithsonian changed no plans after speaking with Iowa State officials." Indeed, Allison expressed surprise at "the flap," since "Atanasoff's role in pioneering use of electronic parts in the central brain of the computer has been clear" among historians.

Brewer notes, however—once again—that the "controversy was ignited by a Smithsonian brochure that called the ENIAC the 'first' computer." He notes, too, that the debate has been complicated and that Iowans were angered by the Smithsonian's acceptance of $4.5 million from a number of computer companies, including Unisys, to help pay for the exhibit. He adds that both "Smithsonian and Unisys officials have denied that money influenced exhibit planning."

A couple of weeks later, Art and I received a letter from John Anderson that was much more specific about the understanding ISU had reached with the museum. In a recent trip to Washington, Anderson had visited Allison and had seen the exhibition as it stood at that point, together with a complete floor plan. He listed six significant changes from the Smithsonian's original plan:

* In the preliminary layout plan, Atanasoff and the Atanasoff-Berry Computer were to have been included in the Pre–World War II portion of the exhibit; they are now included in the World War II section, which highlights how the war honed our society's information technology.
* The work of three men—Howard Aiken, George Stibitz, and Atanasoff—is featured in the portion of the exhibit that shows how computing evolved from their work into the ENIAC.
* The Atanasoff portion of the display will include large photographs of Atanasoff and Berry with the ABC, the original memory drum and a vacuum tube add/subtract mechanism.
* The narrative accompanying the Atanasoff portion of the exhibit acknowledges the ABC as the first electronic computer and that it was the first machine to demonstrate many of the principles of current electronic digital computers, including the use of digital rather than analog signals and regenerative memory.
* Narratives accompanying the memory drum and the vacuum tube add/subtract mechanism detail the significance of the ABC in that it was the first to use electrical capacitance for memory and vacuum tubes to allow "instantaneous processing."
* The narrative accompanying the ENIAC states that Mauchly knew Atanasoff and had seen his computer and that Mauchly derived some of his ideas from the ABC.

Anderson closed this letter with his belief that, while our side did not get everything it wanted, "we have won on all major points, and JVA will be represented in the Smithsonian as a major pioneer in computing."

Of course, a "major point" was missing still: any mention of the court case. However, like Anderson, Art and I were heartened by the progress that had been made, even as we were also convinced that a limit had been reached. Atanasoff would, at long last, be recognized as inventor of the electronic computer, and at least some Atanasoff influence on Mauchly and the ENIAC would be explicitly acknowledged. These were the facts established by the court case, even if the Smithsonian remained unwilling to admit the fact of the court case itself.

In a December 9 letter to Mollenhoff, we said we did not expect to pursue the matter further. But our main purpose in this letter was to thank him for the copies he had sent us of his correspondence with Kennedy, among other documents, and, especially, to congratulate him on his "pivotal part . . . in persuading the Smithsonian to give more space and more credit to Atanasoff than was originally planned."

For, while others had contributed significantly to this outcome, it was Mollenhoff, with his wide range of journalistic and governmental connections—including his most fortuitous friendship with the museum's director—who successfully forced the issue. Those of us privileged to watch from the sidelines could only admire, and marvel at, his know-how and his fortitude. Clearly, what sustained him in the face of the formidable opposition was his strong conviction that he was right—and his long-standing dedication to the right.

Art and I were very happy to have such a person fight this fight in a way that we could not, and to respond to his calls for our help as he proceeded. In this regard, it should be mentioned that Clark Mollenhoff was always careful to credit his sources and to thank them personally. He told us that he particularly appreciated our book, which he referred to often. When he had to answer someone's argument on Atanasoff, he said, he looked in our book and told that person to "read the three paragraphs on page so-and-so." He said he was glad we were on his side.

It had been a pleasure, too, to work with the people at Iowa State, who, like Mollenhoff, always expressed gratitude for our efforts. ISU has continued its promotion of the Atanasoff cause, most recently taking on the huge project of building an exact copy of the Atanasoff-Berry Computer. A campaign to do so had been underway for some time, but the most that was thought affordable was a mock-up model (as first suggested by Art). Ultimately, funds were raised for a true working replica, faithful in every detail. This machine was unveiled in October 1997 at the Washington Press Club. It had given its builders many a challenge and many a surprise at Atanasoff's genius for efficiency and economy in the ABC's tightly integrated design.

In September 1990, Art and I visited the Smithsonian, which had opened its Information Age exhibition on May 6. We found the display on Atanasoff and the Atanasoff-Berry Computer, the last panel in a sector titled "Instantaneous Processing: Origins of the Electronic Computer," quite faithful to John Anderson's depiction of it—with one glaring omission. It seems that sometime after Anderson's visit, what Director Kennedy had called the "other point of view" in his October 5 letter to Mollenhoff had kicked in, one last time, to exert its "powerful influence upon this controversy."

At the top of this two-foot-wide display, captioned "The Electronic Computer," was a photo of the machine (summer 1941) with Berry operating it—its left-right orientation reversed, however. Next down was a photo of a young Atanasoff. Then came the reconstructed add-subtract mechanism (see fig. 11), followed by a photo of the ABC in its final state (see fig. 5) and the actual remaining memory drum (see fig. 6). Lastly, on the "floor" of the display, was propped a photo of Mauchly, Army Ordnance Major General Gladeon M. Barnes, and Eckert, taken on the occasion of the ENIAC dedication in February 1946.

The accompanying text called the Atanasoff-Berry Computer "the first electronic computer." It was not a *calculator*. Indeed, the electromechanical machines in the preceding displays of this sector were also digital *computers*; even the mechanical differential analyzer, in an earlier sector, was an analog *computer*. Nor were any of these machines said to be "experimental," as in the original plans.

The full text on the Atanasoff-Berry Computer read:

> Between 1937 and 1942, Iowa State University Professor John V. Atanasoff and his graduate student Clifford Berry built the first electronic computer. It used some 300 vacuum tubes as well as logic circuits, card readers to input data, and memory drums that stored information as electrical charges. This computer was a special-purpose machine designed to solve systems of simultaneous equations. Although never fully operational, it was a digital binary machine that demonstrated many principles of electronic digital computers, including vacuum tube logic and regenerative memories. Atanasoff left computer development during the war to conduct acoustics research for the U.S. Navy.

The text alongside the ABC's add-subtract mechanism was less satisfactory. It presented this device not as any particular component of the computer—much less as the first binary serial adder—but as an untitled example of vacuum tubes, to be contrasted with the relays of the preceding machines. It did note that because of the speed of the electronic tubes their use in computers ushered in "instantaneous processing."

The text for Atanasoff's memory drum accurately stated that it "stored information as electrical charges that could be read, charged, or refreshed electronically."

It was the text accompanying the bottom photo—of Mauchly, Barnes, and Eckert—that proved so very disappointing in view of what ISU's Anderson had written us. He had said that this text, titled "The ENIAC," stated "that Mauchly knew Atanasoff and had seen his computer and that Mauchly derived some of his ideas from the ABC." Instead, the full passage read:

> In 1943 the U.S. Army funded a proposal by the Moore School of the University of Pennsylvania for a general-purpose digital electronic computer. A team directed by John W. Mauchly and J. Presper Eckert designed and built ENIAC, the Electrical [*sic*] Numerical Integrator and Computer. With some 18,000 vacuum tubes, ENIAC was more flexible than Atanasoff's computer and could be programmed with plug wires to do many different tasks.

We had known there would be no mention of the ENIAC trial, but now there was no mention of Atanasoff's influence, either!

Upon our return to Ann Arbor, I wrote out some reflections on the museum's presentation of the ABC, and especially on this scant introduction to the ENIAC,

tucked in at the end of the "Origins" sector as a transition—the only transition—
to the next, room-sized display of that later machine. I noted, first:

> The Smithsonian has moved a long way from its original (published) position
> that the ENIAC was the first electronic computer, in that it recognizes the ABC
> as such. It has also moved a long way toward recognizing the original enduring
> ideas in the ABC, specifically, "vacuum tube logic and regenerative memories."
> Moreover, it has recognized, at least by implication, that the ABC started the
> computer revolution by stating that instantaneous processing began when com-
> puters were designed to use electronic tubes. Finally, it does not in any way sug-
> gest that the ABC was any less an electronic computer because it was "never
> fully operational." Nor does it use terms like "abandoned" or "incomplete" to
> characterize the final state.

I then lamented the museum's failure to acknowledge the influence of the ABC
on the ENIAC, or on the EDVAC for that matter. I felt it was one thing to omit the
ENIAC trial as an embarrassment and as a highly disruptive facet of the history. But
omitting the bare mention of the Atanasoff-Mauchly connection with regard to the
ENIAC, as represented to John Anderson, was, it seemed to me, inexcusable.

Of course, the ABC still suffered from its placement with, and as a culmination of, the IBM-Harvard Mark I and the Bell Labs Model V (both of which it
actually preceded), rather than separately as the first electronic computer. The
ENIAC also suffered from this initial placement in the nonelectronic sequence,
with the further implication that it sprang from those relay machines. Translating
the "E" of the acronym as *Electrical* rather than *Electronic* only added to the confusion. (At least there was an original nameplate on an ENIAC panel in the next
room that had the name right!)

Eckert's five-minute video, with captions, was a walk-through of a number
of panels of the computer and one of its free-standing function tables. In that brief
presentation, he succeeded in highlighting several critical features of the
machine, together with some of the difficulties the design team had to resolve
under the urgency of the moment. He said nothing about the ENIAC's origins and
named no team members besides himself and Mauchly.

There was also a video of a 1946 newsreel on the ENIAC, a Twentieth Century Fox "Movietone News" feature of that day. Here the original commentary
was replaced by that of a museum spokesman, who, inexplicably, also gave the
acronym as *Electrical* Numerical Integrator and Computer even as the film displayed the nameplate calling the machine *Electronic*.

<<<>>>

What the museum did get right in this one segment of its new exhibition had to be
satisfying, representing as it did at least a partial victory after so much effort by so

many people. As for the overall presentation, Art and I were most struck by its lack of cause-and-effect revelation, especially in a *historical* exhibition. Technological development as a process was left largely to the viewer's imagination, to be gleaned from a series of phenomena only very broadly in chronological order.

Reviewer Hank Burchard, writing in the May 11, 1990, *Washington Post*, puts the matter more bluntly—indeed, scathingly.[14] He had hoped that the exhibition would help "sort out the confusion" of this revolution that "has turned our planet into one great buzzing ball of ideas, images and sounds." Instead, he finds, "the exhibit serves as a brain-battering example of it":

> It's so cluttered you'll miss something if you blink, so noisy you can hardly hear yourself think, and so unfocused you can't tell what you're supposed to be thinking about.

Moreover, Burchard writes, "the show flat fails to live up to its name" Information Age: People, Information & Technology:

> It gives little consideration to the impact of the *information age* on *people*, presents *information* that often fails to inform, seldom explains the principles of the *technology* involved, and scants the awesome implications of it all. [italics in original]

Even the film meant to "explore some of the implications of the information age," Burchard says, is "mainly an artsy melange of quick-cuts of women, men and children spouting opinions." He philosophizes:

> This substitution of streams of words and images for lines of thought is one of the most disheartening phenomena of the computer age, in which "information" is valued by quantity rather than content and the medium often overwhelms the message.

Burchard continues with an explicit example from one of the earlier segments of the exhibition:

> Perhaps the most glaring example of the exhibit's disregard for content is in the "Bombe" section, devoted to the World War II code-cracking projects that allowed the Allies to eavesdrop on enemy communications. Breaking the [German] Enigma code not only shortened the war, it greatly accelerated the computer revolution by bringing many of the best and brightest minds in the world to bear on the problem of high-speed data processing.

For Burchard, the Bombe "was a pivot point in the information age and forms the pivot point of the exhibition." Yet, "the museum's account displays a lack either of scholarship or of candor, because it combines misinformation with disinformation."

An *American-built* Bombe was exhibited, he writes, with no mention of "the Poles whose efforts and sacrifice gave the Allies a crucial head-start on Enigma":

Polish cryptanalysts invented (and named) the Bombe and were using it to read Enigma by 1938. The British further developed the machines before sharing their expertise with U.S. intelligence. What we did, essentially, was fine-tune the Bombe and turn the crank; but most Smithsonian visitors will come away believing the project was mainly an American show.

He concludes, in exasperation, "So much for historicity."

Other reviews were more favorable. The Spring 1990 issue of the *Charles Babbage Institute Newsletter* describes the exhibition overall in terms of what was available to the visitor, with major emphasis on the "more than 40 stations for hands-on use of computers and sophisticated interactive equipment."[15]

Newsweek's reviewer, Jerry Adler, writing in the May 21, 1990, issue, is utterly bedazzled by the "faster and faster" pace of the "bigger and bigger doses" of data "com[ing] at you" as you progress from one information-retrieval station to another.[16] He finds Samuel Morse's telegraph, featured in the show's first display, "an absurdly cumbersome device" at the same time that he also finds it the single artifact in which "the transformation of thought into data is seen most clearly." Adler's philosophizing is a little more "pop"-oriented than Burchard's:

Could [Morse] have imagined that the techniques of electrical data transmission he had just invented would someday be used to tell a man in Washington, D.C., how many RBIs Yogi Berra had in 1954? What hath God wrought, indeed?

A report in the October 1991 *Annals* by David Allison provides some statistics on attendance at the exhibition during its first year: an estimated total of about 1.5 million visitors, 426,000 of whom registered with the network of interactive displays.[17] The most popular of these displays involved the Enigma cipher machine; it was used 314,564 times.

Like others before him, Hank Burchard, in his *Washington Post* review, also questions whether this exhibition, "largely put together and entirely paid for by corporations that sell information, electronics and computers," was uninfluenced by those corporations. He quotes Museum Director Roger Kennedy's explanation that the museum had to seek outside sponsorship because it received "absolutely no federal exhibition funds." The private sponsors, Kennedy said, "have the technology and we didn't have the money." As to influence, however, Burchard has Kennedy adding, "not one of the sponsors ever made any attempt to influence our staff."

Kennedy walks a fine line here. As we saw earlier, the Spring 1989 museum bulletin emphasized the Information Age's dependence on its industrial sponsors. It thanked them heartily not just for money but for "ideas and advice," and it pleaded for others to join in what it termed "truly a cooperative endeavor."

According to a *Washington Post* story just prior to Burchard's, Kennedy had, in an appearance before a House Appropriations Subcommittee, expressed considerable anguish over this very dependence on industry. Kim Masters writes in this April 22, 1990, article:

> Roger Kennedy, director of the National Museum of American History, warned that the current budget process "has left the Smithsonian gasping along." While corporate contributions cover some of the museum's cost, Kennedy asked, "Should every dollar spent for the exhibitions on controversial topics . . . be paid for by corporations? Should every object brought into our collections have to pass the inspection of corporate donors? . . . Is this healthy? I think not."[18]

It seems that, however much Kennedy felt constrained to deny corporate influence—or even any *attempt* at such influence—to the media, he was telling Congress that it had indeed occurred. And it takes no great stretch of imagination to think that one of those "controversial" exhibitions was the Information Age show, at that point set to open in a couple of weeks.

Some four years later, Jacqueline Trescott of the *Washington Post*, in reporting the replacement of Smithsonian secretary Robert McCormick Adams by Ira Michael Heyman, takes note of the continuing funding problem. She writes, in her May 26, 1994, story:

> "We have a resource problem that is significant, both a public and a private resource problem," said Heyman. The Smithsonian is a $458 million-a-year operation, which receives a direct federal appropriation of $342 million and must make up the rest through endowments and private donations.[19]

This situation was not to improve. Corporate engagement in the substance and thrust of Smithsonian exhibitions has become more open, and accepted, as Congress has scrutinized budgets more and more closely and tightened funding more and more severely. Certainly, the storm of protest—from World War II veterans and many others—over the National Air and Space Museum's initial plans for its 50th anniversary "Enola Gay" exhibition exacerbated Congress's astringent mood. On the other hand, the successive rewritings of that show's script, the decision to scrap interpretive material, and, finally, the drastic downscaling under Secretary Heyman brought counterprotests of improper pressure on the institution.

On this note, this recurring concern over the implications of private funding for Smithsonian exhibitions, I want to return to Walter Carlson's article, "Why AFIPS Invested in History," cited at the opening of the present chapter. There I noted Carlson's observation that, as of his writing in 1986, the "input processes" for a history exhibition were assured, in large part through the efforts of the American Federation of Information Processing Societies. The "output market," however, would depend on the ability of the museum to raise the necessary funds.

This latter aspect, the putting together of the actual show over the next four years, entailed a conflict of interest that had evolved as industry grew ever more dominant in information processing. Carlson astutely assesses this evolution in economic terms:

> The simple answer to the question of why AFIPS invested in history—given the benefit of today's 20/20 hindsight—is that there is no economic market for the history of contemporary technology.
>
> . . .
>
> At the outset . . . no market or academic stimulants were available, so action became the responsibility of the nonprofit sector, comprised mainly of academia, government, and the professional societies. When computers and their related information processing technologies burst on the scene, academic and governmental agencies played key roles in creating the fundamental building blocks. The economic driving forces were provided by industry, however, and the scope and health of the information processing profession as we know it today were molded in response to industry's requirements.

Carlson remarks on the initial existence of bias on the part of contributors of documents and artifacts in industry, in government, and in academia. Moreover, he writes, no one in those early days could "afford the time and effort to investigate independently and report objectively" on the developing history. In the end, however, he thinks that the profession has faced up to, and overcome in large measure, this problem of bias, as the history of computing has "become recognized as a scholarly discipline worthy of support."

Unfortunately, the course of events in the ensuing creation of the Information Age exhibition does not bear out Carlson's surmise. Powerful external pressures were brought to bear on the National Museum of American History; moreover, a number of members of this new discipline, especially those the museum relied on, bought into industry's line that recognition should accrue, not to inventors of enduring concepts but to developers of those concepts in the world of commerce.

The need for both materials and money remains a critical issue for the preservers and presenters of the history of the electronic computer—a need that, as Walter Carlson saw, often comes down in turn to the issue of "output" versus "input" in the eyes of prospective donors. I want to report now on the "output" of one other production in which Art and I had some involvement, a production that, like the Smithsonian's, enjoyed partial public support but also had to rely on private sponsorship. This is the Spring 1992 television series, *The Machine that Changed the World*, presented in the United States by WGBH Boston as "A WGBH Boston/BBC TV coproduction in association with NDR Hamburg."

(This film, first titled *The Information Age* after the Smithsonian exhibition on this same history, actually appeared in Germany the previous August and in Britain that November and December. The BBC called it *The Dream Machine*. It appeared in the United States as five one-hour segments, on Mondays from April 6 to May 4, 1992.)

The Machine that Changed the World was a profound disappointment to Art and me, because of what we thought, rightly or wrongly, we had been led to expect after our interaction with its producers, particularly after a nearly six-hour interview here in Ann Arbor by WGBH producer Nancy Linde and BBC producer Fiona Holmes. It is true—as we were reminded later when we expressed our disappointment—Linde did caution us, in the course of that January 25, 1990, interview, that nothing was final at that point. I believe we are justified, however, in being disappointed by the show's many errors and inaccuracies in its depiction of the invention of the electronic computer.

I should make clear right away that we did not feel we had been led to believe that any particular position would be taken on the issues of concern to us: Atanasoff's role and the ENIAC patent trial. All we felt sure of was that those topics were to be treated, and our great letdown was that they were *not*. Atanasoff was not mentioned at all. The sole reference to the court case was a statement in an epilogue to the second segment: "Eckert and Mauchly's patent for the ENIAC was judged invalid in 1971 [*sic*]. Today no one holds a patent for the invention of the computer."

We had discussed Atanasoff at some length with Linde and Holmes and were satisfied that they understood the dispute very well. We also felt that we had argued the case for Atanasoff effectively. As to the trial, I had asked explicitly whether it would be covered, and the response—as we both heard it—had been unequivocally that it would. Linde, in a postseries letter of May 28, 1992, disagreed vehemently with our recollection of this exchange. Her response, she said, had been "quite the opposite."

My recollection remains firm. First, I asked this question because the court case was the one major item left out of the Smithsonian presentation; and, second, I was greatly relieved to understand that it would not be omitted from the television presentation. In any case, I acknowledge that we were cautioned that nothing was yet determined, and I can only protest this omission in the name of historical accuracy.

Linde's letter to us was in reaction to our May 13 letter to the editor of the *Ann Arbor News*, which was reproduced (with our permission) in the May 18 *Ames Daily Tribune* and then somehow came to her attention. She took rather strong exception to our wondering whether PBS and BBC could have come "under the influence of their sole corporate sponsor, Unisys, whose predecessor, Sperry Rand, owned the Eckert-Mauchly patent on the ENIAC and was the loser in the court case that invalidated that potentially lucrative commodity?" She felt this question indicated "the desperate lengths to which you two will go," and she closed her letter with an allusion to what she saw as our "underhanded and libelous tactics."

From our perspective, we saw no reason to suppose that those parties who had pressured the Smithsonian—and earlier, the *Annals of the History of Computing*—would not have pressured PBS and the BBC as they approached this same topic. Museum Director Roger Kennedy's own question to the House Appropriations Subcommittee, "Should every object brought into our collections have to pass the inspection of corporate donors?" was still fresh in our minds when we formulated our question to the newspaper editors. We were also mindful that many reputable columnists and reporters, not to mention senators and representatives and university officials, had expressed concern over the possible influence of Unisys and other corporate sponsors on the Smithsonian presentation.

Equally fresh in our minds was Unisys's recent agreement to pay a record $190 million for corrupt practices in military procurement deals. Paul Mann writes in the September 16, 1991, issue of *Aviation Week & Space Technology*:

> Unisys pleaded guilty Sept. 6 in federal court in Alexandria, Va., to conspiring to defraud the U.S. and to bribery, among other counts. The Justice Dept. won conviction on charges that Unisys and its predecessor, Sperry Corp., bribed Pentagon officials in an influence-peddling scheme to gain a competitive edge in contract awards.[20]

The $190 million, Mann says, was to cover both "criminal fines and civil recoveries in connection with the Operation Ill Wind investigation."

Of course, we do not know that Unisys brought about, or even tried to bring about, the TV series' sidestepping of Atanasoff's work and the patent trial. This is why neither we nor the others made that accusation, but put the matter in the form of questions. It does seem a legitimate concern and one that, as Kennedy indicated, arises because of the necessity of seeking corporate donors for these public enterprises. Moreover, such questions are not meant to impugn reputations, but to call attention to the serious bind that certainly some producers of both public and private television networks have found themselves in because of their dependence on commercial support.

In the case of *The Machine that Changed the World*, the "input" from those on the Atanasoff side was much less than it had been for the Smithsonian exhibition. Unlike the National Museum, WGBH Boston did not circulate progress bulletins to which interested parties might respond, and it did not reveal details of its programs in advance.

(It did advertise for sponsors, at least indirectly, as in a September 11, 1989, *Wall Street Journal* spread that told of WGBH's fund-raising "from corporations and foundations" and cited Unisys and the ACM as already on board for The Information Age series. This ad, "Public Television Sets Sail for the Future," briefly described a total of six "major new series" and named the sponsors procured thus far for each.[21] It also acknowledged the long-term commitments of a number of corporate sponsors and the ongoing support of individuals and of The Corporation for Public Broadcasting and PBS.)

Art was first contacted by associate producer Lauren Seeley in an October 6, 1989, letter. She said that she had seen "the documentary you put together describing the ENIAC" for Boston's Computer Museum and that she would like to have Art's copy of "the original 16mm [Newsreel] material" on which that documentary was based. She also wanted his help in locating the women shown manually programming the machine in that film, as well as others who had worked on it after it was moved to Aberdeen Proving Ground.

Art did send the film, and also copies of our Atanasoff book and the four briefs we had written for Mollenhoff. (She already had a copy of our *Annals* article on the ENIAC.) Mollenhoff himself sent his book and spoke on the phone with Linde several times, beginning as early as August 1989.

Iowa State University's John Anderson also wrote to Linde on November 27, 1989, outlining the history and expressing his concern for Atanasoff's treatment; he sent copies of Allan Mackintosh's *Physics Today* and *Scientific American* articles. Linde responded with her assurance that "the entire series will be balanced and accurate in historical detail."

Curiously, one of the few articles I have in my file for this preseries period is a December 1, 1989, piece from *USA Today* sent to us by Linde after her visit.[22] It was not about the coming TV series but about the striking coincidence of five stellar inventions, including that of the electronic computer by John Atanasoff, all now at the fifty-year mark. Author John Hillkirk writes:

> Consider the technologies that permeate modern society: computers and copiers in our offices, microwave ovens in our kitchens, TVs in our living rooms, high-speed jets for traveling.
>
> Every one of those technologies appeared in 1939. The USA's John Atanasoff built the first computer. Chester Carlson patented his Xerox copier. RCA launched TV at the New York World's Fair. Germans flew the first jet-powered plane. Brits came up with microwave technology to detect enemy planes. No one is sure why so much happened at once. But 1939 certainly was the most important year in modern times for technological breakthroughs. Few of us could make it through the day without using a product dating to that incredible year.

In this *USA Today* "Cover Story," with shots of Atanasoff, Chester Carlson, and an RCA television receiver on the front page, Hillkirk describes each of the five achievements. He ends his write-up of Atanasoff with the comment that "Atanasoff's discovery laid the foundation for ENIAC, the world's first general-purpose computer, introduced in 1946."

(Perhaps not incidentally, 1939 has been singled out for another striking concurrence, this one in the motion picture industry. Television critic Kirk Nice-wonger cites 1939 as "a year of such explosive creativity and imagination that, in retrospect, it seems to have been almost a feat of magic."[23] He names *Gone With the Wind, Mr. Smith Goes to Washington, Stagecoach,* and, for him, "the most beloved" if not the greatest, *The Wizard of Oz.* Other critics cite *Wuthering Heights, Goodbye, Mr. Chips, Dark Victory, Of Mice and Men, The Hound of the Baskervilles,* and *The Hunchback of Notre Dame,* among others.)

All in all, I think that the *USA Today* article, as called to our attention by producer Linde herself, together with the fact that the Smithsonian had (ultimately) credited Atanasoff's invention—and the added fact that President George Bush had, the previous November, conferred the National Medal of Technology on Atanasoff expressly "for inventing the electronic digital computer"—these three circumstances sealed our expectation that this public television series would not overlook him. How mistaken we were!

Whether or not *The Machine that Changed the World* was shaped in part by Unisys, it could not have been more to that sponsor's liking, with regard not just to Atanasoff but also to John von Neumann. An introduction to the series opens with shots of the ENIAC: Art and Herman Goldstine at the multiplier; operators at various locations manually programming the machine, loading cards into the IBM input-output devices, and changing modules; and, again, Art pointing to an array of lights during the public demonstration of 1946.

A narrator's voice says that "45 years ago, there was just one computer" and "people at that time thought that America would only ever need six such machines." No names are given at this juncture—not even that of the machine being shown—nor is it made clear whether the "machine" of the title is this singular behemoth or the computer in general. Rather, the film moves forward, tracing the invention's impact up to the present as a rapid succession of ever "smaller, cheaper, and better" devices.

It is in the first two segments that the errors of greatest concern to us occur: errors of omission and implication but also of commission. Together they cover computer history from the Jacquard punched-card loom of the early nineteenth century through the triumph of the integrated circuit in the Apollo moon landing of 1969. The first segment, "Giant Brains," is "Written, Produced and Directed" by Fiona Holmes of the BBC; the second, "Inventing the Future," by Nancy Linde of WGBH Boston. All five segments acknowledge, at beginning and end, the series' funding by Unisys, by the 90,000 members of the ACM, and by the National Science Foundation.

Holmes's "Giant Brains" has long tracts on Babbage, with his unfinished mechanical analytical engine, and on Konrad Zuse, with his electrical relay computers. Remarkably, the narrator credits Babbage with conceiving of a general-purpose programmable computer; and Zuse with realizing, "by the end of 1941," Babbage's dream of one hundred years earlier, and also with having "solved most of the basic design problems" of a binary computer. But relays were slow, the narrator says, and much faster switching devices were available: namely, vacuum tubes, which were used most commonly in radios but "could be used equally well as lightning-fast switches."

Konrad Zuse himself comes on to explain how his friend Helmut Schreyer persuaded him to take the step into electronic computing, and historian Paul Ceruzzi comes on to explain the on-off switching principle of both the relay and the "thousand-to-two-thousand times faster" vacuum tube. As it happened, however, the narrator continues, the Schreyer-Zuse plan for a computer based on vacuum tubes was rejected by the German high command, which expected to have won the war in the two years needed to build the machine. And so, as Zuse returns to lament, "nothing became of electronic development in Germany." The narrator now observes that "the future of computing would indeed be electronic, but it would be realized elsewhere."

With that, the scene shifts to the United States Army's desperate need for firing tables, which were being ground out at a snail's pace by human "computers." And so it is on to the University of Pennsylvania's Moore School of Electrical Engineering, where "two visionaries thought they had the answer. John Mauchly, a physicist, and a talented 23-year-old engineer, J. Presper Eckert, wanted to build an electronic computer." We are back, then, to the ENIAC as the starting point of the electronic computer revolution, without so much as an allusion to the Atanasoff-Berry Computer.

Now I do not want to take anything away from Zuse and Schreyer, with their brilliant early insights. I want only to point out that Atanasoff's two critical achievements in electronic computing predated theirs as well as Eckert and Mauchly's. Atanasoff's 1939 model, which incorporated an electronic add-subtract mechanism, demonstrated his successful adaptation of vacuum tubes for computing—as against their current use in radios (analog) or in scaling circuits (digital, yes, but limited to *counting on* in the manner of an odometer) (see chaps. 1 and 3). And then his 1942 machine (if not that earlier model) stood as the world's first computer in which vacuum-tube circuits performed complex switching and arithmetic operations.

Schreyer's achievements came later. It was in his 1941 doctoral thesis that he presented several designs for computing circuits based on a combination of special vacuum tubes provided to him and special fast-acting neon tubes. And it was a year or more later still that he actually built a small device using this combination, a binary-decimal/decimal-binary converter. Moreover, even if he and Zuse had been given government support for their vacuum-tube computer, by their own reckoning it would not have been finished before the ABC was finished.

At the same time that this television documentary errs in promoting Schreyer over Atanasoff in pioneering the use of vacuum tubes for computing, it also errs in making light of that critical accomplishment. These faster devices were simply "available," presumably in the physicists' scale-of-two counting circuits. The viewer is told of the worrisome failure rate of vacuum tubes as a challenge to the designers of the ENIAC, but not of the challenge of making them compute in the first place.

Finally, of course, in this process the film also simply bypasses the fully realized Atanasoff vision and its historic role in the conception of the ENIAC and the computers that followed.

The story moves next to the stored-program concept, where, unlike Atanasoff, von Neumann *is* recognized—indeed, as "America's most distinguished mathematician." He is shown to have arrived on the scene after the Moore School team has seen both the need for automatic program storage and how to achieve it. This is accurate enough, as far as it goes. Successively, the narrator, Kay Mauchly Antonelli, Ceruzzi, and Eckert relate how the team saw that the ENIAC's manual programming bottleneck could be overcome in future machines by loading the program for each new problem into the memory in the same digital form as the problem's data. But the concept is left there, as sufficient for the stored-program machines, with no mention of von Neumann's critical further idea for a "substitution instruction" that would render the program self-modifiable. (See chap. 5.)

Von Neumann is pictured and his "First Draft of a Report on the EDVAC" displayed. The narrator observes: "This landmark report became the theoretical blueprint for all future computers. It bore the name of John von Neumann." There is no indication that von Neumann contributed anything new to the concept of the stored program—nor even, in fact, that he addressed that concept. Viewers are left with the impression that Eckert and Mauchly invented the concept as it was applied in the EDVAC and later computers. Von Neumann is seen at best as having written up their ideas. And this, of course, is exactly as Eckert always went on record with regard to von Neumann's role.

There is no further mention of von Neumann: not of his conception, in that same initial report, of the cathode-ray-tube memory as an alternative to the EDVAC's mercury-delay-line memory; nor of the Institute for Advanced Study Computer built in roughly the same time frame as the EDVAC and employing the cathode-ray-tube memory, with its random-access feature. There is no mention, either, of the computers built both in this country and abroad on that IAS model. Finally, there is no mention of the fact that when, as would be noted in the second segment, IBM overtook Remington Rand, it did so *not* on the basis of the Eckert-Mauchly mercury-delay-line model but on the basis of the von Neumann cathode-ray-tube model.

The first segment now shifts from completion of the ENIAC to developments in Britain, which reached fruition before other post-ENIAC machines in the United States. In fact, it devotes considerable space to Alan Turing and to the Colossus, which preceded the ENIAC as well as the EDVAC. It tells of the "first working computer with a stored program" operated at Manchester University in 1948 (the Mark I prototype). And it tells of Maurice Wilkes's "friendly" EDSAC of 1949.

A major problem in this film presentation, at least in its early segments, is its mix of "messages." It shifts from program narrator to scholar to historical figure (or an actor portraying such a figure from the past). The result is in each case an engrossing story, but one that may have been seriously slanted by a "pioneer" whose version of events is highly inaccurate.

For example, in the first segment, the narrator observes that the Moore School lost the race to build the first stored-program computer when, scarcely a month after the ENIAC dedication, Eckert and Mauchly resigned. "The two inventors had applied for a patent on the ENIAC," he explains, because they had recognized the commercial possibilities. But the school's new director of research "demanded that [they] give up their rights to the invention" in order to stay. Eckert then comes on to declare, "We didn't want to do this!" and to mock the director [Irven Travis] as repeatedly asking them to reconsider.

Now, in the first place, they had *not* applied for the ENIAC patent—and would not for another fifteen months. More importantly, the ultimatum given Eckert and Mauchly by Dean Harold Pender on March 22, 1946, not only let them proceed with the ENIAC patent but also let them patent all their further ideas (as for the EDVAC) up until the end of that month (see chap. 7).[24] The first condition of Pender's letter for their *continued employment* was:

> (a) That you execute the University's standard patent release, copy of which is attached hereto, to apply to all work, other than on Contract W-670-ORD-4926 [the ENIAC contract], done by you after March 31, 1946.

This is what Eckert and Mauchly did not want to do!

The preponderance of the TV series' second segment, "Inventing the Future," is devoted to development of the computer industry. Again, it opens with the ENIAC, repeating and enlarging on earlier scenes before turning to the ill-fated business ambitions of that machine's "creators." Due attention is given to the UNIVAC, invented by Eckert and Mauchly but produced commercially by Remington Rand after its takeover of their company. The story continues with IBM's belated decision to go electronic and with its rise to overwhelming command of the field. Then it is on to advances in programming and to invention of the transistor and the integrated circuit. And so to the moon.

Eckert is last seen explaining the narrator's statement that "in 1956, IBM soared past Remington Rand as the largest computer company in the world." Although Eckert is speaking "live" in this 1992 production, he is identified as "V.P., Remington Rand, Retired." Actually, by 1956 Remington Rand had already merged with Sperry Gyroscope to form Sperry Rand, and Eckert had continued on as vice president of the new company, not retiring until 1982. As for the competition with IBM, the year 1956 marked the Sperry Rand-IBM cross-licensing agreement from which Eckert and Mauchly netted their disappointingly small one-half million dollars (see chaps. 5 and 7). Finally, of course, Sperry Rand was succeeded by Sperry and then, with the merger of Sperry and Burroughs, by Unisys.

One of the earliest objectors to *The Machine that Changed the World* was Allen Kirkpatrick, the Control Data attorney who had deposed Mauchly in the Regenerative Memory patent suit (see chap. 2). He phoned Art and me on April 8, 1992, just two days after the airing of the first segment in this country. His chief concern was that somehow the omission of Atanasoff should be remedied. He said he would write to BBC's Fiona Holmes expressing his dismay at the omission, citing our book and Mollenhoff's, and urging remediation in a future segment. He did write to her on April 10; later he sent us a copy of both his letter and her response of April 23.

Like us, Kirkpatrick expected that "there should come a time in the presentation when the litigation over the ENIAC patent would be discussed," at which point "the effect of Atanasoff's work on the patent could be presented, with an explanation of who he was and what he did." But that was not to be.

Holmes replied that she had thought "long and hard about whether Atanasoff among others should be included in this programme. Indeed," she said, "many people think that the omission of the Harvard MK I and Howard Aiken was an even less understandable one." Her argument for excluding Atanasoff rested on the need for a simple "thread of argument" and the decision early on that this thread should be "the development of the stored-programme computer." The first segment, therefore, would concern "the necessary steps" in this development:

> By the mid-thirties Zuse already had a programmable relay machine working satisfactorily in Germany. The next step was a significant increase in speed, and the successful completion of a machine that would give the whole idea validity.
>
> ENIAC was included because it accomplished both of those things, as well as leading directly to the proposal for EDVAC, and thus to the stored programme computer.

This is a strange statement, for Holmes's TV presentation sets the end of 1941, not the mid-thirties, as the point at which Zuse achieved such a relay computer (later named the Z3). As to those earlier efforts, her consulting computer historian, Paul Ceruzzi, writes in Aspray's *Computing Before Computers* that the Z1 of 1938 was "a small prototype," based not on relays at all but on a "purely mechanical approach to calculation"; and that the ensuing relay machine, the Z2, was also "a prototype" that "did not work well" but was impressive enough to secure funding for "a more substantial machine," the Z3.[25]

In her letter to Kirkpatrick, Holmes found Atanasoff's machine lacking the requisite speed. She also found his idea of using vacuum tubes for computing "not really an extraordinary one," since "electronic counters had been in use for some time." "Although Atanasoff was one of the first to begin building an electronic computer in America," she writes, Zuse and Schreyer had proposed one, the British Colossus team was in the process of building one, and, she added, "I think there is evidence that the idea was in John Mauchly's mind before he met Atanasoff."

She has made no distinction between counting and computing circuits, nor between unrealized and realized concepts. Her very choice of words is transparently biased: Atanasoff is minimized as *one of the first to begin* building an electronic computer, while Mauchly is maximized as one who *probably already had the idea* for such a computer.

Finally, Holmes has resorted to the old "unresolvable controversy" argument:

> In the circumstances I could not see how I could include Atanasoff without becoming involved in a contentious argument that I could not resolve, and that would therefore leave the audience puzzled.

I submit that she did "resolve" the argument when she excluded Atanasoff—and that in so doing she left her audience misinformed.

Kirkpatrick tried once more, writing Holmes on July 6 in the hope that Atanasoff's achievements—and those of Aiken, as well—could be explained, albeit briefly, in a series rerun. But that was not to be, either. Among other things, Kirkpatrick argued that, in fact, "the use of tubes in computers was a fundamental and giant step forward," taken earlier by Atanasoff than by Schreyer.

As the series wound down, we received copies of several other letters protesting the omission of Atanasoff and the reduction of a U.S. District Court decision to bare mention in an epilogue. These letters variously reviewed the history; suggested corrective measures; cited Atanasoff's awards and his recognition by the Smithsonian Institution as inventor of the electronic computer; worried about the integrity of public broadcasting; and suggested possible influence by sponsor Unisys. We also learned at this time that Unisys's contribution was $1.9 million.

After WGBH producer Linde responded to us, and BBC producer Holmes responded to Kirkpatrick, the task of answering such concerns seems to have fallen (or risen) to Jon Palfreman, executive producer of the series. He wrote letters to Reid Crawford, Iowa State University's interim vice president for external affairs and attorney at law (May 12); to us (May 29); to the editor of the *Ames Daily Tribune* (published on June 2); and to U.S. Senator Tom Harkin of Iowa (June 9). His June 2 letter, written in response to the Ames paper's publication of ours, is the most comprehensive and in fact includes nearly all the arguments of the others.

Palfreman's defense of the omission of both Atanasoff and the patent trial is best approached from his concluding paragraphs in that letter to the editor.[26]

> I am well aware of how passionately the Burks feel about this issue, but neither the ruling of Judge Larson nor their book has convinced the majority of professionally trained historians of technology who have studied this area. It does not help their case when they perpetrate falsehoods and distortions. There is absolutely no truth to their statement that two of our producers, Nancy Linde and Fiona Holmes, "assured them emphatically" that we would include the ENIAC patent dispute in the series. This was a research trip, one of hundreds of conversations to help determine what would be included.
>
> Moreover, their attempt to impugn our reputation simply because we disagree with them is scandalous. Their suggestions that a sponsor, UNISYS, exerted influence on the content of the series shows the desperate lengths to which they will go. Clearly, they know nothing of how PBS works. Leave aside the fact that PBS rules prevent any contact between the production team and the sponsors. This was an international coproduction between WGBH and the BBC. As executive producer, I had the say as to what was and wasn't included. The problem with the Burks' fantasy is that I was a BBC producer whose salary came from London.
>
> Atanasoff was undoubtedly a great man, but regretfully has become a pawn in the hands of a group of fanatics who use intimidation rather than serious intellectual argument to further their case.

These are very serious charges, not without their own strong element of passion. I have already remarked on both our recall of the Linde-Holmes interview and our reasons for raising the question of possible influence by the major sponsor of the series. (On this latter issue, I do fail to grasp how the executive producer's base with the BBC precluded such influence.)

What is critical here is that these two charges form the sole basis for Palfreman's condemnation of us as fanatics, fantasizers, perpetrators of falsehoods and distortions, and users of intimidation in place of serious intellectual argument. Yet they have nothing to do with the soundness of the Atanasoff case, nor with that of the ENIAC patent case, nor even with our arguments in support of those cases.

Palfreman bases his rejection of Judge Larson's decision on an elementary misconception of the nature of the lawsuit. He writes:

Judge Larson was presented with Sperry's claim that John Mauchly originated the idea of electronic computing, and Honeywell's claim that Mauchly had not thought of electronic digital computing until Atanasoff gave him the idea. Neither Sperry nor Honeywell had anything to gain by emphasizing to Judge Larson that by the time Mauchly visited Atanasoff at Ames in 1940 [*sic*], the idea of electronic computing was "in the air."

He cites the efforts of National Cash Register, Bell Labs, RCA, Eastman Kodak, and MIT to develop electronic computers, as well as the planning for such computers in Germany and Britain.

Palfreman's argument here has the same weakness as Holmes's. Invention, not the idea (even if many were working on it), was at stake. Accordingly, Sperry actually claimed much more for Mauchly than that he originated *the idea* of electronic computing. Similarly, Honeywell did not claim that Mauchly had not *thought of* electronic digital computing before he met Atanasoff, but that he had not *invented* such a computer until he got the technical know-how from Atanasoff.

Judge Larson was clear on these issues. What he ruled in Finding 3—indeed, was led to rule by Mauchly's own testimony—was that Mauchly's broader interest had been in "electrical analog calculating devices," and that he "had not conceived an automatic electronic digital computer" prior to his visit to Ames (see chaps. 3 and 4).[27]

Finally, Honeywell had everything to gain by uncovering any and all electronic computer developments, not just before Mauchly visited Atanasoff, but all the way up to the invention of the ENIAC. This was not a suit between the ENIAC and the ABC, nor between Mauchly and Atanasoff. It was a suit between Honeywell and Sperry Rand over the validity of the ENIAC patent: Honeywell needed to show not only that electronic computing was "in the air" but that it was "on the ground," already invented, before the ENIAC. The Honeywell attorneys were fortunate enough to find the ABC. It was their great additional good fortune that Mauchly had visited Atanasoff and learned from him enough to be charged with derivation.

In this matter of derivation, Palfreman moves from the judge to Art and me. He argues that even if, as he represents our position, "John Mauchly 'stole' some information from Atanasoff, which enabled Eckert and him to build the ENIAC," it is far-fetched to claim that "this act had any influence on subsequent computer history." He writes:

This is a very contentious issue, but let's assume for the sake of argument that John Mauchly did "steal" key technical information from Atanasoff. Did that act "directly influence the ENIAC, immediate successors to the ENIAC, and, indeed, all computers to this day," as the Burks contend? Surely, this implies too great a role for either Mauchly or Atanasoff.

Palfreman claims that Mauchly made little contribution to the ENIAC beyond his initial instigation: "Eckert was the chief designer of the machine," which bore "little similarity" to the ABC. Moreover, he argues, when other teams like the British engineers at Manchester and Cambridge entered the field, they brought their own independent experience to bear on their inventions:

> To retrospectively credit memory devices they used—such as mercury delay lines or CRT's—to Atanasoff's rotating banks of capacitors is a little far-fetched. Are the Burks saying that Maurice Wilkes could not have built the EDSAC because of a visit John Mauchly made to Ames, Iowa, in 1930 [sic]?

Of course, Mauchly did contribute substantially to the design of the ENIAC—and of the EDVAC. He and Eckert were in constant communication. More significantly, Mauchly did pass on to Eckert concepts from the ABC that found expression in both of those machines, concepts that were, indeed, passed on to those "other teams."

Although Palfreman's film does not say so, Wilkes adopted the basic design principle of the EDVAC for the EDSAC: the idea of a regenerative mercury-delay-line memory working in conjunction with a separate arithmetic unit based on a binary adder (see chap. 9). Likewise, the Manchester Mark I, with its cathode-ray-tube memory, used this same design principle of regenerative memory and separate arithmetic unit. The twofold debt of these British designers to Atanasoff (via von Neumann as well as Eckert and Mauchly) is evident, even though his computer's regenerative memory was a capacitor drum.

(Actually, the June 1948 Mark I, as described by S. H. Lavington, was "a small digital computer [built by F. C. Williams and Tom Kilburn] to provide a realistic test for their [earlier] storage invention."[28] Dubbed the "baby MARK I," it served as the prototype for the much enhanced "Manchester MARK I working by April 1949." As we saw in chapter 5, there also ensued the Ferranti MARK I, which in February 1951 became the world's first commercially marketed electronic computer.)

And so we certainly argue that this causal chain exists! As for what Wilkes might have done without Atanasoff's original work, we cannot say. What we can say is that he did in fact design and build an electronic computer that grew from the EDVAC design, which in turn had utilized principles Mauchly had learned on that (1941) visit to Ames.

One further noteworthy aspect of Palfreman's essay is his repeated appeal to the views of "the vast majority of historians of computing and computer experts," even as those views waver somewhat. He offers a definition of *computer*, for example, that he believes "most authorities" agree on: a computer should be programmable; it should be electronic (oddly, because otherwise it "probably would not have changed the world that much"!); and it should have the stored-program facility.

Palfreman recognizes that this definition excludes not just the ABC but also the ENIAC—that, in fact, "by this set of criteria, the first proper computer was the Manchester Mark I." But he excuses the ENIAC, calling now on the view of "most historians" that it is the ENIAC that "deserves the prize." There is the very "achievement of constructing the ENIAC" to consider, plus the fact that it influenced "subsequent computer development in Britain." Of its lack of the stored-program facility, Palfreman asserts, as the show itself has done, that the designers of the ENIAC did understand the concept "by about 1943," even though they could not use it in the ENIAC.

I would just counter that if, indeed, Palfreman's opinion in this history is shared by the "vast majority" of experts, we should bear in mind that vast majorities have been wrong before, both in the realm of science and in the realm of the history of science.

One last puzzlement: in his May 29 letter to us, Palfreman offered a different criterion for determining what should or should not be included in this series. Given time restraints, he wrote, it was decided "that the series would focus on contributions that influenced further development in the field"! Yet Babbage had no such influence, as is clear in the TV series itself; nothing came of electronic development in Germany, as Zuse himself regretted in the film; and the British Colossus was kept under wraps for security reasons for decades, as is also made clear in the film. Only the excluded Atanasoff, among the earliest pioneers, had an immediate and enduring influence on the history.

C.

CLOSING ARGUMENT

TWELVE

AS IT HAPPENED

This is a harshly human story. In the mid-1930s, an associate professor of physics and mathematics at Iowa State College, himself just past thirty years—call him *A*—takes on the task of finding a better way to solve the sets of linear algebraic equations that he and his graduate students repeatedly encounter in their research. The need is not only for faster and more reliable tools than are currently available, but for means to solve much larger sets than have been feasible in the hands of people known at this time as "computers." Indeed, the upper limit for a human computer, working at a desk calculator, has been ten equations in ten unknowns, with an attendant danger that a small (human) error may have spoiled the results.

A aspires to a mechanized solution of sets three times that size. He starts with an exhaustive study of the existing devices, hoping to find one that can be adapted to his purposes. He soon formulates a critical distinction between the analog mode of computation, as in the differential analyzer, and the digital mode, as in the IBM punched-card machines. He comes to realize, ultimately, that he will have to invent his own device if he is to have one. It must be digital, he decides, to deliver the accuracy his problems require. And it must have a much greater capacity than the card machines offer, to handle his long equations.

A machine, which *A* now also terms a "computer," begins to take shape in his mind. Among the digital bases, he chooses the binary, partly because it is the simplest, but also because he has begun to think of computing electronically, with vacuum tubes. Up to this point, vacuum tubes have been used primarily in the analog mode, though physicists have adapted them to certain counting tasks. *A*

371

hopes to interconnect them into stable and reliable computing networks: mechanisms that can receive more than one stream of pulses simultaneously and operate on them arithmetically. The beauty of this idea is that the binary (off/on) application of vacuum tubes fits hand-in-glove with the binary (zero/one) manipulation of numbers.

Moving on to architectural considerations, A comes to see memory and arithmetic as the heart of his computer, and to think of them as separate entities that he will cause to interact. His sets of equations have become sets of vectors to be processed sequentially in pairs, the two members of each pair stored in separate parts of the memory, the occupants of one part brought to bear on the occupants of the other as in the Gaussian elimination procedure. Except that A conceives a variant of the Gaussian method that will allow him to replace the standard multiplication and division operations by repeated additions and subtractions, performed in conjunction with automatic sign detection and place-shifting.

By the fall of 1937, A, a man of uncommon intensity and fierce determination, has been caught up in what can only be called an obsession. And he is stuck! He has settled on using a rotating drum memory, but is stumped for the appropriate memory elements. He conceives of tiny pieces of magnetic material arranged in rings on the drum's surface, but these would be prohibitively expensive in terms of vacuum tubes for amplification. He conceives of small capacitors arranged in rings within, but these would leak off their charges in just a few minutes. He has also settled on using vacuum tubes to perform his additions and subtractions, but is having difficulty with the traditional counting/accumulating approach.

In short, possibilities for the components of his computer have come together in his mind, but the machine refuses to materialize! Until, in utter frustration, he takes a long drive into the winter's night to the door of a tavern on the Illinois side of the Mississippi River. As he will testify later in court, the hours on the road have calmed his nerves, and one or two whiskeys may have cleared his thinking.

A has, quite suddenly, two ground-breaking insights. First, he can use the very cheap capacitors as memory elements if he restores their charges periodically from the arithmetic unit, as, say, upon each rotation of the drum. Second, he can bypass the usual counting procedures by computing through logic, letting his arithmetic devices spew out answers in accord with a table of the possible combinations and outcomes.

It is truly remarkable how this basic conception of the "guts" of A's computer leads to an overall design that brings the regenerative capacitor memory and the electronic arithmetic unit into constant interplay, even in such seemingly extraneous procedures as input-output and base conversion. By the fall of 1939, he is ready to test this fundamental construct with a model, and he has found just the graduate student to join his endeavor. By November, A and student B have produced a model that performs successfully on a pair of twenty-five-binary-digit numbers fed in by a hand-operated probe.

By August of 1940, they have built—or caused to be built in the nearby instrument shop—an angle-iron framework, the two main memory drums, all thirty "add-subtract mechanisms," and the corresponding number of "restore-shift mechanisms." Finally, and also by that August, A has set down on paper a detailed description of the full machine as he envisages it, complete with diagrams, tables, and photographs.

It takes A and B, plus a small crew of talented student assistants, until May of 1942 to finish the computer. They have, of course, been testing out the components in the lab and know that they will work. It is nevertheless very exciting to have them all in place, to feed in a trial set of equations, and to watch the smooth interaction of the various systems. It is very satisfying to note that the two main memory drums work fine, both with each other and with the arithmetic unit, and that the novel electronic mechanisms of that unit also work perfectly.

As do a number of other novel features: the highly efficient base-conversion drum, for example, the timing drum located on the main axle with the other three, and the system of "boosting" voltages for a match between the capacitors in the drums and the vacuum tubes in the arithmetic unit. Indeed, everything hums along most impressively for the solution of small sets of linear equations.

But then a vexing problem arises: as they try larger sets, A and B discover a flaw. Fortunately, this flaw is not in the machine's central apparatus, which holds the key to electronic computing. It is in the binary-card input-output system, the intermediate system for punching and reading equations as the solution algorithm progresses. Indeed, A and B find that the recording portion of the system—the charring of spots on the cards to represent "1s"—works as planned, but the reading portion—the detection of these spots—may err, mistaking a charred spot for a blank, or "0."

The failure rate is infrequent in the extreme, as few as one in ten thousand or a hundred thousand bit spots, they estimate. Yet, given the algorithm's highly repetitive nature, that rate is enough to spoil the results for the large sets of equations A has aimed to solve on his machine.

And now, despite strenuous efforts to overcome this problem, and a strong suspicion that it lies in the card material itself, they are forced to give up—at least temporarily. For their country is at war. B leaves for a draft-deferred job with an electrodynamics company in California, A for war research with the Naval Ordnance Laboratory in Washington, D.C. Their computer is left standing in the Physics Building at Iowa State, finished as planned in every detail, but with a crucial flaw. And so it will stand until 1948, when it is dismantled to make way for other pursuits; only one of the large memory drums and a number of vacuum tubes are rescued by a concerned former student of A's, now on the faculty.

Meanwhile, back in the mid- to late-1930s, another scientist a few years younger than *A*—call him *M*—has been trying to harness his own reams of data. *M* is also an associate professor, the sole member of the physics department at Ursinus College, a small liberal arts school near Philadelphia. He wants to prove his theory that sunspots, or flares, affect Earth's weather in patterns that, if discerned, could lead to better forecasts, both long- and short-range.

From 1936 to 1940, *M* and a few student helpers have run their tabular analyses of meteorological data on keyboard-operated desk machines (a calculator and an adding machine). But now he thinks of a much faster way—not as accurate, he explains later in court, but accurate enough for his purpose. He fashions a different desktop machine, this one a dial-operated harmonic analyzer.

M takes great pride in this device. As he writes *A* in early 1941, his little group has, in just seventy hours, saved 280 hours, or about as long as it took to design and build the new machine! And, at trial, he will give what is perhaps his most enthusiastic testimony, both on his weather theory and on his successful utilization of this twelve-ordinate harmonic analyzer; he will also allude to a further plan, never realized, to build a still more suitable twenty-seven-ordinate machine (twenty-seven days being the period of the Sun's rotation). So far as the history is concerned, however, *M* acknowledges that the harmonic analyzer is an analog, not a digital, device, and that it is electrical, not electronic.

Earlier, *M* has built a small machine that is digital, though not electronic, which he offers (unsuccessfully) to the military as a possible pilot model to be developed for relaying secret messages—first scrambling the English, then unscrambling it at its destination. He has also built a tiny neon flashing device that, mounted as it is on a length of glass tubing, seems primarily intended as a toy railroad signal. He will argue in court that this two-bulb apparatus doubles as a rudimentary electronic binary counter. But he has to admit that all it can count is very carefully administered *current interruptions*—moreover, that it *cannot count beyond one* because it has no means of interconnection with other such "counters."

M does come to realize, by November of 1940, the possibility of computing electronically. He writes to two friends of a hope to build, in a year or so, a keyboard machine that will use vacuum-tube relays to figure sums of squares and cross-products with great precision. Expressing his desire to be the first with such a machine, he remarks that of course its secret lies in the physicists' scaling circuits.

This plan is never executed, either, because *M*'s encounters with *A* lead him to aspire to a much more ambitious computer—*and* because he is able to team up with a brilliant young engineer in that undertaking. *M*'s last attempt to design an electronic desk machine is recorded in a set of notes dated September 21, 1941, that include layout drawings. By now, however, it is three months after he has experienced *A*'s computer firsthand, and in these notes he freely addresses his own ideas as ways in which he might adapt *A*'s components: his capacitor memory, for example, and his add-subtract mechanisms.

M and A have first met in December 1940, in Philadelphia after a session of the AAAS in which M has presented a paper on his harmonic analyzer. On that occasion, A tells M of the digital electronic computer he is building in Iowa and invites him to come out and see it. And so, that June of 1941, after considerable correspondence, M does visit A for several days. A (despite his wife's misgivings) welcomes him heartily and, with grad student B's help, explains and demonstrates his machine. He also lets M read his detailed write-up of it, and discusses this with him at length in his home study. He does not, however, allow M to take away one of his two typewritten copies, in those days before photocopying.

M is then off to the University of Pennsylvania's Moore School of Electrical Engineering for a crash summer course sponsored by the U.S. government to train engineers for defense work. He is already somewhat familiar with that school's differential analyzer, a huge mechanical analog machine for solving differential equations. In fact, A has suggested to him the possibility of devising an electronic digital computer to do the work of the analyzer, both faster and more accurately, and has observed that his own machine could be converted to such an end.

M now has the great good fortune to make the acquaintance of E, the lab assistant in the defense training course who is just embarking on a master's degree and who is already recognized as the Moore School's budding electronics expert. M tells E all about A's computer, together with A's belief that it could be adapted to solve differential equations, and they consider how this might be accomplished.

That fall M leaves Ursinus College to sign on as an instructor at the Moore School. He continues his discussions with E, ultimately—in August of 1942—writing a brief proposal for attacking the solution of differential equations electronically. By this time, the school's analyzer is engaged exclusively in computing trajectories for the compilation of firing tables for the army. In addition, the school has established a center for the numerical computation of such trajectories on desk machines. M sees more than ever the pressing need for an electronic digital computer to solve differential equations—an objective that he might even be able to interest the Moore School in pursuing, say, under army contract.

Both he and E have doubts about A's rotating capacitor memory, which seems to them to detract from the high-speed potential of his electronic arithmetic unit. They turn instead to the counting principle of the desk calculator—and to the decimal system instead of the binary. For E is confident that vacuum-tube decimal counters can be developed to function reliably at 100,000 pulses per second. And this is certainly the way to go at this point: without a memory device that can keep pace with electronic adders, counters that encompass both storage and arithmetic will easily outdistance A's arrangement of separate, interacting facilities.

E, at least, is aware of the earlier reports by a Moore School professor on the possibility of devising a differential analyzer (still analog) with electronic components, and also on the possibility of "ganging" or "chaining" a series of electronic adding machines for the purely digital solution of differential equations. However much, or little, E and M draw on the ideas of this Professor T, who is now serving in the navy, their initial conception of an electronic digital differential analyzer does entail just such a series of adding machines in place of the analyzer's series of integrators.

It is E, then, who will design these very sophisticated "adding machines"—accumulators—to constitute the basic calculating units of the Moore School's computer. Secure in government sponsorship, a team of engineers starts work in June 1943 under the direction of E, with M serving an advisory role. When the ENIAC is dedicated in early 1946, it is hailed as "the world's first electronic computer"; its inventors E and M.

This reputation is intensely fostered, not just by E and M but by a succession of corporations that acquire the E-M rights to the ENIAC patent long before its issuance in 1964. Indeed, this reputation has been firmly established and routinely saluted by October of 1973—when, after a lengthy trial, a U.S. District Court judge declares that patent invalid. This judge, L, finds *both* that the ENIAC was preceded by the electronic computer of another inventor, A, *and* that it was derived from A's computer, now known as the ABC, and from further ideas passed to M by A.

To the surprise and consternation of A's small group of supporters, what would seem momentous news from the business world—all data processing companies have been freed from the very real threat of suits over royalties—is largely ignored in the media. Perhaps it is just this, that the status quo has been preserved, that makes Judge L's decision a non-news item; a ruling in the other direction would have been a bombshell, as every aspect of computing technology fell within the confines of the ENIAC patent.

And now, to the further surprise and consternation of the A side, the fanfare for M and E continues with hardly perceptible change. Articles still celebrate these two men as, if not the inventors of the first computer, at least the progenitors of the modern computer and the launchers of the computer age. In public appearances and interviews, E and M simply overlook the patent case and, when on rare occasions the subject is raised, deride the decision and belittle both the judge and A.

Finally, historians of science do little or nothing to right this wrong. Those who had embraced the original E-M version of events continue to do so, and most of those who are just coming on as historians of the new discipline, computer science, take it up. There is a marked lack of research into the facts of this trial, together with a tendency to iterate the entrenched majority opinion. And so, for years, not only magazines and newspapers but those books that reach the widest audience, reference works and survey histories—sometimes called *consensus* histories—fail even to recognize a "controversy," let alone to countenance the trial's outcome.

<<<>>>

In the courtroom, John Mauchly himself never seriously disputed the first of Judge Earl Larson's two major findings, that of the priority of John Atanasoff's invention.[1] The Electronic Numerical Integrator and Computer was not the first "automatic electronic digital computer," as claimed in the suit, Larson ruled; the Atanasoff-Berry Computer was an earlier "automatic electronic digital computer." Mauchly's own correspondence and notes, both before and after his visit to Iowa, made clear that he considered this new "computing machine" to be just such an invention. And, of course, there was no question of its being "prior."

Judge Larson's decision also spoke to attempts, made to this day, to write off the ABC on the argument that because of the failure of its binary-card system it was "not finished," was "never used," and, indeed, was "abandoned." Although he clearly considered the computer finished as he traced its history, Larson also made clear that its state of completion and its actual use were irrelevant to its status as an invention. Under patent law, the deciding issues were whether it was finished enough to convey its novel principles and whether it functioned well enough to reduce those principles to practice.

On the issue of abandonment, the judge went even further, striking down the ENIAC as derived from an abandoned invention. The critical fact here, he wrote, was that the ideas of the ABC were incorporated in the ENIAC, and ideas so acquired, whether or not the original device was abandoned, do not amount to invention.

Whether under examination by the Honeywell lawyers challenging the ENIAC patent or the Sperry Rand lawyers defending it, Mauchly's testimony centered on this second major ground for invalidation: Larson's finding that the "subject matter" of the ENIAC was derived from "one John Vincent Atanasoff." Although Mauchly himself occasionally lapsed into positive discourses on aspects of the ABC, his defense against the charge of derivation consisted in an outright dismissal of that computer, coupled with a gross exaggeration of his own achievements and aspirations prior to any contact with Atanasoff. In short, he took nothing away from his visit to Iowa, he maintained, because there was nothing that he could use in his own grand scheme—nothing, anyway, that he had not already thought of.

He told, for example, of his great disappointment in Atanasoff's machine, once he had seen it, because it was a special-purpose device—or "gadget," as he termed it—whereas he was intent on building a general-purpose computer. But he had written letters expressing excitement over what he had seen; he had written letters expressing his own goal of an electronic desk calculator with an even more "special" purpose than the ABC's; and he could not produce a shred of evidence for any progress toward any part of any electronic computer before he met Atanasoff, or even before he visited him six months later.

In his decision, Judge Larson detailed Mauchly's early accomplishments. He concluded that while "Mauchly had been broadly interested in electrical analog calculating devices," he "had not conceived an automatic electronic digital computer." Rather, he had derived that invention from discussions with both Atanasoff and his student assistant Clifford Berry, from demonstrations of the computer, and from a review of its written description. As to the conflicting testimony of the two witnesses, it was *Atanasoff's* version of what Mauchly learned in Iowa that the judge found "credible."

The judge's implication that he did not find Mauchly credible is supported by several situations in which, as witness, Mauchly had to back down from initial bold assertions. His harmonic analyzer is a case in point. That device, even though it was nonelectronic and nondigital, should have come off as a positive example of Mauchly's ingenuity. Under cross-examination by attorney Henry Halladay, however, he had begun by insisting that it was entirely his own invention—that he had not encountered any electrical harmonic analyzers in the literature. But, as Halladay produced documents to the contrary, Mauchly had to acknowledge his reliance on earlier designs.

An ironic aspect of this and other similar instances is that the papers used to contradict his testimony came from his own files, brought in under subpoena but clearly not studied by him before he took the stand: in this case, a bibliography of works on harmonic analyzers, including electrical versions, and a Mauchly letter referring to such a device. Moreover, Mauchly hardly helped himself by displaying a jaunty attitude on just such occasions, an attitude that would make his defeat the more memorable in any assessment of his performance: in this case, his declaration at the outset that the harmonic analyzer *was* entirely his own creation because "My children weren't old enough to help"!

Another ironic aspect of Mauchly's testimony is that when he was forced to reverse himself he sometimes conceded far more than was being sought by the examining attorney. When, for example, he was being pressed to say that he had read Atanasoff's descriptive manuscript with some degree of "professional care," he suddenly broke away to explain his "attitude" toward computing back in the days of his trip to Iowa. In one rash statement, he managed to contradict all that he had been claiming for his own progress toward an electronic computer. "I was searching for ideas which might be useful to me in computing," he said of this visit to Atanasoff. "I wasn't even thinking about inventing computing machines"!

Atanasoff, on the other hand, breezed through his own explanations, not just of his electronic computer but of other projects he had conducted at Iowa State: for example, a design that he and graduate student Sam Legvold had worked out for an analog device to help aim antiaircraft fire. On those occasions when Sperry Rand attorneys tried to discredit his testimony, on the basis, say, of an old invoice from his files, another document was always found to confirm Atanasoff's recall of the situation.

Larson's ruling on derivation of the ENIAC was broad. Aside from citing several particular patent claims, he did not specify just how that computer's "subject matter" was derived from Atanasoff. This transfer was, in fact, through electronic switching technology. The add-subtract mechanisms of the ABC's arithmetic unit were the first electronic switching circuits of any complexity. Such circuits were used throughout the ENIAC, as in the high-speed multiplier, the divider/square-rooter, the function tables, and even the accumulators.

To be sure, the ENIAC's electronic switches were more complex than Atanasoff's add-subtract mechanisms, but their further complexity was but a compounding of the same basic technology. Indeed, Atanasoff himself compounded the complexity of his add-subtract mechanisms when he formed his array of thirty of these, together with his co-acting restore-shift mechanisms and carry-borrow circuits, to operate in parallel on whole equations—as vectors.

Another way of stating this matter of derivation is to note that Atanasoff invented the first electronic *computing* element, a notable advance over the *counting* elements of the physicists' scaling circuits. Atanasoff himself preferred to put the matter in terms of his invention of *logic circuits for computing*. In his 1984 *Annals* article, he tells of a pretrial visit to his home by Mauchly and Sperry Rand attorney Laurence Dodds, in which Dodds challenged him to say how the ENIAC was derived from his work.[2] He cited the "interaction of logic circuits in the computing elements" of the ENIAC, he writes, and Dodds agreed that yes, there were such circuits in the ENIAC patent.

There is the further compelling fact that Atanasoff proved the *feasibility* of electronic computing; this is surely part of what Judge Larson had in mind as "subject matter" derived from Atanasoff. It is noteworthy that this fact of proven feasibility entered into the army's decision to finance the ENIAC project. Herman Goldstine, the army's liaison officer for the Moore School computing activities, testified in deposition for the ENIAC case that he had asked Mauchly for some such assurance, and that Mauchly had told him about Atanasoff's "electronic scheme for computation."[3]

Finally, a word needs to be said about the judge's reference to "other ideas" taken by Mauchly from Atanasoff—ideas not incorporated in the ABC. Larson notes, for example, that Mauchly and Atanasoff discussed computing devices at length, and that one of the ideas Mauchly acknowledged drawing from Atanasoff was the categorization of such devices as either digital or analog. Perhaps the most important "other idea" that Atanasoff passed along, in correspondence and in person, was the underlying concept for the ENIAC, that of an electronic digital version of the differential analyzer. It was with this idea that Mauchly first approached the young Moore School master's student, Presper Eckert, for the beginning of a partnership of many years' duration.

<<<>>>

But there is more to this tale of *M* and *E* vis-à-vis *A*, one that evolves, in fact, to encompass *M* and *E* vis-à-vis a fourth computer pioneer—call him *vN*. Even as *E* and *M* wrote their proposal for the ENIAC, they had seen how to move beyond the differential analyzer to a general-purpose, programmable machine. And now, even before they finish building the ENIAC, they see a way to overcome, in their next one, what will surely constitute a serious bottleneck in the ENIAC, the manual setup of programs.

The ENIAC's numerical data for a given problem were to be entered by presetting switches on the read-only function tables and by inserting cards in an IBM card-reader, perhaps more than once per problem run. Its program was to be entered entirely in advance, by hand-plugging jumper cables between units and by hand-setting switches on the face of those units—a process that could take days. By early 1944, *E* has seen not only that the numerical data could be entered much more automatically but that, given a large enough memory, both the numerical data and the program could be entered and stored automatically at the outset.

E writes this concept up, suggesting that the large memory take the form of rotating magnetic drums or disks. At this point, he sees the program as *read-only* for the problem run, just as in the ENIAC, but as *erasable and replaceable* between runs—thus eliminating the ENIAC programming bottleneck.

With this idea, *E* has clearly moved into *A*'s bailiwick. He has left the concept of counters and opted for the separation of storage from arithmetic. At the same time, with this magnetic form of memory—also considered by *A*—he has overcome the difficulty he and *M* saw in *A*'s machine: that a rotating capacitor memory would detract from the speed advantage of an electronic arithmetic unit. Moreover, within a few months, *E* envisions an even better memory, this one to utilize the mercury-delay-line tube he had earlier adapted for use in timing radar signals. Again, *E* expects to have a separate arithmetic unit. *And*, he is aware that this delay-line form of store, unlike the magnetic form, will require regeneration—just as *A*'s capacitor store does.

E discusses these concepts with *M*, but critical decisions remain to be made when, in the late summer of 1944, *vN* enters the picture as a Moore School consultant. *VN*'s imagination is immediately captured by the prospect, conveyed to him at his very first meeting, of a second, better electronic computer based on the interaction of a regenerative mercury-delay-line memory and a binary serial adder. Four further meetings in the spring of 1945 explore various aspects of this next machine, to be called the EDVAC: the design of such an adder, for example, and the number base of the computation together with the matter of base conversion.

VN then goes off to write up these discussions. But he produces an entirely unexpected document, one that is much less a summary of ideas already considered and much more an expansion into new ideas for the projected computer. In his report, *vN* accepts *E*'s idea of a delay-line memory, but he suggests the possibility of a cathode-ray-tube memory as an alternative; he offers some adder designs; and he decides that the computer's number base should be binary, because base conversion could be accomplished simply by storing *it* as a program, too.[4]

VN makes a further suggestion that will become a major and defining aspect of the emerging "stored-program" concept for electronic computers. Whereas *E* has conceived of storing a problem's program at the outset and then reading and executing that program as the problem runs, *vN* has realized that the program, like the numerical data, can be both read *from* and read *into*. He sees that this read-write characteristic of either the mercury-delay-line or the cathode-ray-tube store allows the possibility that a program can be changed not just between problem runs but through *self-modification* during the course of a given run.

This *vN* concept signifies an advance from the read-only constant-address program of the ENIAC to a novel read-write variable-address program that can change its own addresses. It will require a special program language, or code. And *vN* actually presents the first such variable-address program language, including the crucial substitution instruction for altering another instruction by changing its address. He also sets forth the architecture for the projected EDVAC—memory, arithmetic unit, and control—together with the detailed logical design of the first two of these.

VN's report, astounding in so many ways, has a profound and far-reaching impact on the course of computer history. For in June 1945 it is distributed by Army Captain *G*, presumably with *vN*'s approval, to a number of people and institutions in both the United States and England. Titled "First Draft of a Report on the EDVAC" and bearing *vN*'s name as author, it is met with immediate interest, particularly in England, where *vN* is already known as a brilliant mathematical physicist who has consulted there on the statistics of mine-sweeping and the mathematics of explosions.

For *E* and *M*, this report is the source of great bitterness, and not without reason: it carries no acknowledgment of the contributions by the Moore School team—not even those of *E*; it goes out as an unclassified document, so that it can be shared and discussed with others; and it is distributed widely enough to constitute publication, so that contributors of concepts revealed in it have only one year to file for patents on those concepts. To make matters worse for *E* and *M*, that one year expires before *any* of the principals learns that the report will very probably be construed as a barring publication. It is, in fact, nearly *two years* later when an Army Ordnance patent attorney breaks this news, at an April 1947 meeting called by the dean of the Moore School.[5]

The other side of this coin, however, is that *M* had been given the entire academic year *prior to* the issuance of the *vN* report to work with the Ordnance lawyers on patent applications. Moreover, as Judge *L* pointed out in his ENIAC trial decision, *M* had failed to provide the Ordnance attorneys with a copy of the *vN* report when it was first distributed, as he had been assigned to do. If those attorneys had seen the report then, they could have let E and M know of its patent-barring potential. Lastly, vN discovers that E and M are claiming his idea of a cathode-ray-tube memory—which in fact he had revealed soon after he joined the Moore School team.

VN, though expressly uninterested in personal monetary gain, has two top concerns. One is that he be credited with his ideas; the other is that new ideas be spread, in order, as the judge puts it, "to advance the state of the art." This latter, however, does not excuse the distribution of the ideas of others, together with one's own, without their permission, particularly as it is done with no indication that essential ideas emanated from those others.

E and M, for their part, are so interested in monetary gain, as well as credit, that they are willing not just to claim but to patent the ideas of others along with their own. After they leave the Moore School in 1946 to go into business, they take out patents on ideas for the EDVAC that originated with A! Indeed, they patent the heart of A's invention: his idea for binary serial adders and both his idea for and his form of regenerative memory. Moreover, although publication of the vN report seems to preclude their patenting the entire EDVAC, E and M also apply for patents on their own EDVAC-type computers, the BINAC and the UNIVAC. And here, too, as in the ENIAC, they draw on A's fundamental invention of complex electronic switching for use throughout these machines.

In a curious twist at the ENIAC trial, plaintiff H persuades Judge L to rule on the enforceability of all of these non-ENIAC patents. They are presented as part of a package of twenty-five patents and patent applications, all of which had been filed between 1947 and 1955. Two, the BINAC and the UNIVAC systems, are still pending. H's argument for including them in the ENIAC trial is that these twenty-five items entail the same infirmities raised against the ENIAC patent. In the end, on a variety of grounds including prior publication of the vN report and derivation from A, the judge finds the whole package unenforceable.

A, then, although he reaps no compensation and very little public recognition for his contributions to the computer revolution, does have the satisfaction of seeing all of the E and M claims on his work denied in a federal court. He walks away with affirmation of his computer as the world's first electronic computer, and with affirmation of features of it that remain central to all computer design. Those on the side of the late vN have to take their satisfaction, not from any explicit affirmation of his contribution to the stored-program computer, but from the denial of patents in which E and M were claiming that invention as theirs alone.

In the aftermath of the Moore School publication of vN's EDVAC report, two types of electronic stored-program computers emerge to be copied in a number of institutions. Each is based on a separate arithmetic unit working in conjunction with a large regenerative memory: the Moore School's EDVAC-type, with the mercury-delay-line store first suggested by E, and the Institute for Advanced Study's IAS-type, with the cathode-ray-tube store first suggested by vN.

As with Judge L's invalidation of the ENIAC patent, his finding the other E-M patents unenforceable has little public impact in either the scholarly literature or the broader media. Acclaim continues to fall on E and M. A is usually denied or ignored. And the stored-program concept, widely seen as a single phenomenon rather than a two-stage process involving first E and then vN, is usually claimed in its entirety for one or the other by their respective adherents.

Just as we need to consider the credibility of Mauchly and Atanasoff as to derivation of the Electronic Numerical Integrator and Computer, so we need also to consider their credibility as to derivation of the ensuing Electronic Discrete Variable Computer. Here the credibility of Eckert comes in, as well, partly with respect to his ENIAC trial testimony, but more so with respect to his public declarations in the years that followed. And the issue here extends beyond derivation from Atanasoff to derivation from von Neumann.

There is no question that Atanasoff invented the first electronic binary serial adders, and that they worked. He described his add-subtract mechanisms, as he called them, in his 1940 manuscript. This account included a circuit diagram on which the course of the three incoming streams of bits—two from the memory drums, one from the auxiliary carry-borrow drum—could be traced in conjunction with a truth table for binary additions and subtractions and a layout drawing of transactions between the arithmetic unit and the memory.

In the ENIAC patent trial, Atanasoff testified to his adder as one of two major breakthroughs he had made in his evening at a tavern in the winter of 1937–38. He explained how this device computed by logic rather than by enumeration, and he demonstrated it with a small model of his computer's central apparatus. He said that in the course of building the computer itself, he had demonstrated his add-subtract mechanisms to select visitors, but usually without disclosing the design details. One visitor to whom he did make a full disclosure, he said, was John Mauchly, during his 1941 visit.

In the years after the ENIAC trial, Atanasoff told of his add-subtract mechanisms in several interviews, as well as in his own long article in the July 1984 issue of the *Annals of the History of Computing*. All of his accounts of this invention were completely consistent.

Mauchly, as witness, was far from consistent in recalling his experience of Atanasoff's adders. He first testified, in deposition for an earlier lawsuit over the Regenerative Memory patent, that he did not see them in action in Iowa and that he learned only what they were supposed to do, not how or even whether they worked.[6] Indeed, he emphasized to Control Data Corporation attorney Allen Kirkpatrick that he "saw no tests performed" on any aspect of Atanasoff's machine. At the ENIAC trial four years later, however, under probing by Honeywell attorney Halladay, he admitted that he had seen the adders demonstrated and was, in fact, "perfectly convinced" that they worked as intended.

Mauchly had also, in the earlier case, told Kirkpatrick that "of course" he told Eckert about Atanasoff's computer and discussed aspects of it with him. Nevertheless, he and Eckert patented various versions of binary serial adders without reference to Atanasoff's prior invention. Presumably, these devices also figured in their applications for patents on the BINAC and UNIVAC systems.

Mauchly did then testify at the ENIAC trial that he could not recall telling Eckert about Atanasoff's computer, even though it would have been "natural" for him to do so. But now it was Eckert who recalled some such discussion. While he could not be sure that he had learned of any vacuum-tube devices, it is highly probable that if Mauchly told electronics expert Eckert anything at all about the ABC, he would have told him about its absolutely critical electronic adders.

Eckert made an outright claim for the invention of binary serial adders in early 1947 at the Moore School meeting called to sort out the respective contributions of Eckert and Mauchly, on the one hand, and von Neumann, on the other, to the EDVAC. Eckert cited these adders as having been discussed before von Neumann arrived on the scene. And, although von Neumann had included adder designs in his First Draft Report, he indicated that he would not challenge such claims by Eckert and Mauchly. This meeting, then, with no allusion to Atanasoff's prior work, was taken as a green light for them to go ahead with patent applications.

Eckert did, in his interview for the 1986 special issue of *Computerworld*, refer to Atanasoff's adders in response to a question by editor George Harrar.[7] He said that Atanasoff had "instrumented" an adder that he claimed worked. "But," he added, "nobody else knew whether it worked or not. Some of the drawings we examined wouldn't have worked."

This statement would seem to be a dismissal of Atanasoff's circuit drawing of his add-subtract mechanism, but Eckert's timing is uncertain because he could not have seen that drawing before the ENIAC trial. Moreover, here he is, *after the trial*, overlooking the testimony of several witnesses, including Mauchly himself, to the adder's successful operation!

There is also no question that Atanasoff invented the first regenerative memory, and that it, too, worked. He described his capacitor store and its "jogging" operation in his 1940 manuscript; he demonstrated it to visitors; he testified to it at trial as his other major breakthrough in the Illinois tavern; he used a small model to demonstrate it to the court; and he later claimed it in his 1984 *Annals* article and in interviews.[8] Again, he remained completely consistent in all of these accounts.

And, again, both Mauchly and Eckert gave conflicting stories. Neither ever denied that the ABC had an electronically regenerated memory. Mauchly surprised Control Data's Kirkpatrick by readily admitting this in the patent suit over that very invention. As with Atanasoff's add-subtract mechanisms, however, Mauchly stressed to Kirkpatrick that he had not seen the regenerative circuits in action or learned how or whether they worked. But then, at the ENIAC trial, he told of seeing them, with at least the implication that they worked.

In any case, Mauchly told Eckert enough about those circuits to prompt him to describe and praise Atanasoff's "capacitor memory" in a 1953 article and to cite its "regenerative" aspect in particular.[9] Kirkpatrick had also been surprised to find this article, with its attribution of "probably the first" regenerative memory to Atanasoff "earlier than 1942." *And* with its timing: for, earlier that same year, Eckert and Mauchly had received their Regenerative Memory patent that included Atanasoff's rotating electrostatic version of such a memory claimed as their own!

In 1987 Eckert answered Clark Mollenhoff's inquiry about this article by saying that he had conceived the regenerative memory, *independently*, in 1943; Mauchly, he explained, had not told him of that feature of the ABC until late 1943.[10] But why, then, when faced with this same inquiry at the ENIAC trial, by both Halladay and Sperry Rand attorney Thomas Ferrell, did Eckert not assert this claim for independent invention to them? The fact is that, at trial, he acknowledged learning of the rotating capacitor memory in his earliest discussions with Mauchly, in 1941 or 1942. And how, since he clearly knew all about it when he wrote his article, could he justify patenting it anyway, and without the required reference to Atanasoff's priority?

Mauchly, in his deposition for the earlier suit, refused to concede that he had first learned of memory regeneration from Atanasoff. He may have conceived of it himself before his Iowa visit, he suggested, although he had no recollection of doing so. He had never thought much about the question, he said, of when or how he had first learned of memory regeneration.

A strange comment, indeed, for a holder of its patent! But when Kirkpatrick confronted him with Eckert's article ascribing the first such instance to Atanasoff, Mauchly sought to clarify his position: priority of the "mere idea of regeneration of storage" was irrelevant to the particular "means" of achieving it—in this case, the EDVAC's mercury-delay-line memory. Mauchly's difficulty here is that Eckert had not cited Atanasoff for the *idea* but for his *means* of implementing it. Moreover, and quite unaccountably, Mauchly and Eckert had not only patented Atanasoff's form of memory regeneration, along with their own; they had also patented the general idea—clearly Atanasoff's idea—which Mauchly was now calling irrelevant!

Mauchly, not surprisingly, was even less prepared for this deposition than he would be later for testimony in the ENIAC trial. Kirkpatrick had caught him off guard at the very start by revealing, piece by piece, his old correspondence with Atanasoff—letters supplied by Atanasoff, copies of which it turned out Mauchly also had in his own files. He had forgotten Eckert's article, as well, and he had forgotten, and failed to review, the substance of the patent that was the object of this inquiry and that he himself had taken out as joint inventor.

An interesting sidelight to this issue of the *idea* for an invention is that Eckert had raised it at Dean Harold Pender's exploratory meeting. He had asked whether the fact that von Neumann had mentioned the principle of memory regeneration in his Draft Report might preclude the claiming of it in a patent. Ordnance attorney Joseph Church had responded that, yes, that mention would "prevent you from getting any dominant claim." Yet Eckert and Mauchly did, later that year, apply for a patent including that dominant claim—and did receive such a patent, only to lose it at the ENIAC trial. Judge Larson, in fact, cited the Draft Report's disclosure, as well as Atanasoff's priority, in finding the Regenerative Memory patent unenforceable.

The matter of derivation of the EDVAC—and so the BINAC and the UNIVAC—from von Neumann concerns his ideas for program self-modification, program language, and computer architecture. Here the quarrel has been not about patent claims but about credit. And, again, Eckert and Mauchly have been inconsistent in their versions of events, moving in general from conceding at least some of von Neumann's contributions to either fogging the issues or claiming those contributions for themselves.

Originally, in their September 1945 report for the EDVAC project, they credited von Neumann with the concept of modifying a program during a problem run: "Von Neumann has specified that some order symbols be capable of modification by deleting a given part of the order and inserting something else in its place."[11] Later, however, Mauchly spelled out the idea as his own in lectures, both in the Moore School's 1946 summer course and in a 1947 Harvard symposium.[12] And Eckert, in a number of settings, either omitted that portion of the broader stored-program concept or claimed it as his own.

That Eckert-Mauchly progress report also acknowledged von Neumann's contribution of a program language—the first for a stored-program computer. Von Neumann, they said, "has proposed certain instruction codes, and has tested those proposed systems by writing out the coded instructions for specific problems." They said that their own "plan for orders" in this report was "essentially that which von Neumann has proposed." Yet they did not thereafter, as they wrote program codes taking account of program modification requirements, acknowledge this prior work by von Neumann.

As to von Neumann's presentation of a computer architecture in his June 1945 report, Eckert and Mauchly presented the same fundamentals in their September report, but in this case with no attribution to von Neumann. Von Neumann, of course, became famous for that architecture as it was fully developed in the Burks, Goldstine, von Neumann publication, *Preliminary Discussion of the Logical Design of an Electronic Computing Instrument*.[13] Actually, all three of the von Neumann ideas under question here were developed in detail in that June 1946 document.

It is unfortunate that the passages one sees quoted from the Eckert-Mauchly report do not include its clear recognition of von Neumann, either for his idea of a substitution instruction or for his provision of a code implementing such an instruction. Instead, one sees its sweeping—and error-ridden—introductory statement of von Neumann's role: that in his own EDVAC report he "summarized" the spring 1945 Moore School discussions, in the process replacing "the physical structures and devices proposed by Eckert and Mauchly" with "idealized elements."

The truth is that von Neumann originated all of the logical representations of circuits in his Draft Report, almost none of which had been designed yet by anyone anywhere. Moreover, his doing so set a pattern for future circuit design: do the logic first, the electronics second.

The negative "message" of the above passage, vis-à-vis von Neumann, is, of course, one that was often delivered by Eckert and Mauchly in later years, so that its repetition by others is understandable. Eckert, for example, in his 1976 lecture at the Los Alamos conference on the history of computing, cites von Neumann's "translating from electronic circuit terms into neural notation" as an instance of "von Neumann's way of taking credit for the work of others."[14]

It also happens that this September 1945 Eckert-Mauchly report on the EDVAC, prepared for Army Ordnance, was not widely distributed, so that its readership has been limited. The parties who quote or otherwise repeat that negative content may never have seen the full document, and so may be unaware of its strongly positive passages on von Neumann's contribution. (Arthur Burks acquired his copy only at the time of the ENIAC trial, when he was serving as a consultant.)

It should be noted, too, that the bitter contention over credit for the stored-program concept stems in part from the fact that, as an entity, it had no name for years after its particular aspects were understood and utilized. Major attention was focused on hardware advances, not on programming, certainly not on programming theory. When the theorists did come in, much later, it was difficult to sort out the sources of the ideas.

Mention should be made, in passing, of the fact that von Neumann did, in the April 1947 Moore School meeting, freely acknowledge Eckert's invention of the mercury-delay-line memory; and he did relinquish any rights he might have had to binary adders. He explained that he had not written his report on the EDVAC "to stake out claims," and that he now found it "very difficult" that it was a barring publication. Eckert and Mauchly, on the other hand, avoided crediting von Neumann with any of the EDVAC concepts set forth in that report. (It is very fortunate that minutes were taken at this meeting of the contending parties, and that the *Annals* chose to publish them in its April 1985 issue.)

Finally, on the broader matter of derivation from von Neumann, there is the Eckert-Mauchly claim to his idea of a cathode-ray-tube memory. Von Neumann, of course, claimed no more than the *idea*, but he was upset when he learned that Eckert and Mauchly were trying to develop that memory and patent it as of their own conception.

This was particularly nettling because von Neumann had approached RCA at least by early September of 1944 to propose that RCA develop a cathode-ray-tube computer store. A letter written to Aberdeen's Col. Paul Gillon by Moore School Prof. Grist Brainerd on September 13, 1944, attests to that fact. Goldstine, in his 1972 book, quotes Brainerd's remarks on the need for a large "storage capacity" in the machine that was to follow the ENIAC:

> At the present time we know of two principles which might be used as a basis. One is the possible use of iconoscope tubes, concerning which Dr. von Neumann has talked to Dr. [Vladimir] Zworkin of the R.C.A. Research Laboratories, and another of which is the use of storage in a delay line, with which we have some experience.[15]

There is no such evidence that Eckert had thought of using iconoscope tubes for computer memories before von Neumann did—or, more to the point, before von Neumann suggested it to the Moore School group. Indeed, it would seem that had he done so Brainerd would have been claiming that principle, as well as delay lines, for the school.

Von Neumann followed up on his RCA contact, arranging by the end of 1945 for Jan Rajchman to develop and produce a computer memory based on the idea he had formulated in his EDVAC report, for use in the IAS Computer. The June 1946 *Preliminary Discussion* was then written on the assumption that such a store would be available. In the end, however, with one exception, all IAS-type computers used the version of cathode-ray-tube storage invented by Frederic C. Williams, at Manchester University, instead of Rajchman's Selectron tube.

This choice was made at the Institute for Advanced Study because the Selectron was so late, running into many difficulties and not working successfully until after the Williams tube became available. Others followed suit because the Williams version used a standard cathode ray tube, with a simple wire grid on the front, whereas the Selectron was a specially created tube with a highly complicated internal grid structure. Williams's brilliant inventive contribution was his very complex vacuum-tube circuitry to control the writing of bits (the easy part) and the reading of bits (the hard part). Tom Kilburn is usually cited for his assistance in perfecting this invention and for his major role in proving its efficacy in the Manchester Baby Mark I.

Now Eckert, having failed in his own attempt to overcome the inherent design obstacles, still claimed, at the 1947 Moore School meeting, that he and Mauchly had conceived the cathode-ray-tube memory before von Neumann appeared as a consultant. It was another von Neumann idea that had been "obvious" to them. Then, as late as 1976, in his lecture for the Los Alamos conference,

Eckert went so far as to imply that *Williams had usurped* the invention itself from him. There he said:

> I worked on a storage-tube device at the University of Pennsylvania modeled on the ideas of the iconoscope. I showed this work to F. C. Williams, who came over from England when the Moore School Lectures on Computer Design were given in 1946. Williams went back to Manchester and applied for patents on iconoscopic ideas, first in England and then in the U.S.

Mauchly, who had delivered Eckert's Los Alamos lecture in his absence, fielded a question about this Eckert-to-Williams transfer. After providing some background on the 1946 lecture series, he said that Williams and Maurice Wilkes had attended from England [as so-called students], that Howard Aiken had been one of the speakers, but that it had not been possible to get von Neumann. He then said:

> On iconoscopes for storage, Eckert had many ideas, and talked to the attendees about such possibilities. F. C. Williams arrived after the series began, but he and Eckert had private conversations on how CRTs might be used.

The fact is that, whatever ideas Eckert conveyed to Williams, it was Williams who rendered them patentable. Eckert should not have said that "Williams went back to Manchester and applied for patents on iconoscopic ideas," but rather that "Williams went back to Manchester and invented a successful cathode-ray-tube store and applied for patents on it." He could also have added that the idea itself had come from von Neumann!

(Actually, it was not Manchester that Williams "went back to" in 1946 but Malvern, where he had done radar research during the war. He did go back to Manchester University, where he had taught before the war, in January 1947, as chair of electrotechnics.)

Michael Williams, coeditor of that 1946 lecture series (as published in 1985), supports this Eckert claim but without citing Eckert's assertion of it at Los Alamos. In his book (also of 1985), historian Williams finds it "entirely possible" that computer pioneer Williams "got some of his early ideas" for a cathode-ray-tube store from that lecture series, because, he writes, the topic "was mentioned by Eckert in one of the Moore School lectures."[16] He also states there that F. C. Williams *did not attend those lectures*, but he believes that others could have reported to him.

Michael Williams is correct in believing that ideas mentioned in that summer course found their way back to England, and very probably to F. C. Williams among others. It is also the case that a number of other lecturers besides Eckert mentioned the idea of a cathode-ray-tube memory. All did also remark on its challenges, and a variety of approaches were suggested. Eckert himself, in his lectures, commended RCA's Selectron, to which Rajchman devoted his entire lecture, for its potential. Even more significantly, he claimed at that time neither to have originated the basic idea nor to have surmounted its difficulties.

Michael Williams is also correct in saying that F. C. Williams did not attend that July/August course. His name does not appear on the by-invitation-only list of lecturers and students. It seems, rather, that what Eckert and Mauchly were recalling in Los Alamos was Williams's visit to the Moore School that June, at which time Eckert could have discussed the cathode-ray-tube memory with him. The issue in the Los Alamos story is not whether such a discussion occurred but the content of that discussion.

Britisher Mary Croarken, writing in the October 1993 *Annals*, notes Williams's stop at the Moore School prior to the lecture series. In her article, "The Beginnings of the Manchester Computer Phenomenon: People and Influences," she explains that Williams, in his capacity as an editor and contributor to a series of books on electrical engineering, visited MIT's Radiation Laboratory in both November 1945 and June 1946.[17] She says further that he "learned of work being done at both the Radiation Laboratory and the Moore School (which he visited June 21 and 22, 1946) on using cathode-ray tubes as storage devices." She then adds:

> On his return from the US in July 1946, Williams began to study the problem. By October 1946 Williams was able to demonstrate that a single cathode-ray tube could regeneratively store a single binary digit. T. Kilburn . . . began to work with Williams.

After that, Croarken says, it was M. H. A. Newman who, having learned of Williams's success, helped to lure him to Manchester, where he (and Kilburn) continued to develop his storage system. Newman himself, according to S. H. Lavington, had learned of von Neumann's plan for a computer based on the Selectron and was waiting for that tube to be developed when he learned of the Williams tube. Lavington writes in his 1980 book, *Early British Computers*:

> In October 1945 [Professor Max] Newman moved to Manchester University, where he wished to set up a "calculating machine laboratory." His plan was to construct a stored-program computer similar to one being proposed by John von Neumann of Princeton University, using a special storage device called the Selectron tube.[18]

He goes on to cite von Neumann's First Draft Report, RCA's work on the Selectron, and the unexpected prior development of the Williams tube.

Lavington also states that it was Douglas Hartree, himself at Manchester University at the time, who served as the main conduit between the United States and England. Hartree is clearly the link from von Neumann's storage idea to Newman's plan to use it. Among the first to put problems on the ENIAC in 1946,

Hartree had visited the Moore School in 1945 and had received a copy of the von Neumann report. Croarken tells of Newman's own extended visit to the Institute for Advanced Study, from October 24 to December 27, 1946, for discussions with von Neumann.

We cannot be certain how F. C. Williams first learned of the *idea* of a cathode-ray-tube computer memory, whether from a colleague before his June 1946 visit to the Moore School or from Eckert during that visit—or even, as Michael Williams suggests, from colleagues who attended the Moore School lecture series later that summer. The earlier transfer would seem more likely: from Hartree to Newman to Williams, with Newman not anticipating that Williams would pursue a solution, let alone find one so quickly. In any case, the original source was von Neumann, not Eckert. And Eckert had not himself succeeded in developing a patentable entity that he could reveal to Williams.

While Michael Williams overlooks von Neumann's proposal of a cathode-ray-tube store in his First Draft Report, he does correctly state that, whatever the source of "the initial idea," it is F. C. Williams who "deserves the credit for making it a working reality." Eckert and Mauchly, on the other hand, while probably right in recalling that Eckert discussed such a store with F. C. Williams, are certainly wrong to imply that Eckert taught him how to make it work.

Incidentally, contrary to Mauchly's comment, von Neumann *was* a lecturer at the Moore School lecture series of 1946.

I will close this chapter by returning to John V. Atanasoff, inventor of the first electronic computer, in order to pull together all the historic "firsts" encompassed by his machine. These are:

- Complex electronic switching
- Electronic digital computation
- Electronic computation in the binary mode
- Decimal-to-binary and binary-to-decimal base conversion
- Separation of memory and arithmetic in an electronic computer
- Rotating drum memory; actually, two drums interacting with each other and the arithmetic unit
- Capacitor memory elements, representing one linear equation per drum
- Periodic automatic memory regeneration
- Serial binary adders interacting with the rotating memory
- Thirty such adders operating in parallel to achieve vector processing
- Computation on logical rather than counting principles
- A novel variation of the Gaussian algorithm for solving simultaneous linear equations through repeated additions and subtractions

- Sign-detection and shifting mechanisms for a non-restoring arithmetic procedure
- Automatic sequencing and coordination of operations through a central "clock"
- Use of replaceable modular units

I want to note here that while I have shown that many of these features of the ABC were adopted for the ENIAC, for the EDVAC, and for later computers to the present day, I do not claim that *all* of them entered this causal chain. Some aspects were reinvented independently by later designers faced with similar situations. I also freely acknowledge that later applications of the concepts originated by Atanasoff for his computer took increasingly superior form.

I do find it phenomenal that this one pioneer incorporated so many modern features in his computer nearly sixty years ago. I find it phenomenal, as well, that Atanasoff accomplished so much in so little time. In the space of six or seven years, while teaching full-time at Iowa State—and conducting other research projects—he made a thorough investigation of the current technology, conceived the basic principles of an electronic digital computer, built an operating model that reduced those principles to practice, wrote up a detailed plan of the entire machine, completely built every aspect of it, and, again, operated it in such a way as to reduce to practice its basic computing principles.

And I find it phenomenal that he has received so little recognition for his stunning achievement.

THIRTEEN

WRAP-UP

A nd yet we have seen significant progress in righting a great wrong: *righting* through *writing*, primarily. Foremost in this regard, of course, is Judge Earl R. Larson, with his 1973 opinion in the ENIAC patent case.[1] As a legal document, Judge Larson's decision is remarkably straightforward and free of jargon. Its organization is exemplary: the researcher has only to keep in mind that it builds—that each section, while addressing one specific subject, assumes all preceding sections. Indeed, each section is itself a series of sub- and sub-sub-sections, each of which also assumes its predecessors as it carries the argument forward.

Unfortunately, too many critics of Judge Larson's decision have not recognized this cumulative aspect; dipping in here and there, they have come up with what they perceive as contradictions. The most frequently cited "contradiction" has been Larson's ruling, in Finding 4, that Mauchly and Eckert were the "inventors" of the ENIAC, despite his earlier ruling, in Finding 3, that they "derived" the ENIAC from Atanasoff.

Larson's detractors have overlooked both the context of his finding on each of those two issues, derivation and invention, and their compatibility in that context—a compatibility the judge himself elucidated. He was led by his examination of the interactions of Mauchly and Atanasoff to find the ENIAC derived from Atanasoff. But he found Mauchly and Eckert sole inventors of the ENIAC, *subsequently*, in the context of possible *co*invention by members of the "ENIAC design team" at the Moore School. In short, Judge Larson left the ENIAC patent in the names of J. Presper Eckert and John W. Mauchly, so far as the ENIAC's other designers were concerned; but he found that patent invalid because they had derived their invention from John V. Atanasoff.

And so there is no contradiction. I find, instead, a degree of arrogance on the part of the critics of this ultrarational judge, in their implication that as he wrote one section of his decision he had somehow forgotten what he had written in the previous section—especially since he was at pains to explain that the earlier ruling still held, and exactly why it still held.

A second major writing that has helped to set the record straight is the long article, published in the July 1984 issue of the *Annals of the History of Computing*, in which Atanasoff gives his own version of this history.[2] A foreword by Gordon Bell, cofounder (with his wife Gwen) of the Computer Museum, commends this work as "a primary source" on "how science and technology develop, in general, and how the computer was invented, specifically." Bell notes key decisions in the industry that date back to Atanasoff and his computer. He concludes that this article, as it reveals "how Atanasoff himself . . . approaches ideas and problems," provides "an inside view of a creative and brilliant person."

Although focused primarily on his invention of the electronic computer and on the two patent trials in which it figured, Atanasoff's article embraces much more. He tells of his research activities at the Naval Ordnance Laboratory: his invention, during the war, of "pressure sweeps for mines," for which he received the navy's Distinguished Service Award, its highest award to civilians; and his assignments, after the war, to do the acoustical analyses of bomb explosions on Bikini Atoll (1946) and on the island of Helgoland (1947). He tells of his business pursuits after he left the government in 1952.

Atanasoff describes stirringly the visit he and Alice made in 1970 to his father's native Bulgaria, where they were feted as guests of the Bulgarian Academy of Science and given a tour of the country, including his father's village; and where he was awarded Parliament's highest order for scientific achievement, named for the two ninth-century priests, Cyril and Methodius, who invented the Cyrillic alphabet—still the pride of "even communist Bulgaria," Atanasoff notes wryly.

He explains "the patent situation" for the ABC. He describes Mauchly's visits to his division of NOL, as well as to his laboratory in Iowa. And he tells of his difficulties as director of a postwar computer project at NOL, and of its abrupt cancellation.

Atanasoff does, in this article, explain and describe the ABC in considerable detail, together with his analysis of the existing analog and digital devices that convinced him he would have to invent his own computer. He recalls his state of mind as he pondered the challenges and made the critical decisions:

> As I look back at my work in those days, I feel the awe with which I regarded the whole subject of electronic digital computers. I knew of no one who had essayed such a project, and my prospects filled me with foreboding as well as joy.

He also describes the 1939 model and remarks on the surprise of visitors at the amount of "structure" required to obtain his additions and subtractions of binary numbers.

Atanasoff recognizes the contribution of graduate assistant Berry to this venture: "I feel that the choice of Clifford E. Berry was one of the best things that could have happened to the project." He commends Berry for bringing to the task "the requisite mechanical and electronic skills," but also the rarer "vision and inventive skills" that became apparent over time. Atanasoff makes clear that he himself had conceived the makeup of the entire computer in considerable detail before he went looking for someone to help him build it. But Berry *was* inventive in working out specifics, as in developing resistor networks and in developing the binary input-output system; it is for these contributions that Atanasoff wished to acknowledge him.

One of the most engaging tracts in Atanasoff's *Annals* article is his account of a phone call he received from Mauchly in November of 1967, setting up his visit to Atanasoff the following month, along with Sperry Rand attorney Laurence Dodds. The conversation is reproduced from notes made immediately afterward by both Atanasoff and Alice, who was on the extension.

Mauchly starts out by saying that he has been hearing Atanasoff's name a lot lately: at the (August 1967) ACM meeting, he says, and before that from R. K. Richards for his (1966) book. More to the point of this phone call, though, was Mauchly's recent (October) deposition by Control Data's Allen Kirkpatrick for the suit brought by Sperry Rand over the Eckert-Mauchly Regenerative Memory patent.[3] Atanasoff notes that Mauchly said *Kil*patrick throughout. Knowing Mauchly's penchant for plays on words, one has to wonder about this, as he describes his rather harrowing experience at the hands of Kirkpatrick!

Mauchly is not sure Atanasoff will like Dodds when they visit, even though Dodds seems to be a very nice man. "Kilpatrick," he says, seemed so too, at least at first. But "later he put on the thumbscrews, and then he tightened them," Atanasoff quotes. As he recounts his deposition, Mauchly calls the situation "very cloak and dagger." He was quite unprepared, he says, for all the old Mauchly-Atanasoff correspondence "Kilpatrick" showed him.

When Atanasoff expresses an interest in reading the transcript, Mauchly replies, "Maybe you should if you have time to waste." But then he adds, "Maybe you will be mad at me when you see what I said." "—Several things," he says to Atanasoff's query; "perhaps the worst was that when you got into administrative work you lost interest in computers."

Atanasoff seems to have been reassuring on this score and throughout, except for his warning that how the meeting with Dodds would go depended on "what he says and what he wants to know." And, of course, that meeting did not go well for the Sperry Rand side, as Atanasoff seems to have surprised both of them with a staunchness that was new to Mauchly. As for his deposition to Control Data's "Kilpatrick," Mauchly ended his phone call that November day by

saying—aggrievedly, Atanasoff reports—that "he practically accused me of pla-
giarizing everything I've done."

We should also cite Atanasoff for his original paper of 1940, a complete and
detailed presentation of his computer even as its construction was just getting under way.[4] It had a twofold purpose: it was a proposal for securing funding, and it
was a description meant for patent application. The style of this work reminds me
of Judge Larson's in his ENIAC decision: it has the same tightness, the same nut-
shell treatment of complicated material—only more so! And it requires the same
scrutiny to see how everything fits—only more so! In the end, as Gordon Bell has
noted with regard to Atanasoff's *Annals* article, one is rewarded with the firsthand experience of a most remarkable creative process—not to mention a certain
elation in unlocking its riddles.

There is one item in this work that has been neglected but that helps to clear
up a common confusion about what Atanasoff had in mind for this machine, so
often termed a prototype or, even derisively, *only* a prototype. At the very outset,
after indicating "the range of problems in which the solution of systems of linear
algebraic equations constitutes an essential part of the mathematical difficulty,"
he writes:

> The solution of general systems of linear equations with a number of unknowns
> greater than ten is not often attempted. But this is precisely what is needed to
> make approximate methods more effective in the solution of practical problems.
>
> The machine described in this paper has been designed to fill this need. It
> is the hope of the writer that eventually some sort of computational service can
> be provided to solve systems of equations accurately and at low cost for tech-
> nical and research purposes.

This is the first proposal ever made for an electronic computational center.
And it does make clear that this machine, which Atanasoff goes on to call a *computer*, was meant to be a fully realized operating device. Atanasoff reserved the
term *prototype* for the model created in the fall of 1939, both in the courtroom,
where he gave some forty pages of testimony on it, and in his 1984 article.

The 1940 paper was not published until 1973, when Brian Randell included
it in his collection. Atanasoff has been faulted for not having published it closer
to the time he wrote it. It is hard to say just when he might have done so, however, given that he first hoped to patent the computer and then came to believe his
machine had been upstaged by the ENIAC. In any case, for the sake of the history—and Atanasoff's place in it—it is fortunate that he did write it in all its detail, *and* that he preserved it.

A dozen or so scholars and professional writers with no personal involvement whatever in this dispute have proven helpful to the Atanasoff side. Of these,
it seems appropriate to call special attention to W. David Gardner for his three
Datamation articles.[5] In the first two, which appeared within months of Judge

Larson's 1973 decision, Gardner provides one of the best analyses of the ENIAC patent case that I have seen. He does so not only in terms of the ABC and the ENIAC's derivation from it, but also in terms of the antitrust issue, which was actually the issue that enabled plaintiff Honeywell to collect, through the discovery process, so many crucial documents from the Sperry Rand side.

Gardner's third *Datamation* article appeared in 1982. There he offers both a fuller and a more intimate account of Atanasoff's struggle and his achievement. Its theme is that here was an original—even "downright bullheaded"—*thinker*. Gardner has, by this time, come to admire his subject. Yet he manages to evoke the particular qualities that induced Atanasoff to "think" so far ahead of his time: his "unique blend of mathematician and theoretical physicist on his abstract side and laboratory and machine shop handyman on his practical side."

I want also, in passing, merely to make mention of the three treatments of Atanasoff that appeared in 1988: the Clark Mollenhoff book, the Alice and Arthur Burks book, and the Allan Mackintosh article in *Scientific American*.[6] The last of these had an immediate and far-reaching influence; the two books have enjoyed a steady, if slower, impact and, I believe, will endure as source materials.

Finally, we should make special note of the contribution that R. K. Richards made in his 1966 book, his third on electronic digital computing devices.[7] Richards declares: "The ancestry of all electronic digital systems appears to be traceable to a computer which will here be called the Atanasoff-Berry Computer." He further suggests the possible linkage of the ABC to the ENIAC via Mauchly.

It was this book that first alerted the Honeywell and Control Data attorneys to Atanasoff's role in the stories they were investigating. We cannot be sure that they would not have found Atanasoff without Richards's book, because others had—actually through Berry—many years earlier. But Richards certainly opened up the case for them. And he brought with him at least two vital documents, letters elicited from Berry only months before his suicide (in October 1963). The first of these letters described the ABC briefly and told of Mauchly's visit to Ames; the second was a much more detailed account of the computer.

In this regard, we should also salute Berry's widow, Jean, for her 1986 *Annals* article on her husband's career.[8] She quotes his second letter to Richards in full (the first appeared in Atanasoff's article). She also reproduces a 1984 letter she elicited from Robert L. Mather, who, as a fifty-cent-an-hour undergraduate, had worked with Berry on the computer. Mather not only describes the ABC but sets the milieu of the 1930s, noting especially the lack of financial support as compared to today. He laments the serious underfunding of the computer project, which he says forced "too many cost-cutting decisions" in the production stage and then failed to see the invention "through the debugging stage and into useful application."

Mather tells of moving up from "sorting screws and nuts" to "cinching up those waxed-string lacings on the wire bundles" to creating "that chassis with 30 thyratrons" for punching and reading the equations on the binary cards. Engineers on the recent replication project at Iowa State University found Mather a great help in supplying details of the computer. All the wires in those huge bundles were *black*, one of the engineers told Art and me, making their paths and their destinations very hard to keep straight.

The task of writing up one's recollections of long-past events is an arduous one that only a relatively few pioneers undertake of their own volition. Finding them and persuading them to do so is also one of the most difficult tasks in building a reliable history of any era. In the case of the invention of the electronic computer, we have a goodly number of firsthand documentations, some produced voluntarily, some on invitation, and some after considerable prodding. We should be grateful both to the pioneers and to those who have sought them out and, one way or another, induced them to record their memories and their opinions.

Here special mention should be made of the editors and the board of the *Annals of the History of Computing* for the many articles and comments they have secured and published; and also of the editors and writers for *Datamation* for its many timely articles and interviews in addition to those by Gardner. In an entirely different way, our justice system should be credited, as well: by force of law, it has created for posterity an unmatched reservoir of documents, artifacts, testimony, and argument.

Before I ring down the curtain on these writers who have done so much to open up and clarify this early history, I want to cite one other to whom I have not referred previously. This is George L. Hamlin, writing for *On the Surface*, the news organ of the Naval Surface Weapons Center. NSWC was established in 1974 through the merger of the Naval Ordnance Laboratory of White Oak, Maryland, and the Naval Weapons Laboratory of Dahlgren, Virginia. Hamlin, of course, represents the center's interest in promoting Atanasoff as an accomplished alumnus. Nonetheless, he gives a remarkably accurate summary, both of the story and of the invention. His articles are of special interest for their quotations from Atanasoff's colleagues that reflect his style in this post-Iowa period.

Hamlin wrote two substantial articles, each occasioned by an event at Iowa State that he had covered. The first article was "NSWC's J. V. Atanasoff: Recognition Comes Slowly to Computer's Inventor," and the event was a banquet in the fall of 1983, celebrating both the tenth anniversary of Judge Larson's decision and Atanasoff's eightieth birthday.[9] The second article was "More Recognition for Atanasoff," and the event was a series of festivities in the spring of 1988 honoring Atanasoff and announcing the publication of Mollenhoff's book by the Iowa State University Press.[10]

One of George Hamlin's interviewees was Robert Stewart, head of computer science at Iowa State. As a graduate student "on loan" to NOL from ISU after the war, Stewart had worked under Atanasoff on his Helgoland project. He tells Hamlin:

> J.V. was a most unusual individual. The sparks just flew. It was the most exhilarating and yet frustrating period of my life. I was looking for a hero and I found

one. I was trying to put his ideas into practice. The frustration came from the fact
that he kept coming up with better ideas.

You came out of a conversation with him and your head would be aching—
kind of like getting a drink from a fire hose.

More than one former colleague alludes to flying sparks!

Ralph Bennett, Atanasoff's superior at NOL, recalls him as "one of our best
idea men, . . . one of the most creative people we had." But then he indicates,
Hamlin says, "that J.V.'s creativity occasionally crossed the bounds of strict military procedure and frustrated the skipper." Bennett continues:

It was debatable whether Atanasoff or the Admiral would be on my doorstep
Sunday morning—the Admiral to complain about Atanasoff's freewheeling or
Atanasoff to complain about the Admiral's restrictions.

In his 1984 article, Hamlin also quotes Iowa State information officer David
Lendt on the university's efforts at promotion in the decade after the court decision:

We've made some progress. Where we used to get curt notes telling us we must
be mistaken, we're now getting polite letters of apology and interest.

And, in his 1988 article, Hamlin quotes Mollenhoff on the aftermath of the
decision in the ENIAC case:

The ENIAC folks didn't appeal the decision because their lawyers knew it was
pretty clear-cut. But they are still resisting it. When you don't have the resources
for a frontal assault—an appeal—you pick around the edges, and that's what
they're doing.

Hamlin now has Judge Larson "smiling wryly" as he agrees with Mollenhoff:
"Yes, they're still at it. They refer to me as that nutty judge."

Like others, Hamlin remarks on Atanasoff's lack of bitterness. Atanasoff
feels that recognition for his invention is coming, at long last. As for Iowa State's
failure to pursue the patent, he opines that, given the market back then, he "could
not have gotten rich on it": Iowa State "would probably have sold it for, maybe,
$50,000."

Hamlin also records two broad concessions on Atanasoff's part: first, that
"he didn't take up all the slack on his end either," because of his war work, and
second, that "Eckert and Mauchly did do important work beyond his." Atanasoff
concludes, Hamlin writes: "Distinguished men have said there is enough honor
here for everyone, and I agree."

Another very encouraging development has been the recent treatment of this era by major encyclopedias: *Americana* (1996), *Britannica* (1997), *World Book* (1997), and *Academic American* (1997). All four recognize Atanasoff's priority. The first three credit him explicitly with invention of the first electronic computer, then credit Eckert and Mauchly with their subsequent invention of the first general-purpose electronic computer. The fourth, *Academic American*, credits him only with his priority of *ideas*, in "a crude vacuum-tube device," and credits Eckert and Mauchly with invention of the "first electronic digital computer, ENIAC."

Britannica, under the heading "Computers," makes the fullest case for the Atanasoff-Berry Computer as an original invention. It establishes the year 1939 by explaining what the model, or "prototype," demonstrated; and it establishes the year 1942 by citing the novel features of the computer itself, in the context of the electromechanical computers of the day and the general-purpose and stored-program computers that followed.

As to derivation of the ENIAC from the ABC, only *World Book* omits any linkage between the two. *Americana* lets its presentation of the Honeywell-Sperry Rand patent trial and the judge's verdict establish the connection. And *Academic American*, having denied Atanasoff an actual computer, now not only cites the court case but pronounces Atanasoff the "inventor of basic digital techniques that were used in [the ENIAC]."

Again, it is *Britannica* that makes the strongest—and most detailed—case for the ENIAC's derivation from the ABC. In fact, even as it credits Mauchly, Eckert, "and their colleagues at the Moore School" with "a major breakthrough," it takes every opportunity, in a number of different entries, to note the ENIAC's debt to the ABC. Under "Mauchly," for example, it calls him coinventor of the ENIAC, "the first general-purpose electronic computer," which it then characterizes as "a huge machine . . . that incorporated features developed by J. V. Atanasoff."

Britannica also credits the ABC's continuing legacy:

> Atanasoff's computer greatly influenced the future of electronic computing technology. It was the first machine to use electronic means to manipulate binary numbers. Several concepts introduced by Atanasoff remain important in today's computers, including the use of capacitors in dynamic random-access memories, the regeneration of capacitors, and the separation of memory and processing.

Finally, *Britannica* does carefully delineate the British Colossus as next after the ABC in the chronology of electronic computers, describing it as also a special-purpose computer, but created entirely independently of Atanasoff's work.

<<<>>>

I want to look now at the way in which this story has been portrayed for the broader audience, as through publicly supported museum displays and television shows or through intensely promoted private celebrations. These productions have served to sustain the Mauchly-Eckert version of the history, even though the producers have been fully cognizant of the correct version.

In chapter 11, we saw a series of announcements, declarations of intent, and appeals for industry support by the Smithsonian Institution's National Museum of American History as it made plans for the 1990 debut of its Information Age Exhibition. We also saw a number of pleas from Atanasoff proponents urging full recognition of his role in the history, with special stress on the argument that a *federal* court ruling—namely, Judge Larson's decision in the ENIAC patent trial—must be honored by a *federal* museum. In the end, the museum's appeals netted many millions of corporate dollars, including a substantial sum from Unisys, together with appreciable corporate "advice" on the exhibition's content. The Atanasoff proponents' pleas netted his recognition as inventor of the first electronic computer, but no reference to the patent trial or to the Atanasoff influence on the prominently displayed ENIAC and the ensuing computers that had "borrowed" Atanasoff's principles.

We saw Museum Director Roger Kennedy, under prodding from Clark Mollenhoff, complain of the pressure he had come under not to include Atanasoff at all. To his puzzlement, this pressure came not only from industry proper, but from others who advocated a new definition of *invention*, one that, it seemed, excluded anything not brought "fully into existence" by industry. An *invention* had to have become marketable.

We also saw Director Kennedy complain to Congress about a budget so low as to leave the Smithsonian "gasping along," with the unhealthy prospect, he said, of having corporate donors dictate his shows' contents.

A 1994 issue of *The Economist* addressed this problem in "American Museums: Bossy Sponsors."[11] Concerned mainly with public art museums, the article wonders whether these can continue to "justify their charitable status if they behave in much the same way as commercial art galleries." It argues:

> When a business sponsors an exhibition or pays for a new wing, the stage is set for a clash between the values of art and of the marketplace. A museum often has to make difficult choices about where to draw the line between propriety and cupidity, generating revenue and selling out, accepting a helping hand and opening itself to undue influence.

Later the article turns from its art museum examples to the Smithsonian:

> Not even Washington's renowned Smithsonian Institution passed the Caesar's wife test when it organised "Information Age," an ambitious exhibition tracing the history of the computer. The $10m that it cost tó mount was borne entirely by electronics companies and the show was a rapturous valentine to the computer industry.

PBS followed, in 1992, with its own information age series, titled *The Machine that Changed the World*. Here Unisys was the sole corporate sponsor, but, as we saw in chapter 11, the show's producers vehemently denied any Unisys influence on their decision to omit Atanasoff *entirely*, just as the Smithsonian had denied such influence on its severely curtailed recognition of him. PBS did observe, in an epilogue, that the Eckert-Mauchly patent on the ENIAC had been "judged invalid," but failed to state the relevant grounds, namely, Atanasoff's prior computer and its impact on the ENIAC.

Others have begged to differ as to PBS's autonomy. In a May 28, 1998, *New York Review of Books* critique, John Leonard finds that today's public television has strayed far from the original 1967 vision of the Carnegie Commission on Educational Television.[12] What that commission had hoped for, he writes, was:

> a system inclusive of "all that is of human interest and importance which is not at the moment appropriate or available for support by advertising" and "a voice for groups in the community that may otherwise be unheard," paid for by a tax on television sets.

Leonard then cites Congress's Public Broadcasting Act of 1967, which met the spirit of the commission's report but, alas, omitted "any means of funding . . . other than a begging bowl." "And so, from the start," he concludes, "the experiment was corrupted by politics and money."

Yet PBS did take its assigned mission to heart, at least for a time. James Ledbetter, author of one of the books reviewed by Leonard, writes:

> Through the late 1970s, PBS guidelines still tried to keep underwriters from using PBS programming as an advertisement or editorial pronouncement on their industry. "Underwriting of a program will not normally be accepted from an organization having a *direct* and immediate interest in the content of a program," insisted PBS's 1976 underwriting rulebook.[13]

The extremely cynical Ledbetter, who titled his book *Made Possible By . . . : The Death of Public Broadcasting in The United States*, goes on to cite PBS's own startling example, in this same rulebook:

> PBS will not accept a program on the history of the computer by a computer manufacturer. The interest is less that the connection will lead to the potential of control of the content of the program (though this danger may indeed be present), but that the program is so self-serving of the interest of the funder that a reasonable public could conclude that the program is on public television principally because of the existence of the funding or that public television is in fact no different than commercial television, but simply that its advertising of products is more subtle.

James Ledbetter then remarks that "such guidelines seemed quaint, even nostalgic" by the 1990s. "The concern behind the 1976 principles—i.e., that noncommercial television had vital integrity that needed to be safeguarded—had all but evaporated." "PBS," he continues, "broadcast a history of the computer, called *The Machine that Changed the World*, which was paid for in part by a $1.9 million grant from computer manufacturer Unisys." He then tells of other cases of obvious corporate involvement in program content and also of cases in which programs were excluded because they ran counter to corporate interests. He mentions news stories, too, that were suppressed or curtailed because they reflected badly on the sponsors.

PBS's dependence on industry support continues to grow, as evidenced by the longer and longer mini-commercials accompanying the *Made-Possible-By*'s at the start and finish of programs. And PBS is understandably happy about what those added dollars are doing for it. William LaRue, in a July 19, 1998, story for Newhouse News Service, tells of the brilliant lineup of programs to commence in the fall.[14] "When it comes to financial support," he writes, "these are heady days for PBS":

> Meeting with TV critics [at the Television Critics Association summer meeting in Pasadena], PBS President Ervin Duggan noted that the network's operating revenues rose from $188 million in 1995 to $253 million in 1998. Much of that comes from corporate donations, as well as revenues from companion books, videos and cassettes.

By the year 2000, PBS will be spending $165 million on national programming, LaRue adds, as compared to $115 million in 1995.

All of us who watch and support public television can rejoice in this bounty, *except for* the ever-mounting influence the sponsors have on program contents. In his *New York Review* article, John Leonard notes that government support stood at 86 percent of total revenue in 1980, but at only 16 percent in 1995; and that the United States spends just over one dollar per citizen per year on public television. (Leonard cites William F. Baker and George Dessart—in their 1998 book, *Down the Tube*—for the former figures and Ledbetter for the latter.)

A way out of this dilemma, of course, is for PBS to confine itself to "noncontroversial" stories. But, as the Carnegie Commission's report indicates, the public is thereby deprived.

Over the years, there have been a number of celebrations of the ENIAC and of Eckert and Mauchly as its inventors, in most of which Unisys (or its predecessor Sperry Rand or, later, just Sperry) has figured. Perhaps the grandest bash of all was that put on by the University of Pennsylvania in February 1996 for the ENIAC's fiftieth anniversary. Again, just as for the exhibition by the Smithsonian and the documentary by PBS—both public institutions—Unisys was a leading sponsor of the private University of Pennsylvania celebration of 1996.

As a private institution with a public image to maintain, Penn walked a fine line. Marshall Ledger, writing in the October 1982 issue of the *University of Pennsylvania Gazette*, had acknowledged the invalidation of the ENIAC patent by the U.S. District Court, Minneapolis, but with a strong suggestion that Judge Larson was mistaken about the ENIAC's linkage to Atanasoff.[15] Ledger suggested that the Sperry defense had failed to reveal significant evidence of Mauchly's early work, and that the Honeywell offense had won over the judge with its adroit cross-examination of Mauchly. Clearly, however, there would be— could be—no notice of this slice of ENIAC history at the fiftieth birthday celebration. Even acknowledgment of Atanasoff's prior electronic computer would have been uncomfortable for the Penn celebrants. Acknowledgment of the patent trial would have been intolerable, diminishing the ENIAC's sheen disastrously and raising the issue of deception and theft by inventors Mauchly and Eckert.

The event's planners were at pains to ease any ill feeling among the Atanasoff advocates. Art was urged, by phone, to attend, as, indeed, was John V. Atanasoff II. The message was that Penn wanted to "heal the wounds." Art had not attended any of the celebrations since the twenty-fifth anniversary affair in Chicago. His decision not to attend this latest one was cinched when he found his name in the list of "ENIAC Alums" in one of the preliminary mailings:

Dr. Arthur W. Burks
    Logic designer of ENIAC; extensive written work, came down on side of Iowa State in legal patent dispute. Not friendly with Eckert or Mrs. Mauchly. [1946] Moore School lecturer from the Institute for Advanced Study, Princeton.

Besides, one of the several reporters who phoned for stories had rather wryly conveyed his impression that Art "was not very popular at Penn"! Somehow the committee's offer to meet him at the airport rang hollow.

The younger Atanasoff also declined. He told us that he had been asked to say under just what terms he would attend. When he stipulated establishment of the federal court decision, including acknowledgment of Mauchly's 1941 letters praising the ABC and its potential, Penn found this unacceptable. It seemed that any healing was to be on the university's terms.

Speakers at the festivities were careful to qualify their characterizations of the ENIAC's "firstness." Vice President Al Gore, who served as honorary chairman of the celebration, called it "the world's first programmable computer"; university president Judith Rodin called it "the world's first large-scale, general purpose digital computer"; and Philadelphia mayor Edward G. Rendell called it "the world's first large-scale general purpose electronic computer." (President Rodin and Mayor Rendell served as cochairs, along with Unisys chairman and CEO James Unruh.) Others called it the "first super-computer" or the "first all-electronic computer." The word was plainly out that there had been some kind of predecessor that was to go nameless.

A friend told us of a downtown Philadelphia exhibit in conjunction with Penn's anniversary celebration. It included a photograph of the ABC and a write-up of Atanasoff, he said, but made no mention of the court decision, drew no connection to the ENIAC.

I want now to take notice of one other widely publicized promotion of the Eckert-Mauchly cause, namely, a book by *Wall Street Journal* staff writer Scott McCartney.[16] The book's very title, *ENIAC: The Triumphs and Tragedies of the World's First Computer*, reveals its message, as does an early quotation:

> The invention of the computer ranks as one of the greatest achievements of the century, indeed, the millennium. Yet the inventors remain obscure, and the story of how their invention came to be has been largely overlooked.

The major triumph seems to be that Eckert and Mauchly invented the computer; the major tragedy that they did not receive their due fame and fortune. This latter rests on all of the arguments we have seen proposed herein, including the supposed Sperry Rand mishandling of the ENIAC trial and Judge Larson's supposed contradictory findings. But it also emphasizes the factors of wartime urgency and secrecy, followed by postwar business difficulties. McCartney continues in his introduction:

> Once World War II was over, however, the camaraderie of a wartime mission [at the Moore School] splintered into competition and pettiness, and some of the computer's pioneers turned on one another, muddying the whole beauty of its creation. Mauchly and Eckert's success story has a tragic ending. For all their creative genius, the builders of the first computer turned out to be lousy marketers and poor businessmen.

This book has many errors of fact, as it traces the history of the electronic computer and marshals arguments for its invention by Mauchly and Eckert. Our main concern here, of course, is its treatment of Atanasoff and the ABC, but I will cite just one such error that is immediately recognizable from our above presentation of the celebration of the ENIAC's fiftieth, which McCartney has taken to be a *U.S.* affair rather than a Penn affair. He writes in his epilogue:

> In 1996, the United States celebrated the fiftieth anniversary of the unveiling of ENIAC. Vice President Al Gore gave the keynote speech at the University of Pennsylvania. . . . The event was carefully worded to not offend anyone in Iowa, but the bottom line was unmistakable. This was a celebration of the invention of the computer. It was a fitting, and honest, tribute to the pioneers of the computer age.

The author devotes most of chapter 8 to Atanasoff and the ENIAC patent trial. Here is his characterization of the ABC as he explains Atanasoff's statement to Mauchly that his computer would cost only two dollars per digit:

The answer to the two-dollar riddle, of course, was that Atanasoff wasn't using vacuum tubes as the primary electronic components; he was using his semimechanical rotating drum, pimpled with cheap, simple capacitors. So Mauchly's claim of disappointment had some validity, though it wasn't reflected in later letters.

A few pages earlier McCartney had focused on the ABC's "rotating drum pocked with capacitors" as "the key to the Atanasoff machine":

Atanasoff had told [Mauchly] he used tubes, and [his machine] was cheap. The reality was he used capacitors, which were cheap, and employed only a few tubes in the machine, mostly as amplifiers. The problem with that design was that capacitors are slow; they don't let you take advantage of the speed of the tubes. So for Mauchly's purposes, they weren't the answer.

Somehow McCartney has missed the ABC's arithmetic unit altogether, with its thirty thirteen-tube [seven-envelope] serial binary adders; indeed, it is striking that he seems throughout to see computers' memories as their driving force.

This and other errors reveal an amazing misconception of the ABC. McCartney states, for example, that the input and output mechanisms "used electrical charges from capacitors to burn holes in cards," whereas in fact they used sparks from pairs of electrodes triggered by high-voltage gas tubes. Worse yet, he states that "the Atanasoff [*sic*] had no clock, so its internal operations couldn't be coordinated." In chapter 2, we saw Mauchly himself, in his Control Data deposition, describe the overall system of the computer, including its card-punching and -reading mechanisms, and the way in which all operations were coordinated under a program control timed and powered by a sixty-cycle synchronous motor. And, of course, there was the timing drum on the main axle between the two memory drums!

As to the patent trial, McCartney, like so many other writers, believes the "case largely boiled down to one scientist's word against the other," though he goes on to admit that Mauchly's "letters seemed to contradict [his] after-the-fact view of the importance of the [Iowa] visit, and thus bolstered Atanasoff's credibility." He even quotes from Mauchly's September 30, 1941, "devastating" letter in which he asked Atanasoff whether the way would be "open for us [at the Moore School] to build an Atanasoff Calculator (a la *Bush* analyzer) here?" This letter, he concedes, "undercut everything Mauchly had tried to claim about the irrelevance of Atanasoff's work. Mauchly had buried himself."

McCartney's way out of this difficulty is to cite the many differences between the ENIAC and the ABC, such that, he argues, the one could not have been derived from the other; and to claim, as Mauchly always did, that he did not actually use any of Atanasoff's ideas in the ENIAC. McCartney, of course, thinks Judge Larson is wrong in his finding of derivation, "a brutal ruling for Eckert and Mauchly." He then puts forward what he considers the judge's *true* reason for invalidating the ENIAC patent: to "open up the computer industry, let Honeywell, Control Data, and others have access to patent licenses and know-how." Indeed, McCartney sees this move as "the proper thing to do legally, given that Sperry and IBM had engaged in a conspiracy to monopolize the industry," and it was also "clearly the right thing to do for the nation," given that those two firms "would have had a stranglehold [on the industry] at least until 1981—nearly eight more years."

But, the author explains, Larson could not use this 1956 "conspiracy" to open up the industry, and so he found a simple answer: "invalidate the ENIAC patent." Here he concludes:

> Many commentators argued that Judge Larson didn't have all the facts, so he came to the wrong conclusion on the ENIAC patent, or he didn't understand the technology, so he didn't really know what he was doing. But he knew exactly what he was doing: He was breaking a monopoly, freeing computer development to take off in the 1970s and 1980s. *Mauchly and Eckert were just innocent bystanders caught in the cross fire.* [italics added]

It seems almost superfluous to cite this author's resolution of the ENIAC patent trial as a slur on the judge, whose function was not to issue false rulings, even for the good of the nation!

One does not, or should not, accuse someone of "lying" or "stealing ideas" lightly, and should have solid grounds—documented examples—for doing so. I believe I have shown that both John Mauchly and Pres Eckert did engage in such behavior; Eckert to enhance his already formidable achievements and Mauchly to enhance his lesser feats. One should not so accuse someone, either, as a mere exercise, and I believe I have shown that the deceptive practices of Mauchly and Eckert are inextricably entangled in this unfortunate story. Their pronouncements, from the unveiling of the ENIAC onward, have served to propagate and sustain a false version of the history of the electronic computer.

Both Eckert and Mauchly were people who could not let well enough alone, who were not satisfied to be acclaimed for what they really did but needed to have done more. I believe they came, over time, to think they *must have* done more, so great were their creative proclivities—and so reassuring their audiences, so negligible any dissent for a matter of decades.

We have seen a number of instances of false statements by Eckert, some of which seem to reflect an ignorance that he felt no need to monitor, decidedly careless remarks made, nevertheless, to interviewers he knew to be professional writers: his assertions (to Pamela Eblen) that Atanasoff "didn't even have a computer," but only "a couple of counting circuits," and that "Mauchly saw what

Atanasoff had in an hour's time"; or his observations (to *Computerworld*) that Atanasoff's "ideas for storage . . . were never fully instrumented," and that nobody but Atanasoff "knew whether [his add-subtract mechanism] worked or not."[17]

We have also seen Eckert, again in interview situations, make unconscionably rash remarks, not just about Atanasoff but about Judge Earl Larson and his conduct of the ENIAC trial. We saw him call that trial "a farce" (to Clark Mollenhoff) and dismiss Atanasoff as "a liar [who] was paid a lot of money for the testimony he gave."[18] We saw him characterize Larson (to both Eblen and Mollenhoff) as "a nutty judge" and extend this sentiment (for *Computerworld*) to pronounce the entire legal system "nuts."

Lastly, we have seen Eckert make false claims in writing and for publication, quite deliberately, as he did in his paper for the Los Alamos history conference. In 1944, when he first learned of von Neumann's suggestion of a cathode-ray-tube memory, he thought he could figure out how to make it work and was soon claiming the idea itself. When Frederic Williams did unlock its secrets and secure the patents, Eckert seems to have let the matter drop. But some thirty years later at Los Alamos, he gave the impression that he had shown Williams how to design such a memory.[19] Williams, he implied, had patented his, Eckert's, solution to the problem.

Other instances of Eckert's deliberate distortion of the history, also launched years after the fact, related to activities at the Moore School. These pronouncements served to downgrade the role of other members of the ENIAC team—particularly those of his top three lieutenants, so to speak—even as they promoted Eckert's own role. One of the more serious of these is recorded by Nancy Stern, who accepts it as true, indeed, as an illustration of Eckert's "precision as an engineer." In her 1981 book, she quotes him from a 1977 interview:

> In fact in the ENIAC I took every engineer's work and checked every calculation of every resistor in the machine to make sure that it was done correctly. Normally, I wouldn't want to have to do that. But this was the first for a machine with an order of magnitude of 100 times as much stuff as anybody has ever built electronically. And if it was going to work, one had to be 100 times more careful.[20]

It is true that Eckert would not normally have wanted to do this job. Nor did he do it! He assigned it to Art, first with Bob Shaw and then with Kite Sharpless to assist him. They examined the drawings of circuits throughout the machine, checking each configuration of vacuum tubes from the aspect of the driving tube (or tubes), the values of the associated resistors and the lengths of the output wires to the tube (or tubes) being driven. The aim was to make sure the circuit was fulfilling its logical purpose, at the same time that it met the safety factors established by Eckert.

Art has always felt that, as demanding as this assignment was, it gave him—

uniquely—an overview of the entire ENIAC, one that stayed with him ever after. Eckert was right in his argument for doing it: many minor errors were found, each of which had to be corrected. But he distorted the picture when he claimed that only he could be depended upon to do it, let alone that he did it. Of course, the record bears Art out. And Eckert said not a word when Art, in our *Annals* article on the ENIAC, included this task as one of those that he undertook, along with Shaw and Sharpless. Eckert made other objections, but not that one.

(It is because of this assignment, undoubtedly, that Art was able to describe the ENIAC so effectively in our *Annals* article, and that he has been able to respond over the years to writers and others on its details—even to answer questions from Unisys as it prepared an exhibit for presentation in Japan.)

Clearly, Eckert was willing to falsify the history and even to malign other inventors, whether in careless off-the-cuff remarks, in reckless jabs, or in calculated misrepresentations of the facts. And, actually, this approach served him well. As to the passage of the ideas of Atanasoff, in particular, into the ENIAC and the EDVAC, Eckert's remarks were reproduced in the press, and his claims to invention continued to be honored in the broader computing community, as well, despite Judge Larson's findings.

Media attention, of course, has been much more on Mauchly than on Eckert in the matter of derivation from Atanasoff, since he was the one who had the contacts. It should not be overlooked, however, that on the testimony of both Eckert and Mauchly, Eckert did know the source of ideas—Atanasoff—that both he and Mauchly claimed for themselves.

Mauchly, to his credit, did not indulge in personal attacks in the press. The closest he came to accusing Atanasoff of deceptive behavior, I think, was in the ENIAC trial, where he portrayed Atanasoff as withholding information at their first meeting in order to entice him out to Ames to see his machine. The "most" Atanasoff did in Philadelphia, Mauchly testified, was make him "very curious" on several scores, *each* of which he recalled as *the one* designed "to lure me to Iowa." How could Atanasoff compute with vacuum tubes? How could he build a computer for only "$2 per digit"? What was the purpose of his computer, beyond simple arithmetic? What about that "secret teaser," the machine's regenerative memory?[21]

In the end, under prodding by Honeywell attorneys, Mauchly's complaint was not so much that he did not get the answers to these questions as that Atanasoff's answers were a great disappointment. He made the trip to Iowa, he testified, expecting something much more like the "general-purpose," "all-electronic" computer he now claimed—contrary to all the evidence—to have had in mind before he ever met Atanasoff. Indeed, to the extent that it can be said that Mauchly had a strategy at trial, it was simply to belittle Atanasoff's achievements and exaggerate his own.

After the trial, Mauchly mounted this strategy on a grand scale. As the prime player, pitted against just one rival in a contest over invention of the world's first electronic computer, he was approached regularly and often for interviews. If he had slipped into self-contradiction and self-defeating outbursts on the witness stand, he found it easy to leave such difficulties behind at the trial's end.

For Mauchly was subjected to surprisingly few reminders of the facts of the case, brought out by testimony from his own lips and papers from his own files, that had dictated the judge's decision. With the passage of time—and with the encouragement of a computing community loyal to him—it became easier and easier to establish a false story of his progress toward the ENIAC, months, even years, before he happened upon Atanasoff; and to dismiss Atanasoff's computer with devastating characterizations: "just a little piece of junk" (to Mollenhoff), "a crude little machine that wouldn't really do anything" (to *Computerworld*), and "a little gismo" (to Gardner).

As for the judge, although Mauchly expressed surprise at his finding the ENIAC patent invalid (to Gardner), he could excuse him (to Mollenhoff) for his inability to understand "some very important technical evidence"—which remained unspecified. But he also misstated the judge's decision and distorted the history. He claimed at Los Alamos, for example, that Larson had said that because he had visited Atanasoff "for just two or three days in 1941," he had derived all of his "notions about building electronic computers" from him.[22] (He was there for five days, and the judge did not say that.)

In short, the Mauchly response—and that of his adherents—to the ENIAC patent trial has been to construct a *parallel history*, and so to disregard the true history as developed in that trial. "*But Mauchly says, . . .*" as against "*Judge Larson said, . . .*" became the stock rejoinder after the trial, with little or no consideration of the grounds for Larson's findings. (Eckert had only to chime in with unfounded broadsides.)

For me, the most striking aspect of this parallel history is its reversal of roles whereby Mauchly and Eckert are cast as the victims. Blame is then fixed on Atanasoff, the true victim. It is also fixed on the judge. Blame is even fixed on the Sperry Rand defense team, from whom, in fact, Mauchly and Eckert had withheld crucial information about Atanasoff's achievement and Mauchly's acquaintance with it. The loss of the ENIAC patent is then seen as a cruel blow.

Atanasoff's conduct at trial was in sharp contrast to Mauchly's. Faced with the volume of testimony, documentation, and artifacts produced by the Honeywell side, the Sperry Rand attorneys never tried to show that Honeywell's chief witness was lying. They tried instead to challenge his memory of past events. But his memory for those events of thirty or forty years ago proved keen, to the point of evoking odd bits that gave his testimony the ring of truth. And, when pressed to the wall, he could produce the original records to verify his story.

Atanasoff's testimony was of a positive nature, his presence in the courtroom responsive and impressive, as he laid out his own achievements and described his interactions with Mauchly. In the posttrial years, as well, he resisted any temptation to claim more than he did. Although Mauchly had been found not credible by the court, and had become even less forthright after the judgment, Atanasoff limited his remarks to expressing disappointment—and a degree of wonder—that the true history was so slow to emerge.

On one of Art's first visits to Atanasoff, in 1979, I went along. We were both struck by two things: Atanasoff wanted credit for everything he had done, but he did not want credit for anything he had not done! This impression is surely borne out by the way in which he credited Clifford Berry from the start, even assuring him a share of any royalties that might ensue from a patent and, after Berry's death, attaching his name, along with his own, to the machine. Moreover, Atanasoff saw fit to acknowledge the advances made by Eckert and Mauchly, even as they belittled his contribution of the fundamentals on which they built.

We were also struck by the care that Atanasoff took in telling of ideas he had hoped one day to pursue but never did. I recall his telling us that he had had the concept of the transistor as a replacement for the vacuum tube some ten years before anyone started to work on that possibility. He had thought of it in terms of an analogy: "If you could go from a vacuum-tube diode to a vacuum-tube triode, then you should also be able to go from a solid-state [crystal] diode to a solid-state [crystal] triode," that is, to a transistor. But he did not claim to have invented the transistor. Nor did he denigrate the achievement of the three men who did—and received the Nobel Prize. He simply said, a little wistfully, that he had thought of the possibility.

Atanasoff maintained this attitude, which I attribute to a certain pride, through the many Sunday phone conversations we had with him and Alice as we wrote up the details of the ABC for our book. Art was concerned with the technical aspects, I more with the broader concepts and the order in which they developed. We would pose questions one Sunday, and he would make a "memory search" and be ready with answers the next; we would then discuss these answers and pose more questions.

This exercise proved valuable to the builders of the ABC replica at Iowa State, several of whom told us of their reliance on our book for certain details. One, in particular, asked how we knew these things! When we told him of our weekly phone talks with Atanasoff, he was delighted; he could tell the others that these were Atanasoff's own designs, not Art's conjectures!

Atanasoff himself was enthusiastic about this process, remarking that no one had asked him such questions before. We always felt that he was giving honest answers, and of course Art, familiar as he was with vacuum-tube technology, could check the technical explanations against the 1940 description to see that they "fit."

<<<>>>

Art and I have been accused of bestowing a halo on Atanasoff; a devil's tail on Mauchly. Our support for Atanasoff, however, has always centered first on his inventive accomplishments and second on his representation of them. Our criticism of Mauchly has concerned exactly these same elements.

Atanasoff has been faulted for many omissions in this history: not publishing his 1940 paper, not pursuing the patent, not recognizing what he had accomplished for decades, not succeeding in the postwar computer project at the Naval Ordnance Laboratory. We can speculate as to why he handled (or mishandled) these matters as he did. I am inclined to think that he was devastated, first by the flaw in his computer's input-output system that spoiled its results for the large systems of equations that were his goal, and then by news of the ENIAC and Mauchly's word that its principles were entirely different from the ABC's.

But I also see Atanasoff as a man who immersed himself in each successive undertaking with an untoward zeal: who threw himself into the NOL's wartime projects and, after the war, took on the Bikini Atoll and Helgoland studies at the expense of the computer project—and who, when that project was cancelled, moved on to other pursuits. (One can, of course, wonder how much appetite he really had for a new computer project at that stage.)

We can also speculate on the darker questions: Why did Atanasoff entrust Mauchly with all those secrets that he meant to patent? At what point did Mauchly, who surely did not approach Atanasoff with any thought of stealing his ideas, decide, in fact, to claim them? And how did Eckert come to join Mauchly in these claims?

I see Atanasoff as starved for a fellow-physicist who shared his passion for computing devices and appreciated his invention. I see Mauchly and Eckert as readily convincing themselves, in the case of the ENIAC, that their machine so outdistanced Atanasoff's as to allow his role to be brushed aside. Later, when they got to the EDVAC, for which their "borrowings" were more clearly apparent, these two men simply yielded to the call of fame and fortune rather than acknowledge a remote figure who, they realized, was paying no attention whatever.

World War II, of course, with the Moore School's involvement in the production of artillery tables for the army, has to be seen as a huge factor in this scenario. Two novel phenomena were at work: universities were engaging in government research, and the military was funding much of it. It is ironic that, because of Sperry Rand's involvement in the patent suit and Eckert's association as a vice president, the ENIAC is often thought of as a corporate rather than a university or a government enterprise. Actually, no corporation would have risked half a million dollars on such a far-out venture at that time. In short, a war produced the need, a university setting evolved the concept, the army took the chance, and the *public* footed the bill.

From Atanasoff's perspective, other factors entered in. Chief among these was the long delay in the issuance of the ENIAC patent. Not until twenty-two years after he finished work on the ABC could he be shown the ENIAC claims in order to identify those that were really his. But one can wonder here, too, why Atanasoff did not interest himself more in the ENIAC as a physical entity that he might well have looked into. Rather, he seems to have blocked out that part of his life, until corporate lawyers began approaching him and insisting that he take a look.

Yes, there are puzzles, enigmas, in this story. But they are irrelevant to the issue at hand. The fact remains that Atanasoff invented the world's first electronic computer, that it was an astounding collection of original and enduring features, that it had a profound effect on the subsequent history, and, finally, that Atanasoff told the truth with regard to this achievement. The further fact remains that Mauchly and Eckert claimed a preponderance of Atanasoff's ideas—however much they advanced them—and that they resorted to falsehoods, first to protect their patents, and then, when those were lost, to maintain their reputations.

A most regrettable aspect of this whole development has been the failure of a number of influential and supposedly unbiased professional historians to study and address the court proceedings. The need to follow the cardinal rule, *work from original sources whenever possible*, has been largely set aside in this relatively new discipline, the history of computer science.

Allan Bromley, of the University of Sydney, has urged his colleagues on the Mauchly-Eckert side of this very dispute to examine the evidence. In his 1983 article for the *Annals of the History of Computing*, written in response to Art's and mine on the ENIAC in that same journal, Bromley first lauds our tracing of the ENIAC to the work of Atanasoff and to the differential analyzer, then sees our doing so as a needed prod toward the history of ideas. But he adds:

> Theories in this area, as in any other intellectual field, however, stand or fall by the weight of the evidence, and I would welcome seeing those who disagree with the Burkses bring forward the evidence to support their views.[23]

To this day Bromley's invitation has been ignored by "those who disagree." Instead, we have been subjected to our own barrage of falsehoods and irrelevancies, not just by historians but by other concerned scholars. A favorite has been the impugning of our motives—especially Art's—for writing what is depicted as a biased history. A number of people have discounted our support of Atanasoff on the ground that Art harbors a vendetta against Mauchly or a determination to deny Eckert his great accomplishments, or is bitter over a perceived lack of recognition for his own contributions to the ENIAC.

I confess that I find this *ad hominem* attack rather disturbing. Any response from us has to engage the fallacy, as well as protest the absence of real arguments about the issues to which we can respond. No, Art is not motivated by bitterness or hatred, we say, and there is no basis on which to make such bald accusations. They are sheer fabrication, for which their perpetrators' own motives could be challenged.

Art has always credited Eckert and Mauchly, not begrudgingly but often in glowing terms, for their original ideas; and he has always said that he worked on the ENIAC under the direction, particularly, of Eckert. He has also, in accord with his concern for the preservation of this history, stated just what he did contribute to the design of that machine, usually in the context of all the individual contributions. He has been sustained in this regard by the finding of Judge Larson in the ENIAC patent trial, on the basis of the project records and courtroom testimony.

Finally, Art has taken care to reveal the belated effort that he, Kite Sharpless, and Bob Shaw made, at the time of that trial, to be found joint inventors of the ENIAC—an effort that became moot when Larson invalidated the patent.

As I observed earlier, accusing people of prevarication is a delicate matter. It is particularly so when the evidence for such behavior comes decades after the event and when the parties so accused have occupied the public stage not just as upright characters, but as great inventors. People do get upset when someone says, or implies, that Mauchly lied under oath—this is just unthinkable. Challenging Eckert's veracity meets even stronger protest, perhaps because he is seen as the idea man, the inventor, more so than Mauchly, who is seen as the instigator and sounding board.

Expressions of outrage take over the argument. The unrefuted evidence, however, remains intact, and the matter of falsification of this history is an issue that has to be addressed. The process should become easier with the passage of time, as perspective is gained and emotion comes to play a lesser role.

As to Judge Larson's conduct of the ENIAC trial and his conclusions, I submit that the "scholarship" of his critics has been inexcusably shoddy and of incalculable damage both to the academic tradition and to a judge who, in fact, produced a tightly reasoned document in the best tradition of scholarship.

Those of us who have worked for Atanasoff's recognition can take heart in the progress that has been made. His standing as inventor of the first electronic computer is widely accepted, with affirming articles appearing in the nontechnical literature. The August 1998 *National Geographic*, for example, ran a story on Iowa State's replica of the Atanasoff-Berry Computer, "As simple as ABC: A Pioneer Computer is Duplicated."[24]

This piece credits Atanasoff with "using primitive electronics and a binary system of arithmetic" and also with "parallel processing and other hallmarks of modern computers." It notes that a court later found the ABC to be "the fore-runner of all infinitely more complicated computers to come," and it explains that these subsequent machines—"notably ENIAC"—"showed how the [ABC's] devices could be used by the larger world."

Recognition of Atanasoff's direct influence on the ENIAC, through Mauchly, and on its stored-program successors is slower in coming because, I think, it crosses the line into disclosing dishonesty. An outstanding exception here is a July 7, 1997, article by Jeffrey Young in *Forbes*, titled "John Vincent Atanasoff: Father of the Computer?"[25]

This author begins by noting that invention of "the electronic digital computer" is usually credited to Mauchly and Eckert, but then states:

> It's possible that the accepted history is wrong, that Mauchly and Eckert copied the key elements of their machine from another inventor. That other man was John V. Atanasoff.

Young explains the ABC in some detail, even down to the alignment of "cheap paper capacitors" in the memory drums and the rate at which "the capacitor charges were read, regenerated or changed." He further distinguishes the prototype of 1939 from the finished product of 1942.

Young tells of the Atanasoff-Mauchly connection, including Mauchly's Iowa visit in 1941 and Atanasoff's move to war work in 1942. He then states unequivocally:

> Meanwhile Mauchly teamed up with Eckert, took the conceptual underpinnings proven by Atanasoff, revamped them and presented the whole—as their own work—to, ironically, a ballistics team for the Army. The result was ENIAC.

He continues with the Honeywell-Sperry Rand suit and the invalidation of the Mauchly-Eckert patents. And he concludes:

> Atanasoff was a witness—but got nothing out of the case. He didn't even get much recognition for his achievements. Last year, during the 50th anniversary festivities marking the completion of the ENIAC, there was no mention of him.

"History, as it is written," Young opines, "isn't always true."

For many writers, it does seem easier just to call the matter "controversial." Sooner or later, however, the fact must be faced that any controversy rests on what Mauchly and Eckert persisted in claiming, contrary to the trial evidence. Surely the scholarly community will, ultimately, examine that evidence and give Atanasoff his rightful place in this momentous history.

CHRONOLOGY
OF KEY EVENTS

1935–1942:	Atanasoff directs graduate students in several physics research projects at Iowa State College
1936–1941:	Mauchly conducts research on weather periodicity at Ursinus College
1939–1940:	Mauchly builds electrical analog harmonic analyzer for analysis of weather data
November 1939:	Atanasoff demonstrates test model for electronic digital computer for solving large systems of linear algebraic equations
January 1940:	Atanasoff starts to build computer, assisted by graduate student Berry
August 1940:	Atanasoff completes manuscript detailing computer design
December 1940:	Mauchly and Atanasoff first meet at AAAS session in Philadelphia
June 1941:	Mauchly spends five days with Atanasoff at Iowa State, sees demonstrations of computer-in-progress, reads and takes notes on descriptive manuscript
September 1941:	Mauchly joins faculty at University of Pennsylvania's Moore School of Electrical Engineering

May 1942:	Atanasoff's electronic digital computer, later named Atanasoff-Berry Computer, or ABC, is completed by Atanasoff and Berry
August 1942:	Mauchly writes memorandum outlining ideas for an electronic digital differential analyzer
September 1942:	Atanasoff takes war-research position at Naval Ordnance Laboratory
April 1943:	U.S. Army accepts proposal of Eckert and Mauchly for Electronic Numerical Integrator and Computer, or ENIAC, to be built at Moore School
June 1943:	ENIAC project is launched
Late 1943:	First model of electronic digital Colossus code-breaking computer is operational at Bletchley Park, England, but is held secret for thirty years
Spring 1944:	Eckert conceives mercury-delay-line memory for next computer
August 1944:	Von Neumann becomes consultant to Moore School
Early September 1944:	Von Neumann conceives use of cathode-ray-tube memory for next computer
September 18, 1944:	Office of Chairman of (Army) Ordnance issues research and development order for Electronic Discrete Variable Computer, or EDVAC, at Moore School
March and April 1945:	Von Neumann meets with Moore School planners for discussions on EDVAC
June 1945:	Von Neumann's EDVAC report, presenting logical design and program language for modern electronic computer, is distributed by Goldstine
Late 1945–early 1946:	Institute for Advanced Study Computer project gets under way
February 1946:	ENIAC is publicly dedicated
April 1947:	Parties meet at Moore School to discuss patent rights to EDVAC, an electronic digital stored-program computer with mercury-delay-line memory being built at Moore School

June 26, 1947:	Eckert and Mauchly apply for ENIAC patent
June 1948:	"Baby Mark I," an electronic digital stored-program prototype for Manchester Mark I, is operational at Manchester University, England
April 1949:	Manchester Mark I, an electronic digital stored-program computer with cathode-ray-tube memory, is operational
June 1949:	Electronic Delay Storage Automatic Computer, or EDSAC, an electronic digital stored-program computer with mercury-delay-line memory, is operational at Cambridge University, England
1950:	EDVAC, an electronic digital stored-program computer with mercury-delay-line memory, is completed
1951:	Institute for Advanced Study Computer, an electronic digital stored-program computer with cathode-ray-tube memory, is completed
June 1952:	Serial Binary Adder patent is issued to Eckert and Mauchly
February 1953:	Regenerative Memory patent is issued to Eckert and Mauchly
February 8, 1957:	John von Neumann dies at age fifty-three
February 1964:	ENIAC patent is issued to Eckert and Mauchly
June 1, 1971, to March 13, 1972:	ENIAC patent trial (*Honeywell v. Sperry Rand*) is conducted in U.S. District Court, Minneapolis
October 19, 1973:	Judge Larson issues decision in ENIAC trial: finds ABC a prior electronic digital computer; finds ENIAC derived from Atanasoff via Mauchly contacts; finds ENIAC patent invalid; finds Regenerative Memory and Serial Binary Adder patents unenforceable
January 8, 1980:	John W. Mauchly dies at age seventy-two
June 3, 1995:	J. Presper Eckert dies at age seventy-six
June 15, 1995:	John V. Atanasoff dies at age ninety-one
October 31, 2001:	Earl R. Larson dies at age eighty-nine

REFERENCES BY CHAPTER

ALL RISE

1. Alice R. Burks and Arthur W. Burks, *The First Electronic Computer: The Atanasoff Story* (Ann Arbor: University of Michigan Press, 1988).

CHAPTER 1. MAUCHLY ON THE STAND

1. ENIAC trial records. Pretrial depositions, affidavits, complaints, transcripts, exhibits, briefs, and decision. *Honeywell, Inc. v. Sperry Rand Corp. et al.* No. 4–67 Civ. 138. D. Minn. Filed May 26, 1967, decided October 19, 1973. General Services Administration, Federal Records Center, Chicago. Decision published in *U.S. Patent Quarterly* 180 (March 25, 1974): 673–773. Transcript pp. 11824–11834.

2. Ibid., transcript pp. 12191–208.

3. Regenerative Memory trial records. Pretrial depositions, transcript, etc. *Sperry Rand Corp. v. Control Data Corp.* Civ. 15,823 and 15,824. D. Md. Filed April 1, 1964. Out-of-court settlement reached in 1981. Mauchly deposition p. 144.

4. Ibid., Mauchly deposition pp. 91–92.

5. ENIAC trial records, Decision Finding 3.

6. Ibid., Decision Finding 14.

7. John V. Atanasoff, "Computing Machine for the Solution of Large Systems of Linear Algebraic Equations," originally unpublished (1940), in *The Origins of Digital Computers: Selected Papers*, ed. Brian Randell (Berlin: Springer-Verlag, 1973).

8. Alice R. Burks and Arthur W. Burks, *The First Electronic Computer: The Atanasoff Story* (Ann Arbor: University of Michigan Press, 1988).

421

9. Regenerative Memory trial records, Mauchly deposition p. 91.

10. ENIAC trial records, transcript pp. 2053–91.

11. Ibid., transcript p. 2136.

12. ENIAC trial records, Decision Finding 3.

13. ENIAC trial records, transcript pp. 12161–67.

14. John V. Atanasoff, "Computing Machine for the Solution of Large Systems of Linear Algebraic Equations"; ENIAC trial records, Plaintiff's Exhibit PX 455.

15. ENIAC trial records, Atanasoff deposition p. 765.

16. John V. Atanasoff, "Advent of Electronic Digital Computing," *Annals of the History of Computing* 6 (1984): 229–82.

17. Regenerative Memory trial records, Defendant's Pretrial Exhibit 11.

18. Regenerative Memory trial records, Mauchly deposition p. 95.

19. Regenerative Memory trial records, Lura Atanasoff deposition p. 11.

20. Jean R. Berry, "Clifford Edward Berry, 1918–1963: His Role in Early Computers," *Annals of the History of Computing* 8 (1986): 361–69.

21. ENIAC trial records, Decision Finding 3.

22. Regenerative Memory trial records, Mauchly deposition pp. 94, 145, 165, 220, et al.

23. ENIAC trial records, Plaintiff's Exhibit PX 665.

24. ENIAC trial records, Atanasoff deposition pp. 749–51.

25. ENIAC trial records, Plaintiff's Exhibit PX 22420.

26. ENIAC trial records, Atanasoff deposition p. 747.

27. ENIAC trial records, transcript pp. 1971–74.

28. Ibid., transcript p. 11817.

29. Ibid., transcript p. 12140.

30. Ibid., transcript pp. 12140–42.

31. Ibid., transcript p. 12158.

32. Ibid., transcript p. 11817.

33. John W. Mauchly, "The Use of High Speed Vacuum Tube Devices for Calculating," originally unpublished (1942), in *The Origins of Digital Computers*.

34. ENIAC trial records, Decision Finding 14.

CHAPTER 2. MAUCHLY IN DEPOSITION

1. Regenerative Memory trial records. Pretrial depositions, transcript, etc. *Sperry Rand Corp. v. Control Data Corp.*, Mauchly deposition p. 4.

2. Ibid., Mauchly deposition p. 51.

3. Ibid., Mauchly deposition p. 43.

4. Ibid., Mauchly deposition p. 65.

5. Ibid., Mauchly deposition p. 73

6. Ibid., Mauchly deposition pp. 5–83.

7. John W. Mauchly, "The Use of High Speed Vacuum Tube Devices for Calculating," originally unpublished (1942), in *The Origins of Digital Computers: Selected Papers*, ed. Brian Randell (Berlin: Springer-Verlag, 1973); Regenerative Memory trial records, Mauchly deposition pp. 83–84.

8. Ibid., Mauchly deposition pp. 84–86.

9. Ibid., Mauchly deposition pp. 88–89.
10. Ibid., Mauchly deposition pp. 89–94.
11. Ibid., Mauchly deposition p. 144.
12. Ibid., Mauchly deposition pp. 140–45.
13. Ibid., Mauchly deposition pp. 100–102, 190, et al.
14. Ibid., Mauchly deposition pp. 134–35.
15. Ibid., Mauchly deposition p. 94.
16. Ibid., Mauchly deposition pp. 96–101.
17. Ibid., Mauchly deposition pp. 161–71.
18. J. Presper Eckert, "A Survey of Digital Computer Memory Systems," *Proceedings of the Institute of Radio Engineers* 41 (1953): 1393–1406.
19. Regenerative Memory trial records, Mauchly deposition pp. 185–98.
20. ENIAC trial records. Pretrial depositions, affidavits, complaints, transcripts, exhibits, briefs, and decision. *Honeywell, Inc. v. Sperry Rand Corp. et al.*, ENIAC patent cols. 1–2, 32–33, and 36–37.
21. Ibid., ENIAC patent cols. 1 and 2.
22. Regenerative Memory trial records, Mauchly deposition pp. 178–79.
23. Ibid., Mauchly deposition p. 223.
24. Ibid., Mauchly deposition pp. 221–41.
25. ENIAC trial records, Plaintiff's Exhibit PX 675.
26. Ibid., Plaintiff's Exhibit PX 676.
27. Ibid., Plaintiff's Exhibit PX 699.
28. Ibid., Plaintiff's Exhibit PX 712.
29. Ibid., Plaintiff's Exhibit PX 744.
30. Ibid., Plaintiff's Exhibit PX 756.
31. Ibid., Plaintiff's Exhibit PX 778.
32. Ibid., Plaintiff's Exhibit PX 789.
33. Ibid., Plaintiff's Exhibit PX 795.
34. Ibid., Plaintiff's Exhibit PX 808.
35. Ibid., Plaintiff's Exhibit PX 816.
36. Ibid., Plaintiff's Exhibit PX 822.
37. Ibid., Plaintiff's Exhibit PX 870.
38. Ibid., Plaintiff's Exhibit PX 899.
39. Ibid., Plaintiff's Exhibit PX 924.
40. ENIAC trial records, Decision Finding 13.
41. ENIAC trial records, Defendant's Exhibit DX 3361.
42. ENIAC trial records, Plaintiff's Exhibits PX 201.3 and PX 363.5.
43. ENIAC trial records, transcript p. 6545.
44. Ibid., transcript pp. 2128–29.
45. Ibid., transcript pp. 12188–89.
46. Ibid., transcript pp. 6545–46.
47. ENIAC trial records, Defendants Exhibit DX 3361.
48. ENIAC trial records, Decision Finding 13.
49. Regenerative Memory trial records, Defendant's Pretrial Exhibit 11.
50. R. K. Richards, *Electrical Digital Systems* (New York: John Wiley and Sons, 1966).
51. Regenerative Memory trial records, Mauchly deposition pp. 218–20.

52. Ibid., Mauchly deposition pp. 242–47.

53. Ibid., Mauchly deposition pp. 247–54.

54. ENIAC trial records, ENIAC patent cols. 2, 33, and 37.

55. Regenerative Memory trial records, Mauchly deposition pp. 179–90.

56. Ibid., Mauchly deposition pp. 277–78.

57. John V. Atanasoff, "Advent of Electronic Digital Computing," *Annals of the History of Computing* 6 (1984): 229–82.

CHAPTER 3. ATANASOFF AS WITNESS

1. ENIAC trial records. Pretrial depositions, affidavits, complaints, transcripts, exhibits, briefs, and decision. *Honeywell, Inc. v. Sperry Rand Corp. et al.*, transcript pp. 1645–56.

2. Ibid., transcript pp. 1583–84.

3. Ibid., transcript p. 1585.

4. Ibid., transcript p. 2393.

5. Ibid., transcript pp. 1588–89.

6. Ibid., transcript pp. 1590.

7. Ibid., transcript pp. 1591–93.

8. Ibid., transcript p. 2126.

9. Ibid., transcript pp. 1612–13, 1641–43, 1650–51.

10. Ibid., transcript pp. 1637–40.

11. Ibid., transcript pp. 1665–66, 1672–76.

12. Ibid., transcript pp. 1678–88.

13. ENIAC trial records, Plaintiff's Exhibit PX 363.5; John W. Mauchly, "The Use of High Speed Vacuum Tube Devices for Calculating," originally unpublished (1942), in *The Origins of Digital Computers: Selected Papers*, ed. Brian Randell (Berlin: Springer-Verlag, 1973).

14. ENIAC trial records, transcript pp. 2111–16.

15. Ibid., transcript pp. 2141–57.

16. Ibid., transcript pp. 1746–95.

17. ENIAC trial records, Decision Finding 3.

18. ENIAC trial records, transcript pp. 1796–2091.

19. John V. Atanasoff, "Computing Machine for the Solution of Large Systems of Linear Algebraic Equations," originally unpublished (1940), in *The Origins of Digital Computers*.

20. ENIAC trial records, transcript p. 1830.

21. Ibid., transcript pp. 2030–80.

22. Ibid., transcript pp. 2033–34.

23. Ibid., transcript pp. 2073–79.

24. Ibid., transcript pp. 1700–1703.

25. Ibid., transcript p. 1703.

26. Ibid., transcript pp. 2388–2410.

27. Ibid., transcript pp. 2881–82.

28. Ibid., transcript p. 1752.

29. Ibid., transcript pp. 1327–38.

30. Ibid., transcript pp. 2412–14.

31. Ibid., transcript pp. 2870–72.

32. Ibid., transcript pp. 2458–62.

33. Ibid., transcript pp. 2500–2505.

34. Ibid., transcript pp. 2874–75.

35. Ibid., transcript pp. 2479–99, 2505–78.

36. Ibid., transcript pp. 2578–2609.

37. Ibid., transcript pp. 2628–31.

38. Ibid., transcript pp. 2081.

39. Ibid., transcript pp. 2631–54.

40. Ibid., transcript pp. 2655–56.

41. Ibid., transcript pp. 2104–30.

42. Ibid., transcript pp. 2131–37, 2163–68.

43. Ibid., transcript pp. 2418–34.

44. Ibid., transcript pp. 2679–97.

45. ENIAC trial records, Atanasoff deposition pp. 766–79; ENIAC trial records, transcript pp. 2430–34.

46. Ibid., transcript pp. 2697–705.

47. Kathleen R. Mauchly, "John Mauchly's Early Years," *Annals of the History of Computing* 6 (1984): 116–38.

48. ENIAC trial records, transcript pp. 2213–14, 2223–27.

49. Ibid., transcript pp. 2727–31.

50. ENIAC trial records, Decision Finding 3.

51. Ibid., Decision Finding 12.

52. Regenerative Memory trial records. Pretrial depositions, transcript, etc. *Sperry Rand Corp. v. Control Data Corp.*, Legvold deposition.

53. Regenerative Memory trial records, Lura Atanasoff deposition.

54. Regenerative Memory trial records, Atanasoff deposition.

CHAPTER 4.
MAUCHLY BEFORE ATANASOFF

1. John W. Mauchly, "Mauchly: Unpublished Remarks," foreword by Henry Tropp and afterword by Arthur W. Burks and Alice R. Burks, *Annals of the History of Computing* 4 (1982): 245–56.

2. Regenerative Memory trial records. Pretrial depositions, transcript, etc. *Sperry and Corp. v. Control Data Corp.*, Mauchly deposition pp. 53–70.

3. ENIAC trial records. Pretrial depositions, affidavits, complaints, transcripts, exhibits, briefs, and decision. *Honeywell, Inc. v. Sperry Rand Corp. et al.*, Plaintiff's Exhibit PX 665.

4. ENIAC trial records, transcript pp. 11782–90.

5. Ibid., transcript pp. 11743–56 and 11767–82.

6. Ibid., transcript pp. 12128–37.

7. ENIAC trial records, Plaintiff's Exhibit PX 123.

8. ENIAC trial records, transcript pp. 11791–800.

9. Ibid., transcript pp. 12108–28.

10. ENIAC trial records, Plaintiff's Exhibit PX 665.

11. ENIAC trial records, Atanasoff deposition p. 851.

12. ENIAC trial records, transcript pp. 11791–92.

13. Ibid., transcript pp. 11801–803.

14. Ibid., transcript pp. 12173–79.

15. Kathleen R. Mauchly, "John Mauchly's Early Years," *Annals of the History of Computing* 6 (1984): 116–38.

16. John W. Mauchly, "Mauchly: Unpublished Remarks."

17. James McNulty, letter to the editor, *Datamation* 26, no. 11 (1980): 23–24, 26.

18. ENIAC trial records, Kathleen R. Mauchly deposition pp. 291, 292.

19. Pamela L. Eblen, "Verdicts: Who Really Invented the Computer?" *ICP Data Processing Management* (autumn 1984): 14, 16.

CHAPTER 5. LARSON FROM THE BENCH

1. ENIAC trial records. Pretrial depositions, affidavits, complaints, transcripts, exhibits, briefs, and decision. *Honeywell, Inc. v. Sperry Rand Corp. et al.*, Decision Finding 3.

2. John V. Atanasoff, "Computing Machine for the Solution of Large Systems of Linear Algebraic Equations," originally unpublished (1940), in *The Origins of Digital Computers: Selected Papers*, ed. Brian Randell (Berlin: Springer-Verlag, 1973).

3. ENIAC trial records, Decision Finding 4.

4. Ibid., Decision Finding 13.

5. Ibid., Decision Finding 1.

6. Ibid., Decision Finding 2.

7. Ibid., Decision Finding 7.

8. John von Neumann, "First Draft of a Report on the EDVAC," distributed by Moore School of Electrical Engineering, University of Pennsylvania, June 1945, reprinted in Nancy Stern, *From ENIAC to UNIVAC: An Appraisal of the Eckert-Mauchly Computers* (Bedford, Mass.: Digital Press, 1981), pp. 177–246; and in *Papers of John von Neumann on Computing and Computer Theory*, ed. William Aspray and Arthur Burks, vol. 12 of *Charles Babbage Institute Reprint Series for the History of Computing* (Cambridge: MIT Press, 1987).

9. "Minutes of 1947 Patent Conference, Moore School of Electrical Engineering, University of Pennsylvania," originally unpublished (1947), in *Annals of the History of Computing* 7 (1985): 100–16.

10. J. Presper Eckert, "Disclosure of Magnetic Calculating Machine," originally unpublished (1944), in *A History of Computing in the Twentieth Century*, ed. Nicholas Metropolis, Jack Howlett, and Gian-Carlo Rota, lecture series, June 10–15, 1976, at International Research Conference on the History of Computing, Los Alamos Scientific Laboratory, Los Alamos, New Mexico (New York: Academic Press, 1980), pp. 537–39.

11. Arthur W. Burks, "From ENIAC to the Stored Program Computer: Two Revolutions in Computers," lecture, June 1976, in *A History of Computing in the Twentieth Century*.

12. Herman H. Goldstine, *The Computer from Pascal to von Neumann* (Princeton: Princeton University Press, 1972).

13. J. Presper Eckert, "The ENIAC," lecture, June 1976, in *A History of Computing in the Twentieth Century.*

14. Warren S. McCulloch and Walter H. Pitts, "A Logical Calculus of the Ideas Immanent in Nervous Activity," *Bulletin of Mathematical Biophysics* 5 (1943): 115–33.

15. John W. Mauchly, "The ENIAC," lecture, June 1976, in *A History of Computing in the Twentieth Century.*

16. J. Presper Eckert and John W. Mauchly, "Automatic High-Speed Computing, A Progress Report on the EDVAC," unpublished, September 30, 1945.

17. Donald E. Knuth, "Von Neumann's First Computer Program," *Computing Surveys* 2, no. 4 (1970): 247–60.

18. George W. Patterson, ed., *Theory and Techniques for the Design of Electronic Digital Computers*, lecture series, July 8 to August 31, 1946, distributed by Moore School of Electrical Engineering, University of Pennsylvania, 1947–1948, reprinted in *The Moore School Lectures: Theory and Techniques for the Design of Electronic Digital Computers* (as adapted from the Moore School distribution of 1947–1948 and from notes taken by Frank M. Verzuh), vol. 9 of *Charles Babbage Institute Reprint Series for the History of Computing*, ed. Martin Campbell-Kelly and Michael R. Williams (Cambridge: MIT Press, 1985); John W. Mauchly, "The Use of Function Tables with Computing Machines," and "Code and Control II: Machine Design and Instruction Codes," lectures, July 12 and August 9, 1946, Moore School of Electrical Engineering, University of Pennsylvania, in *The Moore School Lectures*, vol. 9 of *Charles Babbage Institute Reprint Series*; J. Presper Eckert, "A Preview of a Digital Computing Machine," lecture, July 15, 1946, Moore School of Electrical Engineering, University of Pennsylvania, in *The Moore School Lectures*, vol. 9 of *Charles Babbage Institute Reprint Series.*

19. ENIAC trial records, Decision Finding 6.

20. Ibid., Decision Finding 10.

21. Ibid., Decision Finding 11.

22. Ibid., Decision Finding 13.

23. ENIAC trial records, Plaintiff's Exhibit PX 822; Plaintiff's Exhibit PX 870.

24. ENIAC trial records, Defendant's Exhibit DX 3361.

25. ENIAC trial records, Decision Finding 12.

26. Ibid., Decision Finding 15.

27. Ibid., Decision Finding 23.

28. John V. Atanasoff, "Advent of Electronic Digital Computing," *Annals of the History of Computing* 6 (1984): 229–82.

29. ENIAC trial records, transcript p. 12213.

30. Ibid., transcript pp. 17493 and 17611.

31. Ibid., transcript pp. 17612–14.

32. ENIAC trial records, Mauchly deposition p. 94.

33. John V. Atanasoff, "Advent of Electronic Digital Computing."

34. John V. Atanasoff, "Computing Machine for the Solution of Large Systems of Linear Algebraic Equations."

35. ENIAC trial records, transcript pp. 2848–57.

36. ENIAC trial records, Decision Finding 14.

37. J. Presper Eckert, "A Survey of Digital Computer Memory Systems," *Proceedings of the Institute of Radio Engineers* 41 (1953): 1393–406.

38. S. H. Lavington, "Computer Development at Manchester University," lecture, June 1976, in *A History of Computing in the Twentieth Century.*

39. Arthur W. Burks, Herman H. Goldstine, and John von Neumann, *Preliminary Discussion of the Logical Design of an Electronic Computing Instrument* (Princeton: Institute for Advanced Study, 1946), reprinted in *Papers of John von Neumann on Computing and Computer Theory.*

CHAPTER 6. BREAKING INTO PRINT

1. John V. Atanasoff, "Computing Machine for the Solution of Large Systems of Linear Algebraic Equations," originally unpublished (1940), in *The Origins of Digital Computers: Selected Papers*, ed. Brian Randell (Berlin: Springer-Verlag, 1973).

2. John W. Mauchly, "The Use of High Speed Vacuum Tube Devices for Calculating," originally unpublished (1942), in *The Origins of Digital Computers.*

3. Sperry Univac, "Who Would Have Thought the Father of Goliath Would Be Introducing David?" advertisement, *Wall Street Journal*, June 5, 1979, 24–25.

4. Alice R. Burks and Arthur W. Burks, *The First Electronic Computer: The Atanasoff Story* (Ann Arbor: University of Michigan Press, 1988).

5. Arthur W. Burks and Alice R. Burks, "The ENIAC: First General-Purpose Electronic Computer," *Annals of the History of Computing* 3 (1981): 310–99. With comments by John V. Atanasoff, J. G. Brainerd, J. Presper Eckert and Kathleen R. Mauchly, Brian Randell, and Konrad Zuse, together with the authors' responses.

6. Kathleen R. Mauchly, "John Mauchly's Early Years," *Annals of the History of Computing* 6 (1984): 116–38.

7. John W. Mauchly, "Mauchly: Unpublished Remarks," foreword by Hentry Tropp and afterword by Arthur W. Burks and Alice R. Burks, *Annals of the History of Computing* 4 (1982): 245–56.

8. John V. Atanasoff, "Advent of Electronic Digital Computing," *Annals of the History of Computing* 6 (1984): 229–82.

9. Marshall Ledger, "The E.N.I.A.C.'s Muddled History," *University of Pennsylvania Gazette* (November 1982): 29–34.

CHAPTER 7. OTHER VOICES

1. Nancy Stern, *From ENIAC to UNIVAC: An Appraisal of the Eckert-Mauchly Computers* (Bedford, Mass.: Digital Press, 1981).

2. ENIAC trial records. Pretrial depositions, affidavits, complaints, transcripts, exhibits, briefs, and decision. *Honeywell, Inc. v. Sperry Rand Corp. et al.*, Decision Finding 3.

3. Ibid., Decision Finding 4.

4. ENIAC trial records, Transcript pp. 12590–95.

5. ENIAC trial records, Finding 12.

6. Brian Randell, ed., *The Origins of Digital Computers: Selected Papers* (Berlin: Springer-Verlag, 1973).

7. Paul E. Ceruzzi, review of *From ENIAC to UNIVAC*, by Nancy Stern, *Science* 214 (1981): 430–31.

8. Henry S. Tropp, review of *From ENIAC to UNIVAC*, by Nancy Stern, *Annals of the History of Computing* 3 (1981): 302.

9. I. Bernard Cohen, review of *From ENIAC to UNIVAC*, by Nancy Stern, *Annals of the History of Computing* 5 (1983): 79–81.

10. Frank Wagner, "Comment: Who 'Invented' the First Electronic Computer?" *Annals of the History of Computing* 2 (1980): 375–76.

11. Nancy Stern, "From ENIAC to UNIVAC: A Case Study in the History of Technology" (Ph.D. Diss., State University of New York at Stony Brook [Ann Arbor, Mich.: University Microfilms thesis number 78–21,846; 1978]); Nancy Stern, "John William Mauchly: 1907–1980," *Annals of the History of Computing* 2 (1980): 100–103.

12. "The Computer at Age 25," editorial, *New York Times*, August 9, 1971.

13. William D. Smith, "Critics Mark 25th Year of the Computer," *New York Times*, August 4, 1971, 43, 49.

14. John Costello, "The Little Known Creators of the Computer," *Nation's Business* (December 1971): 56–62.

15. Richard A. McLaughlin, "ENIAC in Court: What Might Have Happened," *Datamation* 19, no. 6 (1973): 119, 122.

16. W. David Gardner, "How the Judge Looked at the IBM-Sperry Rand ENIAC Pact," *Datamation* 20, no. 1 (1974): 78–80.

17. Pamela L. Eblen, "Verdicts: Who Really Invented the Computer?" *ICP Data Processing Management* (autumn 1984): 14, 16.

18. W. David Gardner, "Will the Inventor of the First Digital Computer Please Stand Up?" *Datamation* 20, no. 2 (1974): 84, 88–90.

19. ENIAC trial records, Finding 1.

20. ENIAC trial records, Plaintiff's Exhibit PX 4258.

21. Gerald W. Brock, *The U.S. Computer Industry* (Cambridge, Mass.: Ballinger Publishing Co., 1975).

22. David J. Kuck, *The Structure of Computers and Computations*, vol. 1 (New York: John Wiley and Sons, 1978).

23. Becky Barna, "He Was an Idea Sparker," *Datamation* 26, no. 3 (1980): 55.

24. Anne Dewees, "Mauchly Was His Own Man," *Datamation* 26, no. 3 (1980): 56, 58.

25. Anne Dewees, "Interview with John Mauchly," *Datamation* 26, no. 3 (1980): 58, 60.

26. J. Presper Eckert, "A Man Not Bound by Tradition," *Datamation* 26, no. 3 (1980): 62.

27. Linda F. Runyan, "A Master of Understatement," *Datamation* 26, no. 5 (1980): 84–85.

28. Alan J. Robinson, letter to the editor, *Datamation* 26, no. 6 (1980): 31.

29. W. David Gardner, "The Independent Inventor," *Datamation* 28, no. 9 (1982): 12–16, 20–22.

30. Patrick Bedard, "The Midnight Ride of John Vincent Atanasoff," *Car and Driver* (June 1984): 192.

31. Alice R. Burks and Arthur W. Burks, *The First Electronic Computer: The Atanasoff Story* (Ann Arbor: University of Michigan Press, 1988).

32. Virginia C. Walker, "To Honor Our Beginnings—ACM '80," *Annals of the History of Computing* 3 (1981): 183–85.

33. James L. Rogers, "Atanasoff Speaks at Digital Computer Museum," *Annals of the History of Computing* 3 (1981): 185–86.

34. Brian Randell, *The Origins of Digital Computers.*

35. Herman H. Goldstine and Adele Goldstine, "The Electronic Numerical Integrator and Computer (ENIAC)," M.T.A.C. 2, no. 15 (1946): 97–110, reprinted in *The Origins of Digital Computers.*

36. John von Neumann, "First Draft of a Report on the EDVAC," distributed by Moore School of Electrical Engineering, University of Pennsylvania, June 1945, reprinted in Nancy Stern, *From ENIAC to UNIVAC*, pp. 177–246; Arthur W. Burks, Herman H. Goldstine, and John von Neumann, *Preliminary Discussion of the Logical Design of an Electronic Computing Instrument* (Princeton: Institute for Advanced Study, 1946).

37. John W. Mauchly, "Preparation of Problems for EDVAC-type Machines," lecture in *Proceedings of a Symposium on Large Scale Digital Calculating Machinery, January 7–10, 1947*, in *Annals of the Computation Laboratory of Harvard University* 16 (1948): 203–207 (Cambridge: Harvard University Press), reprinted in *The Origins of Digital Computers.*

38. Brian Randell, "An Annotated Bibliography on the Origins of Computers," *Annals of the History of Computing* 1 (1979): 101–207.

39. Nicholas Metropolis, Jack Howlett, and Gian-Carlo Rota, ed., *A History of Computing in the Twentieth Century*, lecture series, June 10–15, 1976, at International Research Conference on the History of Computing, Los Alamos Scientific Laboratory, Los Alamos, New Mexico (New York: Academic Press, 1980).

40. J. Presper Eckert, "The ENIAC," lecture, June 1976, in *A History of Computing in the Twentieth Century.*

41. John W. Mauchly, "The ENIAC," lecture, June 1976, in *A History of Computing in the Twentieth Century.*

42. Arthur W. Burks, "From ENIAC to the Stored Program Computer: Two Revolutions in Computers," lecture, June 1976, in *A History of Computing in the Twentieth Century.*

43. ENIAC trial records. Decision, *Honeywell, Inc. v. Sperry Rand Corp. et al., U.S. Patent Quarterly* 180: 673–773.

44. Nancy Stern, "Who Invented the First Electronic Digital Computer?" *Abacus* 1, no. 1 (1983): 7–15.

45. G. Michael Vose, review of *The First Electronic Computer,* by Alice R. Burks and Arthur W. Burks, *Byte* (September 1988): 51–52, 54.

CHAPTER 8. LINES IN THE SAND

1. John W. Mauchly, "Mauchly: Unpublished Remarks," foreword by Henry Tropp and afterword by Arthur W. Burks and Alice R. Burks, *Annals of the History of Computing* 4 (1982): 245–56; Kathleen R. Mauchly, "John Mauchly's Early Years," *Annals of the History of Computing* 6 (1984): 116–38; John V. Atanasoff, "Advent of Electronic Digital Computing," *Annals of the History of Computing* 6 (1984): 229–82.

2. "Who Invented the Electronic General-Purpose Digital Computer?" Condensa-

tions of Kathleen R. Mauchly, "John Mauchly's Early Years," and of Atanasoff, "Advent of Electronic Digital Computing," *Computerworld* (July 9, 1984): ID1–ID16.

3. Joel Shurkin, *Engines of the Mind: A History of the Computer* (New York: W. W. Norton and Co., 1984).

4. "Annals News," *Communications of the ACM* 27, no. 7 (1984): 738.

5. Marshall Ledger, "The Case of the E.N.I.A.C," *University of Pennsylvania Gazette* (October 1982): 30–35.

6. Nancy Stern, review of *Engines of the Mind*, by Joel Shurkin, *Annals of the History of Computing* 6 (1984): 414–16.

7. Fred Hapgood, review of *Engines of the Mind*, by Joel Shurkin, *Science 84* 5, no. 1 (1984): 94, 98.

8. "The Mauchly Legacy: A Revolution Begun in Pfahler Hall," *Ursinus College Bulletin* (March 1985): 4–8.

9. Allan R. Mackintosh, letter to the editor, *Physics Today* (April 1984): 11.

10. Allan R. Mackintosh, "The First Electronic Computer," *Physics Today* (March 1987): 25–32.

11. Evan S. Snyder, letter to the editor, *Physics Today* (December 1987): 13, 15.

12. Philip H. Dorn, review of "Who Invented the First Electronic Digital Computer?" by Nancy Stern, *Annals of the History of Computing* 6 (1984): 186–87.

13. William J. Broad, "Who Should Get the Glory for Inventing the Computer?" *New York Times*, March 22, 1983, 17–18.

14. Simon J. Langlais, "ENIAC: Revisiting the Legend," *American History Illustrated* (October 1985): 48–49.

15. Philip Elmer-DeWitt, "A Birthday Party for ENIAC," *Time*, February 24, 1986, 63.

16. Elsie Atanasoff Whistler, letter to the editor, *Time*, March 24, 1986, 9–10.

17. Eric A. Weiss, review of *Misunderstanding Media*, by Brian Winston, *Annals of the History of Computing* 9 (1987): 105–106.

18. Pamela L. Eblen, "Verdicts: Who Really Invented the Computer?" *ICP Data Processing Management* (autumn 1984): 14, 16.

19. J. Presper Eckert, Keynote Address, ENIAC's 40th Anniversary, February 13, 1986, Computer Museum, Boston, Massachusetts, in *Computer Museum Report* (summer 1986): 3–6.

20. *Celebrating the Computer Age*, a series of articles, *Computerworld* (November 3, 1986): 1–191.

21. J. Presper Eckert, "A Survey of Digital Computer Memory Systems," *Proceedings of the Institute of Radio Engineers* 41 (1953): 1393–406.

22. Michael R. Williams, *A History of Computing Technology* (Englewood Cliffs, N.J.: Prentice-Hall, 1985).

23. Alice R. Burks, "The Story of the First Electronic Computer," *Cobblestone* 5, no. 6 (1984): 20–22; Alice R. Burks, "The ENIAC," *Cobblestone* 5, no. 6 (1984): 23.

24. Charles J. Bashe, "The SSEC in Historical Perspective," *Annals of the History of Computing* 4 (1982): 296–312.

25. William F Aspray, "International Diffusion of Computer Technology, 1945–1955," *Annals of the History of Computing* 8 (1986): 351–60.

26. William F Aspray, ed. and contributor, *Computing Before Computers* (Ames: Iowa State University Press, 1990).

27. Arthur W. Burks and Alice R. Burks, "The ENIAC: First General-Purpose Electronic Computer," *Annals of the History of Computing* 3 (1981): 310–99, comment by Brian Randell.

28. Fred Gruenberger, "What's in a Name?" *Datamation* 25, no. 5 (1979): 231.

29. Alice R. Burks and Arthur W. Burks, *The First Electronic Computer: The Atanasoff Story* (Ann Arbor: University of Michigan Press, 1988).

CHAPTER 9. THE MATTER OF VON NEUMANN

1. J. Presper Eckert, "Disclosure of Magnetic Calculating Machine," originally unpublished (1944), in *A History of Computing in the Twentieth Century*, lecture series, June 10–15, 1976, at International Research Conference on the History of Computing, Los Alamos Scientific Laboratory, Los Alamos, New Mexico (New York: Academic Press, 1980), pp. 537–39.

2. John von Neumann, "First Draft of a Report on the EDVAC," distributed by Moore School of Electrical Engineering, University of Pennsylvania, June 1945, reprinted in Nancy Stern, *From ENIAC to UNIVAC: An Appraisal of the Eckert-Mauchly Computers* (Bedford, Mass.: Digital Press, 1981), pp. 177–246.

3. Michael R. Williams, *A History of Computing Technology* (Englewood Cliffs, N.J.: Prentice-Hall, 1985).

4. Harry D. Huskey, "Harry D. Huskey: The Early Days," *Annals of the History of Computing* 13 (1991): 290–306.

5. Stanley Gill, "Stored Program Concept," in *Encyclopedia of Computer Science*, 3d ed., ed. Anthony Ralston and Edwin D. Reilly (New York: Van Rostrand Reinhold, 1993), pp. 1299–300.

6. Robert F. Rosin, "Von Neumann Machine," in *Encyclopedia of Computer Science*, 3d ed., pp.1425–26.

7. Nicholas Metropolis and J. Worlton, "A Trilogy on Errors in the History of Computing," *Annals of the History of Computing* 2 (1980): 49–59.

8. Maurice V. Wilkes, "Computers Then and Now: Turing Lecture of 1967," *Journal of the Association for Computing Machinery* 15 (1968): 1–7.

9. J. Presper Eckert and John W. Mauchly, "Automatic High-Speed Computing, A Progress Report on the EDVAC," unpublished, September 30, 1945.

10. William F. Aspray, "History of the Stored-Program Concept," *Annals of the History of Computting* 4 (1982): 358–61.

11. Paul E. Ceruzzi, *Reckoners: The Prehistory of the Digital Computer from Relays to the Stored Program Concept, 1935–1945* (Westport, Conn.: Greenwood Press, 1983).

12. Paul E. Ceruzzi, "The von Neumann Architecture," in *Encyclopedia of Computer Science*, 3d ed., pp. 447–48.

13. Nancy Stern, *From ENIAC to UNIVAC: An Appraisal of the Eckert-Mauchly Computers* (Bedford, Mass.: Digital Press, 1981).

14. John von Neumann, "First Draft of a Report on the EDVAC."

15. William F Aspray, *John Von Neumann and the Origins of Modern Computing* (Cambridge: MIT Press,1990).

16. Herman H. Goldstine and John von Neumann, *Planning and Coding of Problems for an Electronic Computing Instrument*, vols. 1–3 (Princeton: Institute for Advanced Study, 1947–1948), reprinted in *Papers of John von Neumann on Computing and Computer Theory*, vol. 12 of *Charles Babbage Institute Reprint Series for the History of Computing* (Cambridge: MIT Press, 1987).

17. Arthur W. Burks, Herman H. Goldstine, and John von Neumann, *Preliminary Discussion of the Logical Design of an Electronic Computing Instrument* (Princeton: Institute for Advanced Study, 1946).

18. William F. Aspray, ed. and contributor, *Computing Before Computers* (Ames: Iowa State University Press, 1990).

19. Herman H. Goldstine, *The Computer from Pascal to von Neumann* (Princeton: Princeton University Press, 1972).

20. J. Presper Eckert, "The ENIAC," lecture, June 1946, in *A History of Computing in the Twentieth Century*.

21. Allan G. Bromley, "What Defines a 'General-Purpose' Computer?" *Annals of the History of Computing* 5 (1983): 303–305.

22. Goldstine and von Neumann, *Planning and Coding of Problems for an Electronic Computing Instrument*, vols. 1–3.

23. Arthur W. Burks, "The Logic of Programming Electronic Digital Computers," *Industrial Mathematics* 1 (1950): 36–52.

24. Donald E. Knuth and Luis Trabb Pardo, "The Early Development of Programming Languages," lecture, June 1976, in *A History of Computing in the Twentieth Century*.

25. Maurice V. Wilkes, David J. Wheeler, and Stanley Gill, *The Preparation of Programs for an Electronic Digital Computer* (Reading, Mass.: Addison-Wesley Publishing Co., 1951).

26. John Mauchly, "Preparation of Problems for EDVAC-type Machines," lecture, in *Annals of the Computation Laboratory of Harvard University* 19 (1948): 203–207 (Cambridge: Harvard University Press), reprinted in *The Origins of Digital Computers: Selected Papers* (Berlin:Springer-Verlag, 1973).

27. "Minutes of 1947 Patent Conference, Moore School of Electrical Engineering, University of Pennsylvania," originally unpublished (1947), in *Annals of the History of Computing* 7 (1985): 100–16.

CHAPTER 10. A HAPPY CONVERGENCE

1. Clark R. Mollenhoff, *Atanasoff: Forgotten Father of the Computer* (Ames: Iowa State University Press, 1988).

2. Alice R. Burks and Arthur W. Burks, *The First Electronic Computer: The Atanasoff Story* (Ann Arbor: University of Michigan Press, 1988).

3. Robert D. McFadden, "Clark R. Mollenhoff, Pulitzer Winner, Dies at 69," *New York Times*, March 4, 1991, D9.

4. ENIAC trial records. Pretrial depositions, affidavits, complaints, transcripts, exhibits, briefs, and decision. *Honeywell, Inc. v. Sperry Rand Corp. et al.*

5. R. K. Richards, *Electrical Digital Systems* (New York: John Wiley and Sons, 1966).

6. John V. Atanasoff, "Advent of Electronic Digital Computing," *Annals of the History of Computing* 6 (1984): 229–82.

7. Regenerative Memory trial records. Pretrial depositions, transcript, etc. *Sperry Rand Corp. v. Control Data Corp.*, Lura Atanasoff deposition, Legvold deposition.

8. J. Presper Eckert, "A Survey of Digital Computer Memory Systems," *Proceedings of the Institute of Radio Engineers* 41 (1953): 1393–406.

9. ENIAC trial records, Decision Finding 0.

10. John W. Mauchly, "Mauchly: Unpublished Remarks," foreword by Henry Tropp and afterword by Arthur W. Burks and Alice R. Burks, *Annals of the History of Computing* 4 (1982): 245–56.

11. Allan R. Mackintosh, "The First Electronic Computer," *Physics Today* (March 1987): 25–32.

12. Kathleen R. Mauchly, "John Mauchly's Early Years," *Annals of the History of Computing* 6 (1984): 116–38.

13. Allan R. Mackintosh, "Dr. Atanasoff's Computer," *Scientific American* 259, no. 2 (1988): 90–96.

14. Alice R. Burks and Arthur W. Burks, "Working in the History of Computers: A Husband-Wife Memoir," *Bosei* (in Japanese) 27, no. 2 (February 1996): 56–63 and no. 3 (March 1996): 44–51.

15. Alice R. Burks and Arthur W. Burks, "Who Invented the Computer? A Memoir of the 1940s," *Michigan Quarterly Review* 36, no. 2 (1997): 222–44.

16. Allan R. Mackintosh, review of *The First Electronic Computer*, by Alice R. Burks and Arthur W. Burks, *Annals of the History of Computing* 10 (1988): 222–23.

17. Saul Rosen, "The Atanasoff Story—Comment on Book Review," *Annals of the History of Computing* 11 (1989): 144–45.

18. Alice R. Burks and Arthur W. Burks, "The Atanasoff Story—A Response," *Annals of the History of Computing* 12 (1990): 68–70.

19. G. Michael Vose, review of *The First Electronic Computer*, by Alice R. Burks and Arthur W. Burks, *Byte* (September 1988): 51–52, 54.

20. Arthur W. Burks, letter to the editor, *Byte* (December 1988): 24.

21. John W. Mauchly Jr., letter to the editor, *Byte* (July 1989): 34, 36.

22. Alice R. Burks and Arthur W. Burks, letter to the editor, *Byte* (December 1989): 36, 38.

23. George Wright, letter to the editor, *Byte* (October 1989): 32; Donald Michie, letter to the editor, *Byte* (January 1990): 36.

24. Jane Pejsa, review of *The First Electronic Computer*, by Alice R. Burks and Arthur W. Burks, *Minneapolis Star Tribune*, July 2, 1989.

25. Lee Loevinger, review of *The First Electronic Computer*, by Alice R. Burks and Arthur W. Burks, and of *Atanasoff*, by Clark R. Mollenhoff, *Jurimetrics Journal* 29, no. 3 (1989): 359–64.

26. Paul E. Ceruzzi, review of *The First Electronic Computer*, by Alice R. Burks and Arthur W. Burks, *Science* 240 (1988): 931–32; Martin Campbell-Kelly, review of *The First Electronic Computer*, by Alice R. Burks and Arthur W. Burks, *ISIS* 79:4:299 (1988): 715–16.

27. Eric A. Weiss, review of *The First Electronic Computer*, by Alice R. Burks and Arthur W. Burks, *Computing Reviews* (April 1989): 199–200.

28. Eric A. Weiss, review of *Atanasoff*, by Clark R. Mollenhoff, and of *The First Electronic Computer*, by Alice R. Burks and Arthur W. Burks, *American Scientist* (July–August 1989): 401.

29. D. E. Ross, review of *Atanasoff*, by Clark R. Mollenhoff, *Computing Reviews* (April 1989): 198–99.

30. A. A. Mullin, review of *Atanasoff*, by Clark R. Mollenhoff, *Mathematical Reviews* 14 (May 1990): 14.

CHAPTER 11. THE PUBLIC EYE

1. *News of the Information Exhibition, A Quarterly Bulletin* 2, no. 2 (Washington, D.C.: Smithsonian Institution, National Museum of American History, 1988).

2. *Information Age: People, Information, & Technology* (Washington, D.C.: Smithsonian Institution, National Museum of American History, 1989).

3. Walter M. Carlson, "Why AFIPS Invested in History," *Annals of the History of Computing* 8 (1986): 270–74.

4. Norm Brewer, "Iowan's Role in Computer Birth Debated," *Des Moines Register*, July 2, 1989, 1A.

5. Norm Brewer, "Smith, Grassley Rise to Defend Iowa Inventor, Warn Smithsonian," *Des Moines Register*, July 4, 1989.

6. Norm Brewer, "Neal Smith Suggests Smithsonian Swayed by Cash in Computer Display," *Des Moines Register*, July 11, 1989, 6A.

7. "Iowa Rep Asks Smithsonian to Give Credit Where it is Due," *USA Today*, July 17, 1989, 4A.

8. "Smithsonian Ducks Trouble in Citing Computer Wizards," *Washington Times*, July 17, 1989, A6.

9. Charles Grassley, "Atanasoff: The Father of the Computer," *Congressional Record*, July 25, 1989, S 8671.

10. Norm Brewer, "Grassley Threatens to Seek Bill to Credit Inventor of Computer," *Des Moines Register*, July 27, 1989.

11. Jack Anderson and Dale Van Atta, "Who Really was Father of Computer?" *Independence Examiner*, August 11, 1989.

12. Stan Augarten, *Bit by Bit: An Illustrated History of Computers* (New York: Ticknor and Fields, 1984); Michael R. Williams, *A History of Computing Technology* (Englewood Cliffs, N.J.: Pretice-Hall, 1985).

13. Norm Brewer, "Smithsonian Exhibit to Recognize 'Father' of Modern Computer," *The Californian*, November 15, 1989, 1B, 7B.

14. Hank Burchard, "Information Overloaded," *Washington Post*, May 11, 1990.

15. "Smithsonian Opens Exhibition on the Information Age," *Charles Babbage Institute Newsletter* 12, no. 3 (1990): 5.

16. Jerry Adler, "Communicating Bit by Bit," *Newsweek*, May 21, 1990, 74–75.

17. David Allison, "National Museum of American History, Smithsonian Institution," *Annals of the History of Computing* 13 (1991): 351.

18. Kim Masters, "Smithsonian Officials Call Budget Shortfall 'Dispiriting, Damaging,'" *Washington Post*, April 22, 1990.

19. Jacqueline Trescott, "Smithsonian Names New Secretary," *Washington Post*, May 26, 1994.

20. Paul Mann, "Unisys Admits Bribery and Fraud, Will Pay Record $190 Million Fine," *Aviation Week and Space Technology* (September 16, 1991): 24–25.

21. WGBH Boston, "Public Television Sets Sail for the Future," advertisement, *Wall Street Journal*, September 11, 1989, B16.

22. John Hillkirk, "Year Saw Birth of Copier, Computer, TV," *USA Today*, December 1, 1989, cover, 1B–2B.

23. Kirk Nicewonger, "Tune in Tonight," *United Features Syndicate*, May 10, 1996.

24. ENIAC trial records. Pretrial depositions, affidavits, complaints, transcripts, exhibits, briefs, and decision. *Honeywell, Inc. v. Sperry Rand Corp. et al.,* Plaintiff's Exhibit PX 479.

25. Paul E. Ceruzzi, "Electionic Calculators," in *Computing Before Computers* ed. William F. Aspray (Ames: Iowa State University Press, 1990).

26. Jon Palfreman, letter to the editor, *Ames Daily Tribune*, June 2, 1992, A6.

27. ENIAC trial records, Decision Finding 3.

28. S. H. Lavington, *Early British Computers: The Story of Vintage Computers and the People Who Built Them* (Manchester, Eng.: Manchester University Press, 1980).

CHAPTER 12. AS IT HAPPENED

1. ENIAC trial records. Pretrial depositions, affidavits, complaints, transcripts, exhibits, briefs, and decision. *Honeywell, Inc. v. Sperry Rand Corp. et al.*

2. John V. Atanasoff, "Advent of Electronic Digital Computing," *Annals of the History of Computing* 6 (1984): 229–82.

3. ENIAC trial records, Goldstine deposition p. 872.

4. John von Neumann, "First Draft of a report on the EDVAC," distributed by Moore School of Electrical Engineering, University of Pennsylvania, June 1945, reprinted in Nancy Stern, *From ENIAC to UNIVAC: An Appaisal of the Eckert-Mauchly Computers* (Bedford, Mass.: Digital Press, 1981), pp. 177–246.

5. "Minutes of 1947 Patent Conference, Moore School of Electrical Engineering, University of Pennsylvania," originally unpublished (1947), in *Annals of the History of Computing* 7 (1985): 100–16.

6. Regenerative Memory trial records. Pretrial depositions, transcript, etc. *Sperry Rand Corp. v. Control Data Corp.*

7. *Celebrating the Computer Age*, a series of articles, *Computerworld* (November 3, 1986): 1–191.

8. John V. Atanasoff, "Computing Machine for the Solution of Large Systems of Linear Algebraic Equations," originally unpublished (1940), in *The Origins of Digital Computers: Selected Papers*, ed. Brian Randell (Berlin: Springer-Verlag, 1973).

9. J. Presper Eckert, "A Survey of Digital Computer Memory Systems," *Proceedings of the Institute of Radio Engineers* 41 (1953): 1393–406.

10. Clark R. Mollenhoff, *Atanasoff: Forgotten Father of the Computer* (Ames: Iowa State University Press, 1988).

11. J. Presper Eckert and John W. Mauchly, "Automatic High-Speed Computing, A Progress Report on the EDVAC," unpublished, September 30, 1945.

12. John W. Mauchly, "The Use of Function Tables with Computing Machines," and "Control and Control II: Machine Design and Instruction Codes," lectures, July 12 and

August 9, 1946, Moore School of Electrical Engineering, University of Pnnsylvania, in *The Moore School Lectures,* vol. 9 of *Charles Babbage Institute Reprint Series* (Cambridge: MIT Press, 1985); Mauchly, "Preparation of Problems for EDVAC-type Machines," lecture, in *Annals of the Computation Laboratory of Harvard University* 19 (1948): 203–207 (Cambridge: Harvard University Press), reprinted in *The Origins of Digital Computers.*

13. Arthur W. Burks, Herman H. Goldstine, and John von Neumann, *Preliminary Discussion of the Logical Design of an Electronic Computing Instrument* (Princeton: Institute for Advanced Study, 1946).

14. J. Presper Eckert, "The ENIAC," lecture, June 1946, in *A History of Computing in the Twentieth Century,* lecture series, June 10–15, 1976, at International Research Conference on the History of Computing, Los Alamos Scientific Laboratory, Los Alamos, New Mexico (New York: Academic Press, 1980).

15. Herman H. Goldstine, *The Computer from Pascal to von Neumann,* (Princeton: Princeton University Press, 1972).

16. Michael R. Williams, *A History of Computing Technology* (Englewood Cliffs, N.J.: Prentice-Hall, 1985).

17. Mary Croarken, "The Beginnings of the Manchester Computer Phenomenon: People and Influences," *Annals of the History of Computing* 15 (1993): 9–16.

18. S. H. Lavington, *Early British Computers: The Story of Vintage Computers and the People Who Built Them* (Manchester, Eng.: Manchester University Press, 1980).

CHAPTER 13. WRAP-UP

1. ENIAC trial records. Pretrial depositions, affidavits, complaints, transcripts, exhibits, briefs, and decision. *Honeywell, Inc. v. Sperry Rand Corp. et al.*

2. John V. Atanasoff, "Advent of Electronic Digital Computing," *Annals of the History of Computing* 6 (1984): 229–82

3. Regenerative Memory trial records. Pretrial depositions, transcript, etc. *Sperry Rand Corp. v. Control Data Corp.*

4. John V. Atanasoff, "Computing Machine for the Solution of Large Systems of Linear Algebraic Equations," originally unpublished (1940), in *The Origins of Digital Computers: Selected Papers,* ed. Brian Randell (Berlin: Springer-Verlag, 1973).

5. W. David Gardner, "How the Judge Looked at the IBM-Sperry Rand ENIAC Pact," *Datamation* 20, no. 1 (1974): 78–80; "Will the Inventor of the First Digital Computer Please Stand Up?" *Datamation* 20, no. 2 (1974): 84, 88–90; "The Independent Inventor," *Datamation* 28, no. 9 (1982): 12–16, 20–22.

6. Clark R. Mollenhoff, *Atanasoff: Forgotten Father of the Computer* (Ames: Iowa State University Press, 1988); Alice R. Burks and Arthur W. Burks, *The First Electronic Computer: The Atanasoff Story* (Ann Arbor: University of Michigan Press, 1988); Allan R. Mackintosh, "Dr. Atanasoff's Computer," *Scientific American* 259, no. 2 (1988): 90–96.

7. R. K. Richards, *Electrical Digital Systems* (New York: John Wiley and Sons, 1966).

8. Jean R. Berry, "Clifford Edward Berry, 1918–1963: His Role in Early Computers," *Annals of the History of Computing* 8 (1986): 361–69.

9. George L. Hamlin, "NSWC's J. V. Atanasoff: Recognition Comes Slowly to Computer's Inventor," *On the Surface: Naval Surface Warfare Center Newsletter* 7, no. 36 (1984): 6–9.

10. George L. Hamlin, "More Recognition for John Atanasoff," *On the Surface: Naval Surface Warfare Center Newsletter* 11, no. 12 (1988): 4–8.

11. "American Museums: Bossy Sponsors," *Economist* (April 30, 1994): 98.

12. John Leonard, "TV: The Mummy's Curse," *New York Review of Books* (May 28, 1998): 26–29.

13. James Ledbetter, *Made Possible By . . . : The Death of Public Broadcasting in the United States*. (London, New York: Verso, 1997).

14. William LaRue, "PBS Plans on Livelier Fall Schedule, *Ann Arbor News*, July 19, 1997, B4.

15. Marshall Ledger, "The Case of the E.N.I.A.C," *University of Pennsylvania Gazette* (October 1982): 30–35.

16. Scott McCartney, *ENIAC: The Triumphs and Tragedies of the World's First Computer* (New York: Walker and Company, 1999).

17. Pamela L. Eblen, "Verdicts: Who Really Invented the Computer?" *ICP Data Processing Management* (autumn 1984): 14, 16; *Celebrating the Computer Age*, a series of articles, *Computerworld* (November 3, 1986): 1–191.

18. Clark R. Mollenhoff, *Atanasoff*.

19. J. Presper Eckert, "The ENIAC," lecture, June 1946, in *A History of Computing in the Twentieth Century*, ed. Nicholas Metropolis, Jack Howlett, and Gian-Carlo Rota, lecture series, June 10–15, 1976, at International Research Conference on the History of Computing, Los Alamos Scientific Laboratory, Los Alamos, New Mexico (New York: Academic Press, 1980).

20. Nancy Stern, *From ENIAC to UNIVAC: An Appraisal of the Eckert-Mauchly Computers* (Bedford, Mass.: Digital Press, 1981).

21. ENIAC trial records.

22. John W. Mauchly, "The ENIAC," lecture, June 1946, in *A History of Computing in the Twentieth Century*.

23. Allan G. Bromley, "What Defines a 'General-Purpose' Computer?" *Annals of the History of Computing* 5 (1983): 303–305.

24. "As Simple as ABC: A Pioneer Computer is Duplicated," *National Geographic* (August 1998).

25. Jeffrey Young, "John Vincent Atanasoff: Father of the Computer?" *Forbes* (July 7, 1997): 335.

BIBLIOGRAPHY

Adler, Jerry. "Communicating Bit by Bit." *Newsweek*, May 21, 1990, 74–75.

Allison, David. 1991. "National Museum of American History, Smithsonian Institution." *Annals of the History of Computing* 13 (1991): 351.

"American Museums: Bossy Sponsors." *Economist* (April 30, 1994): 98.

Anderson, Jack, and Dale Van Atta. "Who Really Was Father of Computer?" *Independence Examiner*, August 11, 1989.

"Annals News." *Communications of the ACM* 27, no. 7 (1984): 738.

Aspray, William F. "History of the Stored-Program Concept." *Annals of the History of Computing* 4 (1982): 358–61.

———. "International Diffusion of Computer Technology, 1945–1955." *Annals of the History of Computing* 8 (1986): 351–60.

———. *John Von Neumann and the Origins of Modern Computing*. Cambridge: MIT Press, 1990.

———, ed. and contributor. *Computing Before Computers*. Ames: Iowa State University Press, 1990.

Aspray, William, and Arthur Burks, eds. *Papers of John von Neumann on Computing and Computer Theory*. In *Charles Babbage Institute Reprint Series for the History of Computing*, vol. 12. Cambridge: MIT Press, 1987.

"As Simple as ABC: A Pioneer Computer Is Duplicated." *National Geographic* (August 1998).

Atanasoff, John V. "Computing Machine for the Solution of Large Systems of Linear Algebraic Equations." Originally unpublished (1940). In *The Origins of Digital Computers: Selected Papers*, edited by Brian Randell, pp. 305–25. Berlin: Springer-Verlag, 1973.

———. "Advent of Electronic Digital Computing." *Annals of the History of Computing* 6 (1984): 229–82.

Augarten, Stan. *Bit by Bit: An Illustrated History of Computers*. New York: Ticknor and Fields 1984.

439

Barna, Becky. "He Was an Idea Sparker." *Datamation* 26, no. 3 (1980): 55.

Bashe, Charles J. "The SSEC in Historical Perspective." *Annals of the History of Computing* 4 (1982): 296–312.

Bedard, Patrick. "The Midnight Ride of John Vincent Atanasoff." *Car and Driver* (June 1984): 192.

Bell, Gwen. "The Director's Letter." *Digital Computer Museum Report: Collections* (January 1982): 1–3.

Berry, Jean R. "Clifford Edward Berry, 1918–1963: His Role in Early Computers." *Annals of the History of Computing* 8 (1986): 361–69.

Brewer, Norm. "Iowan's Role in Computer Birth Debated." *Des Moines Register*, July 2, 1989, 1A.

———. "Smith, Grassley Rise to Defend Iowa Inventor, Warn Smithsonian." *Des Moines Register*, July 4, 1989.

———. "Neal Smith Suggests Smithsonian Swayed by Cash in Computer Display." *Des Moines Register*, July 11, 1989, 6A.

———. "Grassley Threatens to Seek Bill to Credit Inventor of Computer." *Des Moines Register*, July 27, 1989.

———. "Smithsonian Exhibit to Recognize 'Father' of Modern Computer." *Californian*, November 15, 1989, 1B, 7B.

Broad, William J. "Who Should Get the Glory for Inventing the Computer?" *New York Times*, March 22, 1983, 17–18.

Brock, Gerald W. *The U.S. Computer Industry*. Cambridge, Mass.: Ballinger, 1975.

Bromley, Allan G. "What Defines a 'General-Purpose' Computer?" *Annals of the History of Computing* 5 (1983): 303–305.

Burchard, Hank. "Information Overloaded." *Washington Post*, May 11, 1990.

Burks, Alice R. "The Story of the First Electronic Computer." *Cobblestone* 5, no. 6 (1984): 20–22.

———. "The ENIAC." *Cobblestone* 5, no. 6 (1984): 23.

Burks, Alice R., and Arthur W. Burks. *The First Electronic Computer: The Atanasoff Story*. Ann Arbor: University of Michigan Press, 1988. Translated into Japanese by Hiroshi Tsukiyama. Tokyo: Kogyo Chosakai Publishing Co., Ltd., 1998.

———. Letter to the Editor. *Byte* (December 1989): 36, 38.

———. "The Atanasoff Story—A Response." *Annals of the History of Computing* 12 (1990): 68–70.

———. "Working in the History of Computers: A Husband-Wife Memoir." *Bosei* (in Japanese) 27, no. 2 (February 1996): 56–63, and 27, no. 3 (March 1996): 44–51.

———. "Who Invented the Computer? A Memoir of the 1940s." *Michigan Quarterly Review* 36, no. 2 (1997): 222–44.

Burks, Arthur W. "Super Electronic Computing Machine." *Electronic Industries* 5 (1946): 62–67, 96.

———. "Electronic Computing Circuits of the ENIAC." *Proceedings of the Institute of Radio Engineers* 35 (1947): 756–67. Reprinted, with comment by Paul Schneck, in *Proceedings* 85 (1997): 1169–82.

———. "The Logic of Programming Electronic Digital Computers." *Industrial Mathematics* 1 (1950): 36–52.

———. "From ENIAC to the Stored Program Computer: Two Revolutions in Computers." Lecture, International Research Conference on the History of Computing, Los Alamos Scientific Laboratory, Los Alamos, New Mexico (1976). In *A History of Computing in the Twentieth Century*, edited by Nicholas Metropolis, Jack Howlett, and Gian-Carlo Rota, pp. 311–44. New York: Academic Press, 1980.

———. Letter to the Editor. *Byte* (December 24, 1988).

Burks, Arthur W., and Alice R. Burks. "The ENIAC: First General-Purpose Electronic Computer." With comments by John V. Atanasoff, J. G. Brainerd, J. Presper Eckert and Kathleen R. Mauchly, Brian Randell, and Konrad Zuse, together with the authors' responses. *Annals of the History of Computing* 3 (1981): 310–99.

———. Letter to the Editor. *Ann Arbor News*, May 13, 1992. Reproduced in *Ames Daily Tribune*, May 18, 1992.

Burks, Arthur W., Herman H Goldstine, and John von Neumann. *Preliminary Discussion of the Logical Design of an Electronic Computing Instrument*. Princeton: Institute for Advanced Study, 1946. Reprinted *in Papers of John von Neumann on Computing and Computer Theory*, in *Charles Babbage Institute Reprint Series for the History of Computing*, vol. 12, edited by William Aspray and Arthur Burks, pp. 97–142. Cambridge: MIT Press, 1987.

Campbell-Kelly, Martin. Review of *The First Electronic Computer: The Atanasoff Story*, by Alice R. Burks and Arthur W. Burks. *ISIS* 79, no. 4 (1988): 715–16.

Campbell-Kelly, Martin, and Michael R. Williams, eds. *The Moore School Lectures: Theory and Techniques for the Design of Electronic Digital Computers*. Lecture series, July 8 to August 31, 1946, adapted from the Moore School distribution of 1947–1948, edited by George W. Patterson, and from lecture notes taken by Frank M. Verzuh. In *Charles Babbage Institute Reprint Series for the History of Computing*, vol. 9. Cambridge: MIT Press, 1985.

Carlson, Walter M. "Why AFIPS Invested in History." *Annals of the History of Computing* 8 (1986): 270–74.

"Celebrating the Computer Age." A series of articles. *Computerworld* (November 3, 1986): 1–191.

Ceruzzi, Paul E. Review of *From ENIAC to UNIVAC: An Appraisal of the Eckert-Mauchly Computers*, by Nancy Stern. *Science* 214 (1981): 430–31.

———. *Reckoners: The Prehistory of the Digital Computer from Relays to the Stored Program Concept*, 1935–1945. Westport, Conn.: Greenwood Press, 1983.

———. Review of *The First Electronic Computer: The Atanasoff Story*, by Alice R. Burks and Arthur W. Burks. *Science* 240 (1988): 931–32.

———. "Electronic Calculators." In *Computing before Computers*, edited by William F. Aspray, 223–49. Ames: Iowa State University Press, 1990.

———. "The von Neumann Architecture." In *Encyclopedia of Computer Science*, 3d ed., edited by Anthony Ralston and Edwin D. Reilly, pp. 447–48. New York: Van Rostrand Reinhold, 1993.

Cohen, I. Bernard. Review of *From ENIAC to UNIVAC: An Appraisal of the Eckert-Mauchly Computers*, by Nancy Stern. *Annals of the History of Computing* 5 (1983): 79–81.

"The Computer at Age 25." Editorial. *New York Times*, August 9, 1971.

Costello, John. "The Little Known Creators of the Computer." *Nation's Business* (December 1971): 56–62.

Croarken, Mary. "The Beginnings of the Manchester Computer Phenomenon: People and Influences." *Annals of the History of Computing* 15 (1993): 9–16.

Dewees, Anne. "Mauchly Was His Own Man." *Datamation* 26, no. 3 (1980): 56, 58.

———. "Interview with John Mauchly." *Datamation* 26, no. 3 (1980): 58, 60.

Dorn, Philip H. Review of "Who Invented the First Electronic Digital Computer?" by Nancy Stern. *Annals of the History of Computing* 6 (1984): 186–87.

Eblen, Pamela L. "Verdicts: Who Really Invented the Computer?" *ICP Data Processing Management* (autumn 1984): 14, 16.

Eckert, J. Presper. "Disclosure of Magnetic Calculating Machine." Originally unpublished (1944). In *A History of Computing in the Twentieth Century*, edited by Nicholas Metropolis, Jack Howlett, and Gian-Carlo Rota, pp. 537–39. New York: Academic Press, 1980.

———. "A Preview of a Digital Computing Machine." Lecture, Moore School of Electrical Engineering, University of Pennsylvania (1946). In *Theory and Techniques for the Design of Electronic Digital Computers*, edited by George W. Patterson, distributed by the Moore School, 1947–1948. Adapted and reprinted in *Charles Babbage Institute Reprint Series for the History of Computing*, vol. 9, edited by Martin Campbell-Kelly and Michael Williams, pp. 109–26. Cambridge: MIT Press, 1985.

———. "A Survey of Digital Computer Memory Systems." *Proceedings of the Institute of Radio Engineers* 41 (1953): 1,393–406.

———. "The ENIAC." Lecture, International Research Conference on the History of Computing, Los Alamos Scientific Laboratory, Los Alamos, New Mexico (1976). In *A History of Computing in the Twentieth Century*, edited by Nicholas Metropolis, Jack Howlett, and Gian-Carlo Rota, pp. 525–39. New York: Academic Press, 1980.

———. "A Man Not Bound by Tradition." *Datamation* 26, no. 3 (1980): 62.

———. Keynote Address. ENIAC's 40th Anniversary, February 13, 1986, Computer Museum, Boston, Massachusetts. In *Computer Museum Report* (summer 1986): 3–6.

Eckert, J. Presper, and John W Mauchly. "Automatic High-Speed Computing: A Progress Report on the EDVAC." Unpublished, September 30, 1945.

Elmer-DeWitt, Philip. "A Birthday Party for ENIAC." *Time*, February 24, 1986, 63.

ENIAC trial records. Pretrial depositions, affidavits, complaints, transcripts, exhibits, briefs, and decision. *Honeywell, Inc. v. Sperry Rand Corp. et al.* No. 4-67 Civ. 138. D. Minn. Filed May 26, 1967, decided October 19, 1973. General Services Administration, Federal Records Center, Chicago. Decision published in *U.S. Patent Quarterly* 180 (March 25, 1974): 673–773.

Gardner, W. David. "How the Judge Looked at the IBM-Sperry Rand ENIAC Pact." *Datamation* 20, no. 1 (1974): 78–80.

———. "Will the Inventor of the First Digital Computer Please Stand Up?" *Datamation* 20, no. 2 (1974): 84, 88–90.

———. "The Independent Inventor." *Datamation* 28, no. 9 (1982): 12–16, 20–22.

Gill, Stanley. "Stored Program Concept." In *Encyclopedia of Computer Science*, 3d ed., edited by Anthony Ralston and Edwin D.Reilly, pp. 1,299–1,300. New York: Van Rostrand Reinhold, 1993.

Goldstine, Herman H. *The Computer from Pascal to von Neumann*. Princeton: Princeton University Press, 1972.

Goldstine, Herman H., and Adele Goldstine. "The Electronic Numerical Integrator and

Computer (ENIAC)." *M.T.A.C.* 2, no. 15 (1946): 97–110. Reprinted in *The Origins of Digital Computers: Selected Papers*, edited by Brian Randell. Berlin: Springer-Verlag, 1973, pp. 333–47.

Goldstine, Herman H., and John von Neumann. *Planning and Coding of Problems for an Electronic Computing Instrument*, vols. 1–3. Princeton: Institute for Advanced Study, 1947–1948. Reprinted *in Papers of John von Neumann on Computing and Computer Theory*, edited by William Aspray and Arthur Burks, *Charles Babbage Institute Reprint Series for the History of Computing*, vol. 12, pp. 151–306. Cambridge: MIT Press, 1987.

Grassley, Charles. "Atanasoff: The Father of the Computer." *Congressional Record* (July 25, 1989): S 8671.

Gruenberger, Fred. "What's in a Name?" *Datamation* 25, no. 5 (1979): 231.

Hamlin, George L. "NSWC's J. V. Atanasoff: Recognition Comes Slowly to Computer's Inventor." *On the Surface: Naval Surface Warfare Center Newsletter* 7, no. 36 (1984): 6–9.

———. "More Recognition for John Atanasoff." *On the Surface: Naval Surface Warfare Center Newsletter* 11, no. 12 (1988): 4–8.

Hapgood, Fred. Review of *Engines of the Mind: A History of the Computer*, by Joel Shurkin. *Science* 84, no. 1 (1984): 94, 98.

Hillkirk, John. "Year Saw Birth of Copier, Computer, TV." *USA Today*, December 1, 1989, cover, 1B–2B.

Huskey, Harry D. "Harry D. Huskey: The Early Days." *Annals of the History of Computing* 13 (1991): 290–306.

"Iowa Rep Asks Smithsonian to Give Credit Where It Is Due." *USA Today*, July 17, 1989, 4A.

Knuth, Donald E. "Von Neumann's First Computer Program." *Computing Surveys* 2, no. 4 (1970): 247–60.

Knuth, Donald E., and Luis Trabb Pardo. "The Early Development of Programming Languages." Lecture, International Research Conference on the History of Computing, Los Alamos Scientific Laboratory, Los Alamos, New Mexico (1976). In *A History of Computing in the Twentieth Century*, edited by Nicholas Metropolis, Jack Howlett, and Gian-Carlo Rota, pp. 197–273. New York: Academic Press, 1980.

Kuck, David J. *The Structure of Computers and Computations*, vol. 1. New York: John Wiley and Sons, 1978.

Langlais, Simon J. "ENIAC: Revisiting the Legend." *American History Illustrated* (October 1985): 48–49.

LaRue, William. "PBS Plans on Livelier Fall Schedule." *Ann Arbor News*, July 19, 1998, B4.

Lavington, S. H. "Computer Development at Manchester University." Lecture, International Research Conference on the History of Computing, Los Alamos Scientific Laboratory, Los Alamos, New Mexico (1976). In *A History of Computing in the Twentieth Century*, edited by Nicholas Metropolis, Jack Howlett, and Gian-Carlo Rota, pp. 433–43. New York: Academic Press, 1980.

———. *Early British Computers: The Story of Vintage Computers and the People Who Built Them*. Manchester, Eng.: Manchester University Press, 1980.

Ledbetter, James. *Made Possible By . . . : The Death of Public Broadcasting in the United States*. London, New York: Verso, 1997.

Ledger, Marshall. "The Case of the E.N.I.A.C." *University of Pennsylvania Gazette* (October 1982): 30–35.

———. "The E.N.I.A.C.'s Muddled History." *University of Pennsylvania Gazette* (November 1982): 29–34.

Leonard, John. "TV: The Mummy's Curse." *New York Review of Books* (May 28, 1998): 26–29.

Loevinger, Lee. Review of *The First Electronic Computer: The Atanasoff Story*, by Alice R. Burks and Arthur W. Burks, and *Atanasoff: Forgotten Father of the Computer*, by Clark R. Mollenhoff. *Jurimetrics Journal* 29, no. 3 (1989): 359–64.

Mackintosh, Allan R. Letter to the Editor. *Physics Today* (April 1984): 11.

———. "The First Electronic Computer." *Physics Today* (March 1987): 25–32.

———. "Dr. Atanasoff's Computer." *Scientific American* 259, no. 2 (1988): 90–96.

———. Review of *The First Electronic Computer: The Atanasoff Story*, by Alice R. Burks and Arthur W. Burks. *Annals of the History of Computing* 10 (1988): 222–23.

Mann, Paul. "Unisys Admits Bribery and Fraud, Will Pay Record $190 Million Fine." *Aviation Week & Space Technology* (September 16, 1991): 24–25.

Masters, Kim. "Smithsonian Officials Call Budget Shortfall 'Dispiriting, Damaging.'" *Washington Post*, April 22, 1990.

Mauchly, John W. "The Use of High Speed Vacuum Tube Devices for Calculating." Originally unpublished (1942). In *The Origins of Digital Computers: Selected Papers*, edited by Brian Randell, pp. 329–32. Berlin: Springer-Verlag, 1973.

———. "The Use of Function Tables with Computing Machines," and "Code and Control II: Machine Design and Instruction Codes." Lectures, Moore School of Electrical Engineering, University of Pennsylvania (1946). In *Theory and Techniques for the Design of Electronic Digital Computers*, edited by George W. Patterson, distributed by the Moore School, 1947–1948. Adapted and reprinted in *Charles Babbage Institute Reprint Series for the History of Computing*, vol. 9, edited by Martin Campbell-Kelly and Michael Williams, pp. 99–106 and 453–61. Cambridge: MIT Press, 1985.

———. "Preparation of Problems for EDVAC-type Machines." Lecture, Harvard University Symposium on Large Scale Digital Calculating Machinery (1947). In *Annals of the Computation Laboratory of Harvard University* 16 (1948): 203–207. Reprinted in *The Origins of Digital Computers: Selected Papers*, edited by Brian Randell, pp. 365–69. Berlin: Springer-Verlag, 1973.

———. "The ENIAC." Lecture, International Research Conference on the History of Computing, Los Alamos Scientific Laboratory, Los Alamos, New Mexico (1976). In *A History of Computing in the Twentieth Century*, edited by Nicholas Metropolis, Jack Howlett, and Gian-Carlo Rota, pp. 541–50. New York: Academic Press, 1980.

———. "Mauchly: Unpublished Remarks." Foreword by Henry Tropp and Afterword by Arthur W. Burks and Alice R. Burks. *Annals of the History of Computing* 4 (1982): 245–56.

Mauchly, John W., Jr. Letter to the Editor. *Byte* (July 1989): 34, 36.

Mauchly, Kathleen R. "John Mauchly's Early Years." *Annals of the History of Computing* 6 (1984): 116–38.

"The Mauchly Legacy: A Revolution Begun in Pfahler Hall." *Ursinus College Bulletin* (March 1985): 4–8.

McCartney, Scott. *ENIAC: The Triumphs and Tragedies of the World's First Computer.* New York: Walker and Company, 1999.

McCulloch, Warren S., and Walter H. Pitts. "A Logical Calculus of the Ideas Immanent in Nervous Activity." *Bulletin of Mathematical Biophysics* 5 (1943): 115–33.

McFadden, Robert D. "Clark R. Mollenhoff, Pulitzer Winner, Dies at 69." *New York Times*, March 4, 1991, D9.

McLaughlin, Richard A. "ENIAC in Court: What Might Have Happened." *Datamation* 19, no.6 (1973): 119, 122.

McNulty, James. Letter to the Editor. *Datamation* 26, no. 11 (1980): 23–24, 26.

Metropolis, Nicholas, Jack Howlett, and Gian-Carlo Rota, eds. *A History of Computing in the Twentieth Century*. Lecture series, June 10–15, 1976, at International Research Conference on the History of Computing, Los Alamos Scientific Laboratory, Los Alamos, New Mexico. New York: Academic Press, 1980.

Metropolis, Nicholas, and J.Worlton. "A Trilogy on Errors in the History of Computing." *Annals of the History of Computing* 2 (1980): 49–59.

Michie, Donald. Letter to the Editor. *Byte* (January 1990): 36.

Mollenhoff, Clark R. "Court: Computer Iowan's Idea." *Des Moines Sunday Register*, January 27, 1974.

———. *Atanasoff: Forgotten Father of the Computer*. Ames: Iowa State University Press, 1988.

Moore School of Electrical Engineering, University of Pennsylvania. "Minutes of 1947 Patent Conference, Moore School of Electrical Engineering, University of Pennsylvania." Originally unpublished (1947). In *Annals of the History of Computing* 7 (1985): 100–16.

———. *The Moore School Lectures: Theory and Techniques for the Design of Electronic Digital Computers*. Lecture series, July 8 to August 31,1946, ed. George W. Patterson, 1947–1948. Adapted and printed *in Charles Babbage Institute Reprint Series for the History of Computing*, vol. 9, edited by Martin Campbell-Kelly and Michael R. Williams. Cambridge: MIT Press, 1985.

Mullin, A. A. Review of *Atanasoff: Forgotten Father of the Computer*, by Clark R. Mollenhoff. *Mathematical Reviews* (May 1990): 14.

Nicewonger, Kirk. "Tune in Tonight." United Features Syndicate. *Ann Arbor News*, May 10, 1996.

Palfreman, Jon. Letter to the Editor. *Ames Daily Tribune*, June 2, 1992, A6.

Patterson, George W., ed. *The Moore School Lectures: Theory and Techniques for the Design of Electronic Digital Computers*. Lecture series, July 8 to August 31, 1946, distributed by Moore School of Electrical Engineering, University of Pennsylvania, 1947–1948. Adapted and printed in *Charles Babbage Institute Reprint Series for the History of Computing*, vol. 9, edited by Martin Campbell-Kelly and Michael Williams. Cambridge: MIT Press, 1985.

Pejsa, Jane. Review of *The First Electronic Computer: The Atanasoff Story*, by Alice R. Burks and Arthur W. Burks. *Minneapolis Star Tribune*, July 2, 1989.

Ralston, Anthony, and Edwin D. Reilly, eds. *Encyclopedia of Computer Science*, 3d ed. New York: Van Rostrand Reinhold, 1993.

Randell, Brian, ed. *The Origins of Digital Computers: Selected Papers*. Berlin: Springer-Verlag, 1973.

———. "An Annotated Bibliography on the Origins of Computers." *Annals of the History of Computing* 1 (1979): 101–207.

Regenerative Memory trial records. Pretrial depositions, transcript, etc. *Sperry Rand Corp. v. Control Data Corp.* Civ. 15,823 and 15,824. D. Md. Filed April 1, 1964. Out-of-court settlement reached in 1981.

Richards, R. K. *Electrical Digital Systems.* New York: John Wiley and Sons, 1966.

Robinson, Alan J. Letter to the Editor. *Datamation* 26, no. 6 (1980): 31.

Rogers, James L. "Atanasoff Speaks at Digital Computer Museum." *Annals of theHistory of Computing* 3 (1981): 185–86.

Rosen, Saul. "The Atanasoff Story—Comment on Book Review." *Annals of the History of Computing* 11 (1989): 144–45.

Rosin, Robert F. "Von Neumann Machine." In *Encyclopedia of Computer Science,* 3d ed., edited by Anthony Ralston and Edwin D. Reilly, pp. 1,425–26. New York: Van Rostrand Reinhold, 1993.

Ross, D. E. Review of *Atanasoff: Forgotten Father of the Computer,* by Clark R. Mollenhoff. *Computing Reviews* (April 1989): 198–99.

Runyan, Linda F. "A Master of Understatement." *Datamation* 26, no. 5 (1980): 84–85.

Shurkin, Joel. *Engines of the Mind: A History of the Computer.* New York: W. W. Norton, 1984.

Smith, William D. "Critics Mark 25th Year of the Computer." *New York Times,* August 4, 1971, 43, 49.

"Smithsonian Ducks Trouble in Citing Computer Wizards." *Washington Times,* July 17, 1989, A6.

Smithsonian Institution. *News of the Information Exhibition, A Quarterly Bulletin* 2, no. 2. Washington, D. C.: Smithsonian Institution, National Museum of American History, 1988.

———. *Information Age: People, Information, and Technology.* Washington, D. C.: Smithsonian Institution, National Museum of American History, 1989.

"Smithsonian Opens Exhibition on the Information Age." *Charles Babbage Institute Newsletter* 12, no. 3 (1990): 5.

Snyder, Evan S. Letter to the Editor. *Physics Today* (December 1987): 13, 15.

Sperry Univac. "Who Would Have Thought the Father of Goliath Would Be Introducing David?" Advertisement. *Wall Street Journal,* June 5, 1979, 24–25.

Stern, Nancy. "From ENIAC to UNIVAC: A Case Study in the History of Technology." Ph. D. Dissertation, State University of New York at Stony Brook. University Microfilms thesis number 78-21,846, 1978.

———. "John William Mauchly: 1907–1980." *Annals of the History of Computing* 2 (1980): 100–103.

———. *From ENIAC to UNIVAC: An Appraisal of the Eckert-Mauchly Computers.* Bedford, Mass.: Digital Press, 1981.

———. "Who Invented the First Electronic Digital Computer?" *Abacus* 1, no. 1 (1983): 7–15.

———. Review of *Engines of the Mind: A History of the Computer,* by Joel Shurkin. *Annals of the History of Computing* 6 (1984): 414–16.

Trescott, Jacqueline. "Smithsonian Names New Secretary." *Washington Post,* May 26, 1994.

Tropp, Henry S. Review of *From ENIAC to UNIVAC: An Appraisal of the Eckert-Mauchly Computers,* by Nancy Stern. *Annals of the History of Computing* 3 (1981): 302.

von Neumann, John. "First Draft of a Report on the EDVAC." Moore School of Electrical Engineering, University of Pennsylvania, June 1945. Reprinted in Nancy Stern, *From ENIAC to UNIVAC: An Appraisal of the Eckert-Mauchly Computers*. Bedford, Mass.: Digital Press, 1981, pp. 177–246, and in *Papers of John von Neumann on Computing and Computer Theory*, in *Charles Babbage Institute Reprint Series for the History of Computing*, vol. 12, pp. 17–82. Cambridge: MIT Press, 1987.

Vose, G. Michael. Review of *The First Electronic Computer: The Atanasoff Story*, by Alice R. Burks and Arthur W. Burks. *Byte* (September 1988): 51–52, 54.

Wagner, Frank. "Comment: Who 'Invented' the First Electronic Computer?" *Annals of the History of Computing* 2 (1980): 375–76.

Walker, Virginia C. "To Honor Our Beginnings—ACM '80." *Annals of the History of Computing* 3 (1981): 183–85.

Weiss, Eric A. Review of *Misunderstanding Media*, by Brian Winston (Cambridge: Harvard University Press, 1986), *Annals of the History of Computing* 9 (1987): 105–106.

———. Review of *The First Electronic Computer: The Atanasoff Story*, by Alice R. Burks and Arthur W. Burks. *Computing Reviews* (April 1989): 199–200.

———. Review of *Atanasoff: Forgotten Father of the Computer*, by Clark R. Mollenhoff, and *The First Electronic Computer: The Atanasoff Story*, by Alice R. Burks and Arthur W. Burks. *American Scientist* (July–August 1989): 401.

WGBH Boston. "Public Television Sets Sail for the Future." Advertisement. *Wall Street Journal*, September 11, 1989, B16.

Whistler, Elsie Atanasoff. Letter to the Editor. *Time*, March 24, 1986, 9–10.

"Who Invented the Electronic General-Purpose Digital Computer?" Condensations of "John Mauchly's Early Years," by Kathleen R. Mauchly, and "Advent of Electronic Digital Computing," by John V. Atanasoff. *Computerworld* (July 9, 1984): ID1–16.

Wilkes, Maurice V. "Computers Then and Now." Turing Lecture of 1967. In *Journal of the Association for Computing Machinery* 15 (1968): 1–7.

———. "A Tribute to Presper Eckert." Obituary delivered at the International Symposium on Computer Architecture, in Santa Margherita Ligure, Italy (June 24,1995). In *Communications of the Association for Computing Machinery* 38 (1995): 9.

Wilkes, Maurice V., David J. Wheeler, and Stanley Gill. *The Preparation of Programs for an Electronic Digital Computer*. Reading, Mass.: Addison-Wesley, 1951.

Williams, Michael R. *A History of Computing Technology*. Englewood Cliffs, N. J.: Prentice-Hall, 1985.

Wright, George. Letter to the Editor. *Byte* (October 1989): 32.

Young, Jeffrey. "John Vincent Atanasoff: Father of the Computer?" *Forbes* (July 7, 1997): 335.

INDEX

electronic computer, 17, 71, 149,
198, 235, 267–69, 350, 380
hydrogen bomb problem, 152, 157
Mauchly's 1942 memorandum, 67,
71, 84, 120, 220, 233
naming, 71
newsreel, 152, 153, 351, 358
patent. *See* ENIAC patent case
proposal, 120, 350
programming, 71, 380
reference to Atanasoff, 171, 379
replacement for differential analyzer, 67
reputation as first electronic computer, 13, 119, 176, 189, 197, 198,
221–22, 329, 376, 409–10
treatment by PBS, 356, 359–63
treatment by Smithsonian Institution,
14, 328–33, 335–48, 349–51, 401
two-accumulator model, 70, 154,
223, 284
U.S. Army sponsorship, 18, 67, 71,
152–54, 176, 350, 379
vacuum-tube circuits for arithmetic
and control, 33, 48, 379
ENIAC patent case (*Honeywell v.
Sperry Rand*), 23, 33, 51, 80,
145–46, 148–49, 236, 342,
377–79, 393–94
historical significance, 17, 174, 189,
193, 317, 413
Larson's decision
on abandonment of invention,
110, 377
on anticipation by Phelps, 169
on Atanasoff's failure to apply for
patent, 175–77
on Atanasoff's proposal, 41, 147,
149

on Atanasoff's test model, 85–86,
109, 147, 149
on Burks, Sharpless, Shaw petition, 237–38, 310, 414
on coinventors at Moore School,
150–51
on credibility of Atanasoff versus
Mauchly, 43, 148
on definition of pulse, 169–70
on delay before Patent Office, 151,
170–71
on derivation from Atanasoff, 67,
72, 109–10, 117, 146–48, 172
on EDVAC, 144, 178, 386
on ENIAC patent validity, 16, 33,
146
on fraud on Patent Office, 151,
170–73
on infringement of patent, 173
on Mauchly's computing achievements, 109, 148, 149
on Mauchly's Iowa visit, 109,
147–48, 149, 216
on order of events, 149
on placing on sale, 151–52,
153–55
on prior publication, 151–52, 155,
157–59, 178
on prior public use, 151–53
on Regenerative Memory patent,
49, 51, 146, 177–78, 293, 386
on serial adder patents, 33, 293
on Sherman Antitrust Act, 173,
224–25
on 30A patent package, 33,
145–46, 178
on von Neumann's First Draft
Report, 155, 157–59, 172,
290–95